From Creation to Consummation

From Creation to Consummation

Volume II

Gerard Van Groningen

Dordt College Press
Sioux Center, Iowa

Printed in the United States of America

Dordt College Press
498 Fourth Avenue, NE
Sioux Center, Iowa 51250

ISBN: 0-932914-52-7

Contents

I

The Golden Cable Explicated in the Prophets

19

Joel

Setting the Agenda

Part I: Introduction to Prophetic Studies

I. Prophetic Revelation: Divine Revelation

II. Prophetic Revelation's Inclusive Role

Part II: Joel

I. Introductory Comments

II. The Cosmic Kingdom Setting

III. The Revelation of the Covenantal Administration

IV. The Mediatorial Role

V. The Historical and Eschatological Perspectives

19

Joel

Setting the Agenda

Introduction to Prophetic Studies

A brief discussion of prophetic revelation is in order because of the differing views concerning it. It is imperative that the approach taken to it and the explication of it in this study be stated clearly in the context of what has been the understanding of a variety of scholars.[1]

Prophetic Revelation: Divine Revelation

Robert Martin-Achard referred to prophetic conviction as a basis for Isaiah's proclamation and teaching.[2] He did not explain clearly what the source of that conviction was; he may have agreed with C. F. Whitley, who wrote that the basis of prophetic conviction and the message proclaimed was "a personal intuitive knowledge of the mind and purpose of God." Whitley, it should be noted, was not impressed with some scholars' views that the prophetic message was received by prophets who represented a development of prophetic phenomena derived from sources in which ecstasy, visions, and personal experiences were sources of prophetic utterances.[3] Curt Kuhl emphasized that the prophetic material was developed over periods of time; thus the Scriptures present us with collections of items of varying content, in turn composed of subcollections. Some of these collections were derived from prophetic legends, narratives depicting personal experiences, and/or materials such as laments, songs, and promises of salvation.[4] Abraham Heschel insisted that neither a dogmatic view which put sole emphasis on divine revelation nor the pan-psychology view, which stresses prophecy as a human, personal phenomenon, is acceptable. The responses of the prophets in given situations must be considered an integral, constituent part of prophecy.[5] Walther Eichrodt considered the biblical prophetic phenomenon to have roots in nabism, a common feature of Near Eastern religious life. Classical prophecy, as presented by the writing prophets, was less a "psychic phenomenon" but became influenced by a "new experience of the Divine Reality."[6] Claus Westermann is understood to have held the position that the biblical prophets "distinguished rather clearly between their own words and the Word of God."[7] He thus gave allowance for understanding the often repeated phrases, "Yahweh said" or "The Word of Yahweh came . . . " as some kind of revelation. J. Lindblom, attempting to examine the psychological experiences and works of classical prophetism began with a discussion of "The Prophets as Recipients of Divine Revelation." He accepted the biblical statements of Yahweh's Word coming to the prophets as valid expressions of what the prophets and the people believed.[8] Lindblom's efforts to place the prophetic reception of Yahweh's words in a predominantly psychological setting, however, detract from the reality that Yahweh did objectively give "his Word" to the prophets.

A review of what scholars (referred to above) wrote concerning biblical prophecy during the decade of the 1960s, informs us that what Robert R. Wilson wrote ("there is still no scholarly consensus on the questions of the nature and social functions of Israelite prophecy")[9] is correct. Wilson's essay is the first of twenty-one essays in an anthology that was produced to offer the "concerns of critical research and religious use of the prophets." He added that instead of developing one approach, a "dynamic variety of approaches are pursued in the current study of the prophets."[10] Brevard S. Childs, believing that the "witness of the prophets" (as well as those of the psalmists and sages) reflects a unique relationship to Israel's faith and history, finds that a major difficulty in the study of the origins of prophecy is that "the Old Testament does not supply information which is needed for a solution." He states that the Old Testament's interest in prophecy is theological, and this interest must be distilled from the Bible's reconstructed history of Israel.[11] Childs thus reflects an agnostic attitude toward the critical-historical efforts to find the roots of biblical prophecy; his view of whether the prophets received divine revelation, or not, is difficult to discern from his writings. It may be that he follows Gerhard Von Rad (his theological professor) on this subject, as he openly states in regard to other issues.[12]

Old Testament scholars generally considered conservative rather than historical-critical have demonstrated a far greater readiness to consider the prophets as spokesmen for God and thus means of divine revelation. These scholars, mostly aware of what critical students of prophecy have written, give evidence that, as a rule, some aspects of what the critics have written are not to be rejected. But the biblical teaching on prophecy is not fully or correctly presented by these critics. Conservatively oriented scholars do not necessarily include a full discussion on the origin and character of prophetic proclamation; the manner and context of their writings, however, do give insights into their position. For example, William S. Lasor, discussing the prophets during the monarchy, refers to important phrases such as "Yahweh told Moses to say to the people," "Yahweh sent the prophet Elijah," "the command of Yahweh to Jeremiah not to marry."[13] His discussion, however, does include a clear statement on whether all prophecy had its origin from God. Willem Van Gemeren, indicating a readiness to accept various views of critical scholars, does state clearly that prophets "received revelation over a long period of time and in diverse ways."[14] Richard D. Patterson, while discussing at some length the prophet Joel's vitality, spiritual maturity, rich and vivid literary style, genius and originality, faith in God, and contribution to eschatology, states clearly that the prophet "delivered God's message to the people."[15]

The view concerning classical, specifically the writing, prophets whose messages are studied in this book, is as follows. Each man was called by Yahweh; how and when the call came is not recorded for each prophet as it was for Isaiah, Jeremiah, Ezekiel, and Jonah, but that does not preclude their call. It is recorded by some that the word of Yahweh came to them (e.g., Hosea, Micah, Zephaniah). Habakkuk received an oracle; Obadiah and Zechariah received Yahweh's message by vision. These prophets were indeed called in diverse ways, from diverse circumstances. None were altered in terms of personal traits or gifts when they were commissioned and sent to prophesy. Gerhardus Vos has correctly referred to the varied means of the prophets' reception of Yahweh's word they were to proclaim. He explained that these were: (1) speech and hearing, (2) showing and seeing, (3) rapture, (4) bodily effects, and (5) intramental. Whatever the means by which revelation was given, the Spirit of God was deeply involved.[16] Thus the prophetic message was Yahweh's message first of all! The prophets were very conscious that they were spokesmen for God. This divine factor, however, did not preclude or exclude the individual prophet's awareness of his religious/spiritual, social, and cultural situations. In fact, the prophets were so aware of them, that they delivered God's word in such a manner that they gave evidence of their knowing these and often intimated what their personal reactions were.

The context of this revelation Yahweh's spokesmen were to make known by proclamation and writing is often referred to as the theology of the prophets, as if these men were theologians. They were not; rather they were messengers. Hence, it is more appropriate to speak of the message of the prophets.[17] This inclusive message, summarized below, was not a new message. It had been given to and through Moses, Samuel, David, and Solomon. The prophets explicated and applied the message that had been revealed before they were sent to the nation of Israel and the surrounding nations.[18]

Prophetic Revelation's Inclusive Role

Clarification

The message of the prophets, as they expounded and applied previous revelation, included the following in order to clarify Yahweh's word to his people Israel/Judah and the nations.

The prophets communicated an added dimension concerning Yahweh's eschatological purposes and goals. It was not that the prophets were clever politicians, historians, and philosophers who by recalling the past and observing the present were able to foretell what was to take place. Yahweh made known to and through the prophets that his eschatological purposes and goals, revealed in creation and in the proclamation of the protoevangelium, were upheld, were being worked on, and would be fully achieved and realized. Israel's/Judah's unfaithfulness and disobedience notwithstanding, Yahweh would sovereignly continue to rule and direct all people, forces, and events according to his predetermined plan. This eschatological dimension of Yahweh's revelation included a constant reminder of Israel's/Judah's role in the plan of Yahweh. More specifically, the presence, role, and service of the mediator of the covenant was increasingly presented in an eschatological context. And salvation and blessed peace as well as judgment were included in this eschatological dimension of Yahweh's revelation to and through the prophets.

Biblical Understanding of History

The second dimension, closely related to the eschatological, was the historical. The prophets, communicating God's word, did so in their historical context. They were fully aware of their present circumstances from religious/spiritual, social, and/or cultural perspectives. The present was illumined and evaluated in terms of past history and, as they were led to Yahweh to look to the future, they did so in terms of the past and the present. It has been repeatedly pointed out that Yahweh God's revelation was organically, progressively, adaptively given within the crucible of living history. The prophets certainly were aware of their unique and specific role as spokesmen for God in their given *Sitz im Leben*. They never were anachronistic; they spoke to their times and circumstances but as they did so, the past and the future were inseparably related to their contemporary message. Because of the prophets' historical awareness and consciousness, and the applicability of their God-given message to their contemporaries, it is incumbent on readers and scholars of the prophetic word to determine as precisely and clearly as possible the historical context of each prophet's message. Indeed, if biblical theologians are to do their task, carry out their role, and serve other theological disciplines, especially systematic theology, they are duty bound to pay close attention to the historical setting of Yahweh's revelation to and through his spokesmen, the prophets.

Explicating the Golden Cable

The third dimension is the integrating factors that make the prophetic message unified yet widely embracing. Each of the factors to be mentioned provides meaningful material involved in the eventual achievement of the eschatological goals. They also illuminate the historical contexts and processes of the historical dimensions of their messages.

Furthermore, three factors are strands that constitute the Golden Cable, which unites and integrates the entire biblical message and therefore also the entire message of the classical prophets. These factors or strands are Yahweh's cosmic kingdom, his creational/redemptive/restorative/administrative covenant, and the covenant Mediator. These three have been discussed at length in the study preceding this one.[19] A brief statement concerning each follows.

The prophets were definitely kingdom-oriented. They proclaimed that Yahweh God ruled sovereignly over the cosmos that he had created. This cosmic kingdom was given a temporary, limited, but concrete symbolic expression by means of Israel's theocratic monarchy. The symbol was for a time, the cosmic kingdom would endure. All aspects of life, the natural, social, and cultural, were included; all clans, tribes, nations, and races were integral parts of the cosmic kingdom. The prophets therefore addressed Israel/Judah and the surrounding nations, small and large. Their divinely given messages included political, cultural, natural, and social elements, issues, problems, challenges, and roles in the cosmic kingdom under Yahweh God's reign.

The prophets were also very covenant conscious. Some presented their God-given message in such a manner that a covenantal framework is readily discernible. They did not limit their covenant references to the redemptive dimension. They repeatedly presented the creational covenant as the broader context within which the redemptive/restorative covenant functioned. The term *functioned* is used purposely because Yahweh God not only related himself to his cosmic kingdom; he also administered it covenantally. His historic reminders, promises, stipulations, warnings, and assurances of continuity were basic elements of the covenantal relationship and administration. Agents, representatives, and servants in the kingdom were called, appointed, charged, and authorized to serve as specific covenant agents. Specifically set apart as covenant servants were the kings, prophets, and priests/Levites. Even foreign pagan rulers such as Nebuchadnezzar and Cyrus were appointed to serve as Yahweh's covenant agents. Even though the Old Testament contains over 290 direct references to the covenant concept with the term *bĕrît,* some scholars are not hesitant to dismiss the covenantal references in passages if that term is not actually present.[20] The concept, however, is pervasively present, often referred to implicitly by reference to aspects of the covenant. Further evidence of the pervasive presence of the covenant concept, even if the term *bĕrît* is not present, is the increasing number of studies on the covenant attempting to understand and see its role in biblical revelation.[21]

The third strand is the revelation concerning the mediator. The Mediator of creation was the Word, the preincarnate Son of God, who was divinely appointed to also serve as the redeeming/restoring messianic mediator. The concept of the Messiah has been explicated in my previously written study, *Messianic Revelation in the Old Testament.*[22] The narrower view, a royal person, and the broader view, his character, role, results, and types (persons, things, events) were studied. In a sense this messianic mediatorial concept serves as the very core of biblical revelation. But it was never separated from its covenantal and kingdom context. The prophets, aware of what Yahweh God had revealed concerning the messianic mediator, in both the narrower and wider perspectives, continued to uphold this and explicated and applied it more fully. Thus Yahweh God continued to reveal more fully in an ever relevant manner within the historical process the mediator, the covenant, and the kingdom, that is, the Golden Cable.

Interpretation of Prophetic Revelation

The interpretation of prophetic revelation has drawn the attention of many biblical scholars.[23] Much effort has been expended, but there seems to be less agreement as efforts increase. A number of important factors are at the root of this disagreement. First of all, the question of divine involvement, especially the manner and character of this involvement, is answered variously. The character of prophecy is debated: Is it forthtelling (preaching to the present only), is it basically foretelling (prediction), or is it both? And should prophecy be considered a source of specific eschatological events and goals? If so, what was the purpose for the proclamation of these? In this study of the prophets, answers to these questions should become apparent. Choices had to be made; it is impossible to present a unified approach that includes all the major schools of interpretation. The differences are too radical; some are clearly contradictory to others. Dominant guiding factors in this study will be the acceptance of prophetic revelation as an integral part of Yahweh God's revelation, organically and progressively given within the crucible of the historical process. This revelation was realistic and meaningful in every circumstance, regardless of whether the emphasis was on the past, present, or future. (The Golden Cable will be demonstrated to be the unifying and integrating factors.) Furthermore, in this study of the prophets, the interpretation will be influenced by a conscious attempt to submit to the Holy Spirit's illumination and guidance.

Finally, in this study, a detailed discussion of various hermeneutical and exegetical methodologies will not be included. Some of these are helpful, and will be recognized in due course; others are more distracting than directives in understanding the living message given by Yahweh God to and for his people.[24]

JOEL

Introductory Comments

The name *Joel* speaks to Joel's identity. His name is a combination of an abbreviated form of *Yĕhwâ* and *'ĕlōhîm, yôēl,* "Yahweh is God."[25] He was distinguished from the twelve other Joels named in the Bible by reference to his father Pethuel. No other information is known concerning the father. Of Joel it can be said that he was a prophet because *dĕbar yĕhwâ 'ăšer hāyâ 'el yôel* (the word of Yahweh came [or was] to Joel). He received divine communication from Yahweh; he was given a message to proclaim. He was a spokesman for his Lord whose name he bore.

How and when Joel received the word from Yahweh is not revealed. He did not give the time of his prophetic activity. He did not refer to the reign of any ruler, nor was his message related to specifically known dated events. Hence, there has been much debate concerning the time that he prophesied.[26] In my previous work I have stated my preference for the earlier date.[27] It is my considered view that Joel presents a series of important issues in a compact manner; subsequent prophets quote and expand on these.[28] Joel is considered to be a vital prophetic link between Moses, the former prophets, David, and the prophets who functioned in the period between Samuel and the earliest prophets on the one side and on the other such prophets as Hosea and Amos who prophesied in the days of Jeroboam who reigned from 793 to 753.[29] Joel indicated a general awareness of Israel's past and the revelation given to the people. He was given a message to proclaim that stressed major elements that the prophets following him would repeat, explicate, and place in more specific historical and theological contexts.[30] He did this as a gifted man, presenting his message with clarity and authority; his style is one of beauty and fluency and is said to be very different from the stilted style of the semi-rabbinic period (400 B.C.).[31] Others have considered Joel's literary style and structure to be that of a lament to be used in the liturgy of the temple.[32] It is not difficult to find a "lament" in the first part of Joel if a review of Yahweh's chastisement of his people and a call to repentance constitute a lament. It seems doubtful that Yahweh would have Joel give expression to laments in liturgical contexts as a prelude and setting for hope that basically characterizes Joel's message.

The Cosmic Kingdom Setting

A careful biblical-theological study of Joel's prophecy should impress readers, students, and scholars with Joel's expansive vision. Yahweh God gave him a message that truly has the setting of Yahweh's cosmic kingdom. Joel speaks of many and varied aspects of the cosmic kingdom in his message that includes a sincere call to repentance and definite promises of hope.

The Prophetic Call

Attention should be given first of all to the prophet's call to various audiences that are integral parts of Yahweh's cosmic kingdom. Three groups are immediately addressed. They are commanded: *šim'u* (imperative of *šama',* to listen, to hear). First of all, *hazzĕqēnîm* (the elders). Elders were the leaders of the families and clans. They had been an integral part of Israel's social, political, and religious life and functions from the earliest of times of Israel even as an ethnic group. Moses was told to gather and to speak to the elders of Israel; elders were recognized as dignitaries and representatives of Israel while Israel was still in Egyptian bondage (Exod. 3:16, 18; 4:29; 12:21; 17:5, 6). Later, after Israel had been delivered, elders were recognized as representatives and leaders in Israel (18:12; 19:7; 24:9, 14). During Solomon's reign elders were assembled to participate in bringing the ark of the covenant into the temple (1 Kings 8:1, 3). It is true that the kings as shepherds were not addressed by Joel but prophets who did speak to kings also addressed the elders (Isa. 1:4; Jer. 2:8).[33]

The second group called to listen were *kōl yôšĕbê* (all inhabitants). This term referred to all the people, including foreigners. The call was not just to Israelites. Remnants of Canaanite clans had remained in the land; foreigners had been grafted into the families descending from the patriarchs; men from other nations had been included among Israel's military personnel. All these were considered part of the theocratic monarchy that was a local, temporary, and functioning representative of Yahweh's cosmic kingdom.

The third group referred to are the children, the children's children, and their children. This call to instruct children who are integral members of Yahweh's cosmic kingdom and the future leaders of and in it is not a new phenomenon.[34] The command to instruct children in Yahweh's ways and works was an integral aspect of the covenant administration for the continuity of the kingdom and the covenant way of life. Instruction of offspring was referred to when Abraham was informed of the imminent judgment on Sodom and Gomorrah (Gen. 18:19) and again in the context of Israel's deliverance from Egypt (Exod. 12:24–28). The command to instruct children was given by Moses twice on the east bank of the Jordan (Deut. 6:4–9; 11:18–21). Later, Asaph, the psalm writer, reiterated what fathers were to do for their children, and their successors, as teachers of Yahweh God's wondrous word, ways, and works (Ps. 78:1–8). Joel, as the spokesman for Yahweh, standing after the Mosaic and Davidic eras and introducing the classical prophetic era, emphasizes the integral role of children and the important duty of instructing them in matters of Yahweh's kingdom and covenant.

Further indication of the cosmic kingdom setting of Joel's prophecy is his call to various other groups of the inhabitants of the land. He called the drinkers of wine (drunkards?) to weep (1:5); he spoke of mourning like virgins dressed in sackcloth, in deepest sorrow (1:8). The priests (1:9), the farmers, and vineyardists are called to attention. The point to be seriously considered is that Joel was not simply addressing a religious problem and religious leaders. His scope was much wider; it was all-inclusive—as inclusive as Yahweh's cosmic kingdom.

The priests were addressed in a specific and direct manner. According to Mosaic prescription they were to dress in priestly clothes (Exod. 28:1–13), but Joel calls on them to dress in rough, unseemly sackcloth, to give dramatic evidence of mourning (1:13). The priests are to call a fast, summon the elders to the temple, proclaim a fast for the entire assembly. They are to blow the trumpet, sounding an alarm (2:1, 13). They are to lead the people, having assembled them, in weeping and intercession (2:17).

Why were the priests summoned and given directives? Were they specific representatives in Yahweh's cosmic kingdom? The answer is both no and yes. They were not priests commissioned to serve in all nations. They were commissioned to serve especially at the temple in Jerusalem. But this service at the temple was dedicated to Yahweh God, who is Lord of the entire cosmos. And Israel, as a holy nation, had a royal priestly duty that was to extend to all peoples and nations in Yahweh's cosmic kingdom. Israel, under priestly leadership, was to be a priestly people, interceding, sacrificing, serving on behalf of all nations. Thus, the priests in Jerusalem were to represent and serve all peoples and nations because of Israel's unique priestly role on behalf of all nations.

Joel gives specific evidence that Yahweh's concern is for all nations. He prophesied that not only would Judah and Jerusalem have their fortunes restored by a regathering of Israelites to Jerusalem after seventy years of exile, but Yahweh would gather all nations and bring them into judgment in the future (3:4–13 [MT 4:4–13]). Thus Yahweh clearly reveals that he, the cosmic Lord, reigning over the cosmos in its entirety, would have Joel proclaim an all-embracing, cosmic kingdom setting for his prophetic message.

The Inclusive Referential Evidence

It must be clearly understood that Joel's various addresses place before the reader/student a panoramic cosmic kingdom setting. There is no doubt that the religious/spiritual dimension of kingdom life is set forth as all-pervasive, reaching to and appointed to influence all aspects of it. But the religious/spiritual is not to be isolated and distilled from the social, cultural, and natural dimensions of the cosmic kingdom. Because this is true, Joel the prophet has, as it were, a hierarchy, or a framework, which enables him to present the entire cosmic kingdom as the setting for his prophetic message. The following sketch may illuminate more clearly how Joel carried out his task.

Yahweh's Word
Joel the Prophet
The Priests
The People of Israel—including elders, families, children, virgins, farmers, drunkards
All Nations to Assemble and be Judged

This sketch must be considered in the context of (1) Yahweh God's inclusion in his covenant with Abraham that nations were to bless themselves or to be blessed through him (Gen. 12:1–3); (2) Yahweh God's calling Israel his priestly people; and (3) Israel's calling to be a light to the nations. Abraham, Israel, the nations were all integral aspects of Yahweh's cosmic kingdom and were essential elements in Yahweh's eschatological plan and goal.

There are more evidences and indications that the cosmic kingdom was the setting as well as an integral part of the message Joel had to proclaim. Indeed, he had to proclaim a message of judgment that included the call to repentance and a message of hope that directed attention to a glorious future. The people were called to listen, obey, and serve. These activities were not to be considered and carried out in a vacuum or in separation from daily life with all its natural, material, social, and cultural dimensions. Joel proclaimed a message that addressed and involved the totality of the integrated cosmic kingdom of Yahweh. No parts or aspects were to be considered outside Yahweh God's concern and outside the sphere of human life. The theocracy, and later the theocratic monarchy, the earthly symbolic expression and manifestation of Yahweh's eternal cosmic kingdom, involved every dimension of life.[35] Hence, Joel spoke to the inclusive theocratic monarchy as he proclaimed Yahweh God's lordship over every aspect of the cosmic kingdom. Some concrete references should be considered.

Joel called his audience's attention to the locusts that had invaded the land. Which invasion he specifically referred to is not known. Commentators of Joel agree that the appearance of locusts in the land of Canaan was not an unusual phenomenon in the natural, creational sphere of life. Some points should be noted. Joel referred to the various stages of locust development (1:4). He was observant of the natural world around him. He, furthermore, described the result of the locust invasion: vegetation was destroyed. He spoke of the effects on vines and wine, on fig trees with bark stripped off, on grain (specifically wheat and barley), on the pomegranate, palm, and apple trees (1:7–12), on graineries (empty), on moaning cattle and on suffering sheep (1:17, 18). He also realized that this tragic phenomenon in the creational setting was to be considered as a judgment of Yahweh God on people in their cultural, social, and spiritual aspects of life. Joel went on to proclaim that the locust invasion and its results were a harbinger of an even greater and more devastating invasion: a powerful army was to overrun and destroy the land as a greater judgment from God (1:6; 2:1–11).[36] The invading nation would be very fierce; Joel again appeals to the creational dimension, speaking of the lion and lioness that can best describe the character of Yahweh God's agent of judgment (1:6).

Joel, speaking of locusts, lions, invading military forces, various aspects of vegetation, and the land, also addressed the spiritual dimension of life. He referred to the divinely prescribed worship with its officiating priests (1:13) and the sacrificial offerings that did not come in. Indeed, the devastation of the land involving the pastures, cattle, sheep, vineyards, orchards, forests, streams, and even the wild animals (1:7–18, 23) would have a profound effect on worship at Yahweh God's house. But this effect was not to be separated from the spiritual dimension of life. Spiritual as well as physical famine would result because of hard, unrepentant hearts (2:12–14).

As Joel proceeded to develop his God-given message, he spoke of repentance, conversion, and renewed life. He then spoke of the various cosmic kingdom aspects of life. Prosperity would be evident (2:22–26). He spoke of great wonders in the creational dimension of the world (2:30, 31 [MT 3:3, 4]). And he again included the nations as he proclaimed the great events to take place in the future.[37]

Summing up, the main points to be stressed are: (1) Joel, the prophet, was given a message that addressed the people of Israel. (2) The people were afflicted by plagues of locusts that caused severe damage in the creational sphere of life. (3) The basic reason for calamities in the creational sphere of life was Israel's spiritual departure from Yahweh God's will and task for them. (4) The nations to be blessed through Israel's life and service would also suffer because of Israel's dereliction of responsibilities for them. (5) All aspects of life, the natural, the social, the cultural, the spiritual, were presented by Joel as an integrated whole. Each aspect would and did have pervasive effects and influences, for good or evil, on the other aspects. (6) Yahweh God's cosmic kingdom is an integrated unity. Though Israel's sin in particular had devastating effects on all dimensions, the integrated character was not diminished. In fact, because the integrated unity remained, all aspects, or dimensions, were seriously affected by Israel's sinful departure from Yahweh's will as he had made it known to Israel through Mosaic and early prophetic ministries.

The Revelation of the Covenantal Administration

Use of the Term Bĕrît

The term *bĕrît* (covenant) was not used by Joel. We can, nevertheless, speak of Yahweh's covenantal administration of his cosmic kingdom as will be conclusively demonstrated. It is well to remember that the term itself does not always appear when the covenant is clearly referred to.[38] A classic example is the record of Yahweh God covenanting with David (2 Sam. 7); there the term *bĕrît* does not occur but when David referred to how Yahweh God had covenanted with him, he referred to the entire transaction as *bĕrît* (23:5). Psalmists and prophets also used the term to refer to Yahweh's act of binding himself to David and David to himself as covenant. And as will be shown, most prophets organized their messages in such a manner that the covenantal framework is obviously an integrating factor.

The Basic Elements

The basic elements of Yahweh God's covenant, as to both its creational and redemptive/restorative aspects, constitute the very heart and essence of Joel's message. These are all to have come to or will be fully realized in the great *yôm yĕhwâ* (Day of the Lord) (1:15; 2:1, 11, 31 [MT 3:4]; 3:14 [MT 4:14]). On that Day of Yahweh the covenant promise "I am your God; I will be with you" will be completely fulfilled; Joel concluded his prophecy *wayĕhwâ sōkēn bĕṣûyyôn* (Yahweh dwells in Zion) (3:21 [MT 4:21]).[39]

Yahweh God is proclaimed as the sovereign Lord. He has absolute control over all the forces and events in nature. He has brought judgment on all of creation; the locusts are his servants; the damage these have caused is like that of a raging fire in fields and forest. Therefore the prophet cries out *'ēlekâ yĕhwâ 'eqra'* (to you Yahweh I cry) (1:19). Judgment, *miššaddaī,* from the Almighty in the realm of nature has effects on all of life (1:15). The Lord who brings judgment, however, is the one who calls for a return to him because he continues to be the covenant, unchanging Lord of his people. He is still *ḥannûn* (gracious) *wĕrahûm* (and compassionate), *'erek 'appîm* (long of breath or slow to anger), *wĕrab-ḥesed* (and great in covenant love) (2:13). As Yahweh had revealed himself to Moses and Israel after the golden calf debacle at Sinai (Exod. 34:6), so he remained for his people 600 years later.[40] Joel went on to proclaim that the ever-loving God, as a zealous Yahweh (2:18), would continue to contend for the love and devotion of his people. And as in the past, he would bless them *kî higdîl la'aśôt* (surely by great things he does) (2:20, 21). He would continue to be the sovereign Lord in whom the people could rejoice (2:23) for abundant blessings and they would praise him *'ăser 'aśah 'immākem lĕhapelî* (For what he did for you, the extraordinary wonders) (2:26). He would continue to perform miracles (2:30 [MT 3:3]). As he proved to be the sovereign Lord over Egypt in the past, so he continued to be over all nations, Tyre, Sidon, Philistia, Ionia (Greece), Egypt, and Edom (3:2, 4, 6, 19 [MT 4:2, 4, 6, 19]). And in his own time, *gādōl yôm Yĕhwâ* (Great day of Yahweh, 2:11), and *hāyâ bayyôm hahû* (In that day, 3:18]), Yahweh will perform great deeds, with nations (3:12, 19 [MT 4:12, 19]) and in nature (2:10, 11; 3:18 [MT 4:18]).

As Yahweh administers his covenant(s) he continues to call his covenant agents to serve him. Joel, as prophet, served as spokesman. The religious leaders, the priests, were commanded to assemble the people and lead in acts of repentance, fasting, and mourning for sin (1:9, 13, 14; 2:1–15).[41] Elders were called to hear and do their duties (1:2, 14; 2:16). Farmers and vine growers were called to grieve for destroyed harvests. The grasshoppers and the invading nation served Yahweh as he administered his creation/redemptive covenant. Elements in creation likewise would be pressed into service within Yahweh's cosmic kingdom as he continued to execute his plan within the course of history.

Joel's message included covenantal stipulations. We have briefly discussed the command to the elders to have the children instructed (1:3). The children were definitely included in the covenant community. This truth was emphasized by Joel when he commanded that children and infants at their mothers' breasts be included in the gathered assembly to plead for mercy and to remove the ridicule of nations who asked, "Where is their God?" (2:16, 17). The bridegrooms and brides, the parents, elders, and priests—all had to know that Yahweh God was the Lord of all creational forces and events; he it was who called up nations as instruments of judgment upon sinful, unrepentant people.

A second stipulation was to express grief and remorse for the losses sustained and the hunger endured. The people were also called to repent. Joel made it graphic: *šūbû 'aday bĕkol-lĕbabĕkem* (Return to me with all your heart) (2:12). But first *qir'û* (rend, tear apart) your hearts. Outer garments were torn as evidence of extreme grief and pain. Keep your garments whole! Yahweh demands a torn heart (2:13)[42]—as David had confessed, "a broken and a contrite heart" (Ps. 51:17). Indeed, David knew what was required of him as a covenant servant in kingdom service. It should be added that the young people and children had to be taught to do as their parents and leaders were called to do.

A third stipulation was to assemble as a people to hear the message concerning Yahweh's work and intentions. The elders and priests had to take a leading role in these activities of assembling, instruction, and worship. The sacrifices were to be brought (2:1, 14, 15). That worship, including sacrifices, was an integral aspect of covenantal worship had been made very clear through Moses when Israel was at Mount Sinai (cf. the book of Leviticus) and when they were on the east bank of the Jordan (Deut. 12–16).

A fourth covenantal stipulation, though not explicitly referred to, is nevertheless implicitly evident. Abraham had been told that nations were to be blessed through him and they in turn were to bless themselves in their relationships with Abraham and his offspring. Joel does not expressly state that Israel was to be a light to the nations; he does make it clear, however, that Israel was a blight for the nations. The tribulation to come upon Israel would bring anguish to the nations (2:6). Nations had been given reason by Israel itself to scorn them by asking, "Where is their God?" (2:17). In coming times reasons for this scorn would be removed and the nations would no longer be an instrument of judgment (2:19, 20). In fact, they in turn would be judged (3:11, 12 [MT 4:11, 12]). Thus, instead of blessings for the nations by means of Abraham's offspring, they would come under judgment. Israel had failed to be a source of praise and honor to God by the nations. Later prophets would continue to proclaim Israel's responsibilities to the nations. Israel's failure to assume these would bring judgment for all concerned because Yahweh had never withdrawn the command to Abraham's offspring to be a source of blessing. Upon repentance, Israel could be forgiven; nations' penitence for sin and a turning to the Lord would bring salvation and all kingdom blessings to them also.

Another element of the covenant that Joel deals with is the curse of the covenant. Moses spoke of it when he solemnly called Israel to faithfully obey, love, and serve Yahweh (Deut. 11:13). He warned that the curse set before them (11:26) would surely overtake them; Yahweh God's anger would burn against them, and drought, famine, and death would follow (11:17). Later Moses spoke in greater detail about how the covenant curse would be executed. Among various terrible events to happen, Moses warned that locusts would devour what was planted and strip trees bare and that worms would ruin vineyards (28:38–42). Moses had warned of nations plundering Israel and that its sons and daughters would serve their victorious masters (28:32). Joel directed Israel's attention to the execution of these curses upon Israel; indeed, the locusts were a means of executing the curse, as were the nations that overran the descendants of the audience Moses addressed on the east bank of the Jordan.

The element of the covenant that receives the greater emphasis is the promise. The various aspects of the promise, all of which are promises themselves, are set against the background of the curses Israel experienced because of their disobedience by which they broke the covenant, disregarded the stipulations, disobeyed Yahweh's faithful covenant agents, and rebelled against and dishonored their sovereign covenant Lord, even Yahweh God. These promises, moreover, would be realities when—not if—Israel repented and observed all the covenant stipulations. The stipulations were not to be considered conditions; rather, they were instructions, guidelines, which when followed, would have as a consequence the full expression and fruition of those promises. Careful attention must be given to how Joel introduces a series of covenantal blessings.

The verb *wayĕqannē'* (piel form of the denominative term meaning jealous) is prefixed by a waw. There is no specific verb in the perfect that would normally call for the waw to be a waw consecutive and therefore the translation "He became jealous" would be considered correct. The context should give an indication of how the waw should be understood. The preceding verses (2:12–17) call for repentance by the entire community. There is no hint that this turning from sin to Yahweh had actually taken place. So, when one considers that the stipulations had been repeated, but not yet carried out, then the preferred interpretation is that when[43] the stipulations are met in the future, Yahweh God will rise up and exercise his ever-abiding love for his people. His love for them will go on the offensive. So the translation should be *when* Yahweh is jealous. This future sense is supported by what is promised to follow. A past translation—became jealous—should then be followed by already realized promises. And that is surely not what Joel proclaimed. Rather, his message from Yahweh was that covenantal promises would be filled by an active, jealous Lord for an obedient, worshiping, and serving people.

Six specific promises were proclaimed by Joel. Before these are discussed, the following points should be kept in mind. First, the promises refer to realities that had been made known previously by Moses and the earlier, non-writing prophets. Joel clarifies and is more specific on some of these. Second, the preaching and writing prophets succeeding him expand on these promises, as a rule in the context of what Yahweh God would do for his people, who though they may be punished in various ways, will as an obedient people, realize the fulfillment of the promises. Third, the promises are not intended to be understood as being fulfilled in a strictly chronological order. As will be discussed later, there is a historical forward movement. But a promise as it is carried out will not cease when others are being realized. For example, the influence of the poured out Spirit will not cease when wonders in the creational and spiritual realms take place.

The first great promise calls attention to the blessed truth that the sovereign Lord will continue to administer his creation covenant. He will demonstrate his covenantal faithfulness by what he does in the cosmic kingdom's natural/creational and social spheres. He *sōlēah* (active participle of *sālâh,* to send) will be continuously sending grain (staple food), new wine (refreshing beverage), and oil (a basic necessity for a balanced meal). These will be sent in such quantities that the people will be fully satisfied (2:19, 26). Joel expands on Yahweh God's goodness in supplying basic needs for daily life by extolling the great things that are done to meet people's daily natural needs (2:20b, 21). The pastures turn green, the trees and vines bear fruit (2:22). Rain falls, grain harvests fill threshing floors, and wine vats are filled (2:23, 24). All damage done by locusts Yahweh had sent will be compensated for. The people will have every reason to rejoice for what their Yahweh God does for them. Indeed, they will be convinced that Yahweh God continues to administer his creation covenant because they know *kî bĕqereb yìsrâēl 'ānî* (That I am among Israel). And *wìda 'tem* (they will know) that Yahweh is their God. The people will realize that Yahweh God does not forget the heart of his covenant, "I am your God, I am with you" (2:27).

Two more aspects of the first promise are made in this creational context, referring now to the political and social aspects of the creation covenant. The invading and pillaging army of the northern nation that Yahweh had motivated to be his agent of judgment will be pushed away to barren lands or to drown in the sea. Metaphorical language is used to describe the ruinous results of Yahweh's judgment on the enemies of his people (2:20). So, with locusts and invading armies removed, another promise can be realized, *wĕtō yĕbošû 'ammî lĕ'ôlām* (and my people not be ashamed forevermore). The covenant people had been put to shame by impoverishing conditions due to their disobedience. But a good future awaits a repentant, loving, obedient, and serving people. There will be no shame causing natural or national disasters; rather, there will be prosperity and peace as Moses had assured that a faithful covenant people would experience at the hands of, and from the heart of, a never failing, gracious, compassionate and patient cosmic King.

Note should be taken of the term *lĕ'ôlām* (forever).[44] In this context the preferred translation would be "for all time." The Hebrew term can be understood to refer to both time and eternity. Joel, in this context, is stressing that Yahweh God will not, at certain times, capriciously bring on disasters and withhold blessings, causing embarrassment for his people. The certainty of Yahweh God's goodness shown in providing the creational needs of Yahweh's people is stressed. This goodness will be present as long as time continues for a faithful covenant people.

The second great promise is specifically oriented to the spiritual sphere of life and gives reason for covenant people to be assured of their full redemption and their ability and qualification to fulfill the creational spiritual mandate. The descriptive phrase is *wĕhāyâ 'aḥărê-kēn* (and it shall be after this) (2:28 [MT 3:1]). The term *'aḥă rê* should not be understood to convey the thought that once creational blessings have come and are finished, *then* the spiritual will follow. Rather, the term in this context should be understood to say that as Yahweh God continues to administer his creation covenant in a most beneficent manner, he will initiate a greater spiritual epoch in the gracious redemptive/restorative covenant context— *'ešĕpôk 'et rûhî* (I will pour out my Spirit) (2:28 [MT 3:1]). The Spirit of Yahweh had been present and active in time before Joel's proclamation. The Spirit had been present in Joshua (Num. 27:18); Bezalel had been filled with the

Spirit (Exod. 31:3); the Spirit had come upon Balaam (Num. 24:2). The Spirit had come in power upon the anointed Saul (1 Sam. 10:10; 11:6), and then had departed from him (1 Sam. 16:14). The Spirit had come upon David as the anointed (1 Sam. 16:13) and had spoken through him as a poet (2 Sam. 23:2). The Spirit had been a power-giving, enabling, authoritative source for all these men. That the Spirit was also the source of life in creation was celebrated by the psalmist (104:30). And David knew the Spirit was the life giver for the inner man (51:11). The prophetic sons or disciples of Elijah knew of the Spirit's presence and work in Elijah (2 Kings 2:16); Elisha asked for a double portion of the Spirit, who enabled prophetic work (2:9). Considering all these references to the Spirit's presence and activities in the time of Moses, Joshua, Judges, the first kings, and non-writing prophets, one should not be surprised that Joel, speaking for Yahweh, prophesied that the Holy Spirit would not only continue to be present but would extend his presence and influence.

In studies on Joel's prophecy concerning the "outpouring of the Spirit" one can observe variations in interpretations and applications. These need not detain us here. It seems appropriate, however, to make the following explanatory statements.

The term *'ĕspōk* (pour out) conveys the thought of a large, even overwhelming coming out upon whatever object is in the context. And, in contrast to the drought (1:12, 17, 18, 20), there will be an abundance of water—not physical, natural rains but the living water of the Spirit.[45]

The phrase *'āl-kōl bāśār* (upon all flesh) is usually translated "on all people." This is correct, for Joel does not include animal life; this is readily clarified by what follows: it is people from all stratas of life, males and females, older and younger ones.

There is to be specific evidence of the fulfillment of this covenant promise concerning the outpouring of the Spirit. Sons and daughters *nibbĕ'û* (will prophesy). We are again confronted by the connotation and denotation of the term *prophesy.*[46] A careful study of the prophetic phenomenon as recorded in Scripture leads to the conclusion that various levels or intensities of prophetic activity are referred to. And the context of these references gives insight into what type (level or intensity) is referred to. King Saul is said to have prophesied when he was met and included in a group of prophets (1 Sam. 10:10). No specific message was proclaimed; no new message was given. Such had been the case when Moses had, in obedience to Yahweh, consecrated seventy leading elders to be his assistants in hearing and solving disputes among the people (Num. 11:16, 17). These men were to receive the Spirit as Moses had; he had given evidence of the Spirit's presence in his life by proclaiming Yahweh's will for the people. These seventy on whom the Spirit came joined Moses in prophesying (11:25) but joined him only on that day. It would seem obvious that these seventy men joined Moses by repeating what he said and did. Thus these men[47] were confirmed before the people as Moses' qualified assistants.

A further point to be noted is that Moses expressed the desire that all the people of Yahweh were prophets, that is, that they as the seventy elders would repeat, teach, and apply the will of Yahweh God to all areas of life, specifically to areas in which differences existed. Thus, as has been noted by others, Joel prophesies that which Moses had wished would indeed become a reality.[48] Peter, on the day of Pentecost, when he heard the people on whom the Spirit had come declaring the wonders of God, preached that Moses' desire and Joel's prophecy was being fulfilled (Acts 2:11, 16–21).

Joel also referred to old men dreaming dreams and young men seeing visions. Revelation from Yahweh was given at times by dreams and visions. So Yahweh had said when Aaron and Miriam had challenged Moses (Num. 12:1–6). For those who would have women and men be equal in prophetic activity, it should be noted that it is said that old and young men would dream and see visions. The text says that all dreams and visions were channels of revelation. The common experience of dreams and visions could be and was used at times by Yahweh God to give revelation. And it can be said that during Old Testament times, young and older men received revelation from Yahweh. Ezekiel and Daniel were young men. Haggai was older. Thus in Old Testament times, subsequent to Joel's time, this prophecy was fulfilled. What must not be overlooked, however, is that a great, even radical change would take place among God's covenant people. They would become Spirit filled, qualified, and activated, particularly in regard to the communication of Yahweh God's revealed will and truth.[49]

The third great covenantal promise Joel proclaimed referred to what was to be expected, concomitant with the outpouring of the Spirit, in the entire domain of the cosmic kingdom. First mentioned is *wĕnātatû môpĕtîm* (And I will give [or set, cause to happen] wonders) in the heavens and on the earth. Fire, smoke, blood, the darkening of the sun, and the reddening of the moon are referred to as the God-induced wonders in creation (2:30, 31 [MT 3:4, 5]). How literally these references are to be taken can be debated; what must be accepted is that as Jesus himself said, great, unexpected, awe-inspiring phenomena will take place in future eras—not only in the sphere of nature, where Yahweh God administers his creation covenant. There will be wonders in the social and spiritual dimensions of life as well. The miracle of regeneration will become widespread. This will be evidenced by the calling on the name of Yahweh and the giving of salvation to whomsoever calls. Indeed, there will be *pĕlêtâ* (escape) (2:32), a term used when situations of insecurity, disaster, threats of destruction, and death existed. The term can be translated "deliverance" or "salvation" when the dire circumstances in which people existed are removed. Indeed, this deliverance for salvation is to be experienced in the totality of life, not merely for "the soul" or the spiritual aspect of humanity. There will be great cosmic events as redemption and restoration are worked through Yahweh God's administration of the covenant of grace strand of his all-encompassing creation/redemption/restoration covenant.

The fourth great covenantal promise, which later prophets expand on, is the return of covenant people who have been exiled. Yahweh will restore the fortunes (or exile) of Judah and Jerusalem (3:1 [MT 4:1]). Here there is reference to the return from exile after the seventy years of captivity. But Joel refers to other returns also, as Moses had done centuries before (Deut. 30:3–5). Moses had, as Joel, proclaimed a return to the Lord as a prerequisite for this return (30:2). Various nations had invaded Israel and Judah during the period they existed as a monarchy. Tyrians, Sidonians, Philistines, Ionians, and Sabaens are referred to as having captured, enslaved, and maltreated people, young as well as old, from Israel and Judah (3:2b–6 [MT 4:2b–6]). Consider, for example, the Israelite maiden in Naaman's home (2 Kings 5:2). Before the exile took place in 722 (Israel) and 586 (Judah), captives would be returned at various times and in various circumstances. Joel proclaims that Yahweh God does not forget those of his people who have been taken from their homeland. A return could be expected from the earlier exiles as well as from the seventy-year exile later.[50]

The fifth great covenantal promise that Joel proclaimed was the judgment on nations that attacked, exiled, and victimized Yahweh God's covenant people (3:2, 4–6 [MT 4:2, 4–6]; 3:12, 13 [4:12, 13]). Moses had commanded Joshua and the people to exterminate the various Canaanite nations whose cup of iniquity was full (Deut. 7:1, 2). Moses had promised the defeat of enemies (28:7). David, the faithful covenant regal servant, had defeated the invading and afflicting nations and had incorporated them under his reign, thus extending the Israelite domain from the river of Egypt in the south to the great river Euphrates in the north (2 Sam. 8). Thus Yahweh God's promise to Abraham had been fulfilled (Gen. 15:18). David's son Solomon reigned over that entire area (1 Kings 4:21). Joel prophesies that when the covenant people call upon Yahweh's name, receive salvation, and are delivered from enemy nations, some people from these nations would also be included, as had been the situation during the later reign of David and the first years of the reign of Solomon. Later prophets, however, emphatically repeated and expanded on the reality of the promise, as well as the sure fulfillment of it, namely, that enemy nations would be judged[51] and punished; some would be removed[52] and members brought into the covenant community. (A study of the writing prophets will include further reference to this prophecy of Joel.)

The sixth great covenantal promise Joel proclaimed was the assurance of peace. To properly understand Joel's prophecy of universal peace one must consider what Yahweh would o for and among the nations. The fifth promise was that the nations were to receive their punishment (see preceding paragraph). Joel proceeded to proclaim that Yahweh God's people were to be agents of punishment. They were called to turn tools used for gainful labor, plowshares and pruning hooks, into weapons for war. They were to confidently realize their strength (3:9, 10 [4:9, 10]). The nations were to be challenged to assemble and as such receive a due reward for their wickedness. What the assembled nations were to experience is expressed in metaphorical terms taken from agricultural scenes; "swing the sickle . . . trample the grapes" (3:11–13 [MT 4:11–13]).[53] When this judgment takes place, people will be confronted by alternatives. But the outcome will be certain, for Yahweh will roar (metaphor again) as all creation responds to his judging activities (3:14–16a [MT 4:1416a]). These events will be harbingers of the promised peace.

Joel stated it succinctly: *wayĕwâh mahăseh lĕ'ammô wûmă'ôz libēnē yśrāēl* (And Yahweh will be a place of shelter, a refuge for his people and a means of protection [stronghold NIV] for the sons of Israel 3:16b [MT 4:16b]).

Joel then proceeded in metaphorical terms taken again from an agricultural scene—wine, milk, water, in settings of fertile mountainsides, verdant hills, and well-watered valleys (3:18 [MT 4:18])—to present the blessed fulfillment when Yahweh ushers in his reign of peace. Notice again how the creational and redemptive/restorative are integrated into one blessed scene.

Joel added a binary presentation to emphasize the peaceful environment. Egypt and Edom (two bothersome nations at that time, 800 B.C.), representing the parasite satanic kingdom, would be desolate and desert-like but Judah and Jerusalem, representing God's people in a renewed setting, would be settled *lĕ' ôlām* (for all time). They would be a forgiven and pardoned people (3:20, 21 [MT 4:20, 21]) who would know that Yahweh God is King indeed; his residence/throne is Jerusalem, used symbolically to refer to his throne from which Yahweh will reign over his entire cosmic kingdom.

Joel thus concluded his prophecy climactically by emphasizing that Yahweh God was firmly established on his throne, was reigning sovereignly over his cosmic kingdom, and was fulfilling all his promises as he administered it by and according to his creation/redemptive/restorative covenant. Indeed, Yahweh reigns and his covenant is abiding. It will continue throughout all of time.

The Mediatorial Role

We have presented the concept of the Golden Cable in the introductory comments above. It consists of three unifying, integrating strands: the kingdom (which includes the king, throne, reign, and domain), the covenant in its creational/redemptive/restorative entirety, and the mediatorial covenant agent. The question before us in our study of Joel is: Does he proclaim the mediator, that is, the Messiah concerning whom prophetic promises had been given, who was typified by ancestors, other persons, and phenomena such as objects, the tabernacle, the temple, sacrifices, and various great events (the Passover experience and the exodus)?

In my book, *Messianic Revelation in the Old Testament,* I made seven concluding statements. The sixth summary statement is: "There is no direct reference to a personal royal Messiah." That means that Joel did not refer to the narrow view of the Messiah, his royal person. But Joel's prophecy is definitely messianic in the broad view;[54] this includes the giving of specific covenantal blessings and the executing of judgment on covenant breakers and enemies of Yahweh's covenant people. Moses had intimated, Yahweh had promised David, and later prophets clearly and definitely would proclaim that Yahweh's appointed royal agent, the Messiah, would bring in blessedness for Yahweh's people and judgment on all enemies. Indeed, the agent to perform Yahweh's redemptive, judging, and restoring work would be none other than his Anointed One and only Son who was repeatedly promised and typified.

The Historical and Eschatological Perspectives

Joel, the prophet, proclaimed his God-given message within the course of the history of Israel and Judah. He did not indicate whether he was addressing both Israel and Judah directly, but he did objectively refer to both of them by name, Israel (2:27; 3:2 [MT 4:2] and Judah (3:1, 6, 18, 20 [MT 4: 1, 6, 18, 20]). He referred to Jerusalem (3:1, 16, 17, 20 [MT 4:1, 16, 17, 20]). He addressed the people of Zion directly once (2:23) and referred to Zion objectively also (2:1, 15, 32 [MT 3:32]; 3:16, 17, 21 [MT 4:16, 17, 21]). He made reference to the "house of God" (1:14, 16) and spoke to the priests directly (1:13) and of them indirectly (2:17). It seems correct to conclude that Joel was mostly in the area of Judah and Jerusalem. Israel to the north was definitely included in his prophecies, but whether he was actually in its land cannot be said with certainty. The point to be emphasized is that Joel gives sufficient evidence that he lived among the people and was well acquainted with the natural, national, social, and spiritual circumstances of both nations and their neighbors. He was an alert contemporary man; he was historically conscious.

Joel, however was also led by Yahweh God to prophesy from a retrospective vantage point. The covenant people had a past in which Yahweh God had been good to them; they had their land, their central city, their prescription and means for God-honoring worship and service. He called attention to recent, and probably still contemporary, difficult agricultural and economic circumstances. He made it very clear that what had taken place in the past and possibly was happening in the present was determined, directed, and controlled by Yahweh God, who was displeased with his people's responses to him. But, gracious, merciful, patient Yahweh god called the people to repentance and God-honoring worship. The people were assured that Yahweh God loved them then and there in their inherited land. He would demonstrate that love (be jealous), to a repentant, worshiping, and serving people. And what the people did in their contemporary historical circumstances, and continued to do in the future, would influence what would happen in the future.[55] Indeed, Yahweh God was reigning sovereignly, but so doing, he would interact with his people and the nations and deal with them in their historical situation in accordance with attitudes and activities in relation to Yahweh God. The curse of the covenant had been, was, and would continue to be a tragic reality in the lives of disobedient and rebellious people. The promises of continuity of covenant blessings and ever-increasing evidences of Yahweh God's faithfulness stood firm. These would definitely be realities in the lives of a faithful people and their instructed and faithful children. Yahweh God's ways and purposes had been made clear within the past historical processes and would so continue.

Joel's main emphases, after he had referred to the calamities and had uttered the call to repentance, was on the future. He was given a message that would cause people listening to have confidence in the present and hope for the future. They were assured that Yahweh God was moving forward. He was not going to control a cyclical future, that is, that what was, would come again. Yahweh God had a plan, a goal, namely, the coming of the Messiah and the eventual consummation of his cosmic kingdom through the ministry and reign of the Messiah, the administering agent of the covenant. Yahweh God would ever be moving forward; and in this forward movement within the crucible of historical phenomena and events, the curse of the covenant would be executed again, in accordance with whatever the prevailing circumstances might be. But there would be no return to the past. Yahweh God would march on, ever intent on achieving the purpose and the goals of his kingdom according to his covenant means and plan. The very heart of Yahweh God's goal was to usher in the renewed heaven and earth in which his covenant people would realize the completeness, the fullness, the richness, the wonder of covenant promises and kingdom life.[56]

Joel spells out what the main aspects of this covenant kingdom future encompass. He presented an eschatologically oriented future that would unfold in the course of time and history. Each aspect had an enduring, continuing presence and influence. All aspects would not be introduced simultaneously; each newly introduced one would flow forth from or depend on what had been introduced. We have referred to these aspects as covenant promises—and such they are. And Yahweh's promises, correctly understood, will certainly become historical realities with eternal consequences. The following figure illustrates Joel's proclamation of events and realities that Yahweh God includes in his covenantal administration as he moves forward to the attaining of the full realization of his cosmic kingdom.

Covenant of creation continues to be administered and is the context for all other events.

Nations will be sovereignly ruled and dealt with according to their attitudes and activities toward Yahweh and his people.

Six Future Events

Great wonders will be wrought in the heavens and on earth.
The Holy Spirit will be poured out on all flesh.
People calling on Yahweh will be saved.
People of all nations will be brought to the valley of judgment as the gospel is preached to all nations.
Yahweh God's presence among his worshiping, serving people will be increasingly realized.
The consummated cosmic kingdom of Yahweh God.

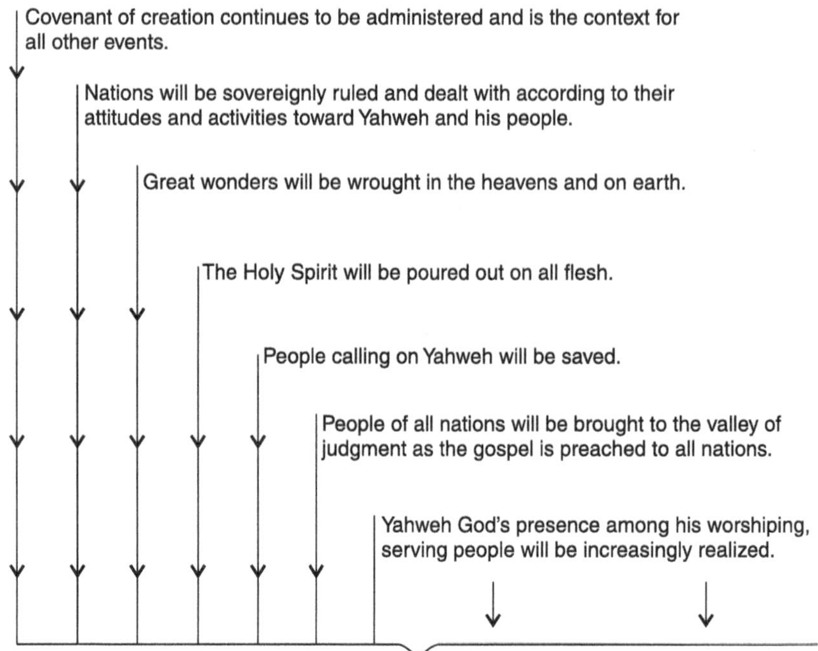

The figure (no figure perfectly presents reality) should not be understood to set forth a specific chronological order, as if each aspect of Yahweh God's ever unfolding plan begins at a certain point in history. It is true that some are indicated in the New Testament as specifically fulfilled. The Holy Spirit was poured out at a specific point in the historical process. People, however, had been calling on god before Pentecost, but a more widespread and effective calling on God was promised after the pentecostal outpouring. So also, nations had been and would continually be dealt with by the reigning Lord. In future times this phenomenon would be more evident, as Daniel recorded some centuries later.

All the promises Joel proclaimed as sure future historical events are to be understood as factors in Yahweh God's ever-present kingdom over which he reigned sovereignly. And these historical kingdom events are to be understood as leading up to and introducing the full realization of Yahweh God's consummated kingdom. What must be clearly understood, however, is that Joel spoke of the Day of Yahweh in terms of contemporary known objects and events.[57] He is not to be understood as prophesying a literal realization of all descriptions and all events. New wine would not actually drip from mountains, nor would the hills literally flow with milk, nor would a fountain in the temple, its size not given but portrayed as large, actually produce so much flowing water it would make a valley of trees fertile (3:18 [MT 4:18]).[58] Joel presented a scene of the consummated cosmic kingdom in terms of gloriously idealistic objects, situations, and events that people of his day could relate to and yet realize they were unattainable in literal, everyday experiences.

Prophets, coming after Joel, were called and equipped by Yahweh God and his Spirit to repeat, amplify, and apply the promises of great things to come that Joel outlined in his prophetic agenda. To be kept in mind is this important reality: Joel prophesied of Yahweh God's covenantal administration of his all-inclusive cosmic kingdom. He in no was intimates that the Israelite monarchy is to be re-instituted in any shape or for any reason before or in the Great Day of the Lord when all Yahweh God's purposes are fully realized.

I have posited the view that Joel proclaimed an agenda for the prophets following him. He prophesied concerning the three strands of the Golden Cable: the cosmic kingdom, the creational/redemptive/restorative covenant, and the mediatorial covenant agent. Sub-themes that developed these strands of the Golden Cable, whether expressed as historical realities, past, present, or future, or stipulations, or promises, or assurances of blessings, or proclamations of the curse, are as follows:

1. Warnings of local, national, cosmic disasters.
2. Calls to repentance, obedience, and trust.
3. Assurances of Yahweh God's zealous love.
4. Abundant blessings in the creational/natural realm.
5. The coming and presence of the Spirit.
6. The renewing of the people and calling on Yahweh.
7. The return and gathering of the covenant people.
8. Judgment on the nations and the inclusion of members of these in Yahweh's people.
9. Assurance of peace.
10. Jerusalem, visited but spared, the symbol of Yahweh's presence, throne, reign; a symbol of the kingdom.
11. Water, living and constant, flowing from the temple in Jerusalem.
12. The Day of Yahweh, with all that it includes.

NOTES

1. The reader is advised to consult what has been written in my book, *Messianic Revelation in the Old Testament* (Grand Rapids: Baker, 1990) under the headings "Prelude" and "An Overview of Prophetic Activity," 414–20. Attention should also be directed to the bibliographical references in notes 1–13. In this study references may be made to views held by some of those authors, but not to all of them.

2. Robert Martin-Achard, *A Light to the Nations,* trans. John P. Smith (Edinburgh: Oliver and Boyd, 1962), 9, 12.

3. C. F. Whitley, *The Prophetic Achievement* (London: Mowbry, 1963), 20.

4. Curt Kuhl, *The Prophets of Israel,* trans. Rudolph J. Ehrlich and John P. Smith (Richmond: John Knox, 1960), 24–28.

5. Abraham Heschel, *The Prophets* (New York: Harper and Row, 1962), xii–xvi.

6. Walther Eichrodt, *Theology of the Old Testament,* vol. 1, trans. J. A. Baker (Philadelphia: Westminster, 1961), 309–53. Gerhard Von Rad's view is similar to that of Eichrodt; cf. his *Old Testament Theology,* vol. 22, trans. D.M.G. Stalker (Edinburgh: Oliver and Boyd, 1965), 6–14.

7. See "Foreword" by Gene M. Tucker in the English translation by H. C. White, *Basic Forms of Prophetic Speech* (Louisville: Westminster/John Knox, 1991), ix–xv. This work first appeared in German in 1960.

8. J. Lindblom, *Prophecy in Ancient Israel* (Oxford: Basil Blackwell, 1962), 108–22. Consider what Lindblom wrote: "The prophets spoke of the divine power of the word, a modern psychologist speaks of suggestion" (115).

9. Robert R. Wilson, "Early Israelite Prophecy," in *Interpreting the Prophets,* ed. James L. Mays and Paul J. Achtemeier (Philadelphia: Fortress, 1987), 1.

10. James L. Mays, in the "Foreword," ibid., ix.

11. Brevard S. Childs, *Biblical Theology of the Old and New Testaments* (Minneapolis: Fortress, 1993), 167–69.

12. Childs also expressed some disagreements with his "esteemed teacher." See, for example, 102; but more often agreement, 110, 115, 122, etc.

13. William Sanford Lasor, "The Prophets During the Monarchy," in *Israel's Apostasy and Restoration* (Grand Rapids: Baker, 1988), 61, 64, 67.

14. Willem Van Gemeren, *Interpreting the Prophetic Word* (Grand Rapids: Zondervan, 1990), 43–45.

15. Richard D. Patterson, "Joel," in *The Expositor's Bible Commentary,* ed. Frank F. Gabelein, 12 vols. (Grand Rapids: Zondervan, 1985), 7:230–34.

16. Gerhardus Vos, *Biblical Theology* (Grand Rapids: Eerdmans, 11th printing, 1980), 216–28.

17. See, for example, Van Gemeren, *Interpreting,* 245–55.

18. It is of interest to pay attention to what Lasor wrote: the nonwriting prophets spoke predominantly to individuals (leaders and kings); the classical prophets as a rule addressed the community. Lasor, "The Prophets," 59.

19. See Gerard Van Groningen, *From Creation to Consummation,* vol. 1 (Sioux Center: Dordt, 1996), chap. 8, part II.

20. See Eichrodt's comments concerning the pervasive presence of the covenant even if the term is not always present. *Theology,* 1:14, 36, 51. For a recent writer who took issue with Eichrodt, and others who agree with his view, see John Stek, "Covenant Overload in Reformed Theology," *Calvin Theological Journal* 29 (April 1994): 12–41. Stek accepted the view of critical scholars who eviscerate the covenant concept and divide its reference to various initial local pagan constructions as models for the biblical covenant.

21. Dispensational theologians are increasingly addressing the issues. See, for example, J. Dwight Pentecost, *Thy Kingdom Come* (Wheaton: Victor, 1990). See index of subjects for numerous references to the Abrahamic, Mosaic, and land covenants. Also see John H. Walton, *Covenant God's Purpose God's Plan* (Grand Rapids: Zondervan, 1994). Walton limits covenant to God's use of it as a means of revelation. Chap. 2, 24–45.

22. Cf. note 1 above.

23. Studies in prophetic interpretation that have influenced my study and research are many and varied. The following have been helpful in various ways (listed in the chronological order in which I consulted them). G. Vos, *Biblical Theology;* Marten J. Wyngaarden, *The Future of the Kingdom in Prophecy and Fulfilment,* initially as a private study, produced in 1934, later published (Grand Rapids: Baker, 1955); Patrick Fairbairn, *The Interpretation of Prophecy,* first published in 1856 in Edinburgh, reprinted (London: The Banner of Truth Trust, 1964); Philip E. Hughes, *Interpreting Prophecy* (Grand Rapids: Eerdmans, 1976); Hans K. LaRondelle, *The Israel of God in Prophecy: Principles of Prophetic Interpretation* (Berrien Springs: Andrews University Press, 1983); Carl D. Amerding and W. Ward Gasque, *A Guide to Biblical Prophecy* (Peabody: Hendrickson, 1989); Walter C. Kaiser, Jr., *Back Toward the Future: Hints for Interpreting Biblical Prophecy* (Grand Rapids: Baker, 1989); Willem Van Gemeren, *Interpreting.* Various commentaries, referred to in notes, as well as specific studies in the prophets and biblical-theological studies (referred to in previous notes) have been helpful to me in varying degrees.

24. While insights can be garnered from a work such as Westermann's *Basic Forms,* it has not been too helpful in many instances in determining what the specific and precise message by a certain prophet in a given situation was. Recently developed methods of exegesis, for example, various types of structural exegesis, rhetorical, or narrative, have given some assistance in certain situations. Consider, for example, how some adherents to dispensationalism have come to realize that the "plain and clear meaning" of a text or passage of Scripture is not derived from a rigid and closed system of grammatical-historical and theological exegesis and/or hermeneutic. Craig A. Blaising, Darrell L. Bock, and other dispensational writers have indicated that recent developments in hermeneutics and literary studies have impelled them to move from classical to revised and on to progressive dispensationalism. See Craig A. Blaising and Darrell L. Bock, *Progressive Dispensationalism* (Wheaton: Bridge Point, 1993), esp. chaps. 2, 3, 57–105. Cf. also *Dispensationalism, Israel and the Church,* ed. Craig A. Blaising and Darrell L. Bock (Grand Rapids: Zondervan, 1992), 30–34, 380, 392–93.

25. See BDB, 222, col. 1. Ebenezer Henderson in *The Twelve Minor Prophets,* reprint (Grand Rapids: Baker, 1980), referred to Jerome's incorrect understanding of the name as meaning "to begin" (92). His preference for the meaning of "begin" could relate to his thinking of Joel as the first of the classical writing prophets.

26. George A. Smith wrote that 'In the history of prophecy, the Book of Joel must be either very early or very late," before 800 B.C. or after 500 B.C. in "The Book of Joel," in *The Expositor's Bible,* ed. W. Robertson Nicole, 6 vols. (Grand Rapids: Eerdmans, 1947), 7:651. Evangelical conservative scholars remain divided on when Joel prophesied. Van Gemeren opted for a late date (*Interpreting*, 120), as did Raymond B. Dillard in "Joel," in *The Minor Prophets*, ed. Thomas E. McComiskey, (Grand Rapids: Baker, 1992), 240–43. See Dillard's listing of dates suggested by various scholars and see also the extensive bibliography on Joel he produced.

27. *Messianic Revelation*, 443–44. Richard D. Patterson, *Joel,* also opted for the earlier date (231–33). Dillard indicates that scholars such as Gerhard C. Aalders, Edward J. Young, and M. Bic also preferred the earlier time, that is, in the ninth-century period of King Joash in Judah. Ibid., 242.

28. C. Von Orelli, for example, wrote that Ezekiel (30:2) was unmistakably dependent on Joel 1:15; 2:1 and Jeremiah (25:30) on Joel 4:11, 16. *The Twelve Minor Prophets,* trans. J. S. Banks, reprint (Minneapolis: Klock & Klock, 1977), 76.

29. Joel's reference to the Greeks (Ionians) (3:6 [MT 4:6]) is believed to be a crucial point in favor of a late date. The Greeks rose to international prominence circa 400 B.C., one hundred years after the date preferred by Dillard and others. But it is known that the Greeks (Ionians) were trading with Phoenicians already in the tenth century B.C. Hence the merchants of Tyre and Sidon could have captured Israelites and sold them to the Greeks as early as the eighth and ninth centuries B.C.

30. Dillard gave a review of various explanations of the agreements in phraseology and concepts between Joel and other prophets: (1) Joel is made up of previous revelation; (2) Joel had an impact on later prophets; (3) Joel used common stock of prophetic idiom, not being dependent on others; (4) each citation must be evaluated in its given circumstances. "Joel," 241. My preference allows for combining explanations 2, 3, and 4.

31. George L. Robinson expressed appreciation for Joel's originality and style in *The Twelve Minor Prophets*, (Grand Rapids: Baker, 1952), 37, 43.

32. See Dillard, "Joel," 243–44. Van Gemeren referred to the possibility of Joel including lament, but seems to opt for an expression of the authenticity of hope (*Interpreting*, 121, 469) (note 65). Douglas Stuart is specific; he entitled the first part orf Joel's prophecy a lament in "Hosea–Jonah," in *Word Biblical Commentary,* vol. 31, ed. David A. Hubbard and Glenn Barker (Waco: Word, 1987), 236. Hans W. Wolff also wrote of an original liturgical lamentation that in the course of transmission to later generations took on the proclivity of sapiential/didactic literature. *Joel and Amos,* trans. S. D. McBride, Jr. (Philadelphia: Fortress, 1977), 9.

33. Dillard, "Joel," 255.

34. Some recent writers have not given sufficient attention, if any, to this call to instruct the children. This is most likely due to the emphasis on Joel's initial proclamation as a lament. Wolff tried to combine the lament with a later instructional character (see note 32 above). Thomas Finley was correct in stating "The Book of Joel has a didactic function." *Joel, Amos, Obadiah,* in *The Wycliffe Exegetical Commentary,* ed. K. Barker (Chicago: Moody, 1990), 19.

35. See my discussion of the theocracy in *From Creation to Consummation,* vol. 1, ibid, chap. 12, part I.

36. The debate concerning whether a second locust invasion was envisaged or not can be found in most commentaries.

37. These future events are discussed more fully in following sections ("Covenantal Administration" and "Eschatological Perspectives").

38. See note 20 above.

39. Wolff posited the Day of Yahweh as Joel's major theological theme. *Joel and Amos,* 12. It seems preferable to say that the Day of Yahweh is presented as the great climactic event in Yahweh's covenantal administration of his cosmic kingdom. Finley attempted to be metaphorical in his statement summing up Joel's message: "two wheels turning on an axle. The wheels are history and eschatology, while the axle is the Day of the Lord." *Joel,* 12. He should have added, the entire cart or wagon is the cosmic kingdom of God and it consists of and is driven by Yahweh's all-inclusive administrative covenant(s).

40. Stuart has correctly stated that Joel is reminding his audience that it is Yahweh and not just any God who is dealing with them. *Hosea-Jonah,* 252.

41. Patterson, commenting on 1:9, points out that priests were mourning because the elements necessary for sacrifice were not coming in from the wasted fields. "Joel," 240. The priests should have been mourning for the sins of the people as they were called to do (Joel 2:17).

42. Theo Laetsch explained Yahweh's demand succinctly. "Be not satisfied with rending your garment with outward symbols and actions, rend, tear, your heart, that deceitful and desperately wicked thing (Jer. 17:9)." *The Minor Prophets* (St. Louis: Concordia, 1956), 121.

43. See Van Gemeren, *Interpreting,* 127. While Van Gemeren is correct in preferring the term *when,* it does not follow, as Dillard has pointed out, that no promise will be fulfilled until after Pentecost. "Joel," 294.

44. The term *lĕ'ôlām* is explained as "No, never again" by Patterson, "Joel," 254. Wolff's comment indicates an "open end" understanding: "v. 27b clearly points to the future." *Joel and Amos,* 65.

45. See Dillard, "Joel," 294.

46. See my classification of types or levels of biblical prophecy, in *Messianic Revelation,* 416–20.

47. Cf. Gerard Van Groningen, "The Sons of the Prophets," *Vox Reformata,* 33 (1979): 23–36.

48. God is going to answer Moses' precepts . . . all Yahweh's people will become prophets. Cf. Dillard, "Joel," 294.

49. The Spirit to be poured on all flesh is to be understood as more than vital power as Wolff intimates in the phrase "Spirit as vital power is on principle the opposite of the feebleness of flesh." *Joel and Amos,* 66. It should not be denied that the Spirit is "empowering."

50. The relevance of this promise for New Testament and contemporary times will be discussed in section E below.

51. Dillard correctly pointed out that the verb *wĕnispottî* from *šāpaṭ* (he judges) appears in the niphal, which "is commonly used in the sense of entering into a judicial proceeding." "Joel," 301.

52. Joel proclaimed that *kōl-haggoîm* (all nations) would be gathered and brought to the valley of *yĕhôšāpàt* (Jehoshaphat). Commentators have discussed which valley would be referred to: Berecah (2 Chron. 20:26) or the Tyropean Valley, just southwest of the temple mount, or the Kidron Valley. Cf. Dillard, ibid., 300–301. It should be noted that there is reference to the valley again in 3:14 [4:14] and it is referred to there twice as *'āmeq heḥārû`s* (the valley of strict decision [BDB, 358]). The term implies judgment rendered. No Valley by that name is known to exist. The name *Jehoshaphat* is derived from a combination of *Yĕhwâ* and *sapāt* (*yĕhwâ* judges). It suggests *Yĕhwâ* pronounced and executed such a valley. It is preferrable to consider the phrase Valley of Jehosphat, Valley of Strict Decision as a metaphor, drawn from a creational and juridical combined setting. The point is: the time and reality of divine judgment on nations is sure to come wherever Yahweh God determines to carry it out as the text (Joel 3:12 [MT 4:12]) states explicitly: "there I will sit to judge all nations on every side" (NIV).

53. Grain was raised in valleys and grapes on the slopes to the valley. Hence the throught of metaphorical language for the valley of Jehoshaphat is supported.

54. Cf. *Messianic Revelation,* 13. See also my discussion of the phrase *'et hammôreh liṣĕdāqâ* (Joel 2:17), translated as "rains in righteousness" (NIV). My conclusion is that "teacher of righteousness" as found in the Dead Sea Scrolls is the preferred translation, 448.

55. Many commentators and biblical theologians correctly understand that Joel was eschatologically oriented. But to say he was predominantly so, is to overstate the case. And the attempt to find future historical fulfillment for Israel as a nation, though repeatedly done, does not result in interpretations and applications that can be accepted with confidence. See, for example, the literal expectations of Charles L. Feinberg, *The Minor Prophets* (Chicago:

Moody, 1948). He wrote of increased rain (cf. Joel 2:23) which he took literally, as falling in recent times but will have grand fulfillment in the future when Israel as a re-gathered nation turnes to the Lord (80). Feinberg, however, considers the outpouring of the Holy Spirit on Pentecost (Acts 2) to be, not a fulfillment, but a pre-filling (82). Robert L. Saucy, considering himself a progressive dispensationalist, to be distinguished from Feinberg as a historic dispensationalist, accepts the position that Pentecost was the fulfillment of Joel's prophecy. Cf. Robert L. Saucy, *The Case for Progressive Dispensationalism* (Grand Rapids: Zondervan, 1993), 178–79.

56. Further study and discussion are certainly required before one could accept Saucy's understanding of Joel 3:17 that Israel as a nation still has a glorious future (248).

57. It is to be doubted that Joel prophesied concerning two distinct, separate "Days of the Lord." Cf. Blaising, *Progressive Dispensationalism,* 294. Blaising acknowledges an interconnection between the terms and themes of Joel's references to the Day of the Lord (Joel 1:15 and Joel 3:14 [MT 4:14]). If Blaising were consistent, he would refer to a third distinct Day of the Lord (2:11). The first time Joel uses the phrase is in the context of the locust plague; the second time is in the context of nations plundering the earth; the third is in an eschatological context. One should not consider these as unconnected and unrelated Days of Yahweh. Rather the first is a metaphorical illustration of the second and the second is a harbinger, a foretaste, of the final Day of Yahweh.

58. Cf. Ezekiel's expanded description of this stream of living water coming from the temple, 47:1–12.

20

Amos and Hosea

Prophets to Israel in the North

Part I: Amos

I. Introductory Comments

II. Israel: Covenant Breakers

III. The Golden Cable

IV. The Eschatological Perspective

Part II: Hosea

I. Introductory Comments

II. Hosea and Gomer, Chapters 1–3

III. Israel: The Prostituting Wife

IV. The Golden Cable

V. Hosea's Eschatology

20

Amos and Hosea

Prophets to Israel in the North

AMOS

Introductory Comments

Amos the Man

Biblical scholars agree that a man by the name of Amos lived and spoke prophetic messages to the people of Israel. It is also agreed that he mainly addressed the leaders and trendsetters in Israel's society. Amos identified himself as *bannōqĕdîm (*one among the sheep raisers) who lived in the area of Tekoa, a small town south of Bethlehem and Jerusalem (1:1). He also made it clear that as a sheep raiser, as a *bôqēr* (herdsman), and as a *bôlem siqĕmîm* (gatherer of figs or a tender of sycamore trees, possibly a type of fig) he was *lò'nābî'. . . wĕ ben nābî'* (not a prophet or a son of a prophet) (7:14). He did, however, intimate that he was aware that he was in a real sense a prophet because he states that he was commanded by Yahweh to go prophesy to *ammî yiśrāēl* (my people Israel). He also made it clear that he had no choice; he had to obey because as a lion roars when it has its prey (3:4), so when Yahweh speaks, he must prophesy. Hence, while not a professional prophet, a member of some guild or group, he is called to be Yahweh's prophetic spokesman.

Further attestation to Amos's prophetic calling and service as a prophet are the visions he received. He wrote that he *ḥāzā* (saw by vision) the words he was to speak (1:1). On four more occasions he saw or was caused to see the message he had to proclaim. The verb *hīs'anî* (hiph. pf. of *rā'â* to see) was used to express the reality that Amos received by vision the messages he was called to proclaim (7:1, 4, 7; 8:1; cf. also 9:1). And as other prophets did before and after him, he became an intercessor on behalf of the people to whom he was not related by tribe or nation (7:3, 5).[1]

The Book

The nine chapters that make up the prophetic book of Amos do not give the impression that Amos proclaimed the material at one time. Nor does a careful study of the text lead to the conclusion that the book is an assortment of short statements, fragments of messages, poems, or prayers. One may add that Amos, possibly on a number of tours into the southern part of Israel to dress sycamore/fig trees and/or to sell the wool of the specific kind of sheep he raised, observed the social, cultural, and spiritual situations there and in that context Yahweh called him to prophesy. His messages, then, given over a period of a few years, were written most likely by Amos himself, or it is possible he had a companion who served as a scribe. So, while the content of the book consists of a series of messages, the themes and style of presentation give strong evidence that there was one author of this unified and integrated prophetic proclamation.[2]

The Times

Amos gave specific information as to the time that he lived and prophesied (1:1). Uzziah was king in Judah; most historians believe 792–740 B.C. are the dates of his reign. Jeroboam II reigned from 793 until 753. Since the dates of earthquakes were not recorded by seismologists as in contemporary times, it is difficult to determine precisely when during the reigns of these two kings Amos began to prophesy.

Jeroboam II, king of Israel, had become militarily strong and therefore succeeded in restoring the boundaries of Israel. Jonah, the prophet, son of Amittai, had prophesied previously that this would become a reality (2 Kings 14:25–28). Elisha had referred to this military success also. The enemy was Syria (Aram) (2 Kings 13:17). Jeroboam was recorded as being Yahweh God's agent to deliver His covenant people from the bitter suffering afflicted on them by the Syrians.

Along with military successes and restoration of tribal properties came material prosperity.[3] Amos made it very clear that this was a reality for many of the Israelites. He spoke of summer and winter houses, of homes adorned with ivory and mansions (3:15; 5:11; 6:4). The women of Samaria had their drinks (4:1); many had gardens, vineyards, and orchards that produced abundantly (4:9; 5:11). They had plenty of materials to bring the required sacrifices (4:4, 5; 5:22). They had their songs and harps (5:23; 6:5) and tables laden with rich foods (6:4, 6) and feasts (6:7). Power and wealth did not bring social justice and cultural advantages to all the people. All the people suffered, in various ways, from spiritual deterioration and corruption. Israel, as a nation, did not live and serve as a covenant people.

Israel: Covenant Breakers

Amos did not use the term *bĕrît* except to refer to a treaty between Tyre and Israel (1:9). That Yahweh's covenant with Israel, as confirmed at Sinai, provides the framework of Amos' prophecy and the basis for Yahweh's judgments against Israel is very evident as one studies the message of Amos.

Israel in the Midst of the Nations

It is not accidental nor purposeless that Amos began his prophecy with two dominant emphases. First, *yĕhwâ messiyyôn yisʾâg* (Yahweh from Zion roars) (1:2). Yahweh, who had spoken from the midst of the fire, thunder, and smoke from Sinai when he confirmed his covenant with Israel (Exod. 19:4–6) was now metaphorically enthroned in the city of David, where the Davidic throne was set, and in Jerusalem where his symbolic throne, the ark of the covenant, resided. Although Israel had been separated from Judah and was no longer under the political rule of the Davidic dynasty, Yahweh as covenant Lord continued to remind Israel that he was their covenant God and Master. He had not withdrawn his covenant prerogatives over them. He continued to claim them as his precious possession, his kingdom, his priestly people, his holy nation. Amos cleverly alluded to these realities as he developed his prophecy.

Having announced that Yahweh has a message for Israel to hear, Amos prophesies judgment on surrounding nations. He did this not merely to imitate the Egyptian priests' execration list (there were eight nations mentioned in this list; Amos also lists eight nations). Commentators have said that Amos had "psychological reasons"; he knew that the best way to get people's attention was to talk about the sins of their neighbors.[4] But there was a basic and definite theological, covenantal reason. Yahweh had placed Abram in the midst of the nations when he had led him from the Ur of the Chaldees and Haran to the land of Canaan. There in the land that served as the land bridge between nations, Abram was given the covenantal stipulation and promise that nations were to be blessed through him and they in turn were to bless themselves in their relationship with Abram (Gen. 12:1–3).[5] So when Amos prophesied concerning judgment on the surrounding nations because of their sins, Israel should have heard the rebuke against them. They had not been a channel of blessing; rather, in their relationship with the nations, reasons for their judgment could be detected. Now it must be understood that Israel was not given a missionizing task with regard to the nations. Israel was not commanded to go preach to the nations. In fact, Amos's messages were not directed to the nations directly, but to Israel. The covenant people had been given a priestly responsibility in the midst of nations (Exod. 19:6). Their holy life before Yahweh, their being a light to the peoples, their serving as a caring covenant people (Isa. 42:6), was to be their means or channel of blessing so that the nations would be drawn to appreciate, join with, and become united with the covenant people.[6]

Amos thus initiated his prophetic proclamation to Israel by reminding Israel of its unique place and role in Yahweh God's cosmic kingdom.

Ignoring Their Election

Not only had Israel not developed its covenantal relationships and responsibilities with the nations; they had also broken their covenantal relationship with Yahweh God their Master. It was not that Yahweh had broken the covenant with them; this reality will receive more attention later.[7] Amos makes express references to Israel's breaking and ignoring of the covenantal life-love bond in several penetrating ways. He directed Israel's attention to their election by Yahweh to be his covenant people who were to love, serve, trust, worship, and walk with him. Amos, however, did not use the term *bāhar* (to choose, elect). He employed phrases that spoke eloquently to Yahweh's election of them to live and serve as his covenant people.

A consideration of Amos 3:1–3 brings the following into perspective. First of all, Yahweh addresses, through Amos, the *běnê yeśrāēl* (sons or children of Israel), who were more directly identified as the *kol-hammišpākâ* (the whole family) that Yahweh had caused to come from the land of Egypt. Amos, by means of these words, places his message in a historical context. He is in effect saying, "Recall your redemption from Egypt, remember what Yahweh did to Egypt and how he brought you to himself" (Exod. 19:3, 4). Second, Yahweh reminded Israel of the covenanting activity at Mount Sinai. He had informed Israel that the whole earth was his—and that included all nations. But Israel was specifically delivered out of Egypt to be Yahweh's treasured possession. Yahweh had confirmed his covenant with Israel as a people. He had elected them. Amos used the term *yādaᶜtî* (I have known) to express an intimate and mutual love relationship. That Israel was to be Yahweh's unique people was emphasized by *raq 'etkem* (only you). The result of choosing and electing was stressed, the intimate knowing of each other. Yahweh had entered into a beautiful marriage with Israel when he had confirmed this covenantal bond with Israel. He had given instructions regarding how Israel was to walk (live, serve, worship) with him. Enoch and Noah had walked with God (Gen. 5:24; 6:9). Abraham, with whom God confirmed his covenant, was commanded to walk before God (17:1). The psalmist sang that covenant people would not be blessed if they walked according to the counsel of the wicked (Ps. 1:1). Thus, the third covenantal reference Yahweh had Amos proclaim came in the form of a rhetorical question (3:3):[8] *Hăyēlěkû šěňayim yaḥdamw betti 'im noᶜādû* (do two walk unitedly if they have not agreed to meet each other). The term *to know* is used in the reflexive sense and therefore is translated "agreed to know each other," or "to meet."[9] The point Amos stressed is that at Sinai Israel had responded with a resounding "we will" (Exod. 19:8; 24:3, 7). So Yahweh had met with Israel; Israel had responded positively that they would be Yahweh's precious possession, his kingdom and priests, his holy nation that would walk with their Redeemer Covenant Lord. Yahweh therefore had every right to expect Israel to walk with him. It would be as natural as a lion lying quietly in its den when it had no prey to protect (3:4); as a bird free to fly because no trap was set for it (3:5); and as a trap remaining unsprung since nothing had touched it (3:5b). Of course, when the trumpet sounded an alarm in a city, the inhabitants were alarmed (3:6a), and of course, when disaster came, Yahweh controlled it (3:6b). Indeed, when Yahweh intends to carry out a plan regarding his people, he makes it known through his spokesmen (3:7). Since one knows and expects causes and effects to be the order of life, why should there be an exception in Yahweh's demands and expectations concerning his covenant people? The covenant had been confirmed and reconfirmed. But Israel ignored and rejected its election as a covenant people; therefore, the sovereign Lord was roaring from Zion/Jerusalem. The King of the universe had a powerful message for his covenant people. Amos was called to be a covenant agent! He *had* to prophesy (1:1, 2; 3:8).

Amos made other references, either veiled or indirect, to Israel's election as a covenant people. They were warned to *hikkôn liqĕra't 'elōhêkâ* (be ready; niph. imp. of *kûn,* to meet your God). This call to be ready, that is, to prepare themselves to come face to face with *their* God comes in the context of Yahweh's charge that Israel had not returned to him (4:11, 12). It was their covenantal duty to return and walk with their Lord. He had chosen them; he had promised blessings but had also warned them concerning the curse of the covenant (Deut. 27, 28). Their election would result in blessings when they walked with their God; their election, if ignored or rejected, would bring the curse upon them as a disobedient, wandering people.

A reference to the very heart-throb of being in covenant with Yahweh comes in Amos' words *wîhî kēn yĕhwā 'ĕlōkê sŏbā'ôt 'etkem* (it will be that Yahweh of hosts [sovereign] will be with you) (5:14). Here is a reference to the covenantal promise given to Abraham (Gen. 17:1–7), to Jacob (28:15), to Moses (Exod. 3:12), to Joshua (Josh. 1:5), to David (2 Sam. 7:9). All these covenantal agents, mediators, servants, had received assurances that Yahweh would be their ever-present God as they carried out their duties for and among Yahweh's elect covenant people. Yahweh, Amos preached, would be with his people, and would have mercy on them when they did not ignore him but responded to their privilege of being Yahweh's elect people.

Another reference to Israel's election is found in Amos's use of the unique phrase *gĕ'on ya'ăqob* (6:8; 8:7). The term *gĕ'on* has been translated "pride or arrogance of Jacob."[10] Some have decided that Jerusalem's fortifications were referred to as the pride because of the parallel phrase referring to fortresses (6:8). But there is no reference to fortifications in 8:7. Could the reference be to Jacob's God of glory?[11] Indeed, Yahweh God cannot be removed from one's understanding of this phrase. Yahweh swears by the "pride." This means that Yahweh emphatically upholds and will deal according to this "pride." As in 3:2, Amos did not give a complete syllogism in 6:8. To have done so, he would have said that Yahweh God stands by what he has done for Jacob; Jacob has not stood by what Yahweh gave them. Therefore, Yahweh will never forget what Jacob, blessed by Yahweh God's specific deed, has done. And what had Yahweh done to set out Jacob as a special people? He had chosen, elected Jacob! Yahweh thus swears by his election of Jacob; he will never forget it. Jacob, however, elected to put his confidence in his own strength, in his fortresses and in his military ability. This understanding of "pride of Jacob" to refer to Yahweh's election of Jacob is clearly expressed in Psalm 47:4: Yahweh chose Jacob's inheritance, and in the parallel phrase, the term *chose, elect* is not repeated, but *pride.* Israel's sin then was that instead of praising Yahweh God for electing them as his covenant people, they turned their legitimate pride into arrogance, self-esteem, and self-sufficiency.[12]

Evidence: Covenant Mandates Violated

Israel, the covenant people, placed as Yahweh's servant among the nations ignored and/or abused its privileged status as an elect people and thus gave definite evidence of itself as a covenant-breaking people. In fact, they were pointedly accused of violating the three creational covenant mandates that had been emphatically and explicitly repeated, expounded, and applied to Israel at Mount Sinai (Exod. 20–Num. 10; Deut. 1–33).

Israel violated the spiritual mandate. The kings, prophets, and priests led the people into gross activities of spiritual adultery. Amos reminded the Israelites they had not left the gods and idols they had had in Egypt. They had shrines for these in the wilderness (5:25, 26). Amos accused them of false worship of golden calves at Bethel and Dan, a worship set up by Jeroboam, son of Nebat (1 Kings 12:25–30). He had also built shrines on high places and appointed non-Levites as priests (12:31–33). Jeroboam II followed his priests and people in the idolatrous worship practices throughout the land (Amos 7:8, 9, 13). Amos was specific in his references. He accused fathers who took their sons with them to the shrines to engage in religious sexual orgies with shrine prostitutes beside altars (2:7b, 8a). They used clothes taken in pledge (collateral for loans to poor people) as bedding at these altars and they drank wine as libations to the gods—wine they had taken as fines (legitimate or not) from people (2:8). The Israelites made the Nazirites, who had vowed not to drink wine (Num. 6:2–4), to drink wine. They forbade the prophets to serve as Yahweh's spokesmen (Amos 2:12). Amaziah, priest of Jeroboam II at Bethel, proved to be a real example of this (7:11, 12). Amos denounced the sin at Bethel and Gilgal where they brought sacrifices, tithes, and offerings at appointed times but in a prideful spirit (4:4, 5). And even if appointed feasts were held, at which burnt and grain offerings (intended to express gratitude) were brought and even if the people also sacrificed choice fellowship offerings, Yahweh would not accept these. Amos was emphatic as he spoke for Yahweh: "I hate, I despise" these acts of worship and the accompanying music and songs that turned Yahweh away (5:21–23; 8:3, 10).

Whenever a people ignore and violate the creational spiritual mandate there are inevitable consequences in regard to keeping and obeying the social and cultural mandates. Life is a unity; all aspects of it are integrated and inseparably interrelated.[13] And difficult as it is to separate the social from the cultural and spiritual misbehavior of the Israelites, Amos can be seen to put emphases on one or the other.

Various scholars have admired Amos because of his call for social justice and righteousness.[14] And indeed, Amos did call for these, in the context of Yahweh's revealed covenant life that included spiritual/religious and cultural obedience.

The specific sins of the surrounding nations that would bring Yahweh God's judgment upon them were largely in the social sphere of life. Damascus, Aram/ Syria, was wantonly cruel with captives and victims; iron sledges with iron teeth, normally used in threshing, were employed to pulverize the people of Gilead (1:3). Gaza was guilty of capturing people and selling them as slaves (1:6); Tyre, who even had a "treaty of brotherhood," sold captives as slaves (1:9). Edom was condemned for unrelenting wrath against Jacob and his descendants (1:11). Ammon, fighting to extend its borders, maltreated and killed pregnant women (1:13); Moab burned the homes of their enemy's king (2:1). But the sin of Judah that Amos singled out was the rejection of Yahweh's covenant law, which covered the cultural, social, and spiritual/religious aspects of life. Note, however, that Amos specifically accused Judah of following false gods (2:4).

Amos, directing his prophetic words of denunciation to Israel because of its violations of the covenant way of life, first calls attention to the violation of the social mandates (2:6b). The people who sought to live according to Yahweh's will, the righteous were enslaved so that the rich could increase their silver, the poor were treated dastardly and considered only what a pair of sandals were worth. Indeed, they accused laborers of stealing ground because they carried away dust on their bodies collected while working. No justice was given these poor, working, disadvantaged people (2:6b, 7). It should be noted that these social sins were committed in the cultural dimension of life.

The women were also singled out as oppressors of the poor and needy. The impression is given by Amos that as the fathers led the sons into spiritual debauchery, the mothers (women) set the tone and provided motivation for the oppression of the poor and needy. These women, referred to as the best fed and pampered cattle in Israel (4:1), called for drinks that their husbands had to provide. Likely as they catered to these demanding women they took the fruit of vines they had confiscated from the poor (2:8b). The men (husbands) seemed to be quite ready to enjoy the opulence that their women displayed in their homes; they had beds inlaid with ivory (imported from the south and east), and dined on choice lambs and fatted calves (6:4, 5).

As the rich and influential leaders and upper-class people lived in luxury, feasted with the best of food and drinks, and made merry with music (6:5, 6) Amos called upon them to hate evil, love good, and maintain justice in the courts where the poor and needy did not receive it. So, emphatically, along with a metaphor of the creational setting, he gave Yahweh's command to practice *mi`spāt wĕsĕdāqâ* (justice and righteousness). This call demanded all of Israel to be right with Yahweh God, to live according to his revealed will, and to apply this will correctly, justly in all areas of life. Righteousness and justice were to fill and penetrate all levels of society as rainwater filled rivers and kept streams (watering the soil) ever flowing (5:24).

The cultural mandate, given when Yahweh God created male and female, commanding them to fill, have dominion over, and cultivate the earth (Gen. 1:28), was not disregarded. In fact, it was carried out in many ways. The land was tilled, crops were raised, sheep and cattle thrived, commerce and business was profitably executed, the political and judicial systems were operating. The arts (e.g., music) were developed, practiced, and enjoyed. The descendants of Cain had been busy in the cultural areas of life (4:20, 21). They, however, did not do so in obedience to Yahweh God. Their development of the material and social-structural aspects of life was for self-gain; violence and bloodshed resulted (4:23; 6:5, 11). Under Jeroboam II, as under Omri and Ahab, cultural development went hand in hand with social oppression and injustice. The cultural advances became advantages for those in places of influence in politics, business, commerce, industry, and the arts. While the heads were intelligent, the hands were crafty, and practices were productive, the hearts of these people were hard, deceitful, and corrupt. Cultural advantages became the means to give expression in the walk of life to satanic influences and participation in the parasite dominion of Satan and his evil cohorts.

Yahweh's Wrath Portrayed

Israel's violating of the three creational covenant mandates demonstrated that they had no desire or intent to be aware of and influenced by Yahweh God's gracious redemptive/restorative covenant. Had Israel been faithful to Yahweh's expanded revealed covenantal way of life as explicated by Moses, that is, the stipulations of the covenant, had Israel been responsive to Yahweh God's electing love and all the promises included in the gracious redemptive/restorative covenant, the king, Jeroboam II, the priests, the prophets, and the influential people of Israel would have sought to respond to Yahweh's covenantal love for them by loving Yahweh, trusting, obeying, serving, and worshiping him. But Israel, violating the redemptive/restorative covenant, as first stated in Eden (Gen. 3:14–19), and repeated, amplified, and applied to Noah, Abraham, Isaac, Jacob, Moses/Israel, Joshua, and David, drew upon themselves the curse of the covenant. Yahweh God, according to his covenantal word, would, in anger and wrath, execute this curse on Israel.

Amos did not use either the term *curse* or *wrath* when speaking of the judgment Yahweh God would visit upon the surrounding nations and Israel.[15] He did make it plain that Yahweh's judgment would come upon each nation because of their repeated sins ("for three . . . even for four"). Fire would descend on Syria's Damascus (1:4), on Philistia's Gaza (1:7), on Tyre (1:10), on Edom's Teman (1:12), on Ammon's Rabbah (1:14), on Moab (2:2), and on Judah (2:5). This fire would be accompanied by the destruction of fortresses, death of kings and rulers, or exile. In regard to Israel, Amos was more detailed in his enumeration of sins and added what blessings Yahweh had given them in the past (e.g., removed the Amorite from the promised land, provided redemption from Egypt, sent prophets, and introduced the Nazrite order to them; 2:9–11). Yahweh's judgment, that is, the execution of the curse of the covenant because of Yahweh's wrath, would be a crushing of Israel to such an extent that even the swiftest, strongest, bravest warrior, soldier, and horseman would not be able to fight but would flee naked (2:13–16).

Amos proceeded to explicate Yahweh's execution of the curse of the covenant. Yahweh would punish Israel (3:2); enemies would overrun the land and plunder even the fortresses (3:11; 6:8, 14), destroy the idols' altars (3:14; 7:9), tear down adorned houses and mansions (3:15; 6:1), and be taken into exile (4:3; 6:7; 7:11, 17). Meanwhile, rain would be withheld (4:3), locusts would devour fig and olive trees (4:9; 7:1), plagues would decimate the population (4:10), and a famine would exist for the word of Yahweh (8:11). These covenant curses, as prophesied by Moses centuries before (Deut. 27:15–26; 28:15–68), were sure to come because Yahweh knew how many and great their sins were (Amos 5:12) and "would never forget anything they have done" (8:7 NIV). Amos summed up his prophetic message by saying that the eyes of the sovereign Lord were on the sinful kingdom and he would destroy it from the face of the earth (9:8a). But then Amos added, "yet I will not totally destroy the house of Jacob" (9:8b). The curse of the covenant would not be absolute. It would be tragic, reaching into all areas of life, the spiritual, social, and cultural. It, however, would be mitigated; Yahweh would preserve a remnant.

The Golden Cable

Amos has elaborated particularly on the sins of Israel, Yahweh's covenant people, and the consequences of these sins; judgment is to be executed. The questions before us now are: Do sin and judgment constitute the totality of his prophetic message? And is this message a unified, integrated message? In reply to the second question, a variety of answers have been offered. A scholar has written that the prophecy as to form is well arranged, plainly composed by Amos, and marked by regularity while the content, with the exception of the conclusion, is of a menacing character.[16] Others have written that the book on first reading seems to be a miscellaneous collection of various prophetic materials.[17] Yet others suggest that the material could be divided into four major sections under titles of Doom, Woes and Lamentations, Visions, and Epilogue.[18] Still others, seeking to apply various approaches to the text of Amos, such as the rhetorical, have suggested alternate divisions.[19] Students can legitimately question whether literary approaches developed in the past four or five decades serve them well in the understanding of the prophetic message.

A general summary of the main aspects of Amos's prophecy includes: (1) judgment against surrounding nations (1:1–2; 5:2); (2) judgment on Israel, who has not remained faithful to Yahweh (2:6–4:13); (3) the call to repentance and declaration of judgment if the call is not heeded (5:11; 7:9; 8:1–9, 10); (4) Amos's confrontation with Amaziah when prophesying concerning the judgment; (5) the eschatological assurances (9:11–15). Uniting and integrating these five aspects of Amos's prophecy is the Golden Cable, which also unites and integrates Amos's prophecy with the entire Old Testament prophetic corpus.

Yahweh is King

The phrase, *Yahweh is king,* does not appear in Amos's prophecy. The reality of Yahweh's kingship, his reign, and his inclusive domain are basic factors in Amos's prophecy. Indeed, Amos speaks from a cosmic kingdom perspective. He does not have a delimited view of the kingdom of God as some scholars would have readers believe.[20] Nor does Amos limit the concept of kingdom primarily to that of Israel/Judah and especially their millennial kingdom.[21]

Consider Amos's references to the kingship of Yahweh God. *Yĕhwâ miṣṣiyyôn yiš'āg* (Yahweh from Zion roars.)[22] Zion was the royal city of David. There the vicegerent, David, had set up his throne to rule as servant king. The verb *roar* brings the lion, proverbial king of the animal world, to mind (1:2; 3:8). Yahweh God exercises his royal prerogatives from Zion/Jerusalem, where the ark of the covenant, the symbol of the heavenly throne is situated. The result of the roar has cosmic effects: pastures and forests on verdant mountaintops dry up. But, more specifically, the nations surrounding Israel are addressed, not as if Yahweh is a foreign invader but the Lord and only rightful Ruler over the nations. Because the kings and peoples of these nations violate Yahweh's kingdom laws, his covenantal social and cultural mandates, he will sovereignly execute judgment on them. Stated simply: these nations are an integral part of Yahweh's cosmic kingdom just as much as Israel is. They will receive divine punishment because of their rebellion against their Creator, Provider, and Ruler. It should also be noted that Amos emphasizes that all nations are under Yahweh's eye and care when he rhetorically asks, "Are not you Israelites the same to me as the Cushites?" (9:7). Indeed, Yahweh God is the Lord over Egypt, Philistia, and Aram.

Amos proclaims the royal characteristics of Yahweh God. His use of the divine name *'ādonây* twenty-four times indicates that the prophet was deeply impressed with the reality of the lordship of Yahweh God over the entire cosmos and all its aspects. As *'ādōnây* Yahweh God is the Lord, owner, master, or governor.[23] Amos elaborates on Yahweh's absolute kingship when he uses the phrase *'ādōnây yĕhwâ 'ĕlōhê haṣṣĕbâ 'ôt* (3:13).[24] Amos used these names when he proclaimed that Israel would certainly receive the punishment it so justly deserved. That no one might even consider that this extreme punishment could or would not be executed, Amos stresses that God is the Owner/Master, he is the covenant Yahweh, he is the strong, Almighty One who reigns sovereignly over all of nature, all the nations, and very specifically over Israel (cf. also 6:8, 14; 9:5, 6).

No reader or student of Scripture should doubt that Amos was proclaiming a message from the Lord, Yahweh, the sovereign God which had as its broadest context the covenant of creation as the administrative means of Yahweh God's cosmic kingdom. The three covenantal mandates divinely given at the time of creation were integral aspects of the covenant. Amos addressed Israel's flagrant violation of Yahweh's demand for the maintaining of the spiritual relationship between them and their covenant Lord and Master. Likewise, as discussed earlier in this chapter, Israel disobeyed and rejected Yahweh God's demand for social and cultural obedience, righteousness, and justice. Hence, Israel defied their king! They refused to acknowledge that they had been called and had been declared Yahweh God's kingdom of priests, a holy nation. They rejected the blessed truth that Yahweh God had taken them as a people to be his precious possession (Exod. 19:4–6). Indeed, Israel rejected Yahweh's kingship, their participation in his kingdom, unilaterally and monergistically established and repeatedly reconfirmed. However, Amos proclaims that Yahweh God maintains his creation/redemptive/restorative covenant even though his chosen people did not.

The Covenant is Maintained

In the preceding discussion of "Israel: Covenant Breakers" (part II, A, of this chapter) Israel's sin as an elect people, called to serve in the midst of the nations, and the consequences of this sin was studied. It became very clear that Yahweh God in wrath executed the curse of the covenant. That he did is evidence that the creational/redemptive/restorative covenant was not abrogated. Yahweh God maintained it. It remains now for us to emphasize the positive dimension of Yahweh's maintaining of the covenant.

Amos made it clear that the personal relationship of the covenantal life-love bond was maintained. Recall that Yahweh emphatically stated, "You only have I chosen of all the families of the earth" (3:2 NIV). That election stood firm and fast. Israel had been, was, and would continue to be Yahweh's chosen people whom he had brought to him as his precious possession (Exod. 19:4, 5). This relationship would not be a simple, objective reality, but would continue as Yahweh God's means of administering his covenant, upholding his stipulations, maintaining his promises, and continuing to work with his vicegerential people toward the realizing of his kingdom purposes and goals.

Consider how Amos called attention to covenantal stipulations, promises, continuity, and goals. How was Israel to respond covenantally? *Dirĕšunî wihēyû* (seek me and live) (5:4b). This is repeated, "Seek Yahweh" (5:6). It was Yahweh's earnest desire that the living relationship would exist between himself and his people. But Israel had its covenantal challenge and responsibility. They had to respond! Yahweh did not call for a seeking of some unknown object or way to fellowship with him. Israel was to worship him according to his revealed will. They were not to go to Bethel and Gilgal, the centers of idol worship, (5:5). These places would be destroyed by the sovereign Creator and Ruler of the cosmic kingdom (5:6b–10). Israel would truly be seeking Yahweh when they worshiped him according to his stipulations for sacrificial offerings, celebrations of the prescribed Sabbath and feasts (5:21–26), and righteous and just living with fellow men (5:14, 15; 6:12; 8:4–6). Indeed, to worship faithfully and to live righteously and justly were divinely prescribed means to seek and to live covenantally as Yahweh God's kingdom vicegerents.

In a unique manner Amos, as an interceding prophet, implored for the continuity of Yahweh's covenantal relationship with Israel. It is in the context of the visions Amos was shown. First, he saw swarms of locusts being prepared to strip the land after the king had had his share of the crop. As Joel had indicated (Joel 1:4), locusts were a plague that would result in lack of food. So Amos cried out, "Forgive, small Jacob cannot survive under such chastisement" (7:2). His plea was addressed to *'ădōnāy yĕhwâ,* covenant Lord and Master. Master Yahweh heard and *niham* (niph. of root form usually translated "be sorry or console," BDB, 636). The basic thought here is that Yahweh as a compassionate God responded when Amos pled.

Master Yahweh responded thus a second time when he spoke of bringing judgment by fire (7:5, 6). Amos, as a covenant agent, pled with Yahweh the covenant Master by addressing God by his covenant name *Yĕhwâ.* And Yahweh God had compassion as the covenant Master. This same compassion was revealed when Moses interceded for an unfaithful, idol-worshiping Israel (Exod. 32–34; cf. esp. 34:6). But when Yahweh indicated to Amos that Israel as a covenant people did not measure up to the plumb line of Yahweh's revealed Torah, Amos did not intercede because Yahweh said the end had come! He would no longer spare Israel. The curse of the covenant had to be executed because of the false sanctuaries and apostate worship that Jeroboam I had introduced and that Jeroboam II maintained as the religion of Israel (7:7–9).

Amos expatiated on what would take place as Yahweh executed the curse of the covenant. Administering the creational covenant, the land would suffer as Egypt's had (8:8); disasters would occur in nature (8:9); feasting would be turned into mourning (8:10); a famine would occur, not of flood but of spiritual nourishment, the Word of Yahweh (8:11, 12). Even lovely young women and strong young men would faint and fall (8:13, 14). The coming disaster would be overwhelming and thorough as Yahweh fixed his eyes upon Israel for evil, for punishment (9:1–4). God, whose name is Yahweh, the sovereign Master of the cosmic kingdom, would indeed execute this judgment (9:5, 6) because Israel by its life, worship, and deeds, was no different than the other nations on whom God's judgment came. The covenant curse upon Israel would be radical in effect and results (9:7–10). Yahweh, by executing the curse, thus maintained his covenant (Deut. 27, 28). Amos went on to prophesy, however, that Yahweh's covenant with David would not be abrogated.

Amos did acknowledge that the covenant with David, which had been declared to be firmly established forever (2 Sam. 7:11–16, 25–29; 23:5; Ps. 89:3, 4),[25] was to undergo a severe time. He referred to David's house, or dynasty, as a *sukkat* (a tent), *hannôpelet* (the fallen one). One must understand that Amos did not say it was gone or removed. It was present, but fallen, uninhabitable, inoperative.[26] But weak and fragile and useless though it may have seemed to be, Yahweh God would reerect and strengthen it. Readers are given a scene with a restored palace with protective walls (9:11b). Further, it was to become the center from which control and blessing would go to all nations, even to people such as the Edomites who were known for their anger toward and hatred for the descendants of Jacob. In this passage, then, Amos takes covenantal concepts expressed by Noah (Gen. 9:26, 27), elaborated to Abraham (Gen. 12:1–3), and confirmed to David. Thus, Amos proclaimed with resounding certainty that Yahweh God, sovereign Owner and Ruler of the cosmic kingdom, would surely continue to administer the affairs of this kingdom according to his eternally established covenant. This kingdom had at its heart, its nerve center, and as its programmatic strategy, the creational/redemptive/restorative covenant with all of its aspects, purposes, goals, and mediatorial agents.

The Mediator is Assured

The preceding statement introduces the third strand of the Golden Cable, the Mediator.

Throughout Yahweh God's covenanting activity in the past, he had chosen, appointed, and designated specific persons to serve as his covenantal agents in various capacities. David, Moses, and Samuel had been prophets in times past; David and Solomon, covenantal kings, called and qualified to serve. Amos was also called and enabled to be a covenant spokesman, hence a type of the covenant Mediator. But Amos drew specific attention to the Mediator who, having been promised to David as his offspring, would be the very one to fully restore, give entrance to, and render purposeful the tent, the house, the dynasty of David.[27] Amos prophesied concerning Jesus Christ to whom the apostle John pointed (John 1:14), and of his gathering people from the nations into the tent, the palace, the kingdom of God according to the apostle James (Acts 15:13–18). Edom is referred to as having a remnant in the Davidic restored tent. This meant that some Edomites would receive the covenantal blessings provided through David's Son, the Mediator. Why was Edom mentioned? Edomites, descendants of Esau, were renown for their perpetual hatred against Jacob's descendants (Amos 1:12). So, if Edomites could participate in the blessing of the covenant Mediator's work, surely all other nations could also. Edom was not referred to "strictly for its own sake, but rather as a synecdoche for the phrase 'all the nations.'"[28] Amos thus speaks directly to the promise to Abraham that through him and his offspring all nations would be blessed and bless themselves (Gen. 12:1–3).

In conclusion, the Golden Cable, consisting of the three strands, the kingdom, the covenant, and Mediator, unites and integrates the prophetic message of Amos. All aspects of this prophecy relate to, derive their significance from, and have meaning in relation to one of the three and so doing, directly or indirectly, implicitly or explicitly, to each of the others also.

The Eschatological Perspective

Amos's Dealings with Joel's Themes

It is appropriate at this point, before discussing the specific eschatological aspects of Amos's prophecy, to inquire concerning Amos's dealing with themes Joel included in his prophetic agenda.[29]

Amos especially referred to and developed the concept of judgment on Israel and the nations. He called for repentance and pointed to the way a covenant people were to live. He referred, if only implicitly, to Yahweh God's continuing elective love. He referred to blessings in the creational/natural realm. He spoke of the inclusion of peoples from all nations in the people of the covenant by means of the Mediator's service. He did not develop all the themes and hardly referred to some of them. This was because Amos was called to preach judgment on wayward, covenant-breaking Israel as he called them to return to Yahweh. This is clearly implied when he prophesied that those involved in David's restored dynasty would possess the remnant of Edom and of all the nations.

Amos's Specific Orientation

A consideration of Amos's contribution to Yahweh's eschatological purposes and program leads one to conclude that he emphasized the following.

The Certainty of the Exile

Israel would surely go into exile. They would be sent north, beyond Damascus, capital of Syria (5:27). This would be done by an enemy overrunning the land, plundering it, and destroying cities and fortresses (3:11, 15; 6:14).

Israel's Continuity

The exile would not destroy all of Israel. Some would be spared. This was stated in terms of a shepherd's experience: two leg bones and a piece of an ear of a lamb would be taken from a lion's mouth (3:12). This was repeated when Amos declared that Yahweh would destroy Israel, the sinful political kingdom, from the face of the earth (9:8), but the house of Jacob, the people, would not be completely obliterated.

The Return from Exile

The exiled people would be brought back; they would rebuild, replant, and make gardens in the land from which they had been taken (9:14). Amos employed two agricultural terms to give expression to what Yahweh would do for his people: *wûnĕ-ta'tîm* (and I will plant them) in their land and *wĕlô' yennatešû 'ôd* (and not pull them up again). Amos assured his audience that there would not be another exile.[30] It can also be understood that Israel would have peace.[31] Some scholars, however, have stated that Amos could not have been referring to Israel's return from exile because Israel's experiences were "not consonant with Amos' prediction." Nor should this prophecy be given a spiritual interpretation, but the reason for this negative view is not always given.[32] John Calvin wrote that it would appear that Amos's prophecy "has never been fulfilled." True, he wrote, the Jews went back to their own country, "but it was only a small number" and they never became a strong ruling nation. So, he asks, in what sense has God promised the blessings described in Amos 9:13–15? His answer was "we come to Christ" because of his reign in God's kingdom. And the abundance of corn and wine refers to the spiritual blessings that abound under the reign of Christ.[33]

We must conclude that Amos was indeed speaking of Israel's return from exile; he stated this explicitly (9:14). And then, in terms from everyday life that his audience understood, he spoke of Yahweh God's covenant blessings that would be their portion. They would have security until God's purposes had been achieved.[34] And Amos had spoken of that in the preceding verses (9:11, 12).

The Fulfillment of the Davidic Covenant

Amos was proclaiming the glorious fulfillment of Yahweh God's promises to David. David's house, dynasty, though fallen and in obscurity, would certainly be raised up and the reign of David's Son would bring blessings to people of all nations. And these blessings would not be only in an abstract spiritual sense. Yahweh God, under the reign of Christ, would be a wonderfully providential God. He would demonstrate that his covenant of creation was functioning; cosmic kingdom blessings, food, drink, homes, security, and peace would be given to his kingdom subjects. Amos thus was speaking of the entire New Testament era that began when David's Son became flesh and tented among men, providing grace, truth, healing, and provisions for daily life under Christ's reign (John 1:14–16). And when we consider what Isaiah would prophesy about the wonderful providential reign of David's Son (Isa. 11), we can rightly say we hear strains of that same message in Amos's final words. The reign of David's Son was assured when a remnant of Israel came out of exile; when a community of Jacob's descendants continued within which the promised Son of David was born, ministered, died, arose, ascended, and then took his place at the Father's right hand. It is under this reign of David's Son that people of all nations will be gathered (Acts 15:16–17a) and the new Israel, made up of all believers in Christ (Gal. 3:28, 29), will prosper. Christ himself said he would build, protect, and keep this Israel, even the universal church (Matt. 16:17–20; Gal. 6:16). Amos's eschatological perspective, presented in four stages, thus covers Israel's exile, the return, Jesus Christ's birth, and the New Testament era from the time of Christ's ministry until his return to usher in the new heavens and new earth (Rev. 21, 22).

HOSEA

Introductory Comments

Relation to Amos

Hosea was the only writing prophet who is considered a native of Israel, the northern tribe of Yahweh God's covenant people.[35] Although the biblical text does not explicitly state he was a northerner, his choice of terms, his intimate knowledge of details about Israel's religious, political, and social situation, his primary addresses to Ephraim, the leading tribe of this northern kingdom, his references to Samaria, Bethel, and Gilgal, all combine to support the view that Hosea spoke to his own national people.[36] He may have been a youth when Amos prophesied in the Bethel region.[37] He is considered to have been a young man when called to marry Gomer and consequently serve as a prophet and did so as one influenced by Amos and prepared to continue that prophetic ministry.[38]

The Times

The prophet identifies the time in which he prophesied. It was during the reign of Jeroboam II in Israel during which time four kings occupied Judah's throne: Uzziah, Jotham, Ahaz, and Hezekiah. Commentators calculate that Hosea prophesied during the final years of Uzziah's reign and the first part of Hezekiah's. The total period is thought to span approximately thirty-eight years.

Culturally Israel was prosperous. But spiritually and socially, the nation was corrupt. Since the three creation mandates are so closely interrelated, the spiritual and the social undoubtedly influenced the cultural life. In fact, Amos referred to offenses executed in the cultural area of life. Hosea had to address Israel's covenant-breaking activities in the context of a wife's prostitution. Israel, Yahweh's bride, had become a prostitute; Yahweh, her husband, was deeply hurt and offended.[39]

Literary Aspects of the Book

Hosea's prophetic material has been considered difficult to interpret due to various literary problems. It has been said that Hosea competes with Job "for the distinction of containing more unintelligible passages than any other book of the Hebrew Bible."[40] The literary structure that seems quite obvious—chapters 1–3, relating to Hosea's personal experiences—is distinctly different from chapters 4 through 14. Scholars have pointed to two specific problems in each section; in the first part, how chapter 3 is related to chapter 1; and there is doubt that a discernible outline can be detected in chapters 4 through 14.[41]

These problems, however, do not in any way cause difficulty in understanding that Israel's covenant breaking was at the heart of Hosea's prophecy. Yahweh's bride, Israel, taken in covenant marriage at Sinai (Exod. 19–24), was unfaithful as a wife. The evidence of this unfaithfulness of Israel is repeatedly described. Meanwhile, Yahweh's covenant faithfulness is set forth clearly.[42]

Hosea and Gomer, Chapters 1–3[43]

The Literary Structure

That chapters 1 to 3 continue to challenge biblical scholars is borne out by the ongoing discussions of these chapters or some aspects of them.[44] There is no known new interpretation of these chapters in recent studies. Hosea is considered by all writers to have a symbolic role that portrays the broken covenantal relationship between Israel and Yahweh. The differences of interpretation center around the specific meaning and intent of the phrase *'ēšet zĕnûnîm,* woman of adulteries (1:2). Should it be taken to mean in this context that (1) Gomer was an active harlot when Hosea was told *lēk qaḥ lêkâ* (go, take to yourself) or (2) was she inclined to harlotry or, (3) was she from a family practicing harlotry but had not yet been so involved herself? Or, (4) had Gomer undergone the Canaanite sexual-sacral fruitfulness ritual, involved in which was her deflowering, or (5) is the question irrelevant because the account is allegorical?[45]

After a careful consideration of the various interpretations offered, it is my conviction that the entire passage, within the wider Old Testament context, presents the view that Gomer was already a practicing harlot.[46] An in-depth consideration of Hosea 1–3 will support the position I espouse.

Hosea's Symbolic Role

One should consider the passage as it is presented. It begins and concludes with a genre that should be recognized as narrative. Narrative exegesis calls for a retelling of the story. God began to speak through Hosea (1:2 NIV).[47] There is no reason to introduce the concepts of allegory or parable. Yahweh God actually communicated with Hosea. And the message he was to proclaim was to be given in the context of his own marriage experience. So the narrative proceeds to relate that Hosea was obedient. He married the prostitute Gomer and then had a son who was to be given the name *Jezreel*—a meaningful name in the historical context of King Jehu's dynasty's sinful reign that was soon to be ended. Then the story continues: Gomer had two more children; they were not fathered by Hosea (2:4) but by Gomer's paramours. These children of adultery were given names expressing the broken relationship between Hosea and Gomer, and between Yahweh and Israel. The broken relationship between Yahweh and Israel was the motivation for Yahweh speaking to and through Hosea. So, in a rhetorical style, the narrative is interrupted to indicate what the real motivation for the entire marriage experience was. Israel, the mother, had to be rebuked and put to shame because Israel, the wife, had forsaken her husband, Yahweh. Once the motivation for Hosea's experience regarding his broken marriage has been rhetorically stated, the narrative continues. Hosea is commanded to retake Gomer, at a price (3:2), and she is to be kept from further adulterous practices (3:3).

Interpreting the Account

The question to be considered now is: Was Israel truly a promiscuous, adulterous people before the time that Yahweh took Israel as his bride at Sinai? If Scripture indicates that Israel was, then Gomer, as an adulterous woman before marriage to Hosea, truly portrays Israel's adulterous spiritual life before Sinai. The biblical evidence is clear. Yahweh took Abram from his idol-worshiping family, clan, and land (Josh. 24:2) and in the process of time Abraham became a faithful, obedient, covenant servant of Yahweh. Yahweh called an idol worshiper and he covenanted with him. Later, when Israel, descended from Abraham, was in Egypt, they adopted Egyptian gods and adapted to the worship of these. Hosea reminded Israel that they sang when delivered from Egypt (Hos. 2:15; cf. Exod. 15) but they soon forgot that song. Within forty days after the Sinai covenanting (marriage) ceremony, Israel was worshiping an Egyptian god and participating in offensive rituals involved in that worship (Exod. 32–34). Amos reminded Israel that though Yahweh had known only them (3:2), they nevertheless carried their Egyptian idols with them in the desert (5:25, 26). Ezekiel, likewise, referred to Israel's premarriage (covenant making) sinfulness (Ezek. 16, 23). The point to be emphasized is that Hosea had to take a woman who was a physical as well as spiritual adulteress to give a definite message that Yahweh God had taken Israel, an idol-worshiping spiritual, social, and cultural adulterous people and covenanted with them—that is, formally, legally, and spiritually he became their husband. Yahweh took a defiled people, thus revealing his grace, mercy, and compassion. Israel had verbally responded three times, "All that Yahweh says we will do" (Exod. 19:8; 24:3, 7). Gomer had responded affirmatively to Hosea as Israel had done to Yahweh. But neither Gomer nor Israel forsook their premarriage adulterous manner of life.

The narrative relates Gomer's unfaithfulness and Hosea's faithfulness in taking her back as bride/wife. The rhetorical part presents the heart of the prophetic message Hosea had to present to Israel. A few cardinal points in this message are as follows. Israel, Yahweh's covenant wife, is rebuked because of her unfaithfulness (2:2). Yahweh no longer functions as her caring and protecting husband. He will punish her, executing the curse of the covenant upon her and her children (2:3–7). Her miserable experiences under this punishment will awaken her to remembering the good life she had living in the covenant bond with Yahweh (2:7b), but she will refuse to acknowledge him as the real source of her good life (2:8). Yahweh will continue to withhold the good cultural, social, and spiritual aspects of a blessed covenant life (2:9-13). Yahweh, however, will not forget her; he will draw her to himself as he did when he took Israel from Egypt (2:14). Israel will again be possessors of the good land (2:15) and will call Yahweh her husband and the renewed troth will eventuate in covenantal blessings for his bride/wife in the spiritual (2:17, 20), social (2:16), and cultural dimensions of covenantal living (2:15, 18). The covenant, in its fullest expression, will be renewed and continued (2:21–23).

The blessings that Hosea briefly outlines are not only reminiscent of what Joel had prophesied; Hosea emphatically repeats and amplifies them. After judgment has been executed, Yahweh God calls for repentance (allures Israel), and assures her of his love and of abundant blessings in the whole of life. Hosea did not explicitly mention the coming of the Holy Spirit, but by implication when he referred to the renewing of the covenant and to the new covenant age to be ushered in the last days, when Israel would seek Yahweh and David their king, that is, the promised messianic king.

Israel: The Prostituting Wife

Hosea elaborates in chapters 4–14 what he first succinctly stated in chapters 1–3. He does not refer to his own marriage situation again, but his prophetic message keeps his experiences implicitly before the reader. Hosea effectively presents

Israel as a covenant-breaking people who had rejected their royal husband, abandoned his promises, violated his stipulations governing the spiritual, social, and cultural covenant life, and refused to acknowledge the binding oath of the covenant and the requirements for the continuity of the covenant.

Hosea commences the amplification of Yahweh's message with a command: *šim'ŭ dĕbar yĕhwâ* (hear the word of Yahweh). The central concept of that word is *rîb* with the inhabitants of the promised land. The noun *rîb* is derived from the verb *rîb,* which speaks of a dispute, a striving with another; in the legal context it speaks of a charge, a "court case." Hosea proceedes to specify how Israel had broken the stipulations of the covenant; hence the legal connotation of the term is stressed. Israel was a law breaker;[48] Yahweh is calling Israel into a judgment setting, that is, Hosea summons Israel to appear in Yahweh's judicial court. Israel must hear the accusations Yahweh has against his covenantal bride.

The Mandates

The spiritual mandate had not been carried out. Israel's relationship with Yahweh was not acknowledged or practiced. Hosea used three terms in his opening explanatory prophetic message:

'ên 'ĕmet wĕ 'ên ḥesed, wĕ da'at 'ĕlōhîm lā'āreṣ (there is "no faithfulness, no covenant love, no knowledge of God in the land." Consider the phrase *no knowledge of God.* Hosea states that Israel had no intimate relationship with their Creator, Redeemer, covenant God. It was not only that they had no intellectual knowledge of their God; they had no living, loving relationship with him. Israel *yisĕkaḥ 'eth 'ośehû* (had forgotten their Maker). Israel had built palaces, put up kings without God's consent, made idols of silver and gold, set up a calf in Samaria, and thus sowed the whirlwind (8:5–14). Their heart was deceitful as evidenced by an increase in altars and the erecting of sacred stones (10:1, 2). Israel-Ephraim had surrounded God with lies and was full of deceit. Israel worshiped Baal and increased their sin against their Redeemer God who had brought them out of Egypt and who lovingly cared for them in the desert. Israel's sin became increasingly heinous as they offered human sacrifices and kissed their calf idols (13:1–6). Yahweh God had not rejected them; this reality will be discussed later. What is to be stressed is that in very close relationship with the lack of acknowledging God was the absence of faithfulness and covenant love.

Yahweh God had remained faithful to Israel; he continued to be their covenant Lord, Israel's husband. Yahweh kept his promises: I will be a God to them and to their children. He had redeemed them and given them the promised land in which each family had received their inheritance. Israel had had no qualms about receiving these covenant promises in full. But Israel had not kept promises in response to Yahweh's overtures. As Gomer had not acknowledged her troth with Hosea and became unfaithful, as evidenced in her adulteries, so Israel had been.

Yahweh God had also continued to demonstrate *ḥesed,* covenantal love, mercy, goodness, kindness, loyalty, mutual liability, solidarity.[49] As Hosea uses the term here, it must be seen as a correlate to acknowledgment and faithfulness. The idea of solidarity, loyalty in expressing love to and for God is certainly to be considered. And if Israel was loyal and in solidarity with God in his revelation of compassion, mercy, and love, these would be demonstrated in everyday life. But because the spiritual mandate was ignored, rejected, and violated, the social and cultural mandates were also.[50]

Hosea, having introduced the heart of Yahweh's legal case against Israel, proceeded to elaborate. He referred to cursing (third commandment), lying (eighth commandment), murder (sixth commandment), stealing (eighth commandment), adultery (seventh commandment), blood shedding (sixth commandment) (4:2). The violations of the three creational mandates, to be obeyed and carried out by redeemed Israel, were evidence of a totally corrupted way of life. Hosea elaborated further on the corrupt manner of life by detailing Israel's physical and spiritual adultery (4:10–18; 5:4; 6:8–10; 7:4–7; 8:9; 10:4, 5, 13; 11:7, 12; 13:1, 2, 10). Israel was guilty of covenantal disobedience in every dimension of life.

The Mediatorial Agents

Yahweh God had ordained that covenant agents, that is, specific people placed in specific offices, were taken from among the people as a whole and were to represent them before God. Even more so, they were to represent Yahweh God to the people. As is well known, the covenantal mediatorial agents were the kings, prophets, and priests. Hosea refers to Israel's disobedience in regard to the office of king. He specifically accuses Israel of setting up kings and choosing princes without Yahweh's consent and approval (8:4). None of these kings called on God (7:7). They were all failures as covenant agents who were to serve as David had. Meanwhile, Israel delighted in their unfaithful kings and drunken, mocking princes with wickedness and lies (7:3–7). Israel, when they realized that their nontheocratic kings failed them, did not turn to their divine sovereign King; rather, they turned to the king of Assyria (5:13), who in time would be Yahweh's agent to destroy them as a nation (8:9, 10). Thus the mediatorial office and the kings who were to faithfully serve in it would be swept away (10:7) and completely destroyed (10:15).

What about the prophets who were Yahweh's appointed covenantal agents to serve as advisers to the kings and as guardians of the theocratic monarchies, Israel and Judah?[51] Hosea was called to serve as spokesman to Israel as a nation and to give Yahweh's word regarding the kings. He does not record having referred to a specific king as Amos had done (Amos 7:13). But he did proclaim Yahweh's word concerning them. To be noted now, however, is that Hosea had to proclaim Yahweh's word concerning prophets. He spoke concerning Moses as a faithful prophet (12:13). He reminded Israel and the prophets what their duty was: to be watchmen over Ephraim/Israel and to relate the visions and parables God gave them (12:10). The tragic reality was that the prophets had become fools (9:7). They stumbled as the people did (4:5) and would be cut to pieces along with Israel (6:5).

The service of the priests, who were to stand between the people and God executing Yahweh's will on behalf of the people, were also unfaithful covenant agents. Hosea addressed them with an imperative statement: *šim'û zō't haccōhă-*

nîm (hear this priests). This imperative is followed by two more; there is a progression in Hosea's call from the priests to all the people and then to the king. The house of Israel, as Yahweh's kingdom of priests (Exod. 19:6), was commanded *haqĕšîbû* (hiph. imperative *qāšab,* to pay attention—indeed, to do so diligently). And the kings were commanded *ha'ăzînû* (to stretch their ears to hear).[52] The priests were called first because Hosea addressed the spiritual prostitution in the hearts of the people of Israel (4:10; 5:4). The priests were to lead the people in obedient worship of Yahweh, in God-honoring sacrificial activities (8:11-13). But the priests had *followed* the adulterous people (4:9) instead of leading them. Hence, Yahweh's word of condemnation is not only against the priests (4:7); Israel, as a nation, was to be rejected as a priestly people. Their covenantal privilege and duty would be removed.

The Curse of the Covenant

Hosea had a very difficult and tragic message from Yahweh God, the faithful "covenant husband," for Israel, Yahweh's unfaithful covenant "bride." The entire nation would have to bear the curse of the covenant. The covenantal mediatorial agents, discussed in the preceding paragraphs, were singled out for punishment. So was the adult population. The people, due to the lack of the knowledge of Yahweh, would be destroyed (4:5, 6; 5:8–12; 9:6; 10:6–10). Their refusal to acknowledge Yahweh as their Redeemer Lord, their rejection of the spiritual, social, and cultural mandates, would have dire results. Hosea said it plainly: "You are destroyed, O Israel" (13:9)—and this is because they were against their Helper, Yahweh God. They had broken Yahweh's covenant with them (8:1) as Adam had done in Eden (6:7).[53]

The curse of the covenant, that is, the destruction of Israel as a nation as it existed in Hosea's time, would come about in various ways. The people as a whole would no longer mediate between Yahweh God and the nations as a priestly nation. Assyria, the very nation Israel appealed to for help when confronted by international military powers (5:13; 7:11; 12:1), would be Yahweh's instrument of punishment (8:9, 10; 10:6; 11:5). The remnant, carried off to Assyria, would continue to violate covenant stipulations by eating unclean food (9:3). As a more tragic consequence of the curse of the covenant on Israel, because *tiškaḥ tôrat 'ĕlōhekâ* (you have forgotten the instruction/law of God), Yahweh *'eškaḥ bōnekā* (I will forget your children). The verb used carries the stronger sense of rejection than the idea of ignore (NIV).[54] Yahweh would turn away from and reject the children of corrupt priests, as he had Eli's sons (1 Sam. 3:11–14). Rejecting the children meant no continuation of the priestly house nor of the covenant priestly people. This rejection of the offspring is definite evidence for the covenantal solidarity Yahweh has placed between parents and children (cf. Ps. 103:17). Parents in Israel did not obey the command to instruct their children and model the covenant way of life for their progeny (Gen. 18:19; Deut. 6:4–9; 11:18–21; Ps. 78:1–8). And the onus of keeping covenant and working for the continuation of it surely rested in the first place with the children.

Another consequence of Yahweh's execution of the curse on Israel would be the removal of all reasons for joy. Israel was forbidden to rejoice (9:1), whether in Yahweh's mandated worship or in pagan ritualistic hilarities.[55] The setting for joy would be removed: the place of worship, the feasts, the activities associated with bringing sacrifices.

Hosea spoke much about the covenant; he symbolized it in his marriage to Gomer. The question to be answered now is: Did Hosea speak of the covenant in the context of the Golden Cable? Did he relate to it, speak of it, and expound on it in isolation from the concepts of kingdom and mediator? Did Hosea's prophetic message have an integral part in the unifying *Mitte* of the Old Testament?

The Golden Cable

The Royal Bridegroom

The term *mamlĕkût* occurs only once in Hosea's prophecy; it is used to refer to Israel as an organized political entity (1:4). The term *melek* (king) appears nineteen times, in the singular and plural. References are to the kings of Assyria and to those of Israel and Judah. As discussed above, Israel's kings were disobedient; they as covenant vicegerents refused to represent Yahweh God, the King of Israel. They rejected their sovereign King's will and way of life for Yahweh's kingdom people. Yes, Israel had wanted a king who would lead them (13:9–11). God gave them Saul and later Jeroboam (1 Kings 11:26–33). Hosea prophesied the time would come, however, that Israel would have no king; and the people would say when experiencing the curse of the covenant, "Even if we had one, what could he do for us?" Israel would also say in that context that they had no king (10:3) because they did not fear *yōre'nû* Yahweh (not fear Yahweh). The term *yārā* could be translated "revered" (NIV) or "worship" (2 Kings 17:41). The tragic reality was that from the very earliest days of Israel's existence as a separate nation the royal and priestly personnel had followed in the way of their first king, Jeroboam, the son of Nebat (1 Kings 12:25–33; 15:25, 26, 34; 16:26). But Israel's kings did not dethrone or remove their sovereign Lord from his eternal throne, nor were they able to demonstrate that Yahweh's kingdom was not a reality. True, Israel did give much evidence of the influence of the parasitic dominion of Satan, effectively demonstrating that the antithesis between Yahweh's cosmic kingdom and the satanic dominion was very deep, wide, and pervasive.

The question before us is: if Hosea proclaimed the presence of Yahweh's cosmic kingdom and the divine sovereign rule over it, how did he do it? There is an abundance of evidence that the prophet did not have to use the terms *melek* and *mamlĕkût* to keep the realities of Yahweh's sovereign lordship over all aspects of life before his audience.

Yahweh, as the Royal Bridegroom, whom Hosea typified, is said to continue his love for Judah but to withdraw it from Israel (1:6, 7). He continues as the sovereign Suzerain who calls his adulterous people into a legal confrontation (4:1). He, as sovereign Ruler over the cosmic kingdom, would bring destruction on Israel; he would raise up a powerful nation, Assyria (5:13; 9:13; 11:5; 14:3). He would continue to control all the forces in the social (2:10, 11), cultural (2:13, 21, 22), and natural (2:3, 6, 12, 15, 18) dimensions of life.[56] Indeed, Hosea continuously held before Israel that they were the people they were because Yahweh, the King of the cosmic kingdom, was their Maker (8:14), their Redeemer (9:10; 11:1; 13:4), their providing God (10:1; 13:5, 6). To graphically depict the kingship of Yahweh, he is metaphorically referred to as the lion, the king of the animal world (5:14; 11:10; 13:7, 8).

Yahweh God, as the awesome, fearsome sovereign Ruler over the cosmic kingdom, continues to set himself forth as a loving Royal Bridegroom. His desire is for his bride to intimately, spiritually respond to him. He will again allure her into the desert, where they initially were married; he will speak tenderly to her (2:14). He desires to be called husband (2:16) and be betrothed to her forever in righteousness, justice, love, and compassion (2:19, 20). It is Yahweh's deepest desire that Israel turn and seek him (2:14, 15). The deepest yearnings of Yahweh's heart are poignantly expressed in the rhetorical question "How can I give you up?" (Yahweh's compassion is aroused, 11:8). He so deeply desires to be God to Israel (Gen. 17:7), the Holy One in their midst (11:9). Truly he longs to redeem them (11:13).

The desire of Yahweh God is the source and motivation for his call to his bride. Through Hosea he called to the priests and people (5:1) so that they would admit their guilt and earnestly seek Yahweh (5:15). The call also went to Judah, who had to know a harvest was appointed for them but that Yahweh would restore them (6:11). He calls his people to sow righteousness, that is, to demonstrate that they are within the will of God in all aspects and relationships of their daily lives (10:12). The sovereign, almighty God, who is the God of renown, calls his people to return, to maintain love and justice, and to wait upon him always (12:6). As Hosea approached the end of his prophecy, the call became very direct: return, Israel, to the Lord your God; take words with you and return. Ask for forgiveness and be graciously received (14:1, 2).

With the call came repeated assurances that only a sovereign Lord of the kingdom could give and carry out. At the close of his prophecy, Hosea speaks for Yahweh: "I will heal their wickedness and love them freely" (14:4). This sums up what Hosea had repeatedly prophesied. Yahweh would show his love even to those called "Not My loved one" (2:23). He would cause the land to produce grain, wine, and oil (2:22). He would come to his people as surely as the sun rises and provides the winter rains (6:3). He would gather them even after they had sold themselves to the nations (8:10). But these assurances of love and blessings were not to be taken without the repeated reminders that the curse of the covenant would be administered if the Royal Bridegroom's desire was thwarted, his call ignored, and his will rejected.

The Covenant Continues

The second strand of the Golden Cable is the covenant. We have dealt at some length with the covenant in preceding parts of this chapter, especially when considering the marriage of Hosea to Gomer as a living metaphor of Yahweh God's marriage covenant with Israel. By way of summary to underscore how Hosea spoke of the covenant as Yahweh God's relationship to his people and as the means by which he administered his kingdom purposes, attention should be given to a few specific passages.

Consider Hosea 2:18, 19. Yahweh said he would make a covenant for his people with beasts, birds, and creatures. He would, as covenant administrator, remove military equipment. Yahweh would do in the future what he had assured before what he would do for an obedient, faithful people (Deut. 8:1–18; 28:1–14; 30:1–20). Indeed, Israel was a covenant-breaking people (Hos. 6:7; 8:1). They had considered the law of the covenant as something alien (8:12).

Consider also Hosea 11:1–4.[57] As a covenant-making and -keeping sovereign Lord, Yahweh had loved and called Israel from Egypt. He taught Ephraim/Israel to walk, holding them up and healing them. He broke Egypt's yoke, the bitter slavery, and with a bond of human kindness and ties of love he led them and fed them. Although Israel paid no attention to these past covenantal deeds of mercy, grace, and love, and although Israel would experience the curse of the covenant, Yahweh God would not forget his binding relationship of life and love with his people. He would heal and love them; he would bless them with life's refreshing blessings (14:4–7).

In summary, it must be emphasized that Hosea's prophetic message cannot be understood or appreciated in its entirety unless it is considered in the broad context of Yahweh's cosmic kingdom and particularly his unique covenant, including its full creational, redemptive, restorative aspects with Israel, the chosen seed of Noah, Abraham, Isaac, and Jacob.

The Mediator is Portrayed

The third strand of the Golden Cable is the Mediator. The mediator, whose messianic task it was to serve as Yahweh's representative and administrator of the covenant within the cosmic kingdom, was referred to and, more particularly, functioned in the context of Hosea's prophecy. Scholars such as Sigmund Mowinckel saw the messianic/mediatorial message in Hosea particularly in the references to David the king,[58] as did George Riggan.[59] The four aspects of Hosea's contribution to the mediatorial message call for some additional discussion.[60]

First of all, careful attention must be given to the role of Yahweh, "the I Am that I Am." It was Yahweh who initiated the formal covenant relationship with Israel as a nation. He took Israel as his bride. He was the husband. He gave his bride, Israel, offspring so that the covenant would continue with and through them. Yahweh dearly loved his people in spite of their spiritual adultery. But the question is:

Does Yahweh refer only to God the Father? Not in the entirety of Scripture. When Jesus the Messiah was incarnate and with his disciples and preaching to the Jewish people, he repeatedly said that he was the "I Am" (John 4:26; 6:35, 51; 8:12; 10:8, 11, 14; 11:25; 14:6; 15:1). And it is Jesus the Messiah who is presented as the Bridegroom of the believing people, the Bride (Rev. 21:1, 2, 9). We must conclude that the second person of the Trinity, the Son, who also appeared as the Angel of the Lord in various contexts, was the One who was carrying out the will of the triune God in the calling of Hosea and the basic source of Hosea's message in deed and word. Pointedly stated: Jesus Christ, who became incarnate, was present and functioning in his preincarnate state. It was he who called Hosea to serve as his prophetic agent and thus Hosea functioned as "the secondary messianic/mediator."

Second, Hosea the prophet, called and equipped, became the mediatorial agent in the course of ever progressing history. His marriage to Gomer had mediatorial significance,[61] particularly in his experiences of pain and grief when she again consorted with her paramours. Hosea typologically gave clarity to the compassion and grace of the Mediator when he obediently went to Gomer while she was living an adulterous life and paid a second dowry and took her back as his wife.

Hosea the mediatorial prophet's intimate relationship with the Great Eternal Mediator is expressed in 6:1–11. Hosea calls on Israel: *lĕkū ẘenāšâbâ'el Yĕhwâ* (Come, [note the imperative] let us return to Yahweh). Here is the call that can be understood as a tender, compassionate plea. Hosea, Yahweh's spokesman, identifies directly with Israel; he is one of them. But his deepest desire is that the living love bond between Israel and Yahweh be restored. He acknowledges that the covenant Bridegroom has given his bride initial experiences of the curse. "He has torn us to pieces," and "He has injured us." But as the good Shepherd he will heal us and bind our wounds (6:1 NIV). This healing can be successful for he will revive us, restore us, and enable us to live in his presence (6:2 NIV). Hosea gave a positive message; the covenant bond can be and will be restored in such a manner that Israel can be refreshingly alive in fellowship with their Great Mediator. Israel, however, is called to respond: *nēdĕ 'â* (let us acknowledge Yahweh); indeed, let us work hard and diligently. Hosea called for Israel to return to her husband as Gomer had returned to him. The results would be an outpouring of covenantal blessings expressed in metaphorical creational terms, like life-giving winter and spring rains. These will come as surely as the sun rises each morning (6:3).

Hosea called Yahweh's bride! Between verses 3 and 4, the second proposition of the syllogism is not stated. "Israel would not listen; she would not return; she would not acknowledge her husband, covenant Lord." The response to this negative reaction came from the loving, yet pained and grieving husband but was actually spoken by the mediatorial prophetic spokesman. Note the plaintiff rhetorical questions: *mâ 'e'ĕśeh hĕkâ* (What can I do with you?). Ephraim/Israel and Judah were addressed. Both were unreliable; as morning mist and dew lasts but a few hours and is gone, so the people disappear from the house of their Bridegroom. The deepest desire of the Mediator was expressed: mercy, intimate knowledge, faithful covenant living, and service. The bringing of sacrifices in formal worship was an offense to Yahweh (6:6, 7) in the context of murders, ambushes, bloodshed, various other crimes, and prostitution (6:5–11).

The tragedy is that the mediatorial spokesman's call was heard but rejected. Then, as Yahweh's mouthpiece, Hosea had to utter words that flowed from the pained and grieving heart of the Great Covenantal Mediator: a harvest is appointed, that is, the end will come. Is there then no future for Yahweh's bride? Yes, there is.

Third, there is to be a future mediatorial messianic agent. He is none other than David. Hosea had indirectly referred to him in the rhetorical section placed within the context of the narrative concerning Hosea's marriage. Hosea spoke of the *rô'š'ehād* (one head [or leader NIV] 1:11 [MT 2:2]).[62] Hosea made it clear who this one head was to be: none other than David their king. Hosea recalled for Israel what Yahweh God had spoken by the mouth of Nathan to David when he had revealed to him what his and his seed's role was to be in the continuing outworking of Yahweh's covenant plan. There was to be a definite future for a recalcitrant covenant bride. Yahweh's covenantal promises to David would definitely be fulfilled. David, the mediatorial king, would die, but David, Yahweh's vicegerent, would never pass away because his progeny, specifically the Son, would be the great mediatorial messianic covenant agent who was even greater than Abraham, Moses, or David, even the Old Testament Yahweh Who came, the Only beloved Son, even Jesus the Mediator.

Fourth, in an unexpected and unique manner Hosea refers to the mediatorial position and who was to occupy it (11:1–11). It was Israel, the child (*na'ar*), whom Yahweh God loved (11:1). Israel, in its infancy stage as a nation, had been called from Egypt and commissioned as Yahweh's bride to be his priestly vicegerent in the world. Yahweh had done all he could to nurture, teach, and train Israel to be what it was called to be (11:3-4). But Israel had refused to listen, submit, and serve (11:2, 5-7). But Yahweh's intent and purpose were not to be thwarted. "How can I give you up? I will not carry out my fierce anger and devastate Ephraim" (11:8, 9a). As the holy God, he will carry out his will and reclaim and resettle his people (11:9b–11). Hosea did not explicate precisely how this was to be done. Matthew, the Gospel writer, gives us the answer. Jesus, who had been taken to Egypt to avoid the envy and murderous intents of Herod, was called out of Egypt to fulfill the royal and priestly task that had been placed before the bride. The bride failed; the Son would not. Israel, as a mediatorial servant, failed miserably, causing Yahweh God pain and grief. The Son would execute the will of the Father; hence he was also called from Egypt.[63]

Hosea's Eschatology

Specific Aspects?

Israel would be reclaimed and resettled in its inherited land. Questions to be answered now are: When was this to take place? How was it to happen? Is this return Hosea's main concern? Does Hosea say less or more about the future than Joel and Amos had prophesied?[64] Hosea repeats most of what Joel prophesied—some parts by implication, other parts more explicitly.

Hosea certainly warned Israel of disasters to come upon them as an unfaithful covenant bride. Moses had warned of judgment to come to an unfaithful people.[65] The curse of the covenant was to be executed locally, nationally, cosmically. But along with the warnings, Hosea spoke of Yahweh's love (2:19, 20; 11:1; 14:4) and blessings in the creational realm (2:21, 22; 10:12; 14:5, 6); he spoke of Yahweh's desire for His people in an assuring manner (6:1–4; 7:1; 11:8–11; 14:4–7).

Hosea, without laying out specifics of Yahweh God's plan for Israel's future, does stress that there would be a return. Stuart states the case when exegeting Hosea 14:7 that the return could be a return to Yahweh or a return from exile.[66] He was correct to emphasize however, that Hosea made it clear that Israel could expect to return to the promised land when the prophet said *wĕhôšabĕtîm 'al bātêham* (and I will cause them to dwell in their houses) (11:11).[67] Hosea thus repeated what he had prophesied before, namely, that Yahweh himself would plant Israel for himself in the land (2:23). Hosea also prophesied that Yahweh's covenant people would be numerous, as the sand on the seashore (1:10), thus fulfilling the promises made to the patriarchs when Yahweh God covenanted with them (Gen. 15:5 [as numerous as the stars]; Gen. 22:17; 32:12). He also spoke of the reunion of Israel and Judah as one people (1:11). This future union is undoubtedly why Hosea interjected references to Judah (1:7; 4:15; 5:5, 12, 13, 14; 6:4, 11; 8:14; 10:11; 11:12; 12:2). This reunion, according to later prophets, would take place when the Holy Spirit would be poured out upon Yahweh's people (Ezek. 37:15–28).

In summing up what Hosea prophesied as certainties for the future, we must conclude that Hosea was very general on specifics concerning the when and how of Yahweh's dealing with Israel. He was emphatic, however, on Yahweh God's continuing covenant love for his people. They would be returned from exile; they would be restored to his favor; they would remove their idols and become a numerous, faithful people. This would take place when the new covenant was instituted by the incarnate Christ and will be fully consummated when he returns to usher in the resurrection, execute the final judgment, bring full redemption from sin and its tragic effects (cf. Paul's reference to this glorious truth, 1 Cor. 15:5), and usher in the renewed heaven and earth. Hosea thus has the entire eschatological program in his prophecy but he does not present many details concerning any specific event.

Evaluating Untenable Views

Finally, a few sentences expressing critiquing several evangelical biblical scholars should be included. First of all, Robert L. Saucy is not to be supported when he apodictically states that the new covenant is to be for Israel only and that Israel, as a provision included in this new covenant, was to be given back their land.[68] Clearly implied here is that Hosea prophesied Israel's return to the land as a New Testament reality. To be more specific, Saucy understands Hosea 2:14–23 to speak of a millennial kingdom in Palestine for Israel. This cannot be supported, as he suggested, by a reference to Jeremiah 31:7–14, 35, 38; 32:37, 38 and Ezekiel 37:15–28. In the light of the book of Hebrews, the new covenant does not refer to Israel as a political entity, a nation, possessing the land for a millennium, and that Gentile nations are outside the pale of the new covenant.

Serious objection should be raised against the view that Hosea's teaching concerning Israel as the bride of Yahweh makes it impossible to consider Israel as the bride of Christ. Israel was the adulterous wife, restored and forgiven. The church, it is posited, is the virgin wife of the Lamb. Hence, Hosea is said to posit a definite distinction between Israel and the church.[69] There is definitely no reason to draw this conclusion from the text of Hosea's prophecy. Hosea prophesied that Yahweh God's bride, Israel, living adulterously, would be rejected and then reclaimed and restored. There is no direct reference to the New Testament church in Hosea. In the New Testament, the church is not presented as the virgin; many passages speak of the church's unfaithfulness. But Christ's redeeming and sanctifying work cleanses the church, removing all past sins and stains. When Christ comes, the bride comes beautifully dressed to meet him (Rev. 21:2). The term *virgin* is not used by John. Paul referred to the church in Corinth as a body of people who had been unfaithful and unsanctified in former days but who, as a redeemed and sanctified people, was cleansed. The church would be presented as a pure virgin bride to Christ. The biblical teaching is that Christ's redemptive work and the Spirit's sanctifying work make pure virgins of those who once were idolatrously adulterous. Indeed, the Corinthian people whom Paul evangelized were as sinful as adulterous Israel. But both, by the grace of Yahweh God, could and would become covenantally pure brides.

NOTES

1. See Gerard Van Groningen, *Messianic Revelation in the Old Testament* (Grand Rapids: Baker, 1990) for a brief summary of Amos the man and his book. Note also the numerous bibliographical sources that were consulted and included in the notes, 464–70.

2. Recent commentaries on Amos have confirmed in various ways my summary. Cf. Francis I. Andersen and David Noel Freedman, "Amos," in *The Anchor Bible,* vol. 24A, gen. eds. William Foxwell Albright and David Noel Freedman (New York: Doubleday, 1989) who wrote "we take the middle ground . . . preparing this commentary . . . convinced with ever increasing force that the text is in better shape than has been generally supposed in modern criticism." The authors find the unity in the "words of Amos," in his life and ministry that moved through various phases, 10. See also 151–78 for their extensive bibliography on Amos. See also the bibliography in Douglas Stuart's commentary, "Hosea–Jonah," in *Word Biblical Commentary,* gen. eds. David A. Hubbard and Glenn W. Barker (Waco: Word, 1987), 274–82. Stuart wrote that Amos used a variety of compositional techniques in conveying the revelations God had given him (285). Stuart's view on the actual writing is that "Amos may himself have" organized his oracles . . . for preservation" or that colleagues or disciples organized Amos's prophetic messages (287). For a succinct evangeli-

cal summary of introductory subjects, background unity, authorship, and date, see Thomas Edward McComisky, "Amos," in *The Expositor's Bible Commentary,* ed. Frank E. Gabelein, 12 vols. (Grand Rapids: Zondervan, 1979–85), 7:2669–75.

3. Gary V. Smith has correctly referred to Israel's political and military power by which control over trade routes was exercised and by legal and illegal means wealth was accumulated. *Amos, A Commentary* (Grand Rapids: Zondervan, 1989). See also Norman H. Snaith, *Amos, Hosea, and Micah* (London: Epworth, 1960), who reminded readers that it had been Omri and Ahab, kings before Jereboam came to the throne, who had developed enlightened trade policies (39, 40).

4. See, for example, Ralph L. Smith, "Amos," in *The Broadman Bible Commentary,* vol. 7, gen. ed. Clifton J. Allen (Nashville: Broadman, 1972), 90.

5. Note the niphal form *nibrĕku* (reflexive) of the verb *bārak* (bless) in Gen. 12:3; 18:18.

6. Gerhardus Vos has correctly written that in the Old Testament state, Israel as a theocracy (and later as a theocratic monarchy) was never intended to be a missionary institution. It was intended to serve as a type of the perfected kingdom of God in which the secular and religious life were fused. *Biblical Theology* (Grand Rapids: Eerdmans, 1980), 125, 126.

7. Chapter 3 will be devoted to a study of all the prophets' messages to the nations.

8. See Hans Walter Wolff, *Joel and Amos,* trans. Walderman Janzen, S. Dean McBride, Jr., and Charles A. Munchow (Philadelphia: Fortress, 1977), 180, on what some critical scholars have said about this verse not included in the original text because it is considered a cumbersome gloss added by later readers. Wolff would accept v. 3 as a supplement to 3:4–6.

9. Note that commentators agree to give expression to the niphal emphasis, Andersen and Friedman, "Amos," have "unless they have arranged to meet" (383); McComiskey, "Amos," (383) "walk together unless they have agreed to do so"; Stuart, *Hosea–Jonah,* "without having met" (323).

10. Stuart, ibid., uses both pride and arrogance (361, 365 NIV) and Andersen and Freedman, "Amos," pride (569), and legitimate pride or detestable arrogance (808).

11. See McComiskey, "Amos," 325; see also Homer Hailey, *A Commentary on the Minor Prophets* (Grand Rapids: Baker, 1972), 120; Ebenezer Henderson, *The Twelve Minor Prophets* (Grand Rapids: Baker, 1980), 175.

12. Theo Laetsch, *Bible Commentary, The Minor Prophets* (St. Louis: Concordia, 1956), wrote that the phrase must be read as "all that Jacob regards as excellent and glorious" (181). Jacob boasted in his election and as the chosen, they could take care of themselves. Hughell E. W. Fasbroke, "The Book of Amos," in *The Interpreter's Bible,* 12 vols., ed. George Arthur Buttrick (New York: Abingdon, 1951–59) correctly states that the term *ga'on* has a double meaning; cf. his exegesis of 6:8, vol. 6, 825, namely, excellency and arrogance. Israel was arrogant in regard to their fortresses and palaces. In his exegesis of Amos 8:7, Fosbroke points out that Amos makes an ironical reference to "the privileged relationship to Yahweh" of which 3:2 had spoken (841). This privileged relationship was Yahweh's election of Jacob.

13. See G. Van Groningen, *From Creation to Consummation,* vol. 1 (Sioux Center: Dordt, 1995), chaps. 3, 4.

14. Note that George Adam Smith, "Amos," in *The Expositor's Bible,* 6 vols., ed. W. Robertson Nicoll (Grand Rapids: Eerdmans, 1947) singled out the social evils in the passage where Amos condemned Israel for its spiritual and cultural sin as well as the social, and of Israel's crimes, in chapters III and VI, 457. Smith elaborated on the lack of morality in Israel, but it was social morality (466). See also Wolff, *Joel and Amos.* He does not omit

reference to Israel's relationship with and worship of Yahweh; he emphasized Amos's call for righteousness and justice in the social dimension, the lack of which destroyed the foundations of "ancient clan life" (104).

15. The NIV has the word *wrath* eight times in 1:3–2:6 but placed the term in brackets to indicate it was not found in the Hebrew text. It has only the phrase *lō'ăšibennû* from the verb *šûb,* to return. Andersen and Freedman translate the phrase, "I will not reverse it" and discuss three interpretations of the phrase. Their correct preference is that the *'ĕnnû* should be translated "it" and could refer back to what Yahweh said when he roared from Zion (1:2). Yahweh's word of judgment will not be reversed or revoked. *Amos* 2:36.

16. C. Von Orelli, *The Twelve Minor Prophets,* trans. J. S. Banks (Minneapolis: Klock and Klock, reprint, 1977), 105–7.

17. Andersen and Freedman, *Amos,* 9.

18. Ibid., 25, 26.

19. Wolff, *Joel and Amos,* 98–100.

20. See, for example, Willem A. Van Gemeren, who wrote that God's kingdom includes "all who cooperate with His rule." *Interpreting the Prophetic Word* (Grand Rapids: Zondervan, 1990), 228.

21. See John F. Walvoord, *The Millennial Kingdom* (Grand Rapids: Zondervan, 1959), who misconceives the view of covenantal theologians, saying they limit the kingdom to the spiritual; he emphasizes the political millennial, 222–23, 296–97. His fellow dispensationalist Dwight Pentecost has a better inclusive understanding set out in *Thy Kingdom Come* (Wheaton: Victor, 1990), 11–19.

22. Hans W. Wolff wrote a carefully phrased discussion of Amos 1:2. He seemed more concerned to discuss the literary form than to discuss the message. He asked, Is it akin to hymnic style? Is it to be assigned to a ritualistic theophany account? Is its origin in the setting of a victory celebration of the old Israelite militia? Or are we to look to Yahweh's coming to Mount Sinai? Wolff finds that there are as many arguments for considering the oracle as having a theophonic form as there are against it. So, what has the reader or student gained? *Joel and Amos,* 118, 119. And what is one to say about his statement that Amos, "being accusatory in approach, presents Yahweh as raging inarticulately through the land, immediately wreaking havoc" (125)?

23. See *Theological Wordbook of the Old Testament,* vol. I, ed. R. Laird Harris (Chicago: Moody, 1980), 12, 13. The title *'ādôn* was given to husbands (e.g., Sarah to Abraham, Gen. 18:12; Ruth to Boaz, Ruth 2:13) to express recognition of headship. The terms most commonly used to translate Amos's use of it are Lord, Sovereign in combination with Yahweh.

24. The NIV translates both *'ădōnây* and *Yĕhwâ* as Lord, while the RSV translated both *Yĕhwâ* and *'ĕlōhī* as God, as does the NASB and the Berkeley Bible.

25. See my study of these passages in *Messianic Revelation,* 288–317.

26. See my discussion of "The Davidic Tent," in ibid., 470–76.

27. See Andersen and Freedman's reference to the debate about the meaning and significance of the phrase *'et sukkat dāvîd* (booth of David). It has been asked if it refers to the realm or to the dynasty of David. No answer was given. In our discussion, the dynasty was considered the major referent, but also, the blessed effects of the reign of the dynasty.

28. See Stuart, *Hosea–Jonah,* 398.

29. See the final paragraph of the preceding chapter.

30. Stuart understands the term *plant,* not *pluck,* to refer to this fact, *Hosea–Jonah,* 399.

31. See G. Smith, *Amos,* 283.

32. See McComiskey, "Amos," 331. He projected the realization of what is stated in 9:15 into a future, earthly millennial kingdom.

33. John Calvin, *Commentaries on the Twelve Minor Prophets,* vol. II, "Joel, Amos, Obadiah," trans. John Owen (Grand Rapids: Eerdmans, 1950), 412, 413.

34. This passage, 9:13–15, either says too little or too much for many biblical interpreters. It says too little for those who see only a reference to Israel's return from the exile. God promises more. It says too much for those who expect a kingdom that would end after a thousand years because Amos used the emphatic *lo,* never.

35. Jonah may also have been. See chap. 3, part 1.

36. See James Luther Mays, *Hosea: A Commentary* (Philadelphia:Westminster, 1969), 1, 2.

37. See my comments on Hosea, "The Man and His Times," in *Messianic Revelation,* 476–78.

38. Von Orrelli, *The Twelve,* 5.

39. See Stuart, *Hosea–Jonah,* 9–11, for a succinct description of conditions in Israel.

40. Andersen and Freedman, *Hosea,* 66.

41. Various commentaries referred to above can be consulted for further details concerning the problematic literary aspects of the book of Hosea. See also the extensive bibliography on "Hosea" that Stuart has included (2–6).

42. It is of interest to note that Walter Brueggemann in his book *Tradition for Crises* (Richmond: John Knox, 1967) introduces his study of the prophets of Israel under the heading of "The Covenant Context of the Prophets of Israel" chap. 1, 133–35. He went on to discuss the prophets in relation to covenant traditions, forms, and institutions. And he posited the question: Were the prophets in reality, as persons, ordained to an office as representatives of or spokesmen for Yahweh's covenant? (106). Brueggemann singles out Hosea as a definite example of stressing that "the covenant Yahweh made with Israel is effective in any kind of circumstance" (123). His emphasis that only certain kinds of persons who had unique experiences could function as covenant servants detracts from his overall helpful discussion.

43. See my study of Hosea and Gomer in *Messianic Revelation,* 478–79.

44. All commentaries discuss these chapters at varying length. References to these will be few because so many points are discussed by all. That essayists continue to appeal to Hosea 1–3 is exemplified by a very recent article by John Goldingay in *Horizons in Biblical Theology* 17, no. 1 (1995), entitled "Hosea 1–3, Genesis 1–4, and a Masculist Interpretation," 37–44. Goldingay emphasizes that masculist interpretation, a parasite on feminist interpretation, has really not been "birthed yet." But he is prepared to initiate labor pangs. He does this as a male who studies texts with an overt "expression of a distinctively male experience." So Goldingay addresses himself to Hosea 1–3 because of the male experience set out in it.

45. See C. Van Leeuwen, *Hosea* (Nijkerk: Callenbach, 1968), who reviews and rebuts all views that would suggest that Gomer was already a practicing prostitute when Hosea took her as wife (30–33). C. Van Gelderen and W. H. Gispen in their commentary, *Het Boek Hosea* (Kampen: Kok, 1953) take the position that Gomer was not referred to directly as a prostitute (*'ĕšet zōnâ*); the plural term *zĕnûnîm* indicates inclination to prostitution. Andersen and Freedman, *Hosea,* stress that adultery refers to breaking the marriage vow and that the main point is not what she was before marriage, but what she became in marriage (163–67).

46. I briefly presented some reasons for this view in my book *Messianic Revelation,* 479.

47. Note the preposition (b) in 1:2a after Hosea introduced his prophecy in 1:1; saying that "the word of Yahweh was to Hosea." He went on to write that within the historical process, Yahweh spoke to him (*wayyō'mer 'mer 'el hō^sēa',* 1:2b). Hosea was called to be the spokesman, agent, by or through whom Yahweh's word was to go to the people.

48. Debate continues whether the Old Testament law was preceded by the prophetic word. The traditional view had been that the law was given in writing at the time of Moses. Julius Wellhausen reversed the order: the law was developed after the prophets had spoken. Ernest W. Nicholson in *God and His People* (Oxford: Clarendon, 1986) has attempted to give a contemporary defense of the Wellhausian position. Brevard S. Childs suggests that this return to Wellhausen was due to "an over-extension of the concept of covenant"; see his *Biblical Theology of the Old and New Testament* (Minneapolis: Fortress, 1993), 174. Childs has upheld the traditional view (cf. his chapter on "Mosaic Traditions," 130–41), to which he refers later when he wrote. "I have argued for the traditional sequence, and found it inconceivable from the broad evidence to reverse the canonical order" (174). He went on, however, to write that the prophets are not to be seen as "simply a commentary on the law" (175).

49. See Francis I. Andersen's chapter entitled "Yahweh, the Kind and Sensitive God" in Peter T. Obrien and David Gad Petersen, *God Who is Rich in Mercy* (Homebush West: Lancer, 1986), who reviewed the various translations of *ḥesed* (41–44) and proceeded to study the use of the term in the many contexts in which it appeared (44–88).

50. Recall that in my previous book, *From Creation to Consummation* (Sioux Center: Dordt, 1996) I have repeatedly emphasized the intimate correlation among the three creation covenant mandates. Reference to this has also been pointed out in the discussion of the Ten Commandments: 1–4 emphasize the spiritual, 5–7 the social, and 8–10 the cultural and the motivation for keeping these mandates of love for Yahweh (Deut. 6:5; 11:1–15). Cf. also Jesus' words as recorded in Matthew 22:34–40.

51. See Edward J. Young, *My Servants the Prophets* (Grand Rapids: Eerdmans, 1952), chap. IV, "Prophecy and the Theocracy," 76–82.

52. See Roy L. Honeycutt, "Hosea," in *The Broadman Bible Commentary,* vol. 7, ed. Clifton J. Allen (Nashville: Broadman, 1972), 26, 27.

53. I am well aware of the ongoing debate about who is referred to—people living in a place called Adam, of whom there is no record of specific covenant breaking, or to Adam in Eden of whom Scripture speaks as a covenant breaker.

54. Stuart, "Hosea," emphasizes that the verb used in Hebrew is to be considered as the opposite of knowing, that is, an obedient knowing (78). See Andersen and Freedman, *Hosea,* who translate the verb "reject," 353.

55. The verb *gîl* can be understood as the singing in pagan rituals. Israel was not to rejoice in that manner but, as called for; cf. Deut. 10:21 and numerous psalms, such as 32, 33, 111, 144:1; 145:1; 146:1; 149:1; 150:1–6.

56. Recall that Hosea elaborates in chaps. 4–14 on what he has proclaimed in chaps. 1–3.

57. See Duane A. Smith, "Kingship and Covenant in Hosea 11:1–4," *Horizons in Biblical Theology* 16, no. 1 (1994): 41–55.

58. Sigmund Mowinkel, *He That Cometh,* trans. G. W. Anderson (Oxford: Basil Blackwell, 1959), 125–54.

59. George Riggan, *Messianic Theology and the Christian Faith* (Philadelphia: Westminster, 1967), 49–52.

60. See "The Messianic Concept in the Book of Hosea," *Messianic Revelation,* 481–88, for an exegetical and biblical-theological study of four aspects of Hosea's contribution to the revelation of the messianic concept.

61. See Ernst Hengstenberg, *Christology of the Old Testament* and *A Commentary on the Messianic Predictions,* 4 vols., reprint (Grand Rapids: Kregel, 1956), 1:165–290.

62. See my discussion of this phrase, and my interaction with various scholars' views, in *Messianic Revelation,* 484–85.

63. See my more detailed exegesis. Ibid., 486–88.

64. See the summary of Joel's prophecy at the close of chap. 19.

65. Umberto Cassuto had correctly pointed out that Hosea reflected knowledge of the Pentateuch; see "The Prophet Hosea and the Book of the Pentateuch," *Biblical and Oriental Studies,* 2 vols. (Jerusalem: Magnes, 1973), vol. 1, 79–100.

66. *Hosea–Joel,* 216.

67. "The covenant restoration blessing of return from exile and repossessing of the land will come to pass for Israel." Ibid., 183. Stuart includes a reference to type 7. In his introduction he listed restoration blessings that had been listed in the Pentateuch, those that Hosea referred to are: (1) renewal of Yahweh's presence; (2) renewal of the covenant; (5) agricultural bounty; (6) restoration of general prosperity; (7) return from exile; and (10) freedom from death and destruction (xli–xlii).

68. Robert L. Saucy, *The Case for Progressive Dispensationalism* (Grand Rapids: Zondervan, 1993), 114.

69. See the *Oxford NIV Scofield Study Bible* (Oxford, 1967), 893. This revised edition repeats what was already written in the original *Scofield Bible,* 1909 (922).

21

Prophetic Revelation to and concerning Non-Israelite Nations

I. Rationale for Including the Non-Israelite Nations

II. The Pentateuchal, Historical, and Early Prophetic References to Nations

III. Later Prophetic Addresses Concerning Nations

IV. Interpretation of the Prophetic Message to the Non-Israelite Nations

V. Conclusion

21

Prophetic Revelation to and concerning Non-Israelite Nations

The Rationale for Inclusion

The Bible is often referred to as a book that presents Israelite/Jewish history and religion. In our studies, however, we have consistently referred to the Bible as the written record of Yahweh God's revelation to all people. This revelation, however, was given primarily to the Israelite/Jewish people. All biblical writers were Jewish, with the exception of Luke, the Greek evangelist and writer of the Gospel of Luke, and the book of the Acts of Apostles. Because God's revelation was given to humanity through Israelite/Jewish agents, and because the Messiah/Christ was promised to come through an Israelite lineage, as he indeed did come, the Bible refers predominantly to the Israelite/Jewish people. The reality that must not be overlooked is that they were never addressed as an isolated and completely separated group of people who had no relationship with the people of other nations. The truth is that as Israel in Old Testament times was called to be a distinct and holy people (Exod. 19:5, 6), they were to be God's agents of revelation and salvation to all peoples, races, tongues, and nations (Isa. 42:6; 49:6; Luke 2:31, 32; Acts 13:47). To serve as such Israel was never to be considered as a unique people with no relationship to and responsibility in regards to all people on earth. Thus, in this study of the history of Yahweh God's revelation we shall see that all peoples are included in the cosmic kingdom, are in a covenantal relationship with Yahweh, and are called to acknowledge the Mediator, receive the benefits that come through him, and believe in him, worship, and serve him.

In our previous studies we have made repeated references to the non-Israelite nations.[1] In this chapter we attempt to draw together what the Old Testament presents as the place and role of all nations and the message that Yahweh God included in his revelation for them.

Specific problems have to be addressed. (1) Did the prophetic messages, as these were addressed to Israel, only include references to the nations, or were the messages also given directly to the nations?[2] (2) If the latter is the case, how were the nations addressed? (3) What actual role did Israel have in Yahweh God's program? (4) Was the message concerning the Messiah, who was to come from Israel, also to be addressed to the nations? That this was the case in New Testament times cannot be doubted (cf. Acts 8:26–40; 10:1–11:18; 13:1–5). In other words, was Old Testament Israel given a missionary task? (5) Was Israel to be kept so distinct and separate that no people of other nations could remain non-Israelite biologically/ethnically if they were incorporated as a living part/member of God's chosen Israelite people? (6) Were non-Israelite people included in Yahweh God's covenant with Israel? If so, was there one covenant or two covenants that presented two ways of life and salvation?[3] These problems will not be addressed one by one, but will be answered as the study progresses. First, we review what has been referred to, that is, what is recorded in Genesis 1:1–Hosea 14:9 and studied in volume I and the first two chapters in volume II. Second, the prophetic address—communicated verbally and by writing—is discussed. We will not follow the time of the prophets chronologically but rather of the nations. Third, we summarize the prophetic message for all nations.

The Pentateuchal, Historical, and Early Prophetic References to Nations

A. The opening chapters of the Old Testament record that God created Adam and Eve and that all of humanity has descended from them. Paul makes a special point of this reality, when addressing the Athenians, he declared, "From one man he (God) made every nation of men, that they should inhabit the earth" (Acts 17:26). The entire Old Testament, as well as the New Testament, keep this truth before the reader/student. While the emphasis is on the seed line of the woman (Gen. 3:15, 16), it is kept in the context of all people. Hence, reference is made to Cain and his progeny when he was banished (4:13–26).

Noah and his family were not isolated. They lived among the wicked peoples of their time (Gen. 6:1–8). Noah preached to them (2 Peter 2:5). Yahweh God destroyed them by means of the flood (Gen. 6:13; 7:17–23). After the flood, his descendants multiplied and were made to spread out on the earth (9:1–11:9).

B. Yahweh God never disowned any person or group of people as his. He had created them; he had made them to be an inherent part of his cosmic kingdom. All people were created, given their times and their determined places (Acts 17:26). Each nation, under Yahweh God's sovereign reign, was given the privilege and responsibility to participate in the cosmic kingdom. All were to obey the spiritual, social, and cultural mandates that had been placed before Adam, Eve, and all their descendants. Hence, it should surprise no one that reference is made to Cain's descendants developing husbandry, metallurgy, and music. The people in the parts of the earth where they lived developed architecture; Noah built the ark; his progeny began building a tower (Gen. 11:1–4). Archaeologists have found evidence that home building had advanced to a high degree in the Ur of the Chaldees by the time Abram was born.

The point to be emphasized is that all people, as they developed into separate races, nations, and linguistic groups, were integral aspects of Yahweh God's cosmic kingdom from the very beginning—from the time of creation! All peoples were Yahweh God's image bearers. All had their time, place, and role under Yahweh God's reign. Though some nations and groups of people came under severe judgment, they were not disowned by Yahweh God, although some were removed from the earth. Rather, because they were his people, he dealt with them when they disbelieved, rejected, and despised him and made substitute deities for their worship and service.

C. Israel in time became a separate and distinct nation. But Israel was not such from the time of creation nor from the time of Noah or even the patriarchs. The woman's redemptive seed line was always present: Adam, Seth, Noah, Shem, Terah, Abraham, Isaac, Jacob, and his offspring. Many historians who have studied and written about the biblical testimony about Israel make a specific point of stressing that Israel must always be considered in the context of its beginnings. F. F. Bruce, writing about Israel, noted that Israel's national history was not lived out in isolation from other peoples. Hence, he entitled his work *Israel and the Nations.*[4] Henri Daniel-Rops introduced his study by referring to Abram's life in the Ur of the Chaldees where his father worshiped other gods. Mesopotamia already had a history dating back fifteen hundred years when Abram migrated from there "about the year two thousand B.C."[5]

John Bright, desiring to present a complete history of Israel, felt compelled to discuss the ancient Orient and "The World of Israel's Beginnings" before he commenced his study of the patriarchs because Israel, as a people, arose from the context of nations when Yahweh God called Abram to leave the Ur of the Chaldees.[6] Walther Eichrodt wrote that "no presentation of Old Testament theology can properly be made without constant reference to it connections with the whole world of Near Eastern religion."[7]

These writers, having their unique perspectives and approaches, and drawing differing conclusions from their studies of Israelite origins, do agree and affirm that Israel, as a nation, came upon the scene of history much later than some other nations. They also agree that Israel arose from within the context of other nations—

those in the lower Mesopotamian Valley. And most agree that Israel emerged as a potential political unit, a nation, when their exodus from Egypt took place. It can be said without fear of contradiction that Yahweh God used nations to give rise to the patriarchs and he made Egypt serve as the maternal source for Israel as a political entity—that is, a nation. The prophet Ezekiel (cf. 6:1–7) employs the imagery of a newborn babe with an uncut umbilical cord and in unwashed condition when it appeared on the scene as a child born from a mixed ancestry. The prophet's reference is clearly to Israel's emergence from Egypt as a "newborn nation."

In view of Israel's emergence and early dependence on other nations, it surely can be said that Israel should have felt a debt to other nations and shown its appreciation to them when Yahweh God chose Israel to be his kingdom-covenantal agent among the nations.

D. Israel had a specific covenantal responsibility to exercise on behalf of all nations because all nations were in a covenantal relationship with God and with all people. This covenantal relationship and responsibility for all nations had been given clear and eloquent expression by Noah.[8] Noah had prophesied that Yahweh God would build the covenant tent with Shem, that Japheth would enlarge it, and even the most unlikely descendant of Ham would be included. They would indeed all be in the covenantal tent! (9:25–27). All of humanity, according to the biblical record, is descended from Noah and his three sons and their wives. Noah had had Yahweh God's covenant confirmed with him (9:8–16) and thus with his sons and all of his descendants.

When Yahweh God called Abram to leave his idol-worshiping home where he was a citizen in the Ur of the Chaldees (11:27–12:3; Josh. 24:2–4), Abram was given wonderful promises. He was to receive a land where he and his descendants would develop into a great nation (Gen. 12:2); other nations would develop from him also (17:6). He would be richly blessed (his possessions became very great, 13:6). He would become famous (his name would become great). These promises were not to be received without accompanying stipulations. He was to be blessed so that he could and would be a blessing. He had to become a channel, an agent, a means of blessing for all nations. Yahweh God specifically stated that all nations were to be blessed through him. The niphal form of the verb *bless* carries both a reflexive and a passive action. The reflexive is dominant and implies two important truths. Abram had to so live, worship, and serve, while obeying the spiritual, social, and cultural mandates, thus demonstrating that he was in reality a covenantal agent in Yahweh's cosmic kingdom, that neighboring peoples and nations beyond his environment would see him as truly a model covenantal kingdom representative. Abram was to commanded to witness verbally only; rather, his entire life was to be a demonstration of a God-honoring, -worshiping, and -serving life. Thus, a great responsibility was placed upon Abram and his progeny. All of their lives, at all times and in all places and circumstances, was to be a positive witness to the nations. This was reemphasized later after Abram had a son with Hagar, Sarah's Egyptian maid, and was commanded to live blamelessly (Gen. 17:1). His entire life was to be lived so that no one could refer to him as an inconsistent witness. His actions were to be continuous testimonies to his covenantal relationship with his Creator, Redeemer, cosmic Lord.

The second important truth emphasized by the niphal form of the verb *bless* was the responsibility placed on the nations. The reflexive aspect certainly calls for the idea of "bless themselves." The nations had the onus placed upon them to relate positively to Abram. They were to consider him a model; they were to model their lives according to Abram's pattern. Thus a mutual responsibility was stressed and was expected to be honored.

That a responsibility was placed on the nations is clearly implied from Yahweh God's statement concerning blessing and cursing. Those who would bless Abram would be blessed. This called for the nations to acknowledge Abram as God's appointed model servant, to honor him as such, to seek his welfare, and to hold him up spiritually, socially, and culturally before God and themselves. Should they not do so, by ignoring, ridiculing, rejecting, hating, and even opposing him, they would be cursed by God.[9] The promises and stipulations given to Abram, and Yahweh God's response to them if acknowledged or disobeyed, is fundamental for the proper understanding of what the psalmists and prophets spoke about nations being either blessed or cursed.

When Yahweh God remembered his covenant with the patriarchs (Exod. 2:24), and confirmed, explicated, and expanded it with the freed Israelite slaves (19:3–24:8), he did not abrogate his covenant/kingdom relationship with the other nations. He specifically stated that Israel was chosen from all the nations to be in a specific bridegroom-bride relationship with him. He went on to say that *kî lî kōl hā'ārez* (to me [is] all the earth) (19:5). In the immediate context all the peoples were referred to. Saying that all the earth was his, God reminded Israel that all the people, in their places, lives, and relationships, were under his ownership and reign. Israel, though chosen from among these nations in all the earth, was not to be separated or removed from them in any way. They were to be a distinct and holy people. They were to be a kingdom, a symbol of Yahweh's cosmic kingdom, and an earthly demonstration of it. As such they were a royal priesthood among the nations. As a priestly nation among the nations, Israel was to serve Yahweh as his representative. Israel had to sacrifice and intercede for, instruct and guide the nations even as the appointed priests were ordained to do within Israel.

Before Israel departed from Sinai, Yahweh God had Moses repeat to Israel that they were to be a unique, separate, and holy nation. They were not to follow the ways of surrounding nations (Lev. 20, 23, 24, 26; 25:44; 26:33, 38, 45). Israel was assured that the Canaanite nations living in the land promised to Abram would be removed because of their iniquities (Gen. 15:16). Those, however, who acknowledged Israel as God's covenantal servant nation could and did become members of Israel (e.g., Rahab, Josh. 6:24, 25; Gibeonites, 9:14–27).

When the theocratic monarchy was firmly established under David and Solomon's reign and their kingdom extended from the river of Egypt to the

Euphrates (2 Sam. 8:1–14; 1 Kings 4:20–25), as Yahweh God had promised to Abraham (Gen. 15:18), various nations became part of the Israelite empire. David and Solomon reigned over them and they brought tribute, especially to Solomon (1 Kings 4:21). David had not only defeated the nations that became part of the extended kingdom; his army included men from various nations (2 Sam. 23:24–39). Thus people from other nations became incorporated into the kingdom of Israel. This fact demonstrated that membership in the theocratic monarchy was not determined strictly along biological lines. In a real sense, by having people of various nations incorporated into Israel indicated that they were representatives, at the very least, that people born outside Israel could indeed become Israelite kingdom participants.

A point that we should stress, however, is that all nations were within the broad parameters of Yahweh God's covenant and under his kingdom rule. Many people from these nations could and did become integral citizens of the Israelite monarchy. Those that did not were in no way absolved from their responsibilities to acknowledge Yahweh God and serve him. The punishment that many nations suffered was due to their rejection of Yahweh God, their opposition to him and his chosen servant covenant nation. In truth, many of the nations were severely punished and even completely uprooted in time as the seven Canaanite nations in the promised land were when Israel conquered and entered it.[10] Yahweh God had assured Abraham the curse would come on those who ridiculed, rejected, and opposed his progeny. Thus the covenantal curse was executed on the Canaanite nations as well as other surrounding nations.

Another point to be stressed, possibly more so than the previous one, is that Israel was aware of Yahweh God's claim on all nations and his heart's desire that all nations know and worship him and thus receive a full and complete redemption. Solomon, in his dedicatory prayer for the newly constructed temple, prayed for the foreigners so that "all the people of the earth may know your name and fear you" (1 Kings 8:41–43). The afflicted psalmist prayed that the nations would fear the name of Yahweh and revere his glory (Ps. 102:15). Other psalmists likewise gave expression to the blessed truth that Yahweh God called and desired all nations to know, love, worship, and serve him. Indeed, some psalmists led Israel in singing that people of all nations were citizens of Yahweh God's kingdom and therefore covenantal agents on his behalf (Pss. 2:1–12; 47:1–9; 67:1–7; 72:8–11; 87:1–7; 102:22; 113:4–9).

E. In our study thus far, references were made to various nations. Abraham fought five maurading kings (Gen. 14) and he and Isaac had dealings with the Philistine king, Abimelech of Gerar (21:22–34; 26:1–33). Egypt had a vital role in the lives of the patriarchs and their descendants (39:1–Exod. 14:31). Joshua conquered the strongholds of the people who had made their residence in Canaan. During the period of the judges, Yahweh God's instruments of judgment on Israel were the people the Israelites had not removed from Canaan; only the tribe of Judah had removed the original inhabitants. The Angel of the Lord informed them that these people left in the land would be "thorns in your sides and their gods will be a snare to you" (Judg. 1:1–2:3). The text states that the nations were left to test Israel, but the Israelites intermarried with them and lived at peace with them (3:1–6). In addition to the nations remaining in the land, surrounding nations were also Yahweh God's instruments of judgment. Those referred to are the people of Aram (3:1–11); the Moabites (3:12–30); the Philistines (3:31; 10:7; 14:1–16:30); Jabin, a Canaanite king (4:1–5:31); the Midianites (6:1–7:25); the Ammonites (10:7–12:7).

The Philistine people, inhabitants of Philistia located on the southwest coast of Canaan, were a dominating people and a cause of much conflict for the Israelites during the 1200–1000 B.C. period. Three important influences were exerted: religiously, their gods, Dagon, Ashteroth, and Baalzebub, were an enticement; culturally, they were superior to Israel; militarily, they were strong, skillful, and determined. King Saul had constant conflict with them. David eventually defeated them and broke their power (2 Sam. 8:1, 12). The Philistines, however, were not completely removed or forgotten, for the prophets referred to them (Isa. 2:6; 9:12; 14:29, 31; Jer. 25:20; 47:1, 4; Ezek. 16:27, 57; 25:15, 16).[11]

Other nations that David defeated and over which he reigned were the people of Moab, Zobah, Aram, Hamath in the north, Edom, and Ammon (2 Sam. 8:1–14). Amos[12] prophesied about and against them years after David had died. The people of Aram (Damascus) threshed Gilead in northeast Israel; these people had been treated cruelly as if they were grain to be harvested by wooden sledges with metal teeth. The Philistines captured the Israelites and sold them as slaves to Edom; the Tyrians, breaking a treaty of brotherhood, had also done so.[13] These neighboring nations violated the creational covenantal social and cultural mandates. The prophetic phrase, "for three sins, even for four," gave poignant expression to the willful disobedience of these nations as they demonstrated their ridicule, lack of respect for, and rejection of Israel as Yahweh God's channel of blessing for them. Their inhuman treatment of Abraham's descendants in the cultural context certainly was an evidence of their cursing Israel and thus calling Yahweh God's covenantal curse upon themselves (Amos 1:3–10).

F. Amos also had a message concerning the nations that can be referred to as the "relative nations."[14] The Moabites and Ammonites were descendants of Moab and Ammon, grandsons of Lot, the nephew of Abraham (Gen. 11:27; 12:4; 13:8; 14:13; 19:37, 38). This relationship placed them in a unique covenantal context. They, nevertheless, were considered to be more hostile than friendly and cooperative as was stated and demonstrated in various ways (Exod. 15:15; Num. 22:1–24:25; Josh. 24:9 [the Balak/Balaam episode]; Num. 25:1–6 [sexual seduction]). But, Moses reminded Israel, after they had bypassed the southern and eastern regions of Moab (cf. Judg. 11:14–18), and had set up camp on its northern plains, just east of the River Jordan, that Israel was not to harass them or make war against them because Yahweh God had given Lot's descendants the land they occupied as their possession (Deut. 2:9). During the time of the judges, Moab fought against and captured some Israelite people and territory (Judg. 3:12–30). Their gods continued to be worshiped by the Israelites (10:6; cf. also 1 Kings 11:7; 2 Kings 17:7–13).

During the time of the kings, Moab was repeatedly at war with Israel. David defeated them (2 Sam. 8:12). Ahab and Jehoshaphat did also (2 Kings 3:1–27). The major prophets prophesied concerning Moab's tragic future. Isaiah spoke of Moab's pride and conceit (16:6) and resultant ruin causing here remnant to flee as fugitives (15:1–16:13). Speaking for Yahweh God, Isaiah's heart cried out for Moab (15:5; 16:11) and he wept for her (16:9). Jeremiah also expressed grief over Moab (48:31, 32, 36) because of her "overweening pride, conceit, arrogance, haughtiness, and insolence" (48:29, 30). She would be destroyed (48:4, 15). Indeed, Moab would come under the judgment of god, the covenant curse, because Moab ridiculed Israel (48:26). Thus God's word to Abram was fulfilled (Gen. 12:3). Zephaniah joined in prophetic denunciation of Moab because Yahweh god hear her insults and therefore it would become as Sodom (2:8, 9). Ezekiel, likewise, prophesied concerning Moab's punishment because of her disrespect for the house of Judah (even though the house of Judah did not deserve it) (25:8–11).

Finally, the question must be asked: Was Moab, within the broader parameters of the covenant Yahweh God made with Abraham, cursed completely as a land and as a nation? What was the psalmist (60:8) singing when he referred to Moab as Yahweh God's washbasin? Moab may have been thought of as a kitchen or bathroom utensil, but as such it was in the covenant household serving a useful purpose. We saw that Isaiah and Jeremiah expressed grief over Moab's sins and resultant curses. This grief can possibly be understood in the context of Moab's covenantal privileges that were abused. Jeremiah pronounced hope for Moab, saying Yahweh would restore her. The Hebrew phrase is emphatically stated: *wĕsabtî šĕbût Môab bĕ' aḥărîm hayyāmîm* (and I will restore the fortunes of Moab in the latter days). This phrase is used by the psalmist when praying for a full salvation and restoration for Israel (14:7). When we consider what the prophets, using this phrase, meant when they spoke of the restoration and continuation of Israel/Judah (cf. Isa. 11:11; Jer. 12:15), one could conclude that there was a future for Moab as a nation.[15] Daniel referred to a deliverance of the three relative nations from the king who would exalt himself above all gods and speak unheard of things about Yahweh God (11:41). In the days of Ezra, circa 450 B.C. however, the remnant of Israel that had returned to their promised land fraternized and intermarried with Moabites and participated in their detestable practices (Ezra 9:1, 2). Writers have pointed out that the name *Moabite* became equivalent to "sinner" and "impious." Historical and archaeological finds seem to conclude that by the second century B.C., the land the Moabites had inhabited had no sedentary occupation until the Nabateans, who were of Arab (Ishmaelite) origins, settled in the land.[16]

In conclusion to our discussion of Moab, it should be stressed that one Moabitess did become an important person in Israel, namely, Ruth, who became an ancestress of David and therefore is in the covenant lineage from which Jesus

Christ was born (Ruth 1–4). And, as to the future of Moab/Moabites, it may be well to understand that the phrase "latter days" might well point to "a messianic expectation."[17]

The second relative nation Amos referred to was Ammon, whose descendants are known as the Ammonites (Gen. 19:38). They lived in the region east of the Jordan River, and of the kingdom of Bashan and Heshbon. They were not in the path of Israel's march from the desert of Sinai to Canaan. But, as in the case with Moab, the Israelites were not to harass the Ammonites as they marched to Canaan. Nor did they invade any part of Ammonite territory when they, under Moses' leadership, conquered Bashan and Heshbon (Num. 21:24). Later, however, when Joshua divided the land east of the Jordan, he allotted half of the Ammonite territory as part of Gad's inheritance (Josh. 13:25).

During the period of the judges, the Ammonites joined the Moabites in attacking Israel and capturing some of her territory (Judg. 3:13). Years later, the Ammonites made war against Israel. Jepthah was raised up to defeat the Ammonites (10, 11).

During Saul's reign over Israel, the Ammonites again attacked Israel and threatened to gouge out the right eye of any Israelite who surrendered and made a treaty with Nahash, king of the Ammonites. King Saul led a victorious army against Nahash (1 Sam. 11:1–11), but he had to continually fight against them (14:47).

The Ammonites, when offered sympathy by David, humiliated David's messengers. David then fought against them; while the Ammonites had hoped to have assistance from the Arameans (Syrians), they did not receive it and were defeated by David's army. It was in this context that David committed adultery with Bathsheba (2 Sam. 10, 11).

The Ammonites were not eliminated by means of the battles they lost. When Solomon reigned over Israel, he took Ammonite women as wives and took Molech their "detestable god" as one to worship also (1 Kings 11:1, 4, 7, 33). During the time of the major prophets, the Ammonites continued to be referred to as enemy people (Jer. 49:1–5). Ezekiel, reproving the Ammonites for their glee when Judah and Jerusalem were plundered by various nations, prophesied that Ammon would be cut off and exterminated (Ezek. 25:1–7). Zephaniah also referred to the taunts of the Ammonites (2:8, 9).

The Ammonites were still present to tempt and influence the covenant people after a remnant returned from exile. Ezra recorded that there was intermarriage and a following after Ammonite deities (Ezra 9:1, 2). Nehemiah relates that the Ammonites joined in a plot to fight against the remnant when they were rebuilding the walls of Jerusalem (Neh. 4:7).

A survey of Ammonite relationships with Israel certainly indicates that they were not willing to be involved with Israel/Judah as a covenant people serving as Yahweh God's mediatorial agents among the nations. As a result, the prophets condemned them and prophesied of their utter extermination (Jer. 49:5; Ezek. 25:7).

Israel/Judah, instead of being a spiritual light and guide to the Ammonites, either joined them in their idolatry or were used by Yahweh God to defeat and punish them.

A final comment: the Jordanian people, now occupying all of the former Ammonite territory, are Arabs, descendants of Ishmael. The capital city, formerly; named Rabbah, is Amman, derived from the name *Ammon.* Some historians have pointed out that when the Arab tribes began their infiltration of Ammonite territory, Ammonite people moved westward and were partially absorbed into the remnant of Israel. This possible historical reality may give a clue to the interpretation of Jeremiah's statement (49:6) that Ammon's fortunes would be restored.[18]

The third relative nation Amos referred to was Edom, the nation descended from Esau, Abraham's grandson.

Amos referred to Edom buying Israelites as slaves (1:6, 9) and to the undying anger raging continually and the unchecked fury against Israel (1:11). According to the patriarchal record, Esau's anger, hatred, and fury against Jacob/Israel arose when Isaac had no special blessing, and especially not the firstborn birthright blessing for him because Jacob had received it when he had deceived his father (Gen. 27:1–45). Esau had previously not shown appreciation for it (25:29–34) but really did want it, especially when he learned that his younger brother had taken advantage of a blind father and had bested him in receiving the birthright. In a real sense, then, we should consider Esau a covenantal son who early on in his life became a covenant breaker. Though he had received covenant blessings, because of his conduct he came under the curse of the covenant. This curse followed him and his descendants for generations.

When Jacob, with his family and possessions, fled from his father-in-law, Laban, he realized he would have to have some sort of relationship with his brother Esau. His attempt to do so, his fear of his brother, and the actual meeting of the two brothers provide an interesting narrative (32:1–33:17). Jacob tried to placate Esau by referring to him as *'ădōnî* (master, lord) and giving him a portion of his possession, which Esau accepted (33:8–11). Jacob, however, was not prepared to continue fellowship with Esau and therefore parted from him (33:12–17). There was no further peaceful interaction between the brothers and their descendants, rather, hatred and hostility on the part of Esau/Edom continued unabated (Amos 1:11).

Moses referred to the Edomites' negative attitude toward Israel when he recounted how they had forbidden Israel to pass through their land on their way to their promised inheritance. The Edomites confirmed this by preparing for military action if Israel should trespass their boundaries (Num. 20:14–23). Moses had had Israel sing about Esau/Edom's terror when reports of the crossing of the Red Sea would reach them (Exod. 15:15). Israel's journey was lengthened because of the detour they had to make around Edom (Num. 21:4; Deut. 2:8; Judg. 11:17, 18). When Moses later addressed Israel on the banks of the River Jordan he reminded Israel of Yahweh God's covenantal assurance to Abraham's grandson's descendants. He spoke of the descendants of Esau as *'ăḥêkem* (your brothers), who in fear of Israel, were not to be provoked to war and whose land would not be part of Israel's possession. Furthermore, whatever Israel took from the Edomites had to be paid for in silver (Deut. 2:3–6). Indeed, Israel had to respect Yahweh God's covenantal concern for the progeny of Esau, Abraham's grandson.

All was not to go well for the covenant-breaking Edomites. Balaam had said in his messianic prophecy, referring to the star and the scepter that would rise from Israel, that God would crush the skull of Moab and conquer Edom/Seir (Num. 24:17, 18). The Edomites eventually gave sufficient reason for having the curse of the covenant applied to them, and that often at the hands of Israelites. Joshua had allotted Judah territory that had a common boundary with Edom (Josh. 15:1, 21). Hence, there was no other territory between the two countries. But this factor also made hostile interactions between them more likely. After he became king, Saul fought against neighboring nations; Moab, Ammon, and Edom are specifically mentioned as receiving punishment, which suggested that these countries were aggressors and thereby demonstrated their readiness to bring curses upon Israel (Gen. 12:3). David also had to take military action against the Edomites; he put Israelite garrisons in their land to maintain peace (2 Sam. 8:12–14; 1 Chron. 18:12, 13). This military action by David (1 Kings 11:14–18) did not preclude some interaction between Israel/Judah and Edom. For an example, there was Doeg, the Edomite, who reported that David was seen at the tabernacle when fleeing from Saul. He indirectly caused the death of many priests (1 Sam. 21:7–22). The kings of Israel and Judah formed an alliance with the king of Edom to fight against Moab (2 Kings 3:4–10). The gods of the Edomites were also attractive; King Amaziah of Judah, after defeating them in battle, brought their gods to Jerusalem, set them up, and worshiped them (2 Chron. 21:14, 20). The general conclusion about the relationship between Israel/Judah and Edom is that the Edomites were repeatedly in rebellion against their brothers to the north (2 Kings 8:22; 2 Chron. 21:10).

Turning to the Psalms, we find a twofold sentiment toward Edom. Asaph called for the defeat and destruction of Edom because of its plotting with other nations against the covenant people and especially their sovereign covenant Lord (Ps. 83:1–18). David, however, after General Joab had led a victorious campaign against the Edomites exulted in the sovereign reign of Yahweh God over all nations. He sang that Yahweh God "will toss his sandal over Edom."[19] In the same context, David sang of Ephraim as God's helmet and Judah as his scepter (Pss. 60:8; 108:9). David went on to sing that Yahweh God would lead him to Edom.[20] David had more than a personal wish; he gave expression to Yahweh God's claim to and reign over the relative nations.

The latter prophets had specific messages concerning Edom. Joel, who presented the overall agenda that prophets following him would develop, had prophesied that when Yahweh God restored the fortunes of Judah and Jerusalem, nations would be gathered for judgment. Edom is singled out as a nation to become a desert waste because "of the violence done to the people of Judah in which Edomites had shed innocent blood" (Joel 3:1, 2, 10). Isaiah, when portraying the work and ultimate blessings that the Shoot or Branch of Jesse, that is, David's Son, would usher in (11:1–16), spoke in terms of past and present experiences. For example, to set forth the blessing of unity he stressed that Ephraim, that is, Israel of the north, would no longer be jealous of Judah or Judah hostile to Ephraim (11:13) and this reunited people would lay hands on Edom, Moab, and the Ammonites. These relative nations would be incorporated into the covenant people of Yahweh God (11:14). Isaiah also prophesied concerning Edom's tragic end as a nation (34:5), when an important city of Edom, Bosrah, experiences a great slaughter as a sacrifice to Yahweh God (34:6). Edom's streams would turn to black pitch and her dust burn as sulfur and pitch, recalling what had happened to Sodom and its sister cities (Gen. 19:23–29; Jer. 49:18), that had been located on the northeastern border of Edom. Total destruction and desolation would be the future of Edom (Isa. 34:11–15) and only thorns, wild animals, and birds, such as owls and falcons would inhabit Edom's land. Later Isaiah again, using picturesque language, described Yahweh's victorious agent coming from Edom, wearing bloodstained garments, to bring salvation to his people (63:1–6).

Jeremiah prophesied that Edom, as well as Ammon and Moab, would be punished, even if circumcised in the flesh, as the people of Judah were, because of their uncircumcised hearts (9:25, 26). The phrase *uncircumcised heart* referred specifically to hardened, rebellious hearts. Recall that Joel had called for a rending of hearts and not merely of outward garments (2:13); Jeremiah had stated it specifically to the people of Judah: "circumcise yourselves to Yahweh by circumcising your hearts;" by this he meant that Judah should put away detestable idols and return to Yahweh (Jer. 4:1–4). Since circumcision was the seal of the covenant (Gen. 17:9–14), the people were implicitly accused of breaking and abusing Yahweh God's covenantal relationship with them.[21] The refusal to do so would cause the cup of God's wrath, the curse of the covenant, to be poured out on peoples of all nations The Philistines, Moabites, Ammonites, and Edomites are mentioned (Jer. 25:15–30). An evidence of this cup of Yahweh's covenant wrath would be Yahweh's delivering them all to Nebuchadnezzar, king of Babylon, who would plunder them and turn their places into desolate haunts for wild animals (27:2–7).

Ezekiel, in the course of his prophetic messages, referred briefly a number of times to Edom. He spoke of the daughters of Edom scorning and despising the people of Judah for their lewd behavior that exceeded that of Sodom and Gomorrah (16:57). In a brief prophecy regarding Edom, Ezekiel referred to Edom's revenge on the house of Judah during the times of its exile. In anger and wrath Yahweh God would stretch his hand against Edom (recall Yahweh God had done so when Israel was delivered from Egypt). Edom's men and animals would be killed and Edom from Teman to Dedan, that is, from north to south, would be laid waste. Ezekiel pronounces that Edom would suffer Yahweh God's vengeance and thereby know that Yahweh is Lord of all (25:12–14; 35:4).[22]

In addition to the brief references Jeremiah and Ezekiel made to Edom, each has included a lengthy statement regarding Esau/Edom/Mount Seir's sins and punishment. These major prophets spoke as Obadiah did. Common themes in these three prophets will be noted as well as some unique to one or two.

Before these common themes are discussed briefly, the question of which of the three was spoken first and their interdependence must be answered. The three prophets do not refer to a specific time that they prophesied. Each is certain that they were speaking the word of the Lord (Jer. 47:9; Ezek. 35:1; Obad. 1). Careful attention to the historical references, or lack of these, and the contexts of each passage would lead one to conclude that Jeremiah's prophecy was prior in time because he did not make direct references to the capture and destruction of Jerusalem in 586 B.C., as Obadiah did (vv. 11–14). Thus, we conclude Jeremiah prophesied against Edom prior to Jerusalem's fall; Obadiah did soon after; and Ezekiel did after Israel had been in exile for some years.[23]

The Edomite people were known specifically for four characteristics. The first of these was wisdom (Jer. 49:7; Obad. 8).[24] Ezekiel implies it when referring to Edomites boasting against Yahweh (Ezek. 35:13). Along with the Edomite sense of their wisdom, they boasted of power, wealth, security, and alliances with other non-Israelite/Judahite countries (Jer. 49:15, 16, 20; Ezek. 35:10; Obad. 3, 7).[25]

These "virtues" led, secondly, to an overwhelming sense of pride (Jer. 49:16; Obad. 3, 4). This pride led, thirdly, to fierce anger, jealousy, and hatred against the progeny of Jacob living in Judah/Jerusalem (Ezek. 49:11). These, in turn, fourthly, motivated the Edomites to repeatedly attack and deal inhumanly with their distant relatives (35:5, 10, 11; Obad. 10, 11, 14). And when Jerusalem was captured and plundered by the Babylonians, the Edomites, in their pride and jealousy, rejoiced over the calamities experienced (Ezek. 35:15; Obad. 12, 13). The psalmist included a reference to the Edomite glee when Jerusalem fell: "Tear it down to its foundations" (Ps. 137:7).

As one considers the sins and vices of Edom that the prophets describe, it becomes very obvious that the Edomites were flagrant covenant breakers and despisers. They developed their cultural propensities, and so would seem to have obeyed the cultural mandate. But when this "obedience" is considered in the context of their horrendous activities in regard to the social and spiritual mandates, one must conclude that they developed their cultural assets to enable them to violate the social and spiritual, that is, their relationship especially with covenantal relatives and their relationship with their ancestor Abraham's covenant God. The Edomites seriously violated the creation covenant, but tragically they utterly rejected the redemptive strand of the covenant. Thus they truly made themselves liable for the full application of the covenant curse. Yahweh God, sovereign Lord over all nations (Jer. 49:19, 20; Ezek. 35:3, 6, 15), would have his day (Obad. 15). Disaster would strike and Edom would suffer complete desolation according to Yahweh God's will (Jer. 49:8, 12, 17). Edom would be as a vineyard that has been so cleanly picked, that not a grape is left for gleaners (49:8, 9; Obad. 5c). Enemies, plunderers, and thieves would thoroughly strip Edom of all its possessions, cities, and land (Jer. 49:10; Obad. 5, 6). Edom would be a ruin, an object of horror, and would be despised (Jer. 49:12, 17; Obad. 2).The prophets stressed that Edom, as a country, would be destroyed forever as a land and nation (Ezek. 35:7–9; Obad. 10). Hence as calamity would come upon Edom, there would be terror and horror, and ruined Edom would be despised (Jer. 49:15, 16; Obad. 2). Jeremiah concludes his prophecy against Edom comparing its warriors to a woman in labor (49:22).

As one studies these prophecies against Edom, who had a covenantal inheritance as a grandson of Abraham, the question arises, Were the sins of Esau/Edom so great that no Edomite could receive mercy and grace? Was there no future at all for any of them? Jeremiah answers saying that Edomite widows and orphans would be spared and can trust in Yahweh (49:11). But there is no assured future for Edom, a nation, a land, as there will be for Jerusalem and Judah. They would be restored (Obad. 17–21), as indeed they were after seventy years of exile.

There is another prophecy that refers to Edom that assures us that Edomites can, and will, participate in Yahweh's great covenant plan to be worked out within the cosmic kingdom. In truth, Edomites will have a share in the redemptive blessings, made sure realities through David's Son, the messianic Mediator of the covenant.

We must consider what Amos prophesied (9:11, 12). Recall that Amos, in his first message, proclaimed that for three, even four transgressions, Edom's cities of Teman and Bosrah would be burned. In the concluding section of his prophecy, Amos proclaimed that not all of Edom would be forever put away.

Amos prophesied that David's royal house, though to fall in time, would be restored, repaired, and built as before (9:11).[26] This rebuilt house would be a "home for all nations that acknowledged (or bore)" the name of Yahweh God. Amos thus prophesied that the Davidic kingdom with its royal Mediator would be inclusive of all people. The apostles, in a council in Jerusalem, after Christ's ascension, the outpouring of the Holy Spirit, and the initial ingathering of Gentile Christians, understood that Amos's prophecy regarding all nations was being fulfilled (Acts 15:12–21). The inclusion of all nations was emphatically stated by Amos when he proclaimed *lĕma'an yîrešû 'et šĕ'ērît 'ĕdom* (so that they may possess the remnant of Edom) (9:12a). The verb *possess* conveyed the blessed truth that even people of the perpetually hating Edomite nation would become integral members of and participants in the believing, loving, serving, and worshiping covenant family of Abraham.[27]

Obadiah had prophesied that as fire destroyed stubble, so the house of Esau would be burned. There would be no survivors of Esau's house (Obad. 13). And it is historically verifiable that the Edomites, as a nation, totally disappeared. Remnants, however, were still present in Jesus' day, for people from Idumea came to see and hear him.[28] Obadiah thus gave a verbal glimpse into the inclusivity of the kingdom of God which he proclaimed as coming (Obad. 15–21). Note especially the last phrase of his prophecy, *wĕhāyēṭâh layhwâh hāmmĕlûkâh* (and the kingdom is the Lord's).[29]

A final comment: Yahweh God's dealing with an obstreperous people such as the Edomites, gives ample evidence of the blessed truth that his is the kingdom, ably administered by means of his covenant of whom the Son of David, the Messiah, is the royal Mediator. Indeed, the Golden Cable unites Yahweh God's revelation as it came to Israel, Judah, relative nations and nonrelative ones.

Later Prophetic Addresses concerning Nations

The Question of Communication

At this point in our study of prophetic addresses concerning the nations, the questions that should be considered are: Did prophets actually go to the nations concerning whom they prophesied? And why were these prophecies included in the Scriptures that deal basically with Yahweh God's revelation to his covenant people, Israel/Judah?

The first question includes uncertainty regarding the actual oral communication of the prophets. If, for example, they were not speaking directly to the nations about whom a message was given, to whom were they communicating?

There should be no doubt in any Bible believer's mind that the book of Jonah is an authentic account of the man Jonah, son of Amittai, who served as a prophet of Yahweh in the days of Jereboam II, 800–750 B.C. He had correctly prophesied that some of the boundaries of Israel would be restored. When commanded by Yahweh, *qûm lēk 'el Ninĕwēh* (arise, go to Nineveh), he disobeyed but later did go (Jon. 1:2; 3:1–3). It is stated clearly "Jonah started into the city. He proclaimed . . ." (3:4). Obadiah does not refer to being sent to Edom, but the manner he addressed the Edomites would certainly indicate that he spoke to them directly. "See, I will make you small . . . you will be utterly despised. The pride of your heart . . ." (Obad. 2, 3). Consider also "you should not look down on your brother" (v. 12). The prophet Nahum spoke directly to Nineveh, "an attacker advances against you, Nineveh, guard . . . , watch, brace yourselves" (2:1). *Hinnî 'ēlēyik nĕ'um yĕhwâ sĕbam'ôt* (Behold, I am against you, declares Yahweh of hosts). When one considers the prophecies of Isaiah against various nations, Babylon (13:1; 21:1ff.), Assyria (14:24ff.), Moab (15:1ff.), Syria (17:1ff.), Arabia (21:13ff.), these were not spoken in the same manner as the prophecy against Jerusalem (22:1–23). The message was addressed directly, personally, as it also was to Tyre, "Be silent you people of the Island and you merchants of Sidon" (23:2). We must conclude on the basis of a direct consideration of the biblical text, that various nations were addressed, even as Israel and Judah were. How the prophets did this is not clear except in the case of Jonah. The possibility of prophets traveling to neighboring nations must be seriously considered. There is also the historical reality that people from various nations were physically present at various times within the boundaries of Israel/Judah and thus could be addressed as representatives of their home countries.[30]

The next question to be answered is: For whom were these prophecies to and against the nations included in the biblical text? Were they basically included for

Israel/Judah to read and know? J. Stek states emphatically that "the narrative concerning this mission, let it be remembered, is addressed to Israel."[31] There is no need to argue with Stek. Israel/Judah had to have the message constantly with and before them. They had been given the mandate to be a blessing to all nations. It must be added, however, that if one takes Stek's statement to mean the nations were not directly or even indirectly given the word of Yahweh concerning them, one must object. Yahweh God had a concern for all nations. This has been positively established in the preceding discussion and will be repeated more specifically in the latter part of this chapter.

Nations Addressed by the Four Major Prophets[32]

Aram

The country of Aram, referred to in the New Testament at times as Syria (Matt. 4:24; Luke 2:2; Acts 15:23), is very often referred to by its capital city, Damascus. Aram was a son of Shem (Gen. 10:22), and was therefore known as a Smite. Aram's territory bordered Canaan on the north (cf. Ezek. 47:16–18). Its capital city was known in Abraham's time (Gen. 14:15); Abraham had a man from Damascus as his chief servant (15:2). Aram was the home country of Balaam (Num. 23:7). In the days of the judges, Cushan-Rishathaim, king of Aram, was Yahweh's agent of punishment when Israel did evil and forgot Yahweh their God. When the Israelites repented, Othniel was raised up to deliver them (Judg. 10:6). Later, in the time of the judges, the Aramean god became attractive to the Israelites. This surely indicated that there was interaction between the Israelites and the Arameans, the latter exerting the greater influence. Years later, David waged a military campaign against Hadadezer, king of the Arameans, and put Israelite garrisons in his country (2 Sam. 8:5). Still later, Rezon, king in Damascus, proved to be a hostile neighbor to King Solomon (1 Kings 11:24, 25). When Asa was king of Judah, he tried to form a treaty with Ben-hadad, king of Aram, with the purpose of trying to break Ben-hadad's treaty with Baasha, king of Israel (1 Kings 15:18). Later, Elijah was commanded to anoint Hazael king over Aram and Jehu king over Israel (1 Kings 19:15). Hazael then attacked Samaria but in time was defeated by Ahab and surrendered to him (1 Kings 20:1–43). Political intrigue and military activities between Israel and Aram continued for decades. Arameans captured Israelites and had them serve as slaves; Naaman had an Israelite slave girl (2 Kings 5:1–19). At times the Israelites gained the upper hand over Aram (14:28).[33] The kings of Judah entered into political and military plots against Aram and Israel in an effort to gain and keep freedom. It was in this context that Isaiah prophesied that the head of Rezin, king of Damascus, would be shattered (Isa. 7:8), after Rezin had been Yahweh God's agent to punish Israel (9:11, 12).[34]

Isaiah included in his prophecies against the nations an unusual oracle against Damascus (17:1–14). He began by proclaiming that Damascus would no longer be a city, but would become a heap of ruins. Its glory and power would be gone.

Then, as the destruction of other Aramean cities is pronounced, a sudden shift is made; Isaiah proclaimed that the glory of Jacob would fade (17:4–6). Israel would turn to their Maker instead of to the Canaanite gods they had served (17:7–9), but it would be too late because they had forgotten God their Savior and Rock (17:10). Isaiah concluded this oracle that began with judgment on Aram, then switched to judgment on Israel, and concluded with a strong statement condemning the raging of nations (17:12–14).

The question has been raised, Why did Isaiah switch from Aram to Israel and then to the nations? The answer can be found in the interactions between Aram and Israel, particularly in Isaiah's time, when the two nations conspired against Jerusalem and the house of David (7:1–9). The raging of these two nations was local evidence of what was transpiring in the broader national context.

Jeremiah included a prophetic message against Damascus/Aram. He referred to a well-known city, Hamath of Arpad, and other commercial and strong military centers. He does not give the reason for tragedies to befall the country; he states in graphic terms how that country would be plundered and weakened (Jer. 49:23–27). We should note that Jeremiah does not prophesy a complete destruction and a wiping away of Aram. This is interesting to note in view of Syria/Damascus continuing to exist as is evidenced by Zechariah (9:1), referring to it as do New Testament writers. And it is continuing to be very much present and active in Mid Eastern politics and economics in the twenty-first century.

Arabia

The home of the Arabians/Arabs was the land between the Red Sea and the Persian Gulf, and between the Syrian desert on the north and the Indian Ocean on the south. The people, comprised of descendants mentioned in the table of nations (Gen. 10) and of Ishmael,[35] were not close neighbors to Israel/Judah. Arabia, however, had many minerals; Ophir and Havilah were cities of Arabia known to be sources of gold (2 Chron. 9:14), plants that produced perfumes and fruits, and various domesticated animals (17:11). There is reference to the Arabians as international business people (Ezek. 27:21). There is no biblical reference to specific religious or military interaction between the countries of Arabia and Israel. An exception could be the queen of Sheba (1 Kings 10:1–10), because geographers believe Sheba was a city in Arabia, from which some Arabian men, who joined a group of raiders, killed King Jehoram and most of his sons (2 Chron. 22:1).

Neither Isaiah (21:13–17), nor Jeremiah (25:24), nor Ezekiel (30:5) gives reasons for the judgment to fall upon Arabia and its people. Isaiah declares that the god of Israel has spoken: Arabians will flee before drawn swords, the pomp of its cities will end, and its warriors will be few (21:13–17). Jeremiah proclaimed that Yahweh's cup of wrath would be drunk by many nations, including the Arabs (25:24). This was prophesied in the context of Jerusalem forced to drink from Yahweh's cup of wrath. This could imply that Jerusalem was as deserving of Yahweh's wrath as any other nation. Ezekiel included Arabia with Cush, Put, Lydia, and the people of the covenant who would fall by the sword. Again, no specific reason was given other than that Arabia was as deserving of Yahweh's judgment as the apostate people of the covenant.

A point of interest to be noted is that the covenant people were not considered in isolation from neighboring nations. The implication could be that had Israel been the theocratic covenant mediatorial nation Yahweh called and placed them to be, judgment would not come upon Israel/Judah nor the nations.

Cush and Put

The countries of Cush and Put are often mentioned together (e.g., Jer. 46:9). Cush and Put were sons of Ham (Gen. 10:6; 1 Chron. 1:8); their countries bordered on the territory of their ancestral brother Mizraim (Egypt). Cush lay between the Nile (cf. Isa. 18:1) and the Red Sea alongside of Upper Egypt (11:11; Ezek. 29:10; Zeph. 3:10), and Put (Phut) on the coast of the Mediterranean Sea west of Egypt.[36] Little is actually said about Phut (Put). Ezekiel spoke of Phut's men serving in Tyre's army, bringing splendor to Tyre. He also proclaimed that Phut, as well as Cush, would fall by the sword because, it seems to be implied, they were allies of Egypt (30:5, 6); Nahum included Phut and Cush as allies of Nineveh (3:9).[37] Cush is referred to a few times more often than Phut. Job knew that topaz from Cush was incomparable (28:19). Isaiah referred to Cush, with Egypt, being stripped naked, as Isaiah had been as "a portent" for them with the result that those nations who looked for support from Cush would, in bewilderment, ask: what has happened to those on whom we relied? (Isa. 20:1–7). The thought expressed is that those Israelites who thought to flee from Assyria would find no refuge or help from Cush.

Egypt

Mizraim, ancestor of Egyptians, was a son of Ham. The Nile River, Egypt's source of life, flowed from south to north through the length of Egypt and emptied into the Mediterranean Sea. Located on the northeast corner of the continent of Africa, it was a close neighbor to the people living in the southwest areas of Asia. In reality, Canaan, also a son of Ham, lived in this southwest Asian area, the very place Yahweh God promised to Abram when he led him to it (Gen. 12:1–9). The history of Egypt has been written and rewritten; to even briefly review it here would take too much space.[38]

Our interest in this study is particularly in the four major prophets' proclamations regarding Egypt. While earlier prophets—Joel, Amos, Hosea, and Micah (the latter a contemporary of Isaiah)—spoke concerning Egypt, their themes, such as Israel/Judah being brought up out of Egypt and Egypt being punished and made desolate, were repeated and expanded by the major prophets. The proclamations, basically theological in character and intent, must be considered in the context of Egypt's historical interactions with the covenant people. Hence, a few incidents should be highlighted.

Abram had found food in Egypt and tension because of Sarai his wife (Gen. 12:1–20). Hagar, Sarai's maid by whom Abram had Ishmael, was an Egyptian (16:1), hence, Arabs, descendants of Ishmael, have Egyptian parentage (25:13–16). Joseph, sold to Potiphar, an Egyptian official, after being imprisoned on false charges, became a high official, or vizier. He brought Jacob, his brothers, and their families to Egypt. Joseph married an Egyptian woman; hence, his two sons were also of Egyptian parentage. Within the boundaries of Egypt, although serving much of 400 years in slavery, Israel was conceived and developed as a potential nation (37:39–50).

Israel's exodus from Egypt was a dramatic deliverance under Yahweh God's providence and the leadership of Moses (Exod. 1:1–15:21). Once Israel was constituted as Yahweh's covenant, theocratic people, they were warned not to do as in Egypt; this was stated in the context of prohibition of sexual immorality (32:4, 6; Lev. 18:3). Throughout the years under the leadership of Moses, Joshua, the judges, and Samuel, Israel was repeatedly reminded that Yahweh God had delivered them from Egypt and they were to be a unique, distinct, and separate people.

Solomon established political relationships with Egypt; he also married an Egyptian princess (1 Kings 3:1). He did not have to do it to acquire Egyptian wisdom, for he had greater wisdom than all the wisdom of Egypt (4:30). The sad result of these social and cultural relationships was spiritual apostasy (11:1–8). When Jeroboam, an Ephramite official under Solomon, rebelled, he fled to Egypt (11:40), and before long, Egypt's king, Shishak, attacked Jerusalem and carried off temple treasures (14:25–28). Later, during the reign of Hoshea, the last king of Israel, Egypt's military aid was vainly sought (2 Kings 17:3–6). When King Hezekiah of Judah was threatened by Sennacherib, the Assyrian supreme commander, he reminded Hezekiah that his dependence on Egypt was like a lame man leaning on a splintered reed that pierces the hand (17:21). It was during Hezekiah's reign that Isaiah prophesied concerning Egypt (Isa. 36:1–37:13).

Isaiah warned Ahaz, a Davidic apostate king of Judah, that Yahweh god would use Egypt in unique ways to harass Judah (7:18), but they were not to fear them for as Yahweh had dealt with them in former times, so he would again (10:24, 26). Isaiah elaborated on Yahweh's dealing with Egypt (19:1–25). This chapter can be divided into three sections. (1) Yahweh reigns over Egypt; riding on a cloud he comes to Egypt (19:1–4). Idols tremble, hearts melt, internecine fighting develops; their plans are frustrated, their mediums and spiritists are useless. Yahweh will bring the Assyrians in to rule over them with cruelty. (2) Conditions in Egypt will be disastrous (19:5–17). There will be no water for parched land, no fishing, no farming, no weaving of flax. The wisdom of the wise will be senseless, leaders will be fools, dizzy and drunk, and people will be terrified. (3) There is a future (19:18–25). Egypt will learn the language of Canaan,[39] there will be an altar to Yahweh in the heart of Egypt, and its people will be saved from oppressors, be healed, and turn to the Lord. Egyptians and Assyrians will join Israel in the worship of Yahweh who will claim "Egypt my people" along with "Israel my inheritance."

The prophecy of a blessed future does not mean that Isaiah did not prophesy Yahweh God's judgment on Egypt. He did; he spoke of Assyrians leading stripped and barefoot Egyptians into slavery (20:4). Isaiah, however, never did prophesy that Egypt would be totally decimated, destroyed, and removed from among the nations.

The psalmists, referring repeatedly to Yahweh's dealing with Egypt at the time of the exodus (Pss. 78:43, 51; 80:8; 81:5; 106:51), expressed confidence that Egyptians and Cushites would submit themselves to God (68:31) and Egyptians (Rahab) would be recorded among those who acknowledged Yahweh (87:4).

Jeremiah prophesied concerning Egypt. The text (46:2) states that he spoke after Pharaoh Neco had been defeated by the Babylonians under the leadership of Nebuchadnezzsar, at Carchemish.[40] On his return from the battle, he captured Josiah's successor, Jehoahaz, and took him as prisoner to Egypt, where he died. Pharaoh Neco exacted tribute from King Jehoiakim who had been placed on Judah's throne by the Egyptian victor (2 Kings 23:25). Egypt did not have a long rule over Judah. Within three years Nebuchadnezzar besieged Jerusalem, defeated Jehoiakim, and took temple treasures and some royal young men to Babylon (Dan. 1:1–7). Egypt was made to retreat and did not threaten Judah/Jerusalem again (2 Kings 24:7).

It was during these three years that Jeremiah prophesied concerning Egypt, especially against Pharaoh Neco and his army. Salient points in the message are as follows: (1) Yahweh God's day of vengeance is coming (46:10). Yahweh, the sovereign King, is on his way (46:18). He will bring punishment on Pharaoh and Egypt's gods (46:20). (2) Nebuchadnezzar is Yahweh God's military agent (46:26). He will bring Egypt's warriors low (46:15), as he comes with a sword of oppression (46:16). (3) Egypt, a beautiful heifer, will be stung by a gadfly (46:20). In sarcasm, Jeremiah roused the Egyptian forces: prepare your shields, harness your horses, polish your spears (46:3, 4). But they are retreating, fleeing in spite of their pride in the Nile and their bragging that they will conquer cities (46:5–8). Charging horses and furiously driven chariots are to no avail on Yahweh's day of vengeance (46:9), and stumbling and falling, there will be no balm or remedies for the people (46:10, 11) who will have to pack for exile (46:19). Egypt's people will be put to shame (46:24) and cry out that Pharaoh Neco is only a loud noise who has missed his opportunity (46:17). (4) Egypt, however, will not be so overwhelmed that it will not continue to exist. In fact, it will continue to be inhabited (46:26). (5) Jacob/Israel, lying between the oncoming of Nebuchadnezzar and the army of Pharaoh Neco, need not fear. Yahweh must discipline them with justice. When in exile (46:27), they can have the assurance that Yahweh God is their covenant Lord, he is with them (46:28). Other nations will be completely destroyed, but Jacob, Yahweh's servant, though scattered, will not be (46:28).

Jeremiah's prophetic word, received from Yahweh, was fulfilled. Egypt was defeated and humbled. It could not withstand the military power of the Babylonians. The people of Jerusalem were slow to understand and quick to forget that Jeremiah had prophesied correctly about Egypt. Twenty-two/-three years later, after Nebuchadnezzar had destroyed Jerusalem, and for a third time deported a large segment (586 B.C.), some of those left behind in the shattered land of Judah assassinated Nebuchadnezzar's appointees to govern over them (40:7–41:15). The rebels, fearing Babylonian reprisal, escaped to Egypt (41:17, 18). The people, the remnant left in the land, asked Jeremiah to seek the will of the Lord (42:1–6). That word was given. The remnant was assured that they need not fear the king of Babylon but to stay in the land and rebuild it (42:7–12). If, however, they departed to Egypt, they would suffer deprivation and be an object of cursing horror, condemnation, and reproach (42:13–22). The rebel leaders refused to heed Yahweh's word from Jeremiah's mouth, and said to him he was lying (43:1, 2). They led the people away to Egypt in disobedience to Yahweh (43:4–7). After their arrival in Tahpanhes, in the delta region of the Nile, and before proceeding to Elephantine,[41] Jeremiah prophesied that Nebuchadnezzar would come and attack Egypt, bringing death and captivity, and destroying Egypt's temples and gods.

Jeremiah's repeated reminders that Yahweh God had brought Israel out of Egypt (2:6; 7:22, 25; 11:4, 7; 16:14; 23:21), made his question to the people very pointed, "why return there?" (2:18).[42] Egypt had nothing to offer after the exodus and Yahweh's covenant confirmation at Sinai (Exod. 19:3–7) that Yahweh God could and would not supply them in their promised land. Those that returned to Egypt never returned; they died there (42:16). Egypt was not the promised land, nor even a part of it!

Ezekiel, prophesying to the exiles in Babylon spoke repeatedly concerning Egypt in the context of the exiles' hopes and disappointments. Using parables in which two great eagles vied for power, he proclaimed that the first eagle, Nebuchadnezzar, had conquered peoples far and wide. The second eagle, the king of Egypt, to whom King Zedekiah appealed for help, breaking his treaty with Babylon, and on whom exiles had placed some hope (17:1–15), would be of no help, even though he had a mighty army and a great horde (17:15). Ezekiel, in a lament, reminded the exiles that Jehoahaz had been led captive to Egypt by Pharaoh Neco. When elders, representing the exiles, came to Ezekiel "to inquire of the Lord," (20:1, 2), Yahweh God's response, by the mouth of Ezekiel, was that he, Yahweh, would not heed the queries of a people whom he had redeemed from Egypt's slavery, vile images, and idols, who rebelled against him in spite of all the gifts Yahweh had given them (20:3–29). As Egypt had been judged (the ten plagues), so Israel/Judah was being judged by the exile for serving idols (20:30–39b). Ezekiel described Israel/Judah's sin by speaking of two adulterous sisters who became prostitutes in Egypt and continued their immoral ways throughout their history (23:1–27). He also told the people that their lewdness and prostitution, begun in Egypt, had to be ended and after suffering the consequences of it, they would know their God was the sovereign Yahweh (23:28–49).

The motivation for Ezekiel pronouncing seven oracles against Egypt (29:1–32:32) was undoubtedly that Yahweh God would not have Israel/Judah's exiles in Babylon consider Egypt to be the means by which they would be liberated and return to Jerusalem and their homeland. The covenant people had to realize that Yahweh God had exiled them. They had to conscientiously consider their rebellion against him, repent, seek forgiveness, and then hope for restoration. Only Yahweh God would restore them. Egypt's Pharaoh, a human potentate, was proud of his strength and dreamed of himself as equal to God and refused to recognize that Yahweh God was Lord over him.[43] The exiles were not to be deceived by such human pretensions.

Note should be taken of what Yahweh God commanded Ezekiel to do: *ben 'ādām śîm pĕnekā 'al par'ōh* (son of man, set your face against Pharaoh) (29:2). "To set the face against" meant to openly and directly confront. Ezekiel was to do this by *hinnābē' 'aliew* (prophesy against him). In this context, the command "to speak to" and "say to" is not to be taken literally, as if Ezekiel went directly to the palace in Egypt.[44] Ezekiel was commanded to prophesy against Egypt verbally in the presence of the elders and the people.

Salient points in the seven oracles Ezekiel proclaimed are as follows: (1) Yahweh God is in charge. He is the King of the cosmos. He determines who rules and who is to be put down. When he stated, "I am against you pharaoh, king of Egypt" (29:3), Pharaoh and all nations will know Yahweh God is *'ădōnāy,* the Master of all (23:8, 19; 30:13). He will destroy idols and images; he will lay Upper Egypt waste, and set fire to Zoan as he pours out his wrath (30:13–19). (2) Pharaoh, believed to be Hophra who reigned from 589 to 570 B.C., was a monster (29:3a), who claimed the Nile River as his, as if he made it (29:3b). In reality he was no more than an unreliable broken reed (29:6b, 7), useless as a support or crutch for a person with two broken arms (30:22). He is to be brought down with hooks in his monstrous jaws (29:4) and there will be no prince in Egypt (30:13). (3) The punishment, executed by a wrathful Yahweh God, will have a tragic effect on all of Egypt (30:3–18). It will become a wasteland (29:9; 30:12); no animals will be able to live there (29:11), cities will be ruined (29:12). Pharaoh's flesh will be spread on the mountains and the land will be drenched with his blood (32:5, 6). Once (31:12) beautiful as a cedar in Lebanon (31:1–9), it will be broken with its branches in ravines. The people will be dispersed among the nations (30:26). Yahweh has an agent to wreak his wrath on Pharaoh and Egypt: it will be Nebuchadnezzar, king of Babylon, who holds the exiles of Jerusalem/Judah captive (29:18, 19; 30:10, 25; 31:12; 32:16). Indeed, it was useless, hopeless, an affront against the sovereign God to look to Egypt for victory and liberation when Egypt was given as a reward to Nebuchadnezzar.[45] (4) Ezekiel did have a word of hope for Egypt. After forty years of defeat, humiliation, and dispersion, Egypt would be restored (29:13, 14).[46] Restored Egypt, however, would be a *mamlākâ šepālâ* (from verb *šāpēl,* be, become low or abased). It would become the lowliest among nations (29:14, 15), never again to rule over nations or to be a source of confidence (29:16).

Daniel made a few references to Egypt. In his prayer of confession, he acknowledged Israel's deliverance from Egypt by the hand of Yahweh (9:13), but Israel had sinned and therefore suffered under the anger and wrath of Yahweh (9:15, 16). In the prophetic chapter 11, Daniel referred to Egypt, where gold, silver, and other riches would be stored for a while, but Egypt would be conquered and lose its treasures (11:8, 42, 43). The interpretation of this eschatological passage has varied considerably. Since Daniel is speaking in an apocalyptic context, it seems wisest to understand him to refer to Egypt as a political power opposing other powers, but not gaining ascendancy because Yahweh God and his representative, the Son of Man, are omnipotent and reign sovereignly.

Finally, Egypt's continuation as a nation, at times indeed a lowly entity, endured. It served as a refuge in the time of Christ as it did in patriarchal times. Jesus, as a babe, was safe in Egypt when Herod sought to kill him (Matt. 2:13–18). Thus Egypt had a role in the covenant administration of Yahweh God's sovereign reign over the cosmos and in the outworking of his plan of redemption.

Tyre

The city of Tyre had an important role in the affairs of Israel. Joshua allotted territory to the tribe of Asher whose northern boundary bordered on the fortified city of Tyre (Josh. 19:29); hence, Israel and Tyre were close neighbors. Tyre was the chief port city of Phoenicia, and maritime activities, launched from Tyre, resulted in Tyrian colonies in Sardenia, Cypress, North Africa (Carthage), Tunisia, and Sicily. These became sources for good commercial activities and wealth for the Phoenecians, especially Tyre.[47]

Hiram, king of Tyre during David and Solomon's reign in Israel, supplied cedar logs and skilled craftsmen to help David build his palace (2 Sam. 5:11; 1 Chron. 14:1). So doing, Hiram gave international recognition to the Davidic throne. But it was to Hiram's advantage to have peaceful relationships with the kingdom of Israel because overland trade routes to Tyre passed through Israelite territory and the Phoenecians depended on Israel for much of its agricultural food (2 Sam. 5:11, 12). Not to be forgotten is that Tyre was a well fortified city (Josh. 19:25; 2 Sam. 24:7). It was to Israel's advantage to have a strong military fortress on its northern boundary.

King Hiram, hearing that Solomon succeeded his father, David, as king, initiated good relationships with him. Commercial agreements were made; the text states that *yikrĕtû bĕrît* (they cut a covenant), (1 Kings 5:1–12; [MT 1 Kings 5:15–26]). Amos later referred to it as a treaty of brotherhood (1:9). When temple building was begun, Solomon depended on Hiram of Tyre for materials and skilled craftsmen (1 Kings 7:13, 14). The chronicler elaborated on the goodwill that King Hiram had toward Solomon (2 Chron. 2:3–16). Strained relationships developed, however, when Solomon, in debt to Hiram for his assistance, gave twenty towns (of Israel's inheritance) to Hiram; upon inspection of these towns, Hiram complained to Solomon that they were really good for nothing (1 Kings 9:10–14). Later, when Hiram's successor Ethbaal, ruled Sidon, it became the capital city, but Tyre remained a strong commercial and business city. Relationships with

Ethbaal, and Phoenecia the country, became closely intertwined when Ahab, king of Israel, married Ethbaal's daughter Jezebel. Through this marital relationship, Phoenecia Baal worship became deeply entrenched in Israel (1 Kings 16:29–33). But the relationship did not remain on friendly terms, because both Joel (3:4–6; [MT 4:4]) and Amos (1:9) spoke of Tyre's capturing Israelites and selling them as slaves. Asaph, the psalmist, referred to the people of Tyre joining in plots and alliances against Israel/Judah (83:7). But other psalmists sing of some Tyrians having their names recorded in Zion (87:4) and of bringing gifts to the messianic King (45:12).

Isaiah, prophesying during the time span (740–680 B.C.), when Uzziah, Jotham, Ahaz, and Hezekiah reigned, gave insights into the affairs of various nations and their impact or influence on the kingdoms of Israel and Judah. Israel was exiled in the earlier part of his lifetime (722 B.C.). His prophecies to and concerning Judah were often proclaimed with an awareness of the international situations at hand. His prophecy concerning Tyre (23:1–18) called for attention to some important factors. First, Isaiah makes direct addresses to various aspects of Phoenecian life. He tells the ship to wail (23:1, 14), Sidon to be ashamed (23:4), the people to be silent (23:2), and for there to be no more reveling (23:12). Because of the proximity of Phoenecian cities to Israel and Judah, it certainly was possible for Isaiah to have spoken his message directly to the people. Second, Tyre/Sidon, Phoenecia, in spite of the wide-ranging business and commercial assets, of its wealth and reputation, would be destroyed to the anguish of its people and colonies (23:3, 4, 9). Third, it is Yahweh who has planned this destruction (23:9, 11, 17). Fourth, Assyrians are Yahweh God's agents (23:13). They will not completely eradicate the cities, for after seventy years of devastation, Phoenecia will be restored Fifth, when restored, she will continue her life of prostitution but will not gain any profit from it (23:15–18a). Yahweh will give what profit she gains to "those who live before Yahweh" (23:18b). This message is in keeping with the repeated promises of Yahweh to his people that they will receive the wealth of the nations (18:7; 60:5–11; Hag. 2:6–9).

Jeremiah repeated what Isaiah had prophesied. Along with other nations, Tyre and Sidon were to drink the cup of Yahweh's wrath (25:17–26). It is interesting to note that Jeremiah said he was sent to the neighboring nations (25:15, 17). Jeremiah prophesied that Nebuchadnezzar, king of Babylon, Yahweh, the Creator's servant would receive various nations from Yahweh. Tyre, Sidon, Moab, Edom, and Ammon are mentioned (27:3–10). In this context, Jeremiah is commanded to send word—not to go, speak directly; the context reveals that Jeremiah was addressing Jerusalem particularly (27:12), and had to give the message of Nebuchadnezzar's victories to the envoys from the nations who had come to Jerusalem (27:3b, 4a). Jeremiah also prophesied that any people who might come to the aid of Tyre and Sidon would be cut off (47:4).

Ezekiel, more than any other prophet, spoke in detail concerning Yahweh God's punishment of Tyre (26:1–28:19). Sidon was also briefly addressed (28:20–26).

Ezekiel's prophecy was given in 587 B.C. From what he said, that the gates of Jerusalem were opened to the nations, it is properly concluded that he spoke soon after Nebuchadnezzar's forces had captured Jerusalem a second time, taken its king, Jehoiachin, who had rebelled against Babylon's rulers, captive, as well as officials, 1,000 artisans and craftsmen, and 7,000 military personnel (2 Kings 24:8–16).

Tyrians, as the Edomites, considered the capture of Jerusalem an occasion for their increasing prosperity (Ezek. 26:2). Therefore Yahweh God had Ezekiel proclaim, "I am against you" (26:3). Sovereign over nations, Yahweh would bring them against Tyre, destroy her, throw her rubble into the sea, and thus allow her to be completely plundered by the attacking nations (26:3–6). Nebuchadnezzar and his army would serve as Yahwah God's primary agent (26:7–14). Reverbations of Tyre's fall would cause trembling among the nations (26:15, 16), and lament as they reflected on Tyre's lost power (26:17, 18). Ezekiel added that when Tyre would be covered by the sea, having had a horrible end, it would not be found again (26:19–21).

Ezekiel was commanded to take up a lament for Tyre, the city that once was the merchant for many people (27:13). As he did, he spoke of Tyre's former beauty, perfectly built structures made of the best timber and decorated with fineries from Egypt and Elishah (Cyprus). He reminisced on Tyre's skilled oarsmen, veteran craftsmen, many ships, and mercenaries from various countries in her armies. He reflected on Tyre's wide-ranging business ventures with countries such as Tarshish, Greece, Aram, Judah, Dedan, Arabia, Sheba, Asshur, and many others (27:4–29). People from these nations would cry bitterly when they considered the horrible end of Tyre (27:30–36).

The king of Tyre was particularly addressed. In his pride he had said he was a god, sitting on the throne of a god (28:2a). Did he think himself wiser than Daniel because of his success in trading (28:3–5)? Because of this self-exaltation of a man, he would be brought down to the pit and die the death of an uncircumcised (unsaved) man (28:6–10). It had been Yahweh God who had placed the king of Tyre in a place of beauty (as Eden was), wealth, power, and prestige (holy mount of God) (28:11–15). But in pride, the king scattered violence, did dishonest trade, and corrupted its wisdom (28:16–18a). Yahweh God, sovereign King of nations, reduced Tyre to ashes (28:18b–19).

Sidon had joined Tyre in sin and in malicious deeds against the covenant people. Therefore, Sidon would suffer the same fate as Tyre (28:20–24).

Yahweh, by the mouth of Ezekiel, revealed that he was very much aware of Tyre and Sidon's violations of the spiritual, social, and cultural covenantal mandates. He also knew how they sought to enhance their own royal status and power by these violations. Therefore, Yahweh god would reveal himself as the truly sovereign One over all nations and their wealth and power. Thus, nations would come to know Yahweh God (28:24). Ezekiel, however, spoke comforting words to his fellow exiles; Yahweh would re-gather them and would reveal himself as holy "among them in the sight of the nations."

The original Tyre was cast into the sea by the Greek army. Nebuchadnezzar had laid siege to Tyre for fifteen years and had not been able to capture and destroy it. Under Alexander the Great, a Greek ruler and victorious army leader, Tyre was defeated and broken down and its rubble was cast into the sea to make a causeway to enable the victorious Greek army to capture the part of Tyre that was situated on an island, just off the coast. Tyre was eventually rebuilt and is referred to by New Testament writers. Jesus withdrew to its regions (Matt. 15:21; Mark 7:24), and when he pronounced judgment on Jerusalem, he said Jerusalem's final punishment would be more severe than that of Tyre and Sidon (Matt. 11:21, 22; Luke 10:13, 14), because Tyrians would be more responsive to his works and deeds than the Jews were.

Assyria

The Assyrian people were of Semitic origin and used a Semitic language. Their home territory was in the upper Mesopotamian region. Nineveh was its capital city. Assyria, as a nation, experienced three periods of international integration. During 1300–1100 B.C., it made various conquests; from 1100 to 900 B.C., Assyrian power was not able to overcome the opposition of people to its west (the time of David, Solomon, Hiram of Tyre). Beginning under the leadership of Tukulti-Ninurto II and his son Ashurbanipal II, Assyria became an international power. The Mesopotamian valley was completely subdued; conquests to the west and southwest were successful.[48] The biblical record relates Assyria's activities with regard to Israel and Judah. Menahem, who had gained Israel's throne by assassinating king Shallum, was defeated by Tiglath-Pileser of Assyria; Israel then had to pay tribute to Assyria (2 Kings 15:17–20). Later the Assyrian king conquered more Israelite territory and deported some Israelites to Assyria (17:29). When Ahaz, the Davidic king of Judah, was threatened by Rezin, king of Aram and Pekah, king of Israel, he made an alliance with Tiglath-Pileser. Ahaz took temple treasures to pay tribute to the Assyrian who obliged and defeated Aram (16:1–9). After Damascus was captured by the Assyrian army, Ahaz went there, saw an altar, made a copy of it, and placed it in front of the temple. The priests offered sacrifices on it (16:10–16).

Hoshea, the last king of Israel, rebelled against Assyria and sought help from Egypt, to no avail. Shalmaneser, who had become king of Assyria, invaded Israel, besieged Samaria for three years, captured it, and deported many Israelites to Assyria and Media (17:1–6). Judah was also made to pay tribute to the Assyrian king. When Ahaz's son, Hezekiah, became king, he successfully rebelled for a while (18:8). But Sennacharib, successor to Shalmaneser, attacked Judah and forced Hezekiah to pay tribute. The Assyrian king tried to capture Jerusalem, but failed because of other military challenges he had to face (1:13–19:37).

Isaiah the prophet was Yahweh God's spokesman during the turbulent years of Ahaz and Hezekiah's reign. Hence, he, more than the other major prophets, spoke concerning the Assyrian kings and their armies. He strongly urged Ahaz not to ally himself with Assyria (16:1–9; Isa. 7:1–8:22), for Assyria's king would sweep with pomp into Judah (8:6-8). This was according to Yahweh's plan; Assyria was to be Yahweh's agent to punish Judah (8:17); Assyria was the rod of Yahweh God's anger (10:5). Isaiah added, however, that the Assyrians with willful pride of heart and haughty look in their eyes, went beyond what Yahweh God called them to do (10:13) and therefore they would be destroyed by disease and fire (10:16; 30:31). Isaiah recorded another specific reason why Yahweh God would destroy Assyria: "the king of Assyria has blasphemed me" (37:6).

Two contemporary minor prophets of Isaiah also included references to Assyria. Hosea, prophesying in the north, referred to Ephraim's (Israel) awareness of his sickness and turning to Assyria for help; Judah did also (Ahaz) (5:13: 7:11–8:9; 12:1). Hosea reminded Israel that the Assyrian king had no cure, for Yahweh would be like a lion, using Assyria, to tear Israel to pieces (5:14). Israel would be taken to Assyria to eat unclean food there (9:3)—yes, carried there as a tribute to the king of Assyria (10:6). This exile to Assyria would be a certainty because Israel refused to repent (11:5, 7). Hosea stated at the close of his prophecy that, "Assyria cannot save us" (14:3); only Yahweh God can heal Israel's waywardness, love them freely, and be as life-refreshing dew to them (14:4, 5).

Micah, in Judah, made a brief reference to Assyria. In a classic messianic passage (5:2–9), Micah declared that the shepherd from the house of David in Bethlehem would rule over Assyria even though Assyria invaded Judah (5:5, 6), and in time, people exiled to Assyria would also return from Assyria (7:12).

Jonah, the son of Amittai, was a native of Gath Hepher, a town in Zebulun in the northern area of Israel.[49] This area had experienced warfare at various times. Jonah's reluctance to preach repentance to Nineveh, Assyria's capital, may have been rooted in his experiences of these invasions Also, as a contemporary of Amos and Hosea, he was undoubtedly aware that they had prophesied that Israel would be exiled beyond Damascus to Assyria (Amos 5:7; Hos. 9:3). Assyria was a wicked nation. Spiritually, Assyrians were polytheistic with animistic and material motifs. Asshur was its chief god and in time the Babylonians' god Marduk was worshiped also. There was a social evil; beer houses thrived as did brothels and free love was practiced widely in public places. Slavery played a very significant role. Culturally, Assyria was quite advanced; militarily, it was well equipped and strong. Inhumane treatment of captives was commonplace; men were flogged alive in the presence of their children; eyes were gouged out; pulling hooks through noses and using thin ropes tied to a larger long rope was the Assyrian method of keeping captives subdued as they were led away into captivity. Yahweh God, directing Assyria to be the rod of his wrath, called for Assyria's repentance. But Jonah did not wish the Assyrians to repent. He fled (Jon. 1:3).

Jonah, a covenant servant of Yahweh, knew the true character of his Lord. Yahweh God had been gracious, compassionate, slow to anger, abounding in love, and hesitant to send calamity to idol-worshiping Israelites (Exod. 32–34). Would he not be the same to a repentant non-Israelite nation (Jon. 4:2, 3)? The king in

Nineveh, hearing Jonah's message from Yahweh, did repent, showed remorse, and called all Assyrians to do so also (3:6–9). Yahweh God spared the repentant Assyrians. He also expressed concern for their children and cattle (4:11).

Nineveh/Assyria's repentance and remorse was not long lasting. It served willingly as Yahweh God's rod of wrath. In cruelty and destruction it went far beyond what was necessary to serve as Yahweh's punishing agent. Hence, another prophet was given an oracle concerning Assyria, specifically concerning Nineveh.

Nahum (whose name means comfort) prophesied that Nineveh would fall and Assyria would be completely defeated. This was fulfilled in 612 B.C. It is reasonable to conclude that Nahum was a contemporary of Zephaniah[50] and of Jeremiah in his earlier years. Yahweh God had indeed been gracious to and slow to anger with Nineveh. Jonah had preached to it sometime between 800 and 750 B.C. Nahum prophesied at least 125 years later. His prophecy was pointed and without mercy for the people of Nineveh/Assyria. Commentators and authors of introductory studies laud Nahum's poetical style; some write of its liturgical character. Some refer to a fiery indignation, akin to animosity and vengeance.[51] Nahum proclaimed a full Old Testament gospel message. His message was not explicitly messianic,[52] but it was at heart a message of consolation to the despondent covenant people in Judah. But he did proclaim that one was coming to preach (1:15 [MT 2:1]). Nahum was truly a comforter. It should also be pointed out that Nahum did not preach repentance, as Jonah had done. It was too late for the Assyrians.

Nahum preached the sovereign King of the cosmos (1:4–6). He spoke of Yahweh as jealous, avenging, full of wrath (1:2). Yahweh, nevertheless, is slow to anger and great in power, a just God who punishes the guilty (1:3). For those who trust in Yahweh, he is good, a refuge, caring for them (1:7).

Nahum addressed Nineveh as *'mennēk yaṣā'* (from you comes [one]) who plots against Yahweh and counsels wickedness) (1:11). Therefore, Yahweh has given a command, *'ālekā* (concerning you) (1:14) you and your allies will be cut off, you will have no descendants, your gods and temples will be destroyed (1:13, 14). Skillfully, powerfully, and passionately Nahum described the battle that would bring defeat, chaos, death, and terror (2:1, 3–13). Note Nahum's *hinnî' 'elayik nĕum yĕhwâ ṣĕba'ôt"* ("Behold, I am against you") (2:13), and then how he elaborates on Nineveh's total destruction (3:1–18). "Nothing can heal your wound" because of your endless cruelty (3:19).

Nahum did comfort those of Israel and Assyria who trusted in Yahweh: *šab yĕhwâ 'et ge'ôn ya'ăqob* (Yahweh will restore the splendor [NIV], [or majesty, excellence, exaltation] of Jacob (2:12 [MT 2:13]). The basic thought is that Jacob was still Yahweh God's elect.[53]

The message of Nahum to Nineveh/Assyria should not be seen to cancel what Isaiah had prophesied. Israel, finally, would be comprised of Egyptians, Assyrians, and a third of Jacob's descendants (19:23–25). In the New Testament era, after the Spirit was poured forth, people of every tribe tongue nation, and race would be anointed among the covenant people of Yahweh.

Elam

In the genealogy of Shem, Elam is mentioned first (Gen. 10:22; 1 Chron. 1:17). His descendants settled in an area to the east of the southern part of the Tigris/Euphrates Valley. It never became an integral part of the Assyrian Empire; it did become a part of the Babylonian Empire. In the time of the ascendancy of the Persian Empire, its capital city, Susa (Dan. 8:2), was located in the central part of what had been the territory of Elam.[54]

The king of Elam, Kedarlaomer, allied with the neighboring kings, attacked countries that were situated just west of the great desert. As they marched southward toward Sodom and Gomorrah, three kings joined the king of these two cities to challenge the invaders. The five kings were defeated; the four invading kings plundered Sodom and Gomorrah and took Lot captive. Abram, in turn, defeated the invaders, rescued Lot, and returned the stolen booty (Gen. 14). The Scriptures do not refer to Elam or Elamites again until the four major prophets do so.[55]

Isaiah was aware of the people of Elam. In his eschatological prophecy he spoke of exiles returning from Elam (11:11). In his prophecy against Babylon, Elam was urged to attack Babylon (21:2), but Isaiah also referred to Elamites taking military action against Jerusalem. Commentators have suggested that Elamite soldiers were mercenaries in the Babylonian army or that Elam was used to refer to Merdia/Persia.[56] Isaiah did not specifically prophesy against Elam as Jeremiah did.

Jeremiah, when prophesying concerning the cup of Yahweh's wrath that all the kings of nations involved in Jerusalem's history would drink, referred to the king of Elam (25:25). In a prophecy about Elam, spoken during the first years of King Zedekiah's reign (the last king to reign in Jerusalem), Jeremiah undoubtedly knew of Elamite archers included in the Babylonian army that would capture Jerusalem. Jeremiah did not give any other reason for the message of destruction that was to overcome Elam. He spoke of Elamites scattered to the four winds; Yahweh in fierce anger would eliminate Elam as a nation (see also Ezek. 32:29). But, Yahweh would continue to reign (have a throne) over the territory of Elam. Indeed, there would be a restoration of Elam's fortunes (Jer. 49:24–39), as was prophesied concerning Moab (48:47) and Ammon (49:6). This prophecy may be considered fulfilled, at least in part later. We read that Elamites were in the throng who heard the apostles preach in the streets of Jerusalem on the day of Pentecost (Acts 2:9).

Babylon

The beginnings of Babylon are considered to date back to the Cushite Nimrod, who named Babylon as one of his kingdom centers (Gen. 10:10). The rebellious and self-serving spirit of the Tower of Babel builders (11:3, 4) characterizes many of the Babylonian people the Old Testament describes. Abram was a native of Ur, located on the lower Tigris River Valley which in time became a city in the southern part of the Babylonian Empire.[57]

Shalmaneser, king of Assyria, ruling over Babylon at the time he captured Samaria and exiled many of the people of Israel to the Mesopotamian valley, took captives from Babylon and other captured areas and settled them in the land of Israel. Hence, the Samaritan people had a partial Babylonian heritage (2 Kings 17:24), and were introduced to Succoth Benoth, one of Babylon's idol gods.

The Babylonians rebelled against the king of Assyria and defeated him in 612 B.C. Prior to this, as Babylon was increasing its power and influence, its envoys were sent to King Hezekiah of Judah, circa 720 B.C. Isaiah rebuked Hezekiah for graciously receiving these Babylonian envoys and prophesied that Jerusalem's treasures would be taken to Babylon (20:12–18; Isa. 39:1–8). This took place in 606, 596, 586 B.C., when Nebuchadnezzar captured Jerusalem when the wicked descendants of godly King Josiah reigned (2 Kings 24:1–25:26). Jehoiachin, one of Judah's kings was taken to Babylon (24:15), as was Zedekiah after he had seen his sons killed and had his eyes gouged out (25:1–7).

Isaiah lived and prophesied before Babylon became a great empire. He was given three prophetic messages; some aspects were directly applicable to his historic situation, others were not. This has lad some scholars to divide the book of Isaiah into at least four distinct prophecies.[58]

Four or five main points found in other oracles are stressed in Isaiah's prophecies against Babylon. It is Yahweh God, covenant Lord of his chosen people, the sovereign Lord and Master in the cosmos and therefore of all nations, who calls for judgment on Babylon. "I have commanded my holy ones, . . . my warriors to carry out my wrath" (13:3). Yahweh Sabaoth is mustering an army for war (13:4). The day of Yahweh, the Sovereign, is near (13:5); it is a day of wrath and cruel anger (13:9). Yahweh said that he would punish for evil, end the arrogance of the haughty, humble the pride of ruthless ones, and make man scarcer than pure gold (13:11–13). When Israel is to be restored, Yahweh will break the rod of the wicked (14:5). He will rise up against her (14:22).

The object of Yahweh God's wrath is Babylon (13:1). Babylon, the jewel of the kingdoms, with her glory will be overthrown like Sodom and Gomorrah (13:19). Babylon the oppressor (14:4), with all her pomp, will be brought down to the grave (14:11). Babylon who said in its heart that it would ascend to heaven and set up a throne above the stars will be brought down to the depths of the pit (14:13–15). Babylon will become nameless, without inhabitants, when Yahweh God sweeps her with the broom of destruction (14:23).

The reasons for Babylon's destructive end are clearly stated. The sin, the evil, the arrogance, the haughtiness, the pride (13:11), the self-exaltation and presumption to reign over the universe (14:13) were revealed as Babylon captured and oppressed nations.

The agent Yahweh will raise up to put a destructive end to Babylon is her neighbor to the east, the Medes, who included the Elamites. Their bows will strike down the young men and there will be no compassion for children (13:18).

The result for the Babylonians will be limp hands, melting hearts, terror, pain, anguish (13:8). Nature will also respond; stars, sun, and moon will not shine (13:10). Infants will be dashed to pieces, houses looted, and wives raped (13:16).

Babylon will be a fallen city (14:12), brought to the grave (14:15). Even the dead bodies will not rest in their graves (14:18–20).

Does Isaiah have a word of hope for Babylon? Not in his first oracle. He does have a message of hope for "Jacob," on whom Yahweh will have compassion (14:1, 2). In fact, in his second oracle against Babylon he says that Israel's lookout, standing on the watchtower, sees the victorious Elamites and Medes represented by a rider in a chariot and exclaims, "Babylon has fallen, has fallen" (21:8, 9). There is deliverance for the people crushed on the threshing floor of Babylon (21:19). Isaiah went on to state that Babylon was brought down by Yahweh, the Holy One, Israel's Creator and King, for Israel, his witnesses' sake (43:12, 14). Later Isaiah repeated the certainty of Babylon's fall (47:1–3). He added that Yahweh God had given his people into their hand, but Babylon had shown no mercy; even on the aged a heavy yoke had been placed. Meanwhile Babylon had asserted it would continue forever, an eternal queen (47:7). Yahweh God, however, had the prophet Isaiah proclaim that Babylon said, trusting in her wickedness, "I am and there is none beside me" (47:10). Babylon had indeed set itself up as god, the lord of life, the master of all nations. Babylon was the archenemy of Yahweh God. Babylon declared itself the incarnation of Satan.

The book of Jeremiah mentions Babylon/Babylonia over 200 times. Many references are in a historical context. Jeremiah lived and prophesied during the rise of the Babylonian Empire and its conquering of many nations. Judah/Jerusalem was invaded three times; Jeremiah experienced each of these. Yahweh God commanded Jeremiah to proclaim his plan for Judah: it was for the Babylonians to attack and conquer Judah and deport most of the leading people who were not killed or who had not fled to other countries.

Jeremiah's task was very difficult. He had to confront Pashur, a priest, who had put him in stocks for a day, with the message that Yahweh God would hand Judah over to the king of Babylon to be either killed or exiled. The wealth of Jerusalem and Judah would be carried off to Babylon (20:1–6). When the last king of Judah, Zedekiah, asked Jeremiah to inquire of Yahweh if he would perform a miracle to make the king of Babylon withdraw from the siege of Jerusalem, Jeremiah's reply was that Yahweh was going to gather the Babylonians within the city of Jerusalem. Yahweh would himself fight against Zedekiah, his people, and in anger, fury and great wrath, strike down those living in the city. Jeremiah went on to preach that those who surrendered to Babylon would live, those who did not would die by sword, famine, and plague (21:1–10; 34:1).

The message of Yahweh turning Jerusalem/Judah over to Babylon was repeated a number of times (22:24; 24:1–7). Nebuchadnezzar was referred to as "my servant" who would perform Yahweh's work of destruction (25:8–10; 27:6–23; 32:26–29). The false prophet Hananiah preached that the yoke of the king of Babylon would be broken, and dramatically put a yoke on Jeremiah and then took it off and broke it. Yahweh's reply was that nations would receive a yoke of iron and would be made to serve Babylon's king (28:2–14). Jeremiah recorded the actual fall of Jerusalem and subsequent events (39:1–40; 52:1–30). The exile into Babylon would last seventy years (29:1–23).

Jeremiah repeatedly referred to why Yahweh God would use Babylon as his agent of punishment. Jerusalem had forsaken her God; the people had followed worthless idols; Judah had exchanged their God for worthless idol gods (2:5, 11, 13, 25). Jeremiah laid other specific charges against the people of Judah and Israel: kings, officials, priests, and prophets provoked Yahweh; they turned their backs to God; they set up idols in the temple, they built high places to Baal; they sacrificed their children to Molech (32:31–35). They violated the covenant (34:18).

Jeremiah had another message for Babylon and the Babylonians. After seventy years of exile for the covenant people (29:10), they would be freed—not by the Babylonians but by the conquerors of Babylon. This was to be announced to the nations; Babylon would be captured, Bel would be put to shame, Marduk would be filled with terror (50:2). An alliance of nations would capture and plunder Babylon (50:9, 10). The king of Babylon was to be punished (50:18), a trap would be set to catch Babylon (50:24). Thus Yahweh God would take vengeance for his temple desecrated by the Babylonians (50:28), and because of all those it slew of Israel (51:49), Babylon would be desecrated and devastated to such an extent that, as Sodom and Gomorrah were obliterated, so would Babylon be; no man would dwell there (50:40; 51:36, 37). Jeremiah emphatically prophesied: a destroyer would come against Babylon, for Yahweh is a God of retribution who will repay in full (51:56).

Habakkuk, the prophet, is believed to have prophesied about the time the Babylonians defeated the Egyptians in the battle of Carchemish; this victory signaled the rise of Babylonian power over other nations.[59] This rise is what Yahweh God referred to when he, in reply to Habakkuk's complaint about the unpunished sin in Judah, said he would do something hard to believe (1:5). The reality was that Yahweh was raising up the Babylonians, ruthless, fearless, dreaded by people who were a law to themselves (1:6, 7). When Habakkuk complained about the Babylonians' wickedness, it exceeded that of Judah (1:12–17), Yahweh revealed to a watching Habakkuk (2:4) that he knew the Babylonians were puffed up, drunken, arrogant, and greedy (2:4, 5).

Habakkuk was called to proclaim five woes against the Babylonians. These woes include further explanations of why they too would be devastated and destroyed (2:6–19). Yahweh, from his throne in his holy dwelling (2:20), would use Babylon to punish Judah and then would carry out the woes on Babylon.

The prophet Ezekiel, a captive exiled to Babylon, used the parable of the two eagles and the vine to illustrate what the king of Babylon had done to rebellious Judah (Ezek. 17:11). The main point Ezekiel made was that Yahweh God used Babylon to punish Judah, who had despised and broken the covenant (17:19, 20). Ezekiel dramatically described how the Babylonians brought the princes to Babylon: with hooks they were pulled into a cage and carried there (19:9). Ezekiel went on to proclaim to the exiles among whom he lived that Babylon's sword that came against Jerusalem was Yahweh God's (21:1–24). Babylon would be Yahweh's agent to bring judgment, as on Judah, so on Tyre (26:7; 29:18):, and on Egypt (29:19; 30:10, 24).

Ezekiel prophesied the downfall of Babylon in a very discreet manner (38:1–39:29). As a captive in Babylon, he avoided saying openly that Babylon would be destroyed, in reality, annihilated as a country. Hooks would be put into the jaws of Babylon's princes, as they had put hooks in their captives. Warriors from Cush, Put, and Persia would wipe out Babylon, just as Babylon had invaded many countries. Ezekiel proclaimed his invasion in terms of the future, when in reality the prophet was describing what Babylon, basking in the glory of its many victories, had already done. Babylon, given the names of Gog and Magog, would fall—and never rise again.[60] The prophet Zechariah, preaching to the returned exiles around 520 B.C., referred to Babylon as a city that still existed, even though the medes and Persians had captured Babylon some eighteen years previous to that (6:10). Historians and archaeologists testify to the eventual destruction of Babylon as a city.[61]

Daniel, a captive in Babylon and eventually an honored official in the Babylonian palace, gave an account of how Darius the Mede captured Babylon and brought about the death of its king, Belshazzar (5:1–30).

Persia-Media

The earlier prophets did not refer to Persia or Media; these countries did not have an international influence in their times. The Medes were referred to first; Isaiah prophesied that Yahweh God would stir up the Medes against Babylon. Their motivation would not be for silver or gold but rather to display their prowess as archers (Isa. 13:17). Jeremiah later prophesied the same, but added that Yahweh God stirred up the Medes to destroy Babylon (51:28, 29). The writer of 2 Kings relates that Shalmaneser was lord of Assyria, having captured Israelites exiled some to the towns of the Medes (17:6; 18:11). It is evident that Media was under the control, at least to an extent, of the Assyrian ruler.[62]

The historical record indicates that Persia became a world empire under Cyrus II the Great circa 550 B.C., after he had had a victory over Astyages of Media, who had been lord over the Persian territory and people. Cyrus captured Babylon in 539 B.C. (Dan. 5:1–31), and the entire Babylonian Empire came under his control. Cambyses, son and successor of Cyrus, conquered Egypt in 525 B.C.; his successor Darius (who was a Mede), (5:31) extended the empire to include part of India. Ahasuerus (Xerxes I) succeeded Darius and reigned from 486 to 465 B.C. Esther became queen to him (Esther 1:1–3; 6:15–18).[63]

King Cyrus, very soon after he gained control of the Babylonian Empire, issued the decree that exiles could return to their home countries (2 Chron. 36:22, 23; Ezra 1:1–8). Cyrus, in that edict, acknowledged that Yahweh, God of heaven, had given him the kingdoms of the earth and that those exiles who wished to rebuild the temple of Yahweh could do so. Whether Cyrus became a true devotee of Yahweh God seems hardly likely because he acknowledged gods of other countries also. It must be emphasized, however, that Cyrus was raised up by Yahweh as his anointed shepherd to carry out his sovereign purposes concerning the covenant people (Isa. 44:28; 45:1–7). Years later, Artaxerxes, successor to Xerxes, royal husband of Esther, continued the policy of assistance to the people of Jerusalem (Ezra 7:1–28). Ezra, in a prayer of confession, acknowledged that Yahweh showed kindness in the sight of the kings of Persia (9:9). Ezra's prayer certainly implies that Yahweh the sovereign God inclined the Persian kings to be favorable to the covenant rebuilders of Jerusalem.

Daniel, Yahweh's servant and prophet in the royal palaces, first in Babylon and later in Susa, recorded that Darius acknowledged Yahweh God as the living God, who endures, whose kingdom cannot be destroyed, and whose dominion will never end (Dan. 6:26). In his visions he was given the message that the kings of Media and Persia would be overcome by a "shaggy goat," the king of Greece (8:20, 21). In another vision Daniel was given revelation concerning the resistance of the Persian kingdom against God and his servant, Michael (10:13). The agent to overthrow the "prince of Persia" would be the "prince of Greece" (10:20).

The sin, wickedness, and resistance of the Median/Persian kings and people to Yahweh God are not described. That Yahweh God's cry of wrath against the Median/Persian Empire was serious cannot be doubted. Media/Persia, however, had served as Yahweh God's special agent to destroy Babylon, to release his people, and to initiate the restoration of the remnant community out of which Jesus Christ would come.

Greece

Greece is the only European country mentioned by name by the Old Testament prophets. Isaiah, in a chapter proclaiming judgment (66:3, 4) and hope for a glorious future (66:10–24) for the person who is humble and contrite in spirit and trembles at Yahweh's word (66:3), that is, assured by Yahweh who sits enthroned in heaven having earth as his footstool (66:1), refers to various people that will hear the fame and see the glory of Yahweh. Greece is mentioned as distant islands of the sea (66:9). Isaiah prophesied that a *'ôt* (sign) would be set among them; a sign is to be set in Greece. Some have suggested that the sign is a banner raised to give a specific signal (cf. Isa. 11:10, 12). Some have suggested it refers to miracles, as the plagues in Egypt (Exod. 10:2; Ps. 78:43). Still others consider the sign to refer to the Messiah, Jesus Christ (Matt. 12:38–40). The basic idea is that the gospel will be presented to and accepted in Greece.

Ezekiel alluded to Greece in a less favorable manner. Greece, in commercial activities with prosperous Tyre, exchanged slaves for Tyrian merchandise. Material possessions were of greater desire and value than the lives of human beings (Ezek. 38:13). The prophet Zechariah, about 580 B.C., proclaimed that Yahweh, using Judah as a bow and Ephraim (Israel) as his arrow, would oppose Greece.

This is said in the context of Zion's king, the Messiah, who comes righteous and bringing salvation, and who proclaims peace to the nations (Zech. 9:9–13).

Daniel, in the interpretation of his vision of a ram and a goat, said that Greece, represented by a shaggy goat, would be divided into four kingdoms, each having less power than the first (Dan. 8:21, 22). Daniel repeated that Greece would defeat the Median/Persian Empire but that Greece itself would have enemies stirred up against her.

In these brief prophecies concerning Greece, little detail is given. What is clearly revealed is that Yahweh God exercises authority over Greece; that Yahweh has Greece as an agent of judgment against the huge empire of the Medes and Persians; that Greece will not continue as a great united empire; and finally, that the Messiah, Jesus Christ, will be presented to her and influence her.

Interpretation of the Prophetic Message to the Non-Israelite Nations

The message the prophets proclaimed to and concerning the non-Israelite nations can be briefly interpreted and summarized as follows.

A. Your king is none other than Yahweh God. He is your Creator, Provider, and Ruler, and he determines the course of your national existence. His loving concern and care for you cannot be doubted. His grace, mercy, and lovingkindness for you are certain and unfailing. You must acknowledge, love, and serve him to enjoy these goodnesses so readily available to you. Repent of your sinful idolatries, your inhumanity among your own people and among and to other nations, and your greed for and misuse of all your cultural advantages. Repent! Believe! Worship! And serve the King of the cosmos, the Redeemer of humanity.

B. Your privilege must be understood. Yahweh God, your Creator and Sustainer, is your covenant Lord. He has bonded himself to you, having created you in his image and likeness. You are his image-bearers; you are called to mirror and represent him in the totality of your lives. It is your privilege to interact with the people, the descendants, biologically, ethnically, and spiritually, Yahweh God's chosen mediatorial agents descended from Noah, Shem, and Abraham. It is your privilege to be part of his cosmic kingdom with all the blessings inherent within it.

C. Your service must always be God-directed and oriented to Yahweh God's chosen people, who were called to serve as a light to the world. You are to honor Yahweh God as he calls you to serve him in relation to Israel and Judah. You are to acknowledge and honor the gifts and tasks Yahweh has given them. And when you are called upon to be my agents of discipline, and at times, severe judgment, you must submit to my commands. Your service is not to be self-serving. You are not to give way to sinful, inhumane practices as you are called up to be my agents of punishment—be it to invade their land, besiege and capture their cities, or take captives into exile. The people of Israel and Judah are deserving judgment; they are objects of my wrath. They are not to be your victims.

D. Your betrayal must be considered from two perspectives. Yahweh's chosen mediatorial people, whom he made to be a theocratic monarchy, have betrayed their sovereign covenant Lord. He redeemed them from slavery in Egypt, led them as they dispossessed the seven nations inhabiting Canaan, and gave them that land as their inheritance. Yahweh placed them in the center of your known world. They were by life and deed to demonstrate to you what kingdom life and service, as Yahweh God ordained it, was to be. They were to be as a city on a hill, shedding light all about them, and to have open gates so you could enter freely and join them in the worship and service of Yahweh. But Israel/Judah betrayed Yahweh God's trust in them. They did not serve him and you as a faithful covenant mediatorial agent.

You, however, are also guilty of betrayal. Yahweh God, your Creator and Sustainer, has been consistently rejected. You made your own deities of wood and stone. You used what Yahweh God gave you to dishonor him. More, you readily influenced the covenant people, Israel and Judah, to adopt your gods and your manner of life. Indeed, you have been betrayed, but you are betrayers yourselves.

E. Your judgment will be severe. Yahweh God, who raised you up to be his servant, will not leave unpunished your idolatries, immorality, greed, and ruthless military, social, and cultural misdeeds. You will be punished as creational covenant breakers. You will be punished for failing to serve Yahweh God as his covenantal mediatorial agents called to discipline and punish his light-bearers to the nations. You will be punished for your glee at misfortunes of other people and for causing unnecessary terror in the hearts of people deserving of my displeasure. You, who have been raised up to discipline and punish will be punished. You will be defeated in battle; you will be overrun by other nations, you will be ruled and forced to pay tribute. Many of you will die; some of you will become extinct as a national entity. As you have given full expression to your ridicule, glee, greed, anger, and wrath, so Yahweh God will make you the objects of his wrath as he raises up other nations to carry it out on you.

F. Your hope can only be based on the character of the sovereign cosmic King who is the unchanging, ever-faithful covenant Lord. His love and care for his image-bearing covenant children can never be doubted. His plan of redemption includes you; the tent of David, restored through the saving work of his Son, is for you to call your home, shelter, and place from which you go forth to serve. Indeed, you can and will be given citizenship in the palace city of the sovereign King from which he administers his inclusive covenant plans and purposes. You who have been bereft of covenantal privileges (e.g., Moab and Ammon), will have your fortunes restored because Yahweh is a faithful covenantal Lord. Indeed, citizens of every country to whom and against whom Yahweh has had his prophets prophesy can be one with a united Israel/Judah. My promises to Israel, Assyria, and Egypt (Isa. 19:23–25), and other nations cannot and will not be revoked. My word concerning the restoration of the "fortunes of Judah and Jerusalem" is sure. Just as sure is Yahweh's word that everyone who calls on the name of Yahweh will be saved (Joel 2:32; 3:1 [MT 3:5; 4:1]).

Conclusion

In conclusion to this study of the prophetic message to non-Israelite nations, it should be noted that not all the major points of the gospel, as revealed in the Old and New Testaments, were proclaimed to the nations. First, they were not explicitly told they were also covenantal people; it was implicit in the messages to and about them. Second, they were not explicitly told that Yahweh was their sovereign King, but they were informed implicitly. The kings of Babylon and Persia openly declared their awareness of Yahweh God as the supreme ruler of the cosmic kingdom (Dan. 3:28, 29; 4:34, 35; 6:25–27). Third, there is no explicit reference either in the messages to and concerning them to the promised messianic covenantal mediator or to the Holy Spirit and his work. Fourth, realizing that there are these omissions of explicit references, the prophetic messages made clear that Yahweh God was and is the sovereign ruler of the cosmic kingdom, that he is a faithful covenant Lord, and that his covenantal mediatorial strategy and method will never fail.

NOTES

1. See Gerard Van Groningen, *Messianic Revelation in the Old Testament* (Grand Rapids: Baker, 1990), esp. 441–63, 567, 613, 672, 73. *From Creation to Consummation,* vol. 1 (Sioux Center: Dordt, 1996) chap. 7. In chapters 19 and 20 of this volume, in a study of Joel, Amos, and Hosea, some extended references were made to the non-Israelite nations because these prophets spoke concerning them.

2. Carl Armerding stated that revelation was always proclaimed to Israel even about other nations. "Habakkuk," in the *Expositor's Bible Commentary,* ed. Frank Gaebelein, 12 vols. (Grand Rapids: Zondervan, 1979–85), 7:494.

3. This question has been raised again recently by Norbert Lohfink, S.J., *The Covenant Never Revoked,* trans. John J. Scullion, S.J. (Mahwah: Paulist, 1991). Although Lohfink specifically addresses himself to the question of the relationship between Christians and Jewish people, the question can be said to relate to Old Testament times and peoples also. Lohfink concludes that there is a "Single Covenant" but a "Twofold Way to Salvation." This he writes must be understood dramatically, for example, while God loves all people, he particularly has regard for the poor, 83–93.

4. F. F. Bruce, *Israel and the Nations*, (Exeter Devon: Paternoster, 1963), 11.

5. Henri Daniel-Rops, *Israel and the Ancient World,* trans. K. Madge (Garden City: Image Books-Doubleday, 1964), 15–17.

6. John Bright, *A History of Israel,* 3rd ed. (Philadelphia: Westminster, 1981), 23–44.

7. Walther Eichrodt, *Theology of the Old Testament,* trans. J. A. Baker (Philadelphia: Westminster, 1961), 25.

8. Gerard Van Groningen, *From Creation to Consummation* Vol. 1 (Sioux Center: Dordt, 1996), chap. 7, esp. pp. 153–156 and the chart that delineates the various aspects of the covenantal relationship of all people.

9. Two verbs are employed to express the concept of cursing. The one used in regard to nations is *qālal.* It does not carry the full sense of an absolute curse as *'āror* does, the verb used to express God's wrath and judgment.

10. A good case can be made for the proposition that Satan induced various Canaanite peoples to inhabit Palestine, to become entrenched there, and develop their religions that would be an eventual snare to the Israelites.

11. The Philistines, (the name *Palestine* is derived from Philistia/Philistines) are recorded to have had a major role in Israel's early national life. Very little, however, has been written about them. J. C. Moyer, in an article on the Philistines, presented some information concerning them. He pointed out that the only comprehensive work has been written about them is by R.A.S. Macalester, *The Philistines,* 1914. But, many references to the Philistines can be found in archaeological reports and in various essays included in biblical dictionaries and encyclopedias. "Philistines," in *The Zondervan Pictorial Encyclopedia of the Bible,* (ZEPB) ed. Merrill C. Tenney and Steven Barabas, 5 vols. (Grand Rapids: Zondervan, 1975), 4:76–77.

12. Cf. chap. 2, part 11, sec. A, where a brief mention was made to Amos's reference to surrounding nations.

13. Damascus/Aram/Syria and Tyre will be discussed more fully when considering the messages of Isaiah, Jeremiah, and Ezekiel in part III of this chapter.

14. The three relative nations, Moab, Ammon, and Edom, will be discussed. The Old Testament also refers to Midian as a relative nation; their ancestral father was a son of Abraham (Gen. 25:2, 4). Moses fled to the land of the Midianites (Exod. 2:15). They were closely identified with Moab (Num. 22:4, 7; 31:7). In the days of Gideon, the Midianites oppressed Israel and were defeated (Judg. 6–8). They joined in a conspiracy against Israel later (1 Kings 11:18). The psalmist, when pleading with Yahweh God to undo the plottings against Israel by nations such as the Edomites, Ishmaelites, Moabites, Hagrites, Gebalites, Ammonites, Amalekites, Philistines, Tyrians, and Assyrians asked that all these people would be deal with as the Midianites were under Gideon (Ps. 83:1–18; cf. also Isa. 9:4; 10:26; Hab. 3:7).

15. Roland K. Harrison wrote an article on Moab and in his bibliography refers only to A. H. Van Zyl, who in 1960 wrote *The Moabites.* Harrison lists a number of articles that refer to studies of the geography and archaeology of the Moabites. "Moab, Moabites," in ZEPB, 4:257–66. Cf. also Harrison's comments in his commentary, *Jeremiah and Lamentations* (Downers Grove: InterVarsity, 1973), 178.

16. Commentators are not agreed on how to interpret the reference to the restoration of Moab's fortunes. Elmer Leslie suggests the phrase was an insertion by an editing scribe, who had the promise to Israel about plans for a good future (29:11) in mind and applied this to Moab also. *Jeremiah* (Nashville: Abingdon, 1954), 289. Theo Laetsch wrote that the Lord in infinite grace and mercy knows, that while Moab's "national existence has ceased forever," where and how to find those individuals (Moabite descendants) chosen by him to be heirs of eternal life. *Bible Commentary—Jeremiah (*St. Louis: Concordia, 1952), 340. John A. Thompson did not try to make an application; he wrote that the prophet "looks to a future day" when Moab's fortune would be restored. *The Book of Jeremiah* (Grand Rapids: Eerdmans, 1980), 713.

17. Harrison, *Jeremiah and Lamentations,* 178.

18. See note 16 above.

19. The importance of the tossing of a sandal on property, as explained in Ruth 4:7, meant that possession was claimed of that property. Derek Kidner, however, suggests that

the psalmist need not be so understood. The picture rather is that of a man coming home and flinging his shoe at a slave or into a corner. *Psalms 1–72* (Cambridge: InterVarsity, 1973), 218. It is difficult to accept this interpretation.

20. Rabbi Samson Raphaeil Hirsch commented that David was expressing his confidence that Edom would be totally subjugated to him. *The Psalms* (New York: Philipp Feldheim, 1960), 415. J. Ridderbos prefers to emphasize that the "I" in the text refers to God. David thus basically gives expression to Yahweh God's sovereign theocratic reign over all the neighboring lands of Israel/Judah. *De Psalmen,* vol. II (Kampen: Kok, 1958), 139–41.

21. See John H. Thompson, *The Book of Jeremiah* (Grand Rapids: Eerdmans, 1980), 215, 216.

22. See Martin H. Woudstra's helpful essay "Edom and Israel in Ezekiel," *Calvin Theological Journal* 3 (1968): 21–35.

23. See the brief but concise review of what various scholars have opined on this matter of the priority in time of the three messages, and a sane conclusion to these by G.C.H. Aalders, *Obadja en Jona* (Kampen: Kok, 1958), 8–12.

24. Recall that one of Job's friends, Eliphas, came from the Edomite city of Teman (Job 2:11; 4:1). Wisdom was repeatedly referred to as a virtue of mankind by Job's friends, but Job insisted wisdom was with God (12:13; 28:28).

25. See Theo Laetsch, *Bible Commentary The Minor Prophets* (St. Louis Concordia, 1956), 196.

26. The term *sukkaṭ* derived from the verb *sākak,* to overshadow or cover or to be woven together, BDB, pp. 696–97, refers specifically to a tent or a booth that had an element of impermanence. David's royal *bayit* (house), (2 Sam. 7:11, 12) had given evidence of being more a temporary booth than a permanent house.

27. Laetsch wrote in his comments on Obadiah 21 that deliverance and salvation were for Edomite individuals also and thus Edom was a type and symbol of the grace of God "evidenced in the preaching of the gospel of salvation unto all people," *Minor Prophets,* 212, 213.

28. Idumea is a Greek form of the Hebrew Edom. Herod the Great, who collaborated with the Romans, was an Idumean.

29. Various biblical commentators have stressed the blessed truth that the kingdom of God will triumph, and their reference is not to the kingdom of Israel. John A. Thompson wrote that the kingdom is described in terms of Israel and Palestine, but "two elements of Obadiah's kingdom hopes are universalized and spiritualized in the book of Revelation." "Obadiah" in *The Interpreters Bible,* ed. George A. Buttrick, 12 vols. (New York: Abingdon, 1951-59), 6:859. Cf. also Laetsch, *Minor Prophets,* 213. Leslie C. Allen reminds his readers of the "diverse eschatological expectations among Christians" and adds, "Certainly the N.T. transmutes the territorial into the celestial, the material into the supernatural." "The Book of Obadiah" in *The Books of Joel, Obadiah, Jonah, and Micah* (Grand Rapids: Eerdmans, 1976), 172. See Robert L. Saucy, who refers to Obadiah 21, along with other passages, to support the view that prophetic hope for world history includes a literal establishment of the millennial kingdom in *The Case for Progressive Dispensationalism* (Grand Rapids: Zondervan, 1993), 296.

30. Various liberally oriented biblical scholars do not address this question of direct personal address; rather, they are more inclined to ask who were the original authors, if these can be discerned, and how and when they were edited. Cf. John Stek, "The Message of the Book of Jonah," *Calvin Theological Journal* 4, no. 1 (1969): 32–35, who allows for a historical writer.

31. Ibid., 32.

32. Isaiah, Jeremiah, and Ezekiel's prophecies concerning Moab, Ammon, and Edom have been discussed in the preceding section.

33. When one reviews the history of Aram, noting particularly the activities in interaction with the covenant people, one can understand Amos speaking against Damascus as he begins his prophecies of judgment against neighboring nations.

34. Ezekiel referred to trade which nations had with Aram (27:18).

35. The Ishmaelites who took Joseph and sold him in Egypt, came from Arabia (Gen. 37:25).

36. Cf. *New Bible Atlas,* ed. D.R.W. Wood (Wheaton: InterVarisity, 1985). 84. Considering where Cush is located, one is confronted with a vexing geographical problem trying to determine where the River Gihon, one of the four rivers flowing from Eden, actually was located (Gen. 2:13).

37. When Egypt and Assyria are considered, the reasons for Cush and Phut's judgment may become more apparent.

38. For a concise review from earliest time until the time of Antiochus's invasion of Egypt in 168, see John Bright, *A History of Israel,* 3rd ed. (Philadelphia: Westminster, 1981). Bright refers repeatedly throughout his work to Egypt's interaction with Israel/Judah and the postexilic Jewish community. The Index of Subjects should be consulted to aid one in locating the parts in which various stages of Egypt's history is discussed.

39. Reference is undoubtedly to some of Egypt's peoples' (five cities) eventual acknowledgment of Yahweh (19:21), Edward J. young, *The Book of Isaiah,* 3 vols. (Grand Rapids: Eerdmans, 1970), 2:34. See also J. Ridderbos, *Het Godswoord Der Profeten,* 4 vols. (Kampen: Kok, 1932, 2:237, rather than to Jesus moving into Egypt and bringing in their language. George Buchanan Gray, *A Critical and Exegetical Commentary on the Book of Isaiah,* 2 vols. (Edinburgh: T & T Clark, 4th Impression, 1956), 1:333. A later critical writer, J. Lindblom expressed the view that before the exile prophets did not speak of a conversion of the Gentiles but after the exile, some expressed vengeance, others expressed the idea that pagan nations would surrender to God. Thus, the book of Isaiah contains both ideas. Lindblom believes postexilic editors reworked Deutero-Isaiah so that both views were included. To accept this view one must join Lindblom and other scholars in the critical-literary dissection of Isaiah's unified book. See *Prophecy in Ancient Israel* (Oxford: Basil Blackwell, 1963), 282–83.

40. Pharaoh Neco was defeated shortly after he had defeated the army Josiah led against him; in this battle, Josiah was killed (2 Kings 23:29, 30; 2 Chron. 35:20–25).

41. See *New Bible Atlas,* map of Egypt, 86.

42. John Thompson comments that this question reflects a motif in the rib pattern, that is, a legal form that reflected a covenant context. *Jeremiah,* 159, 174.

43. Walther Eichrodt wrote that Egypt is to be seen as a chief supporter of resistance to the prophet's preaching of repentance and judgment. *Ezekiel, A Commentary,* trans. Casslett Quin (London: SCM, 1970), 400.

44. See G.C.H. Aalders' discussion of the combination of verbs and prepositions that allow for the idea that Ezekiel had to prophesy against, not to, Pharaoh. *Ezekiel,* 2 vols., (Kampen: Kok, 1957), 2:78.

45. See Eichrodt, *Ezekiel,* 407.

46. Eichrodt, ibid., 406, trying to deal with a seeming contradiction: Egypt defeated, a wasteland–Egypt restored, seeks the solution by injecting a later editor who included the restoration note after Egypt regained national identity.

47. See *New Bible Atlas,* 88.

48. Ibid., 90.

49. The story of Jonah is well known, and commentaries on Jonah are quite numerous and readily available. Special studies have been made. Stek, "Jonah." Phyllis Trible, a student and follower of James Muilenberg, has tried to develop and apply her mentor's literary pursuits in a treatise, *Rhetorical Criticism, Context Method, and the Book of Jonah* (Minneapolis: Fortress, 1994). Her detailed review of how rhetorical criticism arose and how it is to be used certainly raises questions concerning the usefulness and legitimacy of its method in analyzing a prophecy. At the conclusion of 230 pages, in which the artistry of rhetoric was expounded and applied to Jonah's prophecy, she legitimately asked, "Isn't rhetorical analysis so enamored of style that it neglects theology?" Trilbe replied that Jonah's "words abound with theological language," 233, 234. For the reader/student the problem is that rhetocial analysis controlled and overshadowed the message throughout the book. A Bible student, teacher, minister, or common reader is not helped to hear the Lord speaking.

50. See Zeph. 2:13–15: "He (Yahweh) will stretch out his hand . . . and destroy Assyria, leaving Nineveh utterly desolate."

51. George Adam Smith used the heading "The Vengeance of the Lord" for his comments on Nahum 1, "The Book of the Twelve Prophets," in *The Expositor's Bible,* ed. W. Robert Nicoll, 6 vols. (Grand Rapids: Eerdmans, 1947), 4:582, 583. Charles L. Taylor in "The Book of Nahum: Introduction and Exegesis," in *The Interpreters Bible,* ed. George A. Buttrick, 12 vols. (New York: Abingdon, 1951–57), 6:953, wrote that Nahum is ethnically and theologically deficient. More correctly, George L. Robinson wrote that Nahum reveals that Nineveh's destruction is not an act of capricious sovereignty, but the just reward of her iniquities" and "Nahum saw that the kingdom of darkness must fall before the kingdom of light breaks forth." *The Twelve Minor Prophets* (Grand Rapids: Baker, 1952), 114, 115.

52. Ibid., 115.

53. Amos declared that Yahweh would *'āhhâ* the *gĕ'ôn* of Jacob (6:8); in that context Israel's pride, based on its election, is to be understood.

54. *New Bible Atlas,* 90, 91.

55. The name Elam was not uncommon among the people of Israel/Judah. The chronicler, referred to one (1 Chron. 8:24). In Ezra and Nehemiah's time, various men had the name *Elam* (Ezra 2:7, 31; 8:7; 10:2, 26; Neh. 3:12; 7:34; 10:14; 12:42).

56. Joseph A. Alexander stated that Elam was a province of Persia and that Elamites were skillful archers. *Commentary on the Prophecies of Isaiah,* reprint, (Grand Rapids: Zondervan, 1953), 381. Edward J. Young considered it possible that Elamites were mercenaries in the Assyrian army. *Isaiah*, vol. II, 94.

57. See *New Bible Atlas,* 91.

58. All introductory studies discuss this proposal, as do most commentators on Isaiah. Some support the division, others do not. The position taken in this study is that there was one prophet Isaiah, who spoke directly to various situations in his time and was given prophetic messages concerning the future—some were fulfilled within a short time, others within a few centuries, others in the more distant future (e.g., Christ's death).

59. Armerding, *The Expositor's Bible,* 7:493.

60. The interpretation and eschatological application of Ezekiel 38, 39, differ widely among scholars and Bible students. Ralph H. Alexander expresses the view that a restored Israel lying peacefully and secure in their land will experience a final attempt by foreigners to possess the land of Israel. "Ezekiel," in *The Expositor's Bible Commentary,* 6:928.

Craig A. Blaising and Darrell L. Bock, as progressive dispensationalists, take a less literalistic view; they state that apocalyptic passages, such as Ezekiel 38, 39, have a fresh force when referred to in Revelation 20; the names refer to the four corners of the earth; thus there is a shift in imagery. So, while some Old Testament images are not to be taken symbolically, others are. *Progressive Dispensationalism,*(Wheaton: Victor, 1993), 93. G.C.H. Aalders wrote that one is not to look beyond the end of the exile; one is not to look for an eschatological figure or force. Rather, Ezekiel was proclaiming the end of the exile occasioned by the defeat of Babylon. *Ezecael,* II, 213.

61. Cf. Charles Dyer, *The Rise of Babylon* (Wheaton: Tyndale, 1991), 15, 16, who described what he saw of the bleak, undeveloped ruins of Babylon. Saddam Hussein of Iraq had attempted to uncover and rebuild Babylon.

62. The territory of the Medes lay to the east of Assyria. Ecbatana, the Midian capital was situated southeast of Nineveh and north, northeast of Susa, the capital of Persia. See *New Bible Atlas,* 90.

63. Ibid., 94. The ancient countries of Babylon, Assyria, and Persia continue to have much political, social, and religious influence in contemporary times, esp. 1990–2003.

22

Micah's Prophetic Message for Rural Judah

I. Introductory Comments

II. The Kingdom Setting

III. The Covenantal Framework and Administration

IV. The Mediator

22

Micah's Prophetic Message for Rural Judah

Introductory Comments

The prophecy of Micah has undergone intensive as well as extensive studies and analyses,[1] and conclusions drawn from these have demonstrated that the approaches taken to prophecy in general and specifically to this prophecy[2] determine the nature of the conclusions. This is a hermeneutical reality. Since the approaches differ, so do the writers' opinions. In this biblical-theological study, materials discussed in a previous study will not be repeated.[3] In the study that follows, however, some references to times and historical events will be included.

Two initial questions should be addressed. Which of the themes Joel included in his prophetic agenda[4] does Micah refer to and which does he develop? Does he pick up on some themes other predecessors introduced and expounded? As will become evident, Micah elaborated on the themes of the sins of the covenant people, the Messiah, the nature of Yahweh God, and the future of the covenant people. This being said, it should be stressed that Micah does include the other themes Joel and other prophets proclaimed in his prophecy as well.

The second question could be stated in various ways. Is there a structural unity evident? Are there really evidences of a variety of texts and themes brought together over a long period of time, and are these coherently brought together by an editor?[5] Or is there a basic theme that gives the book of Micah a coherent message and therefore a coherent structure?

In this biblical-theological study of Micah it will be made evident that Micah's prophecy, though not following the legal structural form of a covenant, does include the basic elements of the covenant Yahweh God established and repeatedly confirmed.[6] This covenant that Micah elaborates was an integral aspect of the Golden Cable that unites the entire Scriptures; the other strands of the Golden Cable are the kingdom and the Mediator. Within this framework of the Golden Cable, Micah expounded and expatiated on themes included in most of the prophetic messages.

The Kingdom Setting

Micah was not inclined to use the terms *mālak* (to reign) and *melek* (king) in reference to Yahweh God's reign. There is, however, one instance worthy of note (2:13). Micah prophesied that "their king will pass before them, the LORD at their head" (NIV).[7] The preferred explanation is that as Yahweh God, Israel's King, the preincarnate Christ, had gone before his people Israel by cloud and pillar of fire when they were delivered from Egypt and traveled through the wilderness (Exod. 13:21; Num. 9:15–23), so he as King would lead a remnant of Israel from the bondage of the exile to freedom.[8]

That Micah would have the rural, urban, and city people of Judah remember and know that Yahweh God was their king, their master, and their sovereign ruler, cannot be doubted. In fact, he called all peoples, the earth, to hear *šim'û* (imperative form) and to listen to what *'ădōnâi yĕhwâ* [9] had to say (1:2). The term *'ădōnâi,* meaning the master, the ruler over all, appears twice. The concepts of Yahweh the King, his reign, earth, and all its people as his domain clearly indicate that Micah had the cosmic kingdom in its entirety in mind as he prophesied. The King of the cosmic kingdom was speaking through the prophetic voice of Micah, a native of Moresheth, a town in southern rural Judah.

Micah proclaimed that this sovereign ruling King, who had his symbolic and typical throne, the ark of the covenant, in the temple was coming from there and would *dārek* (walk) over the mountains and cause them to split, melt, burn, and flow as molten lava because of his hot, overflowing, burning wrath against rebellious Samaria, capital of Israel, and against Jerusalem, capital of Judah (1:3–7). The sovereign Lord would bring judgment upon his kingdom people as well as on the land he had given them as their promised inheritance. This judgment, executed by Yahweh God the sovereign Lord over his people and the earth, was a theme Micah repeated. Yahweh God was planning disaster against the people (2:3; 7:4) and against all nations disobeying him (4:11: 5:5). When people would call out to Yahweh, he would not answer them (3:4, 7) until his judgment had been executed.

Micah prophesied concerning two other characteristics and activities of Yahweh the sovereign Lord. He spoke of Yahweh God's wrath but he emphasized other realities more. Yahweh God, sovereign covenant Lord is majestic and the source of strength, peace, and security (5:4). He loves justice (6:8; 7:18), and companionship with his people (6:8). He is the wise one, calling for wisdom on the part of the people (6:9); he is the source of hope (7:7) and brings light (7:8). He is a compassionate King who does not remain angry but forgives transgressions and pardons sins. He is the true God, absolutely faithful to covenant promises made to the patriarchs (7:20). In the final verses of the prophecy Micah, asking, *mî 'ēl kāmôkā* (who God like you?), answers by summing up what he had prophesied concerning Yahweh God's beneficent nature and redeeming activities.[10] Thus, Joel's theme of Yahweh God's zealous love was repeated, explicated, and given specific application to rural Judah, who was increasingly harassed and afflicted by neighboring powers in the eighth century B.C., and who heard the rumblings of developing strong nations to the north and east.

Joel had included warnings of disasters, the results of these, and Yahweh's redeeming activities. Indeed, Yahweh God would reveal himself in mighty deeds of judgment, on both Judah and Israel but also on the nations whom Yahweh God would employ to bring judgment on the covenant people (Mic. 5:5, 6; 6:16).

Micah was specific. Yahweh God, coming in power and wrath, was planning disaster (2:2–5). He would make Samaria into a heap of rubble, a bare field, so that a vineyard could be planted there. Idols and the temple in Jerusalem would be thrown into the surrounding valleys (1:5–7). This disaster brought on by the sovereign cosmic King would reach into the areas where Micah prophesied (1:10–14). Yahweh God would bring a conqueror against them. Strange natural phenomena would overtake the covenant people (3:6; cf. Joel 1–2). There would be great misery in the land, no grapes in vineyards, no figs to be picked, bloodshed and bribery would be common, families would be torn apart. All these tragedies would be brought on by Yahweh, Master of his people and sovereign Ruler over all nations and their assets (7:1–6). As Joel had done, Micah also sounds a triumphant note. He will wait and hope on Yahweh God because he knows him as *yišěmā 'ēnî 'ělōhây* (my savior God) who will hear his prophet when he calls (7:7).

Micah could hope, for he had also received the message of Yahweh God's sure intent to deliver, restore, and bless his people. Joel had prophesied that there would be a great deliverance and a wonderful renewing and restoration. Micah repeats, develops, and applies this message of redemption that only the sovereign King of the cosmos could and would bring.

Consider Micah's prophetic words concerning Yahweh God's messages of judgment and deliverance. He states clearly and confidently that Yahweh God is his savior who hears the voice of his servants. Knowing the character of Yahweh, he did not fear the judgments. His God would hear him and deliver. Micah also prophesied regarding Yahweh God, who, as nations gathered against the people,[11] *sām 'yig'ā lēk yěhwâ* (there and then Yahweh would redeem you, 4:10). Yahweh himself would be the *gō'el*, the one who would pay the price and thus redeem his people.[12] Thus Yahweh God, employing the nations as a means of judgment on Israel and Judah, would also bring judgment on these nations. He could and would do so as the sovereign Lord of the cosmic kingdom.

Micah makes it very clear, then, that Yahweh God, the Master, Ruler, King, and Redeemer of the cosmos, has all aspects of it under his providential rule and control. The cosmic King, exercising his reign from his majestic, exalted throne over the cosmos, provides the setting in which he carries out his covenantal administration.

The Covenantal Framework and Administration

We have presented a reasoned case for referring to the entire Old Testament as the King's Covenant Book.[13] And in a consideration of Micah's messianic references, it was demonstrated, in a succinct style, that Micah's prophecy had a covenantal structure.[14] Micah did not follow the order of the aspects of Hittite covenants,[15] but he included a discussion of the major elements that together constitute God's covenant with mankind and particularly with Israel/Judah. The following elements constitute the covenantal message and framework of Micah's prophecy.[16]

As in all covenants, the master introduces himself. It is the covenant-making, -maintaining, and -confirming God who speaks through Micah. By means of a *ḥâzâh* (vision) Yahweh communicates the message of the prophecy (1:1). Note must be taken of the two names of God that appear in the text. It is the word of Yahweh—the God who had said to Moses, I am who I am (Exod. 3:14), who had said to Abraham that he was a shield and great reward to him (Gen. 15:1), and had assured him that he was a God to him and his children (Gen. 17:1). He also had assured Joshua that he would be with him as he had been with Moses (Josh. 1:5). This Yahweh God had assured Moses, and through him, all of Israel encamped at Mount Sinai, that Israel was his precious possession, his holy nation, to serve as a kingdom of priests among the nations (Exod. 19:3–7). Yahweh is also referred to by his name or title, *'ădōnâi,* which can be translated as lord, master, owner.[17] When this term was used to refer to men, it meant either husband or master of the household. *'ădōnâi* has been translated as sovereign Lord (Mic. 1:2). This is certainly a correct translation in the context of Micah's prophecy because the term *sovereign* expresses the concept of sole and powerful ruler over all—and particularly in this context, over Israel/Judah.

Micah presents the sovereign Master in another capacity as well. He, the Lord of the covenant, is the judge. It is his prerogative to call the people with whom he has confirmed his covenant to give an account of themselves. Hence, as Master he functions as judge, setting up court. Yahweh will witness against his people.[18] The summons issues from the *hêkal qodĕšô* (holy temple), in which was the ark, the law of the covenant. Micah was specific: Yahweh Adonai has a *rîb,* a judicial grievance. He is calling his covenant people to come before him and to hear his accusation (6:1, 2). Yahweh, bringing a charge in a legal setting, is not a cold-hearted, loveless master even though he is the plaintiff and judge.[19] Rather, Yahweh the covenant master is holy, righteous, and just. These attributes must come to expression as well as his love, grace, mercy, and compassion.

In many covenants, an historical reference or review is made of what the master has done for the people. Micah does not omit reminding the people of this. Yahweh God had delivered Israel from Egyptian power and slavery and they were given leaders—Moses, Aaron, and Miriam (6:4).[20] King Balak and diviner Balaam had not been successful in their efforts to oppose Israel and the Lord had led them from the Shittim, on the east bank of the Jordan, through the river to Gilgal on the west bank (6:5). Great historical events had demonstrated Yahweh God's faithfulness to his covenant promises. The reality of their possessing of the promised land and dwelling within it was indisputable proof that Yahweh God had done his part.

Implied, if not directly stated, throughout Micah's prophecy were the covenantal stipulations. The accusations particularly imply that stipulations had been broken. Capital cities were not centers of righteousness, justice, and holiness (1:5–7; 3:12; 4:7). The law, a guide for covenantal living, had been ignored, broken, and rejected. Yahweh God was to be heard from and worshiped in his holy temple (1:2, 7); Micah summed up the stipulations in a clear and positive manner. Formal worship was not to be disregarded, but the rhetorical questions concerning appearing before the Lord with offerings (6:6, 7), have been so interpreted by some commentators.[21] Micah did not contradict the Mosaic legislation concerning sacrifices (the book of Leviticus).[22] No sacrifice was acceptable, not even the most precious in life, a son. The prescribed sacrifices were not acceptable when brought with a wrong disposition of the heart and a sinful attitude of the mind and will. Micah, in broader contexts, spoke against Israel's sin of disobeying the will of God in regard to social, cultural, and spiritual aspects of life. There was an enthusiasm for sacrifice (cf. also Isa. 1:10–17), but because a serious departure from other responsibilities was practiced, worship and sacrifices were offensive to Yahweh God.

Micah, in a succinct statement, holds before the covenant people their duty to obey the three creational covenant mandates which are amplified, be it briefly, in the Ten Commandments. Yahweh God has *hīggîd* (3rd person hiph. of *nōgîd*) declared, spoken with power and authority, *mah-tob* (what [is] good) (6:8). What Yahweh declared he also (*dôrēš qal ptc from dāraš*) seeks for and searches out; the participial form of the verb expresses Yahweh's constant and continuous searching out.

Micah called attention to the cultural mandate first. He is not referring directly to the actual activity of ruling over and developing the potentials in the created cosmos but to the attitudes to, conduct in, and personal activities in the cultural realm of life. *'ăśot mišpāt* (doing justice) refers to carrying out the will of the covenant Lord in the cultural aspect of life. The eighth commandment amplifies:

do not steal, do not take into your possession what does not belong to you. And speak the truth, (ninth commandment) in relation to your possessions, to a neighbor or in an official judicial setting. And maintain the proper attitude of heart to material things; do not covet what is not yours. Obey your covenant God in your relationships, among fellow men and women, in regard to material aspects of life.[23]

Micah proceeded to call attention to the social mandate. Again, he did not refer directly to marriage, family, and the needs of widows, orphans, or strangers. The phrase *we'ahăbat ḥesed* (and love mercy) refers directly to personal attitudes to and relationships with especially those who are personally in need. Indeed widows, orphans, as a rule are, but so are victims of crime, disasters, and other catastrophes. To love mercy is also understood as compassion, sympathy, and faithfulness. Make it your heart's desire to maintain such attitudes and relationships, not only to those in need, but in family relationships (5th commandment) in upholding the sanctity of life (6th commandment) and the purity of marriage (7th commandment).

Micah, to give a pertinent expression to the divine command to obey the covenantal spiritual mandate, used a well known biblical phrase "walk with your God." Enoch had done so and God took him away after living 365 years (Gen. 5:24). Noah, righteous and blameless among the people of his time, "walked with God" and, finding favor in God's sight, became the agent of preservation of the human race, (6:8, 9, 13, 14). Abraham, after raising up seed through Hagar, Sarah's Egyptian maid (16:3, 4), was reprimanded by Yahweh God. He commanded him to remember God was "the all sufficient one," and to remember he was to "walk before God and be blameless" (17:2). Yahweh God then graciously confirmed his covenant with Abraham. It is very evident from this passage that walking with God was a covenantal requirement. It was said of Job that he was blameless and upright; he feared God and shunned evil. This was another way of saying Job walked with God and, by doing so, he shunned evil (Job 1). The psalmist picked up on this thought of walking with God by elaborating on how this was to be done: no walking in the counsel of the wicked, no standing and sitting with sinners. Thus one leads a blameless life (Ps. 1). The covenant person would, walking with God, delight in and meditate on what Yahweh God had instructed in the Torah.

Micah, knowing this covenantal spiritual mandate, uses the phrase "to walk with God" to encapsulate all that Yahweh God expected of his covenant people as they lived their lives before him. The spiritual dimension of life that pervasively influences the cultural and social aspects of life had to be recognized.[24] The covenant people had to be in and remain in a definite living relationship with their God in all aspects of life.

To be noted is that Micah added the term *haṣĕnē'a* (hiph. inf. abs. of *ṣāna'*, to be modest, humble). The infinite absolute form of the verb indicates that the walk with God must be of a very defined and precise character. Commentators have used various terms to convey the basic sense of this term, which is a verb used as a noun in an adverbial manner to describe the walk with God. The term basically places emphasis on the character of the one walking with God, hence the terms *careful, wise, modest, humble.*[25] If the heart is right with God, then this relationship will be expressed in the quality and character of one's daily life in constant fellowship with God.

Micah stated the stipulations of the covenant in a very succinct manner. He, however, proclaimed in more detail that the curse of the covenant was to be executed because of disobedience and violations of Yahweh God's covenant requirements.

As if to dramatize the reality of the sin and guilt of Yahweh's covenant people, Micah stressed the judicial setting. Yahweh holds court; he is the prosecutor and judge (1:2; 6:2). Note the language. Yahweh God will witness against his people. He will do that from the holy temple. Yahweh is enthroned in the holy of holies—the ark is the throne with its mercy seat. But mercy will not be shown; Yahweh's judgment, due to his wrath, will issue forth because he has an accusation against his people; he has a judicial case, a real charge against them. They have broken the covenant their forefathers had promised to guard, uphold, keep, obey, carry out (Exod. 19:8; 24:3, 7).

Of what specifically did Micah accuse Yahweh's covenant people? As Samaria had become a center of idolatry in Israel in the north, Jerusalem had become that in Judah (1:5). Idol worship and prostitution are specifically mentioned.[26] The spiritual covenant mandate was ignored and disobeyed. This tragic reality led to other violations in the spiritual, social, and cultural spheres. Leaders and judges took bribes, priests demanded money for their services, and prophets told fortunes for money and did that as they despised justice, distorted what was right, and sought to have Zion thrive on bloodshed and the entire city of Jerusalem with wickedness. These sinful abominations were committed as if Yahweh God supported them as their God in their midst (3:9–11). The social and the cultural mandates were disobeyed and violated as fields and houses were coveted and seized and people were defrauded of their homes and of their inheritances (2:2). People who passed by were stripped of their good robes, women were driven from their homes, and children were robbed of a blessed future (2:8, 9). In the markets and houses of business corrupt business practices thrived. Short ephahs (grain measures smaller than regular size), dishonest scales (weights attached to them to record more than actual weight), and outright lying were commonplace. Honesty and integrity were absent because of the violence of rich men (6:10–12). The breaking of covenantal mandates and the justification for doing so did not keep Micah from openly charging that the covenant people knew what was correct behavior. Yahweh God had showed them what is good (6:8). The accused covenant breakers sinned willingly. They sinned with the proverbial high hand. They sinned defiantly; such sin, because the Lord's word was despised and his commandments broken, had to be punished.[27] The curse of the covenant had to be executed.

Micah intersperses his prophetic messages with Yahweh's statements of what he will do as he brings judgment. The judgment is to be of local and cosmic proportions, which the *'ammîm* (peoples) are called to witness (1:2). Some commentators understand the term *peoples* to refer to all nations; the term *goyîm* (nations), however, does not appear in the text. The term *'ammîm* is mostly used to refer to the covenant people, the inhabitants of both Israel and Judah. The term *'eretz* (land) can refer to the promised land as well as to the entire earth. The introduction (1:1) specifies that the message concerns Samaria and Jerusalem. The succeeding context indicates that Yahweh God has a message for his covenant people in their promised land. They are to experience judgment in the places they live and work that is so great that it will be of cosmic proportions.[28]

Joel had described judgment on the whole land in terms of a locust plague,[29] which was a metaphor for the large nations that Yahweh would employ to punish his covenant people. Micah spoke of mountains melting and valleys splitting apart (1:4). Samaria, Omri, and Ahab's city built on the hill as Jerusalem was, would become a heap of rubble and would no longer be the site for an Asherah cult (2 Kings 13:6; Mic. 1:7) but would continue as a center of prostitution. The disaster would overcome Jerusalem and surrounding towns and villages, causing Micah to weep, wail, and go about barefoot (1:8–14) as the conqueror whom Yahweh would raise up swept through the land (1:15). The disaster that Yahweh God was planning and that was sure to come would result in people losing their fields and houses to iniquitous people (2:1, 2). It would bring calamity, shame, ridicule, and utter ruin (2:3–5). Cosmic judgments would overcome; this is metaphorically portrayed by a Stygian darkness, with vision impossible and the sun setting for the prophets and diviners (3:6, 7). Micah went on to prophesy that the ruin of Zion, the Davidic holy hill, would be so complete that it would become an open, tillable area and the temple mound would be overgrown by trees and bushes (3:12).

The coming disaster, which included natural calamities would, however, include exile to Babylon.[30] Jerusalem would lose its counselors and the people would writhe in pain as a woman in labor as its capture and destruction occurred. All this was to happen at Yahweh's direction as he gave the victorious nations that attacked the means to do so (4:9–13a). The effect of the coming disaster on the people is graphically described by Micah when he proclaims that people will eat and not be satisfied, will save and have nothing, plant but have no harvest, press olives and grapes but have no oil or juice (6:13–16). Families would be severely affected by lack of trust, by betrayal of neighbors and family members (7:5, 6).

As one reads Micah's prophecies concerning the covenant curse to be executed cosmically, nationally, locally, and in family life, one is reminded that he did not prophesy anything new. Moses had spoken of the curses of the covenant to come upon a disbelieving, disobeying, God rejecting covenant people (Deut. 27:15–26; 28:15–68). Israel had experienced disaster during the period of the judges. Prophets preceding Micah, Joel, and Amos had repeatedly warned of certain judgment in the form of various disasters. Indeed, Micah was but a part in the golden cable as he prophesied concerning the covenant curse executed by the Lord of the covenant and cosmos.

All was not hopeless. Micah also spoke of the covenant blessings Yahweh was ready to bestow upon knowing, believing, trusting, loving, worshiping, and serving faithful covenant people. These reminders are also interspersed throughout his prophecy.

First, we must listen to Yahweh as he deals with his people. He comes to them from his dwelling place and in his sovereignty and power over the cosmos makes his presence felt (1:3). He calls out to them. He has not ignored or forgotten them. His call for his people to listen should be seen as rooted in his grace, even if it is a call to the courtroom. Israel and Judah could be acquitted when they repented and pled guilty (1:2). Yahweh called out to his people to rise up and receive the means and power to confront and defeat the nations (4:13).

Yahweh not only called out to his people, he pled with them. He approached them with a searching question: "My people, what have I done to you? How have I burdened you?" Yahweh pleads, "Answer me" (6:3).[31] Yahweh had reminded the people how, as their covenant-making, -affirming, and -keeping Lord, he had redeemed them from slavery in Egypt, gave them covenant agents in the persons of Moses, Aaron, and Miriam, who led them, delivered them from Balak and Balaam, and led them through the desert (6:4, 5).

As Yahweh called[32] and pled by the mouth of Micah, he reminded the covenant people that to hear and listen would lead the people to fear Yahweh's name, for "that is wisdom" (6:9). The Hebrew term *wĕtûšīyyâh* translated wisdom presents the idea of efficient wisdom/and or abiding success. Yahweh God thus reminded the people of Judah and Israel that to fear, that is, stand in awe, worship, and serve him is the sure way to the blessings Yahweh has for his covenant people.

Yahweh God repeated promises heard in the days of Moses and David. He would continue to be a shepherd of his people, even after their dispersal in exile (2:12), and beyond the time of the exile, he would work out his promise to Abraham that he and his offspring would be a blessing to the nations (4:2). Indeed, Yahweh God reassured his covenant people that in spite of judgments experienced, he would redeem them out of the hand of their enemies.[33]

Second, reference was made before to Micah serving as Yahweh God's mouthpiece. A specific blessing, though not acknowledged by most of the covenant people, was the prophetic voice that was active. The prophets were mediatorial agents of the covenant, appointed to address the covenant people. Micah did that. He spoke of being filled with power, with the Spirit of Yahweh, and with justice (3:8) to declare to Jacob's descendants their transgressions and sins.[34] He called on leaders and rulers to listen. They were to recognize that their covenant Lord knew that they despised justice, distorted what was right, and established themselves in power with bloodshed and wickedness (3:9, 10).

This prophetic task was not pleasant; Micah refers to the misery he experiences, comparing himself with fruit pickers who do not find any fruit to pick in the orchards and vineyards (7:1–6). But he would continue to be an obedient spokesman because he watches in hope, knowing Yahweh God is his Savior who hears him while he serves as Yahweh God's prophetic agent (7:7).

It needs to be repeated: Israel/Judah received the blessings of the covenant when the prophetic voice was active, proclaiming the word of Yahweh God. The covenant people were not deprived of hearing the word of their covenant God. That they did not heed it did not remove the blessing; however, ignoring and rejecting Yahweh's word of warning and future blessing would in time result in the curse of the covenant being executed on them.

At this juncture it is helpful to remember that Micah's prophetic voice had competition. Priests who were to teach the revealed will of Yahweh, as Moses had written it, were bribed to teach what the people in their wickedness, corruption, and guilt wished to hear. Likewise, judges accepted bribes and false prophets told fortunes for money (3:11). Micah was outspoken: these false prophets led the people astray when they declared peace for a price (3:5). These prophets were not to be considered a blessing but an implied blessing is stated when Micah warns that there is no future for them, darkness will overtake them, shame and disgrace will cover them because Yahweh God will not answer them and will prove their messages false (3:6, 7). But, the true covenantal agent, the prophet, would continue to speak on behalf of Yahweh God. Thus, the prophetic office and voice would continue and false prophets could not destroy, remove, or undo the faithful prophets' messages.

Third, Micah stated with confidence that another covenant blessing would be the continuing presence of Yahweh God (7:9). Micah spoke on behalf of the covenant people; he identified with them. They were sitting in the darkness of sin and the impending judgment. Micah prophesied: though fallen, sitting in darkness, *yĕhwâ* 'or *lî* ("Yahweh is light to me"). This phrase harks back to the cloud of light that lit up the way as the people journeyed through the desert (Num. 9:16), and also to the glory cloud that filled the tabernacle and temple with light (1 Kings 8:10). The cloud was a manifestation of Yahweh; the cloud indicated Yahweh's presence and where Yahweh was present there was light. This light meant salvation. David had expressed this blessed covenantal reality, singing, "Yahweh is my light and my salvation, whom shall I fear?" (Ps. 27:1). Micah prophesied with power and conviction that though the curse of the covenant would be executed on unfaithful Israel/Judah, Yahweh God would not withdraw his promised presence and gracious salvation.[35]

Fourth, when Yahweh confirmed his covenant with Abraham, he had stated categorically that Abraham was to be a blessing to the nations and that these nations were to bless themselves in their relationship with Abraham. Micah, in hope and assurance, declared that this blessing would continue to be a reality and would be more fully realized in the future. Although in Micah's time many nations gathered against the covenant people and called for their defilement so that the eyes of the nations could gloat over Zion (4:11), they would in time come to this mountain, to the house of Yahweh God and seek to be taught in his ways and walk in his paths (4:2; 7:12).

Covenants were sealed in various ways. The oath sworn to uphold the covenant was a very significant confirming seal. When Yahweh God reconfirmed his covenant with Abraham after he was prepared to sacrifice Isaac in obedience to Yahweh's command we read *bî nišba'ětî ně'um-yěhwâ* (by myself I swear declared Yahweh)[36] (Gen. 22:16). The idea of Yahweh God swearing, and thus giving absolute assurance to what he declares to be essential aspects of his covenantal dealings is repeated often in the Scriptures (24:7; 26:3; 50:24; Deut. 1:8; Ps. 89:3 [MT 4]; Isa. 14:24; 45:23). Micah used that term also when he referred to the *'emet* (faithfulness) to Jacob and the *ḥesed* (mercy) to David that Yahweh God had promised to them (7:20).

It should be stressed, however, that the term *šabā'* (swear) does not necessarily have to be present when Yahweh makes promises or blessings, or pronounces curses. His word is his oath. What Yahweh says is truth; what he promises is sure to be fulfilled; the judgments he pronounced are unalterable when no repentance is evident. The call Micah gave, "hear" (1:2), when he prophesied, "Yahweh says" (2:7), and Yahweh declares (4:6), is equivalent to Yahweh's oath, his word is his oath of assurance.

The presence of witnesses when covenants were made and when aspects of the covenant were referred to was an essential aspect of covenant activity. Speaking for Yahweh God, Micah first of all called for all peoples and nations to know that Yahweh Master would *bōkem lě'ēd* (against you for witness),[37] here to witness against Israel should they become corrupt (cf. Deut. 4:26). Implied in these calls is that Yahweh, the covenant maker, was present when the covenant was established and reconfirmed. Present also was the totality of the cosmic kingdom; it was the setting in which the covenant had been made. The idea of a third party being present and aware of what is agreed upon in a covenant is present in Scripture also (Gen. 31:50). Witness could also be understood in the form of surrendering possessions to confirm an agreement or covenant (21:30) or some aspect of the natural world (31:50; Josh. 24:27). From the references referred to above, it can be deduced that the idea of witness was applicable to those present when agreements/covenants were made and who were called to testify regarding this. But, a witness who had not been present at the initiation, could be called on to hear a later testimony against those who had broken covenant. Micah used the idea of witness in both senses.

The continuity of the covenant is assured by Micah in his prophecy by implied and specific indications. The fact that Yahweh God is the eternal, ever-faithful sovereign king assures us of the continuity of his ever-enduring cosmic kingdom. The covenant is integral to the kingdom; it is an administrative instrument. The kingdom is ruled according to its essential character. All aspects of the kingdom are upheld and unfolded according to and by means of Yahweh God's covenantal relationship to it.

Yahweh God's promises concerning his covenant blessings, as discussed above, give assurance of the continuity. So also his oath/word is ever-enduring. His word will not fail; his oath makes his covenant unchangeable and thus the promised blessings will never fail to be carried out (Mic. 7:20). Micah referred to specific characteristics or virtues of Yahweh God that give assurance that he will carry out what he swore by oath he would be and do as the covenant God of Abraham and Jacob.

mî-'ēl kāmôkâ (Who is a God like you?)[38] (7:18). Yahweh God is unrivaled by any in Scripture.[39] No one can be compared with him. Moses had led the Israelites, when rescued from Pharaoh's army, to sing, "Who among the gods is like you, O LORD, who is like you?" (Exod. 15:11). Yahweh God had demonstrated that he was the sovereign Lord and with wisdom and might had destroyed the enemy. Micah concludes his prophecy, not dwelling on God as a dreadful God, demanding terror and causing horror[40] among the people of Judah as he had done among the vanquished Egyptians. Yahweh God acts very differently toward his chosen people, whom he will pardon and forgive. As incomparable, absolutely unique, as Yahweh God is in power and destructive potential, so he is absolutely incomparable and unique in demonstrating his mercy and grace.

no' sē' 'āwōn (pardon, sin NIV). The verb *nōśē'* is the qal active participle of *nāśā',* to lift, take away, carry off. This is a continuous, ongoing activity of Yahweh God. And what does he take away, carry off? *'āwōn* (variously translated as iniquity, guilt, or sin NIV). The term *iniquity* basically refers to lack of righteousness and justice, virtues demanded in Yahweh's covenant law. An iniquitous person violates Yahweh God's prescription for obedience to the will of God. The term *wickedness* can also be used to express this basic idea. Micah proclaimed with conviction that his incomparable God takes up and carries away the iniquity, sin, and wickedness of his people.

wĕ'ābēr 'al-peša' (and passes by the transgressions). The active participle is used again to express the ongoing act of Yahweh God. He passes by the deeds performed by the iniquitous person. Yahweh God thus graciously deals with the person as well as his or her deeds.

Yahweh knows what the covenant person has done, but does not deal with that person or that person's deeds. He forgives, and as Micah went on to say, he will tread underfoot all transgressions and hurl all iniquities into the depths of the sea. Yahweh God forgives and forgets the reasons why the covenant people would have to endure his wrath for a while. And, whereas many perished, a remnant would continue because of Yahweh God's forgiveness and forgetting of iniquity, wickedness, transgression, and sin.

Micah went on to proclaim why Yahweh God can and does forgive and forget. *lō'-heḥĕzîq lā' ad 'appō* (not he keeps strong always his anger). The hiphil form of the verb *hāzaq* emphasizes the making the character of an object firm, strong, unchanging. But Yahweh God loves his people; his heart is tender and kind toward them. He has great pleasure and joy in demonstrating his basic nature and attitude toward his covenant people—be it only a remnant of them. Yahweh God remembers his attitude and dealings with the patriarchs and will so deal with their covenant offspring. *tittēr 'emet lĕyāqōb* (he will give truth/faithfulness to Jacob).

Jacob had been a deceiving unreliable, man. Yahweh God would continue to be the very opposite to Jacob and his descendants. More, *ḥesed lĕ 'abrāhām* (covenant loving kindness and mercy to Abraham).

A final comment on Micah's doxological conclusion to his prophecy must be made. Micah undoubtedly had Israel's experiences at the Sea of Reeds in mind. Moses had sung, "Who is like Yahweh?" (Exod. 15:13). Yahweh had taken the pursuing Egyptians and cast them underfoot, drowning them in the depths of the sea. Israel was rescued, freed, and ready to proceed. As Yahweh God had dealt with the Egyptians so he deals with the iniquities, transgressions, wickedness, sin, and guilt of his covenant people. The covenant assured Israel in the past of a sure future. So also the remnant would have a sure future.

When studying Micah's prophecy concerning the continuity of the covenant, one is confronted with a number of elements that are integral to an extensive biblical-eschatological panorama.[41]

To place Micah's eschatological references properly within this panorama, the entire scope should be kept before the reader. But before the panorama is sketched out, initial comments are in order.

It was stated at the outset of this study of *From Creation to Consummation* that the eschaton, the completion, the end, was an integral part of Yahweh God's plan and motivation to create. The eschaton was embedded in the very intent, plan, and act of our sovereign God's work of creation.[42]

Throughout the Scriptures terms are used to keep the end, the eschaton, the consummation before the reader. While there is a retrospective aspect, from Genesis 6 on, that is to say, biblical writers were aware that they were recording what was being said and done in the context of prior word and deed revelation. As they did this, there was the consistent future perspective also. There was, then, a continuum, an ever-progressive movement in God's revelation of himself, of his plan for the cosmos and for the people who were created and placed within creation to serve as his vicegerents. The following are such terms and phrases employed to indicate that there was an ongoing movement to the eschaton.

The Scriptures record that Yahweh God said *lō'-'ōsīp* (not be adding, or never again) would he bring a curse upon the ground (Gen. 8:21). He went on to say *'ôd kāl yĕmê hā'ăreṣ* (to all the continuing days of the earth) the order in the created cosmos would always continue. Jeremiah also spoke concerning the fixed, ever-continuing ordinances in the realm of creation (Jer. 31:35, 36). In the context of the ever-continuing order in the cosmos, Noah prophesied how Yahweh God would deal, dividing, leading, and using the sons of Noah and their descendants (Gen. 9:24–27). Jeremiah, prophesying concerning the sure future of Yahweh God's covenant people with the ever-continuing creation, repeatedly uses the phrase *yamin ba'im* (days are coming) (Jer. 31:27, 31, 38).[43]

The phrase *'aḥărîth hayyâmîm* (usuall translated latter days), is found in the Hebrew text often to refer to future times. Jacob prophesied concerning the future of his sons (days to come or latter days) (Gen. 49:1). The term *'aḥărîth* is a feminine plural noun derived from the term *'āḥar* (to stay behind, tarry, or hinder). Other derived terms stress the idea of after, another, last, or end.[44] The phrase *'aḥărîth hayyâ mîm* clearly refers to days that are to come or time in the future or end times.[45]

The term that has been considered to refer to various lengths of future time is *'ôlam* (forever, perpetual, everlasting).[46] Moses used the term seventy times to refer to the perpetuity of statutes and to the "everlasting covenant." The term appears eighty times in the historical books. The psalmists used the term over 150 times to describe, qualify, and quantify (as if this were possible) the joy, praise, and blessings of fellowship with the eternal yet ever-present Lord God whose name is precious, whose throne is steadfast, and whose reign is never-ending. The prophets likewise used the term often to speak of the future, of shorter, longer, and/or enduring periods of time or beyond time. The contexts in which the term was used must be carefully consulted and interpreted to grasp what the prophets proclaimed concerning events as to when and how they would take place.

The series of events that are involved in the ever-unfolding movement toward the biblically presented goal have been outlined in various ways. One way is to set forth the various specific covenanting activities, as in a diagram outlining Yahweh God's confirmation of his creation/redemptive/restorative covenant with Noah.[47] One covenant, established first with Adam and Eve, was continually confirmed, extended, and applied. Some aspects involved in Old Testament administration of the covenant were of a temporary or time-bound nature. For example, the sacrament of circumcision, a sealing of the covenant of redemption, became obsolete when Christ died once for all, because of his shedding of blood, his circumcision (Col. 2:11), in which all believers participate. In like manner the prescribed sacrifices, the tabernacle/temple, the theocracy established at Sinai were all temporary aspects, all were typical of Christ Jesus' presence, ministry, death, and present reign over the entire cosmos. But, because temporary, typical aspects became obsolete, the covenant itself never did—Christ Jesus remains the mediator of the one covenant, creational/redemptive/restorative for all time.

The chart as it appears in volume 1 does not present a complete unfolding of the one covenant. The chart presentation ended with the new covenant, realized at Pentecost. The phrase "after to A.D. 100" should not have been included. The renewed/new covenant of creation/redemption/restoration administration continues until Christ Jesus returns in power and glory. He will then initiate the eternal covenant of peace when he brings forth the new heavens and new earth for all eternity.[48]

To sum up, the covenant Yahweh God established at the time of creation and upheld by adding the second aspect—the redemption/restorative, after Adam and Eve deviated from the way which God set before them—was confirmed with Noah, with Abraham, Isaac, Jacob, Judah, Joshua, Samuel, David; in the postexilic times, at the time of Christ's birth, in his ministry, death, resurrection, and ascension. At Pentecost the same, but renewed/new covenant was confirmed and the eternal covenant of peace would be confirmed at Christ's second coming and will never end.[49]

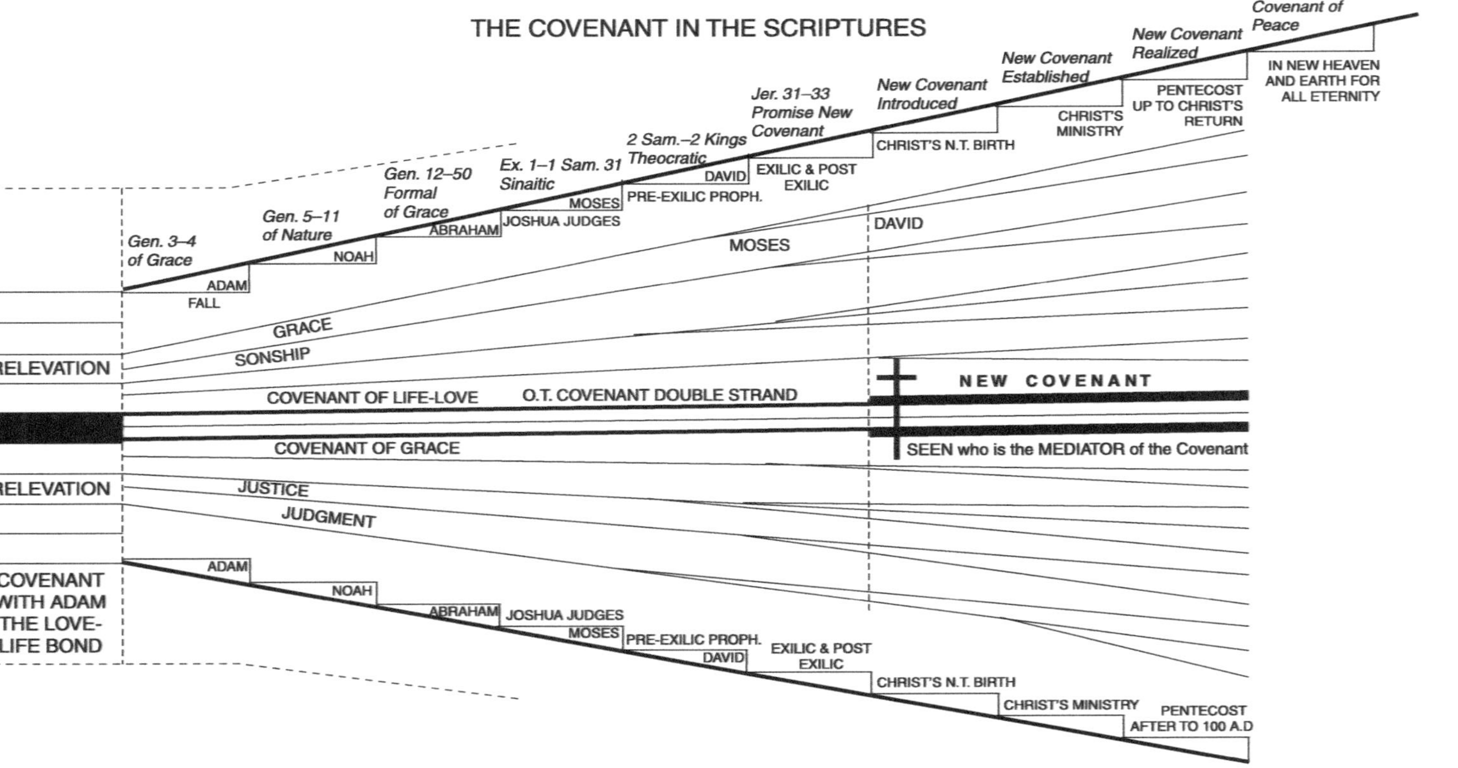
THE COVENANT IN THE SCRIPTURES
Gen. 3–4 of Grace
Gen. 5–11 of Nature
Gen. 12–50 Formal of Grace
Ex. 1–1 Sam. 31 Sinaitic
2 Sam.–2 Kings Theocratic
Jer. 31–33 Promise New Covenant
New Covenant Introduced
New Covenant Established
New Covenant Realized
Covenant of Peace
ADAM
FALL
NOAH
ABRAHAM
JOSHUA JUDGES
MOSES
PRE-EXILIC PROPH.
DAVID
EXILIC & POST EXILIC
CHRIST'S N.T. BIRTH
CHRIST'S MINISTRY
PENTECOST UP TO CHRIST'S RETURN
IN NEW HEAVEN AND EARTH FOR ALL ETERNITY
RELEVATION
GRACE
SONSHIP
MOSES
DAVID
COVENANT OF LIFE-LOVE
O.T. COVENANT DOUBLE STRAND
NEW COVENANT
COVENANT OF GRACE
SEEN who is the MEDIATOR of the Covenant
RELEVATION
JUSTICE
JUDGMENT
COVENANT WITH ADAM THE LOVE-LIFE BOND
ADAM
NOAH
ABRAHAM
JOSHUA JUDGES
MOSES
PRE-EXILIC PROPH.
DAVID
EXILIC & POST EXILIC
CHRIST'S N.T. BIRTH
CHRIST'S MINISTRY
PENTECOST AFTER TO 100 A.D

Micah prophesied during the administrative period of the covenant that had been confirmed with David. But Micah proclaimed, correctly, that the covenant with David was ignored and rejected by a large portion of the people who were specifically intended by Yahweh God to be blessed by and through it.[50] Micah had to warn that the curse, an integral aspect of the covenant also, would be executed as the blessings were withheld. Micah thus reflected Yahweh God's covenantal relationships with the patriarchs, with Israel as a nation, and with David. As he did this, he repeatedly referred to the future unfolding of the covenant, including the return from exile, Christ's birth and ministry, the renewed covenant after Pentecost to be followed by the administration of the eternal covenant of peace initiated at the time of Jesus Christ's return in power and glory.

A second way to set forth the ever-unfolding movement toward the biblically presented goal of Yahweh God is to highlight great historic events that have specific eschatological, that is, future aspects, embedded in them. These high points in history are also interrelated since the succeeding ones always flow out of the preceding ones.[51]

The first great eschatological event in history was Yahweh God's pronouncement in the garden of Eden when he declared that the seed of the woman would crush the head of Satan, and by implication, all of Satan's followers. The second great eschatological event was two-pronged: the deluge and the preservation of Noah and his sons. The third great eschatological event was the calling and directing of Abraham and his seed to Canaan, where he was to live and serve as a blessing to all nations. The fourth great eschatological event was Israel's stay in and exodus from Egypt, followed by the fifth great eschatological event, the inheriting and possessing of the land promised to Abraham. The sixth great eschatological event was the establishing of the Davidic monarchy and David's taking possession of, and his and Solomon's rule over, the land promised to Abraham—from the river of Egypt in the south to the great river, the Euphrates, in the north. The seventh great eschatological event was the exile, specifically the return from the exile. The eighth great eschatological event was the coming of Jesus Christ, his ministry, death, resurrection, and ascension. The ninth great eschatological event was the pouring out of the Holy Spirit and the subsequent gathering of peoples from nations to form the New Testament church, succeeding the *qahal,* assembly of the Old Testament, and incorporating within it all believers, whether Jews or Gentiles. The tenth great eschatological event is to take place when Christ Jesus returns to judge all people, from every tribe, tongue, nation, race, and to usher in the eternally abiding new heavens and earth.

The ten great eschatological events will be highlighted in our further study of Micah and the major prophets.

In the first part of our study of the covenantal framework and administration it was pointed out that Micah, in his unique manner, referred to and applied the main constituent elements of Yahweh God's covenant with his people. He did not present these in a formal, schematic manner. Rather, he included these as he pro-

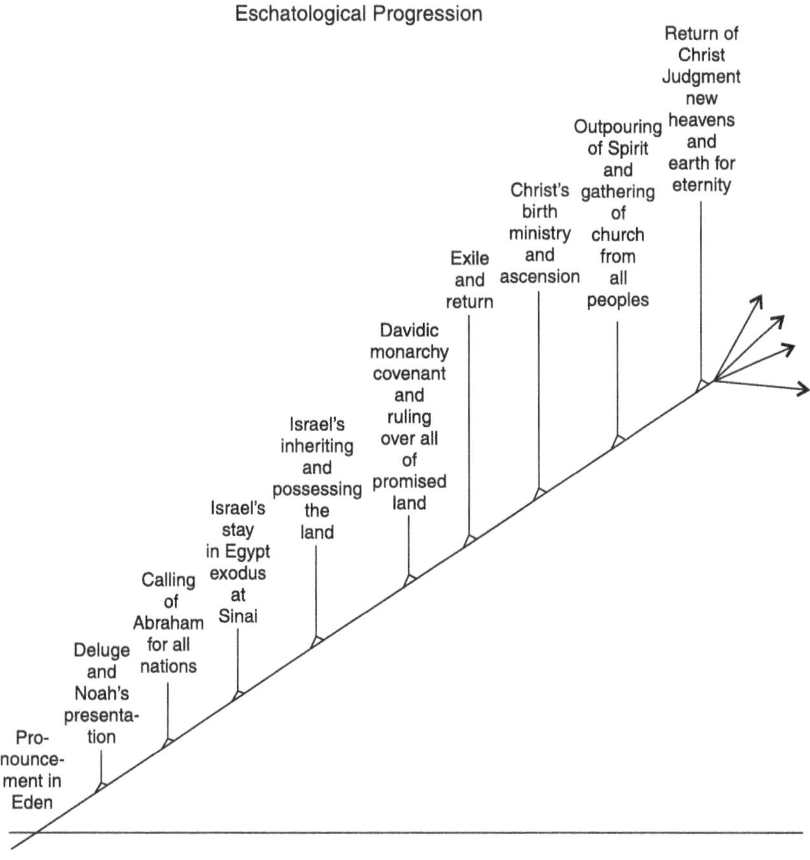

claimed his God-given message, referring them and applying them as he addressed specific issues in their contemporary setting. In regard to the eschatological events, Micah does not refer to them in their historical sequence either, but does allude to some directly and specifically.

The eschatological event, the third, in the course of their occurrence (cf. chart) that Micah refers to is Yahweh God's covenant with Abraham and Jacob (7:20). This reference forms the climax of Micah's prophecy. Why did and does Yahweh God concern himself with Israel/Judah in spite of their rejection of him and his covenant? It is because of the covenant that will not cease. The people broke it repeatedly, Yahweh God will keep it,[52] executing either the blessing or the curse.

Micah referred to the fourth eschatological event also. Yahweh God had informed Abraham that his descendants would be in a strange land 400 years and then come out with great possessions (Gen. 15:13, 14). Micah referred, by implication, to Yahweh God's mercy, grace, and sovereign power displayed in their exodus and wilderness experiences. Yahweh inquired of his people, "What have I done to you?" The answer, "I brought you out of Egypt, redeemed you from slavery, and gave you leaders. I kept Balak from attacking you and brought you into the promised land" (Gilgal) (Mic. 6:4, 5). He assured his people that as he had shown his wonders, the plagues in Egypt and the deliverance at the Red Sea,[53] so he would continue to reveal his sovereign power and rule over all nations (7:15).

Most of Micah's prophecy addressed the tragic situation that existed during the sixth eschatological event—the establishing of the monarchy and Israel/Judah's response to Yahweh God's faithfulness to them. Micah proclaimed that Yahweh God had a case against them, but the people were given an opportunity to plead their case (1:2; 6:1, 2). In the preceding discussion, references were made to the constant ignoring and breaking of Yahweh God's covenant. The people hated good, loved evil, tore the skin off their fellow men, and in extreme cruelty destroyed and did away with them (3:1–3). But Micah also proclaimed that Yahweh God gave them the opportunity to act justly, love mercy, and walk humbly with their God (6:8). And Micah also proclaimed that Yahweh God forgave and forgot sin because of his covenant with the patriarchs (7:20). Then, in spite of many reasons to execute judgment, that is, to exile the covenant people to foreign lands (4:11, 12; 6:1–7:6), grace and mercy would abide then and for all future time.

Micah made it explicit: a conqueror would come, cause much mourning, and exile the people from their homes (1:15, 16). This seventh eschatological event was becoming unavoidable. Because of the despising of justice, bloodshed, bribery, and wickedness (3:9–11), Zion would be plowed like a field, Jerusalem made a heap of rubble, and the temple hill overgrown with brush (3:12). The Assyrians would certainly invade the land. But the exile was not to mean the covenant people would cease to exist. As a nation yes, but the return of a remnant gathered was also a future surety (2:12, 13). As a flock in a pasture, Yahweh God's people would be safely gathered under the leadership of a king[54] who would be under the headship of their Lord God. In these words, Micah could be giving an implied message of a future gathering under the leadership of King Jesus. Micah repeated the assurance of a return from the exile. Again, he spoke of the remnant[55] who, lame and in grief, would be gathered and be under the kingship of the daughter of Zion (4:6–8). This intriguing passage, which holds a tremendous future for the remnant, not the nation, refers to the daughter of Zion/Jerusalem twice. Micah carefully avoids direct reference to the Davidic house; he does not preach that a restored Davidic house will have a representative on a throne exercising kingship over the earth in some distant future. In Scripture, the term *daughter,* refers to coming generations born from the remnant who will be under the dominion of one also born of the daughter. This should be understood as a reference to the Christ to be born[56] of the virgin Mary and, as a descendant of David, to exercise kingship as he gathers his church from all nations.[57]

Micah's message included a more specific reference to this king, the ruler who was to appear and exercise kingship over his people (5:2–5a). Thus he introduces the eighth eschatological event: the coming and reign of the one who is eternal, born in Bethlehem (David's city), who would stand and shepherd the flock, the remnant, the daughter, the bride. He will provide the assured security for his redeemed and restored people.[58] This security and accompanying peace will be worldwide. In proclaiming this great eschatological event, Micah set the stage for the two remaining events implied in this eighth event.

The ninth and tenth eschatological events are so intimately interrelated in Micah's prophecy that care must be taken to understand what is specifically referred to (4:1–5). Micah employs terminology his audience is acquainted with. He spoke of the mountain of the Lord's house as chief of the mountains and people streaming to it. He is undoubtedly holding before his audience the temple on its mountain to which people streamed for the celebration of prescribed festivals. As this was done in the past, so in a greater and more wonderful way would people from all nations come into the house of Yahweh God. They would come, invited and urged to join those walking, according to the will of the Lord, in the paths Yahweh God had delineated in his covenant with his people. This path would be followed by people of all nations. Micah is clearly prophesying, in an eager, expectant, and hopeful manner, how the daughter, the bride, the church, would be established and gathered. Micah did not refer, as Joel did, to the coming of the Holy Spirit when this great gathering and building of the body, the bride, would commence. Micah thus clearly points forward to the ninth eschatological event.

The tenth and final eschatological event is intimated and implied in terms of everyday good life in rural Canaan, for example, every man under his own vine and fig tree, having no fears due to outside threats (4:4). Micah referred to what was to come with the initiating of the covenant of peace.[59] There will be no making of instruments used in warfare, there will be no making of war.[60] People will walk, live, serve Yahweh their God in perfect harmony and peace. Again, it must be repeated, Micah proclaims the consummation, the initiating of the covenant of peace, the eternal rest and well-being of the covenant people in the final state in terms of an exalted, wonderful way of daily life—daily life as rural Judea knew it at its best. As they in their present state could be taught Yahweh's way, and walk in his paths according to Yahweh's proclaimed will (4:2), so they would more fully understand, walk, and serve in the glorious future.[61]

In our study of the covenant, we undertook an extended consideration of how each covenant-making event was really a covenant-confirming event, with previous covenant confirmations and administrations serving as the sources for confirmation as the historical context warranted. These in turn set the stage and provided the basis for future confirmations and administrations. Thus the continuity of the covenant throughout the history of revelation and redemption is demonstrated to be in fact a reality.

In the same manner, we have presented how, as the covenant was repeatedly confirmed, eschatological events took place, or were presented as present or were to become future realities. These eschatological events, each one proceeding from previous ones and progressing to additional ones, demonstrate Yahweh God's progressive revelation in ongoing history and his ever-continuing activities to attain the goals for and final state of perfection in the renewed heavens and earth.

The Mediator

The third strand of the Golden Cable that united the progressive revelation of Yahweh God as it is recorded in the Scriptures is the mediator.

The concept of the covenant mediator can be understood to refer to agents of the covenant who were types, forerunners of the one, only, and real mediator of the covenant: the promised Messiah.

It should be understood that prophets faithful to Yahweh God were agents of the covenant. Hence Micah must be considered such—and he served well. He received the vision concerning Samaria and Jerusalem and proclaimed the message Yahweh God gave him concerning these cities and the countries they represented (1:1; 3:1). He was fully aware that he spoke with power and with the Spirit's guidance as he addressed leaders and rulers, spelling out their injustice, wickedness, and bloodshed (3:8–12). Micah, as a messenger of the covenant, also spoke of his hope for the Lord, his God and Savior (7:7).

There were also unfaithful agents of the covenant, who certainly did not do their mediatorial work as they were called to do. There were the false prophets who led the covenant people astray, proclaiming peace (3:5). Rulers and leaders, none mentioned by name (3:9) except King Ahaz, descendant of David (1:1), under whose reign Micah spoke, were corrupt and unjust, not representing the covenant Lord as was their duty.[62] Priests, also covenant agents, who were to stand as mediating servants between Yahweh God and the people, were unfaithful. They, who were given their livelihood as descendants of Levi, nevertheless charged the people for their priestly work (teaching) (3:11).

Micah, however, presents a sure and strong word of promise for a chastened, exiled, humiliated, and suffering people. The covenant people do not know the thoughts of Yahweh and do not understand his plans to eventually gather them as sheaves, not to be threshed, but by Yahweh's grace and sovereign rule, to be given hooves of bronze. This is a metaphorical reference to means of threshing grain in Micah's day. Animals would be paraded over the threshing floor, covered with grain that had to have the kernels separated from the straw and chaff (4:11–13). Indeed, Yahweh's people would be victorious and devote the wealth of the nations to the Lord.[63]

Micah called for a gathering of troops (5:1a) because of the siege that was sure to come. The king's humiliation, would be afflicted by a stroke of a rod on his cheek. Likely the prophet was referring to the Assyrian assault against Jerusalem under Sennacherib in 701 B.C. (2 Kings 18ff.).[64] But Jerusalem's neighboring small village was no real military threat, it being a grape-growing center. It would play a major role in the future deliverance of Jerusalem and her peace. This small place,

Bethlehem, was the birthplace and home of David. Yahweh God would keep his promise to him. A son would be born to him, a royal dynasty would follow, and an everlasting kingdom would be established (2 Sam. 7:11b–16). This descendant of David would be none other than the one who, from eternity, was destined to be the victorious ruler over Yahweh's covenant people. So, though the people would be abandoned for a while (Mic. 5:3a), the return from the exile was a certainty (5:3b) and from these returned exiles would arise, not a military hero, but a strong and majestic shepherd. This shepherd, the messianic descendant of David the shepherd, would give security and peace. His greatness and majesty would become known throughout the entire cosmos (5:4, 5a).

Throughout most of his prophecy, Micah spoke of Yahweh God who, while performing as judge would execute the curse of the covenant, would also be the only source of hope, deliverance, beneficent reign, and peace. Yahweh would do it through the son of David, his eternal son. This one would be the covenant administrator serving as the covenant Mediator. Indeed, all aspects of the covenant would become sure realities for all time and beyond because of the mediatorial work the son would perform and thus bring into full reality the kingdom of Yahweh God in all its fullness, wonder, majesty, and glory.

NOTES

1. See the extensive bibliography Hans Walter Wolff has produced in his recent updated and revised work on *Micah*, trans. Gary Stansell (Minneapolis: Augsburg, 1990), 27–31. Writers who have published essays since 1990 can be divided into two groups. Those writing in English (British and American) publications have concentrated more on the person of Micah or on some specific issue, such as justice. Cf. Albert M. Pennybacher, who considers Micah the prophet an elder in town and country whose pursuit is justice. "The Two Micah's: Reflections on Integrity in Ministry," *Lexington Theological Review* 27, no. 2 (1992): 33–42. Cf. also Alec Gilmore, "The Voice of the Voiceless," in *The Expository Times* 105, (1994), 10, 303–5. The essay written by Nadav Na'aman, with the title "The House of -no- Shade Shall Take Away Its Tax From You (Micah 1:11)," discusses the literary aspects of Micah 1:8–16 in *Vetus Testamentum* 44, no. 4 (1995), 516–27, is a sample of the many essays in foreign country or language periodicals. Another example is Par Bernard Gosse, "Michee 4:1–5, Isaie 2:1–5 et les redacteurs finaux du livre d'Isaie" *Zeitsschrift das Alteswissenschaft* 105 (Spring): 98–102.

2. See Gerard Van Groningen, *Messianic Revelation in the Old Testament,* reprint (Eugene: Wiph & Stock, 1997), for a concise statement of three groups: (1) the traditional conservative, (2) the critical historical literary, and (3) the covenantalist, 495–99. As is to be expected, there are variations within each group, particularly in the first two.

3. See *MROT* for a review of the time and historical *Sitz im Leben* of Micah, 490–95. Notice should also be taken of the bibliographical references in the footnotes.

4. See conclusion of chap. 19.

5. David Gerald Hagstrom wrote that there are different types of coherence and if there is coherence in this prophecy it has been developed by bringing at least four separate texts into this composite group over "an extended compositional history." Cf. *The Coherence of the Book of Micah, A Literary Analysis,* SBL Dissertation Series 89 (Atlanta: Scholars,

1988). Wolff wrote that "the book of Micah reflects . . .. several centuries . . . only a small part of the prophetic sayings are from Micah of Moresheth." *Micah,* 1. In fact, Wolff concluded that there are evidences of postexilic redactions, 26, 27. Hence the production of the book Micah covered a period from Jothan's reign (742–735 B.C.) up to postexilic times (400 B.C.). Liturgical readings and responses were included, 26, 27. Other recent writers have continued to consider Micah's prophecy to consist of basically three separate documents. J. G. Bosman, writing in "Shrif en Kerk," 16, no. 2 (1995), considers Micah 1–3 to have been written before 722 B.C. because he prophesied the fall of Jerusalem when Samaria fell. The concept of *mispōt* had a basic social injustice reference. When Jerusalem did not fall, but did in 586 B.C., it was for theological reasons. Hence Micah 4–5 includes denunciations of social as well as theological injustice. Micah 6–7, writes Bosman, was revised into its final form in postexilic times, spread out, expanded, "Geregtigheid in die boek Nuga," 219–32. George Pixley did not specifically indicate that Micah's prophecy consisted of three distinct documents; he, however, implies it. He stated that he accepted the literary conclusions of scholars such as Norman Gottwold (*Tribes of Judah*), Bernhard Stade, and Albrecht (*Kliene Schriften*), who all held to literary analysis that concluded Micah's prophecy to consist of at least three parts. He concentrated on Micah 1–3; he interprets these three chapters to present Micah not as a reformer, as Amos was, but as a revolutionary who incited the peasants to revolt against their oppressors. These oppressors had freedom to carry out their social injustice deeds because the government in Jerusalem was not able to exercise a stable control. A commentator, who would wish to be listed among conservative scholars, Ralph L. Smith, "Micah," in *Word Biblical Commentary,* vol. 32 (Waco: Word, 1984), 6, suggested that Leslie Allen could be correct in stating that Micah wrote most of the book except 4:1–4; 4:6–8; 7:8–20. See *Joel, Obadiah, Jonah and Micah* (Grand Rapids: Eerdmans, 1976), 251, 252.

6. See *MROT,* 497, 98.

7. Smith did not discuss this question except to say that the passage is subject to various interpretations. "Micah," 29.

8. See Allen's comments. *Joel, Obadiah, Jonah and Micah,* 303. Wolff also understands the reference to be to Yahweh who breaks through walls, Pss. 80:13 (12); 89:41 (40) and through enemy lines. *Micah,* 85, 86.

9. In the preceding paragraph we referred to the preincarnate Christ as the King. To speak of Yahweh as King does not mean there were two kings. Yahweh, Lord of the covenant, is not to be separated from Jesus Christ, Lord and Mediator of the covenant.

10. It is difficult to accept the literary critical scholars' view that 7:18–20 is a two-part hymn placed at the end of the prophecy by a late redactor for liturgical purposes. Wolff considered the final two chapters to be so arranged that it was given "an antiphonal alternation of voices." *Micah* (Philadelphia: Westminster, 1976), 9. He also considered the book of Micah to be a collection of sayings arranged by a later redactor; 2, 12–15. J.M.P. Smith, at the beginning of the twentieth century, divided 7:14–20 into three strophes, the third (7:18–20) he considered to give expression to the distress that Israel was in when the land was only partly possessed in the days of Ezra and Nehemiah. "Micah," in *The International Critical Commentary,* eds. J.M.P. Smith, William Hayes Ward, and Julius Bewer (Edinburgh: T & T Clark, 1911), 152.

11. Note that Micah not only prophesies regarding the Assyrian invasions but also regarding the future exile to Babylon and the remnant's return from it (4:10).

12. See Ruth 4:4; also Lev. 25:26; Isa. 59:20; Ps. 103:4.

13. Cf. *MROT,* 52–72.

14. Ibid., 495–99. Scholars who had recognized this covenantal structure, including Gerhardus Vos, Walter Brueggeman, John Bright, and Wayne Kobes, are listed in notes 14, 15 on p. 497. It should be noted, however, that many critical scholars continue to question the presence and role of the covenant in the life of Israel, in "Israel's faith" and the role of covenant in prophetic literature. Cf. Brevard S. Childs, *Biblical Theology of the Old and New Testaments: Theological Reflections on the Christian Bible* (Minneapolis: Fortress, 1992), 411–20. More helpful is the discussion by Elmer A. Martens in his book *God's Design: A Focus on Old Testament Theology* (Grand Rapids: Baker, 1981). In a section entitled "The Prophets' Use of Covenant," Martens states that by judging the occurrences of the word covenant (*bĕrît*) the prophets were not much preoccupied with past covenants, 151. Martens proceeds, however, to point out that the prophets, without using the terms too often, were insistent on "the intent of the covenant." A probable reason the term was not used frequently by the prophets, Martens suggests, is that the idea of Israel being a covenant people had "lulled Israel into a false security." 154.

15. Moses did so more closely when he proclaimed and wrote his messages recorded in the book of Deuteronomy.

16. Cf. figure 7 in *MROT,* 498, for themes and textual references.

17. Cf. *'ādôn* in the *Theological Wordbook of the Old Testament,* ed. R. Laird Harris (Chicago: Moody, 1980), vol. 1, 12.

18. Commentators discuss whether Yahweh God is calling all the nations or just Israel/Judah. It seems correct to insist Micah is addressing the latter. He uses the term *ʿammûn*, usually used to refer to the covenant people, not *goîm,* usually used to refer to the nations. Furthermore, in chapter 6 it is clear the reference is to Israel/Judah, brought up from Egypt.

19. Cf. Allen, "Micah," 270.

20. Miriam, the sister of Moses, had had a unique role in Israel's history. As the older sister of Moses she had a vital responsibility in the preservation of baby Moses and being involved in Moses' entrance into the Egyptian palace, where he received indispensable training for his life's tasks (Exod. 2:4; cf. also Heb. 11:23, 24). She was referred to as a prophetess when she led the women of Israel in praising Yahweh God for the deliverance from the Egyptians at the Red Sea (Exod. 15:21). When she was disciplined for her jealousy and rebellion against Moses and put outside the camp for seven days, all of Israel waited until she was restored before moving on (Num. 12:14, 15). Miriam was one of the very few women whose death and burial are recorded in the Old Testament (Num. 20:1). She had been a gift of Yahweh God to the people of Israel, especially to its women, during a crucial period in their history.

21. Delbert Hilliers refers to this view and seems to agree with it to a certain extent. He acknowledged that "holocausts" were devoted to deity but the prophetic objection to sacrifice is religious in the narrower sense—sacrifices are portrayed as useless to God or offensive to him. *Micah,* 79. James L. Mays acknowledges that acceptable sacrifices were not rejected, but that, as other prophets did, a contrast was set up between proper conduct and formal worship. *Micah* (Philadelphia: Westminster, 1976).

22. Norman Snaith, *Amos, Hosea, and Micah* (London: Epworth, reprint, 1960), 103, has correctly written that the sacrifice of the firstborn son was the most precious and costly sacrifice of all. He refers to 2 Kings 3:27, where it is recorded that the king of Moab sacrificed his son. That this was never done in Israel/Judah cannot be said because Ahaz and

Manasseh, of Davidic lineage, sacrificed their son (2 Kings 16:3; 21:6; 2 Chron. 33:6). That it was forbidden in Israel/Judah (Lev. 20:3), Josiah desecrated Topheth so that no one could use it to sacrifice children (2 Kings 23:10).

23. Micah did not refer in detail to the entire cultural mandate, nor do the commandments 8–10. The cultural mandate covers a wide area, including business, industry, commerce, banking, economics, politics, recreation, the arts, technology, education, and other such cultural aspects of life. It is of interest to note that Micah 6:8 receives much attention in English periodicals and journals. Examples are Bernhard W. Anderson "What Does God Require of Us?" *Biblical Review*, vol. xi, 46, 47 and C.F. Dumermuth, "The Good Three-fold Way," *Asia Journal of* Theology, vol. 8:1, 186, 187, and Gilmore, cf. note 1. Rolf P. Knierim in *The Task of Old Testament Theology* (Grand Rapids: Eerdmans, 1995) referred to this passage 616–18, a number of times when discussing the doing of justice, 96; the doing of justice being possible only when "walking humbly with God," 122, when discussing "principles of ethics," 292, and the basic norms of Israel's society's tradition, 444.

24. Allen wrote that the first two requirements of the formula for fulfillment of the covenant are oriented toward a human ethic; they are nevertheless grounded in the revelation of God's character and will. This latent motivation is expressed in a careful walk with God. "Micah," 374.

25. Smith correctly wrote that coming before God called for not what is in our hands but in our hearts. "Micah," 51.

26. Recall that Amos had accused Israel of idolatry and sacred prostitution also (Amos 2:7, 8).

27. To sin with the high hand meant that there was not only knowledge of what the misdeeds were, but that there was specific effort made after thinking, reflecting, planning (cf. Num. 15:30, 31).

28. Thomas Edward McComiskey, joining other commentators, states that *Adonai* Yahweh calls all the nations to hear what his judgment is against all nations. The specific judgment pronounced upon Samaria and Jerusalem included a didactic element that related directly to the future of the nations of the world. "Micah," in *The Expositor's Bible Commentary,* ed. Frank E. Gabelein, 12 vols. (Grand Rapids: Zondervan, 1985), 7:403.

29. Amos had also employed locusts as a metaphor for total destruction (4:9; 7:1).

30. Micah also prophesies concerning the Assyrians invading Israel but not succeeding in the capture of Judah and Jerusalem (5:5b–6).

31. Ebenezer Henderson wrote: "the Israelites are asked, in the kindest and most affecting style, what ground of complaint they had against Jehovah, which could have induced them to act the part they did." "Micah," in *The Twelve Minor Prophets* (Grand Rapids: Baker, 1980), 255. Wolff wrote that these words "are animated more strongly by the keynote of love and courtship than by the desire for self affirmation." *Micah,* 174.

32. The Hebrew text has the phrase *qōl Yĕhwâh lā'îr yēqrâ'* (voice of Yahweh to the city he calls), thus emphasizing that Yahweh is indeed calling to Jerusalem.

33. Micah's prophetic utterances concerning eschatology are discussed in succeeding paragraphs.

34. McComiskey is correct when he writes that the Hebrew term *'ûlām* (but, i.e., but as for me) states Micah's conviction that his prophetic activity stands in sharp contrast to that of the false prophets. "Micah," 418. Calvin wrote of Micah's courageous spirit as he "stands up alone" against a large number of false teachers who appealed to their large numbers. Micah states that he is filled by the power of the Holy Spirit. *Jonah, Micah, Nahum,* vol.

III, *Commentaries on the Twelve Minor Prophets,* trans. John Owens (Grand Rapids: Eerdmans, 1950), 230.

35. Carl F. Keil wrote "In darkness the Lord is light to the faithful . . . who in wrath does not violate his grace" "Micah," in the *Biblical Commentary on the Old Testament: The Twelve Minor Prophets,* vol. 1, trans. J. Marten (Grand Rapids: Eerdmans, 1951), 508.

36. The niphal form of the verb *să' i'* strengthens the thought of *bî,* by myself, because it emphasizes reflexive activity.

37. Cf. R. Smith, "Micah," 16, who understood Yahweh to be a witness, that is, accuser, against the nations.

38. C. F. Keil was correct when he wrote that whether Micah plays on his name is doubtful. "Micah," 514.

39. Henderson, *The Twelve,* 267.

40. Cf. Abraham Heschel, *The Prophets* (New York: Harper and Row, 1962), 289.

41. The study of the major prophets' proclamations, which include many eschatological references, will give occasion to refer to this biblical-eschatological panorama.

42. Cf. Gerard Van Groningen, *From Creation to Consummation*, vol. 1 (Sioux Center: Dordt, 1966), 11, 12.

43. Cf. also Jer. 16:14; 19:6; 23:5, 7; 30:3; 33:14; 48:12; 49:2; 51:52. The context of each reference to the days coming give various indications as to how long a period is referred. Cf. also Isa. 39:6; Mal. 4:1 [3:19].

44. In Proverbs the term is often translated the end: 5:4; 14:12, 13; 19:20; 23:18; 25:8. Cf. also Ps. 37:37, 38.

45. The phrase is found in various contexts. Cf. e.g., Num. 24:14; Deut. 4:30; 31:29; 32:29; Isa. 2:2; Jer. 23:20; 30:24; 48:47; 49:39; Ezek. 38:8, 16; Dan. 8:19, 23; 10:14; Hos. 3:5; Micah 4:1.

46. Cf. how the term was interpreted in the study of God's ever-continuing covenant with David, *From Creation to Consummation,* 1:510–12.

47. Cf. chart on page 148 in vol. 1 of *From Creation to Consummation.*

48. Cf. expanded chart.

49. In the following study of the prophets, reference will be made to some differing views on the time and sequence of the eschatological events. Suffice it to say at this point, that the scriptural presentation of these eschatological events indicates that there is a constant progression toward the final climactic eschatological event. This means that what took place at an earlier time will not be repeated, for that would be retrogression. A specific reference can be made to the theocracy. It was a symbol of the cosmic kingdom and a type of the eternal kingdom ushered in at Christ's return in glory.

50. Allen has described the circumstances in Micah's time. With an influx of material prosperity, a selfish materialism was spawned, a complacent approach to religion to achieve human desires developed, and a disintegration of personal and social values resulted. *Micah,* 240.

51. Cf. the chart, Eschatological Progression.

52. Roland Wolfe made a correct statement when he wrote that the return from exile would not only benefit Israel but would vindicate the faithfulness of God in keeping his promises to Abraham and Jacob. "The Book of Micah," in *The Interpreters Bible,* ed. Nolan B. Harmon, 12 vols. (New York: Abingdon, 1956), 6:949.

53. McComiskey stated correctly that the prophets often cited the exodus as one of the first great acts of redemption and thus Yahweh God demonstrates his faithfulness to his "standard, i.e., the covenant obligations." "Micah," 435.

54. See the discussion of the king in part I of this chapter.

55. Note should be taken of what Micah proclaimed concerning the remnant. The limping ones and the miserable ones among the exiles are to become the remnant, but Micah also referred to the people of Israel (2:12), who as a remnant, would return. Keil correctly points out that only the limping and miserable are mentioned in this passage to express the thought that no one is to be excluded from the future salvation. "Micah," 459, 460.

56. Some commentators omit any discussion of the phrase daughter of Zion/Jerusalem. The term *remnant* they say, is not to be seen as referring to the people in exile but it refers to those who return and are made into a remnant and as such is the repository of God's grace and promise, which will be fulfilled when there is the regathering of Israel in the messianic age. McComiskey, "Micah," 422, 423. See also Craig A. Blaising and Darrell L. Bock, *Progressive Dispensationalism* (Wheaton: Victor, 1993), 225, 226. It is of interest to note also that the term *'ôlām* is not interpreted consistently—it means eternal/forever or for a limited period, e.g., thousand-year millennium.

57. Keil, "Micah," 461.

58. See extended discussion of Micah 5:1–5a in *Messianic Revelation,* 499–508.

59. Cf. elaboration on the covenant of peace in Ezekiel 36, 37, esp. 37:24–28.

60. Cf. Isaiah 11; in this prophetic chapter various eschatological perspectives and events are intertwined and integrated as one glorious future—a future beyond the birth of Christ, the shoot coming up from the stump of Jesse.

61. One can readily understand why believers holding to a postmillennial eschatology consider Micah 5:1–5a, Ezekiel 36, 37, and Isaiah 11 to present an ever-increasing movement to a millennium of peace and prosperity during the New Testament age, that is, the ninth eschatological event.

62. J. Ridderbos has described the sins and wickedness of leaders well in section 4 of his study of Micah, which he entitled "De Zonde van Liedslieden en Volk" (The sin of leaders and people). "Micha," in *Het Godswoord Der Profeten,* 4 vols. (Kampen: Kok, 1930), 1:237–43. Ridderbos reminded readers that Micah indicated at various times that Judah followed their northern kinsmen, Israel (1:5–7, 13; 6:16) in exercising illegitimate power, corrupt influence, idolatry, injustice, and extreme violence. See also *Messianic Revelation* regarding the three messianic offices, 499–501.

63. Micah undoubtedly was calling attention to how broken Egypt supplied the delivered slave people with wealth (Exod. 12:36) so that later they had the means to build a beautiful portable tent of worship (25:1–9; 35:30–36:7).

64. Cf. the discussion of Micah 5:1 by Allen, "Micah," 341, 342.

23

Isaiah's Prophetic Message for Urban Judah

I. Introductory Comments

II. The Covenant in Isaiah

III. The Mediator of the Covenant

IV. The Kingdom in Isaiah's Proclamation

V. Conclusion

23

Isaiah's Prophetic Message for Urban Judah

Introductory Comments

Isaiah and Micah

Isaiah and Micah were contemporaries. Micah was from rural Moresheth, Isaiah was from urban Jerusalem. Both remained in their native setting as they prophesied. They shared the same historical, spiritual, social, and cultural situation. Their messages were in many respects the same. Differences appear as we consider their character and manner of prophesying. Micah, the rural man, reflected his setting but his language was that of a well-prepared spokesman. Isaiah was from a royal family, apparently well educated, and addressed the royal courtiers directly at various times and in various ways. The citizenry of Jerusalem should be considered his audience, as well as possibly some neighboring nations.

The Time of Isaiah's Ministry

Consult the following sketch for an overview of the time references of Isaiah's prophecies.

Overview of Time Reference of Isaiah's Prophecies

Time of Isaiah's Ministry	
740 B.C.	*650 B.C.*
During time of Uzziah (Azariah), Jotham, Ahaz, Hezekiah, and Mannesseh (first part of rule)	
Chapters 1–39, prophesied during his lifetime. Assyria was the dominant empire and Isaiah's prophecies include reference to it. This section of Isaiah has been referred to as the book of judgment.	Chapters 40–66, proclaimed during the Assyrian period. The basic historical reference is to the empire of Babylon and Judah's experiences in exile. This section has been referred to as the book of comfort. It addresses the return from exile, the Messiah's person and work, and the eschaton.

A brief summary of Isaiah's message, his time, his personal history, the unity of his prophecy, and a presentation of how the Isaianic material can be grouped in two specific ways has been carefully surveyed in a previous work.[1]

Previous Messianic Studies

It should also be noted that much of what is included in the actual prophetic message that Isaiah proclaimed has been studied in detail in another work. The messianic passages, in which the Messiah was foretold (4:2–6, 7:1–14; 9:2–7; 11:1–16; 40:1–6a; 41:5–10; 42:18–25; 43:8–13; 44:1–5, 21–23; 44:28–45:13; 48:20; 49:1–12; 50:4–9; 52:13–53:12; 55:1–5; 59:15b–21; 66:1–3)[2] will not be discussed in detail but may be referred to at various times. The prophecies to, for, or against other nations, chapters 12–23, have been studied also.[3]

Themes from Joel's Agenda

The question whether Isaiah picked up and developed the prophetic agenda that Joel presented can be answered in the affirmative. It must be added, however, that Isaiah did not follow it theme by theme. Some of Joel's themes are expanded, others are referred to or implied. Isaiah did include three factors that Joel had not referred to (cf. p. 35, conclusion of chapter I) directly. (1) Isaiah gives historical specifics, for example, persons (Ahaz, Hezekiah, and Cyrus), his own call, and national experience; (2) he prophesied in detail concerning the Messiah; and (3) Isaiah made repeated references to the character, attributes, and virtues of Yahweh God.

Lastly, it will become obvious in this chapter that Isaiah developed the three strands of the Golden Cable that unites the entire biblical record of Yahweh God's revelation.[4] The three strands, or themes, will be studied in the following order: the covenant; the Mediator of the covenant; and the kingdom. The latter will require extensive attention.

The Covenant in Isaiah

A careful exegetical study of Isaiah 1–6 introduces one to the covenant Yahweh God had confirmed, formalized (Exod. 19:4–6), explicated, and applied (cf., e.g., 2 Sam. 7). Isaiah reveals a deep awareness of this privilege Israel/Judah had as Yahweh God's covenant people. This privilege, however, could not be separated from the stipulations that the covenant people were obligated to obey.[5] Moses, addressing Israel in the desert east of the Jordan, had expounded the Torah—the instructions concerning how Israel became a freed people to live covenantally before, with, and for Yahweh God.[6] Isaiah commenced his prophecy calling for witnesses, the heavens and the earth.[7] All that the heavens and the earth included were witnesses to Yahweh God's special relationship with the descendants of Abraham, Isaac, and Jacob, whom he had wondrously and miraculously delivered from slavery in Egypt and providentially led through the wilderness for forty years.[8]

The Judicial Case (Isa. 1–6:13)[9]

Isaiah had received a specific and unique call to be Yahweh God's covenantal spokesman (6:1–13). It came in a vision Isaiah received while in the temple. Yahweh God, in his exalted enthroned state, attended by seraphs (throne attendants), was hailed as the thrice holy, almighty, and glorious one. Isaiah realized his unworthiness to be in the presence of the sovereign King over all (6:5); he, however, was commissioned to be a spokesman for Yahweh in spite of this sense of unworthiness. When assured that his guilt was removed and his sin atoned for, as a forgiven and cleansed man he was prepared to bring Yahweh's message to the covenant people (6:6–8). The message to be proclaimed was to a hardened people (6:9, 10) who had to receive a very difficulty et assuring message: judgment was coming (6:11) but the Davidic stump would abide (6:12).

As the other prophets, Hosea, Amos, and Micah, Isaiah proclaimed that Yahweh God, the covenant Lord had an accusation against his people and was bringing a lawsuit. *Niṣṣāb lārîb Yĕhwâ wĕʿōmēd lādîn ʿammîm* (3:13). The NIV, as do some recent commentators, translates these two phrases as follows: "The LORD takes his place in court, he rises to judge the people." The more specific translation would read, "The LORD has taken his place to contend, he stands to judge his people."[10] Another commentator translated, "Jehovah has appeared to plead, and stands up to judge the nations."[11] The verb *niṣṣāb* conveys the idea of Yahweh God coming forward and standing, firmly, resolutely, and ready. The verb *ʿōmēd* (qal active ptc. of *ʿāmad*) pictures Yahweh God as having taken his stand and continuing in that posture. Clearly, Isaiah was prophesying that Yahweh God had set up a legal court. He had a case against his covenant people. It is in this way that Isaiah's open phrase must be understood, "Hear . . . for Yahweh has spoken" (1:2a).

Isaiah wanted his audience to know that Yahweh God, who was judging them, had a legal right to do so. He had been a faithful sovereign Lord: "I reared children and brought them up" (1:2b). Indeed, Yahweh God had given Abraham many descendants and had brought them out of slavery and given them their land as their inheritance. Isaiah recounted in metaphoric terms how Yahweh had lovingly and carefully brought the people to their land and settled them. He employed the figure of a vineyard, well planted with good vines on a fertile hill that had been cleared of stones. He had provided protection for it (5:1, 2a).[12] He had dealt with them as a loving father does with his children. Taking his children to court, bringing a lawsuit against them in no way detracted from or denigrated the character and position of the sovereign covenant Lord. He remained the exalted one (2:11c, 17c) and the thrice holy and glorious one (6:1–7).

The charges Yahweh God had against his covenant people covered every aspect of life in which Yahweh's promises and blessings were ignored or abused and in which covenant stipulations were violated. The result was that, having forsaken Yahweh, having spurned the Holy One, and having turned their backs on him, Judah proved to be a sinful people and were loaded with guilt. They were a brood of evildoers, parents and children alike (1:2a–4). Their condition, due to rebellion, was incurable (1:5, 6), and their country, its cities, fields, and vineyards, would become as Sodom and Gomorrah (1:7–9). Their worship, if formally according to the law, was corrupt, their sacrifices gave Yahweh no pleasure, their offerings were detestable, their feasts were loathsome and were a burden to Yahweh. Their prayers were rejected because of bloodstained hands (1:10–15). Jerusalem, the city of God, had become a prostitute, a city of murderers led by rebel leaders who kept company with thieves, accepted bribes, and refused to defend the fatherless and widows (1:21–23).

Religiously the people accepted the superstitions of the east and of the Philistines; they worshiped idols they had made and trusted in their treasurers (2:6, 7). Politically, life was misruled by youths and women (3:17). Socially, corruption abounded, the poor were plundered and humiliated. Women demonstrated haughtiness as they flirted and jingled their ankle ornaments (3:14–16). Isaiah summed up Yahweh God's charges with a plaintive request: What more could Yahweh God have done for his people (vineyard)? It is a rhetorical question to which the answer is: nothing. Yahweh had kept his covenant promises. When he looked for good fruit, justice, and righteousness, however, he saw bloodshed and heard cries of distress (5:3–7). Indeed, Judah was a sinful people, loaded with guilt, a brood of evildoers given to corruption, who had forsaken Yahweh, spurned the Holy One of Israel, and turned their backs on him (1:4).

Judah, under the leadership of Jerusalem's rulers, had become a covenant-breaking people. This violation of the life/love bond affected the spiritual, social, and cultural aspects of life. Yahweh God had no alternative but to bring his people into court and pronounce upon them the curse of the covenant[13] that, by the mouth of Isaiah was stated in various ways. There are repeated references to why and how the curses would be executed.

Consider how Isaiah spoke graphically, at times literally, at times symbolically or metaphorically.

1. Isaiah 1:5–12: the people would be beaten, have heads injured, wounds and welts, open sores not cleansed or bandaged. The countryside would be desolate, cities burned, and fields stripped. Jerusalem would be deserted and lonely; their sacrifices would be rejected, their offerings considered offensive, their feast days hated, and their prayers spurned.[14]

2. Isaiah 1:24, 25: *hā'ādôn yĕhwâ ṣĕbā 'ôt* (The Lord, Yahweh the Sovereign One) declared that he would get relief from his foes (the rebelling rulers, 1:23), "avenge myself on my enemies," thoroughly purge away dross and remove impurities. In this proclamation the rulers and their city were referred to as a unit.

3. Isaiah 1:28–31: Isaiah repeated his warning to rebels and sinners who forsake Yahweh that they would be broken and perish. Those living would be ashamed and disgraced because of their animistic worship, but like the fading leaves on a mighty tree or a garden without water, rebels and sinners would learn with an unquenchable fire.[15]

4. Isaiah 2:9–18: the Day of Yahweh that is sure to dawn will bring an end to silver, gold, treasures, horses, chariots, and idols men have made with their fingers. The unforgiven people will be brought low and humbled.

It should not be overlooked that as Isaiah prophesied concerning the bringing low and humbling of the arrogant and proud he repeated that *niśgab yĕhwâ lĕbaddô Payyôm hahû'* (exalted will be only Yahweh in that day). The bringing of judgment would not dishonor or denigrate Yahweh God; rather, he would be honored and exalted in demonstrating his righteousness and justice.

5. Isaiah 2:19–21: the actual response of the sinners and rebels experiencing Yahweh's wrath when he rises in the splendor of his majesty to shake the earth would be that there would be flight to caves in rocks and holes in the ground as idols of silver and gold, once worshiped, would be thrown to rats and bats.

6. Isaiah 3:1–4:1: Isaiah made a specific address concerning the city of Jerusalem and the nation of Judah. He preached that everyday supplies, leaders, rapacious rulers, warriors, and craftsmen would all be taken away.[16] Jerusalem, having become like Sodom, had brought disaster upon itself. The righteous, however, were assured it would be well with them and they would enjoy the fruit of their deeds. That social anarchy was both a cause and result of Yahweh's punishment was uniquely portrayed by Isaiah when he spoke of youth oppressing and women ruling. The description even of those haughty, flirting women is graphic in its elaboration of women's fineries, jewelry, and extravagant clothing. But when the warriors died and the city was in mourning, the women would have their glory taken away. Then they would realize how they really needed men to cover their humiliation and shame.[17]

7. Isaiah 5:8–25. After having uttered the song of the vineyard, in which Yahweh is described as a good vineyardist, who rejoices over what he had done for it, and then discovered it bore only bad fruit, Isaiah challenged the people of Jerusalem and Judah to explain why they responded by producing bad fruit. The people did not answer. Yahweh God, through Isaiah, proclaimed that the vineyard, that is, Jerusalem and Judah, would be destroyed and become a wasteland. They would receive the deserved results of injustice, bloodshed, and unrighteousness. Six woes were expressed. The Hebrew term *hôy* (ah, alas, ha) expressed a lament with pain and sorrow because of the judgment to be executed and experienced. Isaiah repeated much of what he had proclaimed before. Possessions, gotten in greed, would be devastated (5:9, 16). Feasting people, disregarding the work of Yahweh, would go into exile or to their grave; they would be humbled by their just God (5:11–16). People who defied Yahweh with boasting challenges as they carried out deeds of deceit and wickedness would endure pain, grief, and devastation (5:18, 19). So also would those who twisted and overturned the good and just suffer (5:20), and those who considered themselves wise would likewise be judged (5:21). Authorities with responsibilities to uphold and carry out the law, but who accepted bribes and denied justice to the innocent, would perish as straw is burned and a moth is scorched by flames.

Isaiah concluded the series of woe proclamations by reminding the covenant people that Yahweh God's execution of the curse of the covenant was what Yahweh had to do because of their rejection of the Torah (the law) and especially of their rejection of Yahweh God, the Holy One himself (5:24). The agents to be used to bring judgment on the covenant people would be the nations, who would respond with alacrity. They would come swiftly, speedily, well armed, like roaring lions bringing in darkness and distress (5:26–30).

8. Isaiah 6:9–13a: When Isaiah was officially commissioned to prophesy, he was told to go speak to a people who would not understand what they heard, or perceive what they saw because of calloused hearts, a condition exacerbated by Isaiah's preaching.[18] In a real sense Isaiah is prophesying that it is too late for repentance because in answer to Isaiah's query about the length of the hardening, Yahweh God replied that the invasion of Judah, the destruction of Jerusalem, and the exile had to occur first.

In this eighth statement concerning the curse that was sure to come, Isaiah expressed in a climactic manner what was to take place in the future. The previous expressions had hinted or even referred to this catastrophic judgment. He, as Yahweh God's spokesman, had to proclaim in a clear and pointed manner that the warnings Moses had given concerning disasters as a result of covenant breaking (Deut. 29:19–28) were sure to come.

When one considers all the proclamations Isaiah had to utter concerning the curse of the covenant and its sure execution, it could be asked: Was there no grace, no repentance, no forgiveness, no covenant blessings available at all? For answers, consider Isaiah's repeated assurance that there was a covenant way of life, if not for the nation as a whole, surely for people.

1. Isaiah 1:18–19: *lĕkû nâ' wĕniwwākĕhâh* (You come now and let us reason together). The verb *yākâh,* appears only in the hiphal, hophal, niphal, and hithpael. It can be translated as decide, adjudge, reprove, argue with, convict, correct, rebuke, and reason with. Since the translation of the verb has these possibilities, one must consider the context carefully in each instance that it appears.[19] Is this phrase "come now, let us . . ." an indication that Yahweh God is pressing his case in the context of the covenant lawsuit? As was discussed before, Isaiah did speak about Yahweh taking his place in court and arising to judge his people (3:13). The call for witnesses (1:2) supports the idea of Yahweh setting up a lawsuit. Some commentators are hesitant to say that Yahweh is dealing with his people in a lawsuit because mercy is offered, and justice does not rule.[20] What should also be considered is that the verb translated "come" is in the imperative; there is a command here that must be obeyed, but the article *nâ* includes the idea of an invitation to discuss together the accusation Yahweh has made against his people. More, Yahweh intimates that mercy, grace, and forgiveness are available even in Yahweh's courtroom.[21]

In this pericope, then, an essential part of the covenant way of life is to know that Yahweh God is a righteous and just God who is also gracious and merciful to those of his covenant people who heed his call to consider their sins, corruption, and guilt, and confess themwith sincere repentance. Yahweh God assured his people that for covenantly obedient people there was forgiveness, cleansing, and continuity of fellowship. Isaiah repeated this assurance when he preached that Yahweh would thoroughly purge away their dross and remove all their impurities (1:25). That type of covenant life would have judges and counselors who would lead people in covenant living with the result that Jerusalem and all it represented would be characterized by righteousness and faithfulness (1:26). It should be noted that the reference to judges and counselors contributes to the entire setting of the covenant lawsuit; these are necessary in a sinful and iniquitous social order to enhance justice and faithfulness. Indeed, the covenant way of life could be a reality for Yahweh God's people who, knowing their Lord, in fellowship with him, considered their sins, corruption, pollution, and guilt, repented, confessed these, and accepted Yahweh God's gracious and merciful forgiveness and cleansing.

2. Isaiah 2:5: *bêt ya'ăqōb lĕkû wĕnālĕkâh bĕ'ôr yĕhwâ* (house of Jacob, you come and let us walk in the light of Yahweh God). This invitation in reality is from Yahweh God through Isaiah, who identifies with people descended from Jacob the patriarch. This invitation must be seen in the immediate and broader context. In chapter 1 the invitation to receive forgiveness and cleansing was followed by this call to now walk as cleansed people—in the light, that is, the knowledge of Yahweh himself as made available by means "of positive revelation."[22] The immediate context includes the call for nations to go to the house of the God of Jacob where instruction in the way, the Torah, the word of Yahweh, was available (2:2, 3). Since it was a covenant stipulation for Abraham's and Jacob's descendants to be a blessing to the nations (Gen. 12:3; 28:14), it surely was incumbent upon them to so walk in the ways Yahweh had revealed. Indeed, the covenant way of life was

to walk obediently in the light (knowledge) that Yahweh had revealed and thus be a blessing to the nations.[23]

3. Isaiah 2:22: *hidlû lakem min-ha'adam* (cease you from [having confidence] in mankind). There is no Hebrew term in the text translated "confidence," but the context gives assurance that term confidence, or trust, is intended because in the preceding part (2:6–21) Isaiah accused the people of bowing down to handmade idols. He drew attention to their arrogance and pride (2:11, 17), which they demonstrated in their business activities as if they were stately and exalted as the great trees of Lebanon, the oaks of Bashan. Were they really established as lofty mountains and secure in their towers of defense in warfare? Were they prosperous because of the ships they had built to bring in wealth from other parts of the world? The people of Jerusalem and Judah had turned from their covenant Lord who had established and prospered them and had developed attitudes and lifestyles that exalted themselves.

4. Isaiah 5:16, 17: This pericope repeats that Yahweh will be exalted and exhibit himself as the holy God by revealing his righteousness. When Yahweh's people acknowledge their God as he truly is, their lives will be secure and blessed. Isaiah employed a pastoral metaphor to depict the peace and well-being that covenant people would experience in their daily covenant walk with their faithful, sovereign, righteous, and holy God.

Who are set forth as the agents of covenant? Who are going to execute the curse of the covenant and restore the blessings that had been promised and actually realized in previous times? Three should be acknowledged.

First of all, Yahweh God himself, the covenant suzerain or Lord, who had established, upheld, and reconfirmed his covenant with the descendants of Abraham, Isaac, and Jacob would be the one to execute the curse and restore the promised blessings. Despite his covenant people's ignoring and rejecting of him, he would remain the exalted one (2:11, 17; 5:16; 6:1). He is *yĕhwâ ṣĕbā'ôt* (2:12), the sovereign king over the created cosmos and director of all that transpires. His holiness, justice, and righteousness will never be compromised.

Second, the prophet Isaiah was an agent of the covenant.[24] He is not to be considered as an actual executor of the curse nor a dispenser of blessings directly. But as spokesman for Yahweh God, he faithfully proclaimed the message concerning his Lord's work, will, plan, and ability to be the faithful and active suzerain of the covenant. The prophetic word was a means to call to repentance and return as well as to inform the people of Yahweh God's character and plans. Reference to the *rûaḥ* (spirit) appears in Isaiah 1–6.[25] The biblical testimony is that the spoken word is the Spirit's means by which hearts and minds are touched, melted, and changed.

Third, Isaiah made an initial reference to the messianic agent of the covenant using the metaphors of the branch (4:2–6) and the stump (6:13). These two metaphors were used in various contexts in the Old Testament to bring to the attention of the covenant people that Yahweh God had not forgotten his promises concerning the seed of the woman and the descendant of David. Indeed, Jesus Christ, who would appear in time in the course of Yahweh God's unfolding of his redemptive/restorative plan, is the central agent of the covenant.[26]

Covenant consummation was also included in Isaiah's opening prophecy. the phrase "covenant consummation" is used to refer to how Yahweh God, by means of his covenant of creation and by means of his redemptive/restorative covenant, will bring the eschaton to full realization. To be clearly understood, when this phrase is used, is that the covenant, being a bond of life and love, a divinely established relationship between Yahweh God and his created cosmos and particularly with his image bearers, is also the means or the instrument by and through which Yahweh God brings salvation/redemption/restoration as it also serves as his administrative means or instrument in the process of history as it moves on toward the eschaton. Indeed, by keeping his covenant in all its aspects, and particularly through the work of the messianic mediator, all the promises, intentions, and goals included in the covenant will be fully realized. The covenant was and will be Yahweh God's basic means to usher in the renewed and repristinated heavens and earth.

Isaiah referred to this consummation in two contexts (4:2–6; 2:2–5). In contrast to the tragic condition of Judah and Jerusalem when the curse of the covenant is executed (3:1–26), Isaiah employed descriptive terms—*beautiful, glorious, pride,* and *glory*—when referring to what the result of the Branch's presence will be (4:2). But only survivors (the remnant) will experience these after a cleansing and purification has taken place. These will be holy and have their names inscribed as the living ones in Jerusalem (4:3). The cleansing will be done by washing away the filth of the women (so graphically described in chapter 3). The bloodstains, due to the violence that had controlled Jerusalem, would be cleansed. This washing, cleaning, and sanctifying (*qādôš*).[27] The term *rûaḥ* calls for attention. Isaiah employs the term to refer to a personal agent. The Holy Spirit is that agent of the covenant who performs the work of sanctification.[28] The prophecy here must be understood to speak of cleansing, renewal, and sanctification. The end is threatened but the call to holiness was the immediate intent.[29]

Covenant consummation involves much more than the sanctification of covenant people. There is also to be a wonderful development in the realm of nature. Yahweh God will bring forth protection and providential guidance for his people. Isaiah drew upon Israel's experience in the wilderness to express what Yahweh God will continue to do for his people. As there was a cloud by day and a pillar of fire by night for Israel in the wilderness to protect and guide them, so there will be in Yahweh God's own way for Mount Zion (Jerusalem), the city of God, and for the sanctified community. And as the glory of Yahweh God was present among his Old Testament people, first over Mount Sinai and after that in the tabernacle and temple, so it will be as *huppâh* (a cover, or a canopy) over the entire city and its people. All this will be Yahweh's unique accomplishment, for Isaiah said *wĕlārâ yĕhwâ* (Yahweh will create). But Isaiah gave no time reference for these events other than to say *bayyôm hahû'* (in that day). Three specific references are made. First, the mountain of Yahweh's house will become the center. Again, the use of the terms *house, mountains,* and *hills* should not be understood literally. The main intent of the pericope is to emphasize that as the temple was central in Jerusalem, so Yahweh God's dwelling will be. Second, nations will stream toward it to learn Yahweh's Torah, ways, and paths. Third, there will be peace among the nations. The prophet Joel had prophesied about the gathering of the nations also (2:2). The preferred explanation is that Isaiah, employing terms and references his audience was acquainted with, was referring to the future when Christ was to come and, beyond that, to his second coming.[30]

Isaiah, in addition to referring to the covenant as the context for Yahweh God's lawsuit against his disobedient and unfaithful people, indicated that he was aware of various other aspects of the covenant. These should be considered because they give evidence that the covenant was an important factor in Yahweh God's past, present, and future relationships, as well as interactions, with the people who were called into a judicial setting to hear Yahweh God's accusations and judgments.

The Covenant as a Marriage Bond

Isaiah did not use the phrase "Yahweh's covenant with Israel is a marriage bond," nor did he speak specifically of Yahweh's marriage to Israel. He did make indirect references to it and implied it in much of what he proclaimed.

Basic to all that Isaiah prophesies about the relationship of Judah and Jerusalem is the covenanting ceremony that took place at Mount Sinai (Exod. 19–24). Israel, of which Judah was a part, was declared to be Yahweh's *sĕgullâh* (precious possession) of whom he said *'ābi' etkem 'ēlê* (I brought you to myself) (Exod. 19:4, 5). Yahweh God declared his love to and for the people as a bridegroom would to and for his bride. The bride had responded three times, saying she would be a faithful bride (19:8; 24:3, 7). This covenanting ceremony provided the basis for Yahweh God, through Isaiah, to proclaim that he their maker was *bo' ălik* (your husband) (Isa. 54:5). Yahweh God is identified; his name is Yahweh of hosts, he is their *gôēl* (redeemer), the holy one. Isaiah went onto proclaim that the young bride Yahweh had taken would be called back when she was deserted and distressed in spirit. Yes, Yahweh had abandoned her for a short while in anger. He had done so because the bride/wife had become a harlot (1:21).[31] But Yahweh never broke his covenant with his bride. He had never given her a certificate of divorce when he sent her away, that is, exiled her (50:1). Yahweh had very good reasons to divorce his unfaithful bride. In fact, according to Jeremiah (3:8), Yahweh did give the northern tribe a certificate of divorce; Mosaic law allowed for this (Deut. 24:1, 3; Matt. 19:7; Mark 10:4). But, indeed, Yahweh would call her back, take his bride, if only a remnant, as a young man marries a maiden (62:4, 5). Thus the covenant, the marriage, of Yahweh and his people was never removed.

It is necessary, in this context, to remember that even while Israel/Judah was in exile, after many members of the covenant community had been decimated by famine, plague, and warfare, Yahweh God was faithfully keeping his covenant.

The covenant, which included the prescriptions for faithfulness to Yahweh, also included the curse. Thus carrying out the threatened curse was not contrary to covenant keeping on Yahweh's part. But the covenant also included the promised blessings of life and well-being. Thus when Yahweh God's curse had been executed, the promises were again being carried out. The separation having ended, the covenant marriage continued. Yahweh God's grace and mercies became his people's blessed inheritance.

The Sign of the Covenant according to Isaiah

Two terms, *nēs* (standard, ensign, signal, sign) and *'ôt* (sign, mark, token, ensign, standard, miracle, proof, warning),[32] appear in Isaiah's prophesies. Throughout the Old Testament the context in which the terms appear assist us in understanding what is specifically referred to by *ôt,* whether an object, as the luminaries (Gen. 1:19) or a mark Cain received (Gen. 4:15), or a miracle, or plagues (Exod. 7:13), or a warning as Aaron's rod was to rebellious people (Num. 17:5), or tokens as stones in the Jordan (Josh. 4:6), or the plates on the altar (Num. 16:38). A *nēs* was generally considered a rallying point for common action or communication.

It should be understood that the two terms as they appear in Isaiah's prophecies do not always have a clear and direct covenantal reference or an obvious covenantal context. There are, however, instances where the covenant is referred to by a sign or banner.

The term *nēs* appears in the context of Yahweh about to execute the curse of the covenant upon Judah. Yahweh is to lift up the banner (*nēs*) as a signal and a rallying point for the nations as he calls them and directs them to bring darkness and distress to Judah and Jerusalem (Isa. 5:26–30). The banner was thus in effect a sign of the covenant, particularly the curse of the covenant, that would be executed in due time. The banner would also be lifted for the peoples who would be involved in the return of the covenant people, the remnant, from exile. The banner was a sign of the promise included in the covenant of the restoration from the exile and the continuation of the remnant of Israel/Judah.

Isaiah used the term *nēs* (banner) in a personified way also (11:10, 11). The context refers to the stump of Jesse and the Branch. The reference is clearly the promised messianic king, the mediator of the covenant. He will be lifted up to be seen by many and be the rallying point of peoples and nations (11:1–12). Writers differ concerning the fulfillment of this covenant promise. The text is part of a pericope that has an eschatological import. Hence some believe the reference is to the eventual gathering of Jews into one place. Others draw attention to, and correctly, what Isaiah spoke of gathering the *nideḥê* (the niph. of *nādah,* to banish) the banished or exiles of Israel and the *nĕpuṣôt* niph. passive participle of *nāpạs,* to scatter) scattered of Judah. Hence the reference is to the messianic king's activity in returning the exiles to their homeland. This passage should be considered as having a double fulfillment, namely, the return from the exile initially and the lifting up of Christ (John 3:14) in his crucifixion and the subsequent mission activity through which peoples of all nations, Jews included, would be drawn to the Messiah, the mediator of the covenant.[33]

The conclusion to be considered is that the use of *nēs* in various contexts is a sign, banner of the covenant, particularly to aspects of it, the curse, the promise of restoration and continuity, and the messianic royal mediator of the covenant himself.

The term *ôt* (sign) is even more evidently a sign of the covenant in Isaiah's prophecies. It is eminently biblical to speak of the sign of the covenant. Yahweh God declared that the rainbow was a sign of the creation covenant (Gen. 9:13). Circumcision was declared to be a sign of the everlasting covenant made with Abraham (17:7, 11). Moses, quoting Yahweh God, wrote that the Sabbath Israel was to observe was a "sign between me and you for generations to come" (Exod. 31:12). The people were to celebrate the Sabbath as a lasting covenant (31:16) and as a sign that Yahweh God had created the heavens and earth on six days and abstained from work and rested on the seventh day (31:17). Isaiah undoubtedly had these Mosaic injunctions regarding the Sabbath as a sign of the covenant in mind when he addressed the eunuchs to keep the Sabbaths and thus to hold fast to my covenant (Isa. 56:4, 6). It should be kept in mind that when Yahweh God covenanted with Israel at Mount Sinai that keeping the Sabbath holy was one of the then covenantly prescriptions (commandments) for obedient covenant living.

In addition to the rainbow, circumcision, and the Sabbath as signs of the covenant, the promised messianic mediator of the covenant was also a sign. Consider what Isaiah prophesied to Ahaz, a representative of Yahweh God's covenant with David. A sign was given as a surety that Judah would not be overrun by the Assyrian armies (7:1–15). The sign was a babe to be born who would have the name Immanuel, "God with us." This name referred to the very heart of the covenant (Gen. 17:7; Josh. 1:5, 9).[34]

Finally, Isaiah also proclaimed that the covenant was represented by the Spirit, hence the Spirit was also considered a sure evidence of the covenant, indeed, a confirming sign of the covenant (Isa. 59:21). Inseparably related to the covenantal Spirit's presence was the word that Yahweh God gave to speak and that would not ever depart from mouths of covenant people. Thus, the word also is to be understood as a sign of the covenant. Delitzsch pointed out that Isaiah proclaimed a renewal of Yahweh God's covenant with Abraham (Gen. 17:4). He also went on to write that the Spirit of God is also evidence of the New Covenant Yahweh God has made with the church.[35]

The Purpose of the Covenant

The purpose of the covenant as stated by Isaiah was definite. He did not refer directly to various intents of the covenant found elsewhere in Scripture. For example, he did not refer to the covenant Yahweh God confirmed with Noah when Noah and his family were not to be destroyed in the flood (Gen. 6:18). Nor did he refer directly to the covenant Yahweh God confirmed, explicated, and sealed with Israel at Sinai (Exod. 19–24). He did, however, refer to Yahweh God's covenanting with

Abraham. Isaiah prophesied about Abraham, whom Yahweh God had redeemed and whose descendants would keep his name holy (Isa. 29:22–24). The heritage of these descendants of Abraham included Yahweh's call of their ancestor from the Ur of the Chaldees, of their redemption from Egypt because they were chosen to be Yahweh God's servants (41:8–10). Isaiah's audience was called upon to look to Abraham who was called, blessed, and made numerous (51:1–3). Isaiah also quoted the children of Abraham who, when in their misery in exile, said Abraham had forgotten them (63:16). And why was it they were as forgotten descendants of Abraham? The answer is clear. Yahweh God had called Abraham from the Ur of the Chaldees to be a blessing among the nations and the nations were to be blessed through him (Gen. 12:1–3). Isaiah reminded these descendants of Abraham that they were called, led, and kept to be a covenant[36] for the people and a light for the Gentiles (42:6). And why were the exiles to be returned to the land God had shown Abraham? They were to be a covenant for the people (49:8, 9).

Yahweh God's call of and covenanting with Abraham had not been just to bring forth a unique, separated, precious, and holy people (Exod. 19:4–6). This had not been done because Abraham, who had been an idol worshiper (Josh. 24:2), merited it. Nor was it because these descendants were a special possession (the whole earth was the Lord's, Exod. 19:5). Nor were they a chosen covenant people because they were more numerous than other people; they were loved and chosen when they were fewest (Deut. 7:7). Yahweh God kept his covenant of life, love, and blessings with the descendants of Abraham because he called them to be his servant among the nations. And, although the people failed to be that faithful servant, Yahweh God nevertheless brought forth the faithful servant, Jesus Christ, who would be the blessing for all nations. From this perspective Isaiah correctly has been referred to as the "evangelist" among the Old Testament prophets.

The Duration of the Covenant[37]

Isaiah included a prophecy specifically against Ephraim, the leading tribe among the northern tribes, Israel. They had been taken into captivity by Assyria and the people of Jerusalem said they had nothing to fear. They had made a covenant with death (28:15). This is understood to mean that the scoffers in Jerusalem were in effect saying, as in death one has peace, no harm can be done, so we have nothing to fear. Jerusalem's people felt secure. But Yahweh God had Isaiah say that the people's covenant of death would be annulled. The curse of Yahweh's covenant with the people would surely be carried out. A great overwhelming scourge would sweep over the land.[38] But the scourge would end and the blessing of the covenant continue in spite of the people having disobeyed Yahweh God's laws, violated his statues, and broken the everlasting covenant (24:5).

Reference to the everlasting covenant with David was included to assure the people that Yahweh God would surely have it fulfilled in due time (55:3). A Noachic type of flood, earthquakes, quaking mountains, and the removing of hills would not shake or remove his unfailing love, guaranteed in Yahweh God's covenant of peace.[39]

Conclusion

Isaiah's appeal to and confirmation of Yahweh God's covenant of creation and redemptive/restoration came when the people of Judah and Jerusalem were at a critical time in their existence as a nation. They were chosen to be the blessed recipients of all the covenant promises made to Noah, Abraham, Isaac, Jacob, the people at Mount Sinai, and David and his house. They were given the opportunity to live the obedient covenantal life, serving Yahweh God as they carried out the spiritual, social, and cultural mandates. The northern tribes, Israel, had already suffered the curse of the covenant; they had been conquered and exiled by powerful Assyria. Judah was given the opportunity to learn from Israel's folly and tragic fate. Isaiah, the prince, who never seemed to have left Jerusalem, was called and commissioned to address the direct descendants of David, who were reigning, as well as their subjects. Isaiah carried out his task faithfully. He warned the people that because they were in a specific covenant relationship with Yahweh God, they were being judged, as if in a courtroom, for their unfaithfulness and disobedience. They were reminded that they were Yahweh God's wife; he was their faithful husband who would divorce them even if they had to be separated (exiled) for a time. Isaiah reminded the people of Judah that Yahweh God had given them signs of the covenant. He proclaimed that Yahweh God always intended the covenant to be kept because, having been initiated at the time of creation, then expanded and confirmed with Adam, Noah, Abraham, and David, it would not end during the present existence of the cosmos. Indeed, people in covenant with Yahweh could, would, and did break it; Yahweh God would never. He would fulfil his purposes even when he had to execute the curse of the covenant as a purifying and sanctifying means. In Isaiah's time it was not too late for Judah to avoid the execution of the curse as it had been carried out against Israel to the north. There was time for repentance and renewal. Yahweh God knew, of course, that the people of Jerusalem and Judah would continue in their rebellion. But that rebellion would not thwart Yahweh in bringing in the seed of the woman, the seed of Abraham, of Judah and David, the messianic Mediator of the covenant.

The Mediator of the Covenant

Isaiah prophesied extensively concerning the Messiah who, when on earth as the Incarnate One, spoke of his blood as the blood of the covenant (Matt. 26:28) and whom the writer to the Hebrews referred to as the Mediator of the covenant (9:15).

Exegetical Work

In a previously written work Isaiah's prophesies concerning the Messiah have been extensively treated.[40] Isaiah prophesied concerning him as the Virgin's Son (7:1–17), the Ruling Son (9:2–9), the reign of Jesse's Son (11:1–16), the Servant Son (40:1–52:12), the Suffering Son (52:13–53:12), and the Ministering Son

(54–66). There is hardly warrant for repeating the exegetical discussions or the conclusions stated. There are, however, a number of specific issues that should be considered.

The Mediator's Relationship to the Covenant

The question to be answered concerns the Mediator's relationship to the covenant. Does Isaiah give definite information concerning this? A review of the Isaianic passages dealing with the covenant that were studied in part II above will not lead one to conclude that Isaiah specifically prophesied saying that the Messiah to come was the Mediator of the covenant. That omission, however should not lead one to conclude that Isaiah was unaware of this relationship.

First of all, attention should be given to Isaiah's prophecy concerning the son of the virgin who, when born, would be named Immanuel. This prophecy was spoken to Ahaz, a descendant of David and a representative of the covenant seed. Yahweh God had assured David when he covenanted with him (2 Sam. 7:8–16; 23:5) that his descendants would succeed David to the throne. Nathan had spoken Yahweh God's word when David was warned that should he or a descendant do wrong he would be punished. This warning was followed with an assurance of Yahweh God's abiding love (7:14, 15). Isaiah addressed Ahaz, of the Davidic dynasty, when he was not acknowledging or trusting in Yahweh God. It was then that the promised covenant love was demonstrated. Isaiah spoke a comforting and directing word that Ahaz would not accept or obey. But, Yahweh God, nevertheless, stressed that the covenant promises "I am your God," "I will be with you," were sure and abiding realities. The name, Immanuel, to be given to the child, was "the covenant formula." Thus the initial messianic, mediatorial message that Isaiah proclaimed was not only in a covenantal context, it was a specific covenantal message concerning the covenantal Mediator.

Second, the prophecy concerning the child to be born and the son to be given was given a very specific covenantal context. This child/son, whose name would include Mighty God and Everlasting Father, Prince of Peace, was to fulfill Yahweh God's covenant promises to David that his son would reign on his throne forever. Isaiah boldly proclaimed this promise to be fulfilled saying "He will reign on David's throne and over his kingdom . . . from this time on and forever" (9:7 NIV).

Third, in a striking eschatological passage (11:1–16), in the prophecies of the renewed earth (vv. 1–9), the return from exile (vv. 10, 11), and the New Testament gathering of the nations (vv. 12–16)[41] are included. These prophecies refer to the fulfillment of covenant promises given to Noah (Gen. 9:26, 27), Abraham (12:1–3; 17:6) and David (2 Sam. 7:16). And none other than David's descendants identified as the shoot to arise from the stump of Jessie and from his roots a Branch would carry out these promises.[41]

Fourth, Isaiah, when prophesying concerning Yahweh God's Servant (42:1–9; 49:1–7), proclaimed that he would receive the Spirit (as David had) (1 Sam. 16:13), and would reign faithfully, bringing in justice (as David had) (2 Sam. 8:14,

15). More, he would be a covenant for the people and a light to the Gentiles. This assured covenantal promise was fulfilled in the ministry of David's greatest Son, the Lord Jesus Christ (Luke 2:36, 37).

Fifth, in the wonderful passage concerning the glory and suffering of the Servant (Isa. 52:13–53:12) there is the reference again to the fulfillment of the covenant promise that nations would be included in the great work of the covenantal Mediator, the messianic Servant. Isaiah proclaimed it boldly, that the rejected, disfigured, marred, and slaughtered lamb, the Servant, would sprinkle many nations (52:15).

Sixth, in chapters 54 and 55, Isaiah's words are recorded concerning the results of the Mediator's sacrifice and activities. Yahweh God, Israel's/Judah's husband (54:5), would bring his separated bride back to himself because of his unfailing love and assured continuity of the covenant of peace (54:7, 16). The thirsty, hungry, and impoverished are invited to partake of what the great Servant/Shepherd would provide as promised to David (55:1–4). And again there is reference to the inclusion of nations who are summoned to participate in the covenantal promised blessings (55:5).

Seventh, in the Isaianic prophecy that Jesus said was a direct reference to him (61:1–3; cf. Luke 4:18, 19) there is a description of the Spirit-led and -qualified ministry that would bring aliens and foreigners into the daily life of the covenant people who would serve as priests and ministers of Yahweh God and who would be fed and blessed by the wealth and riches of the nations. These messianically blessed people, loving justice, would be members and heirs of the everlasting covenant. And nations and their offspring would acknowledge that Yahweh God blessed them as he had indicated the effect of Abraham obeying and serving Yahweh God would be (61:5–9).

Finally, it should be stressed that the entire book of Isaiah is basically an integrated covenant masterpiece. The Kingship of God, his love for, deeds done on behalf of, and continuing care for the covenant people and their role among the nations, is a major theme.[42] Covenant promises and stipulations are integral aspects of this prophecy, as are the blessings for the obedient and curses to be executed on the unfaithful. The continuity of the covenant made with Noah, Abraham, Moses/Israel, and David is assured through the presence and work of the messianic Mediator. Indeed, the Mediator of the covenant will accomplish the will of Yahweh God. The *qinĕ'at yĕhwâ* (zeal of Yahweh) (9:7[6]; 37:32; 42:13; 59:17; 63:15, 16) is the fundamental reality that gives absolute assurance that the covenant is upheld through the presence, the sacrifice, and reign of the messianic Mediator of the covenant.

Isaiah's Prophecies and the Narrative Genre

Another question to be answered relates to hermeneutics. Specifically, the issue concerns narrative exegesis and theology. The plethora of materials presented in articles, essays, monographs, and books is well nigh impossible to read and digest.[43] The issue of Scripture and narrative was brought to the attention of readers interested in the development of and wide acceptance of evangelicalism in the eighth and ninth decades of the twentieth century. One scholar wrote that recent scholarship considers the importance of the "recognition of the primacy of the narrative genre within Scripture." He then asked how a narrative can serve as a basis of theology.[44] He also wonders if a narrative possesses authority. He went on to write that the narrative quality of Scripture allows the fullness of biblical revelation to be recovered.[45] He also wrote that the Old Testament may be read as a story of a quest for identity among a nomadic people of the ancient Near East. But this narrative must be interpreted correctly within a doctrinal conceptual framework.[46] McGrath believes that the narrative approach to Scripture, rather than regarding Scripture as a composite collection of doctrines, leads to rapprochement between evangelicals and those postliberals who increasingly criticize liberalism's approach to Scripture and the doctrines derived from its basic anthropocentric approach.[47]

When an author makes a careful and in-depth study of the prophetic materials that consider three specific concepts; the kingdom, the covenant, and the Mediator as the core unifying the Scriptures, the question arises whether these can best be understood in their fullest biblical sense in a narrative context. Or should these three comcepts provide the doctrinal framework within which a narrative is to be interpreted and understood? The question now is, in the study of the messianic Mediator as presented in the Old Testament,[48] should much importance be given to the "narrative character" of the material? But a legitimate question at this point is, in regard to the former work and this study: Is the narrative really the context in which the messianic mediatorial prophecies were proclaimed? These questions raise a fundamental problem. How is "narrative" to be defined? What are the ramifications of considering narrative as the context of prophecies?

Narrative theology has been defined as discourse about God in the setting of story and that means that God's purposes are entrammeled in history.[49] But not all scholars are prepared to accept specific and didactic statements concerning this phenomenon that is said to be a major genre of Scripture. One scholar wrote that "there is no consensus concerning the nature, function, and status of narrative."[50] Another writer considered it necessary to write "A Short Apology of Narrative." In this essay human experience is considered the basic aspect of theology and this experience is given in a narrative form.[51] Still another author, working with a definite form-critical presupposition initiates his work with a discussion entitled "From Legenda to Vita" (From Legend to Life).[52] His efforts to place prophetical materials into a narrative context in reality demonstrates that prophecies are not essentially narrations (or stories) in intention content.[53]

It is not the intent of this discussion of narrative/narration to discredit the reality of narratives or stories included in the Old Testament Scriptures. Narratives/narration are present in a variety of contexts; these have been considered, by and large, to give the historical contexts of various biblical persons, events, symbols, metaphors, and verbal presentations. Problems arise when materials that are not essentially narrative are considered as such nevertheless.[54] If and when proper consideration is given to the historical aspects of the Old Testament, the story or narrative genre can and should get proper attention.

Problems arise when narrative/narration is ascribed as a, if not the, dominant genre of Scripture. The first problem relates to the Bible's self-testimony that it is revelatory. God revealed himself in word and deed. Narrative emphasizes the "deed" as the dominant context. This involves, unavoidably, considering the Scriptures more predominantly as anthropocentric. Human experience, insight, and reflection are given undue attention and ascribed to much influence. This in turn leads to the question of biblical authority. Are stories as told, or written, authoritative sources of divine teaching and prescriptions for the Christian life? To consider the Old Testament as basically having the narrative here leads to considering the biblical material as a collection of examples; in reality, it provides much didactic hortatory and doxological materials that do not have a narrative literary quality.

The book of Isaiah has a few passages that give specific historical references. Isaiah saw visions (1:1; 2:1; 6:1; 13:1), the content of which were not related in narrative form. The contexts of the visions were historical, as was the vision related in chapter 6. Isaiah narrated his interaction with king Ahaz (7:11ff.), how he had to symbolize with nakedness what was to happen to Jerusalem (20:1–6) and his interaction with King Hezekiah (37:1–39:7). Thus, the conclusion to be drawn from this is that the prophecies of Isaiah as a whole do not belong to the narrative genre.[55] That does not mean that Isaiah did not on various occasions refer to the historical context in which he prophesied. In fact, some of his prophecies, be they oracles, proclamations, or prophetic reflections (e.g., Isa. 12) may implicitly reveal a general and/or broad context.

The promised Messiah was indeed proclaimed by Isaiah as the covenant agent and mediator. This message, given by prophetic proclamation, was from Yahweh God and did not come to Isaiah by experience, insight, reflection, political situations, or meditation on previously given messages.[56] Yahweh God spoke to and through Isaiah, and at the very core of this divinely given message was he who has been referred to as the Virgin's ruling, reigning, serving, suffering, and ministering Son.[57]

Theological Affirmations Concerning the Son-Mediator

Theological affirmations concerning the mediatorial Son in addition to his covenantal mediatorial position and relationship were proclaimed by Isaiah. He is the covenant mediator. He stands between the Father and the Son and administered the covenant as he did his work in his preincarnate, incarnate, and ascended states. He fulfilled the requirements especially of the redemptive/restorative covenant as he at all times served as administrator of the creation covenant.

The messianic Mediator as descendant of David would be fully human. He would be born of a young woman known in the Jerusalem/Judah area as the virgin. He would be an ordinary boy as he grew up, eating curds and honey (7:14–16).

As a human being, growing up and becoming wise, he, not physically attractive, would be despised and rejected. He, in his human body, would suffer severe punishment, being smitten, afflicted, pierced, and slaughtered as a lamb. He was to be buried, as most other human beings were. This suffering and humiliation that he would suffer as one of humanity was not because of his human sins, transgression, and guilt; rather, he was completely innocent. He was to suffer as a brother to all people for it was the will of the Father to crush him and thus to make him of a guilt offering for sinners (52:14–53:12).

The messianic Mediator would be fully divine even as he was fully human. He was to be conceived by a virgin who had no sexual intercourse with a male partner. He was thus to be born a child, a son, whose name was to be Immanuel, "God with us." He was also to be named Mighty God, Everlasting Father, and Prince of Peace (9:6). When he would come eventually, a voice would call out, "prepare *dērek yěhwâ* (a way for Yahweh) and a *missillâh lē'lōhênu* (an elevated way or highway for our God) (40:3). This proclamation is definitely a prophecy concerning the appearing of the messianic Mediator (John 1:23, 29, 30).

The messianic Mediator of the covenant was heralded as a royal person, a descendant of David's royal house, a king. He will govern increasingly, sitting on David's eternal throne. He will reign eternally in righteousness and justice (Isa. 9:6, 7). Righteousness and faithfulness will give him stability as a belt and waist band (11:5). As the royal Ruler he will bring in a renewed heaven and earth (11:6–9) and will gather his scattered people around him. His reign thus will not only be over his people, but will extend over the totality of the cosmos (11:8, 14, 15). As such he will make one kingdom of Egypt, Assyria, and Israel (11:25). He will reign in righteousness and have rulers serve under him with justice as he renews the earth (32:1, 2). As king he will be highly exalted to such an extent that earthly kings and rulers will stand with mouths shut, amazed at him (52:15). He, as the king, will usher in glory that dispels darkness and brings light to the nations (60:1–3).

The messianic Mediator, human, divine, royal, is also the judge. He is the one who calls Judah to court and weighs the evidence against the people (1:1–3; 3:13, 14). He will judge between nations and usher in peace (2:4). The descendant of David, filled with the Spirit—wisdom, understanding, counsel, power, knowledge, and reverence for Yahweh—will not judge by what he sees or hears.[58] He will judge righteously; the poor and needy will find a true helper in him and the wicked will be put away (11:1–5).

Isaiah also made a number of short, powerful statements concerning the Son also referred to as Yahweh. He is the lawgiver. He is the king. He it is who saves; he is the Savior (33:22). Isaiah did not specify if he was speaking of Yahweh the Father or Yahweh the Son. In the broader context of Isaiah's messages, these ascriptions are given to the messianic Mediator as well as to Yahweh God, the Triune One. In the more immediate context of this pericope (chap. 33), Isaiah was prophesying concerning the distress that awaited Jerusalem/Judah when disasters would come because of the people's disobedience and unfaithfulness. But, Isaiah proclaimed that there is a future for Zion. I will be a peaceful abode; Yahweh, the Mighty One, will be there giving security and waters of life. Recall that the Son to be given was to be named the Mighty One (9:6).

The messianic Mediator, human, divine, royal, judge, is proclaimed by Isaiah to be the Redeemer.[59] Isaiah employed the term *gā'āl* twenty-four times in various forms, especially as a participle, "the redeeming one" (41:14; 43:14; 44:6, 24; 47:4; 48:17; 49:7, 26; 54:5, 8; 58:20; 60:16; 61:16). When used as a verb, to redeem, Jacob his servant, Jerusalem, the covenant people, Israel, are the objects or recipients of redemption.

The term *ga'āl* has the basic sense of payment made of the value assessed or of doing what was necessary to remove debt, guilt, and bring freedom.[60] In everyday life a relative who performed such duties was referred to as the kinsman (Ruth 3:12). The term *gā'āl* applies very appropriately to the human mediator of the covenant, who is a kinsman to the people of God.

The idea of redeem was applied, as mentioned above, to seeming nonpersonal objects, like Jerusalem (Isa. 52:9), and a ransom was to be paid for Zion (1:27). These passages, in their context, speak of the covenant people's redemption and restoration but also of the city that was at the heart of the nation. If and when people were redeemed, restored, and comforted, they would return to their city that was going to be or was actually lying in ruins. The historic context is obviously the return from the exile, when Jerusalem would be rebuilt. Yahweh God would do what was necessary to have the city rebuilt. He would have Babylon defeated and destroyed and have another national power serve as his agent for the "redemption of Jerusalem."[61]

Isaiah's main message, however, was that the covenant people would be redeemed. This redemption was to be carried out in two specific ways. First, the people who were to be exiled would be returned to their homeland and city. Involved in this return to the land was the return to the service and worship of the Lord with an obedient heart. But this spiritual renewal and actual historical return was for the achievement of a far greater goal, namely, the eternal redemption of God's chosen people. Isaiah therefore prophesied concerning the eternal salvation of a faithful covenant people.

Isaiah proclaimed that the redeeming God, who pays the price or does what is necessary to redeem his people, is the Savior (17:10; 19:20; 43:3, 11; 45:15, 21; 49:26; 60:11; 62:11; 63:8). He is the Savior because he saves. The prophets spoke for the people saying, Yahweh, our judge, lawgiver, and king will *yôšîĕnû* (the hiphiel of *yāso'*, cause us to be delivered or saved with the result that freedom and wide space will be given us). Salvation thus does not only mean to be delivered from evil, punishment, ruin, and death, but to be ushered into a new enriching, ever-continuing way of life. This is what is to be understood when Isaiah assured the people that Yahweh God would save them (25:9; 35:4; 45:17; 49:25). In contrast to what Yahweh can and does do as the Mighty One (63:1), the gods people served were unable to do (45:20) as also the people themselves (47:14) or other people (47:15) were unable to do.

The question to be answered specifically is: Who is the redeemer? the savior? Is it Yahweh God the Father, or the messiah Son who is also known as a great redeemer? It was he who confronted Moses in the past as the Angel of the Lord (Exod. 3:2–6). Isaiah proclaimed that it was none other than David's offspring who would come as the Wonderful Counselor, Mighty God, Everlasting Father, Prince of Peace who, reigning eternally with justice and righteousness (Isa. 9:6, 7), would bring redemption, salvation, full restoration, and peace (11:1–16).

It must not be forgotten that Yahweh God, the Father, was ever present as the Messiah Son, the Mediator who accomplished the redeeming, saving, and restoring work. In addition, the chosen covenant people were also called to serve as agents of Yahweh God the Father and the messianic, mediatorial Son, whose Spirit was poured upon them (44:1–7).

The central actor, however, in the redeeming, saving, restoring activities would be the suffering servant (52:13–53:12). He, the highly exalted one (52:13), would become the deeply humiliated servant. He would be the sacrificial lamb, who takes up people's infirmities, carries their sorrows, is smitten and afflicted, is pierced for the transgressions and iniquities of the people (53:4–9). This sacrificial lamb seals the everlasting covenant promised to David (55:3) and who, in the fullness of time (Gal. 4:4) will come and identify himself as the redeeming, healing, restoring, liberating servant (Isa. 61:1–3; Luke 4:16–21).

It must be emphasized at the conclusion of this study of Isaiah's proclamation of the messianic Mediator of the covenant that Isaiah was ever-conscious of the kingdom setting and context of all that he prophesied concerning the covenant (its maker, the people, the aspects of it), and the messianic Mediator. The covenant and its messianic agent were not presented in an historical vacuum, much less in a random progression of events. The kingdom was the context and the overarching and integrating factor.

The Kingdom in Isaiah's Proclamation

Was Isaiah of Royal Lineage?

Jewish tradition has held that Isaiah was of royal birth. Isaiah began his prophecy recording that he was the son of Amoz, whom Jewish rabbis taught was a brother of King Amaziah. His son was Uzziah and Isaiah was a cousin to this king. Commentators, while agreeing that there is no definite evidence to substantiate the royal birth of Isaiah, do agree in various degrees that there are three factors that could support Isaiah's royal character. E. J. Young has written that there is something royal in his nature and bearing.[62] G. W. Grogan wrote that Isaiah certainly had an extensive experience of kings.[63] John D. W. Watts wrote that a "major way the prophetic book thought of God was as King of Heaven." He proceeded to discuss Isaiah as the prophet who set forth the majesty and glory of the divine heavenly king.[64] We should conclude that while there is no substantial evidence that Isaiah himself was of royal birth, he certainly was well acquainted with the concept of royalty and especially of Yahweh his God's royalty, kingship, and kingdom.[65]

The Lexigraphical Evidence

The term *melek* (king) appears often in Isaiah's writings. It is used to refer to those who were reigning in and over nations. It is used to refer to Yahweh God (Isa. 6:5; 32:1; 33:17, 22; 43:15; 44:6). The verb *mālak* (reign), while used extensively to refer to the rule of human kings, is used to refer to the sovereign and active administration of Yahweh God and of his messianic agent (9:7; 24:23; 32:1). The term *mamlākâh* (kingdom) appears in Isaiah's prophecy thirteen times, referring to earthly ones except for the one reference to the kingdom of the Messiah, who will reign over it sitting on David's throne.

The lexigraphical evidence of Yahweh God and the Messiah as king, their reign and kingdom, can be said to be sufficient to support the statement that Isaiah was conscious that Yahweh God and the Messiah were the sovereign rulers of and over the entire cosmos. He, it should be added, was conscious of these glorious truths because Yahweh revealed these to him and he wholeheartedly accepted and believed them.

Isaiah has been referred to as the evangelical prophet of the Old Testament. His name means "The Lord is Salvation," that is, he is the source of salvation.[66] It would seem, however, to be appropriate also to refer to Isaiah as the "kingdom prophet." He proclaimed the king, kingship, and kingdom as he saw these in the vision in which he was called. He proclaimed the messianic Mediator as the royal son of David, and as the royal one who reigned sitting on David's throne (9:7). The theme of Isaiah's message, and the message he would have all heralds proclaim, is "your God reigns" (52:7). It would, however, be wrong to simply place the concepts of save/savior/salvation in juxtaposition to reign, king, kingdom. Rather, they are inextricably integrated. Yahweh God reigns and thus has the authority and is able to save; he is Savior because he is the all-sufficient sovereign King who exercises his authority and power over the entire cosmos and all that is in and part of it.

The term *kingdom* is in reality a composite concept. It consists of four integral aspects: the king, the throne, the reign, and the domain.[67] These four concepts require individual attention.

The Domain of the Kingdom

One can ask, what are the constituent elements of the kingdom domain? Or, precisely, over what does Yahweh God and his messianic Mediator reign?[68]

Isaiah emphasized that Yahweh God reigned over Israel and Judah. The kings in these two nations were representatives of and agents for Yahweh God, who was the sovereign ruler. Consider how Isaiah expressed this. Addressing the covenant people who would experience the tragedies involved in the exile, Isaiah prophesied, "this is what your *'ădônayik yĕhwâ* (sovereign master God), says, "your God who defends his people . . ." (51:22), and then Isaiah called on the heralds among the people to proclaim "*your* God reigns" (52:7). Indeed, Yahweh God reigned over his covenant people whether they were dwelling in their land, were in exile, or were returned from exile. In many other passages, Isaiah spoke it explicitly or implicitly, that Yahweh God was the ruler of his covenant people (6:5; 9:7; 10:11; 32:22; 33:4–6; 43:15; 44:6). They were the very core of Yahweh God's domain. As a theocracy (Exod. 19:1–24:8), they were a symbol, a representative and agent of Yahweh's entire cosmic kingdom.

Israel, alone, did not constitute Yahweh God's domain. The nations were also part of his domain.[69] Consider how Isaiah expressed this in his various messages. Yahweh God, as king, will judge between the nations (2:4; 30:27, 28). Yahweh God as Lord of the nations lifts up a banner for them and whistles for them and they respond (5:26; 11:12). Yahweh God uses the Assyrians as the rod of his anger to punish his people over whom he also reigned (although they do not acknowledge their divine king [10:1–12]). Indeed, Yahweh God considers using a mighty king and nation to serve his purposes (44:28; 45:1, 13). As King of the nations, Yahweh God breaks the rod and sceptre of their ruler (14:4, 5). The nations are as nothing before him (40:17); yet he will sprinkle them (52:15) and have them hasten to know this Yahweh God (55:5). Indeed, Yahweh God will bring them to his holy mountain and to his house of prayer and thus they will bind themselves to Yahweh, to serve and love him (56:6).

Yahweh God's kingship extends beyond the nation of Israel/Judah and all the nations of the world. He is King of the entire cosmos. The cosmos is his cosmic kingdom. Satan may claim he controls the nations and the forces within creation but he can do nothing unless Yahweh God gives him latitude to carry out his satanic designs and activities.[70] Indeed it is Yahweh God, who having created the cosmos, brought forth the ends, that is, the farthest boundaries of the cosmos (40:28). He created the heavens and the earth (42:5; 45:18); he created mankind upon the earth (45:12; 57:16). And as creator he has sustained it and continues to rule over the cosmos in its entirety for his own glory. Isaiah emphasized that the people whom Yahweh had chosen and redeemed had been created for his glory (43:7), but all things in the cosmos are called to give glory to Yahweh (41:12). And they do because Yahweh God reigns over them, enables, and guides, and directs them to do so.

The Throne of the Kingdom

Isaiah prophesied that Yahweh God had created, maintains, and rules over his entire kingdom. It must be emphasized that the writers and prophets of the Old Testament never considered, or presented, Satan as the enthroned one because Yahweh God had been dethroned from his cosmic throne. Isaiah warned would-be rulers, for example, the king of Babylon, not to consider their throne in the heavens above the stars of God (14:12–14). These thrones would not only not be there, but wherever the would-be enthroned ones placed their thrones, Yahweh God, the enthroned one, would topple and destroy them (cf. 14:13–15).

Isaiah spoke graphically about the throne of Yahweh God. He saw it in a vision (6:1–3), *'ădōnây yōšēb 'al kissē'* (Adonay, the Sovereign Master, was sitting on a throne).[71] Yahweh was sitting on it but he is not described.[72] The throne is, however, high and exalted, majesty and splendor surround the throne depicted by the robe filling the scene. The attending seraphs add the concept of authority to the setting of the throne.

The locus of the throne is not stated. Commentators are not agreed whether the vision portrays a palace or temple scene, nor are they agreed as to where Isaiah was when he suddenly saw the vision.[73] These details should not detract from the message: Yahweh God is enthroned in an exalted and majestic setting. And his throne declared that Yahweh God was indeed the King, clothed in splendor and authority. The throne, as seen in the vision, can best be understood to be in the heavens, which the human eye on earth cannot see. But that does not give cause to say that the throne of God and its actual place is imaginary. Isaiah portrayed it as a glorious reality. Yahweh God has his throne room, which also serves as his judgment courtroom.[74]

Isaiah spoke explicitly about David's throne upon which the child to be born, the son to be given, the messianic mediator, was to sit and reign (6:7; 16:5).

In a climactic conclusion to his prophecies, Isaiah, as Yahweh's prophetic spokesman, referred to Yahweh God's throne twice. On behalf of his people, Isaiah called on Yahweh to look down from heaven and to see from his lofty throne, holy and glorious, and from which Yahweh's zealous love, might, tenderness, and compassion issued forth to consider the needs of the children of Abraham (63:15, 16).

This passage demonstrates that the prophet was very conscious that Yahweh God, on his throne, was the only source of hope for a people in distress. And this distress was caused by Yahweh God no longer bestowing grace and mercy on a rebellious people. Yet, the only hope for a rebellious people in distress was at the foot of the throne. And Isaiah had reminded his hearers that Yahweh God would accuse and be angry forever (57:15).[75]

This throne, Isaiah emphatically proclaims as Yahweh's prophet, is the heavens (66:1). The earth is at his feet, a footstool. This passage emphasizes that Yahweh God, having the heavens as his throne, is not to be seen as a localized deity. He is the omnipresent one. The heavens as his throne represents his sovereign universal reign. There is nothing that is not included; all aspects of the created heavens and earth are subject to Yahweh God.

The Reign of the Kingdom

The direct relationship between the throne and the domain of the cosmic kingdom, which includes the covenant people, the nations, and the entire cosmos, is the reign of him who sits on the throne and has earth as his footstool. Recall that Isaiah had proclaimed "your God reigns." This was the message his people had to hear and remember. But they were not to think that this reign was limited to them as a covenant people. As the throne had the entire cosmos under it, so the reign of Yahweh.

The concept "to reign" is expressed by various terms in Isaiah. The verb *māshal* and its derivatives are mostly translated as rule, rulers. It is used once to speak of Yahweh God having dominion (63:19). Other terms that are translated to rule/rulers are *rādâh* (have dominion); *'śar* (to be prince, chief); *ba'al* (be husband, lord, have dominion); and *šāpāt* (to judge, exercise judgment.)[76] When referring to Yahweh God exercising authority, control, supervision, and directing the affairs of the cosmic kingdom, the term *mālak* (reign) or *melek* (king), is used in all instances but one. The noun, *melek* (king), is used predominantly throughout the Old Testament; the verb *mālak* is a denominative translated as "be or become king" and its secondary sense is "to reign." Hence, the concept *melek* concentrates predominantly on the person. God is the King and as such he functions asking, that is, he reigns,[77] and as reigning king he has absolute authority; he has complete ability; he alone is totally in charge of all things, powers, people, and events.

Yahweh God himself, without direct reference to the Messiah, reigns and rules and exercises dominion over all. Examples of this are Yahweh God's stirring strife among Egyptians, who thus weaken their nation; a cruel foreign king will rule over it (19:2–4). In a song of praise Judah sings that though other *ba'als* (lords) ruled over them, they knew that Yahweh God was in reality their true Lord—who was Lord over the human lords (26:13). Yahweh God would raise up Assyria as a rod of his anger. Though it was a godless nation, exercising proud pretensions as if it was the only lord over the universe, Yahweh God has it do his work of judgement on Judah (10:5–15). But Yahweh God will exercise his sovereign rule, sending a wasting and destroying disease on Assyria (10:16–19). Likewise Yahweh, exercising complete dominion, will round up Cyrus the Persian to defeat mighty Babylon (44:24–45:7). Isaiah proclaims Yahweh God's absolute kingship over the entire cosmic kingdom (cf. esp. 45:2, 3, 7, 8). And in the eschaton, all creation will be subject to him as the Almighty reigns gloriously (24:23). This eschatological reign is also ascribed to the messianic mediator.

Isaiah did prophesy about the Messiah's kingship and reign. As David's heir, he would sit upon the throne of this father, reigning over it forever (9:7). The Messiah will also be the royal judge, exercising divinely royal virtues, righteousness, and justice (11:1–3) and will bring peace to the entire cosmos (11:6–9). He will be the sovereign ruling Lord over even the largest nations (11:10–16). And when the eternal kingdom of righteousness is ushered in, the Messiah will exercise kingly power and prerogatives (32:1). The Messiah will be raised up and exalted, and earthly kings seeing him will be dumbfounded before him.

The reign of Yahweh God and the messianic Mediator will be carried out covenantally.[78] The covenant must be considered the administrative as well as the redemptive means and channel. Yahweh God brings redemption and restoration according to his covenant promises and by means of the messianic agent. But the covenant is also the means by which Yahweh God administers the affairs of his cosmic kingdom. He remains absolute Master, carrying out his promises and upholding all the stipulations. He blesses according to the obedient responses he observes; he curses and executes judgment upon those who disobey, rebel, and oppose him. And all the while he carries out his plans in the crucible of history. This reign, at all times, in all places, and for all people is characterized by righteousness and justice. Righteousness relates to Yahweh God's will and plan, which are perfect. Justice related to Yahweh God's applying his perfect will in the course of history (9:7; 11:4; 16:5; 32:1; 33:5; 42:11).

The King of the Kingdom

In Isaiah's prophecies the concept of the kingdom is expressed, as we have discussed, in terms of the domain, the throne, and the reign of Yahweh God. But what are these three aspects if the king who is said to be enthroned as he reigns over the cosmic domain is not present or if he is ignored? Indeed, it is the king himself who provides the legitimacy and reality of all that constitutes the three aspects. Isaiah does not ignore the king. In fact, the sovereign Yahweh God is the central one in Isaiah's prophecies.

Of the varied types of references that Isaiah includes when prophesying, three categories particularly stand out: (1), Yahweh God and the divine messianic Mediator are persons; (2), they are referred to by symbols, metaphors, and images;[79] (3) the virtues, characteristics or attributes of God. Cf. the following sketch:

A Chart to Set Forth Yahweh God the King Mediator as Revealed in Isaiah

Person	*Symbols, Metaphors, Images*	*Virtues, Attributes*
Seen on throne	husband	incomprehensible
Sent by	parent	transcendent
Child	comforter	majestic
Son	inviter	immanent
He, him, his	gatherer	omnipresent
Immanuel	doctor	omniscient
	shepherd	eternal
	farmer/vineyardist	omnipotent
	barber	sovereign
Se	whistler	righteous
	warrior	just
	lawgiver	compassionate
	arbiter	grace

Person	*Symbols, Metaphors, Images*	*Virtues, Attributes*
	judge	love
	destroyer	anger
	stirrer	wrath
	exalted	wisdom
	rider of clouds	understanding
	light	knowledge
	fortress	beauty
	sanctuary	glory
	stone	
	helper	
	redeemer	
	witness	
	sign	
	root	
	branch	
	servant	
	sin bearer	
	lamb	

Isaiah knew his Lord, Yahweh God, as a personal deity. This is proven particularly in the account of the vision he received (Isa. 6:1–13). Isaiah saw Yahweh seated on a throne. The verb *'erĕ'er* (from *'ārâh*) definitely conveys the sense of an actual seeing. Isaiah was not asleep, physically inactive, as when one dreams. Isaiah actually saw into the invisible world.[80] He did not only see the throne and the Lord seated on it, he heard him speak. Isaiah spoke with him. Isaiah heard that he was sent by a personal God. Isaiah was convinced that Yahweh God was a reality, a personal God who could and did refer to himself as "I" (cf. e.g., 1:2, 11, 13, 25; 2:4; 13:3, 11). Yahweh God also referred to himself saying "my people" (40:1), "my servant" (42:1), "compare to me" (40:25). God spoke of himself as "he who created" (43:1). The evidence of Yahweh God, the King, as a truly, real person is strong, plentiful, and expressed in various ways.

The divine messianic covenantal Mediator is a divine person also. He is spoken of as "the child," "the son," and has divine personal names (9:6). He is spoken of in the third person as "he," "him" (11:2), "his" (11:10). Consider particularly 52:13–53:12, where personal references occur repeatedly: "he," twenty-four times; "him," eight times; "his," thirteen times.

The overwhelming evidence in Isaiah's prophecy is that Yahweh God and the divine messianic Mediator were persons who gave Isaiah the strength and courage to carry out a very difficult commission. He knew Yahweh God as "Immanuel," a personal Lord who had sent him, who was ever with him, and whose will would triumph.

Isaiah used a plethora of symbols, metaphors, and images to refer to Yahweh God and also to the messianic Mediator. He was ever-conscious of the reality that as he functioned as Yahweh God's spokesman that the personal God he served was incomprehensible. Hence he employed everyday terminology as he spoke for the living God. Consider some of the ways he referred to his Lord.

Yahweh God is husband (54:5) and *parent* who has reared children (Israel) and raised them (1:2), but they were obstinate and rebellious, going their own way (1:4; 30:1). He nevertheless is concerned for his children (45:11). He remains the *comforter* for them, his people (3:10; 12:1; 40:1; 52:9; 57:18). He continues to *invite* (1:18; 41:1) and to *gather* his people as he reclaims their remnant (11:11). He is their *doctor,* he sees his people's sickness and wounds and cleanses and heals them (1:6; 4:4; 19:22; 53:5; 57:18, 19). He tenderly proves he is a shepherd (40:11).

Isaiah indicated that he knew about everyday life. He spoke of Yahweh God as the *farmer* (5:1, 2) who has his vineyard and garden (56:6, 7). He is also a *barber,* who uses a razor to shave and shame his people (7:20). As a hunter whistles to his dog when prey is detected, Yahweh God is a *whistler,* calling the nations to serve as his punishing agents (5:26; 7:18). But Yahweh God is the *warrior* (42:13) who stirs up his zeal and calls his warriors to carry out his wrath (13:2, 3). Indeed, he is the avenger (35:4). As the *lawgiver* Yahweh God knows who hear and obey him (1:10; 42:4, 21, 24; 51:4). He will be the *arbiter,* reasoning with the accused (1:18), and also the *judge* (2:4; 3:10, 13, 14; 11:3, 4; 33:22; 42:21). Yahweh God who judges in righteousness and with justice is also the *destroyer* of his vineyard (5:5), of great houses (5:9), of the Assyrian nation he had raised up as the rod of his anger (14:25), and of Egypt who would be handed over to a cruel master who Yahweh the *stirrer* has stirred up (19:20; 41:25).

Isaiah also presented Yahweh God as the *exalted one* (2:17; 5:16; 33:5), whose name is exalted (24:15; 25:1). As such he is the only *object of true worship* (1:11–17; 2:2–4), indeed, Egypt, Assyria, and Israel will unitedly worship Yahweh God (19:23; 27:13; 56:6). Yahweh God, the exalted, will be the *rider* of clouds as he approaches Egypt to bring distress (19:1–19) but will be the *light* of Israel (2:5; 10:17) and his justice will become a light (51:4) to which nations will come (60:3, 19). He will be a *fortress* (17:10), a *sanctuary* (8:14); a *stone* (8:14), and a *rock* (8:14; 17:10). Yahweh God is the *helper* of his people (41:10), and he is their *salvation* (12:2; 17:10; 25:9; 45:17; 51:5, 6; 54:8; 59:16; 61:10; 62:11), and their *redeemer* (42:24; 47:4; 48:17; 49:7).

The Messiah, the covenantal mediatorial agent, was also referred to by images, symbols, and metaphors.[81] As discussed above, he is both divine and human. He is the human who is the divinely *anointed* by the Holy Spirit (11:2; 61:1). His divinity is confirmed by his names, Mighty God, Wonderful Counselor, Everlasting Father, and Prince of Peace (9:6). He is also the divine *judge* (11:3, 4) and as a polished arrow he is *slayer* of the wicked (11:4). He is the *light* (60:1) and the *light* for the Gentiles (49:6). A *covenant* for the people (42:6; 49:6), he is the *witness* to the people (55:4). He is their *preacher* (61:1). As the fully human one, he is a *sign,* a *son,* a *child* (7:14; 9:6) who has come as the *root* from David's line (53:2) and also as a *shoot* (53:2) and a *branch* (11:1, 2) from Jesse's lineage. He is the *king* (32:1) yet also *servant* (42:1; 52:13; 53:11). He is the *sin bearer* (53:6, 8) who is slaughtered as a *lamb* (58:7). The messianic covenantal mediator, referred to as the divine and human one, by name, images, symbols, and metaphors has always been, is, and will be *Immanuel* (God with us) (7:14).[82]

Isaiah's prophecies presented the incomprehensible Yahweh God in such a way, by the use of anthropomorphisms and anthropopathisms, that human speakers could present and hearers receive a wide range of glimpses of their sovereign Lord and Redeemer. But Isaiah uttered his own response to the incomprehensibility of the Master of the Universe. When he was called to prophesy that Yahweh God would raise up *kâreš rō'î* (Cyrus my shepherd) and appoint and qualify him (anoint him) to subdue nations and carry out Yahweh God's purposes for Jerusalem and the temple (they were to be rebuilt after the exile), Isaiah made a personal exclamation in response: *'ākēn 'otlâh 'ēl* (truly, you are a God who hides himself). The verb *sātar,* in the hithpael participial form, stresses, with intensity and in a reflexive manner, how Yahweh God is and carries out his purposes among the nations while having a particular purpose in mind: the regathering of the remnant and the reerection of the temple in rebuilt Jerusalem. Prophesying at least 170 years before all this was to take place, Isaiah can only gasp out his amazement and wonder. Yahweh God was, indeed, in person, plan, and use of "shepherds" beyond human comprehension.[83] He had expressed the wonders of God's being and works also when he prophesied concerning the reality of Yahweh God being the Creator (40:12–41:28) and being the Ruler who upholds the cosmos (40:15–17, 22–26). Isaiah made a positive statement—"his understanding no one can fathom" (40:28)—and spoke a rhetorical question—"who has understood the mind of Yahweh or instructed him" (40:12).

The incomprehensibility of Yahweh God for a Spirit-inspired prophet is correlative to the transcendence of Yahweh God and the divine Messiah. Their ways and thoughts are higher than that of human beings (55:9). Two terms are employed. The verb *nišgāb* (be inaccessibly high) (12:4; 33:5) and terms derived from the verbs *rûm* and *rāmam* stress that Yahweh God and his Messiah are far above the earthly, human kings and potentates (24:4). The divine throne is lifted up on high (humanly speaking) (33:5) and therefore, those who love and honor their God exalt, that is, acknowledge and proclaim that he is the high, lifted up, and transcendent deity (2:11, 12; 5:16; 24:15; 25:1).

When Isaiah was called (6:1–13) he received a vision in which he *'ere'eh* (saw, from *rā'âh*) *'ădōnâi* (the Lord) sitting on a throne that was *rām* (high) and *niššâ'* (lifted up). Seraphs, celestial spirits in whose ministry Yahweh's glory and holiness are prominent, surround Yahweh on this throne.[84] Inseparable from Yahweh God's transcendence is his majesty and holiness.

The term *ge'ônō* (from the root *gā'âh,* to rise up, exalted) does not occur but it expresses the majesty of Yahweh God. Isaiah spoke of the splendor,[85] or glory of Yahweh God's majesty (2:10, 11, 21; 24:14). There is, as it were, a piling up of very closely related terms that together express the transcendence, majesty, and splendor of Yahweh God.[86]

The seraphs proclaim, as they antiphonally honor Yahweh God on his throne, that he is *qādôš* (6:3).[87] Various terms are used to translate this term: be hallowed, holy, sanctified, consecrated, and dedicated. But these translations do not express the full range of meaning and application that the term *qādôš* conveys. First of all, a review of how the term is used by Isaiah should be made. It occurs approximately sixty times and is used to describe Yahweh God himself or what is closely related to him. His name, referring to the person of God, is holy (29:23; 57:15) as is his arm (52:10). Places such as his mountain are holy (11:9; 27:13; 56:9; 57:13, 15). The temple is holy (64:11), as is his city (48:2; 52:9) and his throne (63:15). The redeemer is the Holy One (41:14; 43:14; 48:17), hence his people are holy (the remnant, holy ones, 13:3; 62:12). This Holy Redeemer is the Holy Maker of all (45:11). The term *holy* is used often in direct reference to Yahweh God himself. Thus the Holy One is Yahweh the King, Creator, Redeemer, the Spirit (63:10, 11).

The term *holy* is used as can be inferred from the above references in two ways: in reference to God himself and to what is in close relationship to Yahweh God. Gerhardus Vos, in order to draw attention to this dual reference, has written of Yahweh God's majesty holiness and ethical holiness.[88] Majesty holiness sums up what holiness is and means in reference to the person of God.[89] Majesty holiness emphasizes that Yahweh God is separate from all that is created. God is unique; he is distinct. There is no one or anything comparable to him. The holiness of God is correlative with his transcendence and exalted status. It emphasizes his splendor, majesty, and glory. Yahweh God demands and insists that he be known, worshiped, and served as such. Indeed, his holiness is in a real way the reason for giving the first three commandments: no other gods, he alone is God; no form or representation of God, he is transcendent, above human apprehension and comprehension; his name is identical with his holy person; therefore, there is to be no profane use of it. The seraphs attending Yahweh God on his throne were called upon to emphasize the holiness of Yahweh God when he revealed himself in a unique manner, by vision, to Isaiah the prophet.

Isaiah beheld Yahweh God and it was not only his majesty holiness that overwhelmed him, it was also Yahweh God's ethical holiness. This holiness includes the concept of purity—absolute separation from the profane, common, evil, and unclean (i.e., the dirty, filthy, foul, unwashed). Isaiah, the noble prince, the worshiper of Yahweh God, who loved the house of the Lord, suddenly became aware of his own personal being, qualities, and activities. Compared to Yahweh, his Lord, he was unclean, ruined, and unfit to live, having seen the holy, transcendent, majestic, glorious Lord. And he could not imagine how he, a man with unclean lips, could serve and speak for this holy God. His ethics, as known and applied to himself, rendered him a totally and absolutely unfit spokesman. But, Isaiah was assured by the angel's service to him that his sin was atoned for and his guilt taken away (6:6, 7). Thus Isaiah became an ethical holy servant who could serve as Yahweh's prophet. It should be stressed that Isaiah's response to his vision of the holy Yahweh God, indicates that he was aware that Yahweh God's holiness involving also the majesty, as well as the purity, "became the principle of the punishment of sin."[90] Yahweh God upholds his holiness and his majesty. Sin conflicts with it, degrades and undoes it. To fully understand this, it is vitally important to realize that Yahweh God, as the transcendent one, is also the immanent one. It was his good pleasure to create the cosmos and to place humanity, created in his image, as the pivotal point of this created cosmos. In this creating activity Yahweh God, maintaining his majesty holiness, revealed his ethical holiness. He kept himself involved in his creation and particularly with his image bearer agents—man and woman. They were placed in the garden of Eden with a "derivatory holiness." Humanity's deviation removed this holiness. But Yahweh God, nevertheless continued to relate himself as the transcendent, majestic, holy one to certain people and things.[91] Hence Isaiah properly, in his prophecies, repeatedly spoke of Yahweh God as the Holy One of Israel, of his people, and of his city, of his mountain, of his temple, where he, in a specific and gracious way, identified himself with his worshiping and serving redeemed people.

Isaiah's proclamation of Yahweh God's transcendence, holiness, and immanence included the message of Yahweh God's omnipresence. His Lord was not just in the temple or palace. As he was present with his people in Jerusalem, he was present among the nations, guiding, directing, employing them for his own purposes. He is present in Egypt, in Assyria, among all the other nations and he knows all that they plan and do. The Holy One, seeing and knowing all, rejects the unethical even though he may use such to carry out his holy plan.[92]

Closely related to Yahweh God's omnipresence is his omniscience; he is all-knowing. He knows all. Since he is everywhere present, he sees and understands all that is thought, planned, and done. This knowledge of Yahweh is infinite, there are no limits to his understanding of all things past, present, and future. It is his omniscience that makes predictive prophecy a certainty as well as his evaluation of all the past. Yahweh, through Isaiah, assured Ahaz, king of Judah, that though kings planned to invade Judah, that it "will not take place, it will not happen" (7:4–8). And Isaiah spoke on behalf of Yahweh God that before new things spring into being, "I announce them to you" (42:9).

In relation to created time, Yahweh God is eternal. He was before time, he is in and above it and will be beyond it. Isaiah speaks of eternity in mostly anthropomorphic terms. Yahweh God and his messianic son have the name "everlasting Father" (9:6). Speaking of the Creator, who made the ends of the earth, who does not grow tired or weary, Yahweh God is said to be everlasting (40:28). Isaiah proclaimed that there would be never-ending light for his people because their God is the everlasting source (60:19, 20). So also will be their ever-continuing joy (51:11;

61:7) and never-ending salvation (45:17). These, and other great blessed benefits that are never-ending, are that because the King, the ever-reigning covenant Lord is the source of them.

Isaiah's audiences, both hearers and readers, receive the blessed assurance that Yahweh God, who is not confined to or by space and time, made, controls, and directs them. He does this because he is the omnipotent One.[93] Vos wrote that no Hebrew term appears that expressed the full meaning of the concept of the unlimited power of Yahweh God.[94] But the prophet did give expression to it when he spoke of Yahweh God rising to shake the earth (2:19), to scorch the earth (9:19) to drive away the roaring nations as if they were chaff (17:13). Yahweh God weighs the nations and islands as though they are fine dust (40:15). He brings into being and names the starry hosts one by one because of the abundance of his might and the strength of his power (40:26).[95]

A discussion of Yahweh God's omnipotence cannot omit a brief study of the phrase *yĕhwâ śĕba ôt* (Yahweh of hosts).[96] The phrase has engendered much discussion and varying translations. The phrase does not occur before 1 Samuel 1:3 and appears infrequently in the books of the Kings (cf. 1 Kings 18:15; 19:10; 2 Kings 9:14; 19:31). The psalmists used it more frequently (fourteen times). Amos, Isaiah, Jeremiah, Daniel, and Zechariah, reflecting their specific historical contexts, speaking of what Yahweh God can and will bring in judgment and salvation, employ the term to express Yahweh God's unlimited power as he, the King of the universe, executes his reign. Translators are not agreed if the phrase should be translated "sovereign" or "almighty." The Septuagint translated the phrase as "The Lord of all powers" or "The Lord, the All Ruler."[97] Uncertainty on how to translate the phrase has been accentuated by the efforts to translate the divine name *'ădōnâi*. If this name would be consistently translated as Lord, that is, the Master, then some confusion would be eliminated.[98]

Isaiah used the phrase "Lord of Hosts" approximately sixty times. Very seldom did he use it to express distinctly and specifically the personal character of Yahweh God. The term many use to translate the phrase, "Almighty," speaks of Yahweh God in his being. He *is* the strong and mighty One. But the phrase "Yahweh of Hosts" emphasizes Yahweh's relationship with forces outside himself. It emphasizes his strong, powerful, unequaled ability to reign over, control, and direct all the affairs of the cosmos. Yahweh can and does so reign because in his divine person he is almighty. So, as the almighty one he is the Sovereign One, the one who reigns over all. Hence the translation that is basically correct is "the Sovereign One."

Isaiah certainly does emphasize the fact that the omnipotent (all-powerful) King of the universe reigns over all aspects of the universe. As the creator and redeemer he is the sovereign King (Yahweh *šĕbôt*) (47:4). He controls the waves of the seas because of his name (51:15). As sovereign King over the nations, he takes a Persian Cyrus (45:13) and has nations bring gifts to him (18:7). He executes judgment over enemies who exalt themselves (2:12) and he will avenge himself regarding them (1:29). In many and varied ways his and his people's enemies will be punished (10:16, 23, 26, 33; 13:4; 14:22, 23, 24, 26; 17:3; 19:4; 23:9). Israel/Judah will also realize that their sovereign king (5:1; 9:13; 21:10; 37:16) will bring judgment upon them (5:9; 24:12; 39:5), especially against their leaders (3:15). The sovereign King over all will demonstrate his wrath and make the earth tremble (9:19; 13:3; 34:2) but to those who answer his call to worship him (8:13) will have his law as their light (5:24). He will defend and shield Jerusalem (31:4) but will also take away its necessities for daily life when they reject him (3:1). He assures his people that as Lord of Hosts, the Sovereign One, who dwells in Zion gloriously (24:23) and reigns with justice and righteousness (5:16) and will protect and comfort the remnant (1:9; 10:24; 24:23; 25:6; 28:5) because of his zeal (jealous love) for his chosen ones (9:7; 37:32). By his sovereign rule he will unite the nations, Egypt, Assyria, and Israel as his one people, handiwork, and inheritance (19:25).

Isaiah proclaimed that the sovereign King rules in righteousness and with justice. Isaiah spoke of righteous and righteousness often. The term has also been found in various contexts in our preceding studies.[99] Isaiah used the four biblical terms: *śaddîq,* the adjective, usually translated righteous, sometimes as just; *śādaq,* the verb, to be, make, declare righteous; *sedeq,* masculine noun; and *śĕdēqâh,* feminine noun.[100]

Righteousness is predicated of Yahweh God, the sovereign King of the cosmos. The intent of the concepts of righteousness/righteous as applied to God is to direct one to the very nature and heart of holy Yahweh God, the King. His very nature is to be righteous and to reveal it. Righteousness flows from the heart of God because from within the very heart of God his will, his law, comes forth. The law therefore expresses the nature and will of Yahweh God, and he is not, and cannot be or do anything inconsistent with his heart, his will, his revealed law. Thus to say Yahweh God is righteous and that his righteousness is revealed and demonstrated is to declare that Yahweh God never turns away from nor slights his will, his revealed law. Yahweh God never does anything contrary to his own pure heart.

Take notice of how Isaiah speaks of Yahweh God as righteous and reveals his righteousness. In reference to the raising up of Cyrus, prophesied years before that a king was born, Isaiah proclaims that Yahweh God is righteous. He acted according to his heart and will to use Cyrus as the one to free Israel from their bondage in the exile (41:26) and thus be the savior of his people (45:21). The covenant people have nothing to fear because Yahweh God, their Savior/Redeemer, will uphold them with his right hand that performs all that is in accord with Yahweh God's heart and will (41:10). And so he calls them in righteousness, that is, according to his heart's intent (42:6). Isaiah proclaimed the truth powerfully. It pleased Yahweh God to reveal his law as great and glorious so that the deaf could hear and the blind could see how faithful their God was to his own nature and heart. Yahweh revealed himself thus because that is his very nature. He did it for "his own righteousness' sake" (42:21), and therefore he speaks righteousness (45:10). This righteousness of God is and has been revealed in his plan of salvation, which will never fail because righteous Yahweh God never fails. Indeed, salvation flows directly and constantly from the heart of Yahweh God, who never does anything contrary to his nature, his will, his law (36:1; 46:13; 51:6, 8; 57:12).

The messianic mediatorial Son is Yahweh God. The Servant whose heart, will, law, is not in any way different from Yahweh God's is the Righteous One (53:11). His entire being reveals and demonstrates the will of Yahweh God. He carries out the will and the will and the instructions (the law, the Torah) of Yahweh God. He who is also the descendant of David will, as the enthroned one, reigning with or in righteousness (32:1), carry out the will and law of Yahweh God (9:7). And as the Righteous One he will demonstrate his knowledge, readiness, and ability to judge in keeping with the will, the law, the very nature of Yahweh God (11:4). Isaiah assured his audience that the descendant of David would be given support in his judging work because righteousness would be his girdle.[101] Thus he would not only be properly dressed and equipped, but also given strength and stability. The messianic king, highly exalted (52:13) and tragically humbled (52:14; 53:2–9), according to the will of the loving heart of Yahweh God (53:10), would, as the righteous one, cause many people to become righteous.

Isaiah was definite: *bĕda 'tô yaśdîq śaddîq 'abdî lārabîm* (by his knowledge the righteous servant will cause [hiphil impf. second per. sing.] many people to be righteous). The phrase "by his knowledge" has been widely discussed.[102.] It certainly can be stated with assurance that the servant knew what was in the heart of Yahweh God, that he was in full agreement with it, and that, having suffered, he could carry out the will of the loving Father: that many would come into the blessed state of being righteous. To be made righteous thus meant that by what the Righteous Servant had done and knew, he removed the barrier of sin between the heart of Yahweh God and the hearts of sinners. Thus the latter could and would be drawn into a living, loving fellowship with Yahweh God. The heart of Yahweh God and the hearts of cleansed sinners would be drawn into and continue to live in harmonious fellowship for time and eternity.

Yahweh God, the messianic Mediator, and the Holy Spirit had this common heart's desire and intent: to consider the chosen people, as righteous—within the will of God, in heart-to-heart fellowship, and always in service according to the way of life as revealed—that is, the Torah, the law. Consider how often Isaiah spoke of a righteous people in this way (1:27; 13:10; 26:2; 57:1; 58:2; 60:21; 61:3; 62:1). Not only are the people referred to as righteous, their city in which they live, and that represents Yahweh God's dwelling, is called righteous—it is within the will and purposes of Yahweh God (11:16).

In close relationship to Yahweh God's righteousness is his justice.[103] This term by itself is not always clearly understood because the verb *šāpat* is translated as judge and govern. Its derivatives, *šepet, šepôt,* and *mišpāt,* all stress the concept of judge, judgment, and justice.[104] Isaiah used the term *šāpat* to refer to the act of and function of a judge, that is, to judge or to a judge (1:23; 3:2; 11:3; 16:5; 32:1; 40:23; 51:5). These references suffice to demonstrate that Isaiah knew of the important role of judges, their function, and of Yahweh God as judge. Isaiah spoke repeatedly of *mišpāt.*[105] And in the same context that the term *sedeq* appeared (cf. e.g., 9:7; 11:4; 33:5). Hence the distinction between the two terms should be clearly understood.

The terms *righteous* and *righteousness* must be basically understood as referring to character and relationship. Yahweh God is righteous; this is an important and undeniable virtue or attribute of Yahweh God. It refers to a relationship of agreement, of solidarity, of full communal life. A person is righteous when, by faith he or she is in true fellowship with Yahweh God and participates in that righteousness by a declarative act by God. A person can be reckoned, be declared, be, and demonstrate to be in that relationship with righteous Yahweh God. The term *justice,* basically derived from the concept of judge, refers to the activity of applying the will, the Torah, the law of God to whatever circumstance, activity, or person that is being considered. This activity by God is never capriciously carried out. It is always done according to his perfect will. Justice is carried out when sin is considered; there will be a punishment according to God's declared will, or there will be acquittal, a declaration of not guilty, to the repentant, confessing sinner. Justice thus refers to the execution of God's will, Torah, law, in keeping with the righteous character of Yahweh God. Furthermore, rulers demonstrate justice as they carry out their duties according to Yahweh God's will. Judges demonstrate justice when they judge all cases according to Yahweh God's revealed will. A nation demonstrates justice when it carries out the will of righteous Yahweh God in all circumstances and situations in which it finds itself.

Consider some passages in which Isaiah stresses the justice of God. In the first chapter, the term *mišpāt* occurs three times. The prophet calls upon the covenant people whose hands are full of blood, who have been called to wash; he then calls upon them to learn the good or right as revealed and this is followed by the call to seek justice, that is, to apply that good and right (1:15–17). The prophet continues with what can be considered a lament: the faithful city had become a harlot but once she was full of justice—demonstrating that the will of Yahweh God was applied (1:21). Then the hopeful note is sounded. There is redemption but it will be carried out with justice, that is, according to Yahweh God's will (1:27).

Isaiah proclaimed this same message in his song of the vineyard. The house of Israel and the men of Judah did not demonstrate living according to or applying the will/law of God. Instead Yahweh God saw bloodshed (5:7). A disappointed and grieving vineyardist who saw no fruits of justice would not cease from being just—that is, acting according to his righteous character. Punishment will be executed, and in the doing of that, Yahweh *śĕbā'ôt* would be exalted (5:16).

Isaiah emphasized that Yahweh God's justice is not contrary to or inconsistent with his compassion and race (30:18).[106] Yahweh God, Isaiah prophesied, *yĕḥakkeh* (piel impf., 3rd of *hākāh*) is waiting with longing to demonstrate grace. This longing is shown by *yârûm* (qal impf. 3rd per of *rûm,* to rise, be lifted up) and *lĕrahemkem* (piel inf. of *rāham,* to show loving compassion). This longing to demonstrate grace and his compassion is motivated by his *mišpāṭ,* justice. (Yahweh God has a strong desire to give full expression to his will, that is, that sinners repent be redeemed, and be restored. Because he is just, he, according to his very righteous and loving heart longs for the redemption, restoration, and the eternal well-being of his chosen covenant people.

It is in this context that Isaiah's proclamation that it was Yahweh God's *ḥàpēś* (qal per. 3rd per.) delight, that is, it pleased him to crush the mediatorial servant and cause him to suffer (53:10). Yahweh God's justice demanded that sin be punished, that the curse of the covenant be executed. And his justice motivated him to carry away his people's infirmities and sorrows and to heal their wounds. God's justice had to be shown in the punishment of rebellion and sin and in the redemption, restoration, and healing of his covenant people. The mediatorial servant knew that the only way that the two demands of God's will could be met, that is, for justice to be executed, was by his being crushed and having his life made a guilt offering.

In the preceding study of Yahweh God's righteousness and justice, the virtues of love and compassion were briefly discussed. A few words about love is in order. The term *'āhab* (love) appears in reference to Yahweh God only four times. Yahweh God loves justice (61:8). This, as discussed above, stresses that justice flows from the heart of God; to love is to open up one's heart and pour forth what is in it. Yahweh God's heart of love thus comes to expression in justice. Isaiah also referred to Yahweh God's love for his chosen covenant people demonstrated in their exodus from Egypt and wanderings in the desert (63:9). Isaiah here confirms what Moses repeatedly assured Israel when he spoke the messages comprising the book of Deuteronomy (4:13; 7:13; 15:16; 23:5[6]). Isaiah also emphasized that Yahweh God's covenant love is an abiding love. The Lord created and formed his people (Isa. 43:1) into a redeemed people. Isaiah reminded the people, and proved it by what Yahweh God did to other nations to redeem them (43:2, 3). He did this because he loved them, the precious and honored ones in his sight (43:1a). This covenant love is the sure basis for the assurance that Yahweh God is their God and he is with them (43:3).

Isaiah also prophesied concerning *'ăhēbâ* (his loved one). The context clearly refers to Israel's deliverance from Babylon. Their exile will not continue on for may years. Yahweh God has loved one who will be the delivering and restoring agent. Who is this beloved? One commentator calls attention to a parallel passage (42:1, 2). He believes the reference is to the mysterious conqueror, the Servant of the future, a true descendant of Abraham.[107] This interpretation does not give proper credence to the nearer context. Yahweh God, by Isaiah's mouth, had proclaimed that Cyrus, the future Persian king, would be his servant, the shepherd (44:28) and the anointed (*mĕshiăch*) who would subdue nations and open the doors for the covenant people (the remnant) to return from exile (45:1–17). Most commentators state convincingly that the "loved one"[108] is Cyrus, referred to in chapters 44 and 45.[109] This passage informs us that there is a general love of God for people, specifically, for a person who is not called to salvation but certainly to the service of Yahweh God, the omnipotent sovereign King of the universe and of all nations within it.

Isaiah made references to another characteristic (virtue or attribute) of Yahweh God, namely, his anger and wrath. These concepts have to be understood in relation to Yahweh's righteousness, justice, compassion, and love. The first point to emphasize is that anger and wrath are not inconsistent with or contrary to the other divine virtues. The second point to emphasize is that anger and wrath support, strengthen, and provide a greater credence for them. The ignoring, rejection, and violation of righteousness and justice are tests of their reality and genuineness. The spurning of Yahweh God's love and compassion also attacks and challenges their veracity and complete dependability. To react to these wonderful virtues of God in a negative and distrustful way is to go to the very heart of God, from which these flow, in a coarse and rebellious manner. Yahweh God's heart is holy. It cannot and will not tolerate sinful and rebellious men's and women's ignoring, rejection, and violation. Yahweh God must rise up and deal effectively with these. He is motivated by love to maintain pure infinite love. Likewise, his righteousness and justice demand that God remains steadfastly faithful in his upholding and demonstrating them. To do otherwise would be to effectively diminish and even nullify them. Yahweh God, as the sovereign covenant Lord, will maintain himself as absolutely unchanging and unchangeable (Mal. 3:6).

Isaiah had repeatedly referred to the curse of the covenant that would be executed upon covenant breakers. As there were promises of blessing for the repentant, believing, worshiping, and serving people, likewise there would be the curse executed upon those who broke and rejected the covenant. Consider how Isaiah expresses this.[110] In the song of Vineyard (Isa. 5:1–30) the justice and righteousness of Yahweh God are extolled (5:16). What follows then are the proclamations of woe (5:18, 20, 21) because the covenant people have rejected the law and spurned the word of the Holy One (5:24). This accusation against the covenant people is followed by *'al-kēn ḥārâh' ōp-yĕhwâ bĕ 'ammî* (therefore burns the anger of Yahweh against his people [5:25]). Yahweh God's anger is like a fire that burns and removes the objects that have aroused his anger. After prophesying concerning the promised King David, who would reign with justice and righteousness (9:7 [6]) Isaiah prophesied about Yahweh God's anger against his people, who with pride and arrogance, sing they can and will undo whatever punishment is inflicted upon them (9:9, 10). But Yahweh God, who in *'appō* (anger) brings in enemies to punish his people, will not turn away his anger (9:12, 17, 21; 10:4). Isaiah proceeded to use a stronger term to express Yahweh God's reaction to a rebellious people. He said the *bĕ 'ebrāt* (fierce anger) of Sovereign Yahweh would scorch the promised land. Yahweh God's anger would be as a fierce, overflowing fire that burned all in and before it.[111] And while prophesying concerning Yahweh God's anger and wrath came the comforting word that these would end for the covenant people, but would in turn destroy the rod, Assyria, Yahweh had used (10:25). Isaiah went on in a doxological manner to praise Yahweh God for the turning away of his anger (12:1).

Throughout Isaiah's entire prophecy, he spoke of Yahweh God's comfort and blessing for his people. But Isaiah also repeatedly spoke of God's anger and wrath.[112] In his call to all nations, Isaiah proclaims that God's anger and wrath is upon all their armies and he will destroy them (34:2; cf. also 63:5, 6). But he will delay his wrath against his people for his own name's sake (48:9) although he had made his people to drink the cup of his wrath before (51:17, 20).

Isaiah spoke of other virtues/attributes of God. When he prophesied concerning Yahweh God's judgment on Assyria, he said that it is according to God's wisdom, because he has understanding, that the king of Assyria is to be punished (10:13). The term *beḥōkmātî* (root is *ḥākam,* the verb, *ḥākām,* the adjective). The lexicons point out that the term can mean skillful, shrewd, crafty, prudent, and learned. The term *nibunôtî* (to discern, perceive) is used in conjunction with wisdom (10:13). It is the niphal of *bîn* (to be discerning, discreet, and have understanding). These two concepts emphasize that Yahweh God is completely aware of what the circumstances and situations are, who is involved and why, when, and who they are. When this understanding and wisdom is present and active, no mistakes are made and no evil is done. Justice is correctly executed. Wickedness is punished and obedience receives its due acknowledgment. These terms are often used of people; Isaiah complains that sinful covenant breakers lack these (5:13; 6:9; 27:11; 29:14; 47:10). But Yahweh God is wonderful in counsel and magnificent in wisdom.

Isaiah referred to these virtues when he prophesied that Yahweh God's covenant people would receive comfort because her hard service would be completed (in the exilic period) and her sin paid for. Yahweh God is and would be the redeeming and restoring One. He could and would redeem and restore; he had his way of doing these. And as when he had created the cosmos, he needed no counselor or someone who understood his mind (40:1–5; 13:14, 26). So, Yahweh God had, according to his understanding, knowledge, and counsel, prepared the sure redemption and restoration to come. They would certainly be carried out. Yahweh God would not fail.

In the passage in which the Branch from Jesse is proclaimed, it is prophesied that great virtues of Yahweh God will be his because the Spirit of wisdom, understanding, counsel, power, knowledge, and fear of the Lord will rest on him. Two realities should be stressed (1) the virtues of Yahweh God are those of the Spirit also and the divine human descendant of David will also have them; (2) these virtues are mutually correlative and supportive of each other. That is to say, where and when there is wisdom, there is also understanding, counsel, power, knowledge, and fear of the Lord. This reality emphasizes the vital importance and relevance of each virtue. If one is weak or missing, the others are likewise affected.

Two more virtues or attributers that Isaiah ascribed to Yahweh God require attention. These specifically demonstrate that Yahweh God as the righteous, just, angry, wrathful one. Yet he also demonstrates his understanding, knowledge, and wisdom, and is not a cold-hearted, powerful, sovereign God. The terms *beautiful* and *glorious* are ascribed to him. *ṣ̌ĕbî* is the word that conveys the idea of beauty. Babylon was described as the beautiful one (23:9) as was Tyre (23:9).[113] The thought expressed in Isaiah 24:16, translated in the NIV as "glory" is that of beauty (*ṣ̌ĕbî*).[114] From the ends of the earth one hears singing about the beauty of Yahweh, the Righteous One. And in the future Yahweh God, the Sovereign One, will be a beautiful crown for his people and also a diadem of beauty (28:5). The basic thought is that Yahweh God, who is beauty personified, will share this beauty with his redeemed and restored people. And they will know it because, as a beauty queen is crowned to confirm her beauty, so the redeemed covenant people "will wear a crown of beauty" to confirm their partaking in the beauties of Yahweh. And this partaking of beauty is made possible because the Branch of Yahweh (4:2), who is beauty personified, will make those he washes and cleanses a work of beauty (4:4). Thus Yahweh God and his Anointed One, the Branch, are beauty personified and as such, make the redeemed, cleansed, and restored ones works of beauty. This concept of beauty must be seen as very closely related to honor. Closely related to beauty and honor, in turn, is *kābôd* (glory).

The term translated glory appears both as a verb and a noun in the Old Testament and often in Isaiah.[115] It should be apparent that as one studies the many virtues of Yahweh God and the messianic Mediator, the terms *glory* and *glorious* unavoidably appear. The term *kābôd* is most often applied to Yahweh God. Because of the various attributes ascribed to God, such as majesty, splendor, awesomeness, and greatness, it is difficult to define the term specifically, especially as it applies to God. The various terms used to translate it in different circumstances and contexts give evidence of the richness and the wonder that biblical authors sought to express. How can a person, in fellowship with Yahweh God, give proper and full expression of what is seen and heard in a vision such as Isaiah saw (6:1–3)? Isaiah, who heard Yahweh God ascribed three times as holy, is informed that he fills the earth with his glory, radiance, beauty, splendor, awesomeness, and majesty. What Isaiah saw and heard, he proclaimed shall be revealed most fully in due time (35:2; 40:5; 60:1; 66:18). Three points should be stressed: (1) as Yahweh God reveals his glory, he will not give it to another (42:8; 48:11) but (2) men and women were created for Yahweh God's glory (43:7), that is, he created humans as image bearers to reflect and demonstrate his wonderful attributes, and (3) this glory of Yahweh God will be revealed and exhibited in the future when it rises on the righteous and sanctified covenant believers (60:1, 2).

The Continuity of the Kingdom

Several comments must be made. First, the continuity of the covenant was discussed in part II, E. The prophets do not separate these two, as is the time references or the covenant, so it is for the kingdom. Second, the study of Jeremiah, Ezekiel, and Daniel will call for a careful discussion of the future of the covenant and of

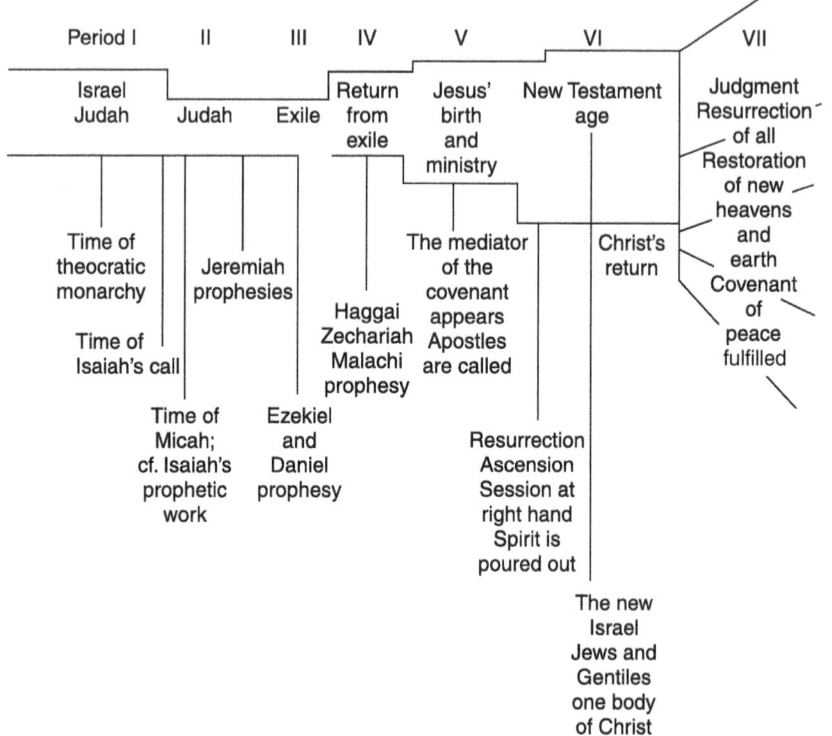

the kingdom. Third, Isaiah was not as specific regarding certain aspects of both the covenant and the kingdom as the prophets were that succeeded him. Isaiah does present an overall view of the future.[116] Fourth, consider Isaiah's presentation as sketched above; clarifying comments will follow.

Period I is the time in which Isaiah was called to prophesy. It was the year Uzziah, king of Judah, died.[117] The first eighteen years of his ministry, Israel to the north of Judah continued as a nation. Isaiah warned King Ahaz of Judah not to rely on Assyria for aid against Aram and Israel. Assyria would threaten Judah (7:8) when Israel would be carried away into exile (10:5ff.). During this Period I Isaiah prophesied concerning events to take place in the future. He prophesied concerning judgment on Judah (chap. 3, Period III), of the regathering of exiles (2:1–5, Period IV), of the messianic descendant of David to be born (7:14; 9:6[5], Period V), and of his reign and restoration of the earth (9:7[6]; 11:1ff., Period VII).

During Period II Isaiah continued to prophesy in Judah after Israel had been carried into exile in 722 B.C. He was particularly active during the reign of Hezekiah (715–688 B.C.). During this period Isaiah prophesied concerning Babylon's capture of Jerusalem (39:5–7) and of Babylon's woes and eventual fall (13:21, Period III). In the latter part of his life (he died during Manasseh's reign) he proclaimed the messages recorded in Isaiah 40–66. He prophesied that the exile in Babylon would end (40:1ff., Period IV) and that their duties as Yahweh God's servant would continue (chap. 44, Period IV). The individual Servant would be present (42:1ff.), and he would minister (61:1ff.), he would suffer and die (52:13–53:12), and call his people to be blessed by the sure mercies of David (55:1ff.). These prophecies spoke of Periods V and VI. As in prophecies proclaimed in the earlier part of his ministry, so in the latter part he combined references to Christ's ministry on earth and his reign after his return (chaps. 56–66, Periods VI and VII).[118]

As Isaiah uttered his prophecies concerning the future of Israel/Judah and the coming and ministry of the messianic Mediator of the covenant and the final restoration of the created cosmos, he did so with the full awareness that Yahweh God, the covenant Lord and sovereign King, gave him these prophecies and that he would carry them out according to his own plan and timetable. These prophecies would all be fulfilled in the context of the ever-continuing cosmic kingdom. What Yahweh God planned and proclaimed through his prophetic servants would surely become realities according to his counsel and plan. Human minds would not always grasp the full and complete intent and timetable (45:15). The message of the continuity and durability of Yahweh God's kingdom is clear. The kingdom of our Lord will abide because its King is true and totally trustworthy.

Conclusion

In conclusion to this study of Isaiah three summary comments should be made. First, Isaiah repeated, expanded, applied, and made some correlative additions to the prophetic theme that Joel had introduced. Second, the Golden Cable is woven throughout Isaiah's prophecy. The theme of kingdom, covenant, and mediator, as a triad, serve as the backbone of the entire prophecy and thus its unity comes to beautiful expression. Third, the gospel in its entirety is set forth. One could do no better than to finish this study of Isaiah than by quoting a biblical scholar. He wrote: "I would contend that if all the other sixty-five books were destroyed, leaving Isaiah's book alone, we would still have all the essential biblical truth in elemental form." We see in this book divine transcendence and immanence, implacable divine justice and unmerited favor; the utter untrustworthiness of any created thing and the absolute dependability of self, the majesty of the Divine King and the suffering of the gentle Savior; substitutionary atonement and the destruction of death; salvation by grace alone and the necessity of holy living on the part of the saved; God the Creator of the cosmos and the Lord of history. No other prophet comes close to this kind of a binding together of biblical thought.[119] Indeed, these biblical-theological themes were expounded by Isaiah as he wove these themes into a beautiful whole, a tapestry, revealing that the three strands of the Golden Cable serve to unite and blend together the core, the stratum, and the seams of the entire prophecy.

NOTES

1. Gerard Van Groningen, *Messianic Revelation in the Old Testament,* reprint (Eugene: Wiph and Stock, 1997), 505–15.

2. Ibid., 516–666.

3. Cf. chapter 3 in this volume.

4. The call for an awareness of the importance of seeing the unity of the Bible is being issued from various sources. Cf., e.g., Daniel P. Fuller, "The Importance of a Unity of the Bible," in *Studies in Old Testament Theology,* ed. R. L. Hubbard, Jr., R. K. Johnston, R. P. Mege (Dallas: Word, 1992), 63–75. Fuller located the Bible's unity in redemptive history (65) and emphasized the historicity of redemptive events (71).

5. Recall how Israel had responded three times, saying, all that Yahweh had said they would do (Exod. 19:8; 24:3, 7).

6. The entire book of Deuteronomy is a repetition of what Yahweh God had declared to be his covenant will for Israel's everyday life, worship, and service. Scholars have attempted to find relationships between what is often referred to as the traditions associated with Moses in books besides the Pentateuch. Efforts to find similarities between Moses and Jeremiah and Ezekiel are referred to by Marten O. O'Kane, who has attempted to find these between Moses and Isaiah. "Isaiah: A Prophet in the Footsteps of Moses," *Journal for the Study of the Old Testament* 69: 29–51.

7. Recall that Micah had called on witnesses (1:2) as had Moses (Deut. 32:1).

8. Walther Eichrodt emphasized that these activities of Yahweh God on behalf of Israel led them to realize and believe that God had set up and developed a special relationship, a bond, a covenant, with them. Eichrodt, however, did not accept the biblical revelation concerning God initiating his covenant with Adam and Eve and reconfirming it with Noah and the patriarchs. He wrote: "Moses, taking over a concept of long standing in secular life based the worship of Yahweh on a covenant agreement." *Theology of the Old Testament,* trans. J. A. Baker (Philadelphia: Westminster, 1961), 36–45.

9. Chapter 1 has been referred to as the introduction to the entire prophecy of Isaiah because it contains the basic themes of Isaiah's ministry. Edward J. Young, *The Book of Isaiah,* 3 vols. in The New International Commentary on the Old Testament (NICOT) (Grand Rapids: Eerdmans, 1965), 1:27. It should be added that chapters 1–6 present the covenantal context and briefly elaborate on themes that are developed more fully in the following six chapters. See John N. Oswalt on the discussion of the location of chapter 6 after the first five chapters that were introduced by the reference to the vision Isaiah received. *The Book of Isaiah, Chapters 1–39* (Grand Rapids: Eerdmans, 1986), 70–80, 171–74.

10. This is R.B.Y. Scott's translation in *Isaiah,* in *The Interpreters Bible,* 12 vols., ed. George Arthur Buttrick (New York: Abingdon, 1956), 5:190.

11. Franz Delitzsch, *Biblical Commentary on the Prophecies of Isaiah,* trans. James Marten, 2 vols. (Grand Rapids: Eerdmans, 1950), 1:140. It is difficult to accept the translation of *'ammîm* in this context as nations because Isaiah is addressing the covenant people in Jerusalem and Judah. And to translate *rîb* as pleading is not acceptable because the following phrase has *lādîn,* "to judge." Two recent writers (as did others) addressed the liter-

ary aspects of Isaiah's prophecy. Paul R. House, discussing the historical context and placement of Isaiah 6 in chapters 1–6 asked, "Is Isaiah 6 basically a call story?" Yes, the chapter records the call of the prophet, but it is also an integral part of chapters 1–6 because it draws the themes of chapters 1–5 together. Cf. "Isaiah's Call and Its Context in Isaiah 1–6," *Criswell Theological Review* 6 (1993): 207–22. Mark R. Rooker in the *Westminster Theological Journal* 58 (1976), quoted C. Seitz of Yale Divinity School, "who had written that the Book of Isaiah consisted of 2 or 3 specific parts was in many ways the greatest historical consensus in this modern period" (303). Rooker, however, by means of linguistic analysis, making a diachronic study of the Hebrew language was aware of a well-known factor that languages change over time (304), but in a careful analysis of four examples found "overwhelming evidence" in support of the view that Isaiah 40–66 was written in the preexilic period. He added that his four examples were not unique but consistent with other examples and features (311). John Oswalt, in an essay in *Trinity Journal* entitled "Judgment and the Full Orbed Gospel," vol. 17, 1996, wrote that the comprehensive theology of Isaiah makes Isaiah the prince of prophets (191) and the prince of biblical theology. This theology has too often been fractured (192). He proceeded to point out that the later part of Isaiah was written with full knowledge of the first part and thus they are not dissimilar books. He also indicated that he hopes to demonstrate that the section 55–66 is designed to synthesize the teachings of the first two sections (1–39 and 40–59), 193.

12. Yeo Hiok-Khong, while preferring to consider the song of the vineyard (Isa. 5:1, 2) as a love song with a funeral mood, acknowledges that others (e.g., Clements, Kaiser, Yee, Williams, Sheppard, Fohrer) consider Isa. 5:1–7 to also be a legal indictment. "Jean Dao," 3 (1995): 77–94. Meanwhile, Hannes Olivier of the University of Stellenbosch (which is located in an environment where many vineyards are cultivated) presented a "more informed reading of Isaiah's "Song of the Vineyard." He did not approach this passage with the intent to rigorously apply literary criticism or historical analysis but rather to focus on the interrelationship of archaeology and history. Hence his title "God, as Friendly Patron: Reflections on Isaiah 5:17," *In Die Skriflig* 30, no. 3 (1996): 293–303.

13. The phrase "curse of the covenant" does not appear in Isaiah 1–6. The punishments and judgments that are pronounced reflect an awareness of the curses that Moses had warned would come as a result of disobedience (cf. Deut. 27:15–26; 28:15–68; 29:16–28; 31:17–22; 32:19–38). Cf. Geoffrey W. Grogan's comments on Isaiah's reminding his audience (hearers/readers) of the spiritual and moral causes of the anarchy and disaster to come; Grogan added, "writers have noted . . . the way of retribution . . . common in the prophets." "Isaiah," in *The Expositor's Bible Commentary,* 12 vols., general ed. Frank R. Gabelein (Grand Rapids: Zondervan, 1986), 6:31, 42.

14. J. Ridderbos, commenting on this passage, 1:5ff, reminds readers that as one considers Isaiah's preaching, it is correct to remember that though the term *bekeering* (conversion) seldom appears in prophecies, the basic intent of speaking of the curses that had and were to be carried out was to move the people "hun zonde te laten" (to leave their sins) and acknowledge that forgiveness was offered. *Jesaja,* in *Het Godswoord der Profeten* (Kampen: Kok, 1932), 2:180.

15. Cf. Young who wrote that the mighty tree (not oak as NIV has) "that stood forth in all its glory and beauty of its foliage, would be fading and a reason for shame because it would easily catch fire" *Isaiah,* 1:92. Attention should be given how Isaiah combines aspects of the cultural and social dimensions of life to highlight the spiritual and moral blight and disaster of the covenant people.

16. Cf. R.B.Y. Scott's comments on the rapacity of the rulers, i.e., elders, princes, magistrates, court officials, and army officers who had betrayed and exploited those under their care. Social injustice as well as idolatry were sure reasons for the curse of the covenant to be carried out. "Isaiah," 190. Cf. also Jason W. Locke, "The Wrath of God in the Book of Isaiah," *Restoration Quarterly* 35, no. 4 (1993): 221–33. Locke discussed topics such as "Causes of God's Wrath," "Purpose of Objects," and "Tools for Disbursing God's Wrath."

17. Delitzsch opined that women prepared to support themselves, did all they could to avoid the reproach of not being married and being childless. *Isaiah,* I:150.

18. See John D. W. Watts, who wrote that the messenger plays an active role in the hardening and dulling so that repentance will not follow. He referred to God hardening Pharaoh's heart as a close parallel (Exod. 8:11). *Word Biblical Commentary, Isaiah 1:33* (Waco: Word, 1985), 24:75.

19. Cf. George Buchanan Gray, who wrote that it is difficult to discover an English equivalent that is etymologically justifiable and suitable to the context. His choice for the niphal use in v. 18 is "reprove one another." He does not prefer to consider a lawsuit as providing the context. *The Book of Isaiah—i–xxxix* (Edinburgh: T & T Clark, 4th printing, 1956), 26–28.

20. Ibid., 27.

21. Cf. Young, *Isaiah,* 756. Cf. also Oswalt, who, when discussing the statement if sins are as scarlet and become white, if red, become like wool, indicate that forgiveness will be given when there is a changed attitude in the judicial setting. *Isaiah 1–33,* 101.

22. Cf. Delitzsch, *Prophecies of Isaiah,* 2:117.

23. Oswalt, *Isaiah 1–33,* 119, wrote that Isaiah used the example of the Gentiles to move God's people to a holy jealousy, that is, if they come to the light, we ought also to do so. It is possible that Isaiah was trying to motivate the covenant people to leave their foolish rebellion by referring to what the nations will do. It seems more in keeping with the thrust of Yahweh's prescription for the covenant people to be a blessing to the nations that this "invitation" to walk in the light was a call to obedient service to Yahweh and all nations.

24. See the introduction to chap. 5 for some comments on the man Isaiah.

25. See succeeding discussion of the term and reference.

26. Cf. *MROT* for a discussion of the branch and the stump, 519–21. For additional discussion of these terms, cf. part III.

27. The term *judgment* could be replaced by *justice;* the idea expressed is that of executing justice. Translators have written fire instead of burning. The term *bāʿēr* is the piel. inf. of *baor,* to burn, hence the Hebrew specifically refers to an intense burning by fire that will cleanse Jerusalem of its violence and resultant bloodshed.

28. The NIV does not translate *rûaḥ* as Holy Spirit, nor does the RSV or the KJV. Oswalt writes that it is not possible to be dogmatic in the interpretation of *rûaḥ, Isaiah,* 148. He preferred to think of the term as referring to a phenomenon such as "spirit of confusion" (Isa. 19:14), but he correctly added that many commentators, both liberally and conservatively oriented, opt for a reference to the Holy Spirit. For reasons to consider reference to be to the Holy Spirit and not to a blast of judgment and fire as Grogan suggests, *Isaiah,* 46, see J. Ridderbos, *Jesaja,* 103–4; Young, *Isaiah,* 1:181–84.

29. Since much of the language used is symbolic, employing terms that Isaiah's audience understood, it is not warranted to speak of this being literally fulfilled in the supposed millennial period after Christ's coming.

30. See the interpretation of Mic. 4:1–5 in chap. 22.

31. The prophet Hosea had also experienced the unfaithfulness of his wife. (Hos. 1–3).

32. Cf. *Theological Wordbook of the Old Testament,* ed. R. Laird Harris (Chicago: Moody, 1980) for a succinct discussion of the term *'ôt* (vol. 1, 18) and the term *nēs* (vol. 2, 583–84).

33. For differing views regarding the application of Isa. 11:10, 12, see Young, *Isaiah,* 1:393–96; Oswalt, *Isaiah 1–33,* 286: "vs. 10 primary focus of the passage seems to be on the historical nation of Israel . . . some great final ingathering." (Note Oswalt's use of the term "seems.") Grogan is definite, the reference is to the end times. "Isaiah," 90.

34. Cf. the study of Isa. 7:1–17 in *Messianic Revelation,* 621–37.

35. *Isaiah,* 2:408.

36. Young pointed out that the term *covenant* as used in 42:6 and 49:8 should not be thought of as a pact or agreement between two parties but as a bestowal of divine grace. *Isaiah,* 3:120.

37. A discussion of the duration of the covenant could include a detailed exposition of Isaiah's eschatology. At this juncture reference will be only to the references of duration; Isaiah's contribution to prophetic eschatology will be discussed in part IV.

38. Cf. Young, *Isaiah,* 2:282, 283, for his comments on the covenant with death.

39. See chap. 26, in which Ezekiel's proclamation concerning the covenant of peace is discussed.

40. Cf. *Messianic Revelation,* 518–664.

41. See discussion in the preceding concerning the Banner, the Root of Jesse, who would gather nations. See also Joel's prophecy concerning in chap. 19.

42. See part IV of this chapter.

43. A sampling of what is on library shelves demonstrates the wide range of subjects involved in narrative/narration aspects of the Scriptures. G. Fackre, "Narration Theology," *Interpretation* 37, no. 83 (1983): 340–52; *Why Narrative? Readings in Narrative Theology,* ed. Stanley Hauerwas and L. Gregory Jones (Grand Rapids: Eerdmans, 1989); Alexander Rofe, *The Prophetical Stories* (Jerusalem: Magnes, 1988); Wesley A. Kort, *Story, Text and Scripture—Literary Interests in Biblical Narrative* (University Park: Pennsylvania University Press, 1988); Hugh White, *A Narration and Discourse in the Book of Genesis* (Cambridge: University Press, 1991); Alister McGrath, *A Passion for Truth* (Downers Grove: InterVarsity, 1996), 105.

44. McGrath, *A Passion for Truth,* 105.

45. Ibid., 107.

46. Ibid., 113.

47. Ibid., 121. It hardly seems correct to posit just two approaches, that of narrative or a collection of doctrines. Many evangelicals take the grammatical, historical, and theological approach and agree that God revealed himself as he communicated his word in a variety of literary styles: history, poetry, liturgical formulas, ethical principles, hymns, letters, maxims, proverbs, and in a love song.

48. As, for example, in the author's work *Messianic Revelation in the Old Testament.*

49. Fackre, "Narration Theology," 343.

50. Kort, *Story,* 4, 9. He also wrote: "I take exception to almost all that is currently being said about these matters—but the topic itself is less controversial." 4. See also Kort's first chapter "Narrative: A Reassessment," 6–23.

51. Johann Baptiste Metz, "A Short Apology of Narrative," trans. D. Smith, in *Why Narrative,* 251–62.

52. Rofe, *Prophetical Stories,* 13–51.

53. The biblical instances of prophetic materials discussed are Macaiah Son of Imlah, the book of Jonah, the Man of God at Bethel, Elijah and Baal, and Jeremiah as evidence of the rise of matyrology. Ibid., 192–213.

54. Narrative theology can be assessed as arising from two specific phenomenon, as mentioned before: treating the Scriptures as predominantly a source book of doctrines and of considering it basically a literary, historical product of national and religious life.

55. This reality does not preclude the efforts that some scholars make to establish that Isaiah's prophesies should be considered to belong to the narrative genre. This can be expected in view of what was done in the past, when form criticism was in its heyday. Continued literary study of the Old Testament has shown that some aspects of form criticism can be useful but not to the extent it was applied. This is the case also with rhetorical criticism, which some have tried to apply too rigorously with the result that emphases on content and some loss of it occurred. This is the case with an over application of rhetorical criticism to the New Testament. Cf. Jeffrey Weima, "What Does Aristotle Have to Do with Paul?, 32 (1997): 458–68.

56. Recall that Walther Eichrodt wrote that Israel became aware of its covenantal relationship to God by means of its experience and reflection on that experience, which was viewed as factual history. *Theology of the Old Testament,* trans. J. A. Baker (Philadelphia: Westminster, 1961), 36–44.

57. Cf. note 40. Carl. E. Amerding, writing on the subject of "Images for Today," presented by Isaiah, did not distinguish between Yahweh God and the Mediator's Son when he wrote "Yahweh as Savior, Healer, Restorer, Cleanser, Branch, Root, Stump, Suffering Servant." These terms all refer quite specifically to the Messiah. Cf. chap. 9 in *Studies in Old Testament Theology* (Dallas: Word, 1992), 177.

58. The question can arise, will the messianic Mediator not judge righteousness according to evidence? Grogan replies that judgment will be made according to inner qualities of character. "Isaiah," 88. This is not a very helpful comment. Oswalt wrote that this statement makes reference to the messianic judge as more than a human character because this judge will go deeper and pierce beneath appearances. *Isaiah,* 1:280–81. Young commented that Isaiah proclaimed that the king who is judge will be judging completely, unlike any other ruler on David's throne, for he will have absolute knowledge and thus be able to execute absolute justice. *Isaiah,* 1:384.

59. Warran C. Young wrote that it is necessary to look to the Old Testament for a full understanding of the concept of redemption. The Greek does not have a specific term and therefore translates the Hebrew terms as *luō,* to loosen; a derived term form *luō* is *latron,* referring to the price paid for loosing. Cf. *Baker Encyclopedia of the Bible,* 2 vols., ed. Walter A. Elwell (Grand Rapids: Baker, 1988), 2:1827–29.

60. Isaiah used the term *pādâh* four times (1:27 in reference to Zion; 29:22 in reference to Abraham; 35:10; 51:11 in reference to people). The verb has the basic sense of ransom, that is, to pay the purchase price.

61. Grogan is correct when he wrote that as God had done great deeds when Egypt's power was destroyed and Israel entered their promised land, so the people would again enter their land and have Jerusalem as their city. "Isaiah," 295.

62. *Isaiah,* 31.

63. Grogan, "Isaiah," 29.

64. John D. W. Watts "Images of Yahweh: God in the Prophets," in *Studies in O.T. Theology,* 136.

65. See this author's comments on "Isaiah's Personal History" in *Messianic Revelation,* 509.

66. Young, *Isaiah,* 1:3.

67. Cf. Ps. 93, which speaks of these four distinct elements.

68. Isaiah did not clearly distinguish between Yahweh God the Father and the messianic Mediator Son as the New Testament does. After the incarnation the Messiah's appearance, presence, and activities are more clearly specified.

69. Cf. the previous chapter, in which the prophetic messages were addressed to and about the nations.

70. See my discussion of Satan's parasite dominion in *From Creation to Consummation,* (*FCTC*) vol. I, chap. 5, part III. "The Parasite Kingdom" (Sioux Center: Dordt, 1996), 102–4.

71. Watts suggested that in visions, the name *'ădōnây* is preferred because it seems to have a special intention. *Isaiah 1–33,* note 1b, 68. In his comment section he suggests that the name, attendants, and setting stress authority, 74. See also Ridderbos, *Het Godswoord,* 2:86.

72. Scott, "Isaiah," 207.

73. Scott, ibid., believes Isaiah was participating as an official prophet in the worship ceremonies; Young states that we have no means of knowing where he was when the vision came to him. *Isaiah,* 1:236. Delitzsch believes Isaiah, in vision, was carried into heaven. *Isaiah,* 1:189. Ridderbos believed Isaiah spoke anthropomorphically as one would who was in a state of ecstasy while in the entrance to the temple in Jerusalem.

74. *Godswoord,* 2:30.

75. See Grogan, "Isaiah," 242, 243, and Young, *Isaiah,* 3:486–89 for exegetical comments on Isaiah 63:15–19 in which Yahweh could be interpreted to be the cause of his covenant people's sin and distress. Readers do well to consider what Yahweh God informed Isaiah when he was called to prophesy to a people who would hear and not understand and whose hearts would become calloused under Isaiah's preaching (6:9, 10).

76. The terms *mašāl, radâh, śar, ba'al, šapat,* while expressing the concept of having authority, do not as a rule, express absolute authority and control.

77. The psalmists stress the royalty, the kingship of Yahweh God, and his exercise of his kingship (Pss. 9:7; 47:8; 93:1; 96:10; 97:1; 99:1).

78. Cf. section II of this chapter, "The Covenant in Isaiah."

79. John D. W. Watts used the term *image* in his chapter 7 on "Images of Yahweh: God in the Prophets," *Studies on Old Testament Theology,* 136–46. He wrote "Images of God proliferate—husband, parent, planter, forester, host, and so on; they are outgrowths of two metaphors: Yahweh is King and Yahweh is the Divine Spirit." 146.

80. Delitzsch wrote that God gave this "by opening an inner sense for the supersensuous whilst the action of the outer sense was suspended." *Isaiah,* 1:189. Young wrote: "In a mysterious manner the power of God came over the prophet . . . with an inner eye he saw what God revealed . . . it was objective . . . not a product of Isaiah's mind." *Isaiah,* 1:236. Scott wrote: "it was the intensified spiritual perception of noble minds" but he went on to say that visions did not originate with men; "they themselves were sure God had spoken to . . . through them." *Isaiah,* 206.

81. Cf. discussion of the covenantal mediator above, part III, esp. D.

82. Various terms employed to reveal the incomprehensible divine One who is also our brother in the flesh speak simultaneously to his two natures, e.g., as servant he is both divine and human, so also as sin bearer.

83. J. Ridderbos, commenting on this passage, wrote that when Isaiah heard the glorious outcome of God's ways with Israel, in holy enthusiasm he exclaimed what Isaiah 45:15 records. Ridderbos added that God, "who conceals himself, not in the sense that he speaks in secret (v. 19) but in the sense that he and his work are cloaked in mystery impenetrable by the human mind." *Isaiah,* in Bible Students Commentary, trans. John Vriend (Grand Rapids: Zondervan, 1985), 412. One should wonder if J. Alec Motyer was correct when he wrote that Isaiah made the exclamation when "the Lord's ways suddenly become clear." *The Prophecy of Isaiah* (Downers Grove: InterVarsity, 1993), 363. John N. Oswalt elaborated on the critical views regarding the context and who the speaker was. He concluded that the nations were speaking at once of "the ineffable transcendence of God and of his revealed presence as Savior of the world, God of Israel, Savior." *The Book of Isaiah, Chapters 40–66* (Grand Rapids: Eerdmans, 1998), 217. The view that the nations spoke this testimony regarding God is very problematic. It is true that Isaiah included a reference to the nations, but not as the speakers but as people included in Yahweh God's salvation purposes. Roger R. Kellar, in an essay entitled "Karl Barth's Treatment of the Old Testament as Expectation," wrote that Barth said "that God is hidden in the O.T. and N.T. means that God is not present to his people as they expect or wish him to be." Kellar added that Barth wrote that for the servants of God, Moses, Jeremiah, the Servant, in their sufferings "had to show that the God who loves Israel is a hidden God from the world and radically at odds with the judgments and values of this world." Cf. *Andrews University Seminary Studies* 35, no. 2 (autumn 1997): 171, 172. It would seem that, if Kellar is correct in understanding Barth, the idea of revelation comes through far less clearly than human views and expectations do. For a Jewish perspective, see Josiah Derby, "Isaiah and Cyrus," *Jewish Biblical Quarterly* 24 (1996): 173–77.

84. Cf. Ridderbos, *Isaiah,* 76.

85. The various terms used, *high, exalted,* are in a real sense synonymous with the terms translated *majesty* and *splendor.*

86. Cf. the author's comments on these terms when writing about the prescriptions for the tabernacle, the palace of the king that was to be built in the desert. *From Creation to Consummation,* 1363.

87. Cf. *FCTC* for a brief discussion of holiness in the context of Yahweh's prescription for the tabernacle, priesthood, and worship. 363–64.

88. Gerhardus Vos, *Biblical Theology,* 11th printing (Grand Rapids: Eerdmans, 1948), 245–50.

89. Eichrodt has written that the definition of "holiness lies not in its elevated moral standard but in the personal quality of God to which it refers." *Theology,* 1:276. Gerhard Von Rad, discussing the first commandment, stated that "this commandment, God's zeal-jealousy and holiness are inseparable in concept." He went on to write that God is "the source of all that is holy" and therefore holiness cannot be deduced in any way "from other human standards of value." *Old Testament Theology,* trans. D.M.C. Stalker (Edinburgh: Oliver and Boyd, 1962), 203–7.

90. Vos, *Biblical Theology,* 248.

91. Ibid.

92. Cf. chap. 23.

93. The term *omnipotent* does not appear in modern translations. It occurs once in the KJV, Rev. 19:6, Lord God omnipotent reigns.

94. Vos, *Biblical Theology,* 238.

95. See E. Young on the interpretation of the Hebrew terms *merōb 'ô nîm wĕ 'ammaṡ kōaḥ Isaiah,* III: 63.

96. The Hebrew word *host* has a variety of references—to armies, spiritual agents, all the stars, and all that exists within the created cosmos, including heaven.

97. Vos, *Biblical Theology,* 239.

98. Translators of the NIV have added to the uncertainty by translating *'ădōnâi* as Sovereign most of the time and *yĕhwâ šĕba'ōt* as God Almighty. Cf. preface of 1978, and 1983 edition, III.

99. Cf. e.g., *FCTC,* vol. 1, 121, note 33:136; 219–20, *MROT,* 550–51. Cf. also Vos, *Biblical Theology,* 250.

100. Joseph Muutuki, a Th.M. candidate at Covenant Theological Seminary, made me more aware when I was his advisor, than I had been, of Isaiah's use of the masculine and feminine forms of the noun. After a careful study and evaluation of the views presented in a long list of bibliographical references, the conclusions reached were that if there were differences in meaning, they were minimal. It is especially evident that the masculine and feminine forms were used interchangeably (cf. Isa. 51:1, 57, the feminine, and 6, 8, masculine).

101. In Old Testament times men in various walks of life wore girdles, sometimes referred to as belts. The girdle consisted of linen, leather, or wool. It was about five inches wide; it was used as an undergarment and as a receptacle for coins, food, knives, and other such objects. A main advantage of the girdle was that it sustained and gave stability to the worker, soldier, and traveler in the narrow, and often weakest, part of one's back.

102. Cf. Oswalt, *Isaiah 40–66,* 403–4. Three views have been set forth: (1) the servant can make many righteous because of the servant's knowing, that is, what he has experienced; (2) by the knowing of him, that by a faith relationship; (3) that the Hebrew root *yd'* can be interpreted as "to humble," thus by his humiliation. Oswalt concludes that the Servant by "a sense of his accomplishment and satisfaction." Ridderbos states that the phrase "by his knowledge" indicates that he is thought of as the *profeet-leeraar* (prophet-teacher). *Jesaja,* 413.

103. The distinction between righteousness and justice has been blurred by two factors: (1) lack of understanding the difference and (2) that some languages, such as Spanish, do not have a specific term for each concept. Also in Dutch, justice is translated into *gerechtigheid* (righteousness).

104. For additional problems in understanding the biblical use and references of these terms, see the essay by Robert Culver on these terms in *The Theological Wordbook of the Old Testament,* ed. R. L. Harris (Chicago: Moody, 1980), 2: 947–49. See also Gerald J. Janzen's essay, "On the Moral Nature of God's Power: Yahweh, and the Sea in Job and Deutero-Isaiah" *Catholic Biblical Quarterly* 56 (July 1994). Janzen referred to *mišpat* and *zedeq* as Yahweh's virtues; i.e., they are evidence of morality. 474.

105. The precise meaning of *mišpāt* in Isaiah is not readily discerned. The context must be consulted in almost all cases to determine whether the most correct translation is judgment or justice. A consultation of Isaiah 9:7 (MT 9:6) reveals confusion; the KJV translated judgment, the 1962 New Dutch translation has *recht* (right); the RSV, NEB, and NIV have justice. The LXX translates *mišpāt as dikaiosione,* which in Arndt and Gingrich's Lexicon is translated uprightness, justice, righteousness. In the *Englishman's Hebrew and Chalic Concordance of the Old Testament* the forty-one appearances of *mišpāt* are translated judgment, except twice it is translated *right* and twice as *ordinance.*

106. Calvin's commentary on Isaiah 30:18 noted that the prophet adds a word of consolation after prophesying concerning the destruction to come. The godly people are not to be thrown into despair. *Isaiah,* 2:366.

107. James B. Smart, *History and Theology in Second Isaiah* (Philadelphia: Westminster, 1965), 158.

108. The NIV incorrectly translates this term as "the Lord's chosen ally."

109. See commentators who consider the prophecy to refer to Cyrus. Oswalt, *Isaiah 40–66:* "the Lord loves him is an expression of the election of Cyrus" and "it is a climactic expression of the chosenness of Cyrus," 276. Motyer, *Isaiah:* "The title is an interesting anticipation of the Cyrus Cylinder account," 380. Grogan, *Isaiah:* "this makes explicit . . . that Cyrus' work would bring down Babylonia," "Cyrus' work is a harbinger of a far greater deliverance" "brought by the mysterious person referred to in 48:16." 430. Ridderbos, *Isaiah:* "Cyrus will capture Babylon," he is referred to as the one the Lord loves; the Lord's favor is with him" (a reference to common grace?). 430. Young, *Isaiah:* "who is the object of Yahweh's love for Israel or Cyrus? Without question, the majority of interpreters refer the passage to Cyrus. Young went on to write that "this love is not saving love but a reference to Yahweh's having him as an object of affection and to serve him in the conquest of Babylon. 3:256, 257.

110. Cf. the discussion in part II, esp. point A.

111. Assyria, Isaiah said, would be Yahweh God's rod of anger (10:5). When Assyrian troops attacked it would be as if a broad stream of molten lava was burning all before it.

112. In addition to the passages discussed, Isaiah referred to anger nineteen more times and to wrath eighteen more times. Cf. essay by Jason W. Locke, "The Wrath of God in the Book of Isaiah," *Restoration Quarterly* 35, no. 4 (1993): 221–233.

113. In the NIV the term is translated jewel, that is, that which is beautiful. The term has also been translated glory, honor, pride.

114. Cf. Young, *Isaiah,* 2: 170, who correctly translated beauty to the righteous.

115. *kābêd* (glory) as a verb is translated as rich, heavy, sore (battle was sore or fierce, Judg. 20:34; 1 Sam. 31:3), to be honorable (Isa. 8:5; 23:8, 9; 43:4) or to honor (43:4; 58:13); to glorify (24:15; 25:3). As an adjective it has been translated as *laden* or *loaded* with iniquity (1:4), *as great* expressing the idea of great weight (of a rank, 32:2) or greatness (of an army, 36:2). As a noun *kābôd* is translated glory. The NIV translated men of glory as "men of rank" almost consistently (5:13).

116. A review of some of the extant literature that presents the attempts to interpret Isaiah's eschatology reveals differences in approaches to and interpretation of Isaiah's prophecies concerning the future. There are specific and concentrated studies such as John Goldingay's essay "What Happens to Mr. Babylon in Isaiah 47, Why and Who Says So?" *Tyndale Bulletin* 47 (1996): 215–43. Yahweh spoke because Mr. Babylon acted like a man who showed no compassion. Steven J. McMichael's essay, "Did Isaiah Foretell Jewish Blindness and Suffering for Not Accepting Jesus of Nazareth as Messiah? A Medieval Perspective," *Biblical Theological Bulletin* 26 (1996): 144–51. McMichael concluded that medieval interpretation of Isaiah shows "how a certain type of exegesis can lead to anti-Judaism." Mark E. Biddle, "The City of Chaos at the New Jerusalem: Isaiah 24–27," in Context," *Perspectives in Religious Studies,* 22 (1995): 5–12. Isaiah, employing a nascent apocalypticism, portrays two cities that cannot exist side by side; Babylon must cease if Jerusalem is to exist. See also Samuel Pagaan, "Apocalyptic Poetry: Isaiah 24–27," *Apuntes* 15 (1995) 14–27. Written in a Hispanic context, Isaiah 24–27 becomes a basic text of hope for the Hispanic church. Isaiah 24–27 is one of the first texts to present the transition from prophecy to apocalyptic, maintaining historical contacts it develops cosmic levels. Robert Chrisholm, "The Everlasting Covenant and the 'City of Chaos': Intentional Ambiguity and Irony in Isaiah 24," *Criswell Theological Review* 6 (1993): 237–53. Since Genesis 1:2 does not mention covenant, the Noachic covenant cannot be broken, and the Sinaitic covenant (Exod. 19) is not eternal, Isaiah's eternal covenant includes all people and Israel.

117. Uzziah (2 Chron. 26) was also known as Azariah (2 Kings 15:1). He reigned fifty-two years, suffered from leprosy, and died in the year 740 B.C.

118. Various commentators reveal views that differ from the view presented in the sketch and explanatory comments because of their eschatological preferences. The passages that speak concerning the future of Israel and Judah are often explained in such a way that the return from the exile also can refer to a regathering of the Jewish people and the establishment of a Jewish theocratic kingdom. This view will be discussed and evaluated in succeeding chapters.

119. John Oswalt, "Judgement and Hope: The Full Orbed Gospel," *Trinity Journal* 17 (1996): 191–202.

24

Habakkuk and Zephaniah

The End is Near

Part I: Habakkuk

I. Introductory Comments

II. The Message of Habakkuk

Part II: Zephaniah

I. Introductory Comments

II. The Three Strands

III. Joel's Themes

24

Habakkuk and Zephaniah

The End is Near

Habakkuk

Introductory Comments

The Redemptive Historical Context

The prophecy of Habakkuk should be dated between 605 and 598 B.C.[1] There are, however, different views that arise from questions concerning whom Habakkuk spoke to in chapter 1—who are the wicked (1:4) and who is referred to by the term *Chaldeans?* Is the NIV correct to write Babylonians? Or is there a reference to the Assyrians as the external threat?[2] These problems, if they be such, do not really have a bearing on the time of Habakkuk. The Assyrian's capital, Nineveh, had been destroyed in 612 B.C. and the Egyptians had been defeated at Carchemish (Jer. 46:2) in 605 B.C. These victories demonstrated that the NeoBabylonian Empire had become the ruling power in the Mideast. Habakkuk, prophesying while Jehoiakim was king of Judah (609–598), referred to the Babylonian presence that was increasingly felt.[3] They had successfully attacked Jerusalem in 606 B.C. and had taken articles from the temple and some members of royal and noble families. Daniel was one of these (2 Kings 23:34–27:7; Dan. 1:1–7). Since Habakkuk was informed that the Babylonians would be Yahweh God's agent of judgment and since they had already been in Jerusalem, Habakkuk had been able to observe the character and methods of the Babylonians.

The Authenticity of the Prophecy

Before 1948 there were various views concerning Habakkuk as the author of the three chapters. One scholar wrote that looking beneath the surface, there are at least four different kinds of material in this, sufficient to raise the question whether all of them are from one hand.[4] J. Ridderbos opined that Habakkuk had not produced the material orally, that the view that a part of the prophecy was produced as Levitical music for the temple was not supported by the text, and that Jewish legends were worthless. He accepted the text as authentic.[5]

The discovery of the Dead Sea Scrolls in 1948 led to a concentrated study of Habakkuk since it was among the first to be photographed and translated.[6] It was noted that chapter 3 was not included. This has led to much speculation and discussion concerning whether it was an authentic part of the prophecy. An acceptable explanation is as follows: the content of chapter 3 gives strong support for its connection with chapters 1 and 2. Furthermore, chapter 3 is included in the LXX, which can be said to be a contemporary document.[7] Of interest is that a scholar, providing a "form-critical reassessment of the structure, genre, and intent of the book," concluded that it has a "coherent structural unity" and its genre is based on the prophetic pronouncement and a petitionary prayer.[8] In response to critical scholars who have tried to indicate that there is a relationship between Ugaritic poetry and Habakkuk, a biblical scholar made an in-depth study of four brief passages that were used to demonstrate such a relationship. He concluded that the "suggested connection between Habakkuk three and Ugaritic mythology does not seem to be well founded."[9]

We must conclude, on the basis of careful exegetical literary and biblical theological studies, that the text of the book of Habakkuk is authentic and provides us with a unique genre of biblical prophecy.[10]

Is Joel's Agenda Followed?

In view of the literary uniqueness of the book of Habakkuk, the question can be raised: Is the message unique, or does it repeat any parts of Joel's agenda? At the conclusion of this study it will be indicated that Habakkuk does indeed expand, to an extent, on some of the themes.

Are the Three Strands of the Golden Cable Present?

The next question to be asked is: Are the three strands of the Golden Cable present, and if so, how are they to be discerned? The term *king* appears once (Hab. 1:10), but *kingdom* does not, neither does the term *bĕrît* (covenant), *mĕšîaḥ* (anointed) does appear (3:13). It will become very apparent that by implication kingdom and covenant are definitely present; in fact, they form the basic and unifying stratus of the entire prophecy.

Does Habakkuk Present a Moral Problem?

The prophecy of Habakkuk is said by some to raise a moral problem. The question is, Is God fair in his governing of the world? The term *theodicy* speaks to this question. Habakkuk has been referred to the "crisis prophet." Does a crisis situation permit a prophet to complain to God and ask "How long do you wait" and "why?" Is it morally permissible to question Yahweh God in such a way at such a time? Or is it evidence of a prophet engaged as a prayer warrior?[11] It is a fact that nothing is known of Habakkuk the man. He is personally completely hidden behind his prophetic message. No other prophet addressed God so openly and boldly. The question confronting readers is, Can situations become so critical that it is legitimate to question God's ways and timetable? In fact, Habakkuk does more than question; he complains to Yahweh God about his tolerance and his lack of dealing with a terrible situation. Is this to be explained by referring to prophetic privilege? Or is it evidence of a close and intimate relationship between the prophet and Yahweh God? This latter will be shown to be a reality.

The Message of Habakkuk

The Kingdom Context

As stated in the previous section, the term *kingdom* does not appear in the text. But we can confidently point out that the idea is certainly present. Aspects of the cosmic kingdom reveal this. The nations are repeatedly referred to. Habakkuk is told to look to the nations and see with amazement what Yahweh God will do employing the Babylonians (1:5, 6) to deal with Habakkuk's people, Judah. Moreover, all nations and peoples will be affected by the Babylonians. This transpires because all nations (3:6), their kings, rulers, and cities (1:10), including "your people" (3:13), are integral parts of Yahweh God's cosmic kingdom.

Habakkuk leaves no doubt that the kingdom includes all of creation. Reference is to the whole earth, over which the Babylonians will sweep under Yahweh God's direction. And consider how Habakkuk expresses the reality of Yahweh God's reign and control over all creation. He brought plagues and pestilence (3:5). He caused mountains and hills to crumble and collapse (3:6). Streams, rivers, the sea, sun and moon, are all part of the kingdom over which Yahweh God reigns (3:5–12). The inclusive cosmic kingdom is under Yahweh God's reign.

Habakkuk knows Yahweh God as King. He addresses him as *'ĕlōhîm* (1:12), God, who is *yĕhwâ,* the covenant Lord (1:12). He refers to Yahweh God as the famous One (3:2), who personally reveals himself by speaking to Habakkuk (2:2) and who has proven in times past that he knows and determines what to do with man's efforts (2:13). Habakkuk proclaims that all that Yahweh God does as King he does as Savior (3:18). His judgments in the earth are for the purpose of saving and redeeming his people even though they will have to suffer severely because they have rejected and rebelled against their covenant Lord.

In this context one must consider how Habakkuk referred to the virtues and character of Yahweh God, King and Savior.

A reading of Habakkuk's prophecy cannot avoid the prophet's proclamation concerning two attributes: Yahweh God's holiness and wrath. These, however, must be considered in the context of the ten other virtues Habakkuk proclaimed.

Habakkuk had lamented that he saw no evidence of Yahweh God's concern about the wickedness so prevalent among Yahweh's people. As a member of the city and nation, he had cried out to Yahweh God that he had to see and endure injustice, wrong, violence, strife, and conflict. It seemed as if ears were closed to his cries and prayers and that there was no divine concern. Then when he learned of Yahweh God's plan to employ the Babylonians as a means of judgment, Habakkuk was shocked and cried out, Yahweh, my God, *qĕdōšî* (my holy one). And he added, your eyes are too pure to use a treacherous, wicked, unrighteous means to bring judgment upon your people, wicked and unrighteous as they are, but not to the extent your chosen agent is. Your instrument of judgment will execute excessive punishment.[12] How can you, as the Holy One, tolerate that?

Habakkuk, as Isaiah had also demonstrated (6:5), had a strong reaction. Isaiah had declared his own unworthiness to stand before and serve the Holy One. Habakkuk, however, fully aware of Yahweh God's holiness, had based his assurance that the sins of his people would be dealt with because of Yahweh God's holiness, purity, and intolerance for sin and wickedness. The very reality of divine holiness had led him to cry out to Yahweh God for justice, correction, and righteousness. Habakkuk, with his concept of holiness, which served as a basis for his cry for justice and righteousness, could not understand why Yahweh God would call upon and use the more treacherous and violent Babylonians. This was contrary to holiness, which connotes purity, separation from sin, maintaining divine sanctity. Hence he is emboldened to address Yahweh God in a most unusual way. He remonstrated with his Lord. Will you not betray, or at least, diminish your holiness using such a means?

After Yahweh God had revealed that he, the Holy One, would severely punish the Babylonians (2:6–19), Habakkuk, in his prayer, recalls that God the Holy One, had come down and dealt with the Egyptians in such a way that the covenant people had been delivered from slavery (3:3). Yahweh God, the Holy One, had employed an idol-worshiping and slave-driving people to give Israel the protection and security required to become numerous enough to become a nation. The Holy One, with pure eyes and intolerance for wickedness, had in the past made a wicked people serve him, gave them the opportunity to either acknowledge the Lord or increase their wickedness. As the Egyptians had increased their wickedness and violence, so the Babylonians would also as servants carrying out Yahweh God's justice.

Habakkuk, in his prayer, referred to the wrath of Yahweh God three times (3:2, 8, 12). When he had not heard or seen a response to his initial cries, he did not fully realize that Yahweh God had the power to hide himself in silence.[13] This silence, Habakkuk later realized, did not indicate that Yahweh God, the Holy One, was not angry or wrathful against all wickedness and violence. The reality was that Yahweh God, in his burning revulsion against these sins, would reveal it whenever he executed judgment, whether on the Babylonians or on Judah. Habakkuk asked the rhetorical question: Was the wrath against streams, the sea, horses, chariots (3:8)?

No, the wrath would, as it had in the past, be executed on the nations as Yahweh God "strode through the earth" (3:12). Indeed, Yahweh God would demonstrate his wrath against his covenant people also (3:12). This would be done according to the divinely determined timetable and not according to that of a concerned, but impatient prophet who has been referred to as complaining and disputatious.[14]

It should be emphasized that Habakkuk's reference to Yahweh God's holiness and wrath does not diminish or put into question the other virtues of Yahweh God, the King in his administration of his cosmic kingdom. Yahweh God's justice is not negated when judgment is postponed; according to the prophet, it will be fully executed. Yahweh God, the eternal and everlasting one, is not beholden to time as people are (1:12). He does not compromise his eternal character when he seems to be tolerant (1:12, 13). He remains as steadfast as a Rock (1:12) in spite of the prophet's wondering about them. Yahweh God is omniscient, he is completely aware of what the Babylonians are like and what they do (1:7–11) and therefore knows how they will serve him as agents of judgment who in turn will be severely judged for being and doing according to their treachery and inhuman violence. Can there be divine mercy for Yahweh God's people when the Babylonians serve as executors of divine justice and judgement? The prophet prays for this and does so in an expectant manner: "in your rage, or wrath, remember mercy." The Hebrew term for mercy here is not *ḥesed,* but *raḥēm* (piel inf. of *rāḥam,* to have compassion). A related term is *rehem* (womb). The thought here is that as a mother is filled with love for the fruit of her womb that is suffering, so the plea is that Yahweh God, while executing his raging wrath, will remember with love and compassion the people to be punished. This does not mean that Habakkuk pleads with Yahweh God to be sparing of his children, but that he upholds in love and pity even while he brings deserved judgment upon the loved one.[15] As the omnipotent one, who can make mountains tremble and seas part, he can and will hear and do as the prophet pleads with his Lord. He concluded his prayer by expressing his confidence that Yahweh God, the sovereign ruler, will do so and so doing, give the prophet strength (3:19).

Habakkuk gave beautiful expression to the overall result of Yahweh God's dealing with sinful humanity in the midst of the created cosmos. He demonstrates his splendor, which is like the sunrise flashing forth rays of light (3:4). And thus the glory of the Lord is known (2:14) as it is spread out over the heavens and given expression in the earth (3:3).

In the preceding study of Yahweh God, the King's personality and virtues, there were references to Habakkuk's awareness of the reign of the King over his cosmos, especially over nations and his own people. The evidence in Habakkuk's proclamation concerning Yahweh God's reign are implied in various instances.

First, in the reply to Habakkuk's first complaint (1:2–4), Yahweh God refers to his reign over Babylon, stating, "I am raising up the Babylonians" (1:6) and he proceeded to tell Habakkuk that he knew what they were like. Habakkuk realized that Yahweh God was King over the Babylonians, for he replied, *lĕmišpāt sanitô*

(For judgment you have set, placed, or appointed him). The sovereignty of Yahweh God is thus expressed—he rules over all.[16]

Second, Yahweh God demonstrated his reign over Habakkuk. He commanded him to write what was revealed concerning Yahweh God's intent to have the Babylonians serve him by being an agent of judgment. The woes that were declared (2:6, 9, 12, 15, 19) made even more clear and definite that reigning Yahweh knew whom he was appointing and what their end was to be. Habakkuk obeyed; he wrote.

Third, Yahweh God had revealed his kingship when the exodus took place. Habakkuk reviews that great event and as he reflected on what the result of a Babylonian invasion would be, he proclaimed his assurance that his reigning Lord would prove to be his savior (3:18).

A point to be stressed at the conclusion of this study on the kingdom as revealed in Habakkuk's prophecy is the reality of judgment to be executed (1:5, 6; 2:4–20). As King, Yahweh God is the judge and what he judges to be the necessary sentence, and the manner of its execution, will certainly eventuate because he is the King of the cosmic kingdom in which his judgments upon Judah and Babylon are and will be executed.

Having studied Habakkuk's proclamation that the cosmic kingdom was the context over which Yahweh God the King reigned and of which he is the supreme Judge, the question that calls for an answer now is, Did Habakkuk refer to the covenant?

Aspects of the Covenant

The term *bĕrît* does not appear in the Hebrew text of Habakkuk and the term *covenant* does not appear in any English text. Do these omissions indicate that Habakkuk was unaware of the covenant, or if he was, did he consider it an unimportant reality or concept?[17]

At this point in our study it may be profitable to repeat a few basic aspects of the concept of covenant. It refers to an established relationship between Yahweh God and the object of his immediate concern, the created cosmos (Gen. 8:22–9:16) and especially with chosen people, such as, Noah (6:18), Abraham (17:1–7), and David. The relationship is a bond of life and love. It is Yahweh God's means for the administration of the cosmos and the means and channel for redemption. As such, the execution of administration and redemption, there are historical backgrounds, indications of who is involved, promises, stipulations, blessings, curses, assurance of continuity, and oaths involved. These are constituent elements. If there is a reference to one or more of the elements, then it should be clear and obvious that the concept of covenant forms the basic stratum, or is referred as a whole, by an aspect that is mentioned.[18]

When one consults various commentaries, it should surprise no one that the term *covenant* appears quite often.[19] Carl E. Amerding referred to Sinaitic covenant history and God's covenant commitment.[20] David W. Baker referred to the covenant repeatedly; he commented on covenant actions, commitments, violations, obedience obligations, promises, covenant God, and God's covenant promises of an eternal relationship.[21] John Calvin preached that the whole church, consisting of the children of Abraham and their righteousness which is by covenant, is not fictitious.[22] C. F. Keil wrote that "the covenant nation received judgment."[23] Edward Marburg referred to the law that is the covenant.[24] O. Palmer Robertson wrote concerning "the covenant nation" and "covenant curses."[25] Maria E. Szeles wrote that in the Torah the response demanded to the covenant was faith, honor, joy, trust.[26]

Commentators referring to the covenant when commenting on Habakkuk's prophecy certainly have read and understood the prophet's message very well. Habakkuk was a covenant agent (more about this later) and understood his Lord's relationship with and his demands of his covenant people. But he also expressed his expectations concerning Yahweh God's response to a disobedient people. He undoubtedly knew the book of Deuteronomy, which had been brought to the people's attention some years earlier. That book called for love for and obedience and reminded covenant people that Yahweh God would not tolerate a rejection of him or his love as revealed in various ways during the history of Israel/Judah.

Habakkuk addressed God by his covenant name, *yĕhwâ* (1:2–4). His complaint to his Lord was basically that the covenant people were disobedient. Violence, injustice, strife, conflict, destruction were everywhere. Unrighteous wicked men prevented the carrying out of justice. Yahweh God's covenant was broken in many ways because the law, a core aspect of the covenant, was ignored and rejected. The result is that the law is *tāpûg* (qal. pf. 3rd per. masc. of *pûg,* to grow numb, be helpless). Covenant law was not upheld; Yahweh God's prescription for blessings in life was not honored. Two factors deeply troubled Habakkuk: (1) the people's disobedience to the covenant law and to Yahweh God; and (2) the covenant Lord's seeming lack of concern and action to uphold his covenant. Why was there no evidence of divine activity to bring in covenant righteousness and justice?

Yahweh God did respond to his bold, lamenting spokesman (1:5–11). The first thing Habakkuk was to do was to read his newspaper. From it he would learn what his sovereign covenant King was doing. He was raising up the Babylonians. They were defeating the Assyrians and Egyptians. They were marching into small countries and pillaging and murdering. They were militarily well equipped. They had no respect for kings nor could fortified cities stop their advances. Yes, the Lord of the cosmos knew what his covenant people were doing and he was preparing an earthly means to execute the covenant curse (Deut. 4:25–28; 28:15, 25; 30:17, 18).

Habakkuk, in response, became disputatious. He addressed Yahweh God, the eternal, holy, rock-steadfast One as not being faithful to himself. How could the eternal, steadfast, holy One tolerate and, in effect, defile himself by using vile means to bring a mitigated curse upon the chosen covenant people (Deut. 7:1–6)?

Yahweh God's patience was displayed even when Habakkuk challenged him to do what was planned (2:1). He would take the stance of a watchman.[27] He would be ready to see and hear that his covenant Lord was carrying out the affairs of the nations in keeping with his covenant plan, purposes, and administration. Habakkuk wanted to know what Yahweh God's response to his rebuke would be.[28] In response, he receives a *ḥāzôn* (vision or revelation).

The revelation Habakkuk received has five parts. First, as covenant documents in past times were written out, Habakkuk is commanded to write Yahweh God's reply and consider it a covenant document for his and the covenant people's benefit.

Second, Habakkuk was told to be patient. He could be certain that at Yahweh God's appointed time, not in Habakkuk's desired time, what was revealed in word would certainly come to pass. It would not delay when the time had come.

Third, Habakkuk was reproved but given a specific covenant message. He should not be as the agent Yahweh God is preparing—puffed up and having desires that are not upright, in keeping with God's desired attitudes (2:4a). Habakkuk is told how to live the tried and true covenant way (2:4b). The *ṣaddîq* (the righteous one) received instruction. He is to be at one with and within the will of God. There is to be no barrier, be it doubt, uncertainty, or whatever, between the righteous God and his covenant servant. The love bond between them was not to be strained by human failings. The covenant man, called to serve, demonstrates *'emûnâh* (faithfulness). And if this is not present, faith itself is lacking. In effect, Habakkuk is instructed that instead of complaining, disputing, and rebuking, he is to exercise faith. Abraham, when uncertain about receiving a son, was assured that in the future he would have a child. Abraham heard the message, believed it, and trusted Yahweh God would keep his word (Gen. 15:2–6). As Abraham, the covenant man, demonstrated his full reliance on Yahweh God, Habakkuk was to do so also. And this was the message he had to proclaim to his people and write for posterity.

Fourth, Habakkuk is given assurance that Yahweh God is fully aware of his agent's character, habits, and activities (2:5). Five woe statements follow. These have been referred to as five mocking statements that express the just recompense that is sure to come.[29] Each woe refers to a characteristic of the Babylonians. These are not "occasional slips, isolated failings."[30] The judgment on Babylon, once it has served Yahweh's purposes, is sure to be executed. The curse of the covenant cannot be avoided.

Fifth, the closing statement of the vision/revelation drew attention first of all to the great contrast between the idols of the Babylonians and Yahweh God, who is in his holy temple and before whom all the earth is called to silence (2:20). Other prophets also called for silence when divine judgment was to be executed (Zeph. 1:7; Zech. 2:17 [14]). This is the case before us in Habakkuk 2:20. Judgment is to be executed upon Babylon. Yahweh God who dwells in his holy temple brings this judgment. Let all of the cosmos keep silence. The creator, ruler, provider, the sovereign king of the cosmos reigns. His will is righteous; his ways are just. Be silent. Believe. Trust. Obey.

The phrase, "Yahweh is in his holy temple," has raised discussion concerning the specific reference to the holy temple. Some commentators do not give a specific answer to the question: Is the holy temple to be understood as the earthly temple situated in Jerusalem or us God's dwelling and throne in heaven?[31]

Some seem to imply that the reference is to the heavenly abode. Suggested texts to consult are Psalm 11:4, which states, "Yahweh is in his holy temple; Yahweh is on his heavenly throne." Reference is also made to Micah 1:2, which states that all peoples, the whole earth, is to listen to Yahweh who is in his holy temple (or dwelling). The call to all peoples is a call to listen to him who is enthroned in heaven.[32] Some commentators refer specifically to the temple in Jerusalem. Appeal is made to passages such as Isaiah 2:3–4, where it is stated the law will go forth from Zion. Habakkuk 2:1 is explained to refer to the day when Yahweh would rebuke nations from Zion.[33]

A careful consideration of the context of Habakkuk 2:20 should lead one to refuse to make a sharp distinction between the earthly and the heavenly. First of all, in the context reference is to Babylon's idol worship; in distinction from that Judah had the sovereign covenant Lord who had chosen Jerusalem's temple as his dwelling. Judah, therefore, was called to remember that their Yahweh God was their covenant Lord who had his throne and sanctuary in their midst. The people of Judah, however, had to keep in mind that the temple in Jerusalem was a symbolic representation of Yahweh God's eternal heavenly temple. Hence the call to silence was directed to the people of Judah because their covenant Lord, dwelling in their midst, sent out his word from there. But Judah, as well as all nations, including especially Babylon, was to listen to and obey the Lord of all the earth.

We must conclude then that this call to silence before him whose dwelling is in the heavens but is symbolized in actual form on Zion's hill is a call to remember and honor Yahweh God, the covenant Lord of Judah and of the entire cosmos. He has made his will known for all nations; let all nations listen to and obey him.

Chapter 3 has been referred to as a prayer, a poem, and a hymn.[34] It has characteristics of all three. The first verses are prayerlike, the historical preference is poetic, and the conclusion is a hymn of confidence. The entire passage, however, is very covenantal! God is addressed by his covenant name *yĕhwâ* (Exod. 3:14). His fame and deeds are well known. The petition is: renew your past covenant deeds (these are poetically referred to in vv. 3–15). These deeds included demonstrations of wrath, the curse of the covenant. But Yahweh had repeatedly demonstrated *raḥîm* (a motherlike compassion and mercy). The prophet's prayer therefore is not that the curse not be executed, but that it be mitigated. And so it would be when Yahweh God remained compassionate and merciful even as he executed the curse. As a covenant Lord he had done so in the past. He had come to the deliverance of Israel from Egypt as he executed his curse on Egypt and revealed mercy to many. He had shown his might and power in creation when he led his people from Egypt, through the sea and desert, and into the promised land. He removed nations from the path of his people as he led them to their promised inheritance. Indeed, Yahweh God had proven to be a faithful covenant promise keeper. He had delivered his people as nations were crushed and nature obeyed him.

The hymn of confidence (3:16–19) expresses the response of a covenant servant of Yahweh God. He acknowledged that calamity was sure to come through the Babylonians. He expressed his personal reaction: his heart pounded, lips quivered, bones weakened, and legs trembled as he realized the reality of the covenant curse to be executed (Deut. 28:15–68). He submitted to it.

The executed curse, bringing devastation to orchards, vineyards, fields, sheep pens, and cattle stalls, did not and would not shake his confidence in his sovereign covenant Lord. Yahweh would always be his strength (3:20). Therefore, he would continue to be joyful and rejoice. Habakkuk did not sing regarding happiness and merriment. Rather, he sang concerning joy which is rooted in a solid assurance of security. He would remain secure in the bonds of covenant love, grace, and mercy. Material blessings would be taken away, but his covenant sovereign Lord would always be Immanuel: God with us.

The Mediator's Presence

The question can be legitimately asked: Is there a clear reference to the covenant mediator in Habakkuk's prophecy as in other prophets' proclamations? There is no reference to David's royal son or sons. There is no reference to the coming king, the royal priest,[35] the deliverer. Habakkuk made no reference to a personal Messiah.[36]

There is, however, the term *mĕšîḥekâ* (your anointed one) in 3:13. This term is widely used to refer to personal messianic mediation. Does the context support that reference in this passage? Various views appear in commentaries.

Habakkuk was describing how Yahweh God demonstrated his sovereign rule and control over the cosmos and over nations (3:12). The prophet employed strong, descriptive language to refer to how the whole cosmos, and especially the environment, the Sinai desert, responded to Yahweh God's presence and activity in delivering Israel from bondage and leading them to Mount Sinai. This interpretation calls for the anointed one to refer to Israel. Those who object to this conclusion maintain that the covenant people are never referred to elsewhere as "the anointed" one. And the question is raised, does the particle *'et* in the Hebrew text indicate the accusative (the anointed one is object of salvation), or should it be interpreted as *with* (salvation comes with the anointed)?

Three other interpretations have been offered. First, it is said that Cyrus is the anointed one. Isaiah had so referred to him (Isa. 44:28; 45:1). This view calls for Habakkuk to prophesy concerning the future deliverance of the remnant from exile. The particle should also be understood as *with.*

Second, Habakkuk had the Davidic dynasty in view. The promise to David that his house would remain eternally is the broader biblical context for this view. Understood is that the "anointed one" is the object of deliverance. This view could include the people over whom the Davidic house ruled.

Third, the ultimate reference can be understood to be the realization of the assured salvation brought in at the coming of the final messianic king.[37]

A consideration of the various explanations does not detract from the fact that the term translated "anointed" refers first of all and basically to the covenant people. Abraham and his seed were called to be covenant agents to bring blessings to the nations (Gen. 12:1–3). Isaiah emphasized that Jacob, father of the covenant people, was Yahweh God's chosen (44:1–5). They were to be blessed with rain and fertility in the land, and have the Spirit poured upon them. It should be emphasized that the salvation of the covenant people included the assurance that the Davidic kingship would continue, particularly through the promised royal one (Gen. 49:8-12). The commentators who preferred to understand the term *měšîḥekâ* to refer to Cyrus should not be completely dismissed. Cyrus was Yahweh God's appointed agent to bring a remnant back to Jerusalem. The context, however, draws attention to Yahweh God's raising up an agent for executing judgment. Babylon, as a nation, was to be this agent in Habakkuk's time. Babylon was to execute the curse of the covenant. And by so doing, the covenant people would be delivered from their evil ways. Through judgment, carried out by Babylon, salvation would be realized. In this way, Babylon should be considered a messianic agent, first of all as Yahweh God's means to execute a mitigated curse and to deliver them from the evil that had led Habakkuk to question why Yahweh God permitted it to exist among the covenant people.

A third mediatorial agent should not be overlooked. It is the prophet himself. His concern for his people because of their wickedness (1:2–4), and his unique manner of interceding for them (1:12–21) was mediatorial activity. His prophetic proclamation had a unique mediatorial significance at that time just before the exile was to take place. His submission to the judgment to come can be understood to anticipate the Mediator's prayer of submission, "not my will but thine be done" (Luke 22:42).

The question was asked in the first part of this study on Habakkuk if any of Joel's prophetic agenda was included by Habakkuk.[38] The answer is yes! In another work it was pointed out that Habakkuk elaborated on the judgment to come and the sure salvation Yahweh God prepared for his people.[39] Habakkuk particularly elaborated on who the agent of judgment was to be, namely, Babylon. Joel made no such specific reference. As Joel had referred to cosmic forces included in Yahweh God's revelation and redeeming activity, Habakkuk referred to this divine activity in a poetic, yet forceful manner. Habakkuk elaborated on Joel's prophesy concerning judgments to come; Joel had referred to present afflictions (e.g., by locusts). Habakkuk made it clear that the time for the execution of a great judgment was near, very near.

Zephaniah

Introductory Comments

Zephaniah the Prophet

It is generally agreed that Zephaniah had a royal ancestry. Hezekiah, who is mentioned as an ancestor (Zeph. 1:1), was the Hezekiah who reigned from 715 to 686 B.C. Since Zephaniah was a great-great grandson, he was most likely a young man when he prophesied. The name Zephaniah means "Yahweh protects." Does the name indicate that at the time he spoke, protection was necessary? It would seem so.

The Historical Redemptive Context

Commentators[40] and other students of Zephaniah's prophecy agree that the major theme of the prophecy is "Yahweh's Day of Wrath," which was soon to come. His message from Yahweh may not have been readily accepted. Other prophets who spoke against the popular, but Yahweh-rejecting lifestyles had been and would be threatened. Jeremiah is a specific case.

The text tells us Zephaniah prophesied during the reign of Josiah, son of Amon,[41] who had reigned for two years and had followed in his father's (Manasseh) evil ways. Zephaniah could have prophesied in the first eighteen years of Josiah's reign before Deuteronomy was found in the temple (2 Kings 22:1–3). It would seem, however, that Zephaniah prophesied later, that is, after that book was found (22:8). Moses had spoken clearly that should the covenant people disobey and depart from the ways Yahweh laid out for his people, the covenant curse would be executed by Yahweh God because of his wrath (Deut. 29:20, 28).[42] Hilkiah the priest and Huldah the prophetess warned the king and people of Jerusalem and Judah that Yahweh God was going to bring great disaster on "this place and the people" (2 Kings 22:16). After Deuteronomy was found in the temple, Josiah, twenty-six years old, renewed the covenant and removed idolatry and wicked priests from his country as well as from Samaria (23:1–25). It was a reformation that came too late. Yahweh God's wrath continued because of the sins of Josiah's grandfather, Manasseh (23:26, 27). The correct conclusion one should draw then is that Zephaniah could and did prophesy after the book had been found. Deuteronomy gave him biblical warrant for his message that there had to be a cleansing of the land and the revival of God honoring worship.

The Authenticity of the Prophecy

Is the prophet Zephaniah the author of the prophecy? Specifically, can one conclude that he actually wrote his prophecies as recorded in the Hebrew Bible? In reply to the first question, R. K. Harrison wrote that literary analysis that would deny various portions of the prophecy to Zephaniah are "based upon entirely subjective considerstions."[43] In regard to the second question, there is not much agreement. The problem is that there is "a remarkable silence" in prophetic literature about the question of composition.[44] Since writing was common in the time of Zephaniah and since he was of royal lineage, he undoubtedly knew how to write and did write himself. There is no evidence of a scribe or a later editor.

Recent studies of the prophecy of Zephaniah by scholars who have not always demonstrated a consistent conservative attitude toward the text of Zephaniah would have us consider the text from various perspectives. Some outrightly posit, others imply, that postexilic redactors provided the final form of Zephaniah; some emphasize that the Josianic context provided the initial elements. Hence these critical scholars contend that the book of Zephaniah was undergoing a formative process over a period of at least a century.[45] The evidence for this position is not established.

Some scholars have emphasized the reformation of the temple during Josiah's time. Singled out specifically is the liturgical renewal; it is posited that Zephaniah contributed to that part of the renewal. Hence, Zephaniah's work must be considered as a liturgical production. One scholar has entitled his study *Zephaniah, A Prophetic Drama.*[46]

It is of interest to note that methods of interpretation that were preferred and emphasized during previous decades receive little or no attention in recent works on Zephaniah.[47]

Conservative scholars have noted that "recent years have witnessed a burgeoning interest in the phenomenon of intertextuality."[48] This term is employed to refer to later prophets making use of what previous prophets have proclaimed. King wrote that the book of Zephaniah "is deserving of an . . . intertextual investigation."[49] Material from Amos, Hosea, Isaiah, and Micah is clearly present; "the parallels are numerous and sometimes striking."[50]

The question has been raised. Since Zephaniah is concerned with matters relative to the Day of the Lord, a time for judgment for sinful people and purification for the redeemed, and uses threats and exhortations, should his work be considered apocalyptic? Other prophetic passages that emphasize divine intervention followed by a golden age of peace and prosperity in connection with judgment day are considered to be apocalyptic (e.g., Isa. 2:1–22; Ezek. 38–48; Zech. 14:1–21). Since Zephaniah also prophesied concerning similar themes, is Zephaniah's work therefore not also apocalyptic? Richard Patterson considered the question and concluded Zephaniah was preapocalyptic.[51]

Recent studies of Zephaniah's prophecy have provided some helpful insights. It must be emphasized, however, that a review of recent authors who have tried to find specific historical events and literary motiefs provide very little evidence for denying that Zephaniah, during the time of Josiah's attempted reforms based on the book of Deuteronomy, prophesied and wrote his prophecy. The structure of the prophecy supports this position. Zephaniah emphasized the judgment that was sure to come. Yahweh's Day of Wrath was very near for Judah (1:1–2:3). It would not bypass the surrounding nations, Philistia, Moab, Ammon, Ethopia, or Assyria (2:4–15). But there would be consolation and comfort for the covenant people to be realized in the future, after the return from exile (3:1–15).

The Canonical Significance and Role of Zephaniah

When raising the question concerning the presence and role of the Golden Cable in prophecies studied in previous chapters, no reference was made to the canonical aspects. To do so in this study of Zephaniah gives occasion to refer to what B. S. Childs has written on this subject. He posits the view that some, maybe a major part, originated before the exile in Josiah's time. But the book, as it comes to us now, was shaped by postexilic redactors who formulated it around the subject of the Day of Yahweh. Thus the unifying theme is the Day of Yahweh, and the leaders of the Old Testament church gave the book its authority and place in the canon.[52]

Serious objection to Childs's view must be taken. Zephaniah, the prophet, inspired by the Spirit of Yahweh God, prophesied and gave the Old Testament and New Testament church an authoritative and trustworthy message from Yahweh God. It therefore had canonical authority, that is, as part of Yahweh God's revelation to Judah, it was part of the canon and had inherent divine authority. It must be added, however, that Childs was correct to refer to a unifying theme. The problem, however, is that the theme he selected is not satisfactory. Zephaniah did emphasize the Day of Yahweh, especially in the first two chapters. But, in agreement with previous prophets, he developed some of the themes they had presented. These themes were aspects of one or all three of the strands of the Golden Cable: the kingdom, the covenant, and the mediator.

The Three Strands

The Kingdom

The term *kingdom* does not appear in the text. That the concept and reality of Yahweh God's kingdom is present cannot be denied, however.

Yahweh God is King of the entire cosmos. The cosmic kingdom includes the earth (1:2; 3:6, 8); animals, birds of the air, and fish of the sea (1:3); houses and vineyards (1:13); silver and gold (1:18); sheep, sheep pens, and shepherds (2:6); pastures (2:7); flocks and herds (2:14); fowls and wild beasts (2:14, 15). The cosmos includes all nations (2:4–15), their merchants (1:11), their wealth (1:13), their cities (1:16), and their lands (2:9). The idols people have made and worship are part of the cosmos (1:4, 5; 2:11). The reign of Yahweh God over his cosmic kingdom is sovereign and supreme. And Judah is included among the nations (1:4), as is the remnant of Israel (3:13, 14). Jerusalem and Zion are also under his reign (3:14, 16). Yahweh God's cosmic domain and sovereign rule over all aspects of the kingdom is beyond a doubt the setting and context of Zephaniah's prophecy.

The term *king* appears once in Zephaniah's proclamation. He prophesied concerning the king of Israel saying, *melek yiśrāèl yĕhwâ bĕgirbēk* (King of Israel is Yahweh [who] is with you). Yahweh God is the King not only of Israel, Judah, and the nations, but also of the cosmos in its entirety. The attributes of the king that Zephaniah stressed are not new or unique to his message. Other prophets, including Moses, had emphasized these. Zephaniah, however, does strongly emphasize the anger and wrath of Yahweh God and these must be considered in correlation with sovereignty. Yahweh God's anger and wrath will be fully executed as he had his prophets say it would. As sovereign, Yahweh God has complete control over every aspect and detail of the cosmos. He has the power, ability, knowledge, and authority to express and execute his anger and wrath fully. In previous studies of prophetic materials the terms *anger* and *wrath* were discussed in detail. Zephaniah, however, does contribute to a fuller and deeper understanding of these concepts. The term *'aph* (anger) appears six times, with qualifying terms, such as *burning* and *fierce* (2:2; 3:8). These indicate the intensity of Yahweh's anger. The phrase, "by the fire of my jealous anger" (3:8), indicates the basic reason for this anger. It is Yahweh's jealousy. Yahweh is righteously jealous; his love has been ignored and rejected. His people have shown love for other gods. Hence the fire of Yahweh's jealousy is white-hot and is expressed with anger. The term *'ebrâh* (1:15, 18) expresses the idea of overflowing. Yahweh's anger or wrath is like a flood that overflows and in so doing destroys. It is like a stream of molten lava, burning, scorching, destroying, ruining everything before it. Another phrase Zephaniah used is *lispōk 'ălêhem za'emî* (to pour upon them my indignation)[53] (3:8). This term, indignation, enables one to understand that Yahweh God has contempt, disgust, abhorrence caused by his disapprobation of that which is mean, disgraceful, or unjust. The disgraceful idols his people chose in place of his love, grace, and mercy struck at Yahweh God's dignity and his complete and full worthiness. Anger and wrath express Yahweh God's response while indignation speaks more directly to what Yahweh God experiences when he is rejected and scorned. Thus when Yahweh God pours out his indignation it comes from his heart, from his inner self.

Reference has been made to the recent interest in intertextuality. Zephaniah was correctly singled out as a case in point. Isaiah prophesied concerning Yahweh God's anger (at times the adjectives *fierce* and *burning* appear) and wrath twenty-nine times in sixty-six chapters. Anger and wrath appear three times in Amos, two times in Hosea, and once in Micah. But the three terms, *anger, wrath, indignation,* appear nine times in Zephaniah's three comparatively short chapters. The time had come when Zephaniah prophesied to put a strong emphasis upon the unavoidable reality of Yahweh God's anger, indignation, and wrath. And the demonstration of these by the sovereign and almighty Yahweh God would be fearful, awesome, and devastating.

Yahweh God was and is the Lord of time. His eternal character does not inhibit his entering into the process of history. He surely reckons with time. Hence, Zephaniah was specific: the day (nineteen times) and the appointed time (two times) were near. The eternal and sovereign King of the cosmos, and specifically of his covenant people, would not postpone the outpouring of his indignation, anger, and wrath. The time was very near. His patience would not be tried much longer.

Zephaniah also held before the nations other attributes of Yahweh God. These were as real and readily demonstrated as his anger, indignation, and wrath. These also would and could be sovereignly revealed and dispensed.

Yahweh God was proclaimed as a calling God, a personal deity whose heart is open and longing for an obedient, loving response from people (2:3). Hear his urgent plea: "Seek Yahweh, righteousness, humility; be obedient to his commands."

The plea comes from the Lord, who *yipqêdêm* (will visit them). He will pay attention to them with care and a real personal interest. Yahweh desires to be recognized as the ever-present, abiding God. But this personal interest does not detract from the reality that he is an awesome Lord, as he destroys idols (2:11). As Zephaniah concluded his prophetic message he reminded the people, be it but a remnant, that Yahweh God was Immanuel, "God with us" (3:15a). Indeed, Yahweh God is a loving Lord who extends his love with delight and joy (3:17).

The Covenant

The word *covenant,* either in Hebrew or in translations, does not appear in the prophecy of Zephaniah. But authors, whether of critical or conservative schools, refer to the covenant in their writings on Zephaniah. They do so correctly.[54]

Yahweh God, the sovereign King, is the covenant suzerain. He spoke with authority. "I will sweep away everything from the face of the earth" (Zeph. 1:2, 3); "I will stretch out my hand against Judah . . . Jerusalem" (1:4); "I will punish the princes and the king's sons" (1:8). These, and other such statements, clearly reveal that Zephaniah would have his hearers and readers think of Yahweh God as the creator, sustainer, judge of the cosmos, the nations, Judah, and Jerusalem.

The domain over which Yahweh God covenantally administered his sovereign rule was the cosmos; he upheld his creation covenant. And he covenantally administered his reign over Judah, its royal Davidic dynasty, and the land with Jerusalem as its capital city. Yahweh God executed his reign with the goal of covenantally administering redemption, restoration, and renewal.

Zephaniah, in the context outlined above, emphasized in particular the stipulations and curses as well as the promises and blessings. He did this by developing the theme of *yôm yĕhwâ haggādôl* (the Day of Yahweh, the great one) (1:7, 14); and *yôm 'Šebrâh hayyômhahû'* (a day of overwhelming wrath, that day) (1:15).

The curse of the covenant, of which Moses had spoken to the people before crossing the Jordan River into the promised inheritance, came in the context of stipulations, calling for loving devotion and obedience to their faithful covenant Lord. Zephaniah's emphasis on the curse of the covenant was certainly apropos because the book of Deuteronomy had come to light and was being read and applied. He was fully aware of how the covenant stipulations were ignored, disobeyed, and rejected.

One writer has summed up the gross violations of the covenant by referring to Zephaniah's calling attention to three specific categories.[55] (1) Social injustice was rampant (1:9; 3:1–3) perpetrated especially by the leaders of the people. (The social mandate and the cultural mandates were flagrantly violated.) (2) Idolatry was very prevalent, it was a violation of the creation covenantal spiritual mandate. This mandate to be faithfully obedient to Yahweh had been repeatedly held before the redeemed and delivered covenant people. (3) These violations of the covenantal mandates and stipulations arose from hearts filled with pride and arrogance (2:8; 3:11).

The cup of Yahweh God's wrath was full (Isa. 51:17). It was to be emptied soon; the great day of wrath was near. Zephaniah knew the attitude of the people; he spoke of the complacent ones (1:12), whether they were priests (1:4), royal persons (1:8), or merchants (1:11), who thought "The Lord will do nothing, either good or bad" (1:12). Zephaniah emphatically warned that the Day of Yahweh was to be a day of wrath, of distress, of anguish, of trouble and ruin; of darkness, gloom, clouds, and blackness (1:14, 15). The day would come with a trumpet blast and a battle cry; fortified cities and military towers would be ruined. People's blood would be shed in the streets (1:16, 17). Gold and silver would not save anyone (1:18). Zephaniah undoubtedly knew of Babylon's army's reputation—the army that was to be Yahweh God's instrument for executing his wrath.

This great day of Yahweh's wrath would concentrate on Judah and Jerusalem, on Yahweh God's covenant people. Zephaniah called Judah, the shameful nation, before the day actually dawned upon them (2:1). Then their land, the earth (1:3), and the whole world would come under this execution of wrath.

It must be understood that the judgment of wrath executed on the covenant people had cosmic involvements. God's people had the great covenantal mandate to cultivate the earth (Gen. 1:26), and this was repeated to Noah (9). Abraham subsequently was commanded to be a blessing to all nations. Hence, from the entire biblical perspective, Yahweh God's covenant people have a pivotal role in the universe, among nations, and among themselves as a covenant community of believing agents under Yahweh God's sovereign rule and direction.[56]

It should also be noted that Zephaniah did address other nations, whom he called to consider that the day of Yahweh's wrath would not only affect Judah. Philistia to the west (2:4–7), Moab and Ammon to the east (2:8–11), Cush to the south (2:12), and Assyria to the north and northeast, would experience the judgment of a wrathful Yahweh God (2:13). Philistia's cities would be ruined and emptied; Moab and Ammon would become like Sodom, a place of weeds and salt pits, and Assyria's capital city, Nineveh, would be a shelter for flocks, and herds, with owls roosting on stripped columns and exposed beams.

Other issues that Zephaniah raises, as do other prophets, call for attention. When will the day of Yahweh God's wrath be implemented? It would seem obvious in view of the nations addressed, Judah, Philistia, Moab, Ammon, Cush, and Assyria, that the time was near. This can be posited from the fact that Babylon, the agent that carried out Yahweh God's wrath, did in reality attack and conquer these nations soon after Zephaniah spoke. There has been historical fulfillment of this prophecy. But the question can be asked, does not Zephaniah present a much greater future period for the carrying out of the curse of the covenant? Does he not prophesy concerning gathering nations and kingdoms, in reality, the whole world (3:8)? It must be clearly understood that the judgment day Zephaniah proclaimed had been preceded by other such times. There had been times of judgment before: on Egypt when the Israelites left; on Israel to the north of Judah. The execution of wrath on Judah was one in a series of such times of judgment. There have been many since. These are all harbingers of the great final day of judgment, which comes when the Lord Jesus returns in glory. Hence, Zephaniah's proclamation referred to the appointed time (2:2), for Judah also has a definite message for all people of all times.

Yahweh God's covenant with Abraham and his descendants included promises and blessings. And these were repeated in various ways. It should be noted who was specifically addressed.

As the shameful nation was addressed (2:1), the humble and obedient were singled out (2:3). These were the ones who did what Yahweh God commanded. They were encouraged to *baqqĕšû* (niph. imp. of *bāqaś,* seek). This term in the form used expresses a seeking of Yahweh with a keen desire. They were urged to seek *ṣedeq* (righteousness), that is, to seek to be in fellowship with Yahweh their covenant God. They were to seek heart-to-heart communion in the manner Yahweh God had held before them. So doing, these people had the possibility[57] of being sheltered when disaster overwhelmed the nation, city, and people. Zephaniah did not assure the humble, obedient, Yahweh-seeking people that they would be spared being involved in what was coming. Rather, in the midst of what was sure to come they could *tiśśātĕrû* (niph. of *śātar,* hide, conceal) escape the judgment. In these words Zephaniah introduced what he spoke about more directly later: *śĕ'erît* (the remnant, a term derived from the verb, *sa'or*). The noun emphasizes that there will be some who have remained. Not all are gone; a residue or representation of what was is still present.

Zephaniah developed the idea of not complete elimination of the covenant people as he repeated that there would be a complete devastation of Judah and particularly Jerusalem. He prophesied woe against it, a city of oppressors, rebellious, defiled, disobedient; rejectors of correction, not trusting or worshiping Yahweh God (3:1, 2). In spite of rapacious officials, arrogant and treacherous prophets, priests profaning and violating the law, Yahweh God remains Immanuel. He is the unchanging righteous and just Lord (3:3–5). The covenant people would not accept correction but were eager to act corruptly even after initial acts of judgment had been inflicted upon them (3:6, 7). The time has come to pour out his wrath (3:8).

Zephaniah followed up this repetition regarding the carrying out of Yahweh's wrath by referring to four deeds Yahweh will accomplish. The prophet did not emphasize that these would be in a sequential order. Whatever the order may be, these will take place.

There will be the purifying of lips so that Yahweh God will be called upon, worshiped, and served. These purified ones are the scattered ones who have been forgiven and sanctified (3:9–11).

There will be a remnant[58] left of Israel, the covenant people, within Jerusalem. These will be a blessed people, meek, humble, truthful, dependable, who will have their needs supplied and can rest without fear (3:12, 13).

There will be singing and joy will well up from the daughter (the people) of Zion.[59] They will be strong (no limp hands) because Yahweh God, their King, is in their midst. He, the one who saves them, quiets them, having taken away their punishment by turning back their enemies, will know Yahweh God's love for them and his delight in them (3:14–18).

There will be a rescuing and gathering. The oppressors will be dealt with so that even the lambs will be free. These gathered ones will have praise and honor as they return home from the exile (3:19–20).

In conclusion to this discussion of the covenant as implied in Zephaniah's prophecy, a question concerning the actual occurrence of the "Day of Yahweh's Outpouring of Wrath," the preservation of the remnant, and the subsequent gathering of the remnant calls for an answer. There was an actual outpouring of Yahweh God's wrath when, in the course of history Judah, as a people, were attacked, defeated, destroyed as a nation, and carried into exile. The curse of the covenant was executed in historical time. This day did prove to be a time of sifting and a remnant of the covenant people remained.

More must be said. Zephaniah also spoke of nations. Salvation was for more groups of people than the scattered people of Israel and Judah.[60] Just as all the nations will be assembled and all kingdoms gathered when Yahweh God pours out his wrath (3:8), so will he purify the lips of the peoples so that along with regathered people (who had been scattered) they would call on the name of Yahweh God (3:9).[61] Zephaniah thus proclaims what actually took place historically at the time of the return from the exile. Telescoped onto the view is the calling of all nations in the New Testament era, and what Zephaniah prophesied concerning the great day of Yahweh God's wrath, the sifting and cleansing of the remnant, is an integral part of Yahweh God's preparation to being in the final judgment. Likewise, his gathering of the remnant is an initial stage in the process of Yahweh God's gathering and cleansing people from all tribes, tongues, races, and nations.

The kingdom of Yahweh God and his covenant endure forever. The curse of the covenant will be executed and the blessings of the covenant will be dispersed through the entire period of time from when Zephaniah prophesied until the Lord Jesus, the Christ, returns in glory, when the resurrection of all flesh takes place, the final judgment is carried out, and the cosmic kingdom is fully restored and renewed.

The Mediator [62]

As with the two other strands of the Golden Cable, kingdom and covenant, so it is also with the third strand, the mediator Messiah. There is no explicit reference to a royal deliverer. Ernst Hengstenberg, however, did not hesitate to write as follows: "the person of the Messiah, although not appearing here [in Zephaniah] stands in the background and forms the invisible center."[63]

In a former work it was set forth that there are two (the narrower and the wider) conceptions of the idea of the Messiah. The first refers specifically to the royal person and the bliss bound up with this God-ordained and -sent king. The second includes promises of salvation and other aspects of the work a divine person fulfills.[64] This second concept is dominant in Zephaniah's prophecy. He emphasized that Yahweh God, the King of the cosmic kingdom, is sovereign Lord over all peoples and nations. The testimony of Scripture throughout is that the Son carries out the will of the Triune God in regard to the covenantal administration of the cosmos and of redemption/restoration. When Zephaniah prophesied concerning the judgment soon to come upon Judah and neighboring nations, he referred to Yahweh God as the judge. Likewise when he prophesied concerning a remnant to be saved and blessed, he referred to Yahweh God. Zephaniah did not distinguish between the Father, Son, and Holy Spirit, the three-in-one God. However, the mediator of the covenant throughout Scripture is the Son. Hence, when covenant stipulations, promises, curses, and blessings are explicated, it is the messianic agent who upholds the stipulations and carries out the promises, the curses, and blessings that Zephaniah proclaimed. As stated elsewhere, Yahweh God exerts kingship through the Messiah (cf. Isa. 9:2–7; [MT 9:1–6]; 11:1–11; Mic. 5:2 [MT 5:1]).[65]

Joel's Themes

Zephaniah did not prophecy concerning any themes not set forth by previous prophets. He did not directly and explicitly take up all the prophetic themes in Joel's agenda. As stated previously, Zephaniah stressed with courage, fortitude, and intensity the theme of judgment to be executed when the day came for Yahweh God's wrath to be poured out. So doing, he implicitly warned the peoples of disasters to come, he called for obedience to the call to seek the Lord. He referred to the divine zeal motivating Yahweh God and spoke concerning the gathering of the remnant. Zephaniah's selective agenda was basically determined by the *Sitz im Leben* of his specific time in the historical process.

It should not be overlooked that Zephaniah, a covenant agent, and in that sense, a type of the Messiah, referred to the three covenant mediatorial offices ordained by Yahweh God. When he prophesied concerning Jerusalem, the earthly seat of the kingdom, he referred to it as a city of oppressors, rebellious and defiled (3:1). He referred to the officials as lions and wolves. He then spoke of the specific covenant agents: the prophets were arrogant and treacherous; the priests were profane and violated the law (3:2). Zephaniah did not refer to the king; Josiah was reigning and was seeking a reformation. From the account of Josiah's effort to bring in a reformation, which included the removal and death of many priests, some cooperated with Josiah and the high priests; one can conclude that Zephaniah's condemnation of covenant agents, especially of the priests, had a wholesome effect (cf. 2 Kings 23:1–24).

NOTES

1. Roland K. Harrison referred to W. F. Albright as being correct in positing this date. *Introduction to the Old Testament* (Grand Rapids: Eerdmans, 1969), 936. It should be kept

in mind that most, but not all, conservative evangelical scholars do not support Harrison's view. Some consider Habakkuk to have prophesied during Josiah's reign (Bullock, Laetsch), and others during Manasseh's reign (e.g., Keil). See Richard D. Patterson, *Nahum, Habakkuk, Zephaniah,* in The Wycliffe Exegetical Commentary series (Chicago: Moody, 1991), 115, 116.

2. See Brevard S. Childs, *Introduction to the Old Testament as Scripture* (Philadelphia: Fortress, 1979) for a discussion of these alternatives, 448, 449. Cf. also J. Alberto Soggin, *Introduction to the Old Testament* (Philadelphia: Westminster, 1976), who wrote that the wickedness mentioned may be that of either Judah or Assyria, 279. If reference is to the Assyrians, Habakkuk would have prophesied earlier than 605 B.C.

3. David W. Baker, *Nahum, Habakkuk, and Zephaniah* (Downers Grove: InterVarsity, 1988), surveys the historical setting in a succinct manner, 44. O. Palmer Robertson gave a summary of Judah's history under kings Hezekiah, Manesseh, Ammon, Josiah, and his sons and grandsons. This review highlights the spiritual degradation in Judah and the failure of reform under Josiah. *The Books of Nahum, Habakkuk, and Zephaniah* (Grand Rapids: Eerdmans, 1990), 1–17.

4. Charles L. Taylor, Jr., "The Book of Habakkuk," in *The Interpreters Bible,* 12 vols., ed. George Arthur Buttrick (New York: Abingdon, 1956), 6: 973, 5–7.

5. J. Ridderbos, *De Kliene Profeten Obadja tot Zefanja* (Kampen: Kok, 1949), 147.

6. Cf. the two works by William H. Brownlee, *The Text of Habakkuk in the Ancient Commentary From Qumran*, vol. 11 in Journal of Biblical Literature Monograph Series (Philadelphia: Society of Biblical Literature, 1959) and *The Midrash Pesher of Habakkuk* (Missoula: Scholars, 1979). See also Robert O. Haak, *Habakkuk* (Leiden: Brill, 1991) in a supplement to *Vetus Testamentum.* Haak provided a summary of early debates, translation efforts, and views concerning the historical setting.

7. Cf. Robertson, *Nahum, Habakkuk,* 38, 39.

8. Marvin A. Sweeney, "Structure, Genre, and Intent of the Book of Habakkuk" *Vetus Testamentum*, 11, no. 1 (1991): 63–83. Cf. also the essay by Michael E. W. Thompson, "Prayer, Oracle, and Theophany: The Book of Habakkuk," *Tyndale Bulletin* 44 no. 1, (1993), 33–53. Thompson demonstrates that there is progression in thought in the laments, oracles, and prayer. He supported the idea of one author who drew from and used wisdom and prophetic (especially Isianic) materials.

9. David Toshio Tsumura, "Ugaritic Poetry and Habkkuk 3," *Tyndale Bulletin* 40, no. 1 (1988). Passages he studied, said to reflect Ugaritic mythology, in which no prophetic poetry appears according to P. C. Craigie, a noted Ugaritologist, are 3:8; 3:9; 3:13b; 3:5, 24–28. But Soggin, *Introduction,* allows for chapter 3 to be borrowed from a Canaanite poem, 278.

10. See Taylor, *Habakkuk,* 978.

11. Peter A. Verhoef, *Krisiswoorde in Krisistije* (Pretoria: N. G. Kerk Uitgewers, n.d.).

12. Cf. Baker, *Habakkuk,* 55.

13. See Maria Eszenyei Szeles, *Wrath and Mercy,* trans. G.A.F. Knight, (Grand Rapids: Eerdmans, 1987), 13.

14. Ibid., 13.

15. Cf. Patterson, *Habakkuk,* 230. See Edward Marbury, *Obadiah and Habakkuk* (Ann Arbor: Sovereign Grace, 1960), 571, 593–94.

16. Cf. Szeles, *Wrath:* "Yahweh is Lord of history who in a sovereign manner directs the fate of his people and brings to their conclusion his inscrutable plans." 7. Also, Yahweh's royal prerogative intervenes and his will is effected. 10.

17. Omission of the term *bĕrît* certainly does not give reason to say it was not present in a discussion of relationships. A classic example is the omission of the terms in 2 Samuel 7. When David referred to what Yahweh had arranged and established, he spoke of the covenant Yahweh God had made with him (2 Sam. 23:5; Ps. 89:3).

18. In literary works, a synedoche refers to a part representing the whole, or the whole representing a part.

19. It was of interest to note that commentaries written by those inclined to be liberal and those inclined to a dispensational eschatology do not, with very few exceptions, refer to the biblical concept of covenant.

20. Carl E. Amerding, "Habakkuk," in *The Expositor's Bible Commentary,* ed. Frank E. Gabelein, vol. 7 (Grand Rapids: Regency, 1985), 521.

21. David W. Baker, "Nahum" wrote "actions . . . demanded by the covenant," 41; "violations of the covenant," 44; "obedience to the covenant . . . covenant obligations," 47; "covenant promise to preserve his people," 60, and "covenant promises are reliable," 61; "an intimate encounter with the covenant God, resulting in ethical living," 65; "He is the covenant God who keeps his promises," 76; "God's covenant promises of an eternal relationship," 77.

22. John Calvin, *Minor Prophets* vol. 4, trans. John Duun, (Grand Rapids: Eerdmans, 1950), 41, 80.

23. Keil, "Habakkuk," 55.

24. Marburg, *Habakkuk,* 265; here is another example of syndoche.

25. Robertson, *Habakkuk,* 145, 153.

26. Syeles, *Wrath,* 18.

27. Commentators have various answers to these questions: "Did Habakkuk go to a military installation? Did he take a stand on the rampart, a part of the city wall? Is the prophet using figurative language to emphasize that he will be carefully watching as he waits for Yahweh God's answer to his complaints so that, as prophet, he knows what to prophesy to the people? Cf., e.g., Theo Laetsch, *Commentary on the Minor Prophets* (St. Louis: Concordia, 1956), 328. Robertson referred to three previous prophets who had taken a watching stance—Moses (Exod. 33:21–23); Balaam (Num. 23:3); and Elijah (1 Kings 19:11)—and who actually awaited a revelation, *Nahum,* 166.

28. The Hebrew term is *tôkaḥtî,* a term derived from *yākaḥ,* to decide or to prove. The noun took on the added nuance of reproof, rebuke, correction.

29. Robertson, *Nahum,* 185. Baker wrote concerning the oracles of woe that were intended to mock Babylon. *Nahum,* 62.

30. Laetsch, *Minor Prophets,* 334. Baker lists these as pillager, plotter, promoter of violence, debaucher, and pagan idolator. *Habakkuk,* 62–68.

31. Marbury, *Habakkuk,* considered the reference to be to both, in fact to all places dedicated to the worship of Yahweh God, 537–49. Rex Mason implies it could refer to the heavenly because *all* the earth is called to silence. *Zephaniah, Habakkuk, Joel* (Sheffield: Academic, 1994), 62. Cf. also Homer Hailey, *Commentary on the Minor Prophets* (Grand Rapids: Baker, 1972). "Reference is "not in the sanctuary at Jerusalem," 288.

32. Cf. Baker, *Nahum,* 678; P. Verhoef, *Krisiswoorde,* 55; Ebenezer Henderson, *The Twelve Minor Prophets* (reprint, Grand Rapids: Baker, 1980), 309, 310. J. Ridderbos, *Kleine Profeten,* 167.

33. Cf. Robertson, *Nahum,* 211.

34. Cf. note 9 regarding possible Ugaritic influences in chap. 3.

35. Timothy Lim has analyzed the Groningen Hypothesis. This hypothesis is based on the Dead Scroll's "Habakkuk Pesher," in which there are references to wicked priests based

on Habakkuk's reference to the crushed leader of wickedness. Lim's conclusion is that the hypothesis's "depiction of six wicked priests in sequential order" is not based on the text but on a "questionable assumption." " The Wicked Priests of the Groningen Hypothesis," *Journal of Biblical Literature* 112–13 (1995): 424.

36. Cf. the author's brief discussion concerning Habakkuk's lack of reference to a personal messiah. *Messianic Revelation in the Old Testament* (Grand Rapids: Baker, 1990), 677, 678.

37. Cf. Robertson, *Nahum,* 237–38; Ridderbos, *Profeten,* 173; Patterson, *Habakkuk,* 247, 248. Some critical commentators regard verse 13 as a later gloss to emphasize what the preceding verse had said, namely, to cleanse the earth of wickedness for the remnant. Szeles, *Wrath,* 110.

38. Cf. Part I, C of this chapter

39. Cf. *MROT,* 678.

40. See Childs, *Introduction* for bibliography. It includes quite a number of non-English titles, 457. See also the author's comments on Zephaniah and the biographical references in the notes. *Messianic Revelation,* 668–70. In this study of Zephaniah, only sources that have appeared since 1988 (when *MROT* was completed) are consulted for introductory comments.

41. Childs wrote that in spite of earlier attempts to discredit what Zephaniah 1:1 records, there is wide agreement among modern scholars in accepting the period of Josiah's reign. There is no agreement when Zephaniah wrote: before or after the attempted reformation. *Introduction,* 458.

42. Herbert Wolf reminded his readers that Leviticus has twenty-six and Deuteronmy fifty-four verses that speak of the curse that would be executed and the wrath of Yahweh God that would be demonstrated as consequence of disobedience. Cf. "The Transcendent Nature of the Covenant Curse Reversals," in *Israel's Apostacy and Restoration,* ed. Avraham Gileadi (Grand Rapids: Baker, 1988), 319.

43. R. K. Harrison, *Introduction to the Old Testament* (Grand Rapids: Eerdmans, 1969), 912. See also Gleason Archer, *A Survey of Old Testament Introduction* (Chicago: Moody, 1964). "Criteria for later dating depend for their validity upon unproved assumptions," 350.

44. Edward J. Young, *My Servants the Prophets* (Grand Rapids: Eerdmans, 1952), 159. Young did refer to a few instances that record a command to prophets to write.

45. See Child's phrases, e.g., "in the earlier and later periods of the book's growth," *Introduction,* 400. Ehud Ben Zvi's work, *A Historical Critical Study of the Book of Zephaniah* (New York: Walter de Gruyter, 1991), is based on the premise that Zephaniah received its final form in postexilic times. Zvi doubts that Zephaniah was a flesh and blood person. Katherine Dell, in a review of Zvi, stated that his work is a backlash against the strong desire to discover the actual words of the prophet. *Vetus Testamentum* 45 (1966): 556–57.

46. Paul R. House, *Zephaniah, A Prophetic Drama* (Worcester: Almond, 1988). Howe's review of genre criticism served as the basis for his evaluation of the text of Zephaniah. See how he dramatized the prophecy, 112–26. Cf. also Adele Berlin, *Zephaniah,* vol. 25A in the Anchor Bible (New York: Doubleday, 1994), who commented on Howe's view, 12. Cf. also Mason, *Zephaniah,* who, quoting Eaton, wrote that the liturgical practice of Zephaniah's time may have influenced the "arrangement, ideas, and language of the composition" 30.

47. Consider, for example, the focus on rhetorical exegesis in the 1970s and 1980s, while in recent works there is hardly any reference to it at all.

48. Greg King, "The Message of Zephaniah: An Urgent Echo," *Andrews University Seminary Studies* 32, no. 2 (1996): 211. Cf. also Szeles, *Wrath.* "His [Zephaniah's] preaching is rooted in the works of his eighth-century predecessors," 63.

49. Ibid., 211.

50. Ibid., 213; references to this phenomenon will be made in subsequent paragraphs.

51. Richard Patterson, "A Literary Look at Nahum, Habakkuk and Zephaniah," *Grace Theological Journal* 11, no. 1 (1990): 12–28.

52. Cf. Childs, *Introduction,* 459–61.

53. The NIV translated the term "wrath"; the KJV, RSV, NEB more correctly translated it "indignation."

54. David Baker, summarizing the message of Zephaniah, referred to the covenant promises, covenant obligations, return to the covenant, commitment to the covenant, *Nahum,* 84–86. Greg King in his essay "The Day of the Lord in Zephaniah," in *Bibliotheca Sacra* 152, (January-March, 1995), included a subheading "The Day of Covenant Implementation," 26. He stressed that the prophets imply a strong connection between the Day of the Lord and the covenant, 27. Robertson, *Nahum,* wrote concerning the covenant relationship, 251; covenantal fidelity, 253; covenantal judgment, 257. Szeles, *Wrath,* referred to the covenant people, 101, 104, and Yahweh's jealous love-passion to protect the covenant, 105.

55. King, "The Message of Zephaniah," 214.

56. Walther Eichrodt addressed this subject of why, or how it came about, that the sin of the covenant people led to judgment on nations and the entire cosmos under the heading of charismatic leaders. His view that the corporate responsibilities of leaders and certain people, that is, Israel and Judah, came to be understood and seen in an ever-evolving manner—personal sin involved communities, community sins involved nations, nations' sins involved the world. See *Theology of the Old Testament,* trans. J. A. Baker (Philadelphia: Westminster, 1961), 374–381. Eichrodt's explanation of what he discerned to be reality, the involvement of cosmic judgment with covenantal judgment, is vitiated by his refusal to acknowledge that the Scripture explicitly states that *Yahweh God has revealed* the source and outworking of human sin according to Yahweh God's enunciated warnings to Adam and Eve and their posterity, the wide-ranging results of their sin.

57. The Hebrew term *'ûlāy* usually translated "perhaps," appears in various contexts to express hope, doubt, or fear.

58. The idea of a remnant was expressed five times by Isaiah; three times by Zephaniah; five times by Amos and Micah. It is Jeremiah who referred to the remnant repeatedly. In the study of Jeremiah the concept will be studied in some detail. Suffice it to say that Zephaniah was speaking of an historical group of survivors who were the ones who had a genuine trust in God. See the essay by Greg A. King, "The Remnant in Zephaniah," *Bibliotheca Sacra* 151 (September–October 1994) 414–27.

59. Larry Lee Walker was not clear when, in his commentary, he said that the daughter of Zion (3:14) refers to "the reassembled remnant of Israel," "the messianic age," "this passage goes beyond the promise of return to the promise of a glorious restoration." "Zephaniah," in *The Expositors Bible Commentary,* vol. 7, ed. F. E. Gabelein (Grand Rapids: Zondervan, 1985), 561–64. Recall that in the study of Micah it was concluded that the daughter of Zion refers to the coming generations born of the remnant. Cf. chap. 22, note 56.

60. Cf. e.g., King, "Day of the Lord" 29. Cf. Zeph. 3:4a—all the peoples of the earth.

61. See the author's discussion of Zeph. 3:9 in *Messianic Revelation,* 672–76.

62. For a fuller discussion of Zephaniah's prophecy concerning the Mediator, see the author's study of Zephaniah in *Messianic Revelation,* 662–76.

63. Ernst Hengstenberg, *Christology of the Old Testament,* trans. Theodore Meyer, 2 vols. (Edinburgh: T & T Clark, 1868), 2:358.

64. Cf. *Messianic Revelation,* 20.

65. Ibid., 676.

25

Jeremiah: Too Late! But Renewal Promised

I. Introductory Comments

II. The Historical Context

III. The Covenant

IV. The Kingdom

V. The Mediator

VI. Summary

25

Jeremiah: Too Late! But Renewal Promised

Introductory Comments

Jeremiah: The Man and the Book

Jeremiah, the man, had a priestly ancestry. He was a descendant of Abiathar, the priest who had opposed the anointing of Solomon to be the king to succeed David. Abiathar then was banished from Jerusalem to an area within the borders of Benjamin's territory (1 Kings 1). Jeremiah, however, is said to be from Anathoth, a village near the northern edge of Jerusalem. Hence he had a unique position and opportunity to observe the situation of and conditions within the city itself. His ancestry and place of residence may have been a factor in the opposition he experienced as a prophet speaking within Jerusalem.

Much has been written about Jeremiah, the man, his times, and his book.[1] In a previous work,[2] the historical context, the Hebrew text, and Jeremiah as a messianic type were surveyed. Attention should continue to be given to problems regarding the text. Has it been properly preserved? Why does the Septuagint include an abbreviated version while the Dead Sea Scrolls reflect a much closer version to the Masoretic text?[3] The authorship of the book really does not require much additional scholarly attention because the text is definite in referring to the prophet as author and to Baruch as his amanuensis (Jer. 36:1–8, 32).

Jeremiah was acquainted with what Moses, the prophet, had spoken and written. This is acknowledged by many scholars. What is a legitimate issue for debate is whether Jeremiah first became acquainted with what Moses had spoken and written in Deuteronomy after the Book of the Law had been found. The correct answer is not difficult to state.

The historical fact is that Jeremiah was born during Manasseh's reign and was about sixteen or seventeen years old when Josiah began to reign in the year 640 B.C. He reigned thirty-one years. In the eighteenth year of his reign (when Jeremiah was approximately thirty-five years old), Josiah decided to repair and renew the temple. Money had been collected to make this possible. When Shaphan, Josiah's secretary, went to Hilkiah the high priest with orders to release the money to pay for the materials needed and to pay the wages of the workmen, Hilkiah informed Shaphan that he had found the Book of the Law (Deuteronomy) (2 Kings 22:1–10). The king's reading of this book gave even greater motivation to the work on the temple. More important, this reading led to a renewal of the covenant (23:1–3).

The question whether Josiah and Jeremiah first learned of the covenant as written by Moses, or not, must be answered as follows. Jeremiah, as a member of a priestly order, was undoubtedly acquainted with the history of the temple, its sacrificial type of worship, and the priesthood. Josiah undoubtedly knew of these also because he was intent on repairing and renewing the temple and restoring proper worship as prescribed in Exodus and Leviticus. Hence it is correct to conclude that Josiah and Jeremiah were acquainted with the Sinaitic covenant. But neither the prophet nor the king was properly acquainted with the renewing and confirming of the covenant by Moses when Israel was camped on the plains of Moab. The Book of the Law, which expanded on the stipulations, warnings, and curses for disobedience, was brought to their attention. They then had the entire corpus of Mosaic writings before them. And it must be added that Jeremiah, in his prophetic proclamations and writings, reflected an intimate knowledge of all that Moses had written.

Jeremiah also reflected more than a passing knowledge of what preceding prophets had proclaimed. He did not repeat them verbatim, but the issues they had raised, he expanded and applied in his own manner and words.[4] Hence the phenomenon of intertextuality is present in Jeremiah. And as will be shown in the conclusion to this chapter, Jeremiah expanded on some of the main themes Joel had included in his prophetic agenda. Jeremiah developed and strengthened the threefold strands of the Golden Cable. As has been demonstrated in a previous work, Jeremiah prophesied concerning the messianic Mediator. Scholarship has largely neglected Jeremiah's prophecy concerning this thematic strand.[5] It will also become clear in the subsequent discussion that Jeremiah also proclaimed the reality of the kingdom.

Prophecies concentrating on the Covenant

Jeremiah can correctly be referred to as the prophet of the covenant. He, as did Elijah long before him, could say, "your people have broken and rejected the covenant" (1 Kings 19:10). Elijah had spoken thus concerning Israel but Jeremiah had to address and deal with Judah, the people who had been spared from exile into Assyria and who had the Davidic dynasty ruling them. Jeremiah referred in various ways to Yahweh God's covenanting activities in the past and he prophesied eloquently concerning the continuity of the covenant in its renewed state. Before an in-depth discussion of Jeremiah's proclamations commences, it is important that the historical context is clearly understood.[6]

The Historical Context

Jeremiah lived and prophesied during a crucial period in the history of the Old Testament covenant people. To understand Jeremiah's message it is important to keep in mind that Jeremiah was born in the decade, 660–650 B.C., during Manasseh's reign. Thus he personally experienced the sharp decline in Judah's political, social, and spiritual areas of life.

The Latter Part of Isaiah's Ministry

One must also keep in mind what happened during the final years of Isaiah's ministry and King Hezekiah's reign. Assyria had invaded, conquered, and exiled the northern kingdom of Israel in 722 B.C. Judah and Jerusalem were spared. Sennacharib, the Assyrian commander, had threatened Jerusalem (2 Kings 18:17–19:13). Hezekiah the king had prayed earnestly that Yahweh God demonstrate to all kingdoms on earth that Yahweh was God alone (19:13–19). Isaiah prophesied that the Assyrian army would not enter Jerusalem because he would defend it for the sake of David his servant (19:20–34).[7] The Assyrian army was decimated and the remaining elements of the Assyrian army returned to Nineveh (19:35, 36).

King Hezekiah became seriously ill. The king prayed fervently for healing and Isaiah prophesied that he would be healed and live (20:1–11). In the latter days of his life, however, Hezekiah made a foolish mistake. He welcomed envoys from Babylon.

The Transition

The relevance of what Hezekiah did in relation to Jeremiah's prophetic ministry and the proper understanding of this ministry is as follows.

First, Yahweh God expressly stated that he would save Jerusalem from destruction by the Baylonians for the sake of his covenant with David (2 Kings 20:6). The Davidic dynasty and its city and country would be kept from conquering armies.[8] Thus, assurance from Yahweh came *when* Hezekiah prayed, turned to Yahweh God for deliverance, and continued to rule the people according to Yahweh's covenant.

Second, Hezekiah made a fatal blunder when, in his pride and foolishness, he received the Babylonian envoys who gave him a gift. The king then showed the envoys "all that was in his storehouse" and "everything found among his treasures." "There was nothing in his palace or in all his kingdom that Hezekiah did not show them" (20:13). Isaiah informed Hezekiah that the time was coming when everything in the palace and storehouse, as well as his descendants, would be carried off to Babylon.

Third, it was at this time that the setting and context of a great and defined transition in the life and affairs of the covenant people were outlined.

The transition referred to is that which takes place with the covenant people as a theocratic nation or *kingdom.* This transition is discerned particularly in the prophetic movement. The first period is from the time of Samuel through the earlier writing prophets. Isaiah is one of these, but in the latter part of his prophetic work he refers to the beginning of the transition. In the first period the possibility of repentance and conversion was clearly stressed. During the second period the call to repentance never ceased but "it acquired a more perfunctory tone."[9] The time for repair was past; a complete regeneration had to take place. And it would commence in due time. This regeneration would never reproduce the theocratic kingdom. Yahweh God had something that far transcended the original structure.[10]

Fourth, in the period between Isaiah's last prophetic ministries and that of Habakkuk, Zephaniah, and Jeremiah, covenant breaking became a way of life. This was during the reign of Manasseh, whose reign is said to have extended for fifty-five years.[11] The brief survey of his wickedness includes references to building high places, erecting altars to Baal and a pole for Asherah, worshiping the stars, building altars in the temple, practicing sorcery and divination, and consulting mediums and spiritists. In a real sense, Manasseh proved to be in league with Satan, who always sought to destroy the messianic seed line. Manasseh sacrificed his own son in the fire, one in the Davidic dynasty. He was said to have committed more evil than the Amorites (21:2–11). The prophetic pronouncements included great disasters to come upon Judah. The time of repentance and conversion was absolutely past. Manasseh is described as turning to the Lord when he was prisoner in Babylon. He was returned to Jerusalem. He attempted a revival of the worship of Yahweh, but it was too late. The people did not follow him. His son Amon continued in the wicked ways of Manasseh (2 Chron. 33:10–23). It was in this historic context that Josiah, the eight-year-old son of Amon, became king. And, recall, it was in the thirteenth year of Josiah's reign that Jeremiah was called to prophesy (Jer. 1:2). The transition to the period of regeneration was complete.

Jeremiah's Call[12]

King Josiah had reigned as king thirteen years (Jer. 1:2) when Jeremiah received the call to serve as prophet and not to carry on in his family's priestly tradition. And since Josiah initiated the temple repair in his eighteenth year (2 Kings 22:3) Jeremiah had already served as a prophet for five years. There is no direct biblical reference to Jeremiah's influence on King Josiah. It is an inviting thought, however, to regard the young king, at age twenty-six, responding to the prophetic message, which included strong and stern warnings concerning Judah's apostacy.

Jeremiah was personally not ready or prepared to receive the call to prophetic service. Although Yahweh God assured him he was conceived and born to be a prophet to the nations (Jer. 1:5), he pled that he was too young and really not a good speaker. Yahweh God assured Jeremiah that the covenant assurance, *I am with you,* was to be reality whenever and wherever he was sent to prophesy. And the assignment he received as a prophet was to have tremendous results for Judah and the nations. They were to be uprooted and torn down, destroyed and overthrown.[13] This message in reality was a statement concerning the curse of the covenant to be executed in due time. To prophesy concerning this certainty was not to make Jeremiah afraid even if opposed and attacked (1:8) because Yahweh God, fulfilling his covenant word, would be with him and rescue him. So Jeremiah was commanded *wĕ' attâh te'ĕzōr mātĕnekā* (and you gird your loins), translated in the NIV as "Get yourself ready" (1:17). The phrase is a Hebrew military term used to describe the soldier dressed and properly fitted to carry his sword.[14] Yahweh God called the prophet to be a warrior who would do as he was commanded and not to be terrified by his audiences. The threefold charge—gird, speak, don't be terrified—clearly implied that "torrid experiences . . . lay ahead."[15] It must be stated emphatically that young Jeremiah actually, in reality, received this call and charge. These words are not to be considered "part of the early poetic level" with a Deuteronomic explanation.[16] Jeremiah was told plainly that in the historical situation in which he was to begin his prophetic work, he had to stand as an impregnable city and a bronze wall as he faced the entire land. His opponents specifically would be the kings of Judah, the officials, the priests, and the people of the land. He would not be accepted, much less loved, as a prophet of judgment.[17]

It must not be overlooked that when Jeremiah was called, he was assured that his message was not only to be one of judgment, that is, of the execution of the curse of the covenant; his commission included two positive terms, to build and to plant. The blessing of the covenant would be realities. The terms, however, do imply a breakdown of the past and the removal of ruins, real necessary endeavors before the rebuilding could commence. Likewise, the remnants of previous produce of the land had to be removed before the planting could begin (1:10c). Thus Jeremiah had to proclaim an end to the present structures and the initiation of the new in the same territory and area. There was not to be a complete end to Yahweh God's covenant, a covenant people, and a covenant way of life. There was to be renewing of the same but adapted to the new historical situation. That was initiated. The removal of the old and failing was a first step in the process of renewing.

The Covenant

Jeremiah was not only covenant conscious, he proclaimed the covenant.[18] He knew the people of Judah and Jerusalem had been chosen and called to be Yahweh God's covenantal agents in the cosmos and especially among all nations and tribes on earth. They were particularly to live, worship, and serve in every aspect of their lives as Yahweh's vicegerents, his prophetic voice, as the priestly intercessor and demonstrator of sanctified living.

Jeremiah, in his prophetic proclamation, indicated that he, and his audience, should honor and praise Yahweh God who had repeatedly covenanted with his people. Jeremiah particularly made reference to no less than six epochs of covenanting activities. It must be clearly understood that these covenanting activities were not proclaimed as instances of new relationships, new stipulations, and new promises. Rather, each covenanting activity set the stage and provided the context for the confirmation of the one covenant as explanations, expansions, and applications were made.

The Creation Covenant[19]

The phrase "creation covenant" is not to be found in the book of Jeremiah. Neither are the phrases "Abrahamic covenant," "Sinaitic covenant," or "Davidic covenant." But that Jeremiah made reference to these is clear and should not be doubted.

Jeremiah used a unique phrase to refer to the creation covenant in his prophetic promise of the sure restoration of the Davidic line (Jer. 33:15). This restoration is sure to come and thus the Davidic covenant will continue as surely as Yahweh God's covenant with the day and the night are not broken but is continued from the time of creation to the very end of time (33:20, 21, 25, 26).[20] That Yahweh God had established his covenant with creation was verified when Yahweh God, confirming his covenant with Noah (Gen. 6:18; 9:1–11), assured him that as long as the earth endured, seasons and day and night would never cease. This covenant of creation was confirmed as covenant with the cosmos in which every living creature is included.

Jeremiah also revealed an awareness of the creation covenant by appealing to or referring to the heavens and the earth.[21] He called upon the heavens to be appalled at the idolatry of the covenant people (Jer. 2:12). He spoke of the earth and heavens being affected by the foolishness of the people (4:21, 23, 26), but what God had created would not be destroyed. The people were accused of worshiping these created aspects of the cosmos (8:2), and not the One who created and controlled them (10:11–13; 32:17). Jeremiah thus repeatedly reminded the covenant people that Yahweh God, having created the heavens and the earth and upheld them, was not to be replaced by these or have them be substitutes for worship. He, Yahweh God, creator and ruler of the heavens and earth, maintained his bond with creation. The covenant people had to continue to be aware of Yahweh God's lordship over all of his creation and because of this close relationship of Yahweh God to the heavens and the earth, Jeremiah, as other prophets, called on these to witness people's transgressions. So doing, Yahweh God would hear this call and be pleased that the heavens and earth were recognized as his handiwork with which he maintained his bond. It must be added, however, that when the people worshiped the heavenly bodies and earthly things, they ignored the Creator and aroused the anger of Yahweh God.

The Redemptive/Restoring Covenant

The phrase "covenant of redemption" refers to Yahweh God's dealing with Adam, Eve, Satan, and their seed as recorded in Genesis 3:14–19.[22] Essential aspects of this covenant, which serves as an integral addition to the one covenant Yahweh God established at the time of creation, are the promises of continuity and blessings of life concerning the role of the seed of the woman. It also included the absolute curse on Satan and a mitigated curse on Adam, Eve, and the ground. Not to be omitted among the essential aspects was the enmity pronounced and established between the seed of the woman and of Satan; thus a definite antithesis was established by Yahweh God.

Jeremiah did not refer directly to it by using the phrase "covenant of redemption/restoration." He certainly did refer to various essential aspects of it.[23]

Jeremiah emphasized the antithesis. He repeatedly referred to the struggle, yes, the battle, between the evil and the good. Evil was very prevalent. Sin against Yahweh God was committed by violating the three creation covenant mandates. There was gross spiritual sin; idols were made and worshiped. Also, gross social and cultural sins were committed. These were evidenced by the ignoring, rejection, and violation of Yahweh God's mandates. Jeremiah, and those who were faithful to Yahweh God, were in stark contrast to the greater majority of the people. Mention of particulars will be made as Jeremiah's references to succeeding covenantal administrations are discussed.

Jeremiah also referred repeatedly to the punishment that Yahweh God would execute on covenant breakers. These punishments were the outworking of the curse that Yahweh God had pronounced in the garden. Later, these judgments and curses were expanded and applied more fully when God covenanted with Abraham and via Moses with Israel. And it must be stated with emphasis, Jeremiah also proclaimed the continuity of victory, even if disaster overcame the people. He proclaimed Yahweh God's readiness to forgive and bless his people with blessings of love and life

This covenant of redemption/restoration, as a renewing and restoring aspect to the one covenant[24] Yahweh God made with his people, was particularly stressed in the later confirmations. Sad to say it has been quite apparent that scholars have been inclined to overlook, ignore, or even reject the biblical revelation of the one covenant Yahweh God established, upheld, and repeatedly expanded as it was applied in the course of progressing history.

The Abrahamic Covenant

Jeremiah referred to Abraham by name only once, in the context of repeating that Yahweh God would keep his covenant that gave absolute assurance that one of David's descendants would rule over the descendants of Abraham, Isaac, and

Jacob (Jer. 33:25). In this context, three administrations of Yahweh's covenant are spoken of: the creation covenant, the covenant with Abraham, and the covenant with David. It is the Abrahamic covenantal administration that serves as the major link between the other two. Yahweh God had promised Abraham, as he had Adam and Eve (Gen. 3:14–16), that he was to have a seed (descendant) and that royalty was to issue forth from his seed line (15:14; 17:6, 16, 19).

Reference has been made in a preceding chapter[25] to the promise to Abraham that he was to be an agent and channel of blessing to all nations (12:1–3; 22:18). But Jeremiah pronounced woes, not blessings, on nations such as Egypt (Jer. 46:14, 20, 28), the Philistines (47:1–7;), Moab (48:1–47), Ammon (49:1–6), Edom (49:7–27), and Babylon (50:1–51:8).[26] The covenant people had failed to be the persistent source of blessing to the nations. Jeremiah made it very clear that these nations had a baneful spiritual influence on the covenant people. These nations had not exercised their opportunities and privileges with respect to the descendants of Abraham. Yahweh God, when calling Abram and covenanting with him, had said that the nations were also to have a responsibility: they were to relate to Abram in such a way that they would be blessed so doing.[27]

A third way Jeremiah draws attention to the Abrahamic covenant is by the way he holds before his audience the covenantal stipulations and promises interrelated with these stipulations. Abraham was called to be obedient, believe, walk with Yahweh God, and be blameless (Gen. 15:6; 17:1). Abraham had been obedient: he went when called and circumcised the male members of his family (chap. 17);[28] he offered his son when commanded; he obeyed Yahweh God's commandments (26:5). He believed the promise of a seed (15:6) and of a land (15:18). After his adulterous action with Hagar, his walk with God and blameless way of life became realities (chaps. 18, 22). But Abraham's descendants, knowing the covenant demands and blessings related, were hardened in disobedience; they forsook Yahweh their God (Jer. 2:17) and said "we will not serve you (2:20).[29] They did not believe; they were called "faithless," more unfaithful than exiled Israel (3:8–10),[30] and they lied about Yahweh God (5:12). They did not walk with God (they strayed so far from me) (2:5, 13). Their life was not blameless; not one person dealt honestly but all were swearing falsely (5:1, 2). The curse that Yahweh God had warned would come upon those holding Abraham and his descendants in disrepute, Jeremiah warned, was to come upon the erring and rebellious offspring of Abraham.

The Sinaitic Covenant

Jeremiah made direct and indirect references to the covenant confirmed with Israel at Mount Sinai. Recall that Yahweh God is said to have brought Israel to himself as a precious possession and she was to be a kingdom of priests and a holy nation. Yahweh God, covenanting with Israel, took her as his "bride"; he was husband to her. Israel had responded, "all that Yahweh says we will do" (Exod. 24:3, 7), and the covenant relationship had then been sealed with the sprinkling of blood (24:8). Metaphorically speaking, the marriage between Yahweh God and his treasured possession (19:5) was truly sealed. Yahweh God was now "legally" husband to his covenant bride (Jer. 3:14; 31:32; cf. also Isa. 54:5; Ezek. 16:32, 45). As husband, Yahweh God had given commandments to govern the husband-wife marriage: the ten commandments. Jeremiah's messages repeatedly stressed that Israel/Judah, the bride, had been unfaithful to her husband. She had made idols to worship (Jer. 1:6; 2:5, 23, 28; 4:1; 5:7; 7:6, 30; 8:2; 9:14; 17:2; 18:4; 19:4; 44:1). In chapter 10 Jeremiah elaborated on the differences between Yahweh God and man-made idols. Idols are a fraud, worthless, objects of mockery (vv. 14, 15). But Yahweh God is the Maker of all things (v. 16). How senseless and foolish these idols were and people who worship these demonstrate their senselessness and foolishness.

In another context, Jeremiah had used the metaphor of a spring of living water (2:13). Yahweh had proven in the desert that he was the source of living water (Exod. 17:1–7 ; Num. 20:1–13). As covenantal head of Israel/Judah, he was also their source of life and provided for their continued livelihood. He, in reality, provided bread, water, and meat in the desert and in a specifically spiritual sense, he was their completely reliable source for life. But the "wife" was unfaithful, she dug her own cisterns that could not produce water, much less provide it as needed. In a real sense, idols were useless cisterns.

Jeremiah, as other prophets preceding him, proclaimed that *lākēn 'od 'ārîb 'ittĕkem* (Therefore, again, I charge you.)[31] This is legal terminology; Yahweh took his "bride" to court and accuses her of being unfaithful to him (Jer. 3:20; 5:11). The reality is, he should divorce her. The grounds were there. Yahweh said, "they have forsaken my law which I set before them; they have not obeyed me or followed my law" (9:13). This charge followed Jeremiah's accusations that the covenant people were a crowd of unfaithful people (9:2). They lie, there is no truth in the land (9:3); there is deception, slandering, lying (9:6). Every aspect of the Sinaitic covenant had been violated. Hence he proclaimed that the covenant from their side was broken (11:1-8). Jeremiah referred specifically to the terms Yahweh God had enunciated when he had brought them out of Egypt and had said, "obey me" (11:1–4).

When Moses had repeated, confirmed, and expanded on some aspects of the Sinaitic covenant when Israel was about to enter the promised inheritance, he had emphasized that Israel/Judah was loved (Deut. 4:37; 7:8, 9, 12, 13; 10:15), chosen (4:37; 7:6; 14:2), and blessed (7:13; 14:29; 15:6, 10, 18; 28:8). This blessing came on a loved and chosen people when they walked with Yahweh their God, obeyed, loved, worshiped, and served him. Moses had also repeatedly reminded the covenant people that a real aspect of the covenant was the curse (11:28; 23:4; 27:15–26; 28:16–19). Jeremiah was strongly reminded of this curse because in his time the book of Deuteronomy had been found and was being read. He reminded the covenant people that Yahweh God, as a spurned husband, would reject his people (Jer. 6:30) and thus demonstrate his anger and wrath (7:20; 21:12; 22:20, 25:24). The curse would definitely come (3:22; 4:1; 6:19, 7:30ff.). Babylon would be Yahweh God's agent for demonstrating the wrath and execution of the curse

(4:16). As Jeremiah proclaimed the tragic message, he said the end had come, there was to be no early summer nor late summer harvest (8:20) and there was to be no healing balm (8:22).[32]

There was, however, a strong reminder in Jeremiah's preaching that Yahweh God had separated from his bride, he had in reality divorced her.[33] But it must be remembered that from God's side, the covenant was everlasting. The covenant promise regarding the land would not be finally fulfilled for Judah as a nation because Judah, as a theocratic nation, would cease to exist for all time. But Yahweh God would keep a remnant (5:18; 7:9; 24:1–7). Hence Jeremiah repeatedly called for individual covenant people to be faithful, to wash evil from their hearts and be saved (4:14). They were to return and be cured of their backsliding (3:22). Jeremiah emphasized that Yahweh God "surely is the salvation of Israel" (3:23). Judah, however, did not respond, it would not listen or answer (7:13).[34] It is in this context that Jeremiah had to tell the people that Yahweh God had commanded him not to pray for this people, not to offer a plea or petition for them nor to plead with him (7:16). Yahweh will not listen to the prophet because it was too late for the covenant with Israel/Judah to be upheld in all of its aspects. The blessings regarding the land, the well-being in the land, the national existence and security was forever ended. But, Yahweh God's covenant would nevertheless be kept, in its different administrative form, that is, with David and with David's son, the Messiah who would be the mediator of the renewed covenant.

The Davidic Covenant

In his prophecies, Jeremiah referred to David by name seventeen times. He referred to David's throne eight times (Jer. 13:13; 17:25; 22:2, 30; 23:5; 29:16; 36:30). David is referred to as Yahweh's servant three times (33:21, 22, 26), reference is made to David's branch two times (23:5; 33:15) and to his descendants (kings) (13:13; 22:30; 33:17, 21, 22; 36:20). Direct reference to Yahweh's covenant with David appears once (33:21). It must be clearly understood that whether Jeremiah spoke of David's throne, his descendants, branch, and servant, these are all terms that have a covenantal context, relevance, and importance.

The following points must be emphasized. First, Jeremiah was fully aware of Yahweh's covenanting activity with David (2 Sam. 7:3–16). Second, Jeremiah never gave as much as a hint that Yahweh's covenant with David and his house would ever cease to be a factor in Yahweh God's dealing with his Old Testament as well as his New Testament people. Third, Jeremiah was fully aware that not all of David's descendants who sat on his throne had been and would be faithful servants and shepherds over Yahweh's covenantal people. He had to denounce the apostate kings. Yahweh warned him that as he, the faithful prophet, spoke Yahweh's messages, the kings and others would fight him but not overcome him (Jer. 1:19). The kings would be disgraced because they worshiped man-made idols (29:26–28) and their bones would therefore be taken from their graves and exposed (8:1–3). The kings and their people violated the Sabbath (17:23) and thus were not a blessing to the nations (17:25, 26). Fourth, Zedekiah, whose name means "Yahweh is righteous," and who was the last of the Davidic house to reign, was directly and explicitly commanded to be a just king. He was told to obey the social mandate by rescuing the oppressed and robbed people (21:11–14) Many of his Davidic predecessors had been guilty of this evil. Thus, the creational spiritual, social, and cultural covenant mandates were broken and the kings did not serve as covenant mediators par excellence. Fifth, Yahweh God upheld his demands for the Davidic kings. They were to reign wisely, do what was just and right (23:5), as David was said to have done (2 Sam. 8:15). And Jeremiah prophesied that such a Davidic king was sure to come. His name would be *Yĕhwâ ṣidĕqēnû* (Yahweh our righteousness) (Jer. 23:6). The anointed one, the Messiah, who was sure to come, would be the fulfillment of Yahweh God's promises to David concerning his everlasting house (2 Sam. 7:16). Sixth, it is important to realize that what Jeremiah proclaimed was in reality a sure reminder that Yahweh God's promises of a victorious seed to Adam and Eve (Gen. 3:15), of a sure seed to Abraham (15:4; 17:16; 22:18), of a ruler to come from Judah (49:10), and of a reigning son of David (2 Sam. 7:12, 13) would surely be fulfilled when Yahweh God would raise up to David a righteous branch, a king, who ruling righteously and justly would be the one saving his covenant people and giving them safety (Jer. 23:5, 6).[35] Seventh, the defiance of the Davidic king, Jehoiakim, who, when the Deuteronomy scroll was read to him, cut and burned it (36:19–31); Yahweh God's turning the weapons of war against King Zedekiah; Nebuchadnezzar's (the king of Babylon) victory over Judah, and their exile to Babylon (21:1–10; 52:1–27) did not in any manner annul Yahweh God's covenant with David.[36]

The Renewed Covenant

The renewed covenant, referred to as the new covenant in the New Testament (Heb. 9:15), is often thought and spoken of as a totally new and different covenant. Various Scripture passages are said to present that view.[37] The writer to the Hebrews used terms such as "first covenant" (9:15) to refer to the Sinaitic/Mosaic covenant but it is well known that it was not the first in time. The "new covenant" is also spoken of as superior (8:6) to the "first covenant." There is biblical basis therefore, it is said, for the view that the New Testament speaks of a second, that is, a completely other, covenant that really has no relationship to the Mosaic/ Sinaitic covenant, because the old covenant is obsolete, aging, and passing away (8:13). Paul is said to have referred to the new covenant (1 Cor. 11:25), as did Luke (22:20), when they referred to Jesus ordaining the sacrament of the Lord's Supper. Matthew, however, writing specifically for a Jewish audience, did not refer to the covenant as new when he quoted Jesus: "this is my blood of the covenant" (Matt. 26:28).

A detailed exegetical and theological study is included in a former work. In that context Jeremiah was surveyed and developed as a context for understanding Jeremiah's prophetic proclamation concerning the Messiah.[38] In this study, the material will be studied in a more specifically kingdom context, that is to say, how does

Jeremiah present the future administration of the covenant as an integral factor of the Golden Cable and especially in relation to the kingdom.?

This distinction, just made above, should be clearly understood. Throughout this study on the three strands of the Golden Cable—kingdom/covenant/mediator—reference has been made to the administrative aspect of the covenant, which was the basic character of the creation covenant and which continued after the salvation-redeeming-restorative aspect was included in the one covenant Yahweh God had established. The second aspect was pronounced and made effective when Yahweh God spoke to Satan the diabolic tempter, and to Adam and Eve who had deviated from God's covenant with them. The mediatorial seed is at the heart of this second strand.[39] But, he had also been the great agent in the establishing of the creation covenant.[40] In the former work Jeremiah's prophetic word concerning the renewed covenant was studied with an emphasis on the mediatorial saving, redeeming, restoring activities.[41] So the question to be answered now is: how did Jeremiah express the relationship of the renewed covenant to the biblical concept of the kingdom? He did this in several ways.[42]

The first comment is negative. The entire new covenant passage, Jeremiah 30:1–33:25, does not have the term *kingdom,* referring directly to the cosmic, theocratic, or Davidic kingdoms. The term *king* appears a few times. It refers to David once as king, who will rule over the remnant (30:9). The remnant is to be a community, the new Israel (31:7). These references appear in an eschatological setting and do not indicate that a specific historic national existence of Israel is envisaged.

Second, Jeremiah, without using the phrase "cosmic kingdom," does refer to it when he stresses the continuity of the kingdom. He stressed that as surely as the creation covenant was established when the cosmic kingdom was created, so surely will the redemptive/restorative covenant continue. Recall that Jeremiah prophesied concerning the sure continuity of the covenant with the day and the night (33:25) (as Yahweh had said when he confirmed the covenant with Noah, Gen. 8:22–9:17). In like manner, the redemptive/restorative covenant would continue. The conclusion one is compelled to acknowledge is that the cosmic kingdom is the context in which the creation and redemptive/restorative covenant, with its renewed features and administrative elements, exists and functions.

Third, Jeremiah's "renewed covenant" passage (Jer. 31:1–33:25) does not refer to a covenant that is entirely new. Rather, the one covenant is to continue in the wider context of the cosmic kingdom. But the redemptive/restorative covenant would receive a changed context and would be administered with some radical changes. The theocratic national setting and context would no longer exist (31:32),[43] but a different setting would be ushered in. This change in administration began with the exile of Judah to Babylon and was completed when Jesus Christ inaugurated the renewed form of the one covenant before his death.

Fourth, the law, spoken by God at Sinai and written on stone when the covenant was confirmed in Moses' time, was an outline for kingdom life in the life of the theocratic nation. This law would always continue. But it would not, according to

Jeremiah, continue to exist and function in a theocratic national setting. The law would be written on the hearts of the renewed covenant community members. The essence of the kingdom's prescribed way of life and service would not change. Once the mediator came and the Holy Spirit was poured out, this kingdom law would be internalized in hearts and no longer be external on slabs of stone. Again, it must be emphasized, the covenant and the kingdom must not be considered as separate and unrelated. It is important to repeat: the law as given in the Old Testament context did not change in essence and demands when the renewed covenant was fully inaugurated. It remained Yahweh's prescription for New Testament kingdom living.

Fifth, the kingdom setting of the renewed covenant is strongly confirmed by the reference to King David's role. Judah and Israel were to return from captivity (30:1–24; 33:1–26) but a human David would not reign over them as a restored theocratic nation. Judah/Israel would not ever be reconstructed as such. But David is nevertheless referred to as king (30:9). He is, however, referred to in such a manner that his dynasty is placed before the audience and readers of the prophet's message. Consider the specific reference to the righteous Branch that is to sprout from David's line (33:15). The effect and blessings of the Davidic sprouted Branch's reign is then described in terms of what a people about to be exiled could understand. There would be a blessed kingdom restoration under the King who would be the covenant Mediator, the messianic offspring of David (2 Sam. 7:16). The kingdom would no longer be national in character. David's sprout would reign as the true Zedekiah, "Yahweh Our Righteousness (Jer. 33:16b), and as the eternal covenant mediatorial Lord restored and perfected.

The sixth and final comment is intended as a summary statement.

Jeremiah was commanded to prophesy that Judah was to go into exile and would cease to exist as a theocratic nation (31:7; 32:1–5, 26–35). But Yahweh God would gather a remnant (31:8, 11, 12; 33:7) and bring them back to their former land; Jerusalem would be rebuilt. Jeremiah continued his prophecy of the return in terms that the people could understand: rebuilding and prospering.

Jeremiah, however, made it very clear that the previous theocratic national order and way of life, as administered and lived under the Sinaitic covenant, would not ever be restored and reinstituted. There was to be a renewing. The covenant, with basic features that were included in the redemptive/restorative covenant and confirmed to Noah, Abraham, and David, would be administered in a new and different way. The offspring of David, the sprout, the Branch, would be its mediatorial agent. In that capacity he would reign over the restored remnant.

The New Testament enlightens us how all this was and is still to be worked out. Christ Jesus, by his death, finally and completely inaugurated the new administration of the one eternal covenant. And this covenant is made with Jews, Gentiles, male and female, bond and free (Gal. 3:28, 29). The new covenant people are one people, one body, the new creation, the New Testament Israel, the church (6:11–16).[44]

The Kingdom

Initial Observations

The idea of kingdom is specifically and definitely biblical and is an Old Testament concept. The Scriptures testify to the reality that Yahweh God founded and established his kingdom when he created the cosmos. Hence it is correct to speak of the cosmic kingdom (Job 38:4; Pss. 47:2; 93:1–4; 97:1, 9; 145:13; Isa. 40:26, 28).[45]

The kingdom and covenant are interrelated and integrated realities in the entire Scriptures. The covenant is basically the administrative agency of the kingdom; that is to say, Yahweh God reigns and provides according to his covenant bond with creation and all that is in it. Hence, as the cosmic kingdom continues eternal from its beginning at the time of creation, so the covenant is, and vice versus.

The cosmic kingdom includes all agents of creation (Gen. 9:8–11). This includes all people. Julius L. Scott has pointed out that Karl Barth was certainly correct when in his *Dogmatics* he wrote that the race, as a whole, is in the covenant and that Israel within the inner circle was called to reach out to all races (1–3).[46] See diagram next page.

This is the biblical presentation of the cosmic kingdom with its covenantal administration, the place of the nations, the role of central governing agents, the Davidic house. The cosmic kingdom with its covenantal administration and mediatorial ruling agent had its beginning at the time of creation.[47] It follows that scholars who insist that the Mosaic covenant is patterned after heathen systems[48] are incorrect.

In this study of Jeremiah's prophetic words concerning "kingdom" it will be demonstrated that Jeremiah was given prophetic revelation concerning the various kingdoms surrounding and involved in Judah/Israel's existence, the theocratic monarchy (kingdom) Judah, and the cosmic kingdom.

Jeremiah's References to the Cosmic Kingdom[49]

As other prophets demonstrated, Jeremiah did not distinguish between the sacred and the secular. The prophets indicated in many ways that they knew, believed, and applied what David had written and sung: The earth is the Lord's, and everything in it

> The world, and all who dwell in it,
> For He founded it upon the seas
> And established it upon the waters (Ps. 24:1, 2).

David asked: Who is this Lord who created all this, who rules over it? Who is it that owns all this? The text says *layĕhwâh* (to Yahweh [the covenant Lord], 24:1) who is praised as *melek hakkābôd* (king of glory, 24:8). As David, and preceding prophets had, Jeremiah standing within the glorious covenant Lord's cosmos, not only attributes it in its entirety to the creator Lord, he freely employs aspects of it

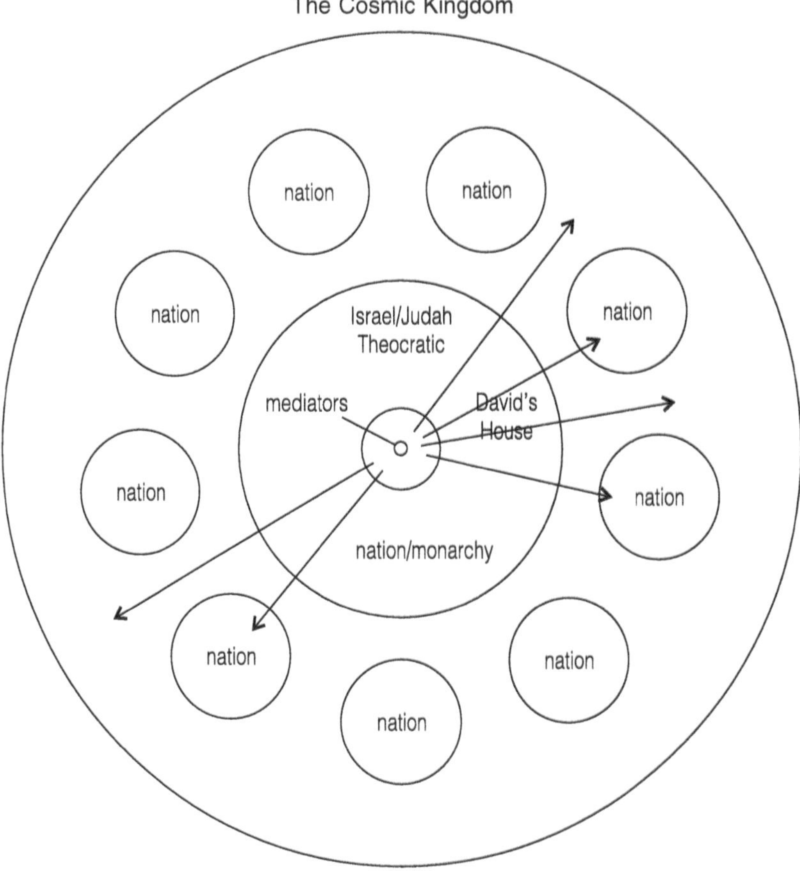

to give color and deeper meaning to the message he is called upon to proclaim: Yahweh will uproot and destroy, tear down and destroy kingdoms, as well as build and plant (Jer. 1:10).

The rejection of the distinction between secular and sacred does not in any way imply that the distinction between the spiritual and material, organic and inorganic, is rejected. The spiritual aspect and dimensions of life as Yahweh God ordained these are very real. These are experienced in every walk of life. The material aspects of the cosmos are likewise sure realities and are to be seen as related to Yahweh God the Creator and Ruler over all. The spiritual and material are interrelated and integrated by Yahweh the Creator in such a way that the spiritual is involved and experienced in the daily involvement with the material. It is in humanity's involvement in the material that the spiritual dimensions of life come to expression in many and varied ways. Yahweh God demands that covenant life and service honors both the spiritual and material aspects of creation.[50]

Jeremiah, as a very conscious cosmic kingdom prophet, employed many material/physical concepts to stress his God-revealed message to Judah. He referred to a boiling pot (1:13) to express national disaster coming and instructed Jeremiah to be as a fortified city, an iron pillar, and a bronze wall as he stood before kings and national leaders to pronounce the coming judgment because of spiritual rebellion against Yahweh God (1:18). Throughout his prophecies he referred to Yahweh God who brought to pass the exodus, with all its involvements (e.g., 2:6; 7:22; 11:4) and how Yahweh gave the promised land. When Jeremiah spoke of the coming disaster he referred to horses, whirlwinds, chariots, eagles (4:13), to a ruined land (4:27), and to the vanity of jewels and the cries of mothers giving birth (4:30, 31). He spoke of trumpets, shepherds, flocks (6:1–3; 10:21) and of sackcloth and ashes to emphasize grief and spiritual despair (6:22). When he prophesied about what would be taken away because of spiritual sins and misuse of material blessings, one can read of failed harvests, of no grapes or figs, of wounds, lack of balm, and physicians (8:13, 23). Jeremiah spoke of the worthless customs of the people who cut down trees and made silver-coated wooden, dead idols who were as speechless as scarecrows in melon patches (10:3–5). In contrast to these idols, Yahweh God is the one who by power and wisdom brought the world into existence and speaks through thunder, clouds, lightning, rain, and wind (10:11–13). To describe the tragedy that the carrying out of judgment brought, Jeremiah prophesied concerning incurable wounds (physical) and tents destroyed, ropes snapped, sons gone, scattered flocks not cared for by senseless shepherds and Judah to become a haunt for jackals (10:19–22). All these afflictions and tragedies in the lives of the people of Judah, described in such daily and earthly experiences, was Yahweh's judgment on the people who broke Yahweh's covenant with these (11:1–17). The spiritual relationship with Yahweh God was to be a deeply personal experience, but this experience was to be revealed and demonstrated in everyday life in the midst of material aspects of the cosmic kingdom. And when people misused the material, they revealed a deep lack of spiritual awareness and relationship with Yahweh God. Hence Jeremiah repeatedly reminded his audience of the integration of the spiritual and material by employing a wide range of material references to give poignant expression to spiritual waywardness, rejection of, and rebellion against Yahweh God.

Jeremiah's References to the Cosmic Nations

Jeremiah revealed another dimension of the cosmic kingdom by the manner in which he prophesied concerning the nations that in one way or another were involved in the life of the covenant people. Details concerning these nations need not be repeated.[51] To be emphasized, however, is the truth that reference to many nations by Jeremiah demonstrated his full awareness of the rich diversity of the cosmic kingdom.

Three important realities in the cosmic kingdom context of the nations must be emphasized. First, all the nations, with various and diverse types of government, reflect aspects of Yahweh God's cosmic kingdom. They were an integral part of it. Thus the divinely implanted structures of government in the cosmic kingdom naturally came to expression in the nations. These nations were not necessarily faithful to nor gave proper expression to the government functioning in the cosmic kingdom. Power and prerogatives were often sorely abused to the detriment of the national kingdoms and too often to many, if not most, of the governed people who constituted the greatest majority of members of any nation. This abuse was often referred to as a reason for judgment to come upon them.

Second, all nations were included in the Noachic covenant, which was a reconfirmation of both dimensions—the creational and the redemptive/restorative of Yahweh God's one covenant.[52] As covenant nations they were inherent participants in the cosmic kingdom and were expected to reflect this covenantal relationship. Many scholars have pointed out how various nations (without realizing it) structured and administered their governments and relationships within their nations in keeping with Yahweh's covenantal administration of the cosmic kingdom.

Third, and a most impressive reality that demonstrated that nations were actually participants in the cosmic kingdom, is Yahweh's rule, control, and use of nations to carry out his will and purposes for the kingdom. All nations, one way or another, made their contribution as they demonstrated their unique ways of life.[53] Jeremiah, as did other prophets, referred to Yahweh, the royal King of all nations, appointing nations to be his agents of judgment to be executed on rebellious nations. Consider how Jeremiah repeatedly referred to Babylon as Yahweh's agent for Judah's destruction and exile but also to Yahweh's judgment to fall on that nation, not for being an agent, but for its arrogant and perverse manner in which the Babylonians carried out their God-given tasks.[54]

Jeremiah's References to the Theocratic Monarchy

Having discussed the reality of the cosmic kingdom as expressed in various ways by Jeremiah and the place and role of nations in the cosmic kingdom, the question to be asked is, how did Jeremiah reveal the theocratic monarchy (i.e., Judah's) place and role to be in the cosmic kingdom?

Jeremiah made mention of Moses once (Jer. 15:1) and the word *Sinai* does not appear at all. But he did make it clear that he had the Sinaitic confirmation of the covenant with Israel as a theocratic nation in mind. He spoke of *habbĕrît hazzō't* (11:3) *bĕyom hôṣî'i 'ôlām mē'eres misraîm* (11:4) (this covenant [which I commanded your fathers] in the day I caused them to go from the land of Egypt). This covenant making is implied in 22:9, and is directly referred to in 31:32 and 34:13. These terms were spelled out in detail in Exodus and Leviticus and explicated and repeated in Numbers and Deuteronomy. These terms covered all aspects of life. Israel, as a kingdom, had to represent, mirror, reflect, bring to concrete expression what Yahweh God intended cosmic kingdom life to be. Israel, as a kingdom, was to be a theocracy with God as their ruling King. Israel was to serve as a model of the cosmic kingdom. Israel's kingdom was not cosmic in extent, but it was to represent specifically what Yahweh God's intent was for the entire cosmic kingdom. Israel was thus to be, as it were, at the heart of the cosmic kingdom. It was to be a blessing to all the nations; it was not only to draw them to participate wholly in it, but also by life and service to demonstrate how all aspects of the created world were integral parts of the cosmic kingdom and thus under Yahweh God's rule. Judah, by obeying and being a faithful covenant agent, could and would serve in this privileged and challenging role. But, Jeremiah had to bring Yahweh God's charge that there was a *qešer* (conspiracy) among the people of Judah (11:9). Judah broke the covenant (11:1–17). The cup of Yahweh God's wrath was to be poured out as he called down the sword on all who lived on the earth (25:15–38). Consequences would be severe. The men of Jeremiah's hometown, Anathoth, who opposed him and sought to destroy him, would not have a remnant left (11:21–23). Drought, famine, and sword (14:1–6), would come; Jerusalem and Judah would be totally ruined. Judah, as a theocratic monarchy, would cease to exist. Yahweh God's covenant would be upheld, however, by preserving a *šĕ'ērît* (remnant) (6:9),[55] which he would forgive (50:20). Thus the theocratic monarchy was to be and actually was finished. From the people who were exiled, a remnant would be spared; these would return to Jerusalem and the land of Judah and exist as a religious community, having the temple, the priesthood, and sacrifices. The law would be upheld for them. The theocratic monarchial kingdom was forever finished. The covenant would continue with David and the cosmic kingdom would continue (33:19–23). The kingdom of Israel (Judah), the symbol and type, was forever removed.[56]

Another important aspect of the kingdom calls for attention. Yahweh God had promised that seed of Abraham and of David, a royal house, would come and exist forever. This promise became an historical and physical reality when David became king of Judah and Israel. Jeremiah, however, records the fall of Jerusalem and the cessation of the reign of the Davidic seed (50:11). But Jeremiah had also prophesied that the Branch of David would reign wisely. This reigning one would be a true Zedekiah (Yahweh is Righteous) (23:3–8). He would come to reign, not over a remnant, not over a restored theocracy,[57] but over the cosmic kingdom. This seed of David would be and is the covenant mediator who is the head of the body, the new Israel (Gal. 6:16), and the king of the cosmic kingdom.

The Remnant

The term *sĕ'ērît* (remnant) appears twice in the Pentateuch. Joseph used it when he made himself known to his brothers. He told them Yahweh God had sent him (he did not say you sold me) to preserve a remnant on earth and to save their lives (Gen. 45:7). The term *remnant* in this context carries the latent idea of salvation. Joseph may not have had in mind that all people related to Jacob's family were to be saved to live, but Jacob's family would be. The covenant family of Jacob is the remnant. Jacob's family was to be preserved. Yahweh God had specific plans for that family. Their deliverance was necessary for Yahweh God to carry out his stated purposes for all nations (12:13).

Moses, speaking to the Israelites on the plains of Moab, before they were to cross the Jordan, spoke of the king of Bashan, who alone was left of the remnant of the Raphaites (Deut. 3:11). The term *remnant* is used here to refer to a very small number, probably only one survivor of the people who had been known as the inhabitants of Rephaim.

The idea of a remnant appears quite often in extrabiblical literature. Gerhard Hasel made an extensive study of the concept as it appeared in ancient literature up through the time of the prophet Isaiah.[58] In a study of the Sumerian Flood Tradition he found the term *remnant* to refer to the seed of mankind by which mankind as a whole was preserved. The remnant idea appeared in Accadian, Babylonian, and Hittite literature, also expressing the thought of life saved for a small remnant for the benefit of mankind.[59] In Egyptian literature survivors of physical illness, civil disorders, war, and natural catastrophes are referred to as *remnant.* In the Ugaretic poem "The Legend of King Keret" the survival of a remnant is the means to preserve life and its existence.[60] It is clearly obvious that the concept of *remnant* was widely known and when Moses used it in Genesis and Deuteronomy, he employed the term that refers to a group of survivors that becomes a nucleus for the continuation of mankind in extrabiblical literature and for the people of God in the Scriptures.[61]

The prophets who preceded Jeremiah employed the term *remnant* to refer to a group of survivors. This group could be understood to be small. Amos used the imagery of what a lion left of a sheep it had devoured—an ear and some bones (Amos 3:12). This remnant would survive the destruction brought on by Assyria. Micah referred to the exiles of Jacob, Israel scattered among the nations (Mic. 5:7, 8), who would nevertheless be regathered (2:12). It would be a remnant of Yahweh's inheritance who received pardon and forgiveness (7:12). Amos also spoke of the remnant as the nucleus of the covenant people whom Yahweh God would preserve when the curse of the covenant was executed by powerful, well-armed enemy nations.

Isaiah's use of the term *remnant* has been widely debated. The Scripture, however, is clear. There would be a small group who survived the Assyrian onslaughts; Isaiah used the metaphor of a hut left in a melon field when the harvest was ended (Isa. 1:8). But this small remnant who are survivors of the covenant people will rely on Israel's Holy One as they return to their mighty God (10:20, 21).[62] Isaiah prophesied that the Root of Jesse, the Branch, would reclaim the remnant of his people left in various nations and gather them as the people united under the messianic reign (11:11, 16). It is of interest to note that Isaiah urged King Hezekiah to pray for the remnant that would survive (31:4) , because this remnant would come from Jerusalem (Judah) and "take root," survive, and bear fruit (31:4, 31, 32). Isaiah clearly prophesied with these words that Yahweh God would preserve a nucleus, or a core, of his covenant people through whom the fulfillment of his covenant promises would be realized.

Jeremiah, more than any other prophet, prophesied concerning a remnant of Judah. The term appears twenty-three times. The people of Jerusalem who would survive the Babylonian siege of Jerusalem would be as few as grapes left on vines that had been picked and had hands pass over the branches to feel a second time for grapes left after the initial picking (Jer. 6:9). But Babylon did leave some people in Jerusalem after it had been captured—these are referred to as a remnant (40:11). This group, however, referred to as a remnant would not serve as the people through whom the covenant promises would come. This remnant would disappear, although the survivors of the Babylonian captive of Jerusalem were referred to as the *šĕʾērît yĕhûdâ* (remnant of Judah) they would disappear from the earth in Egypt (41:11, 15; 42:15, 19; 43:5; 44:7, 12, 14). This group of survivors, a remnant of Judah, when having fled to Egypt, would have Yahweh God watching over them for harm. Having escaped the sword and famine in Jerusalem, they would be destroyed (44:27). But, if a few returned from Egypt to Jerusalem they would become part of the remnant of Judah that would be spared. The remnant of Judah that survived Yahweh's punishment of Babylon would be forgiven and spared (50:20).

Jeremiah prophesied that Yahweh God would gather the remnant of his flock (23:3). When announcing the certainty of the renewed covenant, Yahweh God spoke of his everlasting love for this remnant and called them to sing for joy because Yahweh God saves his people, the remnant of Israel (31:3–9).

Ezekiel spoke of the remnant in the context of the idolaters being slain in Jerusalem. He asked Yahweh God if the entire remnant of Israel was to be destroyed (Ezek. 9:8; 11:13). The inescapable thrust of Ezekiel's prayer is that he realized that very few of the people left in Jerusalem would be spared. Ezekiel did not refer to the exiles, or part of them, as a remnant. Haggai and Zechariah, decades after Ezekiel, did speak of the remnant (Hag. 1:12, 14; 2:2; Zech. 8:6, 11, 12). The 50,000 people who had returned from Babylon to rebuild the altar, the temple, and eventually Jerusalem (Ezra 9:8, 13, 14, 15; Neh. 1:2) were called the remnant.

The main point of the Old Testament testimony concerning the remnant was that when the curse of the covenant was to be, and was executed, there would be a small group of Israelites/Judahites whom Yahweh God would spare. These spared ones were to serve as the nucleus of Yahweh God's covenant people. This core would constitute the community from which the promised Messiah would come. The remnant demonstrated Yahweh God's faithfulness to his covenant promises to Abraham, Isaac, Jacob, Judah, and David that the promised seed of the woman would arise from their progeny.

In the New Testament the concept appears three times. The apostle James, serving as "bishop" of the early church, quoted Amos 9:12. Amos had prophesied that when David's descendant, the Messiah, would come, people from all nations, even from a few surviving Edomites, a remnant of them would be included in the body of believers. Paul, writing to the Romans, quoted Isaiah about the small number of Israelites to be saved (Rom. 9:27). And he went on to write that a remnant of Abraham's seed—of Israel—was chosen by grace. The remnant was represented, he wrote, by a wild olive shoot that would become a fruitful tree. Into this tree the believing Gentiles would be grafted. Thus the remnant of Israel and the believing and redeemed Gentiles would be one fruitful tree. Thus the remnant of Israel/Judah fulfilled its twofold purpose: the Messiah received his humanity through it and it served as the nucleus or core into which believing Gentiles are engrafted. There would then be no remnant but a whole body, composed of Jews and Gentiles (Gal. 3:28, 29).

Summary

Jeremiah proclaimed an abiding covenant in which the promises and obligations emphasized in various administrations were included. This abiding covenant was and is the administrative and redemptive/restorative agency of the ever-abiding cosmic kingdom over which Yahweh God reigns. This cosmic kingdom includes all the aspects: physical, material, organic, inorganic, spiritual. All nations are included in the cosmic kingdom. The theocratic monarchy served as a temporary model, symbol, type from David's time until the exile of Judah. A remnant was preserved through which the eternal mediator, God's Son Jesus Christ, came, fulfilled the covenant demands, and now reigns at the Father's right hand over the cosmic kingdom in its entirety, including the nations and all believing people, regardless of race or ethnicity.

The Mediator

The Three Mediatorial Offices

The covenant kingdom mediatorial agency and offices were represented typically by prophets, priests, and kings. Each had their specific role and authority. Together they pointed forward to the one mediator who was to fill the three offices and carry out the duties involved in each. Adam and Eve, when created, were assigned to carry out the responsibilities and duties of each.[63] The second Adam was to, and did, serve as the one mediator executing the three mediatorial responsibilities. In the period between the first and second Adams, cosmic kingdom and covenantal privileges, responsibilities and duties were to be assumed and executed by people who served as types—reflecting what Adam had had and lost, to a great extent, and pointing to what the perfect mediator would be and do. The prophet Jeremiah prophesied concerning the three and the one mediators.[64]

The Mediatorial Prophet

Jeremiah served as a divinely appointed prophet and prophesied concerning prophets.

Jeremiah, called to prophesy judgment and eventual restoration, lived and worked in a very difficult religious and political context. He proved to be a man of immense courage as he addressed the nation of Judah concerning the judgment that was to be executed within a short span of time. The Babylonians would serve as willing agents to carry out Yahweh God's wrath. Jeremiah was beaten and put in stocks (Jer. 20:2); he was threatened by death in his hometown, Anathoth (11:21) and by the public in the temple courtyard (20:7ff.); he was imprisoned (37:1–21) and thrown into a cistern to die (38:4–6). Faithfully he prophesied as he suffered humiliation and threats of execution. He, in his work and life gave a positive portrait of the future mediatorial prophet.

Jeremiah's humiliation and suffering were accentuated by men who claimed to be prophets also but had messages that were false. They prophesied by Baal (2:8; 23:1, 3), prophesying lies (5:31; 14:14; 27:14). The example of false prophecy of hope for Judah was given by Hananiah whose early death was predicted by Jeremiah (28:1–17). In facing opposition and fearlessly proclaiming Yahweh God's word for Judah, Jeremiah demonstrated a clear and positive portrait of what a mediatorial prophetic agent was, serving as a faithful kingdom and covenant servant.

The Mediatorial Priest

Jeremiah spoke concerning priests no less than forty times. He addressed them personally (Jer. 27:16), telling them not to listen to the false promises of untrustworthy prophets. He knew the priests, Pashur (21:1), Zephaniah (21:1; 29:29; 37:3), Hananiah (28:1), Massaiah (29:25). None of these were faithful to the Lord; Jeremiah accused them of being godless—their wickedness was evident in the temple (23:11). If they, with prophets, claimed to be appointed of God (29:26, 29) or came with an oracle (23:33–40), contradicting the word of the Lord through Jeremiah, they would be forgotten of Yahweh God and he would cast them out of his presence, bringing everlasting disgrace and shame upon them (23:33–40). The priests who had been instructed to uphold Yahweh God's covenant law when they were asked by the people to give Yahweh's will for them (18:18), ruled by their own authority (5:31). Then when Yahweh God in wrath brought disaster from the north, they would be horrified and the prophets would be appalled (4:9). Prophets and priests joined in opposition to Jeremiah but Yahweh God opposed them and they would be punished. Jeremiah recorded the exile of Zephaniah the chief priest.

The blessed truth is that although prophets and priests were unfaithful to Yahweh God, these offices were not to be forgotten or obliterated. With the return from exile, blessings would be restored and Yahweh would satisfy the priests with abundance. These blessings were to come as integral aspects of the renewed covenant, when he, who should have been obeyed by priests who were to be his forerunners and types, came as the perfect high priest, the mediator of the covenant.

The Mediatorial King

Jeremiah demonstrated that he was very much aware of the political circumstances in his time. Politics was woven into the fabric of life. Nations, governments, kings, and officials were deeply involved in the spiritual and social dimensions of the life of the covenant people. These affected the lives, policies, and actions of ruling personnel.

It is of real interest to take notice of which kings Jeremiah spoke. He mentioned King Solomon's contribution to the temple that the Babylonians destroyed (52:20).

He spoke of David by name ten times, of this throne (22:30; 36:30), of the covenant Yahweh had made with him (33:21), of David's descendants (33:20), of the righteous Branch to come from David (23:5), and of David, my (Yahweh's) servant (33:21). Jeremiah spoke of Hezekiah (20:18, 19) who feared Yahweh but because of his son Manasseh's wickedness, death, sword, starvation, and captivity were to be the destroying means of Judah (15:1–4). Jeremiah referred to Davidic kings reigning during his lifetime, Josiah, Jehoachin, Jehoiakim, and Zedekiah. He recalled that the king of Assyria, because of his overkill of Israel, was punished (50:18), and of the roles of Hophra and Neco, Pharaohs of Egypt (44:30; 46:2). Repeatedly he prophesied about Nebuchadnezzar who, as servant of Yahweh (25:9; 43:10), would be Yahweh's agent of severe judgment upon Judah.

All these kings were subject to One who was and is King of the nations. He is the great, mighty, incomparable One, the true and living God, the eternal king Jeremiah proclaimed (10:7, 10). Yahweh God, the Creator, revealed his wisdom and understanding as he "stretched out the heavens" (10:12) and reveals his absolute rule over the cosmic kingdom as he sends lightning, thunder, and rain (10:13). In various finite ways, each ruling king of the nations represented Yahweh God and reflected him. Human kings, however, very often misused their God-given privileges and sometimes in monstrous ways. Some royal members of the Davidic dynasty did also. But David, the head of the dynasty, was assured that of his descendants one would reign righteously and wisely. He is David's Branch whose name is *yĕhwâ śidĕqēnû* (Yahweh our Righteouness). All the royal members of the Davidic dynasty who ruled were ancestors and were to be true types of the Branch. But because many failed, and especially because of Manasseh and his son Amon, the human representative and types were cut off. But promises to David would stand. Yahweh, Jeremiah spoke figuratively, *'aśĕmîaḥ lĕdâwēd śemaḥ* (I will cause to sprout from David a sprout [branch] 33:15). In terms of everyday life the people of Judah understood, Jeremiah proclaimed that this Branch, Yahweh Our Righteousness, was and would be the Savior and security of his people. This is the heart of the redemptive/restorative covenant that stood rock firm throughout the Old Testament times. It would be renewed. This renewal of the covenant would be initiated when the Davidic branch sprouted, that is, when his true royal descendant, the Messiah, the Son of God, became flesh. It would increasingly be realized when the Messiah ministered, suffered, rose from the grave, and ascended to reign at the Father's hand. The renewed covenant would be fully realized when the Messiah comes the second time as Lord and Judge of all people.[65]

Summary

Jeremiah's Prophecy

Jeremiah prophesied that the old order for Israel/Judah was soon to be destroyed and gone forever. The covenant people, as a theocratic monarchy, the holy nation, would cease to exist. But Yahweh's covenant would continue, under a renewed administration, within the cosmic kingdom. And the eternally trustworthy, wise, righteous, ruling, priestly, prophetic descendant of David would be the royal covenantal mediator.

Joel's Agenda

Jeremiah did not strictly follow Joel's agenda nor did he emphasize some of the issues Joel raised. Jeremiah, as had Joel, called for repentance (Jer. 4:1–4) He spoke concerning disasters to come, not so much in figurative terms (e.g., swarms of locusts,) but in realistic terms of what the Babylonians would do. Jeremiah prophesied concerning a blessed future, not so much in terms of Yahweh God's zealous love but in terms of an eventual return and the blessings of the renewed covenant. Joel had prophesied concerning the coming of the Spirit. Jeremiah made no overt reference to it but could be said to imply this when speaking of the internalizing of the law in the hearts of the covenant people. Joel had spoken of Jerusalem spared, Jeremiah prophesied concerning the fall and destruction of the city. Jeremiah expanded Joel's reference to nations by addressing individual nations, and gave hints of some people of these nations becoming members of the new Israel. Joel prophesied concerning abundant blessings in the creational/natural realm of kingdom life. Jeremiah did also to a limited extent but prophesied more concerning the effects and results of judgment.

One very specific reality must be clearly understood. Jeremiah prophesied in a very different context than Joel did. True, Joel spoke of disasters to come; Jeremiah addressed the disastrous events that were beginning to unfold. Jeremiah thus addressed issues very relevant to his times: of disregard for and rebellion against Yahweh God by Davidic kings, priests, and prophets. Hence Jeremiah's personal involvement strongly influenced his attitudes and emotions, and the specific issues he was called by Yahweh God to address.

NOTES

1. From 1988 until the time of writing, additional material has been written but very little, if any, new information has been offered.

2. In 1988 the author spent a few months studying the extant material on the book of Jeremiah. His insights and conclusions have appeared in his book, *Messianic Revelation in the Old Testament* (Grand Rapids: Baker, 1990), 678–89. Reprinted in paperback (Eugene, Ore.: Wiph and Stock, 1997).

3. These literary problems will not receive much attention in this chapter. The intent is to emphasize the biblical-theological contribution it makes to the study of the Golden Cable. Should one wish to consult a critical discussion, cf. John Skinner, *Prophecy and Religion* (reprint, Cambridge: Cambridge University Press, 1955), chap. 6, 89–107.

4. That Jeremiah stood in the line of prophetic proclamation will be referred to in the subsequent study of the message of Jeremiah. In the preceding discussion the concept of intertextuality was introduced. Cf. chap. 24, note 48.

5. Cf. paragraph concerning this in *Messianic Revelation,* 683, and see note 56.

6. Reference has been made to the finding of the Book of the Covenant; the broader national historical context is important for a clear understanding of Jeremiah's prophecies concerning the covenant.

7. 2 Chronicles relates how Hezekiah had not followed in the ways of his father Ahaz who had defied Isaiah and Yahweh God (Isa. 7:1–7). When at the age of twenty-five years, Hezekiah became king, he purified the temple, recommenced the celebration of the Passover, and gathered contributions for worship. It was subsequent to these Yahweh God, honoring activities that Sennacharib threatened Jerusalem (2 Chron. 29:1–31:21).

8. One must keep in mind that Yahweh God's covenant with David included the stipulation of faithful adherence and obedience to the covenant. A curse was included should there be a departure (2 Sam. 7:14).

9. Gerhardus Vos discusses these two periods in a succinct presentation, *Biblical Theology,* 11th printing (Grand Rapids: Eerdmans, 1948, 1980), 189.

10. Vos was definite in his reference to the regenerated kingdom as not in any way allowing for a theocratic kingdom in a millennium. Ibid.

11. Manasseh reigned as co-regent with Hezekiah for approximately ten years and then reigned as a sole regent for forty-five years. Jewish tradition holds that Isaiah was martyred during the reign of Manasseh. See David L. Payne, *The New Layman's Bible Commentary,* ed. G.C.D. Howley, F. F . Bruce, and H. L. Ellison (Grand Rapids: Zondervan, 1979), 763.

12. Jeremiah the prophet, his call, his personality, and his career, were studied at some length in my book, *Messianic Revelation,* 683–89.

13. The Hebrew terms are taken from daily life's experiences; hence no one could say they did not understand what was to take place.

14. See Theodore Laetch's discussion of this phrase. *Jeremiah* (St. Louis: Concordia, 1952), 30.

15. John A. Thompson, *The Book of Jeremiah* (Grand Rapids: Eerdmans, 1980), 156.

16. Brevard S. Childs, *Introduction to the Old Testament as Scripture* (Philadelphia: Fortress, 1997), 347.

17. Charles Feinberg, "Jeremiah," in *The Expositor's Bible Commentary,* ed. Frank E. Gabelein (Grand Rapids: Regency/Zondervan, 1986), 6:386.

18. Jeremiah made repeated references to the covenant; he used the term in various contexts. Gordon Garner found that Jeremiah used the term *bĕrît* twenty-three times, once in relation to the ark of the covenant, six times to agreement to release slaves, ten times to the Sinaitic or Davidic covenant, and six times to the new everlasting covenant. Garner went on to say that this use of the concept covenant provides an essential relationship with Deuteronomy. "Jeremiah and the New Covenant," Tyndale Paper, issued in March 1968, 3.

19. Cf. references and discussion of covenant of creation in *Messianic Revelation,* 56–62, in relation to Jeremiah, 714–18, and especially the author's first volume *From Creation to Consummation* (Sioux Center: Dordt, 1996), 65–72.

20. Cf. the discussion of this reality in O. Palmer Robertson, *The Christ of the Covenants* (Phillipsburg: Presbyterian and Reformed, 1980), 19–21. William J. Dumbrell, *Covenant and Creation* (Nashville: Thomas Nelson, 1984), did not discuss the "irrefragability of the Davidic covenant although he did refer to the passage dealing with God's covenant with the day and night, 172.

21. Cf. Deut. 32:1, Isa. 1:2; 42:5; 51:16.

22. Reference to the seed will be made when discussing the mediator, section iv.

23. Cf. *From Creation,* 1:113–20, where the phrase is discussed at some length. Cf. also note 133.

24. See Dumbrell's discussion on the one covenant in chapter I of his *Covenant and Creation,* 11–43. Note his concluding statement: "There could be only one biblical covenant, of which later biblical covenants are subsets." 43.

25. Cf. chap. 22.

26. Note the three large nations that Yahweh God employed as agents of woe. Philistia, the immediate neighbor, and the three relative nations, Moab, Ammon, and Edom, have propheicies of woe and doom pronounced against them for their idolatry, social injustices, and disobedience to the creational mandates.

27. Recall that the niphal, the reflexive form of the verb *bārak, nibrĕkû,* was employed to emphasize the nations' responsibilities (Gen. 12:3). D. Preman Niles, in his essay, "Called to be a Blessing to the Nations," *Asia Journal of Theology* 12, no. 2 (1998), includes in brackets "will bless themselves" as an acceptable reading. P. F. Payne, in his commentary on Genesis in *The New Layman's Bible Commentary,* ed. G.C.D. Howley, F. F. Bruce, and H. L. Ellison (Grand Rapids: Zondervan, 1979), translates the niphal "by you all the families of earth shall bless themselves," 144.

28. Jeremiah's call to the people to circumcise themselves to the Lord, circumcise your hearts, certainly reflects Yahweh God's command to Abraham to circumcise his family as a sign and seal of the covenant.

29. When referring to Jeremiah 2–6, there is no need to demonstrate that the text is in need of emendation and alterations. Robert Althann in his book, *A Philological Analysis of Jeremiah 4–6 in the Light of Northwest Semitic* (Rome: Biblical Institute, 1983), wrote in the conclusion to his study that his investigation of grammatical and poetic phenomena led to his understanding that the LXX alterations and critical conjectural emending of the text were not to be supported, 303. See also Emanuel Tov's work *The Septuagint Translation of Jeremiah and Baruch* (Missoula: Scholars, 1976). Tov's conclusions include that there were sections of Jeremiah included in the LXX that is a "heterogeneous collection of translations, original and revised." This view would suggest that the LXX is not acceptable as a text of Jeremiah.

30. Cf. the discussion on whether the author of Jer. 3:6–11 misunderstood and misapplied the use of Israel in 3:1–5. J. G. McConville challenged that view. He wrote that "it is not the case that Israel simply refers to Judah. Rather the name is complex and allows the history of the northern kingdom to stand as a warning or threat over Judah." *Judgment and Promise* (Winona Lake: Eisenbrauns, 1993), 38. Care must be taken, however, in accepting some of McConville's views in view of his acceptance of the position that Jeremiah, as a book, was produced over a long period of time and that a final editing process took place at a time not discernible. See his "Conclusions," 173–81.

31. John Bright translated the entire verse, 2:9, as follows: "So—still I must state my case against you—Yahweh's word—to your children's children I will state it." *Jeremiah,* The Anchor Bible, vol. 21 (Garden City: Doubleday, 1965), 10. A. Van Selms commented on the "still" remaining leaders of the past—priests, intellectuals, rulers, and prophets who were charged and on Jeremiah's contemporaries as well as future generations who inherit what the fathers had done. He added "Men kan de trotsenaam van Israeliet niet dragen zonder ook de verantewoordelijkheid van de schuld van Israel op zie nemen" (Men cannot carry the proud name of Israelite without also taking the responsibility for the guilt of Israel), *Jeremiah* (Nykerk: Callenbach, 1972), 1:46.

32. Roland K. Harrison entitled the section 11:1–12:7 "The Prophet and the Covenant." He interpreted this passage as a warning to Judah to be faithful to the historic agreement sealed centuries earlier at Sinai lest the promised judgments be unleashed on her. It seems that Harrison forgot what he wrote, commenting on 8:18–9:1, that the captivity was anticipated. Jeremiah did no more than warn, he prophesied what was sure to come because Judah had repeatedly broken the covenant. *Jeremiah and Lamentations* (Downers Grove: InterVarsity, 1973), 95, 96.

33. Carl F. Keil commented on 3:1–5, writing that, as a divorced woman who had become another man's wife cannot return to her first husband, so Judah, after it had turned away to other gods, "would not be received again by Jahveh."as a theocratic nation, his bride of days gone by. *The Prophecies of Jeremiah,* vol. 1, trans. David Patrick (Grand Rapids: Eerdmans, 1950), 77–78.

34. It seems that Feinberg, in his commentary, "Jeremiah," overlooked what Jeremiah the prophet said, and what Judah should have said (Jer. 3:11–25). Feinberg wrote as if the people had actually "showed the depth of reality of their repentance: they accepted the Lord's offer of pardon" 403, 404. Jeremiah did his utmost to have the people repent; he courageously and emotionally spoke on behalf of his fellow men and women. But, Judah as a people, remained disobedient and faithless. Feinberg acknowledges this when commenting on Yahweh's command not to pray for this people, 430.

35. For an in-depth exegesis of Jeremiah 1–8, cf. *MROT,* 694–707.

36. Cf. what was written in *MROT,* 718, concerning the keeping of previous covenants. See also the discussion of Nebuchadnezzar as the servant reigning according to Yahweh God's will filling the place for a time of the Davidic dynasty, 708-09.

37. Confusion on how to interpret and apply the teaching of the Scriptures concerning the "new" covenant is evident in the commentary by Charles L. Feinberg, "Jeremiah," who insists on holding to a sharp distinction between Israel and the church (which he says was not present in Old Testament times). Feinberg agrees that the "new covenant" is for Jews and Gentiles yet it is to be Israel who is to ratify the covenant after the "full number of Gentiles has come in," 574–76. A footnote in the *Oxford W.W. Scofield Study Bible* expresses the view that this new covenant is contrasted to the old; some features, it is admitted, have been fulfilled for "believers in the present church age but this covenant is to be realized for Israel." Jer. 31:31 is taken to be understood literally. Hence Israel is to benefit from a completely new covenant. Cf. note on 31:32, 783. See also Dwight Pentecost in *Things to Come: A Study in Biblical Eschatology* (Findlay: Dunham, 1958), 124.

38. *MROT,* 707–27.

39. Recall that various biblical interpreters speak only of the covenant of grace. They lift it out of its creational covenantal context and stress that salvation (the covenant of grace) is the factor in God's covenanting with people. A specific example of this can be found in Alistair Reid McEwen's master of theology thesis (Grand Rapids: Calvin Seminary Library, 1987). McEwen had a number of great difficulties to deal with because of various factors. First, he tried to define and understand the idea of covenant by consulting various modern writers, who themselves reveal differences, and his attempt to combine these was not successful. Second, McEwen followed various writers in saying that there was a sharp distinction between obligatory and promissory covenants but as he dealt with the biblical materials he wrote that the obligatory covenants included promises and the promissory covenants included obligations. Third, he consistently referred to covenants (in fact, Yahweh made more than one with Abraham [29–35]) but he wrote that basic elements of preceding

covenants were included in succeeding covenants. Fourth, he chose to write of the covenant Jeremiah prophesied about as the *new* not the renewed, but agreed that this "new covenant" included important elements of previous covenants. Fifth, McEwen relied too heavily on widely divergent sources instead of developing the biblically presented materials by which he should have evaluated the various divergent views. Sixth, McEwen did not give proper attention to the biblical revelation concerning the one covenant Yahweh made but made various alterations in the administration of this one covenant as the historical process unfolded.

40. Cf. chap. 2 of vol. 1, *From Creation to Consummation*, the section on "the Acts of Creation," 24–34. Note statement on page 26, "all that was brought into being came into existence by God's creating word." John 1:1–3 reminds us this creating word was the second person of the Trinity, the Son, Jesus the Christ.

41. Cf. *MROT* After the overview of chaps. 24–32, in which the vision of two baskets of figs and King Nebuchadnezzar's role was explained, passages were studied in which was found the revelation of the messianic concept (30:8, 9, 20, 21, David the king; 31:15, Rachel weeping; 31:22, a woman surrounding a man; 31:31–40, the integral part of the book of comfort; and 33:14–26, continuity of David's house and the Aaronic priesthood).

42. Cf. Thompson's correct comments on Jer. 30:20 and 31:7, *Jeremiah,* 561, 562, 569.

43. The writer of Hebrews commented that the Mosaic/theocratic/national administration of the redemptive/restorative, as set forth in a national theocratic setting, had become obsolete and had passed away (Heb. 8:13).

44. Cf. how Laetsch, *Jeremiah,* presents this understanding of the biblical presentation concerning the people of the new covenant, 247, 248, 255. "This new covenant is made with reunited Judah and Israel, joined by the Gentiles (Jer. 3:16–19; Hos. 1:10, 11; Rom. 9:25; 1 Peter 2:10) who will then form the one holy Christian church." R. K. Harrison in *Jeremiah* wrote that the "new agreement" would not be restricted to the Israelites and he added that the individual (meaning from any nation) was substituted for the nation (Israel) as a whole, 140. Unfortunately Harrison did not include the concept of covenant community with which the new covenant is made.

45. Martin J. Selman wrote that although the concept of the kingdom is thought to be a marginal concept in the Old Testament by some scholars, others regard it as a major concept. He referred to Walther Eichrodt, who had written that the centrality of the covenant in the Old Testament did not obscure the significance of the kingdom. Selman proceeded to indicate that Eichrodt was correct. He gave a detailed study of the book of Chronicles and concluded "the concept of the kingdom and (God's) kingly rule is an important one for the Chronicler" ("Kingdom of God in the O.T.," *Tyndale Bulletin* 40 [1989)]:162–98).

46. Julius L. Scott, "The Covenant in the Theology of Karl Barth," *Scottish Theological Journal* 17 (1964): 182–98.

47. Recall that in vol. 1 the royal position and prerogatives of Adam and Eve were studied. *FCTC,* vol. 1, chap. 3, esp. sections II and IV.

48. Cf. McEwen, who accepted various disparate views and his attempt to correlate these and to harmonize them with scriptural presentations. (Cf. note 39 above.)

49. No attempt will be made to develop these in a chronological order; that is, no attempt will be made to place all the prophecies in the order they were proclaimed. The order in the text will be followed as they are written in the first eleven chapters.

50. A note of application: Christian school education is a vital necessity because it is in this context that children and young people gain an understanding and appreciation of the reality that all aspects of life, the spiritual, material, physical, and psychological aspects are in reality an integrated whole.

51. Cf. chap. 21, in which these nations are discussed.

52. See chap. 7 in vol. I of *FCTC,* especially the chart on p. 155. See also chap 4 in *MROT,* especially 122–28.

53. Cf. chap. 21 for a discussion of these realities.

54. Jeremiah referred to Babylon more than 160 times in his prophecies.

55. Jeremiah repeatedly referred to the remnant. Cf. next section, F, for a discussion of the "remnant" concept.

56. It is difficult to understand the position of scholars who insist that the theocratic monarchy will reappear. The question to be answered is: Why, when once the reality of the cosmic kingdom ruled over by the ascended ruling Jesus Christ is realized, would the symbol, type, preparer for the cosmic kingdom be restored for a millennium? It would be as if a traveler who saw the sign pointing to the city of his destination, arrived there, and then returned to the sign.

57. Jeremiah prophesied concerning the return of the remnant to Jerusalem, to their rebuilding and tilling, to their prosperity and well-being. As a community, not as a nation, they as a covenant community would continue until Jesus Christ had come and the New Testament Israel, consisting of believing Jews and Gentiles, had become a reality.

58. Gerhard F. Hasel, *The Remnant* (Berrien Springs: Andrews University Press, 1972).

59. Ibid. See also conclusion, Part V, 373–80.

60. Ibid., 381.

61. Cf. Raymond Dillard's "Remnant" in *Baker Encyclopedia of the Bible*, vol. 2, ed. Walter A. Elwell (Grand Rapids: Baker, 1988), 1833–36.

62. Hasel stated the case precisely: when Isaiah spoke of the return of the remnant of Israel, he was thinking of a deliverance of such magnitude that can only be performed by Yahweh. The emphasis of Isaiah is on Yahweh's mighty action. *Remnant,* 348.

63. Cf. *MROT,* 32–34, 103.

64. Detailed studies on Jeremiah's prophecies concerning the messianic Mediator are included in *MROT,* 678–729.

65. Hans K. Rondelle in *The Israel of God in Prophecy* (Berrien Springs: Andrews University Press, 1983) made some profoundly correct statements. "It is true that Christ's reign over the church which is effective in inclining the hearts and lives of individual believers (Jews & Gentiles) to obedience of faith, is not yet the glory of the future Messianic kingdom. The second coming brings its own, more glorious consummation of the new covenant in the kingdom of glory. But this greater glory should never lead us to deny the truth and reality of the spiritual fulfillment of Christ's present kingdom (see Rom. 14:14; 1 Cor. 4:20; Col. 1:13)." He went on to refute those who, by disregarding the grammatical, historical principles of exegesis, apply the future of the new covenant as a promise to Israel only, 119.

26

Ezekiel

The Prophet among the Exiles

Part I: Introductory Comments

I. Ezekiel the Man

II. The Time

III. Themes from Joel's Agenda

IV. Golden Cable Strands

Part II: Prophecies of Judgment: Ezekiel 1–32

I. Survey of Prophecies

II. The Kingdom Context

III. The Covenant in Ezekiel's Prophecies

IV. The Mediator

Part III: Prophecies of Restoration: Ezekiel 33:1–48:35

I. Survey of Ezekiel's Prophecies

II. The Covenant

III. The Covenant Mediators

IV. The Kingdom

26

Ezekiel

The Prophet among the Exiles

Ten years ago I wrote "one is easily overwhelmed by the historical, personal, political, literary and theological discussions which have taken place in the eighteenth and nineteenth centuries about Daniel."[1] I must add that the literature produced in the twentieth century about Ezekiel has increased this sense of being overwhelmed.[2]

Introductory Comments

Ezekiel the Man

Ezekiel was born into the priestly family of *bûzî hakkōhēn* (Butzi the priest). Whether he served as a priest in the Jerusalem temple is not known. His references to the cult, temple, and sacrifices indicate he had a specific awareness of these. He was taken as a captive in the second deportation to Babylon by Nebuchadnezzer in 597 B.C. While living among the exiles in a "slave camp" on the banks of the River Chebar, he, a priest, was called to be a prophet.[3] Yahweh God *Adonây*[4] made special arrangements for the covenant people of Judah to hear his word during their catastrophic experiences. Jeremiah prophesied to a remnant left in Jerusalem; Ezekiel did so among the exiled remnant; and Daniel was Yahweh's prophet in the palaces of the kings who ruled and controlled the destiny of the exiled remnant. Yahweh God thus demonstrated his intense desire to keep his word alive among the disinherited[5] covenant people.

The Time

A thorough knowledge of the historical context of a prophet's ministry is important. In a study of the historical progression of Yahweh God's specific revelation, which is unique to biblical-theological studies, the time and context should be clearly understood. So, the question is: is it possible to determine the time and context of Ezekiel's prophetic ministry?

The biblical text is clear as to where Ezekiel was when he received his first revelation from Yahweh God. He was among the exiles *'al nĕhar kĕbar* (by the River Kebar). This was a channel of the Euphrates River that left the river near Babylon and rejoined it about sixty miles south at Warka.[6] Hence, Ezekiel was deep in Babylonian territory.

Ezekiel made two references to the time he received the initial revelation from Yahweh God *Adonây*. It was on the fifth day of the fourth month of the fifth year of King Jehoichin's exile. Jehoichin had reigned only three months when Nebuchadnezzar's officers took him as prisoner to Babylon. This was at the time of the second deportation in 597 B.C. Ezekiel had been in captivity for five years when he received the initial revelation. This was in 592 B.C. During these five years he had undoubtedly come to know and understand the mood and hopes of his fellow exiles. Since Jerusalem was still the capital (if only in name) of the nation of Judah, which had become a vassal state of Babylon, the hope and expectation among the exiles seemed to have been that it was but a matter of time before they would be freed and return to their home, city, and country.

It was Ezekiel's task to convince the exiles that their time in captivity had only begun. He was to inform them in different ways of this reality in the initial five years he had been called to be a prophet. When Jerusalem was sacked in 586 B.C., an escapee arrived in Babylon and informed Ezekiel and the exiles that Jerusalem had fallen and was destroyed. A third deportation of exiles to Babylon followed Jerusalem's fall.[7]

The second reference to time that Ezekiel made was to the thirtieth year (1:1). This thirtieth year was the same as the fifth year of Jehoichin's exile. Since that fifth year was 592 B.C., the thirtieth year was 622 B.C. According to a chronology of the kings' reigns,[8] Josiah began to reign in 640 B.C. And it was the eighteenth year of his reign that the Book of the Law was found in the temple. That would be in 622 B.C. The question of course is: was the finding of the Book of the Law such a momentous event that it became a milestone by which later events were dated?

Another comment that should be made in regard to time concerns the messages that Ezekiel proclaimed. Before the arrival of the escapee in 585 B.C., Ezekiel's message was largely of judgment due to Judah's covenant breaking. After that message was received in 595 B.C., Ezekiel's message was increasingly one of hope and of a glorious restoration in the undetermined future. Hence, it should be kept in mind that in a real sense Ezekiel's work has a bifid character—thirty-two chapters of judgment, and sixteen chapters of hope and of a glorious future.

Themes from Joel's Agenda

Ezekiel did not include all the themes of Joel's agenda. This, in part, was due to the changes in the historical situation. Jerusalem had not been spared. Warnings of local and national disasters to come had become realities and these were referred to only indirectly while these were main ingredients in the context of the people's daily lives. Ezekiel did repeat the call to repentance and gave assurances of Yahweh God's zealous love. He did not prophesy concerning abundant blessings in the creational realm but did give clear preferences to the coming and presence of the Holy Spirit and the renewing of the covenant people. He prophesied concerning judgment to come upon the nations and a renewing of the covenant people. He did not give assurance of a repossessing of the land. But he spoke strong, assuring words concerning a future peace, the covenant of peace that would be fully realized in the Day of Yahweh when an ever-increasing flow of living water would come from the throne of Yahweh God.

Golden Cable Strands

Ezekiel was present at a crucial period in the lives of God's covenant people and was a cardinal spokesman in the progressive revelation of Yahweh God. The question that should be asked is: what precisely did Ezekiel contribute to the three basic concepts or strands of the Golden Cable? Which we have seen unites the entire biblical message.

Ezekiel spoke of kings, but the Hebrew term *malkût* (kingdom) does not appear in his prophecies. Is one to conclude that the concept of the kingdom is no longer a strong strand in the Golden Cable? The term *bĕrît* (covenant) occurs eighteen times; is this frequent enough to consider it a major theme and strand? The term *māšîah* (anointed, messiah) does not appear at all. That Ezekiel prophesied directly or indirectly concerning the messianic Mediator has been clearly demonstrated.[9]

In the study that follows, the role of the three strands as they function in the first thirty-two chapters will be developed. Then, the three strands as they appear in the last sixteen chapters will be studied.

Prophecies of Judgment: Ezekiel 1–32

Survey of Prophecies

Ezekiel Spoke and Wrote

In view of the unique presentation of Ezekiel's prophecies, with the use of metaphors, symbols, and demonstrative yet mystical activities,[10] a survey of the prophecies and prophetic activities will provide the context for the discussion of the theological concepts embedded in these prophecies.

The point to be stressed first of all is that Ezekiel spoke in the first person. Throughout the prophecy he referred to himself with the pronouns *I* and *me*. And being a man from the priestly class in Jerusalem he could undoubtedly write.[11] He was called to be personally involved in his message by acting some of it out.

The Initial Vision (Fifth Year, Fourth Month, Fifth Day)

Ezekiel saw *mar'ôt 'ĕlōhîm* (visions of God) (1:1). Note the plural visions in this introductory statement. This should be understood to mean that Ezekiel had more than one vision. But the use of the plural could also give the sense of magnitude and intensity.

While among the exiles, he had his first overwhelming vision. This vision came to him during the fifth month of the fifth year of King Jehoiachin's exile. Ezekiel had been taken also when many officers were deported (2 Kings 24:10–17). This was in 592 B.C. He saw a great windstorm, with lightning, light, and fire, coming from the north. In the storm were what looked like four living creatures, each appearing as a man, each had four faces, that of a man, a lion, an ox, and an eagle. Each had wings that touched those of the others, giving the appearance of togetherness and unity. Each creature appeared as coals of fire and as flashes of lightning as they streaked back and forth. Beside each creature was a unique wheel that could roll in any direction or lift up from the ground when the creatures rose up. The creatures and the wheels were united by the Spirit. Above the creatures was an awesome expanse, sparkling like ice. As the creatures moved, they sounded like the roar of rushing water and like an army. Through it all was *kĕqôl šadday*[12] (as the voice of Shaddai). From above the expanse that was above the four heads came a voice from one who had the figure of a man surrounded by fire, light, and the glory of Yahweh. Ezekiel fell down at the sight of the vision.

Someone spoke to him (2:1) telling him to stand up and the Spirit helped him.[13] He was addressed as "Son of Man" and as the Spirit lifted him up he was given his prophetic task: go to the rebellious, revolting, stubborn, and obstinate people who were as scorpions. He was not to be afraid. In the continuing vision, he was shown a scroll and told to eat it, it was sweet as honey in his mouth even though it contained words of lament, mourning, and woe. The people who were intelligent enough to understand prophetic language were the house of Israel (3:7), but they would not listen. He, nevertheless, had to speak so he was taken from where he had received the vision and sat overwhelmed among the exiles.[14]

Seven days later Ezekiel received another message (3:16). He simply wrote that Yahweh came to him, addressed him again as Son of Man, and informed him he was made to be *ṣōpeh* (act. ptc. of *ṣāpâh,* to look out, spy, or keep watch). He was to consider himself as duty-bound at all times to convey words of warning to the people[15] and he would suffer severe consequences if he failed to do so. He could be assured of his own salvation when he spoke as commanded (3:21).

Yahweh had his hand upon Ezekiel, that is, God led him to a valley with a plain,[16] where he again received a vision as before of the glory of Yahweh (3:22). The Spirit again raised and instructed him. He was to carry out symbolic activities. He was to tie himself with ropes and was to be dumb, speaking only what Yahweh God instructed him to say. Ezekiel received further instructions on how he was to symbolize the siege of Jerusalem by tying himself with ropes, lying down facing Jerusalem. He was told what to eat and drink (chap. 4). He was also to cut off all his hair, divide the hair into three parts, and keep only a few strands in his garment. One part of his hair represented what fire would burn, another part the dispersion, and a third part death by plagues and famine. Even the few strands that he put in his garment had to be burned. Thus Ezekiel, by deeds, not by word, had to symbolize the destruction of Jerusalem, death, and the exile of the covenant people. They were to be punished in the sight of the nations because of their defiling of the temple and worship of idols. Ezekiel, spokesman for Yahweh God *Adonây,* had to emphasize that the covenant Lord was the one who was to make a ruin of Jerusalem and them a reproach to the nations. In wrath and anger the covenant curse would be executed. Note the specific language: "when I shoot you with deadly and destructive arrows of famine, I will shoot to destroy you." Yahweh's agents would be the means by which he would execute the curse (5:14–17).

It is not clear from the text if the words "the word of the LORD came to me" (6:1; 7:1) are separate prophecies or if what follows this introductory phrase in both instances is a continuation of what had been prophesied before and an explanation for Ezekiel's dramatic activities of eating a scroll (3:3), portraying the siege of Jerusalem, and lying down being tied with ropes (4:1–8).[17] The point should be clear to any reader: Yahweh God *Adonây's* cup of wrath was full and overflowing. The mountains were addressed; the altars to idols on high places would be destroyed and the idolaters also (6:3–7). The three means to be employed were sword, famine, and plague, and thus divine wrath would be spent upon most of the people (6:11–14).

Would every person be cut off? No, grace would also be effective. Yahweh God would spare some, but as captives scattered among the nations (6:9–10)—spared, not dead, but removed from their land and home. Through this divine sparing, Yahweh God *Adonây* would lead this exiled remnant to know that God was Yahweh, the covenant *Adonây* (6:8–10).

The sparing of a remnant in exile would in no way diminish the tragic end that was to come upon "the four corners of the land" (7:2). In anger the covenant people would be judged according to their conduct and evil practices (7:2–4). Ezekiel became dramatic, as Jeremiah had (Jer. 6–8). Consider terms such as the wrath to be expended (four times), the end (three times), the day has arrived, the time is here, doom has fallen. Yahweh God has turned his face away; he will show no pity, there will be no sparing (Ezek. 7:5–22). Wicked nations, coming with chains and shedding blood, would possess the land. And covenant agents would be silenced. The prophets would have no vision, the priests no law to teach, the counsel of elders would be gone, the king and princes would be clothed in despair (7:23–27).

The Second Vision (Sixth Year, Sixth Month, Fifth Day)

Ezekiel had to portray more vividly why Yahweh their God was going to continue to expend his wrath upon Jerusalem. Ezekiel, in visionary experience, saw one like a man and was transported by the Spirit to the temple in Jerusalem (8:1–4). He witnessed four gross idolatrous activities. An image that provoked to jealousy stood at the north entrance to the inner court. He saw a hole in the wall, dug a passage into it, and saw elders committing detestable acts of idolatrous worship. Then at the north entrance to the temple, women were mourning for an idol, Tammuz.[18] An idol had replaced Yahweh God. Ezekiel then witnessed twenty-five men, who had their backs toward Yahweh's house and throne (ark) and were worshiping the sun. Ezekiel then saw the glory of Yahweh move to the entrance of the temple, and six armed men, accompanied by a man in white, were commanded to kill all inhabitants that were not marked on the forehead by the man in white. Ezekiel was distraught at the sight but had to be assured that a few, the marked ones, would be the saved remnant.

The vision continued. Some aspects of the first vision were seen again. The man in white was told to scatter burning coals over the city. The *kĕbôd yĕhwâ* (glory of Yahweh) moved still farther out of the temple (10:1–22). When the coals were scattered by the man in white, the glory of Yahweh moved, with cherubim and wheels going with it, to the entrance of the temple courtyard.

The vision was not yet finished (11:1–24). The Spirit led Ezekiel to the seventy-five men at the east gate, among whom were two leaders who were plotting evil, urging the people in Jerusalem to believe that soon Jerusalem would be free and be rebuilt. In the vision Ezekiel was commanded to prophesy. He had to remind the leaders of their evil and that they would be driven from the city and fall by the sword. One of the false leaders fell dead as a sign of the unavoidable end. But Ezekiel was also commanded to tell the people there would eventually be a return and a cleansing of the city. The final act in the vision was the departure of the glory of Yahweh from the city. The vision ended, the Spirit returned Ezekiel to the exiles and he told the people all he had seen. Jerusalem was sure to fall, and many more people would die or be exiled. But most important, Yahweh God no longer had his throne in Jerusalem. It had become a totally forsaken city.

Ezekiel was then commanded to symbolize the exile (chap. 12) and the deportation of the king to Babylon, but he had to assure the people a remnant would be spared. Chapter 11 ends recording that Ezekiel had to tell the people that soon all that Yahweh had warned would happen. False prophets who spoke of visions and performed divinations were condemned for speaking lies (chap. 13). Idolaters, people with idols in their hearts, were condemned (14:1–11) and their judgment was inescapable, so much so that biblical Noah, Daniel, and Job, if they were living in Jerusalem, would be spared because of their righteous living. There would be no escape for idolaters in Jerusalem from the sword, famine, wild beasts, or the plague but some would be spared by being exiled (14:12–23). Ezekiel proceeded to prophesy concerning Jerusalem, the chosen city, having become useless as a vine is to produce wood. He gave an elaborate allegory concerning Jerusalem, describing her as a foundling who was cared for, loved, and beautiful but unfaithful as a wife (chap. 16). Another allegory referred to two eagles and a vine in which Babylon's king is depicted as coming to and destroying Jerusalem and deporting its king to Babylon, where he would die (17:1–22). The allegory ends by referring to Yahweh maintaining a royal personhood (17:22–24).

Ezekiel was commanded to speak to the people, who were accusing Yahweh of being unfair for punishing persons for the sin of their fathers. His message emphasized that each person would be judged according to his or her own deeds. This message was concluded by a call to repentance, stressing also that Yahweh God takes no pleasure in the death of anyone (chap. 18). Ezekiel was also to utter a lament for the prince who, of royal blood, descendant of David with whom Yahweh God had covenanted, would be uprooted and led with hooks into captivity (chap. 19).

Elders Enquired (Seventh Year, Fifth Month, Tenth Day)

Almost a year after Ezekiel had been taken by vision to Jerusalem and after he had told them of it and had given further explanations by means of prophecy, symbols, metaphors, and allegory, elders who were in captivity with Ezekiel came to him to ask what Yahweh's word was for them. This was on the tenth day of the fifth month of the seventh year of the second deportation, the year 590 B.C.

Ezekiel reviewed Israel's history, stressing how the covenant people had repeatedly been unfaithful and had blasphemed Yahweh their God (20:1–29). Ezekiel proceeded to emphasize that judgment was certainly to come to those who worshiped wood and stone. They would be brought into the "desert of the nations." But Yahweh's grace was also stressed. Yahweh would gather scattered ones and reveal himself as holy to them (20:30–44). Ezekiel prophesied again that Babylon would serve as God's sword of judgment (chap. 21). Again, Ezekiel was told three times to remind the exiles of the sins committed in Jerusalem (chap. 22). Jerusalem and Samaria were two sisters. The sister who represented Jerusalem was much more wicked, engaging in spiritual prostitution, than Samaria. Samaria had been destroyed, surely Jerusalem would be even more so (chap. 23).

The Cooking Pot (Ninth Year, Tenth Month, Tenth Day)

Two years later, in the latter part of the ninth year, 588 B.C., Ezekiel had to inform the exiles that Babylon's king had begun his siege of Jerusalem. It was symbolized by a pot in which flesh was to be thoroughly cooked. The time, Ezekiel stated on behalf of Yahweh, had come for his people's conduct and actions to be judged (24:1–14). Chapter 24 concludes by informing Ezekiel that his wife will die when a fugitive arrives to inform the exiles that Jerusalem had fallen. Ezekiel was not to weep; he could only silently groan when this happened. Ezekiel, the priest/prophet, had to be a sign of Yahweh "losing his bride" by means of destruction and captivity (24:15–27).

Two Issues

Ezekiel continued to receive messages he had to proclaim. These were about people other than Israel/Judah. The content of these messages has been studied in a preceding chapter.[19] Two issues should now be addressed: the dates of these messages and the purpose of these messages.

1. No date for the prophecies against Ammon, Moab, Edom, and Philistia was recorded. These four nations were geographic neighbors to Judah (chap. 25). They were directly affected by Babylon's war against Judah/Jerusalem.[20] But he had an extended prophecy against Tyre, a very influential city (chaps. 26–28). These prophecies were given in the first month of 586 B.C., the eleventh year of captivity. A few months previous to these prophecies against Tyre, on the twelfth day of the tenth month of the tenth year (587 B.C.), Ezekiel gave his prophetic message of defeat for Egypt (chap. 29). Included in this prophecy against Egypt is a prophecy given seventeen years later[21] (29:17–21), in which it is stated that Nebuchadnezzar got no reward from his campaign against Tyre but he did from his campaign against Egypt.[22]

Three months after the first prophecy against Egypt, on the seventh day of the first month of the eleventh year, Ezekiel received word from Yahweh that the arm of Pharaoh, king of Egypt, had been broken and was not restored. Egyptians would also be dispensed among the nations (30:20–28). Less than two months later, Ezekiel prophesied concerning Pharaoh, who had considered himself as the lofty one (31:18), but who would be brought down as Assyria had been. Ezekiel added a lament for Pharaoh (32:1–16). Then fourteen days later, on the fifteenth day of the twelfth month, the twelfth year, Ezekiel was to wail for Egypt who had been brought down as Assyria, Elam, Meshech, and Tubal had been (32:17–37).

During a comparatively short period of time from the ninth year, tenth month, tenth day to the twelfth year, twelfth month, fifteenth day, a period of three years, two months, five days, Ezekiel prophesied to the exiles concerning Jerusalem becoming a cooking pot and Babylon's victories over the nations, the small as well as mighty ones, that were in the greater geographical regions surrounding Jerusalem and Judah.

2. The second issue is closely related to the first one. Three years before the series of prophecies proclaimed in the two-year period reviewed above, the elders had come to inquire of Ezekiel what the word of Yahweh God was. Ezekiel had answered by reminding the elders of Israel's/Judah's rebellion and that judgment was to come by means of Babylon's armies. Ezekiel prepared the exiles for the news of Jerusalem's fall by informing, by means of his prophecies concerning the defeat of nations surrounding Jerusalem/Judah, that Babylon was invincible in its victorious march. The exiles had no reason whatsoever to think that their homeland and city would be spared. Their wickedness could and would not be overlooked or condoned. Wicked as they had been and were, they would suffer as neighboring wicked nations.

The Kingdom Context

The Kingdom Concept

The term *malākâh* (kingdom) appears twice in Ezekiel's prophecy. Once it refers to the nation of Judah (17:14). The kingdom of Judah was brought low when Judah's king and nobles were exiled to Babylon. By means of a treaty with Babylon, the lowly kingdom, what remained of the nation of Judah, could continue. But a royal person of Judah appointed by a Babylon king to reign as a vassal sent representatives to Egypt to seek help. This was rebellion; the lowly kingdom of Judah was soon to be nonexistent.

The term *malākâh* is also used to refer to Egypt (29:14). What was said of Judah, that it was to be brought low, was also said of Egypt. Babylon would cause it to be made lowly. In both instances the term *kingdom* refers to a nation of people that had a king as ruler. These two kingdoms were not powerful and had little influence in the world. But the idea of a national kingdom was nevertheless present: that of a sovereign nation, or a dominion that had a royal person reigning over it. This idea of kingdom included territory, people living in it, and a unique character and place among other nations.

Ezekiel did not use this term to refer to Yahweh God's sovereign cosmic domain.[23] Other passages in Scripture do (Ps. 145:11–13; Dan. 4:3). Among the major prophets, Ezekiel makes the fewest references to the idea of kingdom. This, however, should not be taken to mean that the idea of kingdom was almost foreign and unknown to him. Ezekiel was very kingdom-minded because of his interaction with the King of the cosmos.

The King

Yahweh God was not referred to as the King of the cosmos by Ezekiel. He did use the term *melek* (king) to refer to human rulers, including King Jehoiachin (1:2) and the king of Babylon (also referred to as a king of kings) (26:7), the king of Tyre, and Pharaoh, king of Egypt. There are however, indications of Ezekiel's awareness of Yahweh God as King.

First, consider the names or titles by which Ezekiel speaks of God. The word *'ĕlōhîm* (God) is found twenty-three times in the first thirty-two chapters. It is used in phrases such as God of Israel, Spirit of God, seat of God, heart of God, garden of God, and mountain of God. Ezekiel thus gave expression to his conception of the deity who was sovereign, was related to the Spirit and to Israel. To him the mountains and gardens owed their existence.

Ezekiel also used the term *Yĕhwâ* (usually translated LORD, NIV). This was God's covenant name and title. But of specific importance is that Ezekiel used the term *šadday* (1:24; 10:5). This term refers to God as the all-sufficient One, as in Genesis (17:1; 28:3; 35:11). The term emphasizes God's power and ability to control all aspects and events of life to accomplish his determined purposes. The idea of God that is portrayed by this term is that he is ruler, controller, provider and is therefore the all-sufficient source of whatever is required in any situation.

Various prophets employed the phrase "Lord of Hosts" to give expression to God's sovereignty. Ezekiel does not use that phrase once. Rather, Ezekiel used the term *'ădōnây* with *yĕhwâ*. In the often repeated phrases *'āmar 'ădōnây yĕhwâ* (says the Lord Yahweh) and *wîda 'ĕtem kî 'ănî 'ădōnây yĕhwâ* (and you shall know that I am the sovereign Yahweh) (13:8; 23:49; 24:24: 28:24; 29:16). God's sovereign rule over nations and all events in life is stressed. Yahweh God, the King, absolute Master, strong, firm, superior, had sole mastery over every aspect of life. This sovereign King is not without a domain; he is King of the cosmos. The cosmic kingdom is his.

Second, this sovereign King, Yahweh *Adonây,* has a unique throne (chap. 1). It is a chariot-throne.[24] Scholars have attempted to determine what the details refer to with very little agreement. The chariot-throne moved in any direction that the unusual attendants took it. Some have referred to these "carriers" as cherubim. They have earthly and human resemblances that indicate that the throne, related to the cosmos, is above or over it.[25] The glory and majesty displayed around the chariot-throne indicated its specific relationship to the divine.

This chariot-throne was seen in the vision as coming from the north (1:4). The answers to the question why it was important for Ezekiel and the exiles to know that the chariot-throne came from the north is debated. It has been suggested that the abode of the gods was in the north. This idea came from mythical sources.[26] Some conservative commentators accept this as a possibility, as it demonstrated that Yahweh *Adonây* had conquered the gods that the covenant people had worshiped. It would seem correct to accept the following explanation. The exiles continued to be oriented to Jerusalem, hoping and believing that Jerusalem would soon be liberated and they could return to their home city. But Ezekiel was to make very clear to these exiles that it was Yahweh *Adonây* who came from the north; that is, he as sovereign ruler over the cosmos had brought Babylon in to capture and destroy Jerusalem.[27] The message that had to be known and understood was that Yahweh *Adonây* controlled all aspects of life, including the severe judgment Jerusalem and the covenant people were to experience.

Third, consider Yahweh *Adonây*'s relationship with the prophet Ezekiel. Repeatedly the prophet wrote that the word of Yahweh *Adonây* came to him. Ezekiel by a sovereign king's action was led to say and do the king's business. He had no choice. Obedience was the only course of action that Ezekiel had. His message, conduct, and attitude were to reveal that he was in the service of the King of the cosmos. Obediently Ezekiel spoke and performed as he was commanded. He proclaimed Yahweh *Adonây*'s word of judgment and restoration. He submitted to Yahweh *Adonây*'s Spirit. He was totally controlled by the Spirit when given a vision (2:2; 3:14; 8:8). Ezekiel also referred to the hand of Yahweh *Adonây* coming upon him (1:3; 8:1) and controlling him entirely.[28] The triune sovereign Lord exercised his royal prerogative over the prophet he had called.

Fourth, Ezekiel clearly demonstrated that Yahweh *Adonây* was Lord and Master of all the aspects of the natural created world. The activities Ezekiel was commanded to perform (e.g., to tie himself with rope, how to prepare the food he was to eat, to cut his hair, to dig through a wall, to pack his bags as if to travel), were all evidences of Yahweh *Adonây*'s knowledge of aspects of the natural world and the service these could all perform under his divine reign.

Fifth, Ezekiel proclaimed Yahweh *Adonây*'s reign and sovereign control of the nations. His dealing with them was so that they would know, whether they believed it or not, that God was indeed Yahweh, the covenant Lord (25:10, 17; 28:26; 29:16).

Sixth, Ezekiel did not hesitate to proclaim that the judgment that had come and was to come was at the will, word, and action of Yahweh *Adonây*. He, as prophet, had to instruct the "rebellious house" (2:5, 8) that Yahweh *Adonây* would cut off food (4:16), inflict punishment on Jerusalem in the sight of the nations (5:8), and scatter survivors to the wind (5:10). Yahweh would make Jerusalem a ruin, a reproach, a taunt, and a warning among the nations (5:14). In this way Yahweh *Adonây*'s wrath would be demonstrated (5:13) and no pity would be shown (8:18). Strong words were used to express Yahweh *Adonây*'s intentions regarding Judah as a prostitute on whom Yahweh *Adonây* would bring the blood vengeance of his wrath and jealous anger (16:38).

Seventh, Yahweh *Adonây*, according to Ezekiel, would demonstrate his sovereign control over the people of Israel/Judah and nations when his wrath had been expended (5:13), and he returned a remnant of his people to their homeland (11:17). It would not be just a physical return. There would also be a truly spiritual renewal and return. Yahweh *Adonây* stated it decisively: "I will give them an undivided heart and a new spirit. I will remove from them a heart of stone and give them a heart of flesh" (11:19). This promise of Yahweh God *Adonây* was partially fulfilled in the return of the remnant from exile, more fully in the New Testament era, and will be finally and completely fulfilled when Jesus Christ returns to a renewed creation. Then the eschaton embedded in creation will be fully realized.[29]

The Kingdom's Inclusive Aspects

In this section, the purpose will be to review briefly what is included in the concept of the cosmic kingdom, which is the context and setting of Yahweh *Adonây*'s dealing with the prophet Ezekiel, the covenant people, and the nations.

The Cosmic Kingdom

The phrase "cosmic kingdom" refers to the entire creation. It refers to more than planet earth.[30] It includes all aspects of the created universe. As such it is the kingdom of Yahweh God *Adonây*. He created it, he rules over it, he guides and directs the course of all life and events. Men and women created in his image to mirror, represent, and serve as his highest-ranking agents (Ps. 8) have a unique place and purpose in this kingdom. Yahweh *Adonây*'s call and directive for Ezekiel and his employment of Ezekiel in his unique circumstances highlighted the role and service an image bearer can and does have within the cosmic kingdom. Specifically, Ezekiel was a cosmic kingdom inhabitant and servant. Ezekiel was called by the royal title "Son of Man" (Ps. 8)[31] to give expression to his place, role, and service as a royal cosmic kingdom agent under and for the sovereign Creator and Ruler.

The Theocratic Kingdom

It is very important to keep in mind that to understand the prophetic work and Ezekiel's prophetic ministry, that Judah was referred to as "kingdom." In chapter 17 one can read that Ezekiel was told to use the allegory of two eagles and a vine to speak to the house of Israel (which in this case referred specifically to Judah). The main point of this allegory was to stress that Babylon, an eagle, would break off the top of a cedar (referring to Judah's exile) and take some of the seed (exiles) and plant them in a foreign situation where the seed would become a vine. But the vine reached out to another eagle (Egypt), which led the first eagle to exile the king of Judah to Babylon. Thus, Ezekiel prophesied that the kingdom of Judah would be brought low, unable to rise again.

The main point of the allegory is this: Judah, as other nations, was as a kingdom an integral aspect of the cosmic kingdom. It was specifically a theocratic kingdom[32] and as such it was a type and model of the cosmic kingdom.[33] It was not the entire kingdom over which Yahweh God *Adonây* reigned. That the kingdom of Israel/Judah had a very important and strategic role in the cosmic kingdom must be clearly understood. It was to serve as a model of the cosmic kingdom so that all peoples could have and should have learned the essence, structure, and functioning of Yahweh God *Adonây*'s entire cosmic kingdom. The tragedy was that the theocratic kingdom, instead of serving as a model for the other kingdoms, modeled itself after those surrounding it. As a temporary, pre-Christ kingdom, it was brought low, not to rise again as a kingdom. In a real sense it was really no longer necessary. It had served its typical and metaphorical function. Its record was authoritatively written for all succeeding generations to learn and know essential aspects of the lasting, all-encompassing cosmic kingdom.

Judah's Neighboring Nations

It has been referred to before but a specific point must be stressed. All the kingdoms of the earth are part of the cosmic kingdom of Yahweh God *Adonây*. They all reflect in various ways aspects of the cosmic kingdom. And they all have a role under *Adonây*'s rule and control. Ezekiel made it clear that Babylon was a servant kingdom within the cosmic kingdom of the reigning *Adonây*. It was given the important role to serve as Yahweh God *Adonây*'s instrument to carry out the judgment that the theocratic kingdom deserved because of its rebellion and refusal to serve in its assigned theocratic kingdom role (17:1–22). Assyria had been given that role and task for the northern theocratic kingdom, Israel (Isa. 8:5–10). In truth, all the contemporary kingdoms of Israel/Judah had their role and function in the cosmic kingdom. Israel/Judah was to have been an example, a model, a guide for these so that they could be God-honoring nations serving their cosmic King. As Israel/Judah, the neighboring nations were used by Yahweh God *Adonây* for specific purposes. Many were then removed from the cosmic kingdom scene.[34]

The Covenant in Ezekiel's Prophecies

A proper understanding of Ezekiel calls for a clear understanding of Ezekiel's conception of the covenant, its nature, and its role in Yahweh God *Adonây*'s cosmic kingdom, and specifically with the kingdom of Judah.

The Covenantal Framework[35]

When a writer states that Ezekiel's prophecy reveals a covenantal framework, a reader might expect repeated references to the term *bĕrît* (covenant). Such, however, is not the case.[36] It appears in only four passages in the first thirty-two chapters, (chaps. 16, 17, 20, 30). Ezekiel clearly demonstrated that he was aware of Yahweh God's creation covenant and specific covenant relationship with Abraham, Israel as a theocratic nation, and David. Furthermore, the many references to who Yahweh God is, demands, promises, and the outcome of these, indicate that Ezekiel's prophecies are not only covenant-oriented but covenant-informed.

Ezekiel employed the phrase *wĕhēbē'tî 'etkem bĕmāsōret habbĕrîth* (and I will bring you into the bond of the covenant). (20:37) The term *māsĕret* is a noun derived from the verb *'āsar,* which means to bind or imprison. The term definitely conveys the idea of a binding relationship. When Yahweh God covenanted he bound himself to person(s) and bound them to himself. This bonding was an unbreakable tie. This bond had been established with Adam at the time of creation, with Noah and his progeny after the flood, with Abraham and his seed when he was called from the Ur of the Chaldees and had settled in Canaan, and with Israel as a nation at Mount Sinai. Later when David was king, the bond was personalized with him and his seed while the bond with the nation of Israel continued.

One must consider the verb translated "will bring into" (NIV).[37] Does this phrase suggest that the people, who have been exiled and metaphorically as sheep passed under the shepherd's staff as they entered the fold (20:37a), have been entered into a new bond/relationship? The parallelism in the text suggests that the entering into the bond of the covenant is to be understood as a return into the bond, just as sheep return to their fold at the close of the day. But, scholars have pointed out that Ezekiel later prophesied concerning a new covenant. This raises the question: does Ezekiel consider this new eternal covenant to be distinct from the covenant Yahweh God had established with his people at various times before the exile? A study of Ezekiel's specific references to the covenant in chapters 1 through 32 will serve as a context for an understanding of what Ezekiel specifically referred to in 20:37.

The Covenant Broken

As stated in the preceding, Ezekiel did not verbally refer to the covenant during his first year of prophesying. He had recounted his vision of Yahweh God *Adonây*'s glory and power, of his call to prophesy and to perform prophetic symbolic activities. These provided the context for Ezekiel's initial prophecies concerning the judgment that had fallen upon Judah/Israel and how that judgment was to be further executed. Ezekiel included reference to Yahweh God *Adonây*'s intent to spare some of the people (6:8–10) and to return a remnant (11:18–21). The main theme, however, of chapters 3 through 8 was Israel/Judah's sin. In a real sense one can think of Ezekiel reminding the covenant people of their history of sin.[38] The sure result of this sin was the judgment on the leaders (11:1–15). Ezekiel was to dramatize the exile that had already in part taken place and was to be carried out more fully. Indeed further judgment was to be carried out against Jerusalem (12:1–28). False prophets evidently contradicted Ezekiel's prophetic word (13:1–23).[39] In this historical situation elders came to Ezekiel, it would seem, to hear a positive and comforting message. Yahweh God *Adonây* warned Ezekiel that these elders "had set up idols in their hearts" and "put wicked stumbling blocks before their faces" (14:1–3). There was to be no message of assurance and peace. Judgment upon Jerusalem was sure to come because of their idolatry (14:12–22). The means were the sword, famine, wild beasts, and plagues. As a consequence Jerusalem would be useless as a vine for acquiring lumber (15:1–8).

The elders sitting in front of him gave Ezekiel the setting in which he could elaborate on what Yahweh God *Adonây*'s purposes were. He did so employing an allegory in which the history of the covenant people was clearly set forth. Ezekiel reminded the elders of how Yahweh God *Adonây* had given birth to Israel as a nation, had caused it to grow and become beautiful (16:1–7). When in the course of maturing (ready for love, allegorically speaking) *wā'abô' bĕrît 'otak* (I entered into covenant with you) and *walihĕyî lî* (and you were mine). Ezekiel employed the symbol of marriage. Yahweh God *Adonây* had entered into a lasting and binding marriage relationship with his beautiful bride (16:8). As an adoring husband, Yahweh God *Adonây* continued to beautify his bride. With this reference (16:9–14) Ezekiel summed up all that the Lord had done for Israel from the time of Sinai until Solomon's first years of kingship. But the covenant bride became *hā'iśśah hammĕnā 'āpet* (a wife committing adultery). Ezekiel employed the feminine plural participle of the piel form of the verb *nā'ap* (commit adultery). The form of verb indicated that the covenant wife continually and intensively committed adultery by continuing consistently in idolatrous worship[40] (16:32). And, as a mother, she sacrificed her children to idols (16:36). Thus the seed of the covenant was betrayed; they were not recognized as Yahweh's but as sacrifices for idols.

Ezekiel elaborated on the unfaithfulness of the covenant wife, emphasizing her shamelessness. Jerusalem was worse than Samaria and possibly even than Sodom (16:32–58). He summarized his response to the elders by emphasizing that they, the elders, the people, Jerusalem, had broken the covenant. They had despised Yahweh's oath that he would be a God to them and to their children. Ezekiel, in this chapter, accused the inquirers before him of being unfaithful to the Abrahamic and Sinaitic covenant.

Answering the elders' inquiries, Ezekiel made a specific point of prophesying concerning the Davidic dynasty, and so doing, also referred to the covenant Yahweh God had made with David (2 Sam. 7:8–16). Ezekiel introduced another allegory[41] (7:1–10), added an explanation (17:11–21), and then spoke allegorically again when referring to the future.

First, Ezekiel spoke of a great eagle who came to Lebanon; the reference is to the king of Babylon. Because of Jerusalem's dependence on Lebanon's cedar, which David and Solomon needed, the top of the cedar the eagle broke off was a reference to the Davidic dynasty (17:1–10). Ezekiel explained to the elders that the king of Babylon had gone to Jerusalem, taken King Jehoiachin as an exile, and made a treaty (*bĕrît*) with King Zedekiah, who rebelled against Babylon. Zedekiah was to die in Babylon because he had despised the promise of the king of Babylon involved in their treaty (17:11–18). Thus Zedekiah broke two covenants, one with the king of Babylon and one with the Davidic dynasty (17:19–21).

It must be kept in mind that Ezekiel had been speaking of the covenant people's and their kings' unfaithfulness when he prophesied concerning the judgments they were experiencing (chaps. 3–15). These judgments were the result of the unfaithfulness and sins of the kings and the people. Thus, in chapters 16 and 17 Ezekiel spoke plainly and clearly why the exile had taken place. Yahweh God *Adonây* had remained faithful to the covenant. Moses had warned the covenant people that there was the curse aspect of the covenant (Deut. 27:9–26; 28:15–68). The people, from their side, had despised Yahweh's word and broken off their covenant relationship. Yahweh God *Adonây* maintained the covenant. When Israel/Judah did not remain faithful to the covenant, Yahweh God did by pouring out his covenant wrath[42] on them. Moses had warned he would. The conclusion then must be that while the people despised and broke the covenant, Yahweh God kept covenant with them. He put them away, but he did not forget them. They were still his covenant people and there would be a continuity of the covenant.

The Continuity of the Covenant

Ezekiel did not elaborate to any length on the continuity of the covenant in his prophecies proclaimed before the fall of Jerusalem and the third deportation. There are, however, five indications or references to this continuity even while it may have seemed to the exiles that Yahweh God *Adonây* was not upholding the covenant.[43]

First of all, careful attention should be given to what Ezekiel proclaimed in regard to Yahweh *Adonây*'s real desire. Following a lengthy discussion concerning justice in the execution of punishment, (chap. 18), Ezekiel emphasized that as a result of ancestors' sins, progeny could suffer the consequences. But, in reality, an individual who remained faithful would not die (nor a sinful one who repented). And should a faithful one become unfaithful, former faithfulness would be to no avail.[44]

Commentators have discussed what Ezekiel referred to by "not die" and "shall live." The prophet referred to much more than an assurance of material life. He referred also to forgiveness and the removal of condemnation.[45] But he did not assure anyone that the righteous one would escape the punishment upon the people as a whole, that is, the exile.

The conclusion of this message on corporate, family, and individual moral responsibility is that Yahweh God has no pleasure in executing the covenant curse (18:30–32). Yahweh *Adonây*'s real, heartfelt desire is that sinners repent, confess their sins, and receive a new heart and spirit. Yahweh *Adonây*'s desire is that he pours out the blessing of righteousness upon his covenant people. Yahweh's desire is that the covenant, the bond of love, be upheld and continued. The continuity of the covenant is Yahweh *Adonây*'s desire and since it is, it will surely be so.

Second, Ezekiel inquired whether there would be a remnant left of the people. When he saw (in vision) six men go through Jerusalem slaughtering the unmarked people (9:1–6), Ezekiel cried out asking if the entire remnant would be cut off. Yahweh replied that their violence and provocation to anger gave him no alternative. There is, however, an indication that a remnant of the remnant left in Jerusalem would be spared. They who had the mark given by the man clothed in white would be spared (9:6).

Ezekiel asked about the sparing of a remnant again when the false prophet Pelatiah died (11:1–13). It is clear that Ezekiel was deeply affected by the judgment of Yahweh on the sinful and rebellious members of the covenant people. The question should be understood to express what had been assured before, that there would always be a remnant, 7,000, who would be covenant keepers. Thus there would be the continuity of the covenant promises of life and blessings.

Third, Ezekiel was given the message that there would be a return from exile in due time. Immediately following his second question concerning a remnant, Yahweh *Adonây* had Ezekiel prophesy that although the covenant people had been "sent far away among nations" (11:16), there was a sanctuary for them where they were. Furthermore, Yahweh *Adonây* gave the assurance that he would gather them, bring them back, renew them, and have them realize that Yahweh *Adonây* was their covenant Lord. The covenant formula was repeated: "They will be my people and I will be their God" (11:20).

Fourth, Ezekiel, by direct and indirect references, prophesied that the covenant, the bond of love and life, with its integrally related blessings would continue. There was a reference to the Abrahamic covenant (Gen. 17:1–7; Ezek. 11:20), as well as to the Sinaitic covenant (Exod. 2:24; 6:7; 19:4–6). These are the covenants that were referred to when Ezekiel spoke concerning the covenants made in the days of Israel. The Davidic covenant would also continue even though one of the Davidic dynasty broke the covenant (Ezek. 17:19). Yahweh, by means of an allegory, had Ezekiel prophesy concerning its continuity (17:22–24).

Fifth, Ezekiel gave an assuring message to the elders sitting in front of him that the everlasting covenant Yahweh *Adonây* had made with their forefathers was in reality an everlasting covenant (Gen. 17:7; Ezek. 16:60). The one covenant, once made, would never cease; Yahweh God *Adonây* had Ezekiel prophesy *wahăqimôtî lak bĕrît 'ôlām* (I will cause to continue with you the everlasting covenant).[46]

In conclusion to this study of the covenant in Ezekiel's prophecies given before the fall of Jerusalem, it is important to emphasize again that the covenant was an instrument of administration within the cosmic kingdom as well as a means to work out Yahweh God's redemptive purposes. Yahweh God *Adonây*'s relationship with Judah as well as with the nations and the executing of his will and purposes were all according to the creation/redemptive covenant.

The Mediator

The Covenantal Agent

Ezekiel did not employ the term *messiah* or refer directly to the messianic Mediator. It must be remembered that when a prophet spoke of the covenant, he included, be it indirect or implied, reference to the covenantal agent, the mediator. Yahweh God, in establishing his covenant, always included his mediatorial agent. When the creation covenant was established at the time of creation, the Word was the agent (Ps. 33:6; John 1:1–3).[47] Noah, Abraham, Moses, and David served as covenantal agents when Yahweh God covenanted with them. It bears repeating, to speak of covenant is to also speak of the covenantal mediator.

The Agents

Ezekiel must be considered as referring to the important role covenantal mediators, or agents, had. He knew what his role was, to be Yahweh God's covenantal spokesman. He had to proclaim that the love bond was present, holding, and available. He had to proclaim the curse of the covenant and its tragic outworking. He also proclaimed the covenantal promises, appeals, and assurances as the spokesman for Yahweh God *Adonây,* who sovereignly had established, upheld, and executed the covenant.

Ezekiel was emphatic concerning the tragically devastating results of covenantal agents' unfaithfulness. He referred to prophets, whose duty was to be true spokesmen for Yahweh God their covenant Lord, but who were false. They spoke lies; they gave false messages; they tried to assure the people of good when Yahweh God had already initiated the execution of the covenant curse (Ezek. 13:1–23; 14:9–11). Kings, princes, and leaders were condemned for their unfaithfulness (7:23–27; 11:1–15; 17:11–18). Temple personnel, especially the priests, were tragic violators of Yahweh God's covenantal prescriptions for holy worship (8:3–18).

Ezekiel made it very clear that covenantally appointed and authorized agents were present but did not function as faithful and obedient agents in their roles as priests, prophets, kings, and elders. In reality, they were largely responsible for all the covenant unfaithfulness because they had roles in which they were to represent and serve Yahweh God, their sovereign covenant Lord.

It must not be forgotten that there were those who carried out their covenant duties. Ezekiel did. The king of Babylon carried out Yahweh God's plan against Egypt (29:18, 19; 30:10), and especially against Judah (17:11, 12). Jeremiah had stressed that Nebuchadnezzar, the king of Babylon, was referred to by Yahweh God as *'abdî* (my servant) (Jer. 43:10). This term is at heart loaded with covenantal meaning and responsibilities.

The covenantal agents, priests, prophets, kings, princes, leaders, and counselors were in positions that represented and served as means to exemplify and carry out the role and duties of the one true covenant mediatorial agent, the preincarnate Messiah. It follow that those who were in positions of agents and mediators had tremendous responsibilities, challenges, and opportunities to serve in the cosmic kingdom. And, if in these positions, unfaithfulness, disobedience, and rebellion replaced submission and service, the judgment was most severe. The messianic Mediator was the executor of both the covenant's blessing and curse.

Direct References

The term *mēsîaḥ* (anointed, messiah) does not appear in the prophecies of Ezekiel. There are indirect references, as was pointed out in the preceding paragraphs. In *Messianic Revelation in the Old Testament* the following passages were considered to refer, by type or prefigurement, to the messianic mediator: Ezekiel 1:25–28, the man on the throne; 11:14–21, the *gō'ēl,* redeemer; 16:53–58, atonement to be made by Yahweh; 17:22–24, continuity of the Davidic dynasty; 21:20–27 (MT 21:30–37), the exalted house of David.[48]

Prophecies of Restoration, Ezekiel 33:1–48:35

Survey of Ezekiel's Prophecies

Ezekiel Preparing for Coming Events

In the ninth year of King Jehoichin's exile, 586 B.C., the word of Yahweh came to Ezekiel (24:1). He was informed that the king of Babylon had begun to lay siege to Jerusalem and the prophet had to proclaim that reality by means of the parable of the boiling pot (24:3–8). The parable was followed by an explanation in which Jerusalem was reminded that the people's impure lewdness had not been cleansed because divine efforts to cleanse and heal had been rejected. So the time had come for Yahweh God *Adonây* to act (24:14).

Yahweh God was going to demonstrate to the exiles that he truly was Yahweh God *Adonây.* He ruled! He had all matters under his control. The following are mentioned.

Ezekiel was to lose his wife and not mourn her loss. He was to remain clothed as usual and not to wear mourning clothes but he could groan quietly (24:15–17). He was to symbolize for the people what they were to do when the delight of their eyes and hearts was taken away. This was made clear to them when they asked what Ezekiel was doing. He could not speak in normal conversation, but only what the Lord gave him to speak (3:26, 27).[49] He had Yahweh's word: Jerusalem was no longer to be a stronghold, it would be captured and the temple was to be desecrated. And as Ezekiel was not to mourn the loss of his wife so the exiles were not to mourn the capture of Jerusalem and the destruction of the temple.

Ezekiel was given another assurance: when a messenger arrived to tell of the tragedies in Judah and Jerusalem, he would be given freedom again to speak in normal conversation as well as continue to be Yahweh God *Adonây*'s prophetic spokesman. Following this assurance as recorded in the text are Ezekiel's oracles against neighboring nations, Ammon, Moab, Edom, Philistia, Tyre, and Egypt.[50] These nations were to be judged also because of their disobedience, rebellion, and hostilities against the covenant people. It must be accepted that these prophecies against the nations were given during the time between Ezekiel's wife's death and the fall of Jerusalem. There are two considerations that support this. The date that Ezekiel prophesied against Egypt is recorded; the tenth year, tenth month, twelfth day (29:1). And the exiles had to be assured that Yahweh God *Adonây* was provoked to anger, not only against them, but also against their neighboring nations. And thus, Yahweh God *Adonây* manifested for all to hear and know that he, and he alone, was the king of all nations for they were all real parts of his cosmic kingdom.

Ezekiel: The Watchman

Before the messenger reporting Jerusalem's fall would arrive, Ezekiel again was given instruction concerning his duties and responsibilities. The duties of a watchman were reviewed: to warn the people of an impending attack by means of blowing a trumpet. To fail to do this would bring disaster on the watchman as it would upon those who did not get the warning or who failed to heed the warning when it was given (33:1–6). Ezekiel was reminded that he had been appointed a watchman (3:17; 33:7). As watchman he had to warn the people of the impending disaster and that the wicked individuals should be warned of judgment to come. And as before (18:32) Yahweh God *Adonây* assured Ezekiel he had no pleasure in the death of the wicked but would have them repent and turn from their evil ways (33:11). In reply to accusations that Yahweh God *Adonây* was not just, Ezekiel had to proclaim the justice of the Lord (33:18). This justice would be demonstrated to those who ignored and rejected his gracious call to repentance and life.

The Cycle of Messages

Messages of judgment as well as of restoration were to be given. In these Yahweh God *Adonây*'s justice, grace, mercy, and faithfulness to his word and covenant, and concern for the future of his people and kingdom would be revealed. The cycle of prophecies can be sketched as in the chart below.

1. Judgment had fallen. Jerusalem had been captured. An escapee brought the news and that meant that Ezekiel could speak freely at all times. The people continued to claim the land (33:23, 24), but were reminded they experienced judgment and the land was devastated because of their idolatry (33:25–29). Ezekiel was not to be distracted by the talk of a greedy people who spoke as if they were devoted. The people were obviously impressed by the truthfulness of what Ezekiel had prophesied. He was considered an entertainer (33:30–33).

2. Ezekiel proceeded to pronounce judgment on the unfaithful leaders/shepherds who would be held accountable. Judgment was reserved for them (34:1–10)

3. A gracious restoration would come from Yahweh God *Adonây*'s own hand. He would be the great Shepherd who would gather the sheep, pasture them, and give them rest. The lost would be found, wicked sheep would be destroyed, justice would prevail in the flock. David (progeny) would rule and the covenant of peace would be fully activated. There would be no more plundering by nations and no more famine (34:11–31).

4. A just judgment would be carried out against Edom because of her perpetual hostility and treachery against Israel/Judah. Edom, as a representative of nations

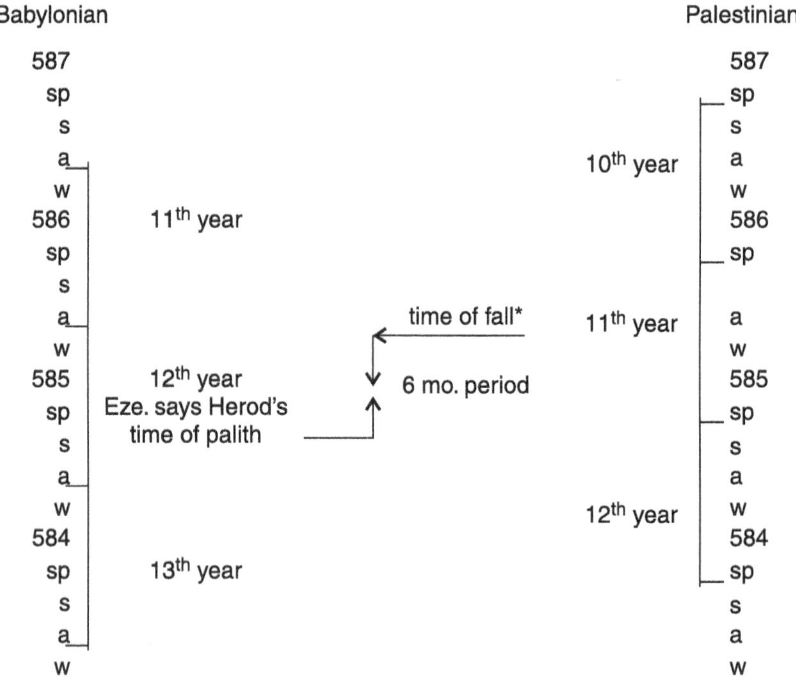

who served well as such because of its attitude and actions against the covenant people, would be made desolate forever. Edom's rejoicing over Israel/Judah's misfortune would surely be rewarded by Yahweh God *Adonây*'s severe treatment.

5. Gracious restoration[51] was again prophesied. Yahweh God *Adonây*'s burning zeal against the nations causes him to speak in his jealous wrath, warning that the afflicting nations would suffer scorn (36:1–7). But the land, addressed as mountains, hills, ravines, and valleys, would again be fruitful and the land and its towns would be reinhabited by people and animals. They would no longer hear the taunts of nations (36:8–15).

Ezekiel went on to remind the covenant people that they had defiled their land with bloodshed and idol worship (36:16–21). The promised restoration that was sure to come was not for the sake of Israel but for Yahweh God *Adonây*'s holy name. What grace! People who profaned their Lord would be restored to demonstrate his holiness (36:22–24). The regathered people would be cleansed, given a new spirit and a heart of flesh, replacing their heart of stone. The renewed people would prosper. Again, this would happen to a people called to be ashamed (36:25–32). The promise of a full and gracious restoration of the people, the land, and towns was repeated and was concluded by the statement, "then they will know I am Yahweh, the faithful, forgiving, restoring LORD" (36:33–38).

The gracious restoration was demonstrated in the vision of dry bones in a valley that came to life by means of the word of Yahweh addressed to them and by the Holy Spirit's activity. "These bones are the whole house of Israel" (37:1–14). This renewal would include a reunification of Israel and Judah. The covenant promise was assured to them. "They will be my people and I will be their God" (37:15–23). David would rule over them; the everlasting covenant of peace would be firmly established and maintained (37:24–28).

6. Severe judgment would be executed on the covenant people's enemies. These enemies are referred to as Gog of the land of Magog, the prince of two cities to the north of Israel, Meshech and Tubal. Gog would come to know that Yahweh God *Adonây* is the sovereign Lord when he attacked the covenant people and would suffer catastrophic loss and be buried in a foreign valley.

Ezekiel, addressing Gog, was basically speaking against Babylon, whose end was sure to come. Living in Babylon among the exiles, Ezekiel employed Gog as a substitute for the king of Babylon (38:1–39:24). The burden of this prophecy against Gog was to assure the exiles that Yahweh God *Adonây* would display his glory among the nations (39:21).

7. A glorious future was depicted. The covenant people would be gathered from the countries of their enemies (39:25–28). The Spirit would be poured on the house of Israel (39:29). And then, twelve years after after the fugitive had arrived to report the fall of Jerusalem and the destruction of the temple, Ezekiel spoke of a restored temple (40:1). This was done in terms of what the covenant people had experienced and knew of their past circumstances.[52] It is helpful to be acquainted with the prescriptions for the tabernacle as recorded in Exodus, the

sacrificial system in Leviticus, the temple built by Solomon (1 Kings 7, 8), and the division of the land as recorded by Joshua (13:1–21:41).

As one studies Ezekiel's reference to the new temple area (Ezek. 40:1–4), the courts and their gates (40:4–37), the sacrifices, places for priests, and the architectural plans for the temple (40:38–42:20), one comes to the realization that what Ezekiel described is symbolic in terms of the past.[53] Ezekiel, in the vision, saw the glory of Yahweh, God of Israel, return. Yahweh God *Adonây* declared that in this temple he would have his throne and live among the Israelites *lĕ' ôlām* (forever).[54] Here there is undoubted reference to the New Testament age (43:1–12).

Ezekiel proceeded to describe the altar and the prescribed burnt offerings and the sprinkling of blood and the system of sacrifices (43:13–25). To interpret this passage literally is contrary to the New Testament's testimony that Christ's shed blood renders all sacrifices and shedding of blood obsolete (Heb. 10:1–18). Some scholars who refer to Ezekiel's sacrifices as symbolic for holiness are very inconsistent with their insistence that Ezekiel 40–48 should be interpreted literally.

Reflecting offices and duties prescribed for the Old Testament temple and worship, Ezekiel again referred to priests and Levites who are to sacrifice fat and blood in the sanctuary in the presence of Yahweh (Ezek. 44:15), who had entered and filled it with his glory (44:4). Prescriptions for the conduct of priests and Levites again reflected the use of the Old Testament revelation to prescribe holiness for those who would serve Yahweh God in the New Testament age.

Ezekiel proceeded to hear in the vision that a specific portion of the land was to be set aside for the sanctuary, priests, and Levites (45:1–6). The prince was to have territory, and to rule according to Old Testament prescriptions for the marketplace (45:7–12)

What Ezekiel proceeded to call for, specific offerings and holy days, gives strong and firm support for the understanding that none of these were to be actualized (45:13–46:24). In terms of Old Testament regulations, worship in the New Testament age is to be carried out in keeping with Yahweh God's call for regularity and sanctity.

Ezekiel described how in a vision he was brought to the entrance of the temple. A small stream of water flowed from under the entrance. This stream of water increased in volume as it flowed away from the temple. No springs in the dry valleys and ravines were present to add to this increase. The ever-increasing water flowing through dry areas gave life. The Dead Sea was purified and provided water for animals, fish, and plants (47:1–12). This passage reflected the work of the Holy Spirit in all of creation, in both Old and New Testament times (Ps. 104:10–18, 28–32) and found a fulfillment on Pentecost (Acts 2).

An important reality in the history of Israel when Canaan was conquered was the dividing of the land and the allotting of territory to each tribe (Josh. 13:8–21:45). Ezekiel clearly indicated that the allocation as in Joshua's time was not to be considered. The twelve tribes are mentioned, but the areas they are allotted are very different (e.g., Reuben received territory on the west side of the Jordan and Ephraim on the east). But all the tribes received an inheritance. Is this to be understood literally, that is, that twelve tribes, plus the Levites, are to actually dwell in the earthly Canaan again? As indicated before, Ezekiel prophesied in terms of what the exiles had known before. But, as one Old Testament scholar wrote correctly, in the Holy Scriptures the land of Canaan is used as a symbol of the heavenly inheritance. The inheriting people in Ezekiel's vision points to the church, the congregation of the new covenant which is renewed and refreshed by the Holy Spirit, symbolized by the Holy Spirit.[55]

Ezekiel concluded his description of the vision by referring to the gates of the city, three on each side, each gate bearing the name of a tribe. Thus each tribe has a wide open gate into the city. And the city *wĕsēm ha'îr miyyôt yĕhwâ sāmmâh* (literally and the name of the city from that day [on] Yahweh is there). The promise of the covenant, "You are mine, I will be with you," will be fully and completely realized.[56]

The conclusion to the survey of Ezekiel's prophecies concerning the gracious restoration is that Yahweh God *Adonây* fulfills his covenant promise. He will always have a people; they will always belong to Yahweh; they will have an inheritance that will never be taken away.

The Covenant

Introductory Comments

A study of the Golden Cable in Ezekiel 33–48 highlights the covenant. In the first thirty-two chapters one thing emerged quite clearly: the people sinned grievously against God's covenant.[57] But Yahweh God *Adonây* maintained his covenant. Often this was demonstrated by executing the covenant curse in anger and wrath against the covenant breakers.[58] There is a dramatic change in Ezekiel's prophecies once Jersualem had fallen. The curse of the covenant had been executed (Deut. 28:15–68, esp. v. 65). He emphasized that the covenant continued, that promises of blessings would flow forth.

Ezekiel's Unique Role

Ezekiel had a unique role throughout the previous prophecies. At the point of transition from prophesying concerning nations (chaps. 25–32) to addressing the exiles again, Ezekiel was personally addressed again.

Ezekiel had a very painful and grievous experience. His wife died on the evening of the day before the fugitive arrived to inform Ezekiel and the exiles that Jerusalem had fallen and was destroyed.[59] There is a clear and distinct message. The delight of Ezekiel's eyes, his wife, was to be taken away; she would suddenly die (24:16). The delight of the exiles' eyes, Jerusalem and the sanctuary, would be taken away. As Ezekiel had to hide his grief, so the exiles were to also hide their grief about their loss. Ezekiel, thus, was to be a sign (24:24) to the exiles. An acute difference, however, must be seen. Ezekiel the prophet had not committed any specific deed, a result of which would be his loss. The exiles would suffer a severe and painful loss due to their sin (24:23). Ezekiel had a tragic burden placed on him; he in person, had to demonstrate how to respond to Yahweh God *Adonây*'s just judgment on a rebellious covenant people. As Yahweh's faithful servant, he had to suffer a double loss: his wife, and as a priest in exile, the sanctuary and Jerusalem.

Ezekiel's role as watchman was repeated and emphatically emphasized.[60] When he, as priest, had received the call to prophesy, he had been instructed to serve as watchman for those covenant people in exile with him. He had been told that he had to warn the people that wickedness would bring death; repentance was the way to life. Former righteousness followed by unrepented sin would not save anyone. Ezekiel would be held accountable for the blood, that is, death due to sin, if he had not given warning of the judgment surely to come on the evil, unrepentant people (3:17–21). Now, as a transition was to come, Ezekiel's message would be affected. No longer would he have to proclaim that Yahweh God *Adonây*'s judgment would fall on Jerusalem, the sanctuary, and the people remaining in the land of Judah. The time had come to emphasize restoration and a new beginning. But one important aspect of his prophetic message was not to be altered, diminished, or dropped. The reality was that Yahweh God *Adonây* repeated and elaborated on his duty as watchman. As a watchman for a city had to sound warning of impending disaster, so Ezekiel as watchman had to continually warn wicked persons that they would die because of their sin (33:7). Ezekiel was to instruct the people that Yahweh God *Adonây* had no pleasure in their death but called all Israel to turn from sin and live.[61] No one was to trust in their righteousness when followed by disobedience but repentance would bring righteousness to the wicked ones. If people would say that their God was unjust, for taking them from the land promised to their forefathers, for not taking former righteousness into account if disobedience followed, the prophetic message was to be unchanged. Yahweh God *Adonây* would be just in judging "each of you according to his own way" (33:20).

Finally, Ezekiel was recognized as a seer; he, as the exiles saw him, had the ability to foresee the future and actually spoke God's word (33:30–33). The exiles encouraged each other to listen to Ezekiel as an entertainer, "as one who sings and plays nice songs beautifully" (33:32). But the exiles would not accept Ezekiel's words as relevant to their lives. In time, however, they would come to know that Ezekiel had been other than a seer, an entertainer. He had been and was a prophet sent by Yahweh God *Adonây* who unhesitatingly had spoken the message he had been given to proclaim.

Covenantal Judgment

Whereas judgment executed in Yahweh God *Adonây*'s wrath was a dominant theme in chapters 2 to 32 and restoration the dominant theme in chapters 33 to 48, judgment is also referred to in the latter part of the prophecies. This is not to be considered strange because of the very nature of the political, social, moral, and spiritual *Sitz im Leben* in which restoration was promised. If indeed restoration was to become a reality, that which had caused destruction and enslavement would have to be dealt with using strong and severe means. Ezekiel prophesied judgment on four specific entities as preludes to full restoration.

When the fugitive from Judah arrived and reported that Jerusalem had fallen, Yahweh God *Adonây* had a specific message for those covenant-breaking residents of ruined Jerusalem. These people, in spite of the calamities they had endured when Jerusalem was captured, continued to insist that they were descendants of Abraham, the one person to whom the land of Canaan had been promised; they were still inheritors and had a claim to the land (33:23, 24). Ezekiel's prophetic message to them was that their covenant-breaking deeds—looking to idols, eating meat with blood, shedding blood, relying on the sword, committing adultery—rendered them guilty and their right to the land was forfeited (33:25).[62] Therefore they would come under the covenant curse. The sword and wild animals would devour them and plagues would cause death for those in strongholds and caves. Yahweh God *Adonây*'s judgment would cause the land to be desolate. The end of Israel's and Judah's claim to the land as their place of residence, work, and worship had come with finality. The land had to be cleansed. It was and would be done by Yahweh God *Adonây* executing the covenant curse (Deut. 27, 28). This curse had to be executed before the covenant could and would be renewed (Deut. 29). Ezekiel repeated the refrain: *weyādĕ'û kî-'ănî yĕhwâ* (Then they shall know that I am Yahweh) (34:27). By means of devastation and destruction, the executing of the covenant curse, the few remaining knew that God *Adonây* was in reality Yahweh, the covenant-keeping sovereign One.

Ezekiel in a prophetic manner pronounced Yahweh God *Adonây*'s covenant curse upon the shepherds of Israel (34:1–10). Isaiah had spoken against the shepherds in a context in which he addressed the *ṣōpāw* (qal act. ptc. of *ṣāpâh,* to look out, watch, be watchman) (Isa. 56:10). Jeremiah had done so repeatedly, addressing leaders still in Jerusalem (Jer. 10:21; 12:10; 23:2; 25:34–36; 50:6). Ezekiel proclaimed the sins of these leaders as the others had done: shepherds used the flocks for their own benefit and well-being; they had not nurtured and strengthened the weak and injured; they had not sought after the straying and lost; they had not given them rest; they ruled harshly and brutally; they scattered the flock. Speaking concerning shepherds, reference was particularly to the kings who had not followed in the ways of David, the good shepherd of Israel, who had shepherded with integrity of heart and with skillful hands (Ps. 78:72).

The curse would be carried out. Yahweh God *Adonây* said that he was against these wicked shepherds and would remove them. They would be held accountable for their taking advantages for themselves at the expense of the flocks. The historical record informs the readers what happened to these robber kings; they were killed, had their eyes gouged out, and were taken into exile.

It should be noted that Ezekiel also included some who were not kings but had the abilities to hinder, harm, and even help destroy the "flock," the covenant people. They were referred to as the "fat ones" in distinction from the lean ones.

Eichrodt has written correctly that the "fat ones" refers to the propertied class in Israel.[63] They were guilty of unbrotherly behavior. The image of the strong sheep pushing the weaker and smaller ones aside so they could not graze and reach clean water gave a clear and realistic presentation of the privileged class. Wantonly spoiling and making good pasture and water unusable were clear evidences of ignoring the maintaining a community of solidarity; antisocial guilt as well as cultic offenses were reasons for the curse of the covenant to be executed.

The kings had their covenantal duties and responsibilities and strong, capable citizens had theirs. Thus judgment came upon the entire community. The weak and lean would suffer even more as members of a cursed community. They suffered before judgment fell, and they suffered when it did. Thus the guilt of the kings and the upper class became even greater because of the added suffering of common people, the weak and helpless.

Edom was again addressed in strong, condemning terms. Ezekiel had addressed Edom in another context (Ezek. 25:12–14). Amos, years before, had condemned Edom for its continual raging anger and fury against his brother Jacob (1:11, 12). Isaiah had addressed the nations, proclaiming that Yahweh was angry with all nations and that his wrath was upon all their armies. They were all to be destroyed (Isa. 34:1–4). Isaiah then proceeded to address Edom on whom judgment would fall in the day of Yahweh's vengeance when God would stretch out over Edom the measuring line of chaos and the plumbline of desolation (NIV) (34:5–15). Jeremiah had given a prophecy against Edom, who inspired terror and who felt secure living in caves in the rocks. Edom would be brought down and Edom's children, relatives, and neighbors would disappear (Jer. 49:7–22). Jeremiah had not specifically singled out Edom's sin against Israel and Judah, but his contemporary, Obadiah, whose prophecy is very similar to what Jeremiah preached, said that destruction would come because of violence against your brother Jacob (v. 10).

It is evident that preceding prophets singled out Edom, as Ezekiel had, as the representative of all the nations that raged against and sought to destroy the covenant people.

Ezekiel made strong dennunciations against Edom. Yahweh God *Adonây* was against Edom; this is the very opposite of the covenant promises of I am your God, I will bless you and your children (Gen. 17:1–7). Edom had not hated bloodshed when they harbored ancient hostility and caused the Israelites to die by the sword when calamity struck (Ezek. 35:5). Because of Edom's attitude and actions against his brother Jacob, Edom would become desolate forever. It must not be forgotten that Edom's forebear, Esau, was a grandson of Abraham to whom the promise of covenantal blessings for his progeny was given. Thus Esau's descendants, the Edomites, had a special position and privilege. But because Edom rejoiced when "the inheritance of the house of Israel became desolate," Yahweh God *Adonây* said that Edom would become desolate likewise. Thus as the curse of the covenant was carried out against Jacob's progeny so would it also against Edom. Edom, as a covenantal brother, would and should have shown the nations how, and led them in relating to Israel, so that all the nations would and could be blessed (Gen. 12:1–3).

The curse of the covenant, as Ezekiel prophesied, would come upon the covenant people residing in the promised land, upon their royal leaders and others in positions of influence, and upon brother Edom. Ezekiel then, using some bizarre, near apocalyptic symbols, addressed Gog of Magog, who was the chief prince of Meshech and Tubal. There is much uncertainty as to whom Ezekiel refers to by the name Gog.[64]

The name *Gog* appears in 1 Chronicles 5:4. The context is the genealogy of Rueben. Ezekiel quite clearly does not refer to this Israelite man. Ezekiel speaks of Gog as "of the land of Magog" (Ezek. 38:2). The name *Magog* appears in Genesis 10:2 and 1 Chronicles 1:5; he was a son of Japheth and grandson of Noah. It is very likely Magog settled in the area just north of where Semitic people settled in the northeastern parts of Asia Minor. Ezekiel gives support for this location when he referred to Gog as the chief prince of Meshech and Tubal, areas probably named after two other sons of Japheth (Gen. 10:2). To be clearly understood is that Ezekiel was addressing areas and its people that were part of the Babylonian Empire. The question to be asked is: why did he address these?

In the context of Ezekiel's prophecies concerning the return and restoration of the covenant people, he prophesied concerning the defeat of its captors. This was Babylon. Ezekiel, living and prophesying in the heartland of Babylon, among the captive exiles, did not address Babylon directly.[65] The Babylonians would not tolerate such preaching. But, to assure the covenant people that they would be freed when their captors were defeated, the prophet referred to a northwestern section of the empire. This was the area north of their homeland. Passage back to their land would be open.

Ezekiel included many details concerning the means of warfare, large regiments of troops, many corpses, and burial in Israel to emphasize the reality of what Yahweh God *Adonây* would do. It was their covenant Lord who would execute the covenant curse upon Babylon[66] as he prepared to restore, be it as remnant, his covenant people to their homeland. Thus, Babylon, the fierce enemy of the covenant people, would be judged in a dramatic and final manner. Babylon stood among the nations as the great opponent of the covenant people.[67]

Covenant Continuation

In the discussion of the execution of the curse of the covenant, no specific reference was made to the continuation of the covenant. It could be assumed that the deportation of Israel and Judah from their covenantally promised land meant that the covenant, broken by the peoples' disobedience, was abrogated by Yahweh God *Adonây* also. But that was not the reality. The execution of the curse of the covenant definitely demonstrated that the covenant was still very much a reality. Repeatedly Ezekiel proclaimed on behalf of Yahweh God *Adonây wĕyādĕ 'û kî 'ănî yĕhwâ* (and they shall know that I am Yahweh) (Ezek. 33:29).[68] Note three specific factors: (1) the name *Yahweh* is the specific covenant name of God *Adonây;* (2) the judgment or curse executed would give knowledge of Yahweh the covenant Lord; and (3) the covenant remained inviolate and was sovereignly administered through judgment, promises, and the fulfillment of these.

Yahweh God *Adonây* assured the continuity of the covenant by declaring what he would do for the sheep scattered by wicked shepherds. He declared that he would keep a people in the salvation/redemption aspect of the covenant. He searched for them, rescued, and looked after them. He would gather them and feed them in rich living conditions. He would help the wounded and weak and execute justice on their behalf (34:11–16). In metaphoric terms Yahweh God *Adonây* demonstrated to the exiles that the covenant would continue. He would be their God and they would be his people. The promises to Abraham would surely be upheld (Gen. 17:1–7). Ezekiel included many aspects of covenant realities as blessings for the remnant of Israel and Judah.

In Yahweh God *Adonây*'s declaration *'īm lō' bĕ' ēš qinĕ'ātî'* (surely in my jealous fury) (Ezek. 36:5) and jealous wrath (36:6) he proclaimed he would deal with the nations that caused the covenant people to suffer scorn. By that same jealous wrath the covenant people, redeemed and restored, would be assured of continuation of covenant life with all its inherent blessings. The covenant people, if only a remnant, would see their land restored as a homeland.[69] Their land would no longer be a scene where they, as a delivered people, would be taunted because of their sins against fellow men nor would they suffer scorn (36:8–15).[70]

A greater blessing that would be realized was the sanctifying of Yahweh God *Adonây*'s holy name that had been defiled by idolatry and bloodshed (36:16–23). This sanctifying would be for the sake of the holy name of Yahweh himself. He had identified himself as the one who gave the land but maintained his ownership of it for the covenant people's sake. As a corollary to their blessing of sanctification was the assurance of the cleansing of the people. Yahweh God *Adonây* assured them *wĕzāraqĕtî 'alêkem mayîm ṭĕhôrîm* (and I will sprinkle them with clean water) and thus cleanse them (the remnant that returned) of their impurities. A new heart of flesh would be given in place of their hearts and Yahweh's Spirit would be given them to enable them to obey their covenant Lord. Thus he would save his people and bless them (36:24–32).

The renewed heart was further assured by the vision of dry bones (37:1–14). Ezekiel was led back and forth in the valley and saw no evidence of life.[71] But life came when the word was prophesied and the Spirit was breathed into the dead. The text is clear: the word and spirit together brought newly regenerated lives. Dead bones thus could become living persons! And these enlivened ones would be numerous (36:37, 38).

The covenant people were assured of one more blessing. They would no longer say or write, "I belong to Judah," or "I belong to Israel" (37:15–17). Judah would be the central one to whom the others would unite (37:19) and thus the gathered people would be made *lĕgôy 'ehed* (one people).[72]

The question concerning the fulfillment of these covenant promises and assurances cannot be answered by a single reference. These promises were to be realized throughout the coming centuries. The promise of return to the land was fulfilled sixty years after Ezekiel prophesied. Physical and natural blessings were realized in various degrees and measures for the returned remnant. The Spirit of God was poured out on Pentecost not in a literal manner, upon dead dry bones, but upon people awaiting the promised Spirit and upon all those who throughout the New Testament age responded to the preached word and submitted to the Spirit's work in their lives. In summary: the covenant would indeed continue for the returned remnant, for the postexilic community, for New Testament believers until Christ's return.

Ezekiel prophesied of the continuity of the covenant in more specific ways. He had, without direct reference, implied the continuity of the creation covenant as made with Adam and repeated to Noah and all his posterity. He had made clear that the covenant with Abraham and the patriarchs and with Israel at Sinai had not been abrogated. These administrations of the covenant had continued and would continue as the context for the fulfillment of two specific covenantal promises and administrations.

In two contexts, assuring words for the exiles were in terms of David, the servant of Yahweh, who would serve as shepherd over the delivered flock and who would be a prince among them (34:23, 24). David would be king over the united people and David, Yahweh's servant, would be their prince forever (36:24, 25).[73]

There should be no doubt that Ezekiel, inspired by the Holy Spirit, wrote about David as king over a gathered, replanted, saved, Spirit-renewed covenant people. Yahweh God had covenanted with David, assuring him he would have an eternal house or dynasty that would rule over the kingdom that would endure forever (2 Sam. 7:11–16). David himself would not so reign, nor would his son Solomon. A contemporary fulfillment of the prophet Nathan's words, or of Ezekiel's words, is not intended by the text. Rather, the promise is to be taken as referring to a real future person who was a member of the royal Davidic dynasty. Ezekiel assured the people that Yahweh God *Adonây* was faithful to his covenant made with David, that the Anointed One, the Messiah, was sure to come, and that he would be the Shepherd of the covenant people. That this prophecy was fulfilled with Jesus' birth and ministry was confirmed when the angels spoke of David's heritage (Luke 2:11), and Jesus referred to himself as the good shepherd (John 10:11). The covenant, made and reconfirmed in Old Testament times, was to continue through all time. Jesus, the Messiah, descendant of David, the covenant redeemer and Lord, was for all time and all people. But, he was to come in time through Abraham's offspring but not just for them. It must not be overlooked that Ezekiel did proclaim that this Davidic descendant was to be the king over and in the midst of the united people of Israel and Judah. The remnant that was to return in due time would be drawn from various tribes and form one united community. And this community would in time be the seed bed for the New Testament church, made up of people from every tribe, tongue, and nation. This church was to become the heart of the kingdom of God and his anointed one, the Christ.

Ezekiel prophesied concerning the future or continuation of the covenant. As he did, he painted a scene in which wonderful events would have a role. A literal interpretation of the portrayal of this scene (Ezek. 37:24–28) is unrealistic.

Reference to David being king over the returned and renewed people as the one shepherd clearly pointed to the future coming of the Messiah. This ruled over people would be an obedient people and would live in the land where Jacob had lived *'ad 'ôlām* (forever).[74] Historically this has not happened; it clearly was not the intent of Ezekiel to proclaim that a united Jewish people would live continually and for all time in that part of the world promised as a dwelling place to the patriarchs. The land, according to Paul, was a first down payment of the entire cosmos (Rom. 4:13); Abraham was promised to be heir of the whole world. Ezekiel referred to this broader concept of the land. Yahweh God *Adonây* gathered (from various lands, and eventually from all peoples) a delivered, redeemed people who are at all times, while living on earth, under the reign of David's son, the Christ, Jesus the Lord. In this context Ezekiel proclaimed that the covenant of peace would be confirmed as an everlasting covenant. He had spoken of the covenant of peace when he spoke of the shepherd who would separate the lean sheep from the fat (Ezek. 34:20–31). In terms of what the people understood, he spoke of a safe dwelling where showers of blessing would water the trees and cause the ground to yield good crops. In that descriptive symbolic context, the people would fully realize the promises made to Abraham: "you are mine and I am your God."

A specific and integral aspect of this covenant of peace would be Yahweh God's sanctuary, which would be among them forever (37:26, 27). This eternal sanctuary was the verification and realization of the promise Yahweh God had made to the patriarchs, namely, that he would be with them as their God. Then an important concluding statement was made: the people will be holy when God's sanctuary is among them forever (37:28).

Three crucial issues call for discussion. First, what was the role of the sanctuary?[75] Recall that the tabernacle was the sanctuary for the Israelites in the desert. It served to demonstrate that Yahweh God was indeed with them; it was his symbolic dwelling place. The people knew it was the place from which Yahweh's word proceeded and where they met him in worship. Solomon built a permanent dwelling, the temple, to serve as the sanctuary. It was, however, as Solomon acknowledged, not able to contain the Lord of heaven and earth (1 Kings 8:27). Yet it was a sure evidence of the infinite God's presence with his people. When the remnant returned to Palestine, the sanctuary had to be rebuilt, for it was to serve as the assurance of the covenant promise, "I will be with you."

The second issue concerns which sanctuary Ezekiel is referring to.[76] The temple Solomon had built as Yahweh God's sanctuary was destroyed. Was he referring to the temple to be rebuilt by the returned remnant? Or to the temple Herod would rebuild? It is clear from Ezekiel's prophecy concerning the new temple that he was not referring to temporary, symbolic sanctuaries that had served as covenant assurances that Yahweh God was in their midst. Was Ezekiel, then, referring to another temple, a physical structure that was to be built in the future? (Ezek. 40–48).

The third issue concerns the temple or sanctuary he described as seen in a vision (40:2). Attempts to describe it in physical terms and measurements are not possible, in spite of efforts some commentators have made. Some parts recall the Solomonic temple. Other parts refer to subsequent events, such as the return of the Glory; Ezekiel had seen it depart in a vision (chap. 43). The Mosaic altar, sacrifices, and priesthood were restored. The land in which the temple was to be restored was redivided in a different way than it had been under Joshua (45:1; 48:1–29). Included in the vision is a call to the princes of Israel to give up their violence and stop dispossessing the people (45:9–12). What had not been a feature of previous sanctuaries was the ever-increasing river flowing from near the altar and giving life to parched areas and the Dead Sea. One must conclude that what Ezekiel saw in the vision gave him assurance that this visionary temple was like, yet very different, from all previous temples. Some parts could be reinstituted, some parts were very different. A river flowing from a rocky hilltop was physically and naturally not to be brought into existence by future builders.

The clues to the understanding of the temple prophecy should be given attention. First, this vision came to Ezekiel twenty years after he had received the vision of the glory of Yahweh God (1:2; 40:1). It came forty years after the first deportation. Was the exile ever going to end? Ezekiel assured the people there was a glorious restoration and future. What could assure the people more convincingly than a presentation of a glorious rebuilt temple? Second, the last phrase of the entire prophecy should be noted: Yahweh God is there! The covenant Lord would not forget his people. He was with them in the wilderness, when the people lived in the land; he was with them in the exile; and he would be with them always! The covenant was permanent! Yahweh God *Adonây*'s covenant bond with his people would never be abrogated or become ineffective. He was their God and would always be with them and their children.

The New Testament gives an explanation that should be of comfort to all believers. The apostle John wrote that the true, abiding, ever present sanctuary that was portrayed by the physical sanctuaries and Ezekiel's visionary sanctuary, was none other then Jesus Christ, who tabernacled among his people and who now on the throne at the Father's right hand is preparing an eternal sanctuary for his people.

A final question arises: is the covenant of peace, with all its inclusions, to be identified with the new covenant of which Jeremiah spoke? Jeremiah's emphasis had been on the initiation of the renewed administration of the covenant. Ezekiel continued to fill out and give fuller assurance of the realities involved in the new covenant.[77]

The Covenant Mediators

In the latter part of Ezekiel's prophecies no new mediators were introduced or referred to. Since reference to covenant agents and mediators were inevitably referred to, because of their close involvement in the covenant life, some are spoken of at some length. It is not necessary to discuss them in this section. It will be helpful to refer to them briefly.

The Prophet Ezekiel

The prophet Ezekiel was a faithful covenant servant. He served as spokesman for Yahweh God *Adonây.* He did not hesitate to prophesy concerning the curse of the covenant nor did he tone down warnings against covenant breaking. He proclaimed with clarity the promises and assurances of the covenant. He involved himself personally in his messages.[78]

The Shepherds: Kings and Prophets

Ezekiel prophesied concerning agents who were called to serve as covenant mediators. He addressed the shepherds, the kings especially, and the unfaithful prophets. He did not hesitate to remind them of their duties and misbehaviors. They neither represented their covenant Lord, Yahweh God *Adonây,* nor did they serve the people as they were called and given the ability to do.[79]

David

David, the first king of united Israel, was referred to as the covenant shepherd. His dynasty was heralded as an everlasting one. In so doing, Ezekiel prophesied that the great covenant servant, the Messiah, would come and faithfully carry out all aspects of the covenant.[80]

Finally, it must be kept in mind that Yahweh God *Adonay* was proclaimed as the covenant Lord. He was specifically declared to be concerned about and for his sheep, the covenant people (34:11–34).

The Kingdom

Introductory Comments

Ezekiel continued to speak of Yahweh God *Adonây* as the Lord of all in various ways as he had done in the initial prophecies.[81] He continued to emphasize that Yahweh was *Adonây,* the Master, that Ezekiel was his agent, that he had complete control over the natural world, that nations were part of the cosmic kingdom over which he ruled with absolute authority and sovereignty. This was especially demonstrated by Ezekiel's proclamation concerning the judgment to be executed over Edom and Babylon (Gog of Magog).

The Biblical Context

Ezekiel's prophecies concerning the kingdom and the king, though not mentioned directly, certainly were in harmony with what the entire Old Testament Scriptures presented. Yahweh God *Adonây* had demonstrated his kingship over the cosmic kingdom in creating it, executing judgment in Noah's time, ending plagues on Egypt, raising up David to be his vicegerent, exiling the covenant-breaking people of Israel and Judah, and employing the nations Assyria and Babylon as his servants. Ezekiel prophesied how the sovereign King of the cosmos would deal with Edom and Babylon and how he would redeem and restore a remnant. As sovereign Lord, the Holy Spirit would bring life so that a disobedient people would become an obedient, worshiping community. Yahweh God was *Adonây,* the Master, the Lord, in his cosmic kingdom and over all aspects of this kingdom.

The Theocratic Monarchy

The question that receives much discussion concerns whether the theocratic monarchy was still, or would be in the future, an integral aspect of the cosmic kingdom. If it would, what would be its role and influence?

Ezekiel spoke of the covenant people as a nation a few times. He spoke of them as a rebellious *gôyîm* (nation) (2:3). Yahweh God *Adonây* would restore them as a nation, having children and no longer hearing the taunts of nations (36:13–15). These people would be a united *nation,* again in the land when the Holy Spirit enlivened them (37:22). Did Ezekiel, employing the term nation prophesy that the theocratic monarchy would continue to be, or in time be, an integral part of the cosmic kingdom? Biblical interpreters are not agreed in answering this question. A number of points must be considered.

Ezekiel prophesied that David would be king in their midst (37:24). It must be recognized that this statement did not intend to say that David, who had died 500 years before, would actually rise up and personally reign. Hence, the prophecy cannot be understood literally. The term *gôy* (nation) was not used consistently as referring to a kingdom ruled over by a monarch.[82]

The promise to the people in exile was that they would be able to return to their homeland. A remnant did but, except for some futile effort in succeeding generations, the remnant never became a theocratic monarchy with a Davidic descendant reigning as king. At most, the remnant became an identifiable religious community under the leadership of priests. The Davidic descendant, Jesus the Messiah, was born in this community.

The light the New Testament sheds is that the theocratic monarchy, or an Israelite/Jewish kingdom, was not mentioned, much less expected. Rather, it refers to the church, a body of Israelite and Gentile members. This body is the people of the new covenant, the covenant of peace, also referred to as the kingdom over which the Messiah, descendant of David, rules with grace and power.[83]

The conclusion that should be accepted is that the theocratic monarchy was a symbol and pointer to the kingdom of the Lord, the cosmic kingdom of which the church is the living body, housing, serving, and worshiping the reigning Christ, who is seated at the Father's right hand.

The Prophetic Vision

Ezekiel had seen the magnitude and glory of Yahweh God *Adonây* in the first vision. He received additional visions: the abominations in the temple court and the departure of the glory presence of Yahweh God *Adonây* (8:4–10:22); the vision of Yahweh God *Adonây* executing judgment on Israel's leaders (11:1–14); and the vision of the promise of restoration (11:15, 25). The Spirit led him to experience the enlivening work in the valley of dry bones (37:1). Then Ezekiel was led to the land of Israel, where from a high mountain he saw a person who had the appearance like bronze and who had a measuring rod in his hand. As the prophet was led through parts of the rebuilt temple in a vision, he saw the glory of God and the radiance of it filling the land.

The survey of these visions leads the reader to see with Ezekiel the glory, majesty, and radiance of the all-seeing and all-knowing sovereign Lord. He came as the sovereign One to bring judgment and cleansing. The majestic glorious one in this vision is on the move; he comes active and ready for action. As the visions progress, the covenant people come under judgment but by the Spirit's power new life is graciously given (chap. 37) and promises of restoration and unification give hope. The final vision breathes hope;[84] it portrays restoration and the rebuilding of a renewed worshiping community. The vision concludes with the covenantal assurance: Yahweh is in the midst of his redeemed and restored people. The exile, a judgment of cleansing and sanctifying, was concluded. The sovereign covenant Lord fulfilled his covenant promise: he was their God; he was with them; they were his people!

NOTES

1. Cf. Gerard Van Groningen *Messianic Revelation in the Old Testament* (*MROT*) (Grand Rapids: Baker, 1990), 730. For a concise review of introductory subjects, consult pp. 730–32 and take specific notice of the bibliographical sources in the notes.

2. Literature produced in the past ten or so years include Leslie Allen, *Ezekiel 20–48, Word Biblical Commentary,* vol. 29 (Dallas: Word, 1990); Daniel Berrigan, Art by Tom Lewis-Barbely, *Ezekiel: Vision in the Dust* (Maryknoll: Orbis, 1997); Michael Lieb, *Children of Ezekiel* (Durham: Duke University Press, 1998).

3. J. Ridderbos wrote that the calling of Ezekiel in his house came in June 593 B.C. Van Ezechiel tot Maleachi, vol. IV in series *God's Woord der Profeten* (Kampen: Kok, 1953), 15. As a priest he was called to be a prophet. Hence C. Hassell Bullock could write that with Ezekiel there was the merging of two spheres, prophetic and cultic. *An Introduction to the Old Testament Prophetic Book* (Chicago: Moody, 1986), 227.

4. Walter Zimmerli commented on Ezekiel's use of the expanded name Yahweh God *Adonay,* which appears 217 times. Zimmerli made a study of the context of the expanded

use. *Commentary on the Book of Ezekiel,* 2 vols. trans. Ronald E. Clement (Philadelphia: Fortress, 1983), 2:556ff.

5. The exiles were disinherited. They lost the promised land, which they never did recover. The land was an important aspect of the covenant but not a central factor. The covenant was maintained without possession of the land as had been the case with Abraham, who had been in covenant with Yahweh but did not possess the land.

6. Cf term *kĕbar* in the *Theological Wordbook of the Old Testament*, ed. R. Laird Harris, Gleason L. Archer, and Bruce K. Waltke (Chicago: Moody, 1980), 1:429. Cf. also Carl G. Rasmussen, *Zondervan NIV Atlas of the Bible* (Grand Rapids: Zondervan, 1989), which includes a reference to Kebar River as a canal in ancient Babylon. It branched off from the Euphrates northwest of Babylon and rejoined it some sixty miles south; 241. Various commentaries discuss the actual locale of the prophet. William H. Brownlee listed seven difficulties with accepting Ezekiel's presence in Babylon and offered five explanations. He also held that the term *gûlâh* (exile) should be read as Gilgal, Ezekiel's hometown in Palestine. Finally, Brownlee asked "Did Ezekiel ever go to Babylon?" He concluded that one would like to affirm it but he also wrongly interpreted Ezek. 29:1–16 when he stated that Ezekiel went to Egypt. *Word Biblical Commentary Ezekiel 1–19* (Waco: Word; 1986), xxii–xxxii. The view set forth by C. C. Torrey in *Psuedo Ezekiel and the Original Prophecy* (New York: Ktav, 1970)—that the prophecy was originally composed in Jerusalem and addressed to the people of Jerusalem and Judah and that it was made over by a Chronicler in the Babylonian exile (xxxvii)—should not be accepted as historically or literarily correct.

7. Much discussion has been raised by the time reference Ezekiel gave for learning of Jerusalem's fall. It was during the twelfth year of his exile, on the fifth day of the tenth month. Since Jerusalem actually fell in 586 B.C., according to the Palestinian calendar, in late 586 B.C., Ezekiel, using the Babylonian calendar refers to the spring of the twelfth year, that is, 585 B.C. The following chart (see page 290) indicates the difference in time references according to the two calendars. Note that there actually was a six-month period between the fall of Jerusalem and the arrival of the escapee.

8. Cf. the listing of kings and their time of reign in the NIV, 503, 504. This listing was adapted from *A Chronology of Hebrew Kings* by Edwin R. Thiele (Grand Rapids: Zondervan, 1977). Different theories on what Ezekiel referred to by "the thirtieth year are: (1) thirty years after the last jubilee year; (2) thirty years after New Babylon came into power; (3) thirtieth year of Jeremiah's seventy-year period; (4) thirtieth year of Ezekiel's life. These and other theories have no credible evidence; the finding of the Book of Law seems to offer the preferable date.

9. Cf. *MROT,* 742–85.

10. Ezekiel has been misunderstood by a number of theologically liberal minded scholars as well as by higher critical authors. His use of bizarre metaphors and symbols reflected the circumstances among the exiles and the religious culture of the world at large in which Yahweh God called him to be a priestly spokesman. Walther Eichrodt, in his commentary *Ezekiel,* trans Caslett Quin (London: SCM, 1965), 26, has stated the case correctly. "Never . . . do we find any trace of mental abnormality or even disease . . . in spite of frequently bizarre symbolic actions and often over strained excitability of his speech." Eichrodt wrote this in response, for, e.g., to Karl Jaspers, "Der Prophet, Hesekiel, Eine Pathographische Studie," in which Ezekiel was explained as a paranoid schizophrenic.

11. The author of the brief introduction to the commentary on Ezekiel in *The NIV Study Bible,* gen. ed., Kenneth Barker (Grand Rapids: Zondervan, 1985), correctly wrote:

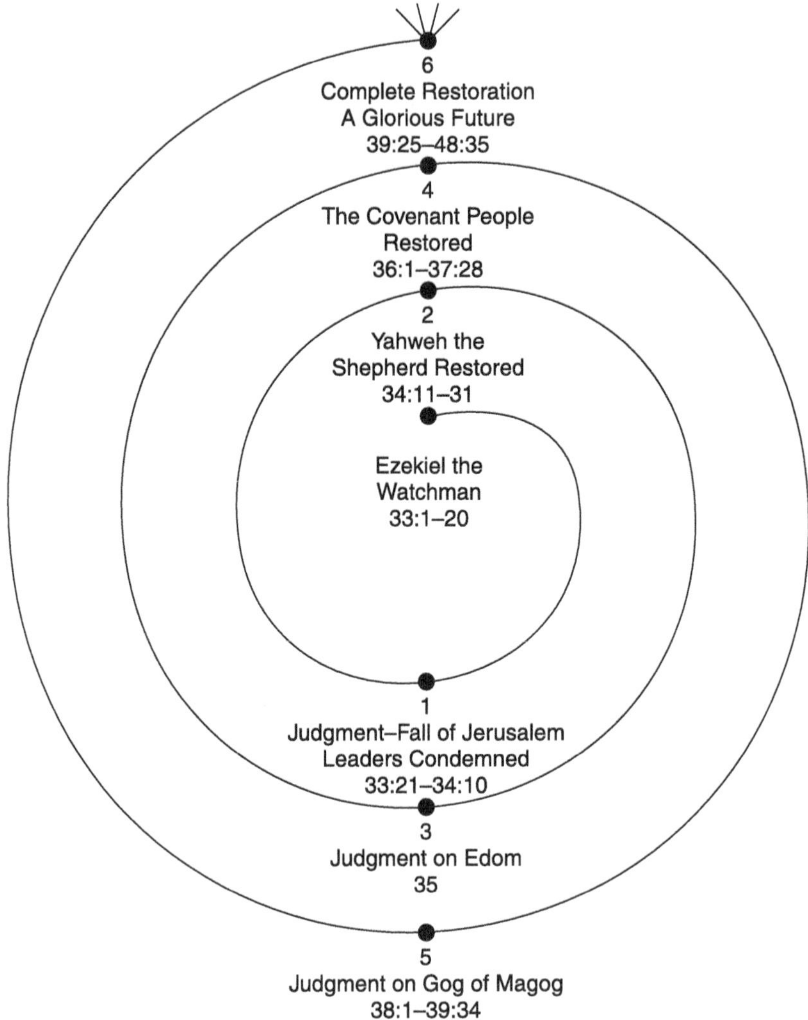

"Ezekiel was obviously a man of broad knowledge . . . of his own national traditions but also of international affairs and history." He also wrote concerning the prophet's acquaintance with the culture of his time, 1226.

12. The Hebrew (*El*) is not in the text. G.C.H. Aalders in *Ezechiel,* vol. 1 (Kampen: Kok, 1955), wrote the reference can be twofold: the sound of thunder is the first but it is also justified to translate "the voice of the Almighty," 52.

13. Moshe Greenberg, *Ezekiel 1–20,* vol. 22 of the Anchor Bible Series, ed. William Foxwell Albright and David Moel Freedman (Garden City: Doubleday, 1983) is incorrect to interpret *rûaḥ* as referring to a sense of vigor or even courage infused into the prophet by the address of God, 62.

14. The text, 3:15, could be understood to indicate that Ezekiel was geographically transported. Ezek. 1:3 stated that Ezekiel was by the River Kebar. There he received the vision. Ezek. 3:15 states *wā'ēbô' 'el hoggâlâh tel 'ābib* (I came to exiles at Tel Abib). Aalders called attention to the imperfect consecutive of the verb, which indicates that the vision was ended and he was with the people again as before the vision. *Ezechiel,* 74.

15. Ralph H. Alexander correctly wrote that the role of a watchman was not reprobative and injurious but corrective and beneficial. "Ezekiel," in *The Expositor's Bible Commentary,* ed. Frank F. Gabelein, vol. 6 (Grand Rapids: Regency, 1986), 765. Daniel Berrigan wrote that the prophet when called to be a watchman had the duties of those who were to walk the ramparts of the city. *Ezekiel: Vision in the Dust,* 104.

16. Cf. John B. Taylor, *Ezekiel* (Downers Grove: InterVarsity, 1974), 72. Later Ezekiel received the vision of dry bones here (chap. 37).

17. Cf. Carl Friederich Keil, *The Prophecies of Ezekiel,* trans. James Marten, vol. 1 (Grand Rapids: Eerdmans, 1950), 93.

18. Tammuz was a well known popular Babylonian deity known in Mesopotamia already in Sumerian times. Tammuz represented dying and reawakening of vegetation in the course of each year. Cf. Eichrodt, *Ezekiel,* 126.

19. Chap. 21.

20. Later Ezekiel gave a second prophecy against Edom (chap. 35).

21. Ezekiel continued to be active among the exiles as a prophet. He received visions in the twenty-fifth year of the exile (40:1). Hence it should not be considered unusual that Ezekiel prophesied two years after that.

22. Why Ezekiel included this later prophecy within the account of the initial prophecy is difficult to understand. Aalders wrote that "kunnen wij moeilyk gissen" (can we hardly guess); he went on, after reviewing what some critical scholars had written, trying to explain the insertion, to say that he would not permit himself to give a judgment. *Ezechiel,* 2:87.

23. See explanation of "cosmic kingdom" in the preceding chapter, part IV.

24. H. L. Ellison, in *Ezekiel: The Man and His Message* (Grand Rapids: Eerdmans, 1956), 22–25 has written a good, concise description of this moving throne.

25. Ellison wrote that this earth is the crown of God's creation. Therefore, it is fitting that the chariot-throne has carriers linked with divine creative and redemptive power here on earth. Ibid., 23.

26. Moshe Greenberg, *Ezekiel,* 42, suggests this as unlikely.

27. Geographically, Babylon was located due east of Judah and Jerusalem but the great desert was between them. The road from Babylon to Jerusalem was therefore in the form of a large arch. Babylonians had to first march north, then westwardly, then south to Jerusalem.

28. H. Veldkamp has given a decisive answer to those who would say that the hand on Ezekiel causing him to fall on his face was evidence of epilepsy and that the prophet was a psychopath. *De Balling Van de Kabaroe* (Franeker: Wever, 1956), 13.

29. Cf. vol. 1, *From Creation to Consummation,* chap. 1, the section entitled "The Eschaton in Creation," 142.

30. Cf. references to the concept of "cosmic kingdom" in vol. 1, *From Creation to Consummation,* 37–41, 72–73, 129–130, and in the preceding chapter, chap. 25, part IV B.

31. Cf. the author's discussion of "Son of Man" in *MROT,* 739.

32. Cf. study of "theocratic kingdom" in *FCTC,* 1:313–44.

33. Ibid., 235.

34. Not all national kingdoms were removed. Egypt stands out as a specific case of continuing endurance.

35. Cf. brief explanation of covenantal framework in *MROT,* 740.

36. Cf. ibid., where it is pointed out that the term *bĕrît* occurs only eighteen times in the entire book, 740.

37. The RSV translated the phrase "I will bring you into the bond of the covenant" as "and I will let you go in by number" following the LXX version in which the word *covenant* is omitted. For a wide-ranging discussion on what commentators have written concerning this phrase, cf. Aalders, *Ezechiel,* 2:327. Also see Greenberg, *Ezekiel 1–20,* who translates obligation instead of bond, 372, 373.

38. Cf. Eichrodt, *Ezekiel.* Ezekiel did not give a history of salvation but of sin, 280.

39. Note that Ezekiel also referred to females who used charms to ensnare the people (13:17–23) and that Yahweh actually enticed false prophets to give false messages (14:9–11).

40. Recall what Ezekiel saw in a vision as recorded in chapter 8. Ezekiel prophesied against the mountains of Israel, chapter 6. Linda B. Hinton in *Basic Bible Commentary,* "Ezekiel and Daniel" (Cokesbury—no further bibliographical information is given) stated that the mountains against which Ezekiel prophesied were places of open sanctuaries for idolatry and other forms of pagan worship, 21.

41. The Hebrew phrase is *wûmĕsôl masâh.* The noun is translated variously as riddle, parable, allegory; the phrase literally translated can be rendered riddling a riddle, parabling a parable, or allegorizing an allegory.

42. Ezekiel referred to Yahweh God *Adonây* pouring out his wrath (7:8; 14:19; 20:8, 13, 21, 33, 34; 21:31; 22:22, 31; 30:15) and spending his wrath (5:13; 6:12; 13:15).

43. Yahweh God upheld the covenant when he executed the curse aspect of it. Andrew Blackwell, *Ezekiel, Prophecy of Hope* (Grand Rapids: Baker, 1965), 122, 123.

44. Greenberg has analyzed Ezekiel's prophecy concerning on whom Yahweh God *Adonay* executes punishment. First he recalls Moses (Deut. 24:10) and shows how Ezekiel inverts the propositions regarding who is punished:

	not fathers for sons		who sins dies
Deut. 24:16	not sons for fathers	Ezek. 18:20	not son for father
	each dies for own sins		not father for son

Ezekiel, 333. Greenberg, 336, analyzed the doctrine of retribution and response:

Doctrine: a. repentance expunges sins
b. God desires repentance
c. reversion expunges past merits
d. not God's ways but yours are perverse

Retort: c' reversion expunges merits
a' repentance expunges past sins
d' not God's ways but yours are perverse

45. Cf., e.g., Eichrodt, *Ezekiel,* 243. Keil refers to blessing of righteousness without giving a clear statement of what these blessings consist of. *Ezekiel,* 1:254. John Wevers pointed out that Ezekiel had to make clear to the exiles that Yahweh did (does) not judge by quantity of sin or righteousness in one's life but by what he finally does and becomes. *Ezekiel* (Greenwood: Attu, 1976), 111. Peter Cragie points out that God does not keep a tally sheet,

so many days of evil, so many of good. The many good will not erase the few evil; all depends on one's relationship to God. *Ezekiel* (Philadelphia: Westminster, 1983), 137.

46. The hiphil form of verb *qûm* expresses continuity, maintaining what had been established (cf. Gen. 6:18). See the discussion of this hiphil form of the verb in *FCTC,* 147.

47. Cf. what the author wrote in *FCTC,* 1:13.

48. See *MROT,* 742–69, for a detailed exegetical study of these passages.

49. Explanations concerning Yahweh causing Ezekiel's tongue to cleave to the roof of his mouth are varied. A good reason for these variations is the seeming contradiction. Ezekiel is told to speak Yahweh's word to the exiles (3:4), and that he would be silent, unable to rebuke the exiles. Aalder's view is that the verbs employed indicate that Ezekiel was personally not to rebuke the exiles. *Ezechiel,* 1:85. Patrick Fairbairn also explained Ezekiel's dumbness as Aalders did. *An Exposition of Ezekiel* (Evansville: Sovereign Grace, 1960), 44. Eichrodt reviewed various views, e.g., Ezekiel had been too vigorous in addressing the people and was punished for it; it indicated a psychological problem. Eichrodt believed that Ezekiel's dumbness only occurred in a short period before the news arrived that Jerusalem had fallen. *Ezekiel,* 76, 77. Alexander wrote that Ezekiel was dumb for seven and a half years, dumb in the sense that he "was restrained from speaking publicly among the people in contrast to the normal vocal ministry of the prophets." *Ezekiel,* 767.

50. In the actual narrative of Ezekiel's life and work as a prophet, it should be noted that 33:1 follows the close of chapter 24. Chapters 25–32 record the prophecies of Ezekiel concerning the nations; cf. chap. 21.

51. Zimmerli, *Ezekiel,* joins 35 and 36:1–15. He considers this a unit, but separates 35 from 25:12–14 because he considers 35 to have been written later when he included events that occurred later. Leslie Allen, in *Ezekiel 20–48,* in *Word Biblical Commentary* (Dallas: Word, 1990), also joins 35 to 36:1–15 stating that 35 serves as a black background to Israel's glorious restoration. Thus Israel and Edom are polarized as negative and positive counterparts, 169, 170.

52. The reading and interpretation of Ezekiel has baffled many commentators and unusual conclusions have been recorded. Cf., e.g., Jon Douglas Levenson, who wrote that two complexes of tradition lie behind Ezekiel's vision (40–48), Zion and Eden. These are primarly mythic and are placed in tension with history. *Theology of the Program of Restoration of Ezekiel 40–48* (Missoula: Scholars, 1996), 161.

53. To conclude, as Alexander does, that much of what Ezekiel described regarding the future is to be taken literally presents insurmountable and inexplicable problems. He attempted to deal with the structure of the temple and the sacrificial system in the light of progressive revelation in the New Testament, but his conclusions cannot be sustained. "Ezekiel," 946–52. To discuss Alexander's efforts point by point would demonstrate discrepancies; to do so would require an unnecessary lengthy discussion.

54. To unite the duration of *'ôlām* to the millennium as Alexander does is arbitrary. His view fits into the millennial scheme he has imposed upon Ezekiel's vision.

55. Aalders, *Ezechiel,* 2:354, e55; 362, e63.

56. William Greenhill concluded his commentary *An Exposition of Ezekiel,* reprint, originally published in 1667 (Avon: Bath, 1994) by writing that "Jehovah *Shāmmâh*" indicates the Lord's great delight in the city. Its citizens in the church and the members thereof refer to the New Testament's reference to the Lamb's throne and that he will feed them and lead them to living water. 831.

57. Cf. Derek Thomas, *God Strengthens* (Durham: Evangelical, 1993), especially his "Focus" on the nature of the covenant in Ezekiel. 121–23.

58. Ezekiel referred to Yahweh's anger and to Yahweh's wrath against the covenant people eighteen times in chaps. 1–32. In contrast, Ezekiel spoke of Yahweh's anger three times in 33–48, against Edom and God and of wrath two times when reference was to what Yahweh God had done in regard to nations and one time in regard to the covenant people's idolatry. Ezek. 36:6, 18, 19.

59. The structure of the text of Ezekiel should be properly understood. Chapter 24 records the death of Ezekiel's wife on the evening of the day before the fugitive arrived, 33:21. The last part of chapter 24 and the first part of chapter 33 record what transpired after his wife died and the next day when the fugitive arrived. This means that if one is to read in actual sequence the events, it would be as follows: Ezekiel is told his wife is to die, he is to grieve in silence (24:15–17). He addressed the exiles in the morning of the day she dies in the evening (29:18). The next morning he spoke to the people explaining that Jerusalem was about to fall and the temple would be desecrated (24:19–27). The Lord then again addressed Ezekiel concerning his duties as a watchman (33:1–20). That same evening he had his tongue loosened (33:22). The next day the fugitive arrived (33:21). Ezekiel's account proceeded after that as it is recorded in chapters 34–48.

60. William H. Brownlee in his essay "Ezekiel's Parable of the Watchman and the Editing of Ezekiel," *Vetus Testamentum* 28, no. 4 (1978): 392–408, made too much of the parable's role in the structure of the book. Having done some editing Brownlee opined that the report concerning the watchman was Ezekiel's "private oracle to himself" but his responsibility as watchman was being "shared with those addressed." Both were responsible "to the nations and then to the house of Israel." Cf. esp. 400. Is this a case of editing the text so that it states what one wishes to read in a text? There should be no doubt that Israel had a responsibility to the nations; Abraham had already been so informed (Gen. 12:1–3).

61. Cf. 18:1–32, which records at length the message of warning to sinners and Yahweh God *Adonây*'s heart wish to have a repentant people.

62. Veldkamp stated the case cryptically. "Geestelijke kinderen van Abraham waren ze echter niet" (Spiritual children of Abraham they surely were not). *De Balling,* 302.

63. *Ezekiel,* 473.

64. Craig Blaising and Darrell Bock refer to Rev. 20:8, which interprets Gog and Magog (both as persons) to represent the whole earth (the four corners of the earth). *Progressive Dispensationalism* (Wheaton: Victor, 1993), 93, 97. These authors refer to Gog and Magog as apocalyptic terms. Willem Van Gemeren wrote that the Gog and Magog motif cannot be restricted to an exclusive historical or eschatological relevance. The kingdom of God evokes acts of hostility and persecution from human kingdoms (who are represented apocalyptically by Gog and Magog). *Interpreting the Prophetic Word* (Grand Rapids: Zondervan, 1990), 334. The note on Ezek. 38:2 in the *Oxford NIV Scofield Study Bible* (New York: Oxford University Press, 1984) states the reference is to powers in the north of Europe, headed by Russia, and that the "prophecy belongs to the yet future day of the Lord." This note, written before the breakup of the USSR, indicates that applying historical references to prophetic persons and places must be done with extreme caution.

65. Note should be taken of Ezekiel's reference to all the neighboring nations, but he did not address Babylon directly (25:1–32:32).

66. Jan G. Aalders in his book *Gog and Magog* (with summary in English) (Kampen: Kok, 1951) presents a case for the fulfillment of the God/Magog prophecy in the time of the Maccabees, 170.

67. Aalders, ibid., sees two fulfillments of this prophecy concerning Gog and Magog. He stresses that there clear and definite historical references to the time of and restoration of the remnant from exile. He also sees a futuristic reference, not in details concerning Israel, but in the final days before Christ's return.

68. This phrase appears more than seventy times, at times with some variations, such as "the nations shall know that I am Yahweh" (36:23; 37:28; 39:7, 23), "all the trees of the field will know . . ." (17:24), "Edom will know Yahweh's vengeance" (25:14), "the Egyptians will know Yahweh is sovereign" (29:6). Through the prophet's presence and prophesying the people would know Yahweh (2:5; 33:33).

69. Ezekiel again addressed the mountains (36:8) on which idolatry had been practiced. These mountains would become sources of blessings; as Ezekiel continued to speak of these blessings it is obvious the whole land was in view (36:9–12). In this manner, Ezekiel, employing references and descriptions they understood, assured the people that covenant blessings would continue.

70. Aalders, *Ezechiel,* has correctly pointed out that the land was addressed in which atrocities had been committed by the covenant people themselves as well as by nations on the inhabitants, 2:187.

71. Daniel Berrigan, *Ezekiel: Vision in the Dust* (Maryknoll: Orbis, 1997), a book that features Tom Lewes-Barbely's art, gives a stark picture of dry bones, shining thigh bones of the aged, skulls of women, and slender bones of children. It was a scene of death, 111–19.

72. The Hebrew term that Ezekiel used was not *'ām* covenant people, but *gôy,* which has a much more inclusive reference.

73. See the detailed study of Ezekiel's prophecy concerning David in *MROT,* 773–83.

74. Aalders, *Ezechiel,* wrote that men would be inclined to deny that the term translated "forever" should not be taken in an absolute way, 2:207. Brian Long, after a study of *'ad 'ôlam,* concluded that the term is used to state the certainty and unchangeableness of a state or activity within the period relevant to the context. "Notes on the Biblical Use of *'ad 'ôlām," Westminster Theological Journal* 41, no. 1 (1972): 54–67.

75. Scholars have written about the relationship between the Gog/Magog prophecy and the new temple. J. Ridderbos, in *Van Ezechiel tot Mateleachi,* vol. 4, *Het God's Woord de Propheten* (Kampen: Kok 1956), wrote there is no direct material connection between Gog/Magog and the temple vision, 192–93.

76. C. L. Feinberg, "The Rebuilding of the Temple," in *Prophecy in the Making,* ed. C. F. Henry (Carol Stream: Creation House, 1971), wrote that impeccable scholars are found on both sides of the interpretation of Ezekiel 40–48. The determining question is: "what saith the Scriptures?" 91. He agreed the basic question is hermeneutical-literal or spiritual interpretation, 92. He considers Ezekiel 40–48 to be a continental divide, 94. He wrote "since all of vs 39 is understood literally, then 40–48 must be also."

77. See the discussion concerning the relationship of the new covenant and the covenant of peace in *MROT,* 775–79.

78. See Part I and Part III, section II B, in the preceding discussion.

79. See Part II, C, 2; Part III, section II, c, in the preceding discussion.

80. See Part II, C, 5; Part III, section D, in the preceding discussion.

81. See Part II, A, B, C.

82. The term *gôy* was applied at times specifically to the descendants of Abraham. And under David, the tribes became a *gôy,* in the sense of being an identifiable ethnic political people. *Gôy* however, was used in other specific ways also—e.g., to people, Gentiles,

heathen. Hence, to employ the term *gôy* as an argument for a full restoration of Israel/Judah as a theocratic monarchy is placing too much emphasis and meaning on the term.

83. Cf. Roderick Campbell, *Israel and the New Covenant* (Philadelphia: Presbyterian and Reformed, 1959), 151–56. Campbell also equates the new temple with the New Testament church and kingdom.

84. E. W. Hengstenberg, *The Prophet Ezekiel,* trans. J. G. Murphy (Edinburgh: T & T Clark, 1874), wrote that the visions recorded in chapters 40–48 stand in relation to that of 1:1–3. The first sets forth anger and judgment, the last healing, 355. The scene of a smitten city was to be overcome by the animating image of a restored city, 359.

27

Daniel: Prophet of the Kingdom

I. Introductory Comments

II. The Kingdom

III. The Covenant

IV. The Mediator

27

Daniel: Prophet of the Kingdom

Introductory Comments

Literature on Daniel

In the 1900s, a careful and serious study was made of the book of Daniel. That study concentrated on what Daniel revealed concerning the promised Messiah.[1] During that study much of the literature available on Daniel was consulted. Since then it has become evident that not all literature was seen; and since then, much more literature on Daniel has been produced. Books, essays, and articles continue to be published.[2] Much is quite technical and some apocalyptic characteristics of Daniel's prophecies continue to attract writers seeking to expound on the eschatology that is considered to be a major theme in the book. Details involved in these aspects of the prophecies will not be given much attention in this present study.

Continued Interest

There are four areas of special interest for scholars who address themselves to the study of Daniel. (1) The historical setting and references to various countries are appealing subjects. The historical setting includes the countries of Palestine, Syria, Assyria, Babylon, Media, and Persia. The specific history and study of these countries, their interaction, and their influence, particularly in relation to the Jewish people in exile and the remnant that returned and their historical experiences until the destruction of Jerusalem and the temple and the widespread dispersion of those who lived in Jerusalem and environments provide much material for scholarly endeavor.[3] The discussion of Nebuchadnezzar's dream also includes specific historical references to Media, Greece, and Rome. (2) The literary aspect of Daniel needs attention.[4] The book obviously consists of two definable parts. Chapters 1 through 6 record the historical experiences of Daniel and his friends, while chapters 7 through 12 deal with Daniel's dreams, prophecies, and prayer.[5] The narratives, the dreams, and the prophecies represent distinct genres of literature and should be recognized as such. The structure of the chapters and the borrowing of foreign words included in the text provide interesting topics for study, as does the presence of the Aramaic. The questions concerning the presence of midrash, court tales, legends, and aretology (references to ethical virtues) in the stories and prophecies require careful attention. It cannot be assumed these must be discovered in the book because of the setting, time, and character of the book.[6] Furthermore, one must be careful not to find myriad of references to some natural phenomena as has been done (e.g., finding fire and meteors to refer to a wide-ranging series of events).[7] (3) The eschatological interest in Daniel can be readily understood because of the apocalyptic elements[8] in the prophecies as well as in Nebuchadnezzar's dreams recorded in chapters 2 and 3. Unique and bizarre objects, experiences, and events are recorded. Daniel uses these to refer to God's plan for his time, but especially regarding God's will and plan for future of the covenant people, the Messiah, and the place and role of the larger and dominant nations. Daniel did not receive a specific, detailed time table for major events and the persons involved even though various writers have endeavored to establish a precise calendar for future events. It must be added that Daniel did assure the people of his time, including Nebuchadnezzar (chap. 3) and Belshazzar (chap. 5), that God was in control and would direct the events that were sure to occur.

Another factor in the continuing and developing interest in eschatology are the nineteenth- and twentieth-century events that have drawn the attention of students of prophecy. Devastating events experienced in the past century in the natural world, such as earthquakes, floods, exploding volcanoes, and shifting climatic patterns have been sources of motivation. In addition the rise and fall of powerful nations, the establishment of the Israeli nation in Palestine, and the influence of large or smaller religious bodies and leaders have inspired efforts to apply Daniel's references to these. (4). The biblical-theological study of the book of Daniel by conservative writers, who do not emphasize the application of Daniel's prophecies to specific historical events, past, present, and future, has not received the attention that is warranted. It is the purpose of this book, as a biblical-theological work, to provide such a study.[9]

Daniel: The Man[10]

Daniel was a teenager when he was taken to Babylon in 606 B.C.[11] He was one of the seed of the kingdom, that is, of royal linage. As such, he was undoubtedly well educated in the courts of the kingdom of Judah. He certainly had been educated in the Scriptures and had the necessary requisites for being known as the seed of the kingdom (Dan. 1:8). In the courts of Babylon, he was educated in the language and literature of the Babylonians (1:4). Thus he became qualified as a dedicated and educated young covenant man and an educated Babylonian courtier. Daniel was thus prepared to serve as Yahweh God's agent in the royal courts of Babylon and Persia. He became Yahweh God's agent of revelation as a writer, recording some of the events that transpired during his life as an exile. He did not return to Jerusalem in 536 B.C., when Cyrus gave the decree that Jerusalem, with its temple, be rebuilt. He remained a spokesman for Yahweh God in the royal palaces as Ezekiel was among the exiles living on the banks of the River Kebar.

The New Testament quoted Jesus as referring to the prophet Daniel (Matt. 24:15). Daniel did not function as other prophets had done. He recorded experiences, interpretation of dreams, visions, and an intercessory prayer. He did not include many biographical details but did refer to himself repeatedly with the pronoun "I" (2:23, 30; 5:17; 6:22; 7:2, 4, 6, 7, 8, 9, 11, 13, 15, 19, 20, 21, 28).[12] Daniel received revelation from God so that he could and did interpret dreams (2:30; chaps. 4, 5). Daniel was recognized as having the Spirit (4:8, 9, 18; 5:11, 14).[13] As a Spirit-filled man he joined other Spirit-inspired Old Testament writers in recording the revelation of Yahweh God. Daniel's writings have a very important role in this progressive divine revelation that came in a very distinct historical period of events in the lives of the Old Testament covenant people. His role was to emphasize the sovereignty of Yahweh God as tremendous changes were taking place, including the conquering of Babylon by Persia; the initiation of Persian rule over the conquered Babylonian Empire, which included Palestine with Jerusalem as its chief city;[14] and the return of Jewish exiles to it.

When referring to Daniel as a prophetic writer, two issues should be clearly understood. The first deals with the question, "Is Daniel also among the prophets?" That the book of Daniel was originally included in the prophetic corpus has been maintained by a wide-ranging group of scholars. It is believed that Daniel was transferred to the Writings by rabbis during strenuous times when revolts against Rome were taking place.[15] Recent scholars, however, have given support for the book of Daniel to be included with the Writings because of its "Wisdom characteristics."[16] There is reference to Daniel being in charge of all the wise men of Babylon (2:48). What should not be forgotten is that Daniel was considered wise because of his prophetic gifts, which enabled him to interpret dreams and to foretell future events in the life of King Nebuchadnezzar and in the future course of nations falling and rising.[17] The conclusion to this issue, on the basis of scriptural evidence, is that Daniel was indeed a prophet as Jesus stated (Matt. 24:14), even though Daniel is not referred to as a prophet in the book of Daniel.

The second issue concerns the actual character of Daniel, specifically as a prophet. Should his intercessory prayer on behalf of the covenant people suffering under the curse of the covenant (9:7, 8) and on behalf of the ruined sanctuary in Jerusalem (9:17) indicate that he was priestly as well as of royal linage but a functioning prophet?[18] Was this priestly aspect in some way related to the apocalyptic materials included in the book of Daniel? It seems correct to conclude that, as

Ezekiel,[19] so Daniel also employed apocalyptic material because of the specific historical situations in which he lived and served prophetically. Daniel produced prophecy that served as a context for his apocalyptic materials. Apocalyptics thus arose from within prophecy. It should be added, that in Daniel's time, 606–530 B.C., apocalyptics had not developed to the extent that it was in the second century B.C., especially in the time of Antioches Epiphanes.[20]

Contributions of Daniel

We have concluded that scripturally it is correct to refer to Daniel as a prophet and his book as prophetic. Two questions arise: did Daniel reveal knowledge of, make reference to, and develop some themes the prophets preceding him did? Specifically, did Daniel refer to and develop some themes in Joel's agenda?

A study of the essays gathered in a recent symposium reveals that scholars find Daniel relating to various Old Testament passages written before his time. E. Koch referred to Ezekiel 17:23; 19:11; 31:6; D. Dimant, in a chapter entitled "Seventy Weeks Chronology," referred to Jeremiah 25:11; 29:10; E. Haag referred to Ezekiel 11:15–21; Job 1:6; 2:1; Psalms 34:73; 91:10–13; Isaiah 41:4.[21] There can be no doubt that conservative and liberal/critical writers find Daniel to be an integral part of the biblical corpus. It is somewhat of a surprise that no reference is made at all to Joel's prophecy, which includes a number of suggestive apocalyptic features, such as swarms of locust (1:4), fire-devouring pastures (1:19), and the earth shaking, sky trembling, sun and moon darkened, stars no longer shining (2:10, 31).

The presence of some or all of Joel's themes[22] has been observed in the prophetic messages delivered after Joel's time. Daniel prophesied in a very different *Sitz im Leben* than Joel did. One must conclude, therefore, that Daniel, in a foreign royal situation, had a basically different message.

Daniel did not emphasize local disasters, but he had much to proclaim about momentous national events. He directly and indirectly called for repentance and obedience to Yahweh God's will, that included assurances of Yahweh God's love for his people. The presence and influence of the Spirit was acknowledged even by heathen rulers. Daniel did not stress the return of the covenant people to Judah/Jerusalem, but prophesied concerning Yahweh God's sovereign reign under which nations would rise and fall. Yet his divine rule over and protection of his covenant people would continue and come to expression in varying and fuller ways. Daniel prophesied concerning judgment on nations and peace for his covenant people. The physical city of Jerusalem was not given much attention but what that city represented for the future certainly did; and as Joel had done in his time and circumstances, so Daniel, in his situation, prophesied concerning the great Day of Yahweh,[23] with all that it includes.

When one asks whether Daniel included references to the three strands of the Golden Cable that unites and develops the revelation of Yahweh God throughout the ages, the answer is a resounding "yes." Daniel contributed much to the kingdom strand, and referred to and implied the importance of the covenant, both the creation and redemption/restorative aspects of it. The concept of the Mediator is integral to his entire prophecy.[24]

The Kingdom

Daniel was a kingdom person. He of all the prophets, due to his preparation, characteristics, challenges, and circumstances, was eminently qualified to serve as a prophet of the kingdom. The kingdom of God is a major theme in his book. Writers representing various schools of interpretation agree. Consider statements as follows. The book of Daniel, despite appearances, shows that "the eternal King is in control."[25] The theme, central to Daniel as in no other book in the Old Testament, is "the kingdom of God."[26] "Daniel witnesses to the final act of God when he will bring in his kingdom."[27] The dominion given the Messiah reaches worldwide sway; this kingdom is not millennial but everlasting.[28] The whole book of Daniel is about the "fading glory of the kingdom of this world as contrasted with the abiding glory of the kingdom of God."[29] The message of Daniel "focuses on the sovereignty of the Creator-Redeemer over the kingdoms of this world."[30]

A very helpful study for pastors and Bible teachers is available; it is entitled *The Lord is King.* In the introduction Daniel is discussed within the biblical prophetic, apocalyptic, and Wisdom tradition.[31] The main theme that unites the book of Daniel is the lordship of Jesus Christ, who is the preincarnate King as well as King over all once he ascended to heaven to sit at the Father's right hand.

The book of Daniel has received much attention as the background to the New Testament teaching on the kingdom of God.[32] One writer wrote that the Daniel passages should be seen as the primary background to the New Testament teaching on the kingdom of God, that Daniel is centrally important to Jesus' thinking, and that Paul's statement in 1 Corinthians 6:2 concerning saints to rule (or judge) the world is commonly thought to be based on Daniel (chaps. 2, 7).[33]

Four central subjects require study as Daniel's prophetic writings concerning the kingdom are considered.

Daniel's Royal Experience

Daniel was born and nurtured in a royal family in Jerusalem and matured in the royal court in Babylon.[34] Hence, he knew the royal life by experience, education, and training. As a youth in exile, he and his young royal friends demonstrated strong royal characteristics in their understanding of a healthy cuisine and of speaking to overseers appointed by King Nebuchadnezzar, who wished and planned to have them serve in a broad royal context. Daniel and his friends did not object to being participants in a royal setting, but did wisely and courteously request they be excused from what was considered to be a specific regal advantage—the enjoyment of eating and drinking what the court offered (1:1–16).

Yahweh God employed the royal family of Judah and its court to prepare Daniel and his friends for kingdom service, both in national palaces and within specific areas of the cosmic kingdom. The text is specific: *nātan lākem hā'ĕlōhîm maddā' 'wĕhaśkēl bĕkōl sēper wĕhākĕmâh* (1:17) (literally, he gave to them, God, knowledge and understanding in every book [or all literature] and practical matters).[35] When Daniel and his friends had been brought to the Babylonian palace, they had been selected because of their good looks, general knowledge, and mental alertness (1:4). These personal qualities were developed, expanded, and strengthened by Yahweh God so that they were able and qualified to study, understand, evaluate, and formulate conclusions concerning Babylonian literature and customs. Thus their training in godliness, as received in the Judean palace, had to be expanded, developed, and used as they learned and were trained in Babylonian literature and culture. Indeed, Daniel was prepared to serve in various royal settings within Yahweh God's cosmic kingdom.[36]

Daniel and his friends were prepared for kingdom service in another very important dimension of their personal lives. They had been taught and learned to pray and to intercede for each other and for themselves. When their lives were in danger as members of the "guild of wise men," Daniel called for intercession (2:18). When that prayer was heard and answered, then a song of praise and thanksgiving was uttered (2:19–23). Daniel fearlessly prayed according to his daily custom (which he had learned as a youth) when the king, with urging from his administration, advisers, and satraps, made a decree that all members of his court should pray only to him, the king. Again, Daniel's prayer was answered (6:6–9, 21, 22). Daniel prayed for his people, confessing their sins and pleading that the covenant curse be lifted after the seventy years of exile (9:4–19).

In addition to the preparation for and exercise of prayer, Daniel and his friends had to learn to and actually exercise trust. They did this when, without fear, they requested a healthy diet, trusting Yahweh God would bless them (1:11–16). The three friends demonstrated faith and trust when they refused to bow before Nebuchadnezzar's image of gold. And their faith and trust was the more severely tested when cast into the fiery furnace (chap. 3). Daniel exhibited great trust in Yahweh God when he was called to interpret and apply the king's dreams and to counsel the king (4:27; 5:23). Daniel demonstrated his unshakable faith and trust in his sovereign Lord when cast into the lions' den and knew that his "God had sent an angel" who had kept the lions' mouths shut (6:22).

Daniel demonstrated his abilities to serve in the palaces of the leading kings in his time. He did this by interpreting dreams and giving wise applications. As Joseph in Pharaoh's courts was enabled by Yahweh God to interpret a king's dream (Gen. 41:15, 16, 28), so Daniel did in the palace of Nebuchadnezzar (Dan. 2:27–45) and Belshazzar (5:17–29). In the interpretation of these dreams, enabled by his sovereign God, Daniel, nevertheless, demonstrated his own royal status and abilities. He gave evidence that he understood the personal affairs of royal persons and their political circumstances. He gave wise advice in the political dimensions of life, and he gave sound guidance, enabling kings not to carry out their threats of death for their so-called wise men, magicians, and astrologers. The point to emphasize is that Daniel, having been prepared for cosmic kingdom service, demonstrated his royal character, status, and abilities as Yahweh God's prophetic servant within the palaces of the empires of the world in his time. And no less did Daniel exhibit these when he received dreams and visions and when explained, understood what was revealed concerning international events to come (chaps. 7, 8, 10, 11).[37]

A truly amazing aspect of Daniel's experiences as a prophet was that he was placed in a high position, had many lavish gifts, and was made ruler over the entire province of Babylon. He was given charge of all of Babylon's wise men, hence they were not in position to advise the king on issues that would be detrimental to the exiles from Israel and Judah. He wisely requested that his three friends, Shadrach, Meschach, and Abednego, be appointed to be administrators over the province of Babylon, the central and influential area of the empire.[38] The terms that appear can be interpreted differently but all stress the high positions Daniel and his friends occupied.[39]

In conclusion to the section on "Daniel's Royal Experiences," it must be stressed that while Jeremiah was with the few left in Jerusalem (who later went to Egypt), and while Ezekiel was in the slave camp among the exiles, Daniel and his friends held important positions of influence in the palaces. Their status was royal. Daniel, particularly, having the position and influence of being second to the king, under the providential rule of sovereign Yahweh God, was truly qualified to be the prophetic spokesman of the kingdom of Yahweh God.

The Revelation of the Kingdom to Kings

The initial problem to be addressed is: how many kings did Daniel serve under, what were their names, and when did they reign?

Nebuchadnezzar is repeatedly referred to in the first five chapters in the book of Daniel. He was king in Babylon from 605 to 562 B.C. His Babylonian armies captured Jerusalem in the first year of his reign. Daniel and his three friends were taken into his court. In 586 B.C. he had his armies attack Jerusalem for a third time; the city was captured and all but destroyed. Daniel spent most of his adult life in the Babylonian royal court, first under Nebuchadnezzar, then under his successors, his son, son-in-law, and grandson.[40]

Belshazzar is referred to as king but he was not *the* royal ruler. His father, Nabonidies, was king from 555 B.C. until 539 B.C. Nonbiblical historical records reveal that Nabonidies spent the last ten years of his reign in Arabia and had "entrusted the kingship" to his son Belshazzar,[41] who served as co-regent with his father until the Babylonian Empire was conquered by the Persian king Cyrus.

Cyrus, king of Persia, ruled from 559 to 530 B.C. He became the ruler of a vast empire. He dethroned king Astyages of Media in 550 B.C., and Media became part of the Persian Empire. Eventually this empire included all the former Babylonian,

Assyrian, Hittite, and Egyptian countries and the eastern part of Greece. According to nonbiblical historical records, Cambyses succeeded Cyrus in 530 B.C. and reigned until 522 B.C.

Darius is the name of a king said to be ruler in the Medio-Persian Empire. Difficult problems are involved in precisely identifying Darius the Mede.[42] The biblical text states that Darius the Mede took over "the kingdom" at the age of sixty-two years (5:30). Darius the Mede is again referred to in 11:1. There is also reference to Darius the son of Xerxes (a Mede by descent) (9:1). According to the chart that lists Persian kings, Darius II was the son and successor of Xerxes II. This Darius II reigned from 423 to 404.[43] Commentators assume that another person by the name of Xerxes was the father of Darius I—Hystaspas, who reigned from 522 to 486 B.C. In view of difficulties in precisely sorting out who Darius the Mede was, the conclusion accepted in this study is that Cyrus reigned until 530 B.C. Darius the Mede was a ruler over a province, probably Media, as co-regent with Cyrus. Darius I Hystaspes, succeeding Cambyses, began to reign in 522 B.C. By this time Daniel would have been 100 years old when Darius I had Daniel thrown into and rescued out of the lions' den.

As we proceed in our study of the revelation of the kingdom of God in the book of Daniel, we will see that kings indicated that they had some perception of the kingdom. The basic truth must be clearly and firmly seen and understood, namely, that Yahweh God was present and sovereignly active in the lives of the four exiles in the courts and also in the lives of kings.[44]

When Daniel was in the service of Nebuchadnezzar for a short time (2:1), the king had his dream concerning the great image and the rock that crushed it. Daniel interpreted the dream when the king's magicians, enchanters, sorcerers, and astrologers were not able to tell what the dream was nor its meaning. The Babylonian gods and their agents proved their uselessness. This gave Daniel the opportunity to represent Yahweh God, who had absolute control over the royal court. Daniel prayed and Yahweh revealed the dream and its interpretation. The courtiers were spared death; Nebuchadnezzar was given the divine plan for four empires.[45] His role was secure and his kingdom was honored to be represented by the pure golden head.[46]

In the interpretation of the dream as he related it to Nebuchadnezzar, Daniel unhesitatingly informed the king that the revealer of dreams and mysteries is in heaven and he is the King. His kingdom is the eternal one; it will never be destroyed (2:44). This kingdom of God will crush all other kingdoms.

The response of Nebuchadnezzar was an acknowledgment of Yahweh God as the supreme Lord of kings. Daniel was rewarded by being placed in a high position and given lavish gifts (2:48). It would seem that the king's honoring of Daniel was indirectly an honoring of the God whom Daniel represented and served.[47]

Nebuchadnezzar received a second revelation of Yahweh God's kingship (3:1–30). Daniel was not involved in this event, his three friends were. They refused to bow down to the large golden image the king had made and erected.

Their confession was brief and clear: "the God we serve is able to save us from the blazing furnace and from your hand." Their declaration of knowledge of and trust in God involved the following truths: (1) our God is greater than you, Nebuchadnezzar, even if you and your kingdom are represented by gold; (2) our God is Lord in and over his cosmic kingdom, which includes a fiery blazing furnace; (3) our God can save us, if that is his will and purpose; (4) we trust him with our lives even though we are at your mercy. These words of faith and trust were followed by Yahweh God's demonstration of ruling within a blazing furnace. Under Yahweh God's control, the ropes that were used to tie the three friends were consumed, but their clothes were not singed[48] or made to smell of smoke.

The question to be answered if possible is: who was the fourth man the king's advisers saw walking in the furnace with the three friends of Daniel? He was described by the Babylonians as one who "looks like a son of the gods" (3:25). What the Babylonians did not know, much less understand, was that here before them was a divine epiphany—an appearance of the divine one.[49] This divine one had appeared in the burning bush to Moses (Exod. 3:4). Thus Yahweh God kept his covenant promise, "I will be with you,"[50] in Babylon as he had done in Egypt.

The entire event impressed Nebuchadnezzar to such an extent that he exclaimed, *bĕrîk 'ĕlōhăhôn* (pass. ptc. of *bŭrak*, bless [Aramaic]), "blessed be the God"[51] of the three friends. It should be noted that this was an objective exclamation. "Those three have a god that blesses them." He did not acknowledge that Yahweh God was such for him personally even though Yahweh God's kingship affected him and his kingdom in a most dramatic manner.

The book of Daniel records a third revelation of Yahweh God's kingship and of his rule over the cosmic kingdom (chap. 4). There are four parts to this account: (1) Nebuchadnezzar's dream (4:4–18); (2) the interpretation of the dream by Daniel (4:19–27); (3) the fulfillment of the dream (4:28–33); (4) Nebuchadnezzar's response (1:1–3; 4:34–36).

In the dream, or with images and visions passing through his mind (4:5), Nebuchadnezzar saw an enormous tree (4:10), which was a source of beauty, fruit, and shelter for every creature (4:12). A holy messenger from heaven commanded that the tree be cut down, with only its stump and its roots left to be exposed to the weather (4:13–15). The stump took on the person of a man (4:16), whose mind was to become that of an animal. In this dream he saw three other factors: (1) the wise men failed him in interpreting (4:6, 7); (2) Daniel, given a new name in honor of the Babylonian god, appeared and was asked to interpret the dream; (3) Daniel was said to have the spirit of the gods (4:8).[52] Up to this point the king did not acknowledge the God of Daniel but did acknowledge that a Most High Ruler over the kingdom of men is the dispenser of whatever he wishes. In these words Nebuchadnezzar did acknowledge that "there is a God who reigns over all," but he indicated that this God was not his.

Daniel interpreted the dream (4:19–27). Daniel, in spite of a sense of terror, with urging from the king, informed Nebuchadnezzar that he was that tree (4:22). The

Most High (Yahweh God), who rules over all aspects of his cosmic kingdom, which included all the kingdoms on the earth, was to demonstrate that Nebuchadnezzar was under his control. The king was to become mad, to be driven away from people to live with wild animals and eat grass like cattle.

The dream was fulfilled. A year after he had had the dream, he was glorying in his achievements. A voice from heaven informed him that the Most High Ruler had to be acknowledged. Until he, the king did that, he would be driven mad and made to live with the animals in the field (4:31, 32). His authority was to be taken away. This happened (4:33). Nebuchadnezzar himself acknowledged it.[53]

After seven years the king's sanity was restored (4:34, 36). He had looked up to the heavens; he then praised, honored, and glorified the Most High. Now the king made a personal statement. He realized Yahweh God has an eternal dominion, or kingdom, in which all peoples are included (4:34, 35). He was restored to his throne; he acknowledged that the proud one is humbled (4:37), because this King of heaven does what is right (in keeping with God's will) and just (carries out what is right) (4:36, 37). The sincerity[54] of Nebuchadnezzar was demonstrated when he made a kingdomwide proclamation that the Most High God performs wonders and miracles; this God has an eternal kingdom; his rule is from generation to generation. The terms that Nebuchadnezzar used definitely refer to the cosmic kingdom. Daniel and his three friends gave no evidence that they disagreed with the Babylonian's understanding of Yahweh God's kingship and his actual rule over a kingdom that endures from generation to generation.

The revelation of Yahweh God's kingdom to Belshazzar, who reigned as co-regent with Nabonidies, was given at his last great banquet.[55] During the feasting, the king ordered that the golden goblets from the temple in Jerusalem be used for drinking wine. As the drinking went on and praise was rendered to the Babylonian idols of "bronze, iron, wood, and stone" (5:3, 4), Yahweh God revealed his just judgment on Belshazzar and his court by the handwriting on the wall (5:5). The Babylonian wise men were unable to interpret the writing, but the queen reminded her husband of Daniel's abilities because the spirit of the holy gods was in him (5:10–12). Daniel testified concerning the "Most High God" who had been acknowledged by Nebuchadnezzar (5:18–21). Daniel accused Belshazzar of opposing this Lord of heaven and defiling and dishonoring him by the way he used the temple treasures (5:22, 23). Belshazzar heard that God had numbered the days of his reign and his kingdom would cease. The response did not acknowledge the revelation concerning Yahweh God as king over all, but Daniel was promoted to become the third highest ruler in the kingdom (5:29). But the kingdom of Belshazzar became part of Cyrus's empire. It is not recorded if Daniel held that position.

Cyrus is referred to three times in the book of Daniel, and each time it is in reference to Daniel (1:21; 6:28, 10:1). Daniel is recorded as prospering during the reign of Cyrus; this implies that Daniel, as the prophetic servant of Yahweh God, was free to serve and worship his Lord, the King of the cosmic domain. Daniel is recorded as having received a vision during Cyrus's third year as king of the entire

Persian Empire. This revelation to Daniel was not reported to Cyrus and there is no evidence that it had any influence on him. But, it must not be forgotten that Cyrus was referred to as an appointed shepherd and as Yahweh God's *mešîah* (anointed) (Isa. 44:28, 45:1). It was Cyrus's divinely appointed task and privilege to decree that Israel's/Judah's exiles could return to Jerusalem. As he made the decree public, he made it known *mamlĕkût hā'āre`s nātan lî Yĕhwâ'ĕlōkê haššāmayîm* (the kingdoms of the earth given to me "by" Yahweh God of the heavens) (Ezra 1:2). Cyrus made known he was fully aware of who the covenant Lord of Israel/Judah was, that covenant people lived by the covenant promise of Yahweh, "I am your God, I will be with you" (1:3). Cyrus thus gave a definite expression of his knowledge of Yahweh God's lordship over the cosmic kingdom, and his decree indicated that Cyrus knew he had no alternative but to serve Yahweh God. Cyrus, however, never expressed a living covenantal relationship with Yahweh God. Cyrus was content to recognize who his benefactor was. He, however, gave no evidence of worshiping the Most High One, the Lord of heaven and earth.

King Darius, who had Daniel thrown into the lions' den, knew that Daniel was a servant of "the living God" (6:20), and harbored the hope that this living God exercised his lordship over the lions. And when he learned from Daniel that Yahweh God *šelah malăkêh* (sent an angel) to shut the lions' mouth (6:2 [MT 6:23]); he was overjoyed. He then published a decree for all the nations in his kingdom, irrespective of what language they spoke, that all had to fear and reverence (i.e., worship) the God of Daniel, the living God whose kingdom cannot be destroyed and whose reign (dominion) will never end (6:25–27).

The conclusion that one must unavoidably make after consulting the text is that Daniel was a pivotal means in Yahweh God's revelation of himself as the Most High One, who reigned and controlled kings, nations, administrations, lions, and the historic events that occurred in the prophet's lifetime.

The Sovereignty of Yahweh God

The terms *sovereign/sovereignty* appear seven times in the NIV but do not appear in the KJV, AV, RSV. The term used in these is *Most High* or *Highest. Sovereignty* appears once in the NASB (5:18), where it is ascribed to Nebuchadnezzar along with the terms *greatness, glory,* and *splendor.* The term used in the Hebrew Bible is the Aramaic adjective *'elây,* in text *'illây'â* (a plural of intensity), translated "Most High." The idea is that as Nebuchadnezzar was above all the "kings" and "rulers" of the countries he had conquered, so Yahweh God was above and Lord over all gods and kingdoms. Daniel used this term undoubtedly because the pagans he addressed understood this term.

It is not incorrect to translate the Aramaic term as Most High as it appears in Daniel 4:24; 5:18, 21; 7:25. It can be used to express the two concepts that should be understood to have a close affinity but are nevertheless distinct. The term *Most High* can be understood to refer to the deity that has all authority; he has the authority over all "gods," or all kingdoms and cosmic affairs. The "Most High has the right" to exercise this authority. The term *Most High* can be understood to refer to the actual exercise of authority, that is, the actual reign over all kingdoms, and indeed, over the entire cosmos. The term *sovereign* specifically refers to this divine reign over all creation, the cosmic kingdom, which includes all that is involved on earth and in the heavens. It means that Yahweh God is all-powerful,[56] he is able to do what he has the right (authority) to do.

Yahweh God's sovereignty was dramatically revealed in the lives of Daniel and his friends. Yahweh God reigned supremely in their lives when they were prepared for royal service in Nebuchadnezzar's palace and kingdom. In matters such as diet, general physical appearance, gaining knowledge and understanding of literature, visions, dreams, Yahweh God overruled the pagan court even as he used aspects of it (Dan. 1).

Yahweh God proved his supreme reign over the fire, clothes, and lives of the three friends who refused to worship Nebuchadnezzar's image and were cast into a blazing furnace (Dan. 3). Likewise Yahweh God's sovereignty over lions was demonstrated when the aged Daniel was cast into their den (Dan. 6).

These experiences of the young men demonstrated that the sovereignty of Yahweh God was magnificently and powerfully exercised. Yahweh God could and did undo and even reverse the intentions, abilities, and activities of powerful men and forces in nature.[57] The deities worshiped in the Babylonian and the Persian Median empires were powerless in the presence of Yahweh God and his sovereign reign over all aspects of the cosmic kingdom. The book of Daniel beautifully and powerfully declares that Yahweh God reigns. Daniel may not have employed the phrase as Isaiah did, "Your God reigns" (Isa. 52:7), but he proclaimed it as he recorded events that transpired in the course of the exile, and particularly in the royal courts of rulers over great and powerful empires.

Yahweh God revealed his sovereign rule over earthly kingdoms and their kings in Daniel's dreams and visions as he had also done through the king's dreams and the interpretation of these by Daniel (Dan. 2, 4). The second part of the book of Daniel, chapters 7 through 12, begin recording *dānàyi'l ḥēlem hăzâh weḥezĕwēy rē'šēh* (Daniel [had] a dream and saw visions [in his] head) (7:1). Three comments should be made. (1) The means of revelation were by dreams and visions to Daniel. The term *vision* was employed more than *dream* (7:1, 15; 8:1; 10:1); *mār'eh,* also a term for vision emphasizing the seeing from *rā'âh* [to see]). The dream usually referred to a recipient's complete physical inactive role while the recipient of a vision was active in thought and often with speech. Daniel records that what he dreamed gave him visions in his head. (2) The time that Daniel received the revelation was after he had interpreted Nebuchadnezzar's dreams (chaps. 2, 4). It was when Belshazzar had begun to reign thirteen years after Nebuchadnezzar's death. The Babylonian empire's "glory and might had begun to wane."[58] (3) The dreams and visions of Daniel and the interpretations of these recorded in chapter 7 through 12 are not to be understood as new revelation, but they are added as fuller explanations of what had been revealed to Nebuchadnezzar by dreams.[59] And the historical events recorded in chapters 3, 5, and 6 should continue to be considered as presentations of what was occurring in the Babylonian and Persian empires. The religious, social, and political environment continued to be hostile, at least to quite a degree, for those among the covenant people who continued to strive to be faithful to their covenant Lord and their covenant heritage.

As this biblical-theological study of Daniel proceeds, emphasizing the unifying roles of the kingdom, covenant, and mediator in the book, no specific and detailed effort will be made to find and posit detailed references to nations and events. The semiapocalyptic character of chapters 7 through 12 should caution any interpreter not to press for details.

There are two specific parts in chapter 7 that record Daniel's dream/visions in his head during Belshazzar's first year of reigning as a vice regent. In the first part Daniel records what he actually saw. Four great beasts, one like a lion, one like a bear, one like a leopard, and a terrible appearing one with large iron teeth, ten horns, and a small horn, arose from a sea churned up by a great wind (7:2–8).[60] The little horn looked like a man and spoke boastfully. Daniel saw more. The Ancient of Days took his throne, which was a flaming fire with a river of fire flowing from it. Thousands attended him as the books were opened (7:9, 10). Daniel heard the boastful words of the horn and saw that the beast was slain while the other beasts were stripped of authority for a while (7:11, 12). The one who received authority, glory, and sovereign power from the Ancient of Days was worshiped. He had the everlasting kingdom that will not end (7:13, 14).

The interpretation that Daniel received was similar to what he had told Nebuchadnezzar when interpreting his dream. There are four beasts representing four kingdoms; the fourth would be more warlike, vicious, and destructive than the other three. The saints will suffer under the ruler of this kingdom (7:24, 25). The great comforting message was that these kingdoms would not endure; their sovereignty, power, and greatness would be given to the saints, the members of the ever-enduring kingdom of the Son of Man given him by the Ancient of Days. These saints will obey and worship their everlasting king.

The message of the vision Daniel received was that Yahweh God, the Most High, reigns sovereignly as king over heaven and earth, namely, the cosmic kingdom. Opposition will be present in various forms and to various degrees. Yahweh God and the Son of Man, however, reign supremely and sovereignly; the powerful nations are part of his cosmic kingdom. These nations rise and fall; the kingdom of the Ancient of Days and Son of Man is present and always will endure. The sovereignty, glory, and power of the king of the cosmic kingdom were, are, and will always be everlasting.[61]

Two years later *ḥāzôn nirâh* (a vision was seen; *nirâh* is imph. pf. of *rā'âh,* to see). Daniel had a "follow-up vision" (8:1). In this vision he saw himself in a royal setting, which was a fortified city.[62] The reference to his historical environment is of interest particularly in view of what he sees and understands as the vision is revealed to him. The main theme has a strong political message; namely, what about nations that will arise and exert political and military power? Daniel, informed and inspired by divine revelation, expressed views concerning Yahweh God's sovereign controlling reign in, during, and over the international historical scene. In this historical context, this second vision must be understood.

The scene that appeared by vision to Daniel had a ram with two horns that charged with power in various directions (8:3, 4). Daniel is told that the ram represents Media and Persia (8:20). He also saw a shaggy goat with a one horn arise from the west; with a violent destructive rage the goat attacked the ram, shattered his two horns, and trampled him in invincible power. Its one horn was broken and four horns grew in its place (8:5–8). Daniel was informed that this shaggy goat represented Greece (8:21). One of the four horns set itself up as the great Prince and caused havoc with sacrificial practices and the sanctuary (8:9–14).[63] This Grecian war lord who defeated the hosts of heaven (thought to refer to believers) set himself up as the "Prince of the Host" (8:11), in place of Yahweh God of host. He took a stand against the Prince of princes but would eventually be destroyed by a nonhuman power (8:23–25).

Daniel was deeply troubled by what was revealed to him in the two visions (7:28; 8:27). He was in a unique and what could be considered a precarious position. He was a prophet, a spokesman and mediating agent representing Yahweh God. He was also a high-ranking, influential statesman living and working in the very heart of a powerful nation that would eventually be destroyed. But he was not to make the messages known.

In this second vision there is no repetition of how Yahweh God, the Ancient of Days, and the One like the Son of Man were sovereignly ruling and controlling all the national and international events. It is stated, however, that a voice commanded Gabriel the great messenger angel to explain to Daniel what the vision meant and that it certainly would be fulfilled in the future. Yahweh God was and would be in complete control and demonstrate his sovereignty in the rise and fall of powerful, ruthless, and seeming invincible kings on earth.

After receiving his two visions, Daniel, troubled, prayed and fasted in sackcloth and ashes. This time of prayer came within a year after he had the vision in which the goat with two horns arose. He was told it represented the nation of Media and Persia. It was the first year of Darius, who was made ruler over Babylon; he was the Median king whose reign coincided with the reign of Cyrus, who had become the supreme king over the entire empire that then had been formed, including the Egyptian, Assyrian, Babylonian, Median, and Persian empires. Darius, according to the biblical text, became king over the Babylonian part of the Persian Empire. Some commentators wrote that he began this reign in 539 B.C.[64]

Daniel had witnessed the fall of the Babylonian Empire and the rise of the Median-Persian power and rule. It had been revealed to him that this rule would continue for a long time. What was to be the experience of the covenant people? He referred to Jeremiah (25:11, 12), who had prophesied that the covenant people would be in exile for a period of seventy years. The seventy years would be completed soon. He and others had been exiled in 606 B.C. In two or three years' time the seventy-year period would be fulfilled.

This became a matter of prayer. He called upon *yĕhwâ 'ĕlōhî* (Yahweh my God),[65] whom he addressed praying, *'ânnâ'* (I beseech) *'adōnâi hā'ēl haggadôl* (Sovereign One, the Great God) (Dan. 9:4) and *wĕhannôrâ'* (niph. ptc. of *yārê'*, to fear, the one to be feared). Some translators prefer to refer to Yahweh God in this context as the "awesome One."[66] Daniel, in prayer, as in his dreams/visions and prophecies understood and confessed that Yahweh God was sovereign. He was a covenant-keeping God.[67] He is righteous (9:7); merciful and forgiving (9:9); wrathful and angry (9:16).

Daniel received an immediate reply to his covenantal prayer through the great archangel, the messenger Gabriel. He was assured that a decree would come to restore and rebuild Jerusalem (9:25). Gabriel did not specify when but it is known that Cyrus did give the decree seventy years after the exile began.[68] What Gabriel did speak about was the coming of the Messiah, his death, and the eventual destruction of Jerusalem and the temple within it. The heart, the central reality, of the covenant was not the restoration of Jerusalem and the temple. These symbolic features, city and temple, would eventually disappear when the Messiah would come. It is difficult to decipher precisely when the living temple, the Messiah would come.[69]

The visions that Daniel received according to chapters 7 and 8 had a prophetic aspect. Daniel was given revelation concerning the large nations of Babylon, Media-Persia, and Greece. Then, after his covenantal prayer, he was given the prophetic message concerning the Messiah, his time of appearing, his death, and the end of the temple era. Daniel had a message for his people and all subsequent hearers (and readers). Even though nations rise and fall, Yahweh God's kingdom does not even totter. He sovereignly rules as he guides national and international events and does so that in the appointed time, the Messiah comes and ministers according to his divine promises and plan.

The emphasis changes in chapters 10 through 12 from that of chapters 7 through 9. Commentators disagree whether these chapters record actual historical events. Some of what is written seems so real regarding what actually transpired 350 years later that they insist the material was written when or shortly after the events referred to happened, in 173–165 B.C. For those scholars history did not become prophecy even though the literary form employed would so suggest. The biblical text, however, demands that chapters 10 through 12 be considered prophecy.[70] These prophecies were given at a crucial time in the history of the covenant people. They were given to comfort the covenant people and to assure them Yahweh God was sovereignly carrying out his determined purpose.[71]

Daniel recorded that the prophetic message he received was in the third year of Cyrus's reign, 535 B.C. Exiles had begun to return to Jerusalem according to the decree that Cyrus had issued, permitting Jewish exiles to return to Jerusalem to rebuild their temple (10:1; Ezra 1:2–11). Daniel received revelation concerning a conflict that was waged in the spiritual realm that had direct implications for the national scene. The ancient antithesis established when Adam and Eve were tempted by Satan in Paradise came to the foreground in a strong way. Daniel was made aware of this.[72] Critical thinkers and scholars relegate Daniel's experiences to the realm of mythology. It must be stressed, however, that a conflict was waged in the spiritual realm at this important juncture in history. The exiles were returning to Jerusalem so that in time the promised Son of the woman would come forth through the restored community of the seed of Abraham and David.

When Daniel was outside the city of Susa, standing on the banks of the Tigris River, he was confronted by a humanlike heavenly person.[73] Daniel's companions were overwhelmed by terror, even though they did not see the vision because of their nearness to a heavenly being.[74] Daniel was also overcome; he "had no strength left" (10:8). Was Daniel confronted by a theophany? The text speaks of a man (10:4), who did not have divine power to prevent his being detained (10:13). But Daniel had his mouth opened, enabling him to speak (10:16), and was given strength (10:18, 19). Could an angel do this for Daniel? Daniel's account is not specific regarding the presence of two figures: an angel in the form of a man and the Lord.[75]

The message Daniel was given had the following main points: (1) Daniel was assured that he was highly esteemed (10:19) and that his prayers were heard. In response to these, the heavenly messenger came. (2) The messenger was opposed and detained (could God be detained?). He had been confronted and resisted by the prince of the king of Persia. Undoubtedly, the reference is to an evil spirit representing that king (10:13a). Michael, the warrior archangel, came to help the messenger. It really seems correct to believe that the two archangels, Gabriel and Michael, were resisted by a satanic power. There had been a spiritual conflict fought in which Yahweh God's angelic servants overcame the satanic efforts. Here one is reminded of the antithesis that is ever present between Yahweh God and the Son on the one side and satanic powers on the other.(3) The Persian representative will not continue to exert power and have control over the destinies of the covenant people. Another country's princely (satanic?) power will rise and rule. Hence there will be in addition to the spiritual antithesis a conflict in the world of the evil representatives of two national powers, Persia and Greece. This was a prophetic message that referred to great changes in the international context. (4) Yahweh God has his plan; it is written in the Book of Truth (10:21). His plan will be carried out. He is the only Sovereign One. (5) Daniel is informed that the overthrow of Babylon was accomplished by Yahweh God working through his archangel, Michael (11:1). (6) Implied in 10:1–11:1 is that the evil prince representing the Persian king sought to thwart the return of the covenant people to Jerusalem. Implied is that Cyrus had opposition to his issuing the decree for the return to Jerusalem and the rebuilding of the temple. It certainly is correct to say that Satan did his utmost to prevent a community returning to and living in Jerusalem, through which the seed of the woman, the descendant of David, the Branch, would come, according to

Yahweh God's plan. The antithesis was as sharply defined as ever. The outcome was definite: Yahweh God, demonstrating his sovereign power, authority, and rule, would so direct the fortunes of powerful nations that his plan for the redemption of his people, through the seed of the woman, would surely become a reality.

Daniel received additional prophetic information (11:2–12:4). This prophetic message was not to be publicized but sealed up in writing (12:4). It concerned what the covenant people would experience wherever they were in the Persian Empire. After a series of kings in Persia had reigned the empire would be broken and political power will be transferred. This was fulfilled when Greece conquered Persia (11:2–4). Transition is made in the prophecy from a united Greece to a divided nation. Two of the four Grecian empires would become dominant; the king in the south refers to the Ptolemaic regime and the one in the north to the Seleucid regime.[76]

The prophecy recorded in Daniel 11:2–12:4 presents a number of salient points: (1) The historical context in which the covenant people will live is described in some detail. Life will be tumultuous for them. (2) National and international circumstances happen not by chance; there is a concentrated effort, in the spiritual as well as the earthly spheres, to bring stress and if possible destruction to the covenant community. (3) Not only will there be much warfare, there will be powers who seek to enthrone themselves and exercise worldwide reign under which the worship of and service for Yahweh God are made extremely difficult. (4) The salvation of Yahweh God's people is never to be in doubt.[77] (5) Yahweh God will triumph because he is the sovereign King and Ruler of the cosmos. All nations are under his rule; none of that can or will thwart him (12:1–4).[78]

At the conclusion of our study of the sovereignty of Yahweh God, it should be clearly stated again that divine sovereignty is the overall theme of the book of Daniel.[79] Yahweh God's sovereignty was revealed in unique names—The Highest, The Most High. It was exercised in the lives of Daniel's three friends and spectacularly so in the life, abilities to interpret dreams, the reception of prophecies via dreams and visions, and the prayerful life of Daniel. Divine sovereignty was exercised when Nebuchadnezzar dreamed and his dream (chap. 4) was fulfilled. Likewise, Yahweh God's sovereignty as the only Lord and King in heaven and earth was revealed and exercised when Daniel received prophetic revelation, in dreams and visions, concerning the rise and fall of nations and their role in the lives of the covenant people. This sovereignty comes to even clearer expression as the eschatological issues of Yahweh God's cosmic kingdom are studied.

Eschatological Kingdom Issues

The literary means to present and convey the kingdom realities Yahweh God had in his plan for his covenant people calls for careful examination. Daniel did not speak forthrightly and write in careful, detailed exposition. The times and circumstances in which he lived and worked were such that he had to be discreet in his explanation of his visions and in the proclamation of the prophetic messages he received from Yahweh God.

A listing of Daniel's unique terms, symbols, metaphors, and time references include beasts, horns, blazing fire, river of fire, the Ancient of Days, the Son of Man, court, books, set times, beautiful land, starry hosts, 2,003 evenings and mornings, time of wrath, master of intrigue, time of the end, appointed time, seventy sevens, sixty-two sevens, one seven, a man with eyes like flaming torches, Michael, four winds of heaven, royal escort, metal images, tax collector, contemptible person, heart bent on evil, holy covenant, abomination that causes desolation, temple fortress, multitudes who sleep in the dust, for a time, times, and half a time—all these things will be completed, and the end of the 1,035 days.

These and other references to appearances of unusual persons/angels, as well as descriptions of these and of events to come certainly give reason to think of apocalypticism. There should be no doubt that Daniel resorted to apocalyptic terms and phrases. Daniel's literary presentation of the messages he was to proclaim calls for discretion in one's effort to interpret and understand them.

A legitimate twofold question arises. The first question concerns why apocalyptic elements are used. Times and circumstances called for an unusual manner of presentation. Daniel employed these elements because he had to present messages from Yahweh God to the covenant communities, those in exile, and those who would, and had, returned to Jerusalem; that would not be readily understood by the Babylonians, Medians, and Persians. He had to be careful, as Ezekiel had been (Ezek. 38, 39), not to irritate or inflame their captors and rulers. Daniel did not want to arouse hostility and conflict.

The second question pertains to the needs of the covenant people in exile and those who may have been struggling in Jerusalem, having returned there and now experiencing opposition. These people needed encouragement, hope, and motivation to continue to be patient and be assured that Yahweh their God had not forgotten them. In spite of contemporary situations, there was a sovereignly ordained future. Yahweh God would carry out his plan. This would be done in unusual ways at times; unexpected help would come forth. The apocalyptic elements were really not new for those who knew and understood what former prophets had proclaimed. These had shown they had knowledge of Moses and his instructions and of David's kingdom and dynasty. With unique terms and phrases these were brought to the attention of Daniel and his audiences (when he was permitted to publicize them). Thus the people were given assurance and hope within their own unique circumstances.

There have been many attempts made to identify which eschatological events are referred to by Daniel. Recall that eschatological, as a term, means "word about the end." Daniel referred to the *kālâ* (the end, a completion) (9:27).[80] Consummation is a term that implies a process that began at creation and is completed at a specific time; when the process is completed, that which came forth from the process remains. The process had and continues to have progressive stages. Certain specific events signal the arrival of each stage in the process.

In our study of the prophecies of Micah, specific attention was given to the stages in the "Eschatological Progression."[81] The book of Daniel, in various ways, refers to the great initiation of the process by speaking of the eternal dominion that endures from generation to generation in which Yahweh God demonstrates his power.[82] Daniel made reference to Moses, who was so integrally involved in an important stage (Israel's exodus from Egypt and the confirming of the covenant with Israel as a theocracy [9:11, 13]). Daniel made no reference to the promise to Israel regarding the land nor to David's reign and that of his dynasty. The eschatological stages in the process referred to above set the stage for what Daniel did concentrate on. As he did this, he was careful not to present an established time table, a specific schedule of when various stages in the process would take place. He referred to periods of time, but did not specify precisely when each time period would arrive.

It was during the period of the exile and the first years of the return from exile that Daniel spoke and wrote concerning future events. Daniel acknowledged that the covenant people had been exiled because of their rebellion, refusal to listen, and wickedness (9:5, 6). He also recorded that when he had concluded his prayer of confession and submission he was given a message concerning the future of the covenant people, Jerusalem, and the Messiah (9:25).

In revelations previous to when he prayed, especially in the contexts of dreams recorded in chapters 2 and 4, he had been told about the future of the various large empires, the Babylonian, Medio-Persian, Greek, and Roman. The rise and fall of these nations provided the international environment and context for the more specific future events regarding the covenant people and the Messiah. No dates or time periods were recorded for the rise, duration, or fall of these nations. What is recorded, as will be studied under another heading, was the sovereign lordship of Yahweh God and the Messiah over the nations. This was intimated already in the dream Daniel interpreted for Nebuchadnezzar; in this dream a rock had crushed the great image which represented the four nations (2:34, 35, 44, 45).

Daniel's prophecies concentrated to quite an extent on what Yahweh God's plan was for the last part of the exilic period and the continued dispersion of many of the covenant people. Daniel prophesied about the events to take place in the 500 years to come, the period plus-minus 535–500 B.C. It was to be a time of political upheavals. The covenant people were to be caught up in these. These events were presented in Daniel's vision of the four beasts (7:1–27), in the vision of the two beasts (8:1–26), and in the vision of the kings of the south and the north (11:2–45).[83] These visions also included some features of events to take place in the future beyond the 500-year period before the Messiah was to appear. It must be stressed that Daniel did not provide information by which specific time tables or schedules could be determined.

Daniel prophesied concerning the coming of the Messiah, his ministry, death, resurrection, and ascension. Again, no specific time table was presented. The great opponent, who was recorded as oppressing the saints (7:25), would have power for an indefinite period, referred to as "a time, times and half a time." When this period of quite some length (as it seems to be described) was to begin and end was not revealed.

Daniel did not prophesy directly or explicitly concerning the pouring out of the Holy Spirit and the gathering of people from all nations to form the New Testament body of Christ, the church. He did record that the time would come when neither the temple nor the sacrificial system would continue. He referred to a number of days (12:11, 12), but there is no indication of when these days would begin or end. From historical accounts one can learn when these events occurred: it was when the Romans destroyed the temple and caused a widespread dispersion of the Jewish people.

Daniel made one more reference, in a general way, to a time period. He prophesied concerning the end of time on earth when the resurrection will occur and the final judgment will take place. But again, Daniel did not give any information as to when these final events were to take place.

Concluding this review of what was prophesied concerning the exile, the end of the exile for some, the continued dispersion of many people, the rise and fall of great nations, the opposition to and oppression of people of faith, the coming of the Messiah and his death, the ascension, and the destruction of the temple when sacrifices were discontinued, it must be affirmed: Daniel did not provide information that could be used to establish a specific schedule of events, or a time table for these.

It must be emphasized that Daniel did prophesy concerning the kingdom of God. The term *kingdom* appears thirty-five times in the NIV translation of Daniel; *dominion* five times; and *realm* once. In almost all instances the terms refer to the combination of king, throne, reign, domain, the basic aspects of what is included in the concept of "kingdom."

Daniel, however, must not be understood to speak and write of one specific entity when employing the term *kingdom*. There are three specific referents; these three are also in some contexts included together as one kingdom. (1) Daniel referred to earthly, human, secular kingdoms, represented by gold, silver, bronze, and iron (2:31–43), or by goat and ram (8:19–21), or by a tree (both Nebuchadnezzar as king and his kingdom) (4:19–22). (2) The kingdom is that of the Lord Jesus Christ. When he would ascend and sit at the Father's right hand, he would be given the kingdom, to reign over it and to bring his own into it (7:14–27).[84] (3) The cosmic kingdom, established at the time of creation, is eternal, ever-enduring, never-ending kingdom spoken of and written by Daniel. The cosmic kingdom includes all of creation, all nations, all peoples, and certainly all covenant people who know, love, worship, obey, and serve their triune God. Daniel has this all-inclusive cosmic kingdom as the context for his messages. And it was from the mouths of pagan kings that recognition was given of this ever-enduring kingdom. It must be clearly understood that as all secular kingdoms were included in the cosmic kingdom, so also the kingdom that is referred to as the messianic kingdom was included. But this kingdom has a specific and unique place and role in the cosmic kingdom. It represents it and is the dominant ruling, controlling force in the cosmic kingdom.

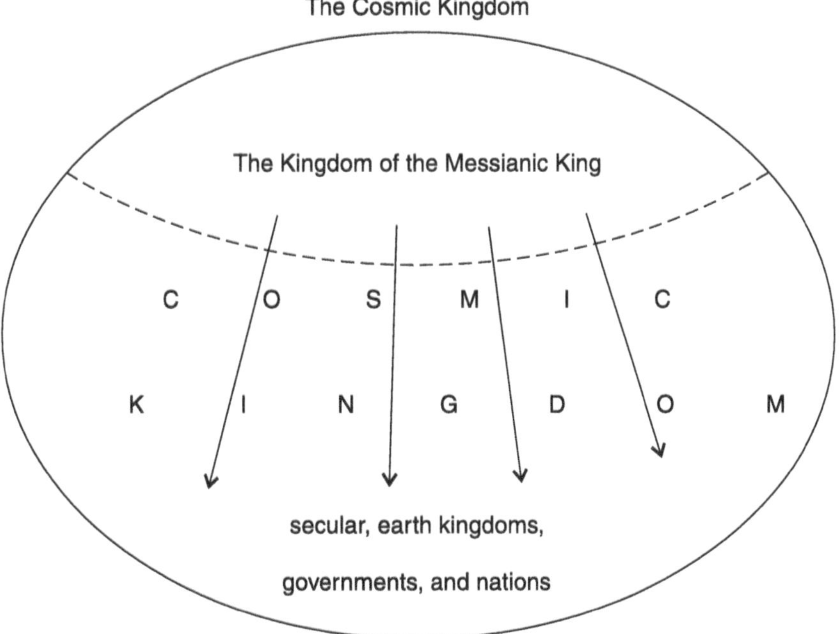

The following diagram could assist the reader to grasp and understand that there is one enduring cosmic kingdom which is inclusive of all kingdoms.

In summing up, the following should be kept in mind. The cosmic kingdom includes all that is present in space. The heavens are part of it as they declare the glory of God. The geographic areas of all nations, past, present, and future combined, occupy the earthly part of the cosmic kingdom. The areas covered by oceans, seas, and other bodies of water are included. The space taken up by stars and planets, and the space between these, also must be considered as the space of the cosmic kingdom. There is no area in Yahweh God's created cosmos that is outside the limits of Yahweh God's kingdom.

As the cosmic kingdom includes all space, so also it is ever-enduring. It was begun when Yahweh God created. The secular kingdoms of which Daniel prophesied were present for a comparatively short period of time. This is also to be said of any nation, whatever type of government it may have. This ever-enduring kingdom is under the reign of the Messiah from the time of his ascension and will be until the very end of the present age.

One more glorious truth must be stated. Those whom the Messiah claims as his redeemed, restored people will be the very heart and core of the enduring cosmic kingdom.

The Covenant

The Covenant Upheld

Daniel used the term *bĕrît* six times and, as will become evident, he may have had more than one referent (9:4, 27; 11:22, 28, 30, 32). That the covenant had an important role in Daniel's life and service should not be doubted. Theologically considered, since Daniel emphasized the kingdom, he consistently implied the presence and role of the covenant.

Israel, as a theocratic monarchy/kingdom, had the covenant confirmed to them (Exod. 19–24). Yahweh God had confirmed the bond of love and life with the descendants of Noah and the patriarchs, and David. He maintained the covenant.[85] "At the heart of Israel's life is the covenant."[86]

The wonderful and abiding elements of the covenant were the assuring promises: I am your God, and the God of your children (Gen. 17:7). I am with you, I will watch over you, I will not leave you (28:15). You will be my treasured possession and be for me a kingdom of priests and a holy nation (19:5, 6). These promises had been sealed by the sprinkling of blood (24:7, 8). Daniel undoubtedly had these elements in mind when he referred to Yahweh my God. Yahweh was the specific covenant name (3:14). Daniel claimed Yahweh as "my God" and made it very clear that his covenant God was great and awesome. More, Yahweh God was confessed to be a faithful God because *šōmēr habbĕrît* (act. ptc. of *šāmar,* to keep, to uphold the covenant). Daniel knew that his God was continually keeping his bond of love with his people (Dan. 9:4). As the covenant-keeping God, he was righteous, always doing all things according to God's revealed will (9:7).

Another sure and abiding aspect of the covenant was the revealed body of instruction, the Torah. The core of this instruction was the commands and laws (9:5, 10, 11), which had to be known and obeyed. Daniel indicated that this covenant was an integral aspect of his life with all its varied experiences.

Indirect References

Daniel's and his three friend's experiences in the initial period of their stay in the Babylonian palaces revealed their knowledge of and obedience to the covenant stipulations concerning food and drink. Faithfulness and courage were demonstrated by the young covenant servants of Yahweh God. They refused to defile themselves (1:8).[87] Their faithfulness was rewarded. Eating healthy food, in accordance with covenant rules, they were blessed and acknowledged by their Babylonian lords to be very fit for royal service.

The three young friends who refused to worship Nebuchadnezzar's image of gold, when threatened, demonstrated covenantal assurance and courage. They confessed that Yahweh God could save and rescue them from death in the fiery furnace (3:17). Covenantal protection was given. The Angel of the Lord came and was with them. In the blazing furnace they were not singed, much less burned to death. The assurance that Yahweh God would be with his servants, watch over them, and never leave them was wonderfully demonstrated. The statement, "they trusted in him (Yahweh) . . . and were willing to give up their lives" rather than be idolaters (3:28), was the occasion for their demonstration.

Daniel proved his covenant faithfulness and steadfastness as an administrator in the Persian Empire. He was trustworthy; he was neither corrupt nor negligent (6:4). He exhibited in his life and work that Yahweh God's bond of love, with its integral promises and requirements, was a powerful influence in his life. When he was cast into the lions' den, he was not attacked. Yahweh's angel, not specifically identified as Michael or as the Angel of the Lord (the preincarnate Son) protected him by proving Yahweh's powerful influence in the cosmic kingdom. The lions' mouths were kept shut. It was none other than the Persian king who voiced the covenant promise: the living God performs signs and wonders as he rescues and saves his faithful obedient servant (6:26, 27).

Direct References

Daniel made a direct reference to the everlasting covenant when he prayed concerning the fulfillment of the seventy-year period of captivity (9:1–3). He acknowledged that his people had sinned, done wrong, been wicked, rebelled, turned away from Yahweh God's instructions and commands, and refused to listen to the prophets. Baldwin correctly wrote that Daniel, using terms that were not synonymous, brought "out different aspects of Israel's wrongheadedness."[88] This wickedness was all the more grievous because Yahweh, their great and awesome God, always kept and remained faithful to the covenant. The contrast between what a merciful and loving God continually does and what the people God covenanted with consistently do is stark; it is tragic. Daniel confessed that Yahweh God was righteous, while the people were covered by shame. Their shame was that they were exiled and scattered.

Daniel referred to what Moses had warned. A breaking and ignoring of the covenant would bring the curse and sworn judgments upon the people (Deut. 27:15–26; 28:15–68). Daniel was fully aware of the basic components of the covenant. Yahweh God was the suzerain, the people were his vassals. Promises were given to and carried out for a faithful and obedient covenant people. Stipulations, laws, commands followed the promises; a violation of these would bring the curse, which, in a real sense, was an assurance that Yahweh God kept his covenant faithfully. Daniel was explicit: curses and judgments came upon the people, a great disaster (Dan. 9:11–14), because their Yahweh God was righteous "in everything he does." But this righteous God was also Yahweh the unchanging I am that I am (Exod. 3:14), who was compassionate, gracious, slow to anger, abounding in love, faithful, forgiving wickedness and sin (34:6). The Psalmist had sung of these virtues (Pss. 103:7–10; 145:8–10). Jonah knew Yahweh God would demonstrate these virtues to a repentant Nineveh (4:2). And on the basis of Yahweh God's covenantal virtues Daniel concluded his prayer with two supplications.

wĕʻattâh ʻădōnaî ʼĕlōhênû (and now our sovereign God) who delivered Israel from Egypt and made himself known for all time, turn away your anger and wrath (Dan. 9:15, 16). This anger and wrath were the motivations for the destruction of Jerusalem and the exile of the people. Scorn had been brought upon the people; this reflected on Yahweh also because of the bond he had with his people. Daniel did not mention the people, but pled for the restoration of Jerusalem, his city, his holy hill. It was here that Yahweh God had his earthly house; it was here that Yahweh God fulfilled his covenant promise: he had put his name, his presence, there (2 Sam. 7:13; 1 Kings 8:29).[89] It was here that Yahweh God's people realized to the fullest extent possible that the covenant promise "I am with you" was a fulfilled reality. The central thrust of this first petition Daniel uttered was that Yahweh God, the sovereign covenant Lord, be honored in the restoration of his palace city, this earthly symbol of his heavenly dwelling and throne.

Daniel's second petition followed *wĕʻattâh šĕmaʻ* (imper. of *sāmaʻ*, to hear) *ʼĕlōhênû ʼel lĕpillat ʻabdikâ* (our God the prayer of your servant). It was a plea to be heard by Yahweh God. The thrust of the plea was not for the people specifically. Rather, it was an emphatic repetition of the first plea: consider your name (Dan. 9:18), your city and your people who bear your name (9:19). Covenant promises and blessings were inextricably bound to the city of David, Yahweh's palatial city. Daniel was convinced: when Yahweh God returns to and restores Jerusalem, with its temple, then the covenant people will be restored also!

Daniel's covenantal prayer was heard, in fact, as he was praying, Gabriel the archangel, the messenger from Yahweh God, assured him he was heard. Daniel was assured that he was esteemed (9:23). His prayer of confession and petition validated this esteem. But the response Daniel received did not refer specifically to Jerusalem although it was involved. The response Daniel received consisted of the following.

First, the figure of seventy should be kept in mind. It was in Daniel's mind (9:1, 2). It was a lead off-point. But seventy is not to be the limit, the final count (9:24a). The figure seventy "sevens" is of greater importance.[90]

Second, a decree would be issued that Jerusalem would be restored and rebuilt. This decree was issued within a year or two, at the most, after Daniel's prayer. The date of the issuing of the decree was 536 B.C.

Third, three references to "sevens" presents a unique challenge[91] to interpreters. Seventy "sevens" equals 490. This is less than the time of Cyrus's decree until Christ's birth or death. A precise literal application is not correct.[92] The additional references to seven "sevens" and sixty-two "sevens" which divide the seventy "sevens" period presents additional problems. But what seems clear is that there is a reference to the Messiah's death after the end of the sixty-ninth year, specifically during the middle of the seventieth (the last seven, 9:27). It would seem correct to conclude that the end of the last "seven" refers symbolically to the destruction of Jerusalem.[93]

Fourth, the Anointed One, when he comes and performs his ministry will *wĕhigĕbîr* (hiph. pf. of *gābor*) *bĕrît lārabbîm* (and he will make strong, confirm the covenant). There will be no making of a new covenant because the terms employed clearly emphasize that what was present will be made stronger, confirmed, in a real sense, completed. The covenant referred to is the covenant first pronounced in a brief statement to Adam and Eve (Gen. 3:14–16); confirmed to the patriarchs, David, and by the prophets (especially Isa. 52:12–53:12), the Anointed One, the Messiah.[94] Confirming the covenant had this effect: transgression was finished, sin ended, wickedness atoned for, and everlasting righteousness was brought in (Dan. 9:24).

Fifth, in summing up one must conclude that Daniel was assured that Jerusalem would be fully rebuilt, with walls, moats, in times of trouble;[95] this is referred to by the seven "sevens." The Anointed One, the Messiah, would come, and fulfill the promised covenant in his death. The destruction of Jerusalem, at the end of the last sixty-third "seven" would end all sacrifices. The rebuilt city and temple would be destroyed and left in ruins.

Daniel made references to the agents of the covenant in various seemingly obtuse ways. Reference now is not to the messianic Mediator. The ruler, or prince (9:25), who destroys Jerusalem without his specific intent and knowledge, confirms and fulfills the covenant.

In the final "great vision" Daniel referred to the *bĕrît* (covenant). In each case, the covenant does not stand alone in the text. There is a *nĕgîd bĕrît* (prince of the covenant) (11:22) and the phrase *'al bĕrît gōdĕs* (11:28, 30) and *wĕmarĕsî'ê bĕrît* (11:32) (violators of the holy covenant). The challenge to be faced is, if possible, to understand which covenant is referred to and who the persons involved are.

The context of these references to covenant is the great opposition and wars between the kings of the south (Ptolamaic) and the kings of the north (Seleucid). The Greek conquest of the Persian Empire led to its division into the four kingdoms that would constitute the entire Grecian Empire. Daniel saw the king of the south would have a victory over the king of the north and be filled with pride as he slaughtered many of his enemies (11:11, 12). But the king of the north would regain power and do as he pleased when he invaded the south and coastal countries (11:13–19). His successor would not last but a contemptible nonroyal person would come to power and wreak havoc. In this context Daniel saw "a prince of the covenant destroyed" (11:22). This king of the north was becoming ever richer and stronger; he would successfully invade countries to the south and return to his own country with great wealth (11:23–28). There and then he would be against the holy covenant (11:28). When this king of the north again invades the south and returns to his place, he will vent his fury against "the holy covenant" but show favoritism to those who forsake "the holy covenant." He will corrupt with flattery those who violated the covenant (11:29–32). Then Daniel adds: but *wĕ' ām yōdĕ'ê 'ĕlōhâw* (and the people knowing their God) will strongly work against this king (11:32).

The pivotal question is: to which covenant did Daniel refer? The answers given to this question are quite consistent. Commentators interpret the reference to be to the covenant Yahweh God made with Israel at Sinai. Hence the prince of the covenant refers to a priest or leader among the people and to people who remained faithful to the covenant.[96] The covenant is understood to refer not only to faithful people, but also to Judah and Jerusalem and its inhabitants.[97]

Daniel, in this vision, was given further revelation concerning the covenant of which he had referred to in his prayer. The covenant would be maintained; it would be represented by a leader(s); it would be violated by covenant people suffering persecution; it would be kept strongly, faithfully, by a "remnant" of the remnant. The covenant Yahweh God had made and repeatedly confirmed would be kept and maintained during the severest persecution.[98] Daniel prophesied of this assurance when he proclaimed (and wrote) that faithful covenant people will have their names written in the "Book of Life." They will be delivered. They will be resurrected to everlasting life. Those unfaithful will awake and arise "to shame and everlasting contempt." The covenant blessings will be realities for the faithful, the covenant curse will be executed upon covenant breakers.

The kingdom of Yahweh God was/is the major theme of the book of Daniel. And since the covenant was/is the administrative and redemptive/restorative means by which the kingdom is sovereignly upheld and ruled, it follows that Daniel could not omit references to it. In reality, he demonstrated the vital and pivotal role of the covenant within the kingdom of Yahweh God. Indeed, Yahweh God was ever faithful to every aspect of this covenant and carried it out as assured to the "faithful keepers" and to the covenant breakers.

The Mediator[99]

Three subjects call for attention: Daniel as a messianic type, the term *māšîah* (messiah), and prophetic references to a person.

Daniel as Type

Daniel, as a person, was an attractive man. Nothing is known regarding his physical appearance. There is no reference to him as a married man or of having a family. When yet a youth he gained the trust and admiration of the high-ranking officials as well as their envy. Daniel had great abilities; he studied and learned much; he was astute in his political roles. As a covenant agent and servant he performed his duties in royal arenas flawlessly. He served as a prophet, interpreting dreams and visions, counseling kings, receiving revelations, and publicizing them. He was a passionate intercessor on behalf of his people and pled with Yahweh concerning promises given through fellow prophets. In his character, role, and work, he can be said to have been an effective covenant messianic agent. Thus, it is not out of order to refer to Daniel as a type of the Messiah.[100]

The **Māšîah**

The term *māšîah* (Anointed One) appears twice in Daniel's prophecies, both times in the same context (9:25, 26). Gabriel, the archangel, Yahweh God's special messenger informs Daniel that the Anointed will come, will be cut off, and will confirm the covenant (9:27). These words were part of the answer Daniel received in reply to his prayer when in effect he asked: how long will the exile last? (9:4–19).[101] That the term itself appears only in this context should not lead anyone to conclude that Daniel's prophecies include scant references to the Mediator of the covenant. As a review is made of various specific passages, it will become clear that the "Anointed One," the Messiah, the messianic Mediator, had a very key and influential role in Daniel's prophecies concerning the nations and the covenant people.

Prophecies concerning the Coming Messiah

Daniel 2 records Nebuchadnezzar's dream of the great image consisting of gold, silver, bronze, and iron/clay. A rock cut out, not by human hands (2:34), that was part of a mountain (2:45), crushed the iron/clay feet. So doing, it crushed the entire image and the scene that is presented is that what was represented by the gold, silver, and bronze has no lasting influence. What does continue is what Yahweh God was setting up in the times of the four kingdoms' destruction. He was setting up a kingdom that will never be destroyed (2:44). This rock stands for the sovereignty and power of God establishing a lasting kingdom.[102] The kingdom of God is thus represented by a rock that is known for is durability.

Daniel, in this passage, did not give any indication that the rock denoted a personal Messiah. In Christian tradition the conviction was that the man Jesus initiated the "ultimate downfall of worldly empires and the establishment of God's rule."[103] The question this view raises is whether the reference is to a kingdom on earth or to the heavenly glory realm of Christ, the kingdom of Christ Jesus.[104]

We must agree that Daniel, in his interpretation of the king's dream, did not specifically identify the Messiah. He was definite that the God of heaven would set up an everlasting kingdom. This presentation of the kingdom that removes all earthly kingdoms and brings to expression Yahweh God's all-encompassing rule lays the groundwork and provides the context for further revelation in which the Messiah is more specifically and graphically portrayed.

Two passages that are not prophetic but historical present Yahweh God, the sovereign King of the cosmos, bringing deliverance through two "unique agents." The three friends of Daniel, after refusing to worship Nebuchadnezzar's image, were thrown into a blazing hot furnace (3:1–21). When the king looked into the furnace he saw a fourth being, whom he referred to as looking like a "son of the gods." To be noted is that Nebuchadnezzar recognized the presence of deity in the furnace but could not specifically identify the divine one. He did acknowledge that the three friends were servants of the "Most High God." By this phrase he undoubtedly expressed his belief that of all the existing gods, this delivering God was the greatest, above all others, including the gods he acknowledged and worshiped.[105]

The question to be answered is: can the fourth being in the furnace, who was seen as deity, be specifically identified? Nebuchadnezzar referred to it as an angel sent by the God of the three friends (3:28). Commentators have given four identifications.[106]

The first reference mentioned is to the Angel of the Lord who in other biblical passages was the preincarnate Christ. Thus Nebuchadnezzar saw the Messiah in the form of an angel and referred to him as one of "the sons of the gods."

The three other references are less specific. A few conservative commentators took the phrase "son of gods" to refer to deity, using phrases such as "of the race of gods" and "divine companion." The critical liberal commentators consider the passage to have been edited with apocryphal insertions or as a story of a martyr group that was added later.

The biblical testimony is that God was present in a theophany in which the preincarnate Christ was the deity. He was present as the "Angel of the Lord," having been sent by God. This was also Daniel's testimony when, having been cast into the lions' den, he was delivered (6:22). The only proper answer to the question—who was with the three friends in the furnace and with Daniel in the lions' den?—is the preincarnate Christ, who is the mediatorial agent of Yahweh God's covenant with his people. He is the messianic Deliverer.

Daniel, in chapter 7, records what he experienced during the first year of Belshazzar's reign.[107] Thus Daniel received a revelation by means of a dream and visions (7:1) that was similar to the one Nebuchadnezzar had received in the second year of his reign, which had begun during the last few years of the sixth century B.C. Hence, about fifty-five years had passed. Dramatic events were to take place within the present decade. Daniel was given assurance that Yahweh God was sovereignly in charge. The dream/visions contain five specific parts.

Four beasts were seen coming out of the sea churned up by the four winds of heaven. These beasts with unique appendages looked like a lion, a bear, and a leopard. The fourth beast was terrifying, powerful, having iron teeth and ten horns (7:3–8). Daniel was given an explanation of these beasts: they represented four kingdoms (7:17–25).

In contrast to these beasts, Daniel received in the visions the scene of thrones.[108] The Ancient of Days took his seat among these (7:9). The description of him included white clothing and hair. His throne and its wheels were burning fire and a river of fire flowed out before him. Many thousands attended him. Once the court was seated "the books were opened." This Ancient of Days was God, seen in the vision as dignified, venerable, majestic, who has complete control over the nations represented by the beasts.[109]

In close relationship to the Ancient of Days, God was one "like a son of man" coming with the clouds of heaven. In the presence of the Ancient of Days he received authority, glory, and sovereign power. He was given an everlasting dominion.[110] Who is this one like the son of man?[111] He is referred to as a celestial being, an angelic being, and like a human being. It must be concluded that the phrase "son of man" does not refer to a weak and frail human. In Psalm 8 the phrase refers to one who is a ruler, a royal person.[112] Ezekiel was called son of man as a prophet called to speak for Yahweh God. Jesus referred to himself as the Son of man (Matt. 24:27, 30; 25:31). He said this one would come on the clouds of heaven

(Mark 13:26), and thus identified himself with the one like a son of man coming with the clouds of heaven (Dan. 7:13).

In Daniel's interpretation of the dream he related that one aspect of the fourth beast would arise and speak against Yahweh God and oppress the saints (7:21, 25). A reference to the duration of this oppression is said to be "for a time, times, and half a time" (7:25). The term *saints* refers to the faithful covenant people who are members of the everlasting dominion given by the Ancient of Days to the one like the Son of man. These saints would suffer under the king to follow the ten represented by the ten horns of the fourth beast. This period of oppression would last for a specific period of time.[113] Most commentators conclude that this king refers to Antiochus Epiphanes, who was very much opposed to the Messiah; he was an antichrist.

The dominion or kingdom that will never be destroyed (7:14), which was given to the Messiah by the Ancient of Days, is eternal. The Messiah is definitely presented as the one who reigns, rules, controls, and directs all affairs that the "antiking" seeks to alter or remove; "set times and laws." This kingdom is the inheritance of the saints (7:27). Thus Daniel's dreams/visions project a glorious future for the covenant people. Oppression will last for a time but it is under the reign of Yahweh God and the Messiah forever. Nations will rise and fall; they may exert great power for a while. Yet the kingdom of the Messiah will never fail or be destroyed. It endures forever.

Two years after Daniel received the revelation recorded in chapter 7, he received another vision. Additional revelation was given concerning the second and third worldly empires as presented in chapters 2 and 7 and by implication concerning the kingdom of God because it is under the sovereign reign of God that nations rise and fall.

Not many commentators believe that Daniel 8 contains messianic/mediatorial references. One could say that since the sanctuary represents Yahweh God's presence that it also represents the Messiah typically. Christ in the New Testament is spoken of as Yahweh God's temple among his people (John 1:14).[114]

Commentators are not agreed either on how to answer the question: does Daniel prophesy concerning the Messiah in chapter 9?[115] After a careful study of this passage, and consulting a wide selection of commentaries, this conclusion was stated: Yahweh will send his appointed Anointed One who will fulfill all the promises of the covenant by his atoning death. The messianic concept is revealed and explicated: the Messiah is to come as Ruler. He will carry out his atoning work and will render typical aspects such as physical Jerusalem and the temple; because the sacrificial rituals are fulfilled, they are therefore obsolete.[116]

As is the case with the prophecy recorded in chapter 9, so it also is regarding chapters 10 through 12. Some scholars consider that the man in linen (Dan. 10:5; 12:7) is the Messiah or that Michael the archangel should be identified as the Messiah (10:13, 21; 12:1). The evidence for these views is too scant to be considered creditable. The conclusion should be: neither the Messiah nor his works are referred to directly.[117]

In conclusion to this study on Daniel and his contribution to the presence and relevance of the three concepts that form the cable that united the Old Testament revelation, it must be stated again that the kingdom of Yahweh God is the central and inclusive concept. The kingdoms of this world, great, powerful, and expansive though they are, rise and fall under the sovereign reign of Yahweh God. And this is done by Yahweh God as the covenant keeper. He reigns and carries out the affairs of his cosmic kingdom in keeping with his administrative/redemptive/restorative covenant. The covenant mediator, the Messiah, is the agent who effectively and efficiently carries out his regal prerogative and responsibilities in such a way that the covenant is progressively revealed and the cosmic kingdom of God is enhanced and more firmly established. In the context of the cosmic kingdom, the kingdom of Christ comes to the fore and serves as representative of and functioning power within the eternal cosmic kingdom.

NOTES

1. Gerard Van Groningen, *Messianic Revelation in the Old Testament* (*MROT*), (Grand Rapids: Baker, 1990), 788–846.

2. Mention can be made of the book by John E. Goldingay, *Word Biblical Commentary: Daniel,* vol. 30 (Dallas: Word, 1989). An extensive bibliography is included, xxi–xxv; xli–lii, and also at the head of each chapter. In his introduction Goldingay presents a succinct but complete review of the history of the book's interpretation, xxv–xl. Another recently produced commentary is by Tremper Longman, III, *Daniel: The NIV Application Commentary* (Grand Rapids: Zondervan, 1999). Some works on Daniel appearing during the decade of 1990s include Alvin Bernard, who wrote that as a Seventh-Day Adventist he had been committed to their set of doctrines. But, a study of the book of Daniel led him to understand that Daniel's prophecies were fulfilled by Christ during his first coming and in the time soon after his ministry on earth. *Insights Into the Book of Daniel*, (St. Louis: Bernard, 1993); *The Book of Daniel in the Light of New Findings,* ed. A. S. Van Der Wouda (Leuven-Louvain [Belguim]: Leuven University Press, 1993); *Solving Riddles and Untying Knots,* ed. Ziony Zevit, Seymour Getin, and Michael Sokoloff (Winona Lake: Eisenbrauns, 1995) (a symposium in Semitic Studies, including essays on the book of Daniel).

Writers dealing with eschatological issues who refer to Daniel's prophecies are Craig Blaising and Darrell Bock, *Dispensationalism, Israel and the Church* (Grand Rapids: Zondervan, 1992). Also by these authors, *Progressive Dispensationalism* (Wheaton: Victor, 1993).

The periodical index available to me listed 367 essays, chapters in symposiums, and articles in periodicals that have been published on Daniel since 1980.

3. One wonders if Goldingay was correct when he wrote "whether the stories are history or fiction, the visions actual prophecy or quasi prophecy written by Daniel or someone else" or when they were written, "makes surprisingly little difference in the book's exegesis." *Daniel,* xl. It seems that Goldingay does not consider the historical aspect to be really important for exegesis. The Antiochian scholars taught it was and contemporary biblical theologians stress its importance. It bears repetition that a well-orbed biblical-theological study, which emphasizes the history of revelation and redemption, calls for careful attention to the historical setting of this revelation.

4. No effort will be made to present arguments against the position that Daniel was the last of canonical Hebrew Scriptures to have been written in the period 175–164 B.C. Cf. Robert A. Anderson, *Signs and Wonders* (Grand Rapids: Eerdmans, 1984), xiii, who assumes that the book refers to specific events that occurred 350 years after the historical person, Daniel, died. Anderson and many nonconservative authors discount much of the prophetic character of the book of Daniel. Anderson follows what scholars such as Arthur Jeffrey wrote in the introduction to his exegetical work on Daniel in "The Book of Daniel," in *The Expositor's Bible,* ed. George A. Buttrick (Nashville: Abingdon, 1956). Jeffrey, in a concise review of the historical period from 333 B.C., the time of Alexander's death, to 175 B.C., referred to Alexander's initiating the Hellenization of the Orient, which also affected the Jewish people. Jeffrey wrote that Daniel was written during the time of persecution by Antioches IV Epiphanes, whose territory included Jerusalem. The name *Daniel* was taken as a symbolic name (meaning "God hath given decision") from the Ugaritic legend of Daniel, 341–44. Stanislav Sagert, in his essay "Poetic Structures in the Hebrew Section of the Book of Daniel," in *Solving Riddles,* wrote that "characteristics of Hebrew poetry from the later biblical period have not been clearly observed and defined," 261. He assumed that the book of Daniel was received in its final form circa 165 B.C., 261. Segert wrote that a lack of preexilic poetic characteristics and the heavy impact of Aramaic influences suggest characteristics of this date, 202–4. Another literary question deals with the LXX dealing with Daniel. P. W. Coxon wrote that opinions differ on the origin and development of that idiosyncratic text (LXX on Daniel). He preferred to work with the traditions lying behind the so-called Theodotionic version, as do other more recent scholars. "Nebuchadnezzar's Madness," *New Findings,* 213. For this study, the Masoretic text, as it has been accepted for centuries, will serve as the proper and basic text.

Readers and students who wish to read a rebuttal against a late date of Daniel, can be helped by Robert Dick Wilson, *Studies in the Book of Daniel* (a classic defense of the historicity and integrity of Daniel's prophecies), paperback edition (Grand Rapids: Baker, 1979). The first edition was published in 1917. G. K. Beale, in his *The Use of Daniel in Jewish Apocalpyptic Literature and in the Revelation of St. John* (Lanham: University Press, 1984), reveals the problem a scholar has when working with texts written by critical writers when he himself holds to the traditional early date of Daniel (cf. 10, note 15).

5. The threefold division that Gleason Archer, Jr., and Ronald Youngblood present in the *NIV Study Bible* (Grand Rapids: Zondervan, 1985), namely, the Prologue, (chap. 1); The account of the Nations of the World (chaps. 2–7); and the Destiny of the Nation of Israel (chaps. 8–12), suggest a specific eschatological approach to the book.

6. Goldingay has not demonstrated that these are constituent features of the stories in chapters 1–6. He added that to characterize the stories as such does not necessarily declare they are unhistorical. *Daniel,* 6, 7.

7. Consider what Isaac Newton wrote (1642–1727) in his *Observations Upon the Prophecies of Daniel and the Apocalypse of St. John,* reprint (Cave Junction: Oregon Institute of Science and Medicine, 1991), 18, 19.

8. For a nonconservative approach to and discussion of apocalyptic literature, consult the twenty-four page "Introduction to Apocalyptic Literature" in J. J. Collin's *Daniel* (Grand Rapids: Eerdmans, 1984).

9. Reference is to Van Groningen's writings, *Messianic Revelation in the Old Testament* and *From Creation to Consummation,* vols. 1 and 2. One should not conclude that good, reliable commentaries on Daniel are missing. Reliable conservative exegetical works

include G.C.H. Aalders, *Daniel* (Kampen: Kok, 1962); Gleason L. Archer, "Daniel," in *The Expositor's Bible Commentary,* vol. 7, ed. F. C. Gabelein (Grand Rapids: Zondervan, 1985); Joyce C. Baldwin, *Daniel* (Leicester: InterVarsity, 1978); C.F. Keil, *The Book of Daniel,* trans. M. G. Easton, (Grand Rapids: Eerdmans, 1949); Edward J. Young, *The Prophecy of Daniel* (Grand Rapids: Eerdmans, 1949). A number of special studies on topics introduced in the book of Daniel have also continued to appear, as have essays in periodicals.

10. In *MROT,* a survey is given of Daniel the man, as exile, statesman, prophet, and type of Christ, 789–91.

11. Daniel was judged to be fourteen or fifteen years old; hence he was born circa 620 B.C. Cf. Young, *Daniel,* 39, 40. Young wrote that there is no evidence that the Babylonians made Daniel and his young friends eunuchs.

12. Daniel made more references to himself in chapters 8–12. Branson L. Woodard Jr. wrote that the book of Daniel displays "presumptuous monarchs, crafty soothsayers, a worldly-wise queen, zealous Hebrews and a supernaturally wise Daniel." Woodard discounts the Maccabean theory regarding the time when the book was written but accepts that a "sixth century prophet composed the book, creating a unified presentation of historic events. "Literary Strategies and Authorship in the Book of Daniel," *Journal of Evangelical Theological Society* 37, no. 1:1 (1994): 39–53.

13. The texts refer to the spirit as the one of the holy gods. B. Becking correctly pointed out that Daniel received this "qualification from persons who are not Israelites." Cf. "A Divine Spirit in You," in *New Findings*, 515–16. Non-Israelites recognized the presence of the Holy Spirit, but according to their religious perception, attributed the spirit to their "holy gods."

14. P. R. Davies has raised the issue of "Reading Daniel Sociologically." Cf. *New Findings.* He called for a distinction between a "functionalist approach," which considers the functions of parts within the whole system, or a synchronic approach, in which history reveals a tendency to stability, 346. Two basic issues must be considered, namely, the relationship between literature and social reality (347) and the actual social setting of Daniel. It seems to this author that the sociological reading of Daniel does not offer many insights due to the lack of detail concerning Daniel's social setting. This problem is severely complicated by liberal scholars who do not accept the sixth-century Daniel as the author of the book and who question whether there was a historic person named Daniel. Cf. Woodard's reference to M. Sternberg, who wrote in *The Poetics of Biblical Narrative*, (Bloomington: Indiana University Press, 1985), that the historical person and author as writer must be carefully distinguished. Cf. *Literary Strategies,* note 4, 40. It would seem that a sociological study becomes well nigh impossible since the historic person and the later writer must be carefully distinguished. The writer was believed to have lived at least 300 years later than the historical person, whose social setting is to be examined.

15. Michal A. Knibb, in an essay "You Are Indeed Wiser Than Daniel," *New Findings,* 399–411, reviewed what K. Koch wrote in "Is Daniel also Among the Prophets?" in *Interpreting the Prophets,* ed. J. L. Mays and P. J. Achtemeier (Philadelphia: n.p., 1985). Koch had written that the earliest literary evidence for Daniel being included in the Writings was in the Babylonian Talmud, written between the fifth and eighth centuries A.D.

16. Cf. Knibb on this; Gerhard Von Rad brought this view into prominence, 401. Knibb wrote in the conclusion of this article that "Daniel is not a prophetic book," 41.

17. Ezek. 28:4 implies Daniel was wise because of his prophetic gifts.

18. Davies wrote: "Daniel is no priest, yet he intercedes, in the absence of the temple, he is a priestly figure" and "Daniel reflects a priestly perspective." "Reading Daniel Sociologically," *New Findings,* 359, 360.

19. Ezekiel was of priestly linage, yet was called to be a prophet; this reveals his "sacredotal training" and propensities in the apocalyptic aspects of the book of Ezekiel, esp. chaps. 1, 40–48.

20. The undeveloped apocalyptic materials in Daniel support the view that Daniel was written centuries before the Maccabean period, when much more developed apocalyptic materials were produced.

21. These biblical references often are employed to suggest Daniel's dependence on or use of these. There are nine pages of Old Testament Biblical references in the last part of the book *New Findings;* a half page of New Testament references is included. I. Frohlich, in an essay also included in *New Findings,* 266–70, has attempted to find a correlation between Daniel and Deutero-Isaiah. To do this he had to concede that a good part of Daniel reflects the Persian period and had to also place part of Isaiah in that period. Notice should also be taken of essays written on the relationship of the prophecy of Daniel to the book of Revelation. Cf. Gregory Beale, "The Danielic Background for Revelation 13–18," *Tyndale Bulletin,* no. 31 (1980): 163–70. Cf. also Wilbur Wallace, "The Coming of the Kingdom, a Survey of the Book of Revelation," *Presbyterion* 8, no. 1 (1982): 13–70, which made numerous textual references to Daniel and wrote such statements as follows: "No doubt John was aware that he was seeing the same eschatological event about which Daniel had written, and was filling in dramatic details," 19. Kenneth L. Barker, in an essay, "Premillennialism in the Book of Daniel," *Master's Seminary Journal* 4 (Spring 1993) appealed to the book of Revelation for orientation for his discussion of Daniel 2:31–45; 7:1–27; 9:24–27. The main point is: Neither Daniel, nor any other of the prophets, when speaking/writing of the future of the kingdom refer to a thousand-year reign by the Messiah who returns to earth to accomplish what he was not able to do the first time, namely, establish a worldwide kingdom ruled from a throne in Jerusalem.

22. Cf. conclusion of chap. 19 in *FCTC,* vol. II.

23. Daniel did not use the phrase *yôm yĕhwâ* (Day of the Lord), but prophesied about events that other prophets had spoken about as being part of that great day.

24. Cf. *MROT,* 787–846.

25. Desmond Ford, *Daniel* (Nashville: Southern Publishing Association, 1978), 25 (with a Seventh Day Adventist approach).

26. Goldingay, *Daniel,* commentary, 330. He also wrote that the Aramaic of 2:4–7:28, "is a form of Imperial Aramaic, the international language of the Middle East through much of O.T. times." xxv. Since this is so, Daniel must be rescued from three kinds of friends who are "actually foes that imperil its being heard: 1) those who preoccupy themselves with merely historical questions; 2) those who have turned Daniel into a children's story book; 3) those who treat the visions as a mere coded preview of events to unfold in the Middle East. ix, x. A careful and helpful study on "The Aramaic of Daniel" was written by Kenneth O. Kitchen. Cf. Tyndale booklet *Notes on Some Problems in the Book of Daniel* (London: Tyndale, 1965), 31–79. Kitchen concluded, in response to those who hold that the use of Aramaic reflects a second-century date for the writing of Daniel, that it is obscurantist to exclude dogmatically sixth- to fifth- (or fourth-) century date as far as the Aramaic is concerned, 79.

27. Norman W. Porteous, *Daniel, A Commentary* (London: SCM, 1965), 21. Porteous is a representative of the critical historical/literary school of thought.

28. Rousas John Rushdoony, *Thy Kingdom Come* (Garden Grove: Presbyterian and Reformed, 1975), 56, represents a theonomic postmillennial position.

29. Herman Veldkamp, *Dreams and Dictators,* trans. Theodore Plantinga (St. Catherines: Paideia, 1978), 141, wrote from a Reformed/Presbyterian amillennial perspective.

30. Willem A. Van Gemeren, *Interpreting the Prophetic Word* (Grand Rapids: Zondervan, 1990), 342.

31. Ronald S. Wallace, *The Lord is King* (Downers Grove: InterVarsity, 1979), 23–29.

32. The question has been raised concerning the precise meaning of the preposition *of* in the phrase "kingdom of God." Is *of* a preposition referring to origin, that is, established by God, or is it referring to the kingdom ruled by God? There is no warrant for making the distinction since the kingdom is both established and ruled by God.

33. Cf. D. Wenham, "The Kingdom of God and Daniel," *The Expository Time* 98, no. 5 (1987): 132–34. Wenham referred to G. R. Beasley Murray's work, *Jesus and the Kingdom of God*, (Grand Rapids: Eerdmans, 1956), which takes Daniel as background to the New Testament seriously, (cf. note 2, 34).

34. Cf. what is written in the preceding, Part I. Section C. 1.

35. The Hebrew term *haśkēl* is the hip inf. absolute of *śākal,* to be prudent, have insight, and used as a substantive (noun). Cf. G.C.H. Aalders, *Daniel* (Kampen: Kok, 1962), 45, who referred to 1:4, where the term *maskîlîm* is translated "showing aptitude for every kind of learning."

36. This passage in Daniel provides great insights and valuable directives for a well-rounded liberal arts education as well as for learning and training for specialized areas of kingdom service.

37. Daniel's dreams and visions are discussed in section II, C, 1.

38. The passage in Daniel that records Daniel's and his three friends' promotions are written in Aramaic. The use of Aramaic should not be considered as evidence that the material in 2:4–7:28 was written in the second century B.C., as F. H. Polak accepts in "Daniel Tales in Their Aramaic Literary Mileau," *New Findings,* 249–65. Kenneth Kitchen, having reviewed the use of the so-called loan words and the orthography and phonetics of the Aramaic in Daniel, concluded that we have no right to assume the Aramaic of Daniel requires a second-century date for the original composition of the Aramaic text, 67. Cf. "The Aramaic of Daniel," in *Notes on Some Problems,* 31–79. See also Richard D. Patterson, "Holding on to Daniel's Court Tales," *Journal of Evangelical Theology* 36, no. 4, (1993): 445–54, who wrote that his study shows "that based on literary genre" the extreme position that views all of Daniel to have been written in the second century B.C. "is manifestly in error." 246.

39. The texts read *rabbî* (make great). Nebuchadnezzar the king made Daniel great, *has-ˇlĕmēh* (made him a man of great power) that is, governor or viceregent, *wĕrab-signîn 'al kōl hakîmîe bābel* (and made him chief [president] over all the wise men of babel). Cf. Kiel, *Daniel,* 113. R. H. Charles wrote that Dan. 2:44b defined Daniel's position. He "was in the gate of the king" and was the grand vizier over the wise men. The three friends had like rank with satraps, deputies, governors, and other high officials, but "Daniel stood . . . in a unique position of rank and authority next to the king himself." *A Critical and Exegetical Commentary on the Book of Daniel* (Oxford: Clarendon, 1929), 55.

40. Daniel made no reference to these three relatives who were successors within a period of six years. Nabonidies, not of royal ancestry, but a high official in the Babylonian court, took the throne of Babylon.

41. Cf. Goldingay, *Daniel,* 106.

42. Cf. Louis F. Hartman's chart of the kings who ruled Babylon, Media, and Persia. *The Book of Daniel*, vol. 23 in the Anchor Bible Series, ed. W. F. Albright and D. M. Freedman (Garden City: Doubleday, 1978), 30. See also H. H. Rowley, *Darius the Mede and the Four World Empires* (Cardiff: University of Wales Press, 1959). Rowley concluded that Darius the Mede is fictitious, 53, after reviewing the possibilities that Darius referred to kings by

other names. Cf. also D. J. Wiseman, "Darius the Mede," in *Notes,* 11–16. He evaluated Rowley's conclusions and concluded that, on the basis of an interpretation of Dan. 6:28, Darius the Mede could be another name for Cyrus, 15, 16.

43. Daniel was born in 620 ± , hence he was gone 200 years later when Darius II became king.

44. Cf. what R. B. Kruschevitz wrote: "all the court narratives, including Daniel 7 seem to say that God was active in the lives of individual Jews and even Babylonian kings." "Nebuchadnezzar as the Head of Gold: Politics and History in the Book of Daniel," *Perspectives in Relgious Studies* 24 (Winter 1997). Kruschewitz revealed his view of the authorship of Daniel when he wrote that the perspective of the original author was not changed by the second-century interpretation, 403. And he wrote that chapter 11 gives a detailed report about the relationship between the Seleucids and Ptolemics: 411. This view is contrary to what the Scriptures present, namely, Daniel prophesied concerning what was to take place three to four centuries later.

45. The most widely accepted view among conservative interpreters is that these empires were represented: the golden head, the Babylonian; the silver chest, Median-Persian; by the bronze belly and thighs, the Greek; and iron/clay legs and feet, the Romans. The interpreters who do not accept prophetic revelation concerning the future refer to the Babylonian, Median, Persian, and Greek empires; these were present by 200 B.C., when the book of Daniel was finally completed according to their historical interpretation. Cf. Rowley, *Darius . . .. Four Empires,* who concluded that the first empire was the Neo-Babylonian, the fourth the Greek, the second the Median, and the third the Persian.

Both the conservative and liberal critical views are not without difficulties; efforts to present alternatives are made. E.g., John Walton, in his essay "The Four Kingdoms of Daniel," *Journal of the Evangelical Theological Society* 29, no. 1, (March 1986): 25–36, explains difficulties he has with Young's (conservative) and Rowley's positions. He wonders if Robert Gurney's position, developed in an essay "The Four Kingdoms of Daniel 2 & 7," *Themelios* 2 (1977); that Darius the Mede ruled over the Median at the same time that the Babylonian Empire still existed, is a probable solution. Thus the four are the Babylonian, Median, Persian, and Greek. Gurney's position, Walton stresses, is not based on the liberal critical interpretation of the book of Daniel.

46. Cf. Goldingay, *Daniel,* "the golden splendor of Nebuchadnezzar's empire is God-given," 58.

47. Cf. Baldwin's comments regarding this. *Daniel,* 94.

48. Various commentators have written as Aalders has (translated): the bonds must have been destroyed immediately by the fire, enabling the men to walk about without any hindrance. *Daniel*, 82, 83.

49. Cf. Andre Lococque, *The Book of Daniel,* trans. David Pellaver (Atlanta: John Knox, 1979), 66.

50. Cf. Goldingay, *Daniel,* 74.

51. NIV translates "praise be to God" Jerusalem Bible, NASB, RSV translate more correctly, "blessed be."

52. See essay by B. Becking, "A Divine Spirit is in You," in *New Findings,* 515–19. Becking discussed how to translate *Elohim* as plural for the Babylonians and as singular for Daniel.

53. P. W. Coxen, in his essay "Nebuchadnezzar's Madness," *New Findings,* 211–22, consulted various writings such as the Palestianian Targums, the LXX, and the Theodotion-Daniel, and found Babylonian cultural coloring in them. Coxen concluded that Nebuchad-

nezzar, stripped of his empirical splendor and human dignity, was "forced to assume the role of the early Enkidu, the primordial savage man whose habitat was the steppe and whose company were the wild asses." These new findings may find some analogies with pagan literature, but one must be assured that a correct reading of the biblical text does not lead to positing pagan motifs into the text.

54. G. L. Archer acknowledged that chapter 4 was composed under the authority of a pagan, that the king spoke as one intellectually convinced, but can hardly be said to "have had a genuine heart conversion." "Daniel," 58. There is no evidence on the basis of a written text that one can so judge the king's heart.

55. During Belshazzar's first year of reign and during his third year, Daniel had a dream and a vision; the content and meaning of these were not reported to King Belshazzar.

56. Cf. Longman's brief discussion of the sovereignty of God, *Daniel,* 20.

57. Cf. essay by Zdranko Stefanovic, "Daniel: A Book of Significant Reversals," *Andrews University Seminary Studies* 30 (Summer 1992): 139–50. The writer correctly referred to thematic reversals in the "historical section of Daniel." Examples given are: (1) the Hebrews had a ten-day test and later demonstrated a tenfold superiority in acumen (chap. 1); (2) Daniel's wisdom succeeds when wise men's fails (chap. 2); (3) Nebuchadnezzar demanded false obeisance but at the close praised the Most High God (chap. 3). These reversals, and others recorded, reveal that Yahweh God "was fully able to act on behalf of his faithful ones even in their captivity and distress in Babylon." 141.

58. Cf. Young, *Daniel,* 141.

59. Richard D. Patterson in his essay "The Key Role of Daniel 7," *Grace Theological Journal* 12 (Fall 1992): 245–61, has presented a study of the relationship of Daniel's visions and dreams recorded in chaps. 7–12 to that recorded in chaps 1–6. He has included three "tables" in which he portrays the similarities in the various parts of the book of Daniel. His main point was to demonstrate "the unity and composition of the book of Daniel," 245. A questionable effort by Patterson is his bringing John's Revelation (the book) into a relationship in such a way that Daniel is believed to set the stage for a premillennial view of the kingdom, 256–61. Cf. also Longman, *Daniel*, who wrote that the apocalyptic chapters continue the theme in the first six chapters, 177.

60. John J. Collins, in his essay "Stirring up the Great Sea, The Religio-Historical Backgrounds of Daniel 7," *New Findings,* 121–36, reviewed the liberal search for pagan sources from which Daniel drew his scene. Herman Gunkel had "claimed to have found its prototype in the Babylonian creation story, the Enuma Elish. This view eventually was rejected because the Ugaritic texts discovered in 1929 seemed to serve better than Enuma Elish. Since then, claims that Daniel 7 has a Mesopotamian background, "the underworld," has been suggested. Collins suggested that whoever composed Daniel 7 "was a creative author, not a mere copiest," 124. He, nevertheless turned to the Ugaritic myths again and stated that though there are "important differences between Daniel 7 and the Ugaritic myth," 127, the main ingredients for Dan. 7 are to be found in ancient myths, 128, both Babylonian and Ugaritic. Collins wrote that the author of Dan. 7 depended on these myths to more adequately depict the terrible struggle between Antiochus Epiphanes and the Jews circa 175 +/- B.C. A real problem Collins presents is that he views the time Dan. 7 was written was over 350 years (+/-) later than Daniel actually recorded his vision in writing.

Andre Lacocque, in an attempt to update the discussion of the authorship of the apocalypticism of Daniel, considers the book to be a "complex amalgamation" of popular lore, renaissance of mythological imagery, mantic wisdom, prophetic imagination, scribalism, pietism, and apocalyptic eschatology. These features reflect stances of dualism, determinism, and priestly interests. Jewish Hasidism in its early stages also had influence. Cf. "The Socio-Spiritual Formative Mileau of Daniel Apocalypsy," *New Findings,* 316–43. Lococque exhibits a strong denial of Daniel's prophetic gifts and role during the period of international upheavals.

It is unfortunate that critical writers on Daniel ignore what has been written concerning the impact the study of the Daniel manuscripts discovered among the Dead Sea Scrolls has had. Cf. Gerhard Hasel's essay, "The Dead Sea Scrolls Have Provided a Wealth of New Material for Reassessing Opinons regarding the Book of Daniel," *Ministry,* 1979, 9–11. Hasel wrote that scholars holding to the late composition of the book of Daniel (167–164) have a difficult problem because the Scrolls date from the third century B.C. to circa A.D. 67. He referred to S. R. Driver, who argued that the Dead Sea Scrolls had to be dated later because, in so doing, the late date of Daniel could be maintained.

61. This is the *conclusion* emphasized by many commentators, cf. e.g., Baldwin, *Daniel,* 137; "the Most High is the reigning king in heaven and earth. There is no opposition to his rule." Keil, *Daniel,* "the everlasting kingdom is simply placed over against the kingdoms of this world," 269; Longman, *Daniel,* "the; major theme is, in spite of present circumstances, God will win," 202. It is difficult to follow Archer, "Daniel," who concluded that Daniel can be understood to pave the way for the battle of Armegeddon and return to reign as conquering king over all the earth (in the millennium).

62. Daniel continued to indicate his royal setting; he was in *habbîrâh* (variously translated as castle, palace, fortress, citadel). Goldingay points out that Daniel was in Susa, the fortress city, *Daniel,* 196.

63. Many commentators see the vision concerning the shaggy goat fulfilled by Antiochus who was defeated in time by Judas Maccabaeus (Dan. 8:23–25).

64. Cf., e.g., Baldwin, *Daniel,* 164, and Longman, *Daniel;* Hartman, *Daniel,* sets the date in 538. 240.

65. Daniel called on him who is the true God of heaven and earth. Cf. Young, *Daniel,* 184.

66. Cf. NASV, but RSV translated "terrible," and KJV, "dreadful."

67. The covenant in Daniel is studied in the following section, III.

68. Readers are again reminded that the seventy years can refer to the period between the first exile, 606 B.C., and the decree to return, 536 B.C., or to the destruction of the temple in 586 B.C. and its completed rebuilding in 516 B.C.

69. A brief study of the Messiah is made in section IV.

70. Cf. Baldwin's discussion in *Daniel,* 182–85.

71. Readers of Daniel 10–12 can receive aid in understanding these chapters by consulting commentators such as Baldwin, *Daniel;* Longman, *Daniel;* E. J. Young, *Daniel.* For an effort to present a combination of what critical and conservative scholars have written, see Goldingay, *Daniel,* on these chapters.

72. Cf. the study of the antithesis' origin and development in the author's *FCTC,* vol. 1, chap. 5, II, A.

73. Babylon was located on the east bank of the Euphrates River but Susa, capital city of Persia, was 150 miles east of Babylon and about 100 miles east of the Tigris River. The Ulai Canal (Dan. 8:2), may have been a waterway connected with the Tigris River. Daniel records that he was in Susa in vision. Scholars have debated whether Daniel was ever in Susa, other than by vision.

74. Cf. Keil, *Daniel,* 414.

75. Cf. Longman, *Daniel,* 250, for a discussion of this phenomenon. Young wrote that the "majestic Person here presented is none other than the Lord Himself." He added that it was an appearance of the preincarnate eternal son. *Daniel,* 225. For intertextual discussions concerning Daniel, Ezekiel, and the book of Revelation, consult commentaries listed above in various end notes.

76. Consult commentators such as Aalders, *Daniel,* 256–316; Goldingay, *Daniel,* 294–309; Longman, *Daniel,* 273–85; Lacocque, *Daniel,* 215–33; Young, *Daniel,* 231–53; for studies on how Daniel's prophecies were historically fulfilled in the subsequent three centuries. Note particularly how all consider Antiochus to be referred to as the king who exalts himself (11:36–39).

77. Cf. Wallace, *The Lord is King.* "The main point of the book of Daniel is that none of the elect will be lost." 194. Cf. also Keil, *Daniel,* "every one whom God has ordained to life, all genuine members of the people of God" will be in the Book of Life; they will receive the promised salvation, 480.

78. Cf. discussion of divine sovereignty and human responsibility by Longman, *Daniel,* 289–92.

79. Recall that Longman stressed this in his introduction to his commentary on *Daniel,* 20.

80. The Greek word for end is *eschaton,* meaning specifically "the last thing." Cf. study of these terms in *FCTC,* 1:11, 12.

81. Cf. chap. 22, Part III, B. Cf. also the sketch, which highlights the stages from the time of Isaiah's call when Judah's theocratic monarchy was still strong up to the end time, chap. 23; Part IV, G.

82. These words were spoken by Nebuchadnezzar and quoted by Daniel as absolute truth (4:34, 35). Darius spoke similarly (6:26, 27).

83. Archer wrote that Dan. 11:36–39 contains strikingly accurate predictions of the whole sweep of events from the reign of Cyrus" to the unsuccessful effort of Antiochus Epiphanes to stamp out the Jewish faith." "Daniel," 143. Once the prophecy was fulfilled, the time could be determined but not before because Daniel did not give the time for these events.

84. Dwight J. Pentecost, and others holding to the eschatological position he advocates, consider Daniel to be referring to Christ's second advent when he is supposedly to reign on earth during the millennium. *Thy Kingdom Come* (Wheaton: Victor, 1990), 305, 325. Here is a real problem: Daniel never referred to a millennium or to the Messiah reigning on earth. Pentecost misunderstands Rev. 20, and reads this misunderstanding into Daniel's prophecies as also into Isaiah's, Jeremiah's, and Ezekiel's and some of the Minor Prophets' messages.

85. Cf. Lacocque, *Daniel,* 178. This author, in the brief reference to the covenant, made more reference to the law, because Daniel referred to it four times, 9:5, 10, 11, 13. Young specified "that the law is to be regarded as an administration of the covenant of grace. *Daniel,* 16. Keil quoted the text, covenant of mercy (*ḥesed*) which has roots in Deut. 7:21. *Daniel,* 327. Archer referred to "their covenant with God" rather than God's covenant with his people. "Daniel," 108.

86. Consult the detailed chart that exhibits the covenantal epochs of both the creation and the redemptive covenant in *From Creation to Consummation,* 1:148, and in this volume, chap. 22, III.

87. Some commentators refer to what the Babylonian royal diet involved: no distinction between clean and unclean animals, no taboo on pigs. Horse was eaten, cf., e.g., Balwin, *Daniel,* 83.

88. Note the Hebrew terms Daniel used to describe the covenant people's religious response *ḥāṭṭā'* (offense against God), *'āwôn* (perversion), *mārad* (rebellion), *rāsâ* (guilt). Baldwin, *Daniel,* 165.

89. Goldingay referred to the special focus on Jerusalem (and Judah) because it was Judah who had remained faithful to David and the city continued to be the embodiment of Israel after the exile. *Daniel,* 247. There is an element of truth expressed here, but the emphasis in the prayer is on Yahweh's honor.

90. Commentators have used much paper and ink to interpret the "seventy sevens." Baldwin has presented a review of present-day interpretations. She cautions against predicting an exact time for any future event. *Daniel,* 172–78.

91. Cf. Keil's discussion on what seven refers to—days, weeks, or years. He concluded years is the only possible reference. *Daniel,* 338. Van Gemeren: "The exact identification of 'sevens' is open to interpretation. The emphasis is on the events and the certainty of the progression of redemption." *Interpreting,* 394.

92. Cf. Baldwin's succinct discussion of how to interpret the numbers. She concluded after reviewing efforts to give precise dates and pointing out irreconcilable problems involved, that "it is better to be consistent and to keep a symbolic interpretation of all the numbers." *Daniel,* 176. Cf. also Young, *Daniel,* 206. But cf. Archer, who made a rather torturous attempt to do so. *Daniel,* 112–18.

93. It is inconsistent to apply the last "three and half" of the last seven to an indefinitely long period between Christ's death and his second coming on earth. This position has been referred to as the gap theory or the unexpected "church age." For discussion of these views, cf., e.g., Aalders, *Daniel,* 214–34; Baldwin, *Daniel,* 172–78; Young, *Daniel,* discusses the parenthesis interpretation, 194. Lacocque's reference to the author's (he refers to a late author of Daniel) "factitious chronology" may be one way out of attempting to discover what Daniel was given to reveal, but Lacocque's entire approach to the authorship of the book of Daniel renders his interpretation of Dan. 9:24–27 unacceptable. *Daniel,* 177–80, 187–99.

94. Cf. Young, *Daniel,* 212. Baldwin, however, considers that the "prince who is to come" is an enemy of Yahweh's cause and he "forces an agreement by means of superior strength" (possibly referring to the Roman destruction of the temple, A.D. 70). *Daniel,* 121.

95. Cf. Archer, "Daniel," 113.

96. Cf. Baldwin, *Daniel,* 192–96.

97. Cf. Young, *Daniel,* 242; Keil, *Daniel,* who stresses the theocracy, 458–59; Goldingay, *Daniel,* covenant people, 279. It is of interest to note that Archer did not discuss the covenant. "Daniel," 135–39.

98. Cf. commentators referred to in preceding notes who without exception write concerning the fulfillment of this prophecy in the times of the Selucid dominance over Judah and Jerusalem.

99. Daniel's prophecies regarding the messianic Mediator, the Messiah, was discussed at some length in a previously written work. *MROT,* 788–846. Some salient points developed in that work will be briefly reviewed and some materials written since 1990 will be added.

100. Cf. *MROT,* 788–91. Note the comments that Daniel's life experiences were typical, at the very least by analogy, 791.

101. Cf. discussion of the term *māšîah* in *MROT,* 830, 837.

102. Goldingay, *Daniel,* 52.

103. Ibid., 60.

104. Cf. *MROT,* 806–7. To gain a fuller understanding of the author's interpretation and conclusion, consult the entire discussion, *MROT,* 708–807.

105. Goldingay, *Daniel:* "Nebuchadnezzar alone sees a divine being," 71.

106. Cf. *MROT,* 807–10 for an evaluation of each.

107. Historical records indicate that Belshazzar was co-regent with Nabonides. This co-regency commenced in 549 B.C., ten years before Babylon fell. Cf. Hartman and Dillela, *Daniel,* 30.

108. The beasts represented national authorities and power. In contrast, the thrones represented heavenly authority and power. This could be referred to as a reversal, or as antithetical.

109. See discussion of the Ancient of eays in *MROT,* 811–13. Take note of comments in notes.

110. Again the question in regard to the Son of Man appearing, is: does the scene take place in heaven or on earth? Cf. *MROT,* 812. Longman, when discussing the appearance of the one like the son of man, concludes that he cannot decide whether the scene is heavenly or earthly. *Daniel*, 186.

111. Cf. Bruce Chilton, "The Son of Man, Who Is He?" *Bible Review* 12, 96 (1996). "This visionary passage forms the heart of the book of Daniel."

112. Cf. discussion in *MROT,* 814–16.

113. The precise period of time referred to is difficult to determine. Archer considers "time" to refer to a year, "Daniel," 94. Young, *Daniel,* reviewed various interpretations and concluded that "this period . . . apparently stands for a period of testing and judgment which for the sake of God's people, the elect, will be shortened." Young did not give a specific time of duration, 162. Goldingay, *Daniel,* concluded that "for a time, and for a longer time, and yet more time" was a promise that a limit was set to this. 187.

114. Cf. *MROT,* 818–24.

115. Cf. discussion of parts of chap. 9 in the preceding sections of this chapter.

116. Cf. *MROT,* esp. 839.

117. Cf. ibid., 843.

II

The Golden Cable Explicated in the Postexilic Literature

28

The Challenge in Understanding Postexilic Literature

I. Common Confusion among the General Public

II. Possible Procedures for Study

28

The Challenge in Understanding Postexilic Literature

Common Confusion among the General Public

The General Public

This chapter is intended to address the challenge of understanding postexilic literature.[1] There are various reasons that could be stated as to why it is necessary to commence a study of postexilic literature with this introductory chapter. Among these reasons are the following. It has been observed that this literature has been the most neglected portion of the Old Testament. There is no book of the Bible that presents a unified historical overview of the postexilic period. The restored community is present but its relation to the preexilic times, events, and artifacts is not clearly and specifically spelled out.[2] There is also the question of the goals of the restored community. And it could be added that there is no evidence for the precise dating of some of the writings. The authors of the historical books do not give much data concerning their specific time.[3]

The Liberal Contribution to This Confusion

Various biblical scholars who do not consider the Scriptures to be divinely inspired, authoritative, inerrant, or infallible, have attempted to present the postexilic literature as a record strictly of human thought which sought to determine the purposes of God. This was presented in a diversity of patterns. Those scholars who considered the "Law of Moses" to have been written, or at least edited and finalized, during the postexilic period have exacerbated confusion to varying degrees. It was claimed that a Deuteronomic author rewrote, edited, and finalized the historical books of the Old Testament and did so as they were influenced by their "restored *Sitz im Leben.*" It was pontifically asserted that the Deutero-Isaiah (40–66) was written during this first postexilic period to engender hope.[4] And as has been referred to in the previous chapter, the book of Daniel has been dated in this period also.

The liberal critical dealing with postexilic literature has contributed to the lack of interest on the part of the public for various reasons. The first is that the literature has been made even more complicated than the biblical presentation. Furthermore, the material as it came and comes from the liberal critic's corner lacks relevance to contemporary readers. The reality for any general reader is that this biblical literature, as it is in the Old Testament, with historical repetition and isolated anecdotes, genealogies, and descriptions of building activities, do not lead to devotional reading except for some passages.

The Influence of the Apocalyptic Environment

After the exiles returned from captivity, they experienced social and political opposition and in time were involved in military situations. Apocalyptic interests and writings developed. The prophecies of Ezekiel and especially Daniel were available and lent to esoteric thinking and writings. Of the commonly accepted postexilic literature, only the prophecy of Zechariah includes much apocalyptic material, which is difficult to interpret and understand. The other material, though not apocalyptic, recorded the historical setting for esoteric thinking. The point to be stressed is that the inspired writers wrote as they were led, but they were in an environment that was not socially, politically, or militarily stable.

Possible Procedures for Study

The Historical Period

The historical time period that is covered by postexilic literature can be set out in two ways.

First, consider the actual time the authors lived. Haggai, the first to prophesy and write, is considered by various commentators to have been an old priest when he wrote in 520 B.C.[5] Due to the uncertainty, as demonstrated by various conservative authors concerning the actual times of Ezra, Nehemiah, and Malachi, one must be careful not to be apodictic about their specific time. One wrote that Malachi could have preceded Ezra and Nehemiah; the time span of these three could be from before 458 B.C. to 333 B.C.[6] Others wrote that Malachi could have been a contemporary of Nehemiah and likely wrote after Nehemiah returned to Persia or during Nehemiah's second time in Jerusalem, after 433 B.C.[7] We can conclude, then, that the actual time period in which the authors lived is from 610 B.C. (approximate time Haggai became a priest) to 430 B.C. (approximate time that Malachi wrote), or a total of 180 years.

Second, consider only the time period during which the prophets wrote. Since Haggai began to prophesy (and probably write) in 520 B.C. and Malachi prophesied (and probably write) in 430 B.C., the actual writing period was ninety years. During these years the rebuilding of the temple was completed and though Jerusalem was inhabited it was not securely established until the walls were rebuilt in Nehemiah's time.

In what order is one to consider the prophets to have spoken?[8] According to the dates given by Haggai and Zechariah, Zechariah began to prophesy before Haggai had given his third and fourth messages.[9] Zechariah prophesied again (and wrote) two years after he concluded the account of the visions with their prelude (1:1–8) and postlude (chaps. 7, 8). The prophecies of Zechariah recorded in chapters 9 through 14 were given in the time of Esther's experience in the palace of King Xerxes of Persia, in the years 492–475 B.C.[10]

As mentioned before, there is no agreement in regard to the order Ezra, Nehemiah, and Malachi were active in the restored covenant community. A common assumption is that Ezra was first; he wrote the book of Ezra and 1 and 2 Chronicles.[11] Then Nehemiah wrote about twenty years later, followed soon after by Malachi.

Order in Which Books Were Written

Haggai 1, 2 522 B.C.
Zechariah 1–6 522 B.C.
Zechariah 7, 8 516 B.C.
Esther 475 B.C.
Zechariah 9–14 474 B.C.
Ezra 450 B.C.
1 & 2 Chronicles 445 B.C.
Nehemiah 435 B.C.
Malachi 430 B.C.

Order of History of Revelation

1 & 2 Chronicles creation to 538 B.C.
Ezra 1–6 536 B.C.
Haggai 1, 2 522 B.C.
Zechariah 1–6 522 B.C.
Zechariah 7, 8 516 B.C.
Esther 475 B.C.
Zechariah 9–14 474 B.C.
Ezra 7–10 450 B.C.
Nehemiah 435 B.C.
Malachi 430 B.C.

In a biblical-theological study such as this book is, it is of vital importance that the historical period and context be clearly understood because Yahweh God revealed himself, his purposes, and his plan through the activities and lives of people as well as by means of the historical events in which groups of people and nations were directly involved.[12] In the preceding paragraphs the order in which the prophets and other writers wrote was described. In the following study, one could choose to follow the chronological order that the various authors appeared on the scene of history. To do so would involve either a reversion to authors discussed before or to repetition.

The Historical Sequence of Actual Revelation

If one limits one's study to the actual revelatory redemptive events recorded in postexilic literature as occurring in the ninety years of scribal activity, the order would be as follows. First would be a study of Haggai's preaching and the spiritual motivation to continue rebuilding the temple, followed by Zechariah's preaching to stimulate rebuilding and to remember to live covenantally (1–8). Then would follow the study of Yahweh's redemptive activity in the context of Mordecai and Esther, and Zechariah's assuring prophecies (9–14). Yahweh's guidance of and instruction and revelation through Ezra and Nehemiah would follow and Malachi's prophecies would be the last to be considered.

The postexilic writers, led, guided, inspired by the Spirit, placed their contemporary lives and experiences in the context of their predecessors. They reminded their audiences and readers that what was revealed and done in their time was a continuation of what Yahweh God had revealed and done from the beginning of time. Hence the Chronicler began with Adam, then to Noah and his sons, on to Abraham's family followed by Jacob's. Details concerning the royal houses of Saul and David were reviewed, especially of David, the covenant promises given him, his royal court, and death (1 Chron. 11:1–29:30). Solomon's temple-building activity and its dedication were described in detail. Then followed the recording of the division of the covenant people into two nations, the affairs of the royal families, and eventual exile because of the disobedience and sin of the people. The chronicler concluded his writings by briefly referring to the exile and Cyrus's decree permitting exiles to return to their homeland and Jerusalem their city (2 Chron. 1:1–36:23). Ezra began his book by picking up on Cyrus's edict and a description of who actually returned, how the altar was rebuilt, and how the rebuilding of the temple was begun (Ezra 1:1–4; 5). Ezra then introduced Haggai and Zechariah (5:1).

The chronicler's "review of what Yahweh God had revealed and done" is important for this study on the Golden Cable because the three concepts, kingdom, covenant, and mediator, are set forth as dominant elements in Yahweh God's revelation to his covenant people in their restored context.

The Procedure to Be Followed

The conclusion to this chapter then is that a study of 1 and 2 Chronicles, and of Ezra 1:1–4:5 should be considered first. Thus the context in which the further revelation concerning the kingdom, covenant, and mediator occurred is unfolded.

NOTES

1. Postexilic literature includes Haggai, Zechariah, Malachi, Esther, Ezra, Nehemiah, and 1 and 2 Chronicles.

2. A personal note: in the thirty-five years I served as a professor of Old Testament Studies I was continually made aware of how college and seminary students were mostly ignorant of what these postexilic books contained and, therefore, had no clear conception of their place and purpose in the Bible.

3. In 1946 J. Stafford Wright published a pamphlet entitled *The Date of Ezra's Coming to Jerusalem* (London: Tyndale). A reading of Wright's presentation gives some evidence that the Scriptures were not precise in referring to times and events. See Peter Ackroyd, *Exile and Restoration* (London: SCM, 1968), 236.

4. Ibid. A cursory look at Ackroyd's "Contents, VII–IX" presents a lineup of these critical liberal approaches. Cf. also what the author wrote in a previous work, *Messianic Revelation in the Old Testament (MROT)* (Grand Rapids: Baker, 1990), 848. See note 1, in which other critical writers are mentioned.

5. Joyce Baldwin in *Haggai, Zechariah, Malachi* (Downers Grove: InterVarsity, 1972), wrote that Haggai 2:3 implies he had seen Solomon's temple before it was destroyed in 586 B.C.

6. Ibid., 212. See Brevard Childs, *Introduction to the Old Testament as Scripture* (Philadelphia: Fortress, 1979) on the relation of Ezra and Nehemiah; he considered them as contemporaries and that they interacted, 634, 635.

7. See John Stek and Herbert Wolf in the *NIV Study Bible,* gen. ed. Kenneth Barker, (Grand Rapids: Zondervan, 1985), 1423.

8. The assumption is that the writing followed directly after the prophecy was spoken.

9. Haggai's dates are, second year, sixth month, first day of Darius's reign; he gave his first prophecy. Then the second year, seventh month, twenty first day, he gave his second prophecy (Hag. 1:1; 2:1). Then in the second year, in the ninth month, on the twenty fourth day, Haggai gave two messages (2:1, 10). Zechariah recorded that he first prophesied in the second year of Darius in the eighth month (Zech. 1:1, 7). Zechariah's visions began during the eleventh month of that same second year of Darius' reign.

10. The relationship between Xerxes's command to destroy the Jews and Zechariah's last prophecies will be developed more fully in a later chapter.

11. C.F. Keil wrote, when he reviewed the discussion concerning the author of the books of Chronicles, that these were not written before the time of Ezra because there is reference to Zeruabbel's progeny. *The Book of Chronicles,* trans. Andrew Harper (Grand Rapids: Eerdmans, n.d.), 22.

12. It is of interest to note that Brevard S. Childs, in his biblical-theological study, *Biblical Theology of the Old and New Testament: Theological Reflection on the Christian Bible* (Minneapolis: Fortress, 1993), has two references to 1 and 2 Chronicles, three to Ezra, and two to Nehemiah and only in the historical part regarding the origin of these writings, 159, 163.

29

The Golden Cable in 1 and 2 Chronicles

I. Introductory Comments

II. The Covenant

III. The Kingdom

IV. The Mediator

V. Conclusion

29

The Golden Cable in 1 and 2 Chronicles

Introductory Comments

Specific Studies on 1 and 2 Chronicles

John W. Kleinig wrote that the "Cinderella of the Hebrew Bible has at last emerged from years of obscurity and scorn." Though Chronicles is "not yet the belle of the academic ball" it has begun to receive long overdue attention.[1] He pointed out that Wellhausen's attention to 1 and 2 Chronicles in the nineteenth century was eclipsed by Deuteronomistic emphases, and this in turn waned until the decades of the 1990s. He hailed two scholarly writers who have opened up the minds of the scholarly world to 1 and 2 Chronicles.[2]

While it is true that 1 and 2 Chronicles have not received the scholarly attention that other biblical books have, it seems incorrect to point to only Japhet and Williamson as influential writers. Kleinig may have selected these because of their critical approach to and development of their views regarding these books. One wonders why he did not include Jacob M. Myers as a third influential author who wrote with a very critical perspective.[3]

There are some authors who have written from a generally conservative perspective. Five could be mentioned. While they are not agreed on various major points, they do encourage readers to consider 1 and 2 Chronicles as reliable, authoritative sources of divine revelation.[4]

Varying Views concerning Authorship

In the preceding chapter Ezra was mentioned as the likely author of 1 and 2 Chronicles. We have referred to the evidence that one author is considered as the writer of these books who did not write before the time of Ezra.[5] Ancient Jewish tradition considered Ezra to be the author of Chronicles. Some scholars suggest that Ezra is considered the single editor of the writings of various authors.[6] A commentator wrote that the vast majority of Old Testament scholarship has assumed that the greater part of 1 and 2 Chronicles is the work of one author. Not wishing to refer to a person by name, the author was referred to as The Chronicler.[7] In this chapter, the term *Chronicler* will be used predominantly instead of Ezra. Since there is no final positive evidence concerning who the author is, one must be careful not to be dogmatic when assuming Ezra was the author. When, however, one considers the purpose of writing the books of Chronicles, one can find reasonable support for Ezra as author. One reason is that the historical situation in the 450–400 B.C. period called for the assurances that 1 and 2 Chronicles presented to a harried people.[8]

The Purpose of 1 and 2 Chronicles

A consultation of various sources discussing the purpose the writer of Chronicles had in mind can be helpful but also somewhat disconcerting. Consider what has been written: (1) The writer/editors were of the same school as the author of the Priests' Code, which had covered only the worship of Israel before the nation entered the promised land. The Chronicler carried on the description of worship requirements while he simultaneously stressed the divine rule of God.[9] (2) Another writer concluded that the Chronicler was setting forth "principles" that he had uncovered in selected parts of the history of the covenant people. He is said to give evidence of "inventive storytelling," thus creating the effect he sought to produce.[10] (3) Still another writer wrote that considerable disagreement remains concerning the Chronicler's aim in writing his history. He rejected the critical assumption that the author "has cloaked his real intentions behind some tendentious handling of the sources." If one, however, takes the Chronicler at face value, then it is clear that the aim was to remind the restored community of God" that his eternal covenant continued to demand an obedient response to the divine law.[11] (4) A fourth writer, considering particularly "some characteristic themes," suggested that the Chronicler intended to assure the community that there was a definite continuity of the people, of the Davidic kingship, and of the temple and its worship.[12] (5) Another author, who dealt with purpose, emphasized the theological foundations that had to be brought to the attention of the restored and developing community. He listed seven foundational theological realities: (1) the theocratic character of Israel; (2) the place of David; (3) liturgy and Levites; (4) the united Israel, excluding the Samaritans; (5) eschatological perspectives; (6) emphasis on the antithesis; (7) the Holy Name.[13] There should be no doubt that one can, upon studying 1 and 2 Chronicles, agree that the Chronicler intended to emphasize these somewhat disparate themes. A scholar, who spent much concentrated study on 1 and 2 Chronicles, summed up the purpose of the Chronicler as follows: "The Chronicler wrote for the restored community. The burning issue was the question of continuity with the past."[14] Finally one can refer to John Goldingay, who considered "the Chronicler as a theologian." He posited the view that the Chronicler's main intent was to push the postexilic community to a proper realization of divine mandates concerning worship, purity, and obedience.[15]

A review of the content of 1 and 2 Chronicles assists one to more clearly see and understand what the Chronicler, under divine inspiration, communicated to the postexilic community. Note the sections: genealogies, the first three kings, the faithful and unfaithful Davidic kings in Judah, and finally the result of covenant breaking although seven kings had kept and obeyed the covenant.

Sketch I

1 Chronicles 1–9:34	Genealogies
1 Chronicles 9:35–10:14	Saul's genealogy, reign, death
1 Chronicles 11:1–29:30	David's reign (Hebron), Jerusalem, temple preparation
2 Chronicles 1:1–9:30	Solomon's reign and temple-building activities
2 Chronicles 10:1–14:1	Rehoboam and Abijah—covenant breakers
2 Chronicles 14:1–21:3	Asa, Jehoshaphat—covenant keepers
2 Chronicles 21:4–22:9	Jehoram, Ahaziah—covenant breakers
2 Chronicles 22:10–27:9	Joash, Uzziah, Jotham—quite faithful
2 Chronicles 28:1–27	Ahaz—covenant breaker
2 Chronicles 29:1–32:33	Hezekiah—covenant keeper
2 Chronicles 33:1–25	Manasseh, Amon—covenant breakers
2 Chronicles 34:1–35:27	Josiah—covenant keeper
2 Chronicles 36:1–14	Jehoahaz, Jehoiakim, Jehoiachin, Zedekiah—covenant breakers
2 Chronicles 36:15–21	Fall of Jerusalem—exile
2 Chronicles 36:22, 23	Cyrus's edict for return

Sketch II

Genealogies	1 Chronicles 1:1–9:34
Saul	1 Chronicles 9:35–10:14 genealogy, reign, death
David	1 Chronicles 11:1–29:30—reign in Hebron, Jerusalem, temple preparation
Solomon	2 Chronicles 1:1–9:30—reign, temple building, other activities
Covenant Keepers	*Covenant Breakers*
2 Chronicles 14:1–21:3 Jehoshaphat, Asa	2 Chronicles 10:1–14:1 Rehoboam, Abijah

2 Chronicles 22:10–27:9 Joash, Uzziah, Jotham	2 Chronicles 21:4–22:9 Jehoram, Ahaziah
2 Chronicles 29:1–32:30 Hezekiah	2 Chronicles 28:1–27 Ahaz
2 Chronicles 34:1–35:27 Josiah	2 Chronicles 33:1–25 Manasseh, Amos
	2 Chronicles 36:1–4 Jehoahaz, Jehoiakim, Jehoiachin, Zadok
	2 Chronicles 36:15–21 Fall of Jerusalem
	2 Chronicles 36:21, 22 Cyrus's edict

My personal continued study of the Old Testament Scriptures led me to realize, as referred to often in preceding chapters, that the author intended to demonstrate to the restored community that the Golden Cable's three strands that unite with the entire revelation of God, held firmly. These three strands provided unity to the prophetic messages and these also so function in postexilic revelation.[16]

Unity in the Presentation of History

A few comments should be included in the introductory section on the unity of the presentation of Israel's history. First of all, it should be remembered that no Old Testament writer intended to write a complete history of Israel. Second, the intent of the Old Testament writers was to present the specific revelation of Yahweh God particularly to the nation of Israel. Third, only those aspects of Israel's history were recorded that provided specific contexts for Yahweh God's revelation. Fourth, the writers of 1 and 2 Kings wrote in the historical context of their unique time. The Chronicler presented historical realities that were specifically relevant for the returned, restored, and struggling community as it faced its challenges approximately ninety to a hundred years after the return from Babylon. Fifth, there was no specific need to repeat verbatim all that had previously been recorded. In the later historical *Sitz im Leben* some aspects were repeated and others that had not been included previously were included because the historical situation at the time called for these. Sixth, it can therefore be considered, with confidence, that there are no contradictions or unnecessary omissions in the two biblical presentations of Israel's history. The two accounts are complementary; together they provide a fuller account, be it still partial, of Israel's history. Indeed, there is a real unity in the biblical presentation of the historical context in which the progressive revelation of Yahweh God was given.[17]

The Covenant

Most of the scholars referred to in the preceding section point out that the covenant is a major theme in 1 and 2 Chronicles.[18] Because of what had happened in the preceding 150 years the question undoubtedly came to mind: Is Yahweh

God's covenant with us still upheld and in force? Are we still Yahweh God's specific and unique covenant people? Are we correct to think and speak of Yahweh God as our covenant God who embraces us in his love? Does he still have great promises for us to be realized in the days and years to come?

The Term **Bĕrît** *in Political Contexts*

The term *bĕrît* appears thirteen times in 1 Chronicles and seventeen times in 2 Chronicles. It appears in different contexts and thus translators have employed various terms such as *compact* (NIV) or *pact* (Jerusalem Bible) to refer to the political agreement worked out between David and the people of northern Israel after Saul, their king, had died in battle with the Philistines (1 Chron. 10:8; 11:3). The terms *league* and *treaty* also appear. An instance of this is when the discussions between King Asa of Judah and King Benhadad of Syria are recorded. Benhadad had made a treaty with Baasha of northern Israel, and Asa sought to bribe the Syrian king with treasures from the temple so as to induce the Syrian king to break his treaty with Baasha (2 Chron. 16:3). The restored community could thus be reminded that political relationships could be made binding either in an acceptable covenant manner or in a situation of political intrigue. They, however, received repeated reminders of what the concept of covenant was intended to convey concerning the binding relationship between Yahweh God and his people. They also had to be instructed in honesty and faithfulness when making agreements in their turbulent times.

The Priests' Initiated Covenants

The term *bĕrît* appears three times in the recording of a tragic period in the history of Judah. It was when Queen Athaliah, daughter of Ahab, king of Israel, and wife of Judah's king Jehoram, vented her rage against the Davidic house. Her son, Ahaziah, had followed Jehoram as king and was killed. Athaliah then tried to kill the entire royal house of Judah. But the priest Jehoiada hid one son, Joash. When still very young, he was made a child-king, and he ruled under the skillful guidance of the priest Jehoiada. As priest he led the making of three covenants at the time Joash was made king and thus restored the throne to David's house. The first covenant was basically a binding agreement with Jehoiada and the military commanders in Judah (2 Chron. 23:1). Then the second covenant was set up between the assembly of the people and the child-king (23:3). The third covenant, initiated by Jehoiada the priest, was between himself, the child-king, and the people; in this covenant it was established that they, the three together bound by their covenants, would be Yahweh God's people (23:16).[19]

The biblical-theological significance of this account as recorded by the Chronicler must not be overlooked. First of all, it must be emphatically stated that the three covenants are not to be considered new and isolated covenants. They are signs, or better, strong reminders of the covenant God had made with the patriarchs, with Israel, and particularly with David. In a real sense, there was a renewing of the one, eternal covenant. Second, it is important to realize that the

Chronicler records that a high priest led in this covenant-renewing activity. This was of particular importance for the restored community in Jerusalem and Judah. The people were without a Davidic king; the Persian king ruled over them. The high priest, however, could function as a covenant-renewing and -maintaining agent in the absence of an anointed ruling Davidic king. Yahweh God's eternal covenant, as upheld throughout history, was continuing to be maintained and remained in force.

The Abrahamic Covenant

The Chronicler reminded his community of how there had been a second placing of the ark of the covenant in a tent.[20] When David had become king over all Israel, and had established Jerusalem as the royal city, he prepared a tent for the ark of the covenant (15). When the ark was placed in the tent (16:1), he ordered Asaph and his choir to sing a psalm of thanksgiving which he had obviously arranged by using parts of three psalms.[21]

David was a covenant-conscious king. He wanted his people to know and remember that Yahweh God had confirmed his covenant with Abraham, their forefather. When the covenant was confirmed Yahweh God had assured Abraham of three realities: he would have a seed, he would have a place to live and worship, and his covenant Lord would be with him and his progeny. David claimed these promises for himself and for his people when he became king over all Israel.

The Chronicler included this reference to the Abrahamic covenant, confirmed with Isaac and Jacob (16:16). The restored community was reminded that as great changes took place, as when Israel had to make a new beginning under David, Yahweh God's covenant with Abraham was upheld and in force for the restored community. Yahweh God had not forgotten; he had not permitted the covenant with Abraham and his progeny to lapse. As David had sung, Asaph had sung, so the restored people were called to sing *zikĕrû lê 'ôlām bĕrîthô* (Yehwah our God remembers forever his covenant) (16:14, 17), specifically, confirmed *'et 'abrāhām . . . yishāq . . . ya ' ăbqōb* (with Abraham . . . Isaac . . . Jacob).

The Davidic Covenant

The restored community, experiencing a number of challenging problems,[22] did not have their own king, that is, a Davidic dynastic king, reigning over them to represent, lead, and protect them. The Persian king ruled over them. His throne and presence were far away. In these circumstances the question could very reasonably and understandably be raised: Is Yahweh God's covenant with David abrogated and forgotten? The Chronicler is led to give the community assurance that the same covenant made with their forbears, the patriarchs, was still upheld and applicable in their time. The promise of the eternal dynasty was not forgotten.

David received much attention from the Chronicler. In this study, his role as a covenant man will be discussed in this section, his specific role as a kingdom man and as a mediatorial agent will be discussed in parts III and IV of this chapter.

An important truth that the restored community had to remember was that Yahweh God had established and confirmed an eternal covenant with David.[23] The people had to be reminded of who David was. The Chronicler singled out David's ancestors from among Judah's descendants. Hezron, a son, became a direct ancestor of David through his son Ram's descendants Amminadal, Nashon, Salmon, Boaz, Obed, and Jesse. David was Jesse's seventh son (1 Chron 2:3–17). David's ancestry was firmly established. He was definitely of the tribe of Judah of whom father Jacob had prophesied that through and from him a royal ruling son was to eventually come forth (Gen. 49:8–12). The Chronicler then "carefully traced down to the Chronicler's own time" David's genealogy.[24] This genealogy goes to the approximate year of 420 B.C.[25] Questions have been raised as to why the "list of Davidides" was stretched over eight generations beyond the exile. Was it that Davidic nobility played a prominent role in the restoration? Was it an expression of hope for a future political restoration? The text is silent in regard to these questions in this part of the Chronicler's account.[26]

The Chronicler directly and specifically referred to the covenant Yahweh God had made with David. He did so in the context of what Jehoram, a Davidide, did. He was the firstborn son of Jehoshaphat the king of whom it was written he did right in the eyes of the Lord (2 Chron. 20:32). But son Jehoram married Athaliah, Ahab's daughter; and when he had firmly established himself as king he killed all his brothers and some princes in Judah also (21:4). Then by way of introducing how Yahweh God kept his covenant with David, "to maintain a lamp for him and his descendants forever" (21:7), the Chronicler recounted how Yahweh God struck down Jehoram with a lingering disease so that he died after reigning only eight years (21:14, 15).

This account was a strong and lucid reminder that Yahweh God was a faithful covenant keeper. Although no descendant of David was on an earthly theocratic throne, it was not meant to be understood that the covenant had elapsed or was abrogated. During very dark days, in the time of Jehoram and Athaliah, Yahweh God had kept his covenant; he kept a lamp burning and bright. This covenant was still upheld; it was in force. The promised descendant was to come, but he was not named in this context.

David established himself as a covenant man; he kept covenant and worked out the requirements of the covenant in regard to the cult. When Yahweh God confirmed his covenant with David, he was not specifically commanded to deal with the ark of the covenant, a home for it, and the personnel to be involved in the temple and the worship to be rendered in it. David knew that his sovereign covenant Lord should have a permanent residing place (1 Chron. 17:1, 2). And, as also recorded in 2 Samuel 7:1–8, the Chronicler briefly recounted that not David but his son was to build the temple of the Lord (17:14). David, however, had the worship of Yahweh God continue before the tabernacle he had erected in Jerusalem under the leadership of Zadok the high priest and his fellow priests. These priests and Levites carried out their duties as Yahweh God had instructed Moses they should. Levitical personnel also were ordered to supply the musical aspects of worship (15:16–22).

David, the covenant man, was not content and at ease. Since his son was to build the temple, he had all the preparations made for this. Foreigners were ordered to assist (1 Chron. 22:1), and provide supplies (22:4). He divided the Levites into their prescribed orders, as Moses had done (Num. 4). He organized musicians, sons of Asaph, Heman and Jeduthan, to accompany the proclamation of the word.

The Chronicler also included what Solomon did once he became king. He carried out all that David had planned. Thus God-honoring worship was instituted and provision for its continuity was in place.

The question has been implicitly raised: why did the Chronicler include the material recording David's activities in regard to the temple and all that was involved with it? One writer wrote that the Chronicler wished to "legitimate the proper order of temple personnel, especially in times of national and cultic renewal."[27] Another wrote that the Chronicler wanted to evoke the proper response within the restored community—a prayerful response that breathes joyful faith and single humility.[28]

It should be obvious to anyone who studies the historical situation of the post-exilic community that, as it sought to rebuild, reestablish, and renew their cult they would be well served to be reminded of what Moses had prescribed and how these prescriptions stood as legitimate directors and guidelines for all time. David and Solomon, faithful covenant servants, had the conviction that Yahweh God demanded full obedience to his requirements for worship. So David and Solomon had obediently carried out Yahweh God's will in their specific and unique historical situation. It had been a time of new beginnings in the theocratic context. What Moses, under Yahweh God, had prescribed for desert wanderers, for inheritors of the promised land, was not only relevant for but was required to be carried out in a kingdom context. Even though the theocratic kingdom had ceased to exist Yahweh God's covenantal demands for worship were not abrogated but were always to be carried out. They could be, they should be, and would be a covenant community that was called to worship as the covenant Lord had revealed centuries before.

The Ark of the Covenant

In the preceding paragraphs reference was made to David's desire to be a faithful, worshiping, covenant king. Hence, he considered the need for a dwelling place, the prescribing of personnel to lead in worship, and the appointing of personnel for various other priestly aspects of worship. At the very core of all these prescriptions and preparations for proper covenant worship was the *'ārôn bĕrît yĕhwâ* (the ark of the covenant Yahweh [1 Chron. 15:25]).

The ark of the covenant had played an important role when Moses was given the prescription for the tabernacle and its furnishings (Exod. 25, 26, 30, 31, 37, 39, 40). Aaron was to approach it, only on the Day of Atonement (Lev. 16:2). It was referred to when procedures were given for moving from place to place in the desert (Num. 3:31; 4:5). Reference was made to Moses appearing before it to speak with Yahweh (7:1, 4). The ark of the covenant was to lead the people in the desert when moving and halting and moving again (10:33, 35). When the ark did not accompany the military in desert warfare, the Israelites were defeated (14:44). When Moses recounted what Yahweh had required and done for Israel before they entered the promised land, he referred to the ark a number of times (Deut. 10:18; 31:9, 25, 26). These deuteronomic references were reminders that the ark and the law of Yahweh were not to be separated. In the account of Israel's preparing to enter the promised land, the ark had an important role (Josh. 3:4, 6; 7:6; 8:33). In the time of Samuel the role of the ark was repeatedly referred to. It was captured by the enemy and returned in an unusual manner (1 Sam. 4:6). David had an active role in bringing the ark to Jerusalem (2 Sam. 6) and it went along with him when he fled from Absalom (15:24–29). When Solomon had built the temple, the ark of the covenant was brought into it (1 Kings 8:1–9, 21).

The Chronicler did not refer to the earlier part of the ark's place and role in the life of Israel. The first reference to it is when he referred to David appointing men in charge of the music once the ark was placed in the temple (1 Chron. 6:31). The Chronicler retold with some detail why and how David brought the ark into Jerusalem (13:1–14; 15:1–16:43).

Three questions call for answers. The first that requires a clear reply is: How is the ark described? The answer lies in the term used to refer to it. It was the *hā 'ārôn* (the ark) that had been given rest by David (6:31). It was the *'ārôn 'ēlōhênû* (ark of our God), according to David (13:3–14; 15:1, 2), and the *'ārôn yĕhwâ* (ark of Yahweh) [15:3, 12]) but in that same context he referred to the *'ārôn 'ĕlōhîm* (ark of God [15:15]) after he referred to the *'ārôn yĕhwâ 'ĕlōhâ yi`srāēl* (the ark of Yahweh God of Israel. The Chronicler continued to refer interchangeably to the ark of God and the ark of Yahweh (16:4, 6), in the latter instance he referred to the *'ārôn bĕrîth hā'ĕlōhîm* (the ark of the covenant of the God). Moses had referred to the ark repeatedly by the phrase *hā'ārôn 'et hā 'ēdat* (the ark of the testimony). The tabernacle was also repeatedly referred to by the term testimony (*hā 'ēdut bĕ 'ôhel* [Exod. 30:36; 38:21]). The Chronicler also referred to the tent of the testimony (2 Chron. 24:6). Considering the various terms employed to refer to the ark (the Hebrew terms literally mean a box, chest, or coffin); it was Yahweh God's unique chest with a specific covering and made to contain objects that were reminiscent of what Yahweh God had said and done.

The second question to be answered is: What was the purpose of "the ark?"[29] An immediate answer could be: to represent the covenant Yahweh God had confirmed with Israel, and with David particularly.[30] This statement is true, but it requires explanation. (1) The covenant referred to the bond of life and love Yahweh God had established with his people. The ark thus spoke of Yahweh God's constant presence with his people. The ark represented Yahweh God himself. It had a definite sacramental message.[31] (2) It served as a symbol of Yahweh God's throne. Yahweh God was the King of Israel. This was to be emphatically presented, believed, and obeyed (2 Sam. 6:2; 1 Chron. 13:6). This throne represented sovereignty and power, as depicted by the cherubim. It was a throne that had mercy as its seat and grace as a dominant virtue. (3) The ark containing the two tablets of stone, referred to as the "testimony," kept the declared laws of Yahweh in the midst of the people. The manna and Aaron's rod were in it to serve as messages of Yahweh God's wonderful provisions for his people. (4) The ark was a constant reminder that Yahweh God was a redeeming sovereign Lord. This was demonstrated particularly on the Day of Atonement when the high priest was to sprinkle bull and goat blood as a symbol of Yahweh God cleansing his people from their sin (Lev. 16:2, 13, 14, 15, 30).

The Chronicler recounted what role the ark had had in David's reign, and its place in the temple and in the worship of Yahweh God. The ark was a central and very significant part of Israel's covenantal, spiritual, worshiping heritage.

The third question is: Where was the ark when the Chronicler wrote concerning it? The answer has to be: it was not in the rebuilt temple.[32] There was no indication anyone knew what had become of it. Jeremiah had prophesied while the Solomonic temple still stood that a future time when true faithful shepherds led the covenant people, there would be no calling for the ark; it would not enter their minds or be remembered. It would not be missed or replaced (Jer. 3:16). Commentators have offered various interpretations. Maybe Jeremiah was prophesying concerning the future kingdom of Christ. Another proposed that when Judah and Israel were united, the people of Judah would no longer boast of the ark as their specific blessing.[33]

The ark of the covenant, the chest with cherubim on it, the written law, and the Torah was irretrievably lost. The restored community, however, had to remember their history and heritage. They were a covenant people. Yahweh God's covenant, with all of its aspects, was not abrogated. All that the ark had signified was still a precious certainty for them. They would, however, be called upon to exercise their faith and obedience as a covenant people without the aid of a visual symbol. The restored covenant community, reminded of their heritage, had to demonstrate that the maturation process expected of them was taking place.

David's Royal Progeny and Covenant Renewal

Four references to covenant keeping by David's ruling descendants should be mentioned. The Chronicler continually reminded his contemporaries of the history of their royal house.

First, the Chronicler did not hesitate to recount how unfaithful Davidides had broken the covenant through their disobedience and idol worship. Apostasy characterized the life of King Rehoboam, son of Solomon. Under him, the northern tribes had seceded and he reigned over Judah, Simeon, and Benjamin, the tribes that constituted the kingdom of Judah. When his southern kingdom was established he had become strong. He *'āzab 'et tôrâh yĕhwâ wĕkol yiśrăēl immo* (forsook the Torah—Yahweh and all Israel with him). When Rehoboam and his people[34] forsook the Torah of Yahweh, he rejected the covenant Yahweh God had confirmed with David. The Torah was, it must be remembered, the body of instructions for covenant life, service, and worship. Yahweh God punished Rehoboam at the hand of Shishak of Egypt (2 Chron. 12:1–4).[35] After the prophet Shemaiah proclaimed that Yahweh had abandoned them, the king and princes *yikkānĕ 'û* (humbled themselves) and confessed that *śaddiq yĕhwâ* (Yahweh is righteous) [12:6]). The Chronicler concluded that *bihûdâh hāyâh dĕbarim tôbîm* (in Judah were good things).[36] Abijah, Rehoboam's son, did not continue with "good things." He committed the sins of his father and his heart was not right with Yahweh (1 Kings 15:3). The Chronicler, however, wrote that the priests remained faithful to Yahweh (2 Chron. 13:10–12), and Abijah was quoted as saying, "God is with us," reciting the covenant phrase stressing Yahweh God's promise. Jehoram, son-in-law of King Ahab of Israel, was a tragic covenant breaker; he killed all his royal brothers and some princes (21:4–20). Ahaziah, son of Jehoram, continued the covenant breaking of Jehoram (22:1–9). This covenant breaking continued by Athaliah and by Joash in his later years as king. Amaziah, his son, did not wholeheartedly follow in the ways of David (25:2). Some generations after Amaziah, Ahaz was not faithful to the covenant (28:1–25), nor was his grandson Manasseh (33:1–20), nor Amon, Manasseh's son (33:21–24). The last kings of Judah, Jehoahaz, Jehoiakim, Jehoiachin, and Zedekiah, were covenant breakers. Judah was destroyed because of the sins of unfaithful kings. The Chronicler did not spare the covenant-breaking descendants of David. Yahweh God was proclaimed to the restored community as a faithful covenant Lord who carried out the curse of the covenant. The Chronicler, however, did not omit reference to faithful kings.

Second, the Chronicler wrote in some detail about Asa and his son Jehoshaphat (13:1–21:3). Asa brought in reforms but was not always wise and faithful and he died from a disease in his feet. His son Jehoshaphat followed in the ways of David. Yahweh was with him and established the kingdom of Judah under him (17:3–5). Jehoshaphat's heart was devoted to the ways of Yahweh; he ruled wisely, and powerfully and gained victories. He did not hesitate to pray for guidance and success (20:1–29). He became rich and before his death he gave gifts to his sons. Jehoram, his oldest son, succeeded him; he did not follow in his father's ways; rather, he followed Ahab, Jezebel, and Athaliah of Israel.

Third, the Chronicler recorded how Joash, Amaziah, and Uzziah were inconsistent in their following in David's footsteps. They did some good things, but did not wholeheartedly serve as faithful covenant kings. Their descendant Hezekiah, however, was recorded as a model covenant-keeping servant. Hezekiah rejected the ways of his sinful father Ahaz, who had shut the doors of the temple and set up altars in Jerusalem's streets for worship of other gods. The Chronicler recorded that Ahaz had provoked Yahweh the God of the Fathers to anger (28:24, 25). Hezekiah was presented as following in the footsteps of David. He demonstrated what a covenant-obeying king of David's house should be and do.[37]

The Chronicler recounted how Hezekiah had restored and purified the temple. He gathered the Levites, commanding them to consecrate themselves and the temple. The king informed them, *'attâh 'im lĕbibî likĕrôt bĕrît layhwâh 'ĕlōhê yîsrāēl* (and now it is in my heart[38] to be cutting covenant with Yahweh God of Israel [29:10]). Hezekiah was intent on renewing the covenant Yahweh God had confirmed with Israel at Mount Sinai and with David and Solomon. An integral aspect of the covenant, the love/life bond, was the presence of Yahweh God (symbolized by the temple) and his worship by the people, led by the priests and Levites. Hezekiah also restored the celebration of the Passover (30:1–26). Under Hezekiah, a cleansing of the land became a reality (31:1). He had contributions gathered for the renewed temple and worship (31:2–26). The Chronicler confirmed what the writer of 2 Kings 18:3–6 had written, that Hezekiah was a great king; there was "none like him." He was indeed a second "Saint David."[39] The Chronicler did not expand on the circumstances in which King Hezekiah led; the repatriated community may have known these. The point to consider is: covenant renewing and upholding in its aspects must be realities in whatever circumstance pertains.

Fourth, the Chronicler devoted two chapters to young King Josiah. His reign followed that of his extremely wicked grandfather, Manasseh, and wicked father Amon. While at a young age, sixteen, he sought the God of David (2 Chron. 34:3), and when he was twenty years old he purged Jerusalem and Judah (34:3b, 7). When he was twenty-six years old, he gave orders to repair the temple (34:8–13). During this repair work the Book of the Covenant was recovered. When Josiah learned what this covenant book contained about the curse to come on unfaithful covenant people because of the sins of his immediate forbears, he called together the leaders and the people and read to them what was written in Deuteronomy. It was confirmed by the prophetess Huldah that the curse detailed in the Book of the Covenant was surely to be executed. He had been assured that the curse would not be executed in his lifetime because he humbled himself (34:23, 27; nevertheless he *yikĕrôt 'et habbĕrîth liphnê yĕhwâ* (he cut, i.e., renewed the covenant before, as in the presence of Yahweh). It was not just a formal ceremony. He vowed to follow Yahweh, to do what was involved in covenant life. He would obey (34:29-31). He did more; *wayya'ămēd'ēt kōl hannimĕṣā' bîrûsalayîm* (and he caused to stand all those present in Jerusalem). Commentators have translated this phrase in various ways.[40] The point is, Josiah made all those present vow that they would obey all that the covenant required. The Chronicler then added that they did not fail to follow Yahweh. Furthermore, Josiah had an unusual feast of the Passover on which the Chronicler commented that the Passover had not been observed in such a way since the days of Samuel (35:18).

It should be repeated: the Chronicler reviewed portions of the history of the kings of Judah, emphasizing the failures and the positive service of David's royal descendants. All were evaluated according to the demands of Yahweh God's covenant and declared good or evil according to the obedience rendered. This obedience was particularly emphasized in relation to the worship of the covenant Lord. This worship included the presence of the house of Yahweh (the temple), the service conducted according to stipulations, and the daily service for and walk with Yahweh God. The restored community had a meaningful covenantal heritage. It was theirs to know, appreciate, love, and work out accordingly.

Yahweh God Remembers His Everlasting Covenant

An important point to emphasize is that the Chronicler would have the people of his time know, and keep in remembrance, that the covenant referred to was Yahweh God's covenant. David, in his psalm of thanks, had sung that Yahweh God remembers his covenant forever to thousand generations (1 Chron. 16:15). He specified that this remembered covenant was the very one Yahweh God had made with Abraham, Isaac, and Jacob. The Chronicler stressed that Yahweh God's remembering would never end. He remembers forever; therefore, his covenant would never end; it was an everlasting bond of love and life, which included all the elements of the covenant.[41]

Solomon followed his father David. When the temple had been built and the ark of the covenant was placed in it he included a meaningful reference to the covenant Yahweh had made with Israel (2 Chron. 6:11). Solomon confessed that there is no God like Yahweh God in heaven or on earth: *šōmēr habbĕrît wĕhaḥesed* (keeping, act. ptc. of *šāmar)*, indicating continuity, the covenant, and love.[42] He, in this context, also referred to Yahweh God keeping his promise to David (6:16), and this promise included the *ḥesed* promised to him (6:42).

Again, it bears repeating. The Chronicler's audience was given reminders that Yahweh God's covenant continued for all time and in all circumstances. What Yahweh God had covenanted from the very beginning, confirmed with Noah, the patriarchs, David, and Solomon, was very much a real love/life bond with them. Yahweh God was their covenant Lord; they were his covenant people.

The Seed/People of the Covenant

Legitimate questions can be asked of the Chronicler, namely, was his main interest to address the people whose forefathers were citizens of the nation of Judah?[43] Or did the Chronicler, acknowledging that the covenant people had existed for years as two separate nations, basically consider the postexilic community to represent all the tribes? That is, did the Chronicler consider the community to be one people? The evidence as recorded in the text clearly reveals that the Chronicler considered Israel to have been one people,[44] people of the one covenant Yahweh God had confirmed with the patriarchs and with David and Solomon.

It has been pointed out by most commentators on 1 and 2 Chronicles that the Chronicler referred to the northern nation only when it was necessary to indicate its effect on the southern kingdom. A quick overview of the two books reveals the following. The first nine chapters record partial genealogies of Abraham and the twelve sons of Jacob. The family of Judah is set out in greater detail than the others (1 Chron. 2:3–4:23). The family of Levi receives more attention than the others also (6:1–80). These two tribes had been given greater covenant roles and responsibilities in the life, service, and worship of the Israelites. Up to the time of the schism (after Solomon's time), they had functioned accordingly. Neither David's house nor the Levitical priesthood functioned in the northern kingdom; the men who were kings and priests there were not covenantally appointed, hence the Chronicler did not include them in the "covenantal genealogy." David received the most attention (10:1–29:30). His role in the organization of personnel for temple service and the preparation for the building of the temple was emphasized as a reminder to the postexilic community of their covenantal heritage. David's dynasty was reviewed in 2 Chronicles. All those who reigned are discussed. Faithful kings received most attention: Asa (14:2–16:14), Jehoshaphat (17:1–23:4), Joash (22:16–24:27), Hezekiah (29:1–32:33), and Josiah (34:1–36:1).

The Chronicler evidently was inspired by Yahweh God to record that the covenant Lord had maintained the seed of the woman (Gen. 3:15), of Noah via Shem (1 Chron. 1:17–27), of Abraham (1:28–2:1), of Judah (2:2–55; 4:1–21), of David (3:1–9), and of his dynasty (3:10–16). The Chronicler made a point of tracing David's seed line right up to the time he wrote (3:17–24).

The Chronicler did not record what took place after Jerusalem's fall and Cyrus's edict permitting exiles to return to Jerusalem and Palestine (2 Chron. 36:15–23). Hence he did not record who returned. Ezra, who is believed to have been a contemporary of the Chronicler (if not the Chronicler himself), did provide a partial list; most of those he mentioned were from Judah, Benjamin, and Levi (Ezra 2:1-63). No mention is made of descendants of most tribes, but the Chronicler recorded that some men from Asher, Manasseh, and Zebulun had humbled themselves and heeded Hezekiah's call to come to Jerusalem (2 Chron. 30:11). Likewise, after the northern kingdom had been exiled, men from Ephraim, Manasseh, and the remnant of Israel assisted in the temple's repair under Josiah (34:9).

On the basis of specific tribes referred to by the Chronicler and his fellow writers, the postexilic community consisted predominantly of people who had been, or were descendants of, the tribes of Judah, Simeon, and Benjamin—the preexilic nation of Judah. There are, however, some passages in postexilic writings that could give evidence that most if not all of the thirteen tribes were represented in the postexilic covenant community. Yahweh God had maintained his covenant and a remnant of his covenant people.

The Kingdom

In the Chronicler's writings the covenant Yahweh God had established and reconfirmed repeatedly is the dominant theme of the three in the Golden Cable. He wanted to impress upon the postexilic community that had been in surrounding countries for eighty to ninety years that Yahweh upheld his covenant with them. They were descendants of their covenant forebears. They were strongly reminded of their covenant heritage. The question now is: since the covenant was an integral aspect of the cosmic kingdom and of the theocratic kingdom, did the covenant continue to function within a kingdom context? After all, the theocratic monarchy no longer existed. Was the covenant then upheld in a nontheocratic kingdom context? In a vacuum, as it were?

The Theocratic Kingdom under the Davidic Dynasty

One commentator on Chronicles referred to the theocratic monarchy as the kingdom of God. The temple Solomon built was called a blueprint for God's kingdom. Jehoshaphat was named God's Royal Lamp.[45] There is a definite effort made to identify the temple and the Davidic kings with the kingdom of God. Yet it is not clear how these are to be understood as related.

There should be no doubt that the Chronicler was concerned to remind the postexilic community concerning the theocratic monarchy over which David and his royal followers had reigned. This monarchy had a basic theocratic character in that Yahweh God was its sovereign King. He had given the kingdom to David and his successors. But Yahweh God had removed the royal house from the throne of Judah. In reality, Yahweh God had removed the theocratic monarchy from the face of the earth. The Chronicler wrote "God handed all of them over to Nebuchadnezzar, king of Babylon" (2 Chron. 36:17). The writer of 2 Kings 21:12–15 had stated it clearly: due to the sins of Judah, Yahweh God would wipe out Jerusalem. Nebuchadnezzar carried out Yahweh's word.

The Restored Temple

The temple had been an integral aspect of the theocratic monarchy. David had prepared for it to be built. Solomon, his son, had built it. It, in a real sense, had been Yahweh God's palace; the ark of the covenant in it was Yahweh God's throne.[46] When Nebuchadnezzar destroyed Jerusalem, the temple was also destroyed. The ark/throne completely disappeared. The symbol of Yahweh God's reign was gone. The city and nation in which the symbol had resided was gone. The theocratic monarchy, Judah/Israel, as a kingdom no longer existed. David's dynasty no longer reigned. The Chronicler did not give any hope to the postexilic community that the theocratic monarchy would be restored.

Prior to the time that the Chronicler wrote, the temple had been rebuilt.[47] He had referred extensively to the building of the Solomonic temple.[48] The point to stress now is that the symbol of Yahweh God's throne, the ark of the covenant, was no longer present. Did that mean that Yahweh God no longer reigned? That he was not the restored community's King?

The temple continued to be the symbol of Yahweh God's covenantal presence. It would function as such until after Jesus Christ's ascension and the temple's total destruction by the Romans in A.D. 70. What did continue, without a break, was the covenant. And it should be kept in mind that the covenant was established and reconfirmed repeatedly before the theocratic monarchy was formed. Yahweh God had exercised his sovereign guidance, rule, and control over Israel when the people were still in Egypt, when wandering in the desert, and when conquering and possessing the promised land as their inheritance. The Chronicler definitely conveyed the message that Yahweh God had been faithful to his people as their sovereign King throughout all time—whatever the circumstances had been.

Yahweh God's Continued Reign

The Chronicler did not use the phrase "the cosmic kingdom." He did, however, give much evidence of the reality that Yahweh God was the sovereign Lord of the entire creation and ruled over every aspect of it. A survey of some references will give ample evidence of this.

King Saul had been an unfaithful covenant vicegerent.[49] He ignored the word of Yahweh God. He consulted the witch of Endor for guidance (1 Sam. 28:7–19). The Chronicler stated cryptically that he did not seek Yahweh. Therefore *wayĕmîtēhû* (hiph. impf. of *mût,* he caused him to die). Yahweh demonstrated that he was sovereign over life and death. Yahweh directed the events on the battlefield between the Philistines and Israel.

The Chronicler wrote that David knew Yahweh had established him as king. King Hiram's contribution to the materials for building the temple led David to this conviction. Yahweh God had inclined the king of Tyre, a noncovenant king, to assist David (1 Chron. 14:1, 2). David, in a psalm of thanks, expressed Yahweh God's lordship over the cosmic kingdom. He sang that all nations should hear of Yahweh God's wonderful acts and his judgments in the earth (16:8–14). All nations were to fear, for he made the heavens (vv. 16, 20) and he reigns. All should call upon him because he is a God of strength, of glory, of splendor and majesty, of holiness and love. It must be repeated with emphasis: the Chronicler held before the postexilic community that their covenant Lord was the King of the cosmos and they were his kingdom people; they were to acknowledge, praise, serve, proclaim, and worship him as such.

As David had come close to the end of his life, and he had witnessed how the people of Israel had contributed in preparation for the building of the temple, he prayed a beautiful prayer. A commentator has written that David had ransacked the theological dictionary, "piling up terms for God's sovereign power."[50] David acknowledged that Yahweh God owns the world; he is its king, he is the source of human wealth, and he gives power to human beings to do his will (28:11, 12).

One phrase requires attention in the context of discussing the kingdom: *kî—kol baššamāyîm wûbā'areś lĕkî yĕhwâ hammamĕlākôh* (because all in the heavens and in the earth "are" to you Yahweh the kingdom). The term *kingdom* stands as the term that includes all of heaven and earth over which Yahweh God reigns. He reigns over the cosmos; the cosmos is his kingdom. He owns it; he rules over it; he dispenses to men parts of it for purposes that fulfill his claim to glory and honor.[51] For David, the more wondrous and assuring reality was that he as king of the theocratic monarchy was under the reign, guidance, provision, and love of Yahweh God, who had created and upheld the universe.

Before David died, he counseled and admonished his son Solomon, who was to reign after he died, that he acknowledge, seek, and serve "the God of your fathers" (28:9). Solomon, seeking Hiram's help, stated that his God was greater than all other gods (2 Chron. 2:5). Hiram, not a devoted servant of Yahweh God, did, however, acknowledge that Yahweh God *'āsâh* (made) the heavens and the earth and that it was Yahweh who had given the throne to Solomon.

Another foreign king was brought to the attention of the restored community. The Chronicler wrote that Solomon's son Rehoboam *'āzab 'et tôrâh yĕhwâ* (forsook the law [revealed will] of Yahweh). The prophet Shemiah told Rehoboam that since he had forsaken Yahweh, Yahweh would abandon him to Shishak, king of Egypt. The account tells of Shishak's entering Jerusalem but not totally destroying the city because Yahweh's anger turned from humbled Rehoboam. The message is clear: Yahweh God had final control over Jerusalem and over Shishak, one of the most powerful rulers at the time.

A member of the Davidic dynasty who remained faithful to Yahweh God expressed in clear words that he served the God of his fathers *môšal bĕkol mamlĕkôt haggôyîm* (who was the ruler, act. ptc. of *māšal,* to rule, over the kingdom of peoples/nations). Jehoshaphat confessed in prayer that Yahweh God had power and might, making him invincible. As Yahweh God had demonstrated his invincible reign when Israel conquered the promised land, so Jehoshaphat was assured he was the Lord who would give victory over the Moabites, Ammonites, Meunites, and Edomites (2 Chron. 20:1–12).

Another clear evidence of Yahweh God's kingship over the cosmic kingdom is recorded in 2 Chronicles 36:22–23. Yahweh God had proclaimed by Jeremiah that the exile was to last for seventy years. At the end of that period, Cyrus, king of Persia, made a declaration that the temple was to be rebuilt and anyone wishing to work on that could go back to Jerusalem. It should be understood that Cyrus was not aware of Jeremiah's prophecy. He, however, acknowledged Yahweh God as having given him all the kingdoms of the earth and he *pāqad 'ālây libĕnôt lô bayet* (appointed me to build to him a house). In Ezra 1:1 it is stated *hê'îr yĕhwâ 'et—rûah kōreš* (Yahweh caused to rouse—hiph. pf. of *'ûr,* to rouse oneself). Yahweh God had stirred the heart or had awakened Cyrus to the task of rebuilding the temple and proclaiming an edict permitting exiles to return to Jerusalem. None other than the King of the universe, the Ruler over all, and the knower and controller of hearts, minds, and actions of earthly kings, was again revealed to the covenant community existing in Jerusalem and former Judah and Israel.

The restored community had to know and believe that Yahweh God, who had established and reconfirmed his covenant repeatedly, was their eternal King. The theocratic monarchy, which had been a realistic symbol of the cosmic kingdom, was gone for all time. But that which it had symbolized and represented was an ever-abiding eternal kingdom. As the covenant that had been established at the time of creation, and the redemptive covenant that was inaugurated after the fall, was an integral, eternal part of it, so was the kingdom context within which the covenant operated. The restored community, with its temple in Jerusalem, was not only a covenant community, they were a kingdom community kept and provided for by the everlasting Adonai, Yahweh God!

The Mediator

The Narrower and Wider Conceptions

In a previously published book, I called attention to a distinction scholars have made when explaining and applying the idea of the anointed One, the Messiah, the mediator; namely, the narrower and wider conceptions. The narrower emphasized the person, a royal and serving person representing Yahweh God, the Father and the Son. This person could be either the Son, the promised anointed One, the Christ, or a royal person typifying and representing him. The wider conception was understood to include the promises, qualifications, activities, goals, and results of the anointed One.[52]

The Chronicler used the terms *anoint* as a verb (2 Chron. 22:7) and the *anointed one,* an adjectival form as a noun, twice—once to refer to prophets (1 Chron. 16:22) and once to refer to David (2 Chron. 6:42). Prophets and David served as mediators between Yahweh God and the covenant community. The prophets spoke on behalf of Yahweh God, and David (and his progeny) ruled under Yahweh God.

David's and Solomon's Royal Position

David and Solomon received more attention from the Chronicler than any other persons did. These men were covenantal vicegerents—they were not vice-regents. They did not reign in Yahweh God's stead but under him. As such, both were mediators who stood between Yahweh God and the people.

Cyrus, Yahweh's Servant

The Chronicler referred briefly to Cyrus, king of Persia. He had prepared and published the edict giving the exiles freedom to return to their homeland. Isaiah had prophesied that Yahweh God would consider and call Cyrus to be his undershepherd who would proclaim "let Jerusalem be rebuilt." Isaiah had proceeded to refer to Cyrus as Yahweh God's "anointed." Cyrus would be commissioned and enabled for the sake of Jacob, Yahweh's chosen servant (Isa. 44:28–45:5). The Chronicler records that Yahweh God influenced Cyrus to carry out what Isaiah had prophesied. Cyrus was truly a mediator who typified Christ, even though Cyrus did not personally know Yahweh God's person, plan, and goals (45:2, 3).

The Eschatological Dimension

The Chronicler made no mention that David's dynasty would be resurrected at the time he wrote.[53] In the genealogical listings he had referred to the royal line present after the exile (1 Chron. 3:17–24). The reason for this was undoubtedly that the restored community would be assured that David's progeny were still alive and with them. It was of great eschatological relevance and importance that the people were assured that the dynasty of David was present and recognized. Yahweh God's promise to David stood—his house, kingdom, and throne would endure forever (2 Sam. 7:16). Although there was no theocratic monarchy that David could actually reign over, an earthly kingdom, the Davidic kingship continued. His great eternal descendant, the messianic Mediator, the eternal royal One, the everlasting anointed One, the Christ, even in his preincarnate state, was reigning with the Father.

Conclusion

The three strands of the Golden Cable are integrated and form a continuous presentation[54] of what Yahweh God, the eternal King, did on behalf of his covenant people. The restored postexilic community was given strong reminders of what their heritage was and continued to be. Yahweh God's eternal covenant included them; Yahweh God administered his cosmic kingdom, ever mindful of his covenant people who were redeemed through the redemptive aspect of the eternal covenant. This administration involved nations which, in various ways, were employed by Yahweh God to be a means of judgment and blessing to the people. This covenantal administration was often executed directly by human agents, called and appointed by Yahweh God.

NOTES

1. In the previous chapter I wrote that the postexilic literature was not well known and that little attention had been given to it. John W. Klienig has attempted to demonstrate that 1 and 2 Chronicles have received some attention in recent decades. He listed sixty- six titles written between 1900 and 1989, but these either discussed nonpressing issues or did not make an impact in the scholarly community.

2. Kleinig referred to Sara Japhet, *The Ideology of the Book of Chronicles and Its Place in Biblical Thought,* trans. Anna Barber (New York: Peter Lang, 1994 [1989]). Japhet had published various essays previous to publishing the book. In an essay entitled "The Historical Reliability of Chronicles," *Journal for the Study of the Old Testament* 33 (1985), she pointed out what Spinoza and De Wette, by early 1800 wrote; the latter "directly aimed at disproving the reliability of Chronicles." 83. She reviewed a rather long list of critical scholars who did not consider Chronicles to be historically reliable. She concluded, "we are still looking forward to a broadening study . . . that will enlighten our use of the book of Chronicles as a source for the history of Israel," 99. Japhet, a Jewish scholar, is obviously most interested in the history of Israel rather than in what Chronicles adds to the recorded history of divine revelation. He also referred to G.H.M. Williamson, *1 and 2 Chronicles, The New Century Bible Commentary* (Grand Rapids: Eerdmans, 1982). Although both of these were written in the 1980s, they, along with essays written by these authors, came to a fuller attention in the decade of the 1990s.

3. Jacob M. Myers, *1 and 2 Chronicles,* Anchor Bible, vol. 12 (Garden City: Doubleday, 1965).

Recently various writers have written essays dealing with some aspects of 1 and 2 Chronicles, e.g., Simon J. De Vries, "Festive Ideology in Chronicles," in *Problems in Biblical Theology,* ed. Henry T. C. Sun and Keith L. Eades (Grand Rapids: Eerdmans, 1997), 104–24, stated that 1 and 2 Chronicles was composed in the fourth century B.C.E. He employed a type of literary criticism to produce four schemes that he considered forming a narrative framework. The fourth scheme was the "Festival" he referred to in chaps. 7, 15, 29, 30, 33 in 2 Chronicles. One could question if five festivals scattered throughout the book provide a scheme. De Vries was correct when he wrote that these five festivals were not merely descriptive but were prescriptive for the postexilic community: 124. A Jewish essayist, Ehud Ben Zvi, studied various Jewish sources, e.g., Esdras, the Testament of Moses, the Ascension of Moses, 4 Maccabees, Baruch, the Prayer of Manasseh, Qumran documents, and writings of Pluto and Josephus and searched for references to 1 and 2 Chronicles. He concluded that he found little reference to 1 and 2 Chronicles, and also concluded the authors did not consider 1 and 2 Chronicles to have much, if any, authority. He wrote that Deuteronomic writings, 1 Samuel–2 Kings, were considered more authoritative. Zvi's essay: "The Authority of 1–2 Chronicles" *Journal for the Study of the Psudepigraphy* 3 (1988): 55–88.

4. The five authors with a generally conservative perspective are: Leslie C. Allen, *The Communicators Commentary 1, 2 Chronicles* (Waco: Word, 1987); Roddy L. Braan, *1 Chronicles Word Bible Commentary,* vol. 14, (Waco: Word, 1968); Raymond Dillard, *2 Chronicles, Word Biblical Commentary,* vol. 16 (Waco: Word, 1987); John Goldingay, "The Chronicler as a Theologian," *Biblical Theological Bulletin* 5 (1995): 99–126; and Michal Wilcox, *The Message of Chronicles* (Downers Grove: InterVarsity, 1987).

5. Cf. note 10 in chapter 28. See the comments concerning Ezra as author in *MROT*, 916. The critical scholar, Edward L. Curtis, wrote in *The Books of Chronicles,* ICC series (Edinburgh: T & T Clark, 1910) that there are three reasons why it is correct to assume that Ezra is the author: (1) the ending of 2 Chronicles and the beginning of Ezra are the same; (2) both books have the same general character; (3) both books exhibit a degree of similar linguistic peculiarities; 2–5.

6. A careful scholar, Leslie C. Allen, wrote after considering various times suggested by scholars for the writing of 1 and 2 Chronicles, that he prefers the time to have been sometime during the fourth century, but he did not name the author. *1 and 2 Chronicles* in *The Communicator's Commentary,* vol. 10 (Waco: Word, 1987), 18. A. Noordtzy, in *Kronieken,* vol. 2, (Kampen: Kok, 1938), after a careful consideration of a wide range of views wrote that he cannot accept the view that 1 and 2 Chronicles (as well as Ezra and Nehemiah) could have been written before 400 B.C., most likely 300 B.C. after the Persian Empire had fallen. 29. I. W. Slotki wrote that since 1 Chronicles 3:19–24 enumerates "six or more generations after Zerubbabel lived, the book could not have been written earlier than 350 B.C., but Ezra could have begun the book and it was really written later by a priest or Levite. *Chronicles* (London: Soncino, 1952), XI. H.G.M. Williamson wrote in *1 and 2 Chronicles,* in *The New Century Bible* (Grand Rapids: Eerdmans, 1982) that he preferred a Levitical scholar who wrote about a century later than Ezra did. 17. Michael Wilcox, *The Message of Chronicles* (Downers Grove: InterVarsity, 1987), supports Williamson's position. 13.

7. Cf. Roddy Braun, *1 Chronicles,* in *Word Biblical Commentary,* vol. 14, xix.

8. Cf. chap. 30, in which the historical context of Ezra is discussed.

9. Curtis, *Chronicles,* 8, 9. Curtis's position is vitiated by his acceptance of the "four document hypothesis" as developed by Wellhausen and his associates.

10. Wilcox, *Message,* 16, 17. It is unfortunate that Wilcox presents the view that the Chronicler was not always reliable in his handling of historical realities. Because the writer of 1 and 2 Kings did not include all details of Israel/Judah's history does not mean that the details he and chronicler added were invented.

11. Brevard S. Childs, *Introduction to the Old Testament as Scripture* (Philadelphia: Fortress, 1979), 643, 644. Childs's reference to the covenant and the law is laudable; his

position concerning a very late date and his view of the Chronicler's use of sources raise questions and detract from his position concerning the covenant and obedience to the law. 645.

12. Williamson, *1 & 2 Chronicles,* 24–28.

13. Roubos, *1 Kronieken,* 11–15.

14. See Raymond Dillard's summary of 1 and 2 Chronicles in the *NIV Study Bible,* gen. ed. K. Barker (Grand Rapids: Zondervan, 1985), 578–80.

15. Goldingay, "Chronicler-Theologian."

16. In my previous work, *MROT,* while concentrating on the messianic concept revealed in 1 and 2 Chronicles, I referred to three themes the Chronicler stressed: the covenant, the temple, and the royal house. 615–619. In this work developing the three strands, the three I stressed previously will be included in the broader and inclusive approach and an understanding of postexilic literature.

17. C. F. Keil wrote that neither the genealogical material nor the history of the twelve tribes was given a perfect review. It was the intent of the Chronicler, according to Keil, to teach how the Lord rewarded fidelity to his covenant and therefore the writer selected certain parts of Israel's history by which he would remind the restored community how faithful maintenance of communion with their covenant God would assure fulfillment of the gracious promises made in times past. *The Books of Chronicles,* trans. Andrew Harper (Grand Rapids: Eerdmans, n.d.), 1, 2.

It should be understood that those who apply historical criticism to the biblical text usually bring confusion and uncertainty, e.g., Roland E. Murphy, "Reflections on a Critical Biblical Theology," in *Problems in Biblical Theology,* ed. Henry T. C. Sun and Keith L. Eades (Grand Rapids: Eerdmans, 1997), is correct to write that historical criticism, in biblical studies, has received a generous share of criticism. 265. One reason is that it can never reach its goal, which is to approximate the precise historical past, 265–74 (of course not: no accepting of an inspired record) yet he wrote concerning the wrong-headedness of putting aside the assured results of historical criticism. 272.

18. Japhet refers to the covenant in various contexts but always, as a subpoint under what she considered to be the major themes. Cf. her outline, *Ideology* ii–iii. She referred to the covenant as a relationship described by "choseness." 87. In various contexts she referred to the covenant, especially the covenant with David. In her concluding chapter she wrote that the covenant relationship is an everlasting and unchangeable bond. This bond covenant was part of the very blueprint of creation, part of the world's natural order. 50. R. Mark Shipp in "Remember His Covenant Forever," in a study of the Chronicler's use of the Psalms, *Restoration Quarterly* 35, no. 1 (1993): 29–39, argued that the Chronicler intentionally appropriated and strategically placed quotations from and/or references to the Psalms, 30. The quotations stressed reminders of Yahweh God's promises of faithfulness to his covenant. The Chronicler placed these reminders in contexts of corporate temple worship, temple dedication, crises, persecution, and deliverance, so that the restored community "could rely on God for covenant faithfulness because he is good." 31.

19. Wilcox, *Chronicles,* presented a concise summary of this covenanting action. 209.

20. Moses had been the first to place the ark of the covenant in the newly constructed tabernacle (Exod. 40:21).

21. The psalm, as recorded in 1 Chron. 16 includes parts of Psalms 105:1–15; 106:1, 46, 47; and 90:1–13. In the Book of Psalms no authors are mentioned for Psalms 105 and 106. Moses is the author of Psalm 90.

22. These problems will be discussed in the following chapter.

23. The Chronicler briefly but succinctly recorded Yahweh's making the covenant with David (1 Chron. 17), but the tenor of the covenant is not mentioned in this context. Cf. Allen, *1 Chron.,* 19, who wrote that David was Judah's most favorite son and that David is the key to Judean history and hopes.

24. Braun, *1 Chronicles.* Cf. his genealogical sketch, 52.

25. Ibid., 55.

26. H. W. Nel, in "The Davidic Covenant in 1 and 2 Chronicles, A New Theme for an Old Song," *In Die Skriflig* 28, no. 3 (1994), wrote that he considered 1 and 2 Chronicles to have their origin in discussions by a group of exegetes who, while in exile, met annually during the so-called Kallah month (the month of assembly). Their main subject was "the chosen people" and David's lineage in regard to kingship. They also discussed the Cult. 429–44. Nel did not indicate sources for his views, though he included a bibliography, which does not readily lend itself to include reference to the "Kallah Exegesis Group." He is correct, however, to stress that the Davidic covenant is an integral theme throughout the Chronicler's writings.

27. See essay by John W. Wright, "The Legacy of David in Chronicles: The Narrative Function of 1 Chronicles 23–27," *Journal of Biblical Literature* 110, no. 2 (1991): 233–34.

28. Williamson, *1 and 2 Chronicles,* 185.

29. See my brief discussion of the ark of the testimony in *From Creation to Consummation,* vol. 1 (Sioux Center: Dordt, 1996), 359–60, 442–43. Also Marten H. Woudstra, *The Ark of the Covenant from Conquest to Kingship* (Phillipsburg: Presbyterian and Reformed, 1965).

30. Cf. Wilcox, *Chronicles,* who presented four features concerning the ark: (1) its characteristics; (2) the attention it deserves; (3) the truth enshrined; and (4) the promises concealed in it, 65–75.

31. Cf. J. B. Payne, "The Ark of the Covenant," in *The Zondervan Pictorial Encyclopedia of the Bible,* ed. Merrill C. Tenney, vol. 1 (Grand Rapids: Zondervan, 1975), 367.

32. Payne, "Ark," referred to Josephus, *War,* vol. 5, who had written that the ark was not in the rebuilt temple. Payne added that today's Jewish synagogues are equipped with "arks" located on the side that faces "toward Jerusalem." 310.

33. Cf. John Calvin, *The Prophet Jeremiah,* vol. 1, trans. John Owens (Grand Rapids: Eerdmans, 1950), 182, 183.

34. The phrase *kol yi`srāēl* should be understood to refer to the three tribes, Judah, Simeon, and Benjamin. The northern tribes, known as Israel as a rule in distinction from the southern tribes, had also rejected the Torah under the leadership of Jereboam, who had appointed his own priests for high places and for the goat and calf idols (2 Chron. 11:13). It should be noted that the text refers to Levites and priests, as well as to some people in the northern tribes who remained faithful to Yahweh and migrated to Judah (2 Chron 11:17) Japhet presents a detailed discussion. Cf. "The People of Israel," chap. 3. She wrote that the use of "all Israel" and not just "Israel" to indicate the northern kingdom shows that the expression was used flexibly, depending on the context. 276.

35. J. W. Slotki wrote, "Neglect of God's Law by Rehoboam and his subjects had its sequel in an attack upon the land by the King of Egypt." *Chronicles* (London: Soncino, 1952), 213.

36. A commentator translated the term *dĕbarim* (some things). Allen, *Chronicles*, 267. Roubus wrote that the keeping of the king "*rust vooral op de dĕbarîm tôbîm*" (rest especially on the good *things*). *Kronieken II,* 132.

37. Wilcox, *Chronicler,* "Hezekiah went right back to David and Solomon, to the roots of his kingdom's life and worship," 245. Williamson, emphasizing the temple work of Hezekiah, wrote that Hezekiah was a "second Solomon," *1, 2 Chronicles,* 350. Allen stated

that the purpose of the Chronicler's account of Hezekiah's work was to remind the restored community that though Yahweh God had been angry with their forefathers, they were still heirs of the prophetic message so they should not be negligent but get on with the work of being faithful to Yahweh God. *1, 2 Chronicles*, 373.

38. Keil, *Chronicles,* wrote explaining the term *kārat* (cut) and *lĕbibî* (to the heart). "Hezekiah wishes to make a covenant . . . i.e., to renew the covenant with Yahweh by restoring his worship." 449.

39. W.A.L. Elmslie, in "The First and Second Book of Chronicles, " *The Interpreters Bible,* 12 vols., ed. G. W. Buttrick (Nashville: Abingdon, 1954), 3:519.

40. The term *wayya'amēd* is the hiph. of *'am̄ad,* to stand, translated, "cause to stand," "pledge," "vow." The term *hannimăṣā'* is the niphal ptc. of *māṣa',* usually translated "to attain" or "find." The Chronicler used the term to refer to those present in Jerusalem.

41. David referred one of the aspects of the covenant—the place to live in the inherited land of Canaan (1 Chron. 15:18).

42. The NIV translated the three terms "you who keep your covenant of love." Myers, *II Chronicles,* translated "who keeps covenant faith," 32. Elmslie translated the phrase "who keepest covenant and showest mercy" (injecting showest), 456. Allen translated "you who keep your covenant and mercy," *Chronicles,* 225

43. Williamson has written that since the early days of critical study of Chronicles, it has been recognized that these books "contain a distinctive approach to the question of Israel as the people of God." It seems that it is an overstatement to say that the Jewish people at the time lacked a precise definition of the extent of their own community. *Chronicles,* 24.

44. Braun, *1 Chronicles,* wrote that the Chronicler's strongest statement of his "all Israel" theme includes "groups of warriors from all tribes of Israel, north and south" who came to transfer the kingdom of Saul to David. 171.

45. Allen, *Chronicles,* The Kingdom Come, 1 Chron.17:1–20:8. 120. A Blueprint, 2 Chron. 8:1–9:31. 242–50. God's Royal Lamp, 2 Chron. 21:1–23:21. 313–23.

46. Cf. discussion of the ark of the covenant in Part II, Ezra 1:1–6:22.

47. Cf. study of Haggai and Zechariah 1–8:23, chap. 30.

48. Cf. 1 Chron. 22–2 Chron. 7:22.

49. Keil, *Chronicles,* wrote that Saul's death sentence was given by Yahweh as the judge. 173. Roubos suggested that the Chronicler may not have read the account in 1 Sam. 25 properly because it was stated there that Saul had asked Yahweh for guidance and did not receive a reply. Roubos wrote "nog harder klinkt" (still harder sounds) that the Chronicler wrote "Hij deed him sterven" (he caused him to die). *Kronieken I,*. 178.

50. Allen, *Chronicles,* 191.

51. Commentators disappoint any reader who looks for a discussion of the term *kingdom.* Some, e.g., Curtis, Myers, and Roubos, do not refer to it at all. Allen, Braun, and Williamson refer to the term but do not explain or apply it.

52. *MROT,* 19, 20.

53. This positive statement is made knowing that some scholars studying 1 and 2 Chronicles have written that belief in and longing for a messianic Davidic monarchy are central to Chronicles and that the entire orientation of the book in fact is eschatological. As Japhet wrote, these efforts were and are not too successful. *Ideology of Chronicles,* 493–501.

54. A reminder: the various themes that Roubos saw in 1 and 2 Chronicles (cf. note 13) and that were selected as the dominant themes: (1) *Yhwh,* the God of Israel; (2) the worship of *Yhwh;* (3) The people of Israel; (4) kingship; (5) the hope of redemption (*Ideology, I–III*) are essential elements of the three strands.

30

The Golden Cable Upheld in Early Postexilic Times

I. The Historical Context

II. Haggai's Prophecy

III. Zechariah 1–8

30

The Golden Cable Upheld in Early Postexilic Times

The Historical Context

This chapter covers the historical period from the time of Cyrus's edict permitting the Israelite exiles to return to Jerusalem and surrounding areas. The time was 538 B.C. to 514 B.C., when Zechariah prophesied in response to queries he received after the temple was rebuilt.

Ezra's Account

A reader of Ezra's entire book will soon realize that Ezra did not personally witness what he wrote in the first six chapters. Chapters 7–10 record Ezra's personal experiences. The authorship and reliability of Ezra are subjects that call for study and discussion.

The question of authorship has given rise to various opinions.[1] A reading of a scholar's work, such as that of Peter Ackroyd, leads one to wonder if Ezra wrote only part of the book ascribed to him and if he did, did he write in 398 B.C.?[2] Or was there an historical person known as the Chronicler who wrote or edited works of others?[3] Or was Ezra, the scribe, the author of Ezra–Nehemiah and 1 and 2 Chronicles? This was the view held by W. F. Albright.[4] That there are differences in the conclusions arrived at by scholars is believed to be due to the reality that the authorship of Ezra and Nehemiah is one of the most difficult problems in Old Testament research.[5] The view accepted in this study is that Ezra was the author of the book of Ezra. He employed sources when he wrote the first six chapters. A review of literary style and historical circumstances in which Ezra was involved, according to chapters 7 through 10, present convincing evidence for Ezra the scribe as author of the book of Ezra.[6]

The reliability of Ezra's account is inextricably bound up with the question of authorship. Since I prefer the view that Ezra himself was the author of the book, I consider his work to be reliable. He was a Spirit-inspired author who recorded why the exiles, under leadership of certain personnel, returned to Jerusalem.

The reliability of Ezra has been questioned for several reasons. Writers have wondered if his literary style, vocabulary, and references to historical events give cause for doubt.[7] A writer who entitled his essay, "The Myth of the Empty Land," has stated a much stronger case against the reliability of Ezra.[8] He posited a parallel between the Israelite occupation of Canaan under Joshua that called for the purification of the land by eliminating the pagan inhabitants. This purification had to be repeated by the exiles, who were returning to a land that was not empty of settled inhabitants. The author wrote that "for many generations scholars, as well as ordinary readers of the Bible, have tended to take the literature at face value." But the essayist considers the writings under Ezra's name as "reflections of cultic theology." These were written in conjunction with an attempt to set forth the value of the temple.[9]

It would seem far more preferable to accept the account written by Ezra as reliable. It presents an historical account, be it largely in an anecdotal style, of what transpired over a period of approximately a hundred years, from 538 B.C., when Cyrus issued his edict, up to the time of the city's complete restoration and the purifying of the covenant community by the removal of noncovenantal wives.

As indicated in the preceding paragraphs, Ezra's writings should be considered historically as a reliable account. Cyrus did issue the edict permitting the return of the exiles to Jerusalem to rebuild the temple. The king indicated that treasures taken years before were returned. He listed what these were (Ezra 1:7–11). He listed the names of people, basically leaders of the exiles and those who accompanied them (2:1–60). Temple servants were particularly singled out, even those who could not find their family records (2:61–63). All the people who returned did not settle in Jerusalem; after they gave their gifts for the temple to be rebuilt they went to settle "in their towns" (2:68–70). The altar was rebuilt in its former place, sacrifices were offered on it, and the rebuilding of the temple was begun. There was joy when the foundations were laid but sadness and loud weeping by the older returnees who remembered the Solomonic temple's structure and beauty (3:1–13). Ezra then recorded how opposition had arisen and increased, during the time of Cyrus and of his successor Darius. People who had lived in the land, and were basically enemies of Judah and Benjamin, initiated this opposition. Their offer to help rebuild the temple was rejected by the "political leaders," Zerrubbabel, and the cultic leader (priest Joshua). This help was rejected because they were syncretistic worshipers (2 Kings 17:27–40). By 536 B.C. the rebuilding had stopped. Ezra recorded how the prophet Haggai was instrumental in the continuation of the rebuilding. Cyrus was gone. Tattenai, governor under Darius of an extended area which included Judah/Benjamin, wrote a letter in which he requested Darius to issue an edict to stop rebuilding. The king, however, ordered the opponents to help pay expenses involved in rebuilding. Darius's edict was based on Cyrus's earlier edict (Ezra 4:1–6:12). This edict from Darius provided the historical context in which the prophets Haggai and Zechariah prophesied.

Before delving into a study of the books of Haggai and Zechariah, some questions should be answered. It has been stated that Ezra introduced the historical setting for the work of Haggai and Zechariah.[10] Does this historical account present a clear and acceptable setting and reason for the prophet's messages? The answer is definite: he did. Ezra recorded the edict for the exiles to return; he gave the names and functions of those who returned. Ezra recorded the initial efforts to rebuild and the opposition to it.

The second question is: Did Ezra present a theological as well as historical context for the prophets? Jeremiah had prophesied concerning the return and rebuilding (Jer. 29, 30). It had been the word of the Lord that Jerusalem was to be rebuilt (30:18). And Yahweh God had demonstrated his sovereign rule over Cyrus by moving him to issue the edict that the temple was to be rebuilt (Ezra 2).

The third question, closely related to the second one, is: did Ezra contribute, explicitly or implicitly, to the three strands of the Golden Cable? If the presence of the terms *kingdom, covenant, mediator,* is to be considered the only evidence, then one must admit that these terms are not always stated explicitly. When, however, the content of Ezra 1–6 is carefully studied, then one must conclude that Ezra joined in the continued development of the Golden Cable. It can be said he did so in a positive manner. And he did so by unobtrusively integrating the three strands.[11]

Ezra presented his message in a kingdom context (1:2). Yahweh God was the sovereign King who moved his servants to work in a mediatorial role on behalf of his covenant people—the remnant that returned to Jerusalem and the areas of Judah and Benjamin. Cyrus and Darius, kings of Persia and rulers over Jerusalem and environs, issued decrees that brought the remnant back, according to Yahweh God's purposes. They also, as agents of Yahweh God, provided the material means (1:9–11; 3:7), which are all aspects of the cosmic kingdom, for the rebuilding of the temple and for the resuming of covenant worship (3:3; 6:16–23). This divinely ordained reality of restoring covenant worship by the covenant community proved the context for five covenant agents, mediators representing Yahweh God to perform their roles.

Zerubabbel, a Davidic descendant, served as the political leader and had much influence over the community. Shesbazzar, referred to as *hatrĕšata'*[12] (a Persian term meaning governor) (2:63), was the one with whom Cyrus' treasurer entrusted the treasurer of the temple (1:11). Shesbazzar may have been another name for Zerubbabel, or he may have been an assistant to him.[13] The third covenant agent-mediator was Jeshua, a descendant of the Aaronic priesthood. And as mentioned before, Haggai and Zechariah were given the prophetic role and task to proclaim Yahweh God's word to a fearful and hesitant covenant people (5:1). These prophets inspired Zerubbabel and Joshua to initiate the continued building of the temple.

Zerubbabel had an important role; he was a member of the Davidic dynasty. He, with the high priest Joshua, had to exert leadership. Yahweh God had covenanted with David, as will be referred to later. It is important to remember that Yahweh God had also covenanted with the Aaronic house. When Yahweh God had covenanted with Israel he called for the building of the tabernacle—where his presence would be symbolized and the covenant promise, "I am with you," would be realized. In that context Aaron and his sons were ordered as priests (Exod. 28). Their dress and paraphernalia were carefully prescribed. These prescriptions were concluded by the statement, "This is to be a lasting ordinance for Aaron and his descendants" (28:43). This priesthood, conferred upon Aaron and his progeny, was an integral aspect of Yahweh God's covenant with Israel. This became very evident when the curse of the covenant fell upon Nadab and Abihu because of their unfaithfulness as priests (Lev. 10:1–3). Eleazar and Ithamar continued the Aaronic priesthood.

Later, when Israel was prepared to cross the river Jordan, quite a number of Israel's men committed immorality with Moabite women. They broke covenant by committing this disobedient deed. One Israelite man boldly took a Moabite woman into his tent. Phinehas, son of Eleazar, grandson of Aaron, in jealousy for faithful covenant living and especially for the honor of God, killed both the adulterers. In response to this sanctifying deed Yahweh God declared that he, Yahweh God, *"nōtēn lô 'et bĕrîtî sālôm"* (I am giving to him my covenant of peace) and it was to be *bĕrît bĕhunnat 'ôlām* (a covenant of a lasting priesthood). Thus the priesthood was a confirmed covenant with Aaron's descendants. The priestly lineage extended to Joshua, compatriot of Zerubbabel. He was the son of the high priest Jehozadak (Hag. 1:1), who had been deported as an exile to Babylon. Jehozadak was a direct descendant of Eleazar. Hence Joshua was a priest who held a specific covenant role as high priest. It was altogether fitting that Joshua took a leading role as high priest by covenant in the restoration of the temple and the prescribed worship in it.

The thrust of Ezra's message (chaps. 1–6) was that Yahweh God, sovereign Ruler of his cosmic kingdom, moved kings and leaders to build the temple so that Yahweh God's symbolic dwelling would be rebuilt, that the covenant people could reinstitute worship according to Mosaic and Davidic instructions, and that divinely appointed men could serve as Yahweh God's mediatorial agents, carrying out the tasks of rulers (kings), priests, and prophets. The sovereign role of Yahweh God was likewise demonstrated in the thwarting of the two efforts of opponents to hinder the covenant people from carrying out their duties in regard to the temple, the house of Yahweh God, and the worship of him.

The Prophetic References

The prophets Haggai and Zechariah present information concerning the time that they prophesied. What they proclaimed and wrote confirmed what Ezra had written. Opposition to temple rebuilding had halted that work. As Ezra had written, Haggai and Zechariah had urged the people to continue to rebuild. Haggai gave the precise date that Yahweh God's word came to him, Zechariah the prophet, and Joshua the high priest. It was during the second year of Darius, the first day of the sixth month. This was in 521 B.C.

Haggai was the first to prophesy.[14] Zechariah took up the message. The question has been raised whether there was a personality clash. Was there jealousy?[15] Pieter Verhoef wrote that one could assume that Haggai died after prophesying. Many scholars maintain Haggai was an old man and Zechariah was a young man when the call came to them to prophesy.[16]

Haggai called for Jerusalem workers to gather timber from the mountains for the rebuilding of the temple (1:7). It is stated explicitly: the voice of Yahweh God was obeyed (1:12); the work of rebuilding was begun (1:14).

Zechariah gave the precise date he began to prophesy. It was in the eighth month of Darius's second year as king. Haggai proclaimed two more messages after Zechariah commenced his prophesying (2:10, 20). Though Zechariah did not refer directly to the lack of attention to the house of Yahweh God, his initial message and the visions certainly do support the claim that Zechariah continued to prophesy during the initial days of rebuilding activities. The visions included references to aspects of the temple (Zech. 2:1–13; 4:1–14), to the high priest (3:1–10), and to the social and political circumstances of that historical period (1:7–17; 5:1–11; 6:1–8).[17]

The Prophetic Agenda

"Jewish history began a new chapter in 539 B.C." when Cyrus established himself as king of a new world empire.[18] It certainly is true that a great change took place under Cyrus in Jewish history. The theocratic monarchy was gone for all time; the Davidic human dynasty was no longer reigning; many of the "people of Israel and Judah" remained living in dispersion. In this context, the question is very relevant: Did the prophetic agenda change? Specifically, does the agenda as Joel had set it out provide the basic elements of postexilic prophetic proclamation?[19]

A review of Joel's agenda and of the content of postexilic prophetic proclamation will bring the following to one's attention. There is no emphasis on local, national, or cosmic disasters[20] or on judgment coming on nations, the inclusion of members of these nations in Yahweh's people, and living water constantly flowing from the temple in Jerusalem.[21] The postexilic prophets do add to the prophetic agenda and strong references to renewal of worship, messianic hope, and eschatological emphases. Joel's agenda did not include these as dominant themes but they did develop as prophecy continued and developed in the context of Israel/Judah's checkered history and their eventual removal as nations from the scene of history.

Haggai's Prophecy

Introductory Comments

Scholars have written that Haggai, very likely a priest, lived the greater part of his life in Babylon. He may have seen the Solomonic temple before it was destroyed.[22] He is said to identify himself with rebuilding the temple.[23] One scholar wrote that Haggai was far more concerned that his people understood the guaranteed character of Yahweh God's promises under which the temple could be rebuilt. The remnant in Jerusalem had to understand that the way of postponement, indifference, and slothfulness led to disastrous consequences.[24]

Haggai's message, given in four short prophecies within a period of three months and twenty-four days, aroused the leaders, Zerubbabel and Joshua, to stir up the people to continue to rebuild the temple. He challenged the people and assured them with comforting words (1:2–15); he held before the people the glory of Yahweh's house (2:1–9), and he encouraged them with assurances of blessings for an obedient and sanctified people (2:10–19). Finally, he proclaimed with conviction that the promises regarding David's progeny would be fulfilled (2:20–23). These four prophecies held before the fearful and hesitant people the absolute assurance that Yahweh God's kingdom was a reality, his covenant was steadfast, and the promises concerning the messianic mediator were being fulfilled.

The Kingdom

The King

The King of the kingdom was none other than *yĕhwâ šĕbā'ôt* (Yahweh of Hosts). In Haggai's four short prophecies this reference to the God of the restored remnant appears fourteen times. I have discussed what the term *šĕbā'ôt* means in various contexts. The most correct translation is *sovereign.* It refers to the absolute unchanging reign of Yahweh God over the entire cosmic kingdom, including all aspects of it. The term *sovereign* includes the ideas of all-authoritative and all-powerful. Haggai was called by Yahweh God to proclaim that the God who called him to prophesy and gave him the messages for his contemporaries was the absolute and only sovereign Lord. He reigned over the restored community and over their opposition. The restored community had nothing to fear. They could and should proceed with their rebuilding task with full confidence and assurance that their covenant Lord was in complete control. He reigned, as always, consistently according to his established and revealed will and purposes.

As the sovereign King he was fully aware of what was transpiring in the restored remnant community. He knew what the opposition was and did to the hearts, minds, wills, and hands of the people. He knew their situation very well. He had given them time, from 536–522 B.C., to realize that fear had made them disobedient. But under his sovereign rule Yahweh God's purposes were to be realized.[25] He called two men to serve as his spokesmen. There is no evidence that they had been aware of their prophetic office and task. Yahweh God gave these. Haggai had no choice. He evidently was fully aware of what the people were doing—building their own houses and attempting to be successful in vocations (1:3–9). Yahweh God, the sovereign Lord, opened Haggai's mouth! He gave him a prophetic task and message. Yahweh God spoke through Haggai (1:3). But Haggai had to do the actual speaking.[26]

The Cosmic Kingdom

Haggai never referred to the theocratic monarchy that had existed from the time of King Saul until the final exile. He did not proclaim its reestablishment. He did not prophesy that the *nation* of Israel would be restored.[27] He certainly prophesied concerning Yahweh God's sovereign rule over the cosmos. He did in various ways.

In the natural material aspect of the cosmos, Yahweh God knows where building material is to be acquired: in the mountains (Hag. 1:8). He commands the people to get the timber. Meanwhile he demonstrates his sovereign rule over the people's houses, food, and clothes for which the people labored but could not control. Yahweh God blew these away. He knew of the holes in many pockets through which he dispossessed people of what monetary gain they hoped to have (1:5–9).[28] There was no seed in the barns, and vines, trees, and pomegranates in the fields did not bear crops. Yahweh God the King of the cosmos withheld these (2:19). He struck the work of their hands with blight and mildew[29] and withheld rain though hail fell to ruin what little did grow (2:17). These occurrences in nature controlled and ruled over by Yahweh God certainly do indicate that Yahweh God, King of the cosmic kingdom, has every aspect of it not only under his control; he reigns over every aspect of the natural and human dimensions of the cosmic kingdom. To ascribe such disasters to Satan is to ignore Yahweh God's sovereign kingship and to reject his bringing judgment by these disasters upon a disobedient and/or rebellious people.[30]

Haggai prophesied concerning Yahweh God shaking the heavens and the earth. The King of the cosmos rules over all the powers in the nation and world. Military power, represented by horses, chariots, and riders, meets disaster under Yahweh God's reign. The wealth found in the world belongs to Yahweh God. Yahweh's spokesman proclaimed *lî hakkeseph we lî hazzāhāb nĕ'um yĕhwâ šĕb ā'ôt* (to me the silver and the gold is mine oracles Yahweh of Hosts) (2:8). Yahweh God owns the riches in the cosmos and makes them available for his glory, which will be evident when the gold and silver is used to beautify the rebuilt temple.

The nations are integral aspects of Yahweh God's cosmic kingdom. He can, has, and will shake nations, causing them to give up their wealth (2:7). He will *hāpaklî kissē* of *mamlākōt* (overturn throne of kingdoms) and *hišmadtî hōzeq* (shatters power of kingdoms) (2:22). The sovereign ruler of the nations can, does, and will carry out holy war[31] against those who oppose him, his people, and his work.[32]

Sufficient evidence has been presented from Haggai's prophecy that he has held up the kingdom of God as the all-inclusive context and setting of his prophecies. His hearers had to know at all times that their God, Yahweh, was the sovereign King over them, their lives, their possessions, their work, and their future. The remnant was not given even a hint that they would again become a nation. They were *assured* they were Yahweh God's community.

The Royal Community

The remnant living and struggling in their homeland was not, politically, a legal entity, a nation, much less a kingdom with a ruler on their throne. They did have a very special heritage. They were descendants of a people who had been citizens of a theocratic monarchy. That heritage had, in a specific manner, been taken away. But the promises regarding a royal person who was to come from and through them were not abrogated. The promised royal mediator would surely come.

While not legally a royal entity, a kingdom, the remnant had to know and consider themselves to be a royal community within the cosmic kingdom. They were the cosmic King's chosen people through whom he would fulfill his promises and purposes. Until the promised descendant of David, the Messiah, came, Yahweh God's presence among them as their Lord had to be symbolized and typified by the rebuilt temple. In a real sense, the temple had to serve in a twofold manner. It was the symbolic royal dwelling of Yahweh God the cosmic King and it was the house of worship. The temple was to be the symbolic meeting place of the king and his royal family, the people who were the descendants of the patriarchs, Abraham, Isaac, and Jacob.[33]

The Covenant

The Hebrew term *bĕrît* does not appear in Haggai's prophecies. *kārat* (to cut), very often used when covenanting activities took place, does appear. Hence some translations have promise (2:5) or translate the verb *kārat* as covenanted.[34] Here is a case where, as elsewhere, the term *bĕrît* does not appear but what was involved in the covenant making and in the covenant itself is clearly present.[35]

The phrase "I am with you" (1:13; 2:4) is a covenantal phrase Yahweh God spoke when covenanting with Abraham, "I will be your/their God" (Gen. 17:7, 8) and with Jacob (28:15). This covenant made with Abraham and his descendants had not been annulled, as it may have seemed.[36] Yahweh God repeated what he had said to Abraham, "I will bless you" (Hag. 2:19).

The covenanting activity at Mount Sinai is reflected in various ways in Haggai's prophecies. The remnant of the covenant people were fulfilling the cultural mandate; they tilled the ground, and they built houses; however, they did this in disobedience to what Yahweh God had demanded of his covenant people when at Sinai. They were to prepare a "tent of meeting" to symbolize and represent their covenant God's presence and thus prepare a proper place for worship. The rebuilding of the temple was covenantal duty.[37] Fear caused by opposition led to covenant disobedience. The people were given strong covenantal demands: "Be strong and work" (2:4). This language is also reminiscent of what Yahweh God proclaimed to Joshua (Josh. 1:5, 6).

Haggai reminded the remnant that an obedient, working people had the covenantal assurance that Yahweh God's Spirit remained among them. The reference is definitely to the Holy Spirit, who had been present with Moses and Aaron and the people at and after Mount Sinai. When the tabernacle was to be prepared at Mount Sinai and after the covenanting activities, as recorded in Exodus 19:1–24:18, had been completed, which included the giving of the ten commandments, the Holy Spirit had been given to Bezalel to enable him to skillfully and knowledgeably make artistic design for the tabernacle (31:2–42; 35:31–33). And while in the desert the Spirit of God had told Moses that the Spirit that was on him would be given to seventy men to assist him (Num. 11:17–29), Caleb, one of the spies, followed the Spirit in him (14:24). Joshua had the Spirit who enabled him to obey and carry out Yahweh God's covenantal demands (Deut. 34:4).

The Holy Spirit had been a definite reality in the lives of leaders and workers in Israel after they had left Egypt. The Holy Spirit had been a covenant gift and asset. The people who were commanded to rebuild the temple and to carry out the laws given for worship and service to Yahweh God had the same covenant blessings as the people centuries before had had. Zechariah emphasized that the Spirit of Yahweh God would be the people's great enabler (4:6). The covenant was in force; its requirements could be met and executed in the remnant community as it had been in the people who had been redeemed from Egypt and called to covenant life and service.

The law, an integral aspect of the covenant, had to be known and obeyed. Haggai implies that it was with the Spirit's aid that the law proclaimed at Sinai was heard and obeyed to the extent that it was by the influence of the Holy Spirit. In the same way, the restored exilic community could live a sanctified life with the Spirit working in them.

The question that arises reading Haggai 2 is: When Yahweh God promised to supply the rich material for building a house to be filled with glory (Hag. 2:6–9), does Haggai's third message, given two months later, call for strict obedience on the part of all individuals as well as the community as a whole, to keep even the details of the law (2:10–14)? Note that the question is addressed specifically to the priests. It was their duty, as covenant servants, to tend to the purity of the people. The answer is in the affirmative. Haggai accused the priests and the people of bringing defilement (2:14). The illustrations Haggai gave of meat being defiled and people being defiled due to contacting a dead person emphasized how the people needed sanctification and holiness. A believing and God-serving covenant people, by nature defiled, needed the law of the covenant to guide them. The Holy Spirit would remain among the restored community (2:5) to bring forth sanctification and holiness. Faithful adherence to and keeping of all aspects of the covenant was absolute requirements for receiving Yahweh God's rich provisions for the rebuilt temple to be truly filled with glory.[38]

Haggai's prophecies called for the covenant people's attention to Yahweh God's covenant requirements. The people had a responsibility. They had to respond to the demands and dictates of their covenant Lord. Haggai had raised questions in his initial message and he followed these up by quoting Yahweh God their sovereign Lord; "Give careful thought to your ways" (1:5). A restored, redeemed covenant people were basically accused of not walking in the covenant way nor working according to Yahweh God's demands. Haggai repeated this call to careful thinking (1:15; 2:18). It was a call to self-examination and evaluation of various aspects of life. If blessings were not received, was a withholding of them due to disobedience? Haggai definitely implies this is the case. Yahweh God promised and assured the blessings of the covenant, materials for rebuilding his house, daily necessities for livelihood, and abundant harvests from grain fields, vineyards, and orchards.[39] The restored community had but to reflect on the history of Yahweh God's dealing with a people redeemed from Egypt and given their promised inheritance. Indeed! Think deeply about your heritage. Remember that Yahweh God remains faithful to his covenant demands and promises.

Haggai had made brief references implicitly and indirectly to Yahweh God's covenant with Abraham. He drew much attention to the covenant made with Israel at Sinai that included the giving of the law and the requirements for a symbolic dwelling, the tabernacle. The building of Yahweh God's house was a main theme for Haggai. This factor introduced the covenant Yahweh God had made with David. David had wanted to build this house (2 Sam. 7:1–5). He was not to build it; he could prepare for it. The heart and continuing thrust of Yahweh God's covenanting activity with David was his house, progeny, dynasty, a ruling Son.

When Haggai made direct and indirect references to temple rebuilding, he was unavoidably bringing Yahweh God's covenanting with David to the attention of his hearers. Haggai had to proclaim Yahweh God's assuring word that his covenant with David was an abiding reality. David's national throne was not occupied. It was gone for all time. But the basic thrust of the Davidic covenant was not abrogated. David's dynasty would not disappear from the scene of history.

In this context of referring to the Davidic covenant, the three strands of the Golden Cable really come to the fore. David had been king over the theocratic monarchy, symbolically representing the cosmic kingdom. David became king under Yahweh God's guidance in fulfillment of the prophecy made by Jacob that a descendant of Judah would rule (Gen. 49:8–12). Yahweh God kept that promise and covenanted with David that this covenant was to be eternal; it would never end. Hence David became the mediator, symbolically and typically, of the mediator to come in the future.

The Mediator

Reference was made in various preceding contexts to the prophets and priests serving as mediatorial agents. Joshua, the high priest, had his role in stirring up the people in regard to temple activity. Haggai the prophet spoke Yahweh God's word. Zerubabbel, a descendant of David, was given the role of governor (Hag. 1:1). He governed under the reign of Cyrus and Darius. He, however, represented Yahweh God's divine rule over his people.

A previous study includes a detailed exegesis and biblical-theological presentation of Haggai's prophecies concerning the Messiah.[40] Repetition is not warranted, however, in the context of a study of the kingdom and covenant in this book, it is necessary to address at least three issues.

The first issue that Haggai raised is the role of nations and their contribution to Yahweh's redemptive activities (2:6–9). A specific question has been raised: to what does the phrase *wûbā'û hemdat Kāl-haggôîm* (and shall come the ??? of all nations.") Does the term *hemdat* have messianic mediatorial significance? The textual context must be seriously considered first of all.

Yahweh God had Haggai ask the question of those who had seen the glory of the former temple, the Solomonic temple. Some had because Ezra referred to the sorrow of those who had seen it and now approximately seventy years later saw the beginning of the second temple (Ezra 3:12). Haggai went on to ask if the temple being rebuilt seemed like nothing (Hag. 2:3). This question surely implied that the second temple lacked much compared to the first one. In spite of this lack, Joshua and Zeruababbel are commanded to be strong and the people are also (2:4) because Yahweh God, as he had covenanted before, was with them. Yahweh God's presence was to be the source of strength and encouragement to proceed with building. But, what about material for building a house of glory for their covenant Lord? Yahweh assured them he would provide. The house would be filled with *kābôd* (glory). When Yahweh God had entered the tabernacle, it was filled with glory (Exod. 40:34, 35). The presence of Yahweh God in the rebuilt temple would make it glorious. But, though this reality can be implied, the text speaks of *kesep* and *zāhāb* (silver and gold), that is earthly, yet rich, materials that would contribute to the glory of the temple.

Where was this gold and silver to come from? They were to come from the nations that Yahweh God would deal with in his sovereign power. He was to demonstrate his power and authority in his own time. The Hebrew phrase that refers to the future is unique and difficult to translate. Some translations have "in a little while" (NIV) or "in just a little while longer"[41] or "again and for one time, in a short while."[42] The point communicated is clear: Yahweh God will supply "treasures"[43] held by nations when he shakes them. He had shaken Egypt and provisions for the tabernacle had been showered upon the Israelite nation. The international scene was not too stable. Would changes in it bring treasures to the restored community? No definite answer was given to this.

Haggai proceeded to proclaim that a greater glory would fill this rebuilt temple than the one in the first temple. This greater glory, in this context, refers to the presence of the covenant Lord, the "I Am" who was with them (2:4). He would bring great glory, he said, "*bammāgôm hazzeh 'ettēn šālôm* (in this place I will give peace). The messianic mediatorial thrust is present. The treasures to be supplied come from the hand of the great I AM." As he supplies he is present. Ezekiel's assurance is in effect repeated: "*Yĕhwâ sāmmâh* (Yahweh is there)."

In conclusion to this first point, a negative statement must be made. The treasures of the nations is often mistranslated to read "the desired of the nations." This phrase has led some students to interpret the concept of desire as referring to the Messiah.[44] Whereas I have pointed out that there is an implicit reference to the presence of the mediator, it is incorrect to imply that nations are desiring the Messiah.[45]

The second issue pertains to Zerubabbel. He served as governor of Judah. Haggai's fourth message was particularly for him (2:21). The first part of the message repeated what had been prophesied before concerning the glory that would fill the temple: Yahweh God would shake all the nations and the required materials for rebuilding the temple would come from the nations (2:7). Zerubabbel had to hear that Yahweh God would carry out a greater shaking: the heavens and the earth would be shaken. By this shaking royal thrones would be removed, the power of foreign kingdoms would be shattered, and their military means would be decimated (1:21, 22).

The message that followed was addressed directly to Zerubabbel. Yahweh God addresses him as *'abdî* (my servant). This term has appeared repeatedly in regard to an anointed one. He is told he is the chosen one. The interpretation of what Haggai (2:21) proclaimed has given rise to various views.

The liberal critical scholars are quite certain that Haggai was expressing his own personal view and hope. The phrase used by Haggai, *nĕum yĕhwâ šĕb ā 'ôt* (decares Yahweh the sovereign One), is explained as a prophetic effort to give authority to his view. One commentator wrote that Haggai "appears so anxious to be recognized as a veritable ambassador of the Almighty."[46] Haggai is interpreted to prophesy that Zerubabbel, a Davidic dynastic member, will soon become king in the restored community. David's theocratic throne would be restored. The Judean community would again be a kingdom with a Davidide ruling over it. He would be able to do so because foreign nations would be overthrown (2:22). Haggai is thought to reflect the international problems the Persian Empire had to face.

A somewhat less specific view than that which called for Zerubabbel to become king is that the theocratic rule will continue among the nations. This is to be an expectation, but how it will become a recognized reality is not explained.[47]

The prophecy should leave no doubt that Zerubbabel received a message from Yahweh God through the prophet Haggai. He was Yahweh God's chosen representative of the Davidic dynasty. He had a position of authority. This is conveyed by the term *kaḥōtām* (seal or signet ring). The noun is derived from the verb, *ḥātam* (to seal, affix seal, seal up). The basic concept is that of attestation to a specific pronounced truth or deed. It meant to ratify what was said or done. There was to be no doubt concerning the veracity and reliability of what was said or done if sealed by the ring. The bearer of this "sealing" considered it a precious possession. It was not a mere ornament. It represented an authority, one who gave rights and confirmed agreements and proclamations.

Since Zerubabbel was set to be like (take note of כ, like) a signet ring, he was definitely not the authoritative person himself. He represented that authoritative person. In the context it must be understood that he was confirmed by Yahweh God to represent the Davidic dynasty. As such, he was assured that he was valuable and precious in Yahweh God's eyes and plan.[48] But Zerababbel was not the main, central, important reality; the Davidic dynasty was. Yahweh God's promise to David that he would have an eternal house was not abrogated. The presence of Zerubabbel was Yahweh God's confirmation of the sovereignty of David though it existed in a sphere of humiliation.[49]

The third issue is closely related to the role of Zerubabbel. Briefly stated, it is a question of eschatology. Is there a message here for the future? Is the basic message that there is a renewal of the promise of salvation?[50] There is salvation for Yahweh God's people in the future. But Haggai gave more than that. He made it clear that the Davidic house would continue. Zerubabbel was chosen as Yahweh God's seal bearer to assure that the One who was to reign forever was to come. The specific time is not stated or even implied. What is assured is that Yahweh God, sovereign Lord of all nations, will cause nations to fall but the Davidic dynasty would certainly endure. It did not require an earthly throne. That, however, did not indicate that the promised One to come was not to reign and would not appear as the one who would reign in a realistic manner in the future. Zerubabbel's name was inserted as "a contemporary figure into the age when God's benign and universal rule will prevail. . . . Haggai, by using a living individual . . . bridges the gap between the present and the future."[51] He was not apocalyptic as he proclaimed this eschatological message.

Conclusion

Our study of Haggai has demonstrated clearly that the prophet continued to develop three strands of the Golden Cable. He prophesied in difficult political, social, international, and religious circumstances. His messages that highlighted the concepts of kingdom, covenant, and mediator gave inspiration and motivation to a fearful and uncertain covenant community. The people were inspired to build the temple, the very symbol of their covenant Lord's presence among them. The temple spoke eloquently of their sovereign King's rule, his bond with his people, and the role that the mediators, Joshua and Zerubabbel, carried out. The Golden Cable proved to be the tie that bound the restored community to its heritage of the past, its present role in Yahweh God's ever-unfolding plan and purposes, and its pivotal part in the continuity of the messianic mediators represented by the Davidic dynasty's administrative and redemptive role for then and for the future.

Zechariah 1–8

Introductory Comments

Zechariah's relationship to Haggai has been referred to in a preceding section.[52] He was a young man of priestly descent whose interest in the temple made him a likely prophetic messenger in the context of the rebuilding of the temple.

Zechariah's role in prophecy was diverse. He prophesied concerning the sure involvement of Yahweh God in the lives of the restored community who had a momentous task, rebuilding the temple, in their troubled *Sitz im Leben.* They had opposition; they lacked sufficient materials. The restored community was not unanimous on the appearance of the temple being rebuilt. The older members of the priesthood, Levitical groups, and family heads grieved while other praised Yahweh for the humble beginnings of the rebuilding. Once the temple was near completion, or possibly completed, Zechariah had to address the community concerning religious (cultic) issues (chaps. 7, 8). Years later, in turbulent times,[53] he was called to bring encouraging messages concerning the sure future of the kingdom and the role of the mediator. Zechariah proved to be a resourceful and faithful prophet among the people of the restored remnant covenant community.[54]

The structure of the first eight chapters calls for attention: 1:1–6 records his first prophecy; 1:7–6:8 records his visions; 6:9–15 records an historical postlude; 7:1–8:23 records his messages to an uncertain people as they commence life with a rebuilt temple in their midst. The following sketch could assist in visualizing the structure of Zechariah 1–8.

In the study of Zechariah 1–8 the three strands of the Golden Cable will not be considered seriatum. Rather, each section will be studied to determine its relevance

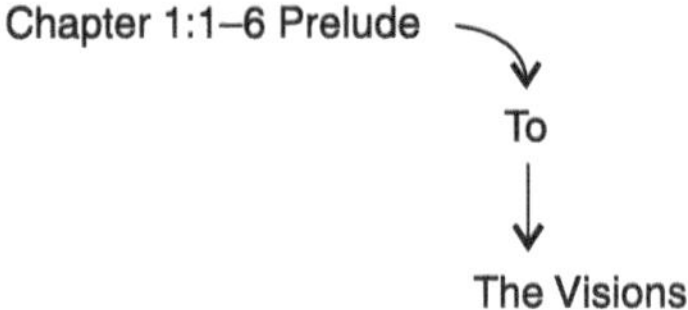

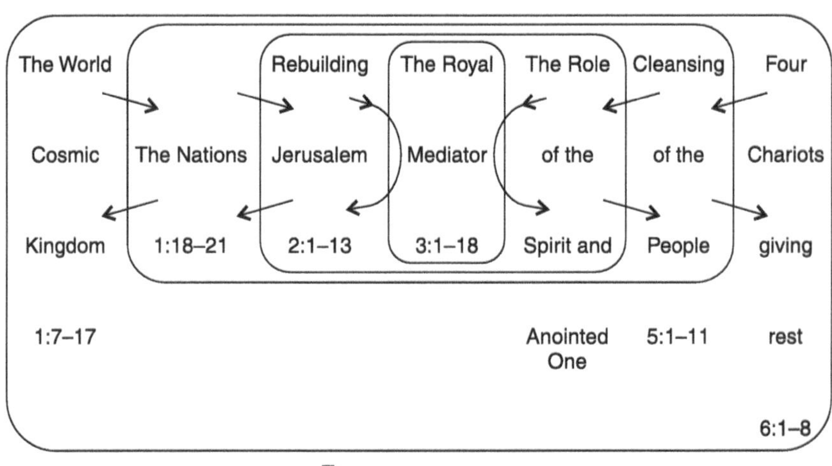

To

Chapter 6:9–15—Interlude—High Priest Crowned

To

Chapter 7 to 8, Postlude

Addressing an uncertain people

and contribution to each strand and to the Golden Cable as a whole. This procedure may call for some seeming repetition but the progress of revelation can be demonstrated more effectively through this procedure.

Zechariah's Prophetic Prelude: 1:1–6

Zechariah has been understood to issue a call to repentance in his opening statement. There should be no doubt that Zechariah called upon the people to return to the Lord.[55] A commentator summed up the message of the prelude: Zechariah is making a plea for a wholehearted response to the Lord's invitation to return to him. It should become immediately apparent upon a reading of this prelude that the context of the call to repentance was specific. A strong reminder was given that the covenant Yahweh God had kept for centuries was still very much in force. Evidence for this is as follows.

Zechariah proclaims *qāsap yĕhwâ 'al-'ăbôtĕkem* (Yahweh was full of wrath against your fathers). Moses,[56] when renewing the covenant on the plains of Moab, had warned of Yahweh God's anger and wrath should his covenant people disobey him and break the covenant. The history of Israel/Judah is filled with accounts of covenant breaking. Idolatry and injustice, sins against God and fellowmen, marked the lives of most forefathers. The covenant people provoked Yahweh God their covenant sovereign Lord to anger and wrath. The people of Israel and Judah suffered under the judgment of Yahweh God (2 Kings 17:7–23; 2 Chron. 36:15–17).[57]

Zechariah was correct when he reminded the people of their forefathers' unfaithfulness. He was not exaggerating the reality of Yahweh God's execution of the covenant curse. Moses and the prophets repeatedly warned that Yahweh God's patience would not last forever. The prophets Jeremiah, Ezekiel, and Daniel had emphatically proclaimed that the fathers in Israel/Judah were responsible for their destruction of Jerusalem and the death of many by means of the sword, famine, and disease. These had come at the hand of an angry and wrathful covenant God. Zechariah could, therefore, legitimately ask the rhetorical question: *'ăbôtêkem 'ayyēh*[58] *hem* (your fathers where they?) (1:5).

They are gone! The prophets who warned them are no longer here. Why not? Because Yahweh God said "*'ak dĕbāray wĕhuqqay . . . hiśśîgû*" (1:6) (Did not my words and statutes overtake . . . your fathers?) Indeed, they had.

Zechariah, in this first message, stressed the following.

First, Yahweh God, the sovereign Lord, had been in complete and total charge in upholding this covenant with the fathers when he executed the curse of the covenant upon them.

Second, Yahweh God had faithfully and repeatedly warned the covenant fathers that their sins would bring the curse upon them. He had had the earlier prophets proclaim, "Turn from your wicked ways." The call to repentance had not been heeded. The fathers would not listen or obey.

Third, Yahweh God's covenant was an abiding, bonded relationship. The descendants of the cursed fathers could receive blessings from their covenant

Lord. Repentance and turning to their covenant Lord, as covenant people was the only pathway to these blessings.

The responses to Zechariah's message are recorded. *wayyâsûbû* (and they returned). The leaders and the people did what was demanded of them as a covenant people.[59] They did more: they confessed Yahweh God, their sovereign covenant Lord, had been faithful. He had done to the fathers as they deserved. He had kept covenant with them. Zechariah's preaching emphasized what Haggai had preached. The response of the people was obedience. They continued the rebuilding of the temple (Ezra 6:14).

Zechariah's Visions

Vision 1, 1:7–17

The time of this first vision was about three months after Zechariah's initial message and two months after Haggai's last prophecy. The rebuilding of the temple may have just begun (Hag. 1:14). The people evidently needed assurance that they were working according to Yahweh God's plans. Zechariah assured them that Yahweh God had said, *šābtî* (I have returned).[60] Yahweh had kept his promise: you return and I return to you (Zech. 1:3). The response to Zechariah's initial message had been positive. The people were in need of encouragement but also of specific instruction concerning Yahweh God's purposes and ways of continuing to work out the covenant promises he had made for a glorious future. The temple had to be rebuilt as well as Jerusalem and surrounding towns. This would provide the setting for the fulfillment of covenant promises concerning the seed of the woman, even David's son, who was to reign eternally.

In the immediate environment, the people experienced opposition. On the international scene the situation seemed difficult because of national forces firmly entrenched. Was there really a future, a sure hope, for the responsive covenant community in a hostile world?[61] Zechariah's vision gave specific and concrete evidence that Yahweh God, the sovereign Lord was reigning. He was carrying out his purposes.

The vision(s) Zechariah saw came from Yahweh God. The text states *hâyâh dĕbar-yĕhwâ 'el-zĕkaryâ* (the word of Yahweh came to Zechariah). The vision(s) brought divine revelation. The phrase *ra'îtî hallayelâ* (I saw in the night) must be understood literally. Zechariah was not dreaming. He saw a scene; he was conscious of what he saw and heard during the night.

The scene in the vision was a valley with myrtle trees. Horsemen on horses of various colors were standing behind a rider on a red horse. The colors of the horses may not have any significance beyond indicating they were to be differentiated.[62] The rider on the red horse served as a spokesman. Included in the scene are two angels, the one who spoke with and interpreted for Zechariah and the Angel of the Lord. This latter one in biblical contexts is none other than the second person of the Trinity. In the conversation between the four it is not readily discerned who is speaking to whom.[63] The vision can more readily be understood if the conversation is understood as follows. Seeing the horses, Zechariah asked the angel, "What are these horses?" He answered, "I will show you." The man on the red horse interjects, saying, "Yahweh sent them throughout the earth" (v. 10). The four horsemen then addressed the Angel of the Lord saying, "the whole world is at rest and peace" (v. 11). The Angel of the Lord then addressed Yahweh, the sovereign Lord. He asked how long mercy would be withheld from those with whom he had been angry (v. 12). The Angel of the Lord, evidently knowing the answer to his query spoke kind and comforting words to the angel speaking with Zechariah (v. 13). He commanded Zechariah to proclaim Yahweh God's word.

The first vision presents a student/reader with the following. First, the cosmic kingdom is the context. Nations are involved; they are at rest and peace. They seem to have control of the affairs of all nations and communities such as the postexilic.

Second, the restored community, the remnant of the covenant people, must be aware that they are an integral part of Yahweh God's cosmic kingdom. They are to know and accept their role in it.[64]

Third, the Angel of the Lord, the preincarnate Christ, is personally and actively involved in the affairs of the cosmic kingdom. He is especially concerned about the well-being of the restored community and Yahweh God's relationship with them. He pleads for mercy to be demonstrated replacing the anger so evident for seventy years.

Fourth, the restored remnant learned that Yahweh God the sovereign Lord was jealous for his people. His love is positive; he will defend, uphold, and prosper his covenant people. The house of the Lord, the temple, will be rebuilt.

Fifth, Yahweh God's anger continues—not against the restored community, but against the nations that consider themselves secure and in charge of all cosmic affairs.

Sixth, there is a good future for an obedient and serving people. They will know Yahweh's comfort; they will know they are his chosen people.

Seventh, Yahweh God's sovereign authority and rule over the cosmos provides assurance of security and prosperity. The role of the Mediator, interceding and making promises, gives courage and motivation.

Vision 2, 1:18–21 (MT 2:1–4)

This second vision follows very closely on the first one. Zechariah "raised his eyes." He received a new scene.[65] The interpreting angel was still there. Zechariah now saw four horns that the angel explained as representing the nations that *zĕrû* (niph. pf. of *zārah,* to scatter)[66] Judah, Israel, and the nations. The horn represented power, often brute power, willfully demonstrated. The number 4 has raised questions. Were not Assyria and Babylon two nations that had scattered the covenant people? The figure 4 can be understood as the totality of opposition.[67] The two powerful nations that had been used by Yahweh God to execute the covenant curse upon Israel and Judah represented all the opposition that the covenant people had experienced in the years of the theocratic nation's existence. These nations, in a real way, represented the dominion of Satan, they were, nevertheless, under Yahweh God's authority and reign. Once they had carried out their God-given task, their role within the cosmic kingdom would end. Yahweh God would deal decisively with them.

Yahweh God then had Zechariah see the second main part of the vision. There were four horns but also four *hârâšîm* (smiths). Was it natural to think of an ironworker dealing with horns of bulls? Translators have preferred to translate the term as *craftsmen.* But what did craftsmen represent in contrast to powerful horns? The text records that the craftsmen had come on the scene to *hahărid* (hiph. inf. construct of *hārad*) terrify[68] them. The term *hārad* can also mean to tremble, quake. The thought of driving in terror with the result of a complete rout is present. The following verb *yăddat* (piel. inf. of *yādâ,* to cast down) emphasizes that complete destruction would come upon the nations opposing the covenant people.

The message of this second vision is clear. First, the powerful nations used to disperse the covenant people are under the reign of Yahweh God, the ruling Sovereign over the cosmic kingdom. Yahweh God raises up means of judgment; he uses means to bring them down and annihilate them.

Second, Yahweh God does not always employ power, political or military, to bring judgment on the enemies of the covenant people. He brings in craftsmen, ironworkers, and builders to undo the opposition and cause it to dissipate.

Third, Yahweh God gave a strong motivation to the hesitant community. It is not by military power that such powers can be overthrown. Rather, doing positive work is the means. The restored community had been allowed to return to rebuild Jerusalem and the temple. That rebuilding would thwart the opposition and throw it into disarray.[69]

Fourth, Yahweh God reigns over all aspects of his cosmic kingdom. The covenant community, an integral part of that kingdom, is secured when covenant people obey and carry out Yahweh God's will.

Vision 3, 2:1–5 (MT 2:5–9)

This third vision is introduced also with the formula "I raised my eyes." Zechariah saw a number of different participants. He himself was outside Jerusalem but the city became a central factor. Zechariah saw a man with a measuring line. He was going to measure the width and length of the walls to be built. The idea conveyed is that if the temple was to be built, Jerusalem the city had to be properly defended. Walls were necessary for this defense and security. But the immediate rebuilding of the walls was not part of Yahweh God's plan.

A second angel entered the scene. He had a message for the man with the measuring line. The angel who had talked with Zechariah was leaving him and the second angel urged this first angel to run to the man with the measuring line. The message he had to hear was: forget about men building walls. Jerusalem does not need them. It will receive a wall of fire. This second angel was definite: "I will be the wall of fire around it." This angel was the preincarnate Christ, who had been a pillar of fire and a cloud of shade for the Israelites in the desert. The forefathers had been defended, protected, and guided as a nomadic people. As the history of redemption unfolded the descendants of the desert people had a city that would be defended, protected, and exist securely by that same cloud of fire that would serve as a wall. That protecting wall would extend much farther than a wall built by man. It would encircle a great number of people and livestock that were included in the city.

One more important reality must be stressed. As the tabernacle and temple (Solomonic, 1 Kings 5:14) had been filled with glory, so Jerusalem, expanded, extensive, surrounded by the wall of fire, would have the glory of the Lord within it. This was a very definite covenant assurance. Yahweh God did not say, "I will be with you" this time. Rather, that assuring word was now expressed in more graphic terms. "I will be the glory within it." This meant that Jerusalem's inhabitants would not only have Yahweh God with them, they would be surrounded by the glorious presence of their Lord. Vision 3 emphasized the following cardinal points. First, Yahweh God's plan for his people was far more extensive than that of men. Yahweh God had a wonderful future for his people within the cosmic kingdom.

Second, the people had to think of more than themselves. They had to think cosmically. Their livestock was part of their kingdom heritage. Their role in regard to the nations was very significant. They were to be the nucleus to which all nations of the cosmic kingdom could be drawn and attached.

Third, the people had to know that they as builders were not to set limits on their efforts. They were to realize that Yahweh God would not encircle them with man-made walls. His people had to think and plan for great results from their presence and efforts as they rebuilt their city and surrounding towns.

Fourth, this third vision was the context for a prophetic message that had to be made known far beyond Jerusalem and the surrounding towns (Zech. 2:6–13 [MT 2:10–17]).[70] Since this third vision is closely related to the first two, it can be rightly said that the prophetic proclamation follows directly from the first three visions.[71] So, following the scene of the world at rest, of the powerful nations being thrown down, and of Jerusalem and environments being extended because of the great increase in population and livestock and Yahweh being present in glory, Zechariah must send forth a prophetic message.

The first challenge is to determine who spoke. As mentioned, Zechariah was the prophetic spokesman. He spoke for Yahweh God *nĕūm-yehwâ* (declares Yahweh, 2:16 [MT 2:10).

Zechariah adds *kī kōh 'āmar yĕhwâ šĕbam'ôt* for thus says Yahweh of hosts (2:8, [MT 2:12]). Through Zechariah *nĕum yĕhwâ* (Yahweh declared, 2:10 [MT 2:14]) his word to all covenant people wherever they were, and to the nations.

Various commentators have made a strong case for referring to a third speaker. Yahweh God spoke. Zechariah spoke Yahweh's word. The third speaker's presence became evident especially in the words "For I am coming, I will live among you; you will know that Yahweh God of hosts has sent me to you" (2:10, 11 [MT 2:14, 15]). This third speaker is the preincarnate Christ, who appeared as the Angel of the Lord and had instructed the angel to tell the young man with the measuring line to stop measuring. This same Angel of the Lord had interceded for the scattered exiles (1:11). It was the preincarnate Christ who is also Yahweh of Hosts. He is the second person of the Trinity. He performs great redemptive events. He is the agent of divine judgment, and he gathers and unites his people drawn from all nations. The second challenge is to understand who were to be recipients of the prophet's message.

The preferred understanding of this verse (2:8 [MT 2:12]) is as follows.[72] Zechariah was calling to the people scattered far and wide (2:16). He is calling because Yahweh has sent him to go for glory[73] to the nations. Yahweh had Zechariah proclaim that he, Yahweh God, would be the glory within Jerusalem, ever-expanding the city (vision 2). The city would experience increasing glory as the nations listened and joined the multitude dwelling in Jerusalem.

The text is specific. The prophetic message is first of all for the daughter of Zion (2:10 [MT 2:14]). In some passages the daughter of Zion refers to the coming generations born of the remnant (cf. chap. 22, note 56). Zechariah, however, had a far more inclusive audience in mind. He was addressing those who had returned to Jerusalem, to the city of David, to Zion. He also addressed those still in Babylon, "who live in the daughter of Babylon" (2:7 [MT 2:11]). They were directly called to flee from the north (Persia, which included Babylon) (2:6 [MT 2:10]). Yahweh had scattered them to Persia, Babylon, and beyond (to the four winds). So the address to those in Babylon was to be heard in a far greater area.[74] Zechariah added that nations were to be recipients, for they were to be joined with Yahweh and become his people (2:22 [MT 2:15]). Indeed, the nations Yahweh God had used to scatter the covenant people would be humbled under his hand so effectively that slaves would be able to plunder them (2:9 [MT 2:13]). This humbling would surely come because of what the nations had done to the apple of Yahweh's eye, his covenant people. They had served his purpose in executing the curse of the covenant upon the covenant people. They in turn would be humbled.[75] These humbled nations, integral aspects of Yahweh God's cosmic kingdom, were graciously given the reality of becoming integral living members of Yahweh God's eternal redemptive covenant.

The third challenge is to understand the eschatological perspective of the message (2:6–13 [MT 2:10–17]). There should be no doubt that Zechariah presented a number of future perspectives.[76]

First, he had called *hôy hôy,* which can be understood to mean woe or ho, or hey.[77] It is an exhortation to pay attention to the call for action. It was addressed specifically to the covenant people who had remained in Babylon. International upheavals were on the horizon.

The call to flee and escape implies Jerusalem and environs would not be greatly influenced by the upheavals. Judah would be a safe and secure place to live because of the presence of Yahweh God the Father and the preincarnate Christ. We must conclude that the first eschatological perspective draws attention to what is to transpire in the not so distant future.

The second eschatological event that Zechariah held before his audience was the coming of the New Testament era, particularly the first few decades of it. The preincarnate Christ said, "I am coming and will live among you" (2:10, 11 [MT 2:14, 15]). This prophecy was dramatically fulfilled when Christ was born and lived among the covenant people.

The third eschatological event has a few aspects to it. The nations are to be joined and become a real and living part of the covenant people. This was phenomenally demonstrated on Pentecost Sunday when people, having come from various parts of western Asia, were given the message of redemption and received the Holy Spirit. Thus God's covenant promises were fulfilled.[78] This was not just on one occasion, but continued on as missionary activity commenced and was carried out from then on. The ascension of Christ to reign at the Father's right hand is implicitly referred to in "The Lord will inherit Judah as his portion in the holy land and will again choose Jerusalem." His rousing from his holy dwelling thus initiates the birth, ministry, and ascension of Christ.

The fourth eschatological perspective is implied in the events referred to in the preceding paragraph. Christ Jesus will reign over the cosmic kingdom from the time of his ascension until he has fulfilled all the aspects of the Father's plan and submits himself to God (1 Cor. 15:25–28).[79]

Finally, the prophetic message for the restored exiles was clearly that they had been restored for a definite purpose. They were not restored as a favor to themselves. Rather, they had an important and crucial role. They had a definite part in Yahweh God's plan to have the Messiah become incarnate within a covenant community; the restored exiles were to reinitiate that community and to develop it so that in the fullness of time Christ would come and give a renewed kingdom perspective. Thus the restored community had a vital role in the unfolding of Yahweh God's plan to bring in the consummation. This community had to realize they had a place and role in the movement from creation to the consummation.

Vision 4, 3:1–10

The fourth vision answers the question why the restored exilic community has the important role it is given in Yahweh God's plans to finally usher in the consummation. Zechariah has to know and proclaim that the community is chosen, forgiven, sanctified, and commissioned to serve in Yahweh God's plan.

The scene is dramatic; a court drama is succinctly developed.[80] The judge, the defendant, the accuser, the court's personnel are present and carry out their assigned roles.

The participants in the drama have to be understood. Joshua, the high priest, represented the people before the Lord. Part of the official role of the priesthood was to represent Yahweh God before the people, particularly in their worship. This role of representing Yahweh God before the people demanded that the priest be clothed in pure, sacred priestly garments, "to give dignity and honor" (Exod. 28:2). Joshua the high priest, however, was dressed in black, sooty, vile clothes. These represented the people's (and the priesthood's) sins and the curse of the covenant on them. The exile had been a fire that charred and blackened the covenant people even more than their sins. The wages of sin were fire and its destruction. But Joshua, and the people he represented, had not been burned up. They were rescued, plucked from the fire. They had received what they could not do for themselves. They had been delivered from a powerful nation just as Israel centuries before had been rescued and delivered from Egypt.

The second character in the drama was the judge before whom Joshua (and the people) stood as guilty offenders. The judge was the Angel of the Lord, who was in reality the preincarnate Messiah.[81] He is also the sovereign One; he exercises his authority in the court scene. The idea of a court held by God was referred to by various prophets in various contexts of Israel's history. Isaiah implied it when he called for adjudication regarding sins as scarlet which, when removed, results in the sinner becoming white as snow (Isa. 1:18). Amos called for a court drama (3:1, 2), as did Micah (1:2). Zechariah adds to the court scene by referring directly to an accuser. In other prophetic contexts, it could be understood that Yahweh God was the accuser, accusing his people of breaking the covenant. Zechariah proclaims that, Satan, adversary of Yahweh God, is the accuser.

The accuser of Joshua and the people he represented was *haśśāṭān* (the Satan). The Hebrew term has as its basic meaning the idea of adversary or it can refer to one who opposes.[82] In the vision Satan stands at the right side of Joshua, the place, as a rule, where the defender stood. Satan had a definite role in Joshua and the people becoming covenant breakers. He was in a real sense a basic cause of the blackness of the high priest. If he were consistent, he would not be accusing, prosecuting Joshua, but defending him. The vision portrays Satan as a very untrustworthy "friend" of Joshua. He double-crossed Joshua. He prosecuted instead of defended him. The main point is Satan had much to do with Joshua's priestly garments becoming blackened.

The fourth reference was to those courtiers who served the Judge.[83] They carried out the orders of the Judge. They removed the filthy garments from Joshua. Zechariah had referred to angel messengers as present in the first three visions. In this fourth vision angels were present to serve in the application of Yahweh God's gracious work of forgiving sinners and making them righteous in his presence. This activity by angels was portrayed symbolically by their removing the filthy garments and the putting on of rich garments. Angels are referred to in the New Testament as "ministering spirits sent forth to serve those who will inherit salvation" (Heb. 1:14).[84]

Finally, Zechariah the prophet who was given the vision also became an active participant. This involvement of Zechariah is clear evidence that he did not receive this message in a dream—which would have meant he was asleep, not alert or able to participate. In this vision Zechariah spoke up: if Joshua is to be redressed in pure garments, his turban, filthy as it was, should also be removed. A clean one should be given. The high priest represented Yahweh God, the sovereign King of his people.[85]

The message given in this vision was of great significance for the restored remnant community.

First, they were assured that they were the people whom Yahweh God had chosen. The phrase *habbōhēr bĭrušālem* (the choosing one of Jerusalem) stresses Yahweh God's continuing delight[86] and love for Jerusalem, which continues to be his chosen city. Jerusalem, that had been forsaken and ruined, continued to be the elect city. Jerusalem must be understood as a metaphor for all the people dwelling in it. Zechariah had emphasized this glorious truth twice before (1:17; 2:12).

Second, Satan's accusations, true as they were, did not affect Yahweh God's love for and election of his covenant people. Satan was rebuked. He was put, with finality, in his place.[87] Yahweh God would not tolerate anyone or anything standing in his way and opposing him as he carried out his plan in which the covenant community had a vital role.

Third, this vision highlights the antithesis that Yahweh God had placed between Satan and his seed and the woman's seed. Satan was continuing his efforts to uphold his parasite dominion; his accusations against Joshua demonstrate this. He accused Yahweh God of not having a faithful people. If that were indeed the case, Satan would triumph.[88] The triumph of Yahweh God's reign over his cosmic kingdom and his keeping covenant with the woman's, Abraham's, and David's seed are positively demonstrated.

Fourth, Yahweh God's grace and love shine forth brilliantly. Joshua and the people he represents are a forgiven people. Their past sins and the punishment for them are forgotten. The removal of the filthy clothes and turban and the dressing in rich clothes (3:4) beautifully demonstrate that the people were declared righteous before their covenant Lord. The pure garments declared that they were sanctified.

Fifth, the righteous and sanctified people were given a twofold charge and two promises. The Hebrew grammatical terms and structure reveal how Yahweh God will deal with his people. They were given clear and definite instructions. The conjunction *'im* introduces both instructions. How is the term *'im* to be understood? Most commentators translate it as *if,* which tends to stress conditionality. But the term can also be translated *when,* which stresses contingency. Yahweh God thus proclaimed when you walk in my ways and keep my requirements—what then? The adverb *gam* (then) introduced what would follow: they would have a role in Yahweh God's house,[89] that is, his plan, and they would be included among his sanctified servants. They would be given honorable positions of service in Yahweh God's "cosmic kingdom and in his redemptive reign." They would be given great privileges but not without meeting their responsibilities. Justified (declared righteous) and sanctified covenant people are faithful, obedient, serving, and worshiping people according to Yahweh God's revealed will. They were to demonstrate utter commitment to Yahweh God's will, intentions, and revealed character.[90]

Sixth, the vision included a messianic prophecy. Joshua, who represented the people before Yahweh God, was upheld as a type and forerunner of the Messiah. Two statements call for clarification. Who were the associates seated before him and symbolic of things to come? The most acceptable interpretation is that reference is to the priests under Joshua's authority and leadership. The entire priesthood was a type of the priesthood of the Messiah and his role as such. And second, does Zechariah refer to the Messiah as the Branch (3:8)? Undoubtedly so! In Scripture the Branch is a reference to Christ (Isa. 4:2; 11:1; Jer. 23:5; 33:15). And what is meant by the stone with seven eyes set before Joshua (Zech. 3:9)? The stone complemented the Branch. It gave another perspective of the promised Messiah, the messianic Mediator. Commentators and some biblical theologians have suggested various interpretations but these do not always do justice to what the Messiah, often referred to as the stone, represents and does (cf. Ps. 118:22, 23; Isa. 8:13–15; Dan. 2:35, 45; Matt. 21:42; Eph. 2:19–22; 1 Peter 2:7, 8).[91] The Messiah, as stone, speaks of unity (headstone) and stability (cornerstone). This stone with eyes in it (not on it) spoke intelligibily and omnisciently. The restored community, rebuilding the temple, had to be reminded that their Lord was the unity and the stability of their work, service, and worship. And he knew what they needed.

Seventh, an engraving on the stone would give assurance of the removal of sin from the land and bring in prosperity for its inhabitants (Zech. 3:9b, 10). Just what was referred to by the engraving of the stone is difficult to say. The text literally reads, "I will engrave its engraving."[92] Did the engraving refer to a preparation of it as a beautiful and costly stone?[93] Does this engraving of the stone represent a permanent result of God's work for his own people?[94] Is there an implied reference to the relationship between the Messiah and the Holy Spirit who is referred to elsewhere by seven eyes (4:10), or seven spirits (Rev. 1:4) and lighting seven golden lampstands (1:12)? It would seem so particularly because the removal of sin and the prosperity to be enjoyed (Zech. 3:10) are the result of Christ's and the Spirit's work.

Finally, as in previous visions, the message in vision 4 presents an eschatological perspective. The forgiveness and cleansing experienced by the restored community is a beginning of and an assurance of an abiding redemptive work that will become the blessing of future generations. Everyone will be able to invite his neighbor to share in the ever-present and expanding work of the messianic Mediator and the Holy Spirit.

Vision 5, 4:1–14

The fifth vision picks up on what the fourth vision introduced: the presence and the role of the Holy Spirit and how he is involved in the person and role of the messianic Mediator. Zechariah recorded that it was as if he had slept when the angel who talked with him roused him (cf. 1:8). He, as prophet, would receive more of the message Yahweh God had for the restored community. It was still involved with the challenge of rebuilding the temple and laying groundwork for the unfolding of Yahweh God's plan to continue his redemptive work and unfold further aspects of his redemptive reign.

It is difficult to determine the specific setting. The candelabra suggests the interior of the temple, but the olive trees and the oil receptacles do not.

In a vision various aspects that are not usually closely associated can be brought into close proximity to each other and made mutually dependent.

The text, Zechariah 4:2, in Hebrew is far more challenging than the simplified English text in the NIV.[95] The sketch gives a more elaborate presentation of what the text seems to record. The text speaks of channels from the olive trees to two bowls, one on each side of the candelabra. Channels from each bowl conduct oil to each of the seven lamps. Hence the lamps are supplied oil from both sides—from the two trees and then from the two bowls.

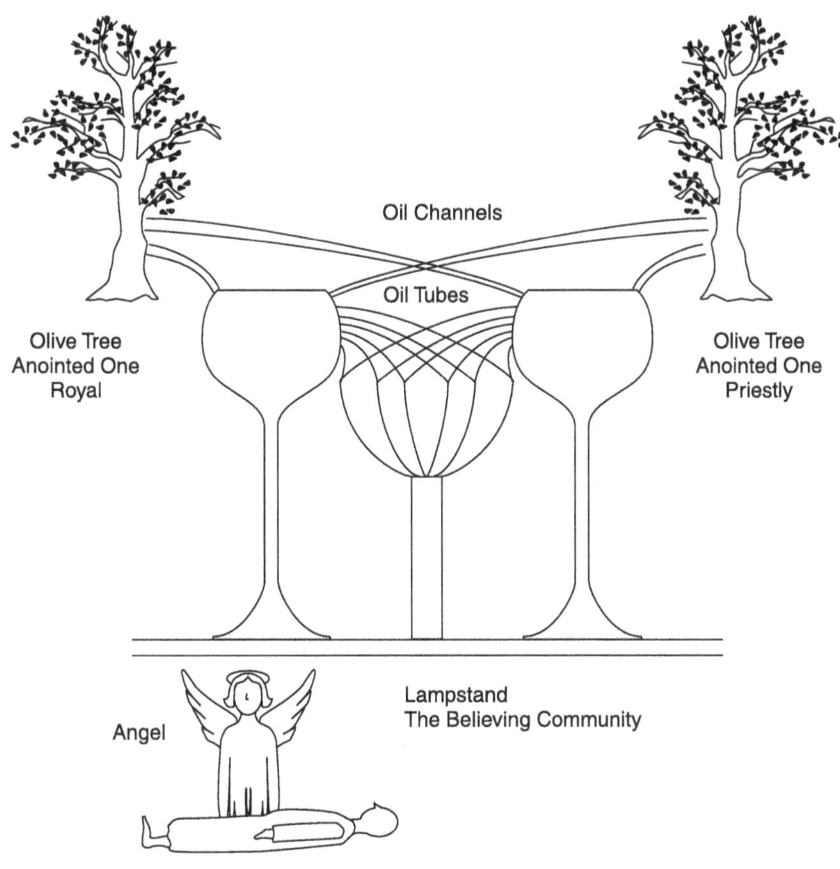

Zechariah inquired about the meaning, saying, *mâh 'ēlleh 'ădōnî* (what these, my Lord). Zechariah did not receive a specific answer regarding these. One can question what Zechariah was referring to. After some discussion, he specifically inquired about the trees. But the angel talking with Zechariah immediately stressed the central message of the vision. The message, the word, was specifically for Zerubabbel; Yahweh God supplied the means required for building the temple. The basic need was not for physical ability and power that any builder would think necessary. The first and greatest need was the Holy Spirit represented by the olive oil (4:6). With the Spirit's presence and aid, opposition (mighty mountain) would disappear. On level ground he would be able to complete the temple; this was represented by the reference to the capstone of the temple being put in place (4:7–9).

Zechariah evidently understood that the candelabra represented the restored community and that the Holy Spirit lit and enabled the community to carry out the work of rebuilding the temple under Zerubabbel's leadership. He could not, however, understand the presence and purpose of the olive trees (4:11). The answer was brief but direct. They are the two anointed[96] who are standing in the presence of *'ădōnî kōl hā'ārez* (the Lord of the earth).

The message was particularly for Zerubabbel, the descendant of David, who had the authority to serve as the leader and director of the task of rebuilding the temple. The first point to emphasize then is that Yahweh God was upholding his covenant promise to David. His house would be the central agent in the unfolding of Yahweh God's redemptive work through the Davidic seed. Zerubabbel was of that line, a direct link between David and the Messiah to come.

The second point that must be emphasized is that all the human might, power, and abilities of David's dynasty was very inadequate to carry out Yahweh God's specific redemptive plan and sovereign reign over Israel and the nations. Even the greatest power on earth could not accomplish the all-encompassing kingdom program that Yahweh God willed.

The third point emphatically states that the Holy Spirit's presence, power, and influence is an absolute requirement in the lives of the forgiven, redeemed members of the restored community. And that was particularly true of Zerubabbel.

The fourth point to emphasize is that the completion of the rebuilding of the temple, a type of the Messiah to come, could be and would be recognized by the entire community. They could and would make known far and wide "God bless it." That phrase meant the completion was enabled by Yahweh God who gave his Spirit.

The fifth point of the message strongly set out the immediate source of the Holy Spirit who enabled the community. Oil was the wonderful, enabling power substance in the cosmos. It was the very proper symbol of the Holy Spirit. Olive oil was known in Zechariah's and Zerubabbel's time to be the most desired oil. The oil was taken from olive trees. Zechariah asked what these trees represented. The answer was astounding. It was very apropos for then and for all ages. One tree represented the royal office of the Messiah; the other one represented the priestly office of the Messiah. Neither tree on its own supplied sufficient and efficient oil! The royal task (to reign and judge) and the priestly task (to sacrifice, make atonement, and intercede) together supplied the power and ability to carry out Yahweh God's will. It is not enough in common parlance to say and believe Jesus reigns or to say Jesus saves. It is the reigning royal Christ who redeems; it is the redeeming one who reigns. The Holy Spirit comes from the Messiah who is both Lord/King and Savior/Priest.

The final point to stress is that the Holy Spirit does not accomplish great deeds as soon as he begins to exert his influence. He initiates his work in small ways. Hence the warning not to despise the day of small beginnings (4:10). But these small beginnings must not be interpreted to mean that the Holy Spirit is limited. In the message he is represented by the seven eyes (3:9), in the stone. He sees and knows all that is and transpires. And the Holy Spirit serves as the eyes of and communicator to the Messiah, the king and priest.

Conclusion: the vision emphasized that Yahweh God's plan and purpose would be accomplished by humans who were empowered and led by the Holy Spirit who came from the reigning and redeeming Messiah.

Vision 6, 5:1–11

The first issue to be settled is: does chapter 5 record one vision or two? Commentators differ in answering this question.[97] Why two visions? There are two introductions. Zechariah wrote: "I looked again" (5:1), that is, after seeing the lampstand and trees, and then the angel told him to look up. In the first view he saw a flying scroll, in the second, an ephah with a woman inside it.[98] These differences, however, do not rule out that Zechariah saw one vision with two specific parts. Both had the same message presented in two unique ways.

It is important to understand that the flying scroll was *hayyōsē't* (the one going) over the entire land (5:37). The Hebrew term for land could be translated earth, that is, over all the earth. In this context, reference is to the area where the restored community had taken up their residence. The import of the flying scroll is that the eighth and ninth commandments, concerning stealing and speaking falsehood, were highlighted. Idolatry was not a prevalent sin, but social sins were. People violated Yahweh God's law that spoke directly to everyday life. And the lawbreakers were condemned according to what was written on both sides of the scroll. Not only were they to be condemned, they were to be banished. Their homes would be destroyed (5:4).

The second part of the vision speaks concerning these banished sins. They are referred to as iniquity and represented by a woman who is named wickedness. The point is: a purifying and sanctifying work was to be effected among the people who had been forgiven and sanctified (vision 4), and among whom the Holy Spirit was present to motivate and empower them to work. Sin and wickedness would continue to try to be present; the woman (wickedness) would attempt to get out of the ephah and remain in the land. But the angel forced her into the container and sealed it. Two women, with wings, took up the ephah and carried it to Babylon, where the woman in the ephah could inhabit a house (not a temple) built for her.

A number of specific points should be emphasized. First, sin and wickedness are incompatible with forgiveness and sanctification. They must be separated and kept apart. They cannot reside together. The temple and the house for wickedness are absolutely contradictory. Those who rebuild the temple may not and cannot dwell in the house of sin and wickedness.

Second, the antithesis is again presented as an absolute reality. Since the experience in Paradise, the unbridgeable gulf between righteousness and wickedness was fixed. This antithesis came to expression repeatedly in the lives of the covenant people. Many had succumbed to the wiles of the evil one. As a prostitute cleverly plies her trade so also the woman in the basket. The women who built a house for her were to continue their efforts to pollute the restored community.

Third, there is a latent and clearly implied message for those exiles who remained in Babylon. They had been called to escape from Babylon, where sin and wickedness were established (2:9, 10). Their place was in Jerusalem and they had to take up their role in rebuilding the temple. They had to come to where the preincarnate Christ and the Holy Spirit were present in a unique and powerful way. Jerusalem was the place of full life; Babylon was the place of wickedness, punishment, and destruction. This reality had been set forth in the second vision. Forgiven, sanctified, and dedicated temple/kingdom builders effectively challenged the power of wicked nations and destroyed them.

Fourth, this vision, with its two parts presents an eschatological perspective. Cleansing from and victory over sin and wickedness is a certain reality for the covenant people who have been forgiven, and sanctified and who obediently serve. The community in Zechariah's day did not realize the full effects of the presence of the Angel of the Lord (the preincarnate Christ) and of the Holy Spirit. But their continued presence and influence would in time cause sin and wickedness to be completely banished. The restored community had a reminder of what would be fully realized in time.

Fifth, the full import of this vision will not be grasped unless the conviction is present in one's heart and mind that Yahweh God certainly was reigning and had full control over the affairs of the cosmos in Zechariah's time. He gave Zechariah the message and ability to proclaim it. The message was definite. Satan, sin, wickedness, in whatever form and way they appear, will not triumph. Yahweh God had his plan and purpose. He caused these to be made known and had movements made that would lead to a full realization of his reign over the cosmic kingdom and especially over his covenant community. And the role of the messianic Mediator and his Spirit cannot be ignored. They are powerfully effective.

Vision 7, 6:1–8

The seventh vision correlates with the first vision. There are differences. In this seventh vision chariots are seen coming from between two mountains of bronze. Since Zechariah received the vision in the area of Jerusalem, commentators opine that the two mountains represented are the Mount of Olives and Mount Zion. The significance of these is not revealed except to suggest that the chariots come from a place of security and strength. Another difference to be noted is that the color of the horses pulling the chariots differs from those that were ridden in vision 1.[99] Another difference is that in vision 1 the report of the horsemen was that the world controlled by nations was at rest and had peace. In vision 7 the horses and chariots come from standing in the presence of the cosmic king, Yahweh God (6:5). They go forth from the divine presence as *ruhôt haššāmayîm* (spirits of heaven). These were agents commissioned to bring judgment. Those going north, the red ones and likely the dappled, are bringing rest to Yahweh God's Spirit in the north, that is, in Persia and Babylon. Judgement will fall on them. It was not a secure place for the dispersed to remain.

The message in vision 7 stresses some important biblical tenets. First, Yahweh God, the sovereign Ruler of the cosmos, has his agents who are eager to serve him. They strain to go over all the earth to do his bidding.

Second, these agents are basically spiritual. They do not go out with military equipment. The message of vision 2 had already emphasized this reality.

Third, the basic spiritual character of the agent did not mean they would not bring judgment. They will do so, and effectively. Under Yahweh God's reign they will overcome powerful opposition and destroy the forces that seek to bring disaster upon Yahweh God's covenant people.

Fourth, the eschatological perspective of the previous visions is definitely implied. Although there is no direct reference to the Davidic dynasty or to the promised Messiah, he is at the heart of the great plan of Yahweh God the cosmic King. He represented by the stone with seven eyes (seeing agents, the Spirit and his assistants),[100] performs his work of redemption and judgment through the Spirit who penetrates all people and works in all circumstances of life. The execution of judgment was taking place in Zechariah's time and would continue until, in the eschaton, Yahweh God's plan is fully carried out and his purposes completely fulfilled.

Fifth, as implied in previous specific points, the triune God is held before the restored community. Yahweh God, the Angel of the Lord, the preincarnate Christ, and the Spirit are together the sovereign (Lord of Hosts), Ruler, Redeemer, and empowering and enabling sanctifying Spirit.

Zechariah's Mandate (6:9–15)

Zechariah 6:9–15 does not record a vision.[101] Rather, the text makes it clear that Zechariah, the prophet, received a message, in reality, a mandate. What he was to do, however, was closely related to what had been revealed in the visions. The role of Joshua and of Zerubabbel was further demonstrated, in the context of the rebuilding of the temple.

Zechariah, the prophet, had to become involved in the temple scene. Gold and silver had been brought from Babylon by some men and had been taken to the home of Josiah who may have been the leader of the group, perhaps part of a caravan.[102]

Zechariah was told to make a *'ăṭārôt* (crown, the Hebrew noun is derived from the verb *'āṭar,* which means to surround). It had royal significance but it was to be placed on the head of Joshua the high priest.[103] Zechariah was commanded to inform the crowned high priest that the person whose name was Branch would extend his work and thus complete the rebuilding of the temple. This was clearly a reference to Zerubabbel. Zechariah was further informed that the crowned high priest would be priest on the throne (v. 13). The Branch, the temple builder, clothed in royal garments, would sit and rule on this throne (v. 13a). The text can only be understood to say that Joshua the high priest would be united with the Branch, David's royal descendant, represented at that time by Zerubabbel.[104] It must not be understood that the two men became one person. The text implies the two would remain distinct persons and that a counsel of peace would exist between them (v. 13a). The message is that the office of high priest and the office of royalty could not be seen or considered as separate and distinct. The high priest was royal; the Branch, the rebuilder, was also high priest. The offices cannot be separated or be seen to function independently of each other.

This unity and harmonious functioning by the royal One, the Branch, and the high priest, had been depicted in vision 5. Both the priestly and royal "trees," the anointed ones, united to qualify and empower the restored community. In the prophetic message Zechariah received, he proclaimed that the twofold source of power produced unity, harmony, and peace.

Zechariah also had to proclaim that under the influence of the priest/king, more help would arrive from distant places to assist in the rebuilding of the temple (v. 15a).

Three specific additional points must be noted. First, the crown that had been made and set on Joshua the high priest's head had to be given to the men who had brought the gold and silver. They, however, had to place it in the temple where it would serve as a *lăzekkārôn* (remembrance; root term is *zāker,* to remember). A threefold reason has been given for the crown to be placed in the temple: (1) to perpetuate the giving of the gold and silver by the men who came from Babylon; (2) to guard it "against profanation," that is, a misuse of it; and (3) to serve a symbolic and prophetic meaning of other nations coming and assisting in building the temple of Yahweh God.[105]

The second additional point is that the help from those from far away, that is, the covenant people still in dispersion and members of other nations, is to confirm that Yahweh God had spoken. He had revealed this to Zechariah and the prophet had proclaimed it. The fact that people would assist was thus definite evidence of Zechariah truly speaking on behalf of Yahweh God.

The third additional point is that Yahweh God, via Zechariah, placed a strong challenge before, and responsibility on all workers, leaders, local workmen, and those coming from afar. They had to *šamô 'a* (inf. absolute of *šāma,* to hear). The form of the verb conveys the strongest possible emphasis on hearing. In common parlance it meant that strict and uninterrupted hearing would take place so that full and complete obedience would be rendered to *tišmĕ'un* (that what was heard). Unconditional obedience to Yahweh God was called for.

In conclusion to this study of the mandate given to Zechariah, one must realize that it is of utmost importance that the messianic message be heard and understood.[106] Joshua and Zerubabbel, the Branch, are representatives and types of the promised and sure to come messianic Mediator. He was already present in and through these two leaders as the preincarnate Lord. Through their agency the temple was rebuilt. Through their agency the covenant body was united, motivated, and productive. The eschatological perspective is clearly presented. The preincarnate mediator was at work preparing for his eventual coming and work in the fullness of time. Then he would no longer be present through types. He would be present in and through the lives of redeemed of Spirit-led and -filled believers.

The Postlude to Zechariah's Initial Prophetic Work (Zechariah 7–8)

Zechariah 7–8 records prophetic messages the prophet proclaimed almost two years after the visions and the mandate had been received. The occasion was a request from the people of Bethel (7:1–3). They had sent messengers to the priest at the temple concerning the continuation of fasting. The text states that these Bethel people sent their messengers to *lĕḥallôt 'et pĕnê yĕhwâ.* This is a unique Hebrew phrase. The verb is the piel inf. construct of *hālâh* that basically can convey one of two intentions. It can mean to appease or pacify one who is angry; it can also mean to ask a favor with the hope of gaining success. The context of this phrase leads one to conclude that the Bethel people were not only tired of fasting but also felt that since they had returned and the rebuilding of the temple was proceeding well, Yahweh God's anger, as expressed by the exile, should no longer be considered present. Why fast if divine anger was no longer necessary? Why fast when the exile was past and there was a return to normal life? Implied was this complaint: Yahweh God, you seem to desire that we working people continue to see ourselves under your anger. You seem to want us to mourn when we have reason to be happy.

The response of the sovereign Lord, who knew the hearts and minds of the people, was in the form of a question: When you did fast and mourn for seventy years, were you demonstrating faithful covenant living and worship? The question implies a rebuke! You fasted and mourned but you also feasted, by eating and drinking. You did for your own sake. Your mourning and fasting was not done with a sense of sorrow for having been covenant breakers. Before the exile you enjoyed the everyday blessings of covenant life (7:6, 7). Do you not want to return to enjoying the blessings, thinking you have paid your dues? You are self-seeking. You are not determined to honor me.

Yahweh God had the prophet press upon the hearts and minds of the restored community that they had to demonstrate a real and deep desire to be faithful covenant people. They had to give real evidence of carrying out important aspects of the covenant's social mandate. Justice, mercy, and compassion were to replace the oppression of the widows, the fatherless, the stranger, and the poor. Their hearts had to be cleansed; they had to be circumcised (Deut. 10:16; 30:6; Jer. 4:4). Hearts, attitudes, and thoughts would demonstrate a truly circumcised heart and a covenantal way of life.

Zechariah reminded the people that Yahweh God's anger had been aroused because of their forefathers' disobedience in spite of what the earlier prophets had prophesied. Anger and exile came as consequences of hard hearts. Can you expect grace, mercy, compassion, and freedom to celebrate, when the sins of forefathers are still present in your lives? Can you expect and ask for covenant blessings when you refuse to face and carry out covenantal requirements and duties?

What conclusions should be drawn from a study of Zechariah 7? Some commentators conclude that Zechariah exhorted the people to put away the fasts that the exile had made necessary.[107] The text has no statement to that effect. Rather, the prophet held the covenant requirements before the people—including possibly Babylonians who had joined the returned exiles.[108] True, the fasting on the fifth month may no longer be necessary for faithful covenant people. That certainly is the thrust of what Zechariah proclaimed (Zech. 8:1–23).

After the introductory statement, (8:12), nine proclamations are introduced by *kōh 'amār yĕhwâ* (thus says Yahweh). The term *sĕbā' ôt* appears seventeen times in chapter 8. Zechariah had used it twenty-five times in chapters 1 through 7. The continued use of the term certainly emphasizes that Yahweh God was the sovereign King of the restored community but also over every aspect of their lives. In reality, the prophet emphasized the sovereign and almighty kingship of Yahweh God over the entire cosmic kingdom. The kingdom with all its aspects, nature, nations, armies, earthly kings, and heavenly bodies, were not only controlled by Yahweh God; as King he reigned over them. Thus by his power and wisdom he guided and directed all events and aspects.

Zechariah, emphasizing the sovereign reign of Yahweh God, also stressed his faithful covenant keeping. Yahweh God maintains his covenantal love for his people and assures them of many covenantal blessings.

Zechariah proclaimed that Yahweh God would remind his people, that is, the people (8:6) who were working on the temple, whose hands had to remain strong (8:9), that he loved them. This love was not a general emotive attitude. Yahweh God said he was jealous with a great jealousy and it was with a burning "ardor" that he demonstrated this jealous love. In jealous love Yahweh chose, defended, and kept his covenant people secure. The restored community was not ever to doubt but to always be assured of Yahweh God's ever strong and actively demonstrated love for his people. Zechariah was not proclaiming a new reality. Yahweh God's people had been assured of this repeatedly (Exod. 20:3; 34:14; Deut. 4:24; 5:8; 6:15; 29:18, 19; 32:16, 21). Ezekiel had prophesied concerning Yahweh God's love (Ezek. 5:13; 16:8–14; 23:35).

Yahweh God's jealousy would be demonstrated to the covenant community in various ways. He would return to and dwell in Jerusalem and it would be a city of truth and holiness (Zech. 8:3). The city would become a safe and secure dwelling for older people and children (8:4–6). Other dispersed people would be saved and restored and Yahweh God would demonstrate his righteousness and faithfulness to them (8:7, 8). He would protect them as they built the temple (8:9–11), and would give them prosperity on the ground, in vineyards and orchards. As the sovereign King of the cosmos he would provide moisture (8:12). As they worked with strong hands they would be safe and a blessing among the nations (8:13). Yahweh God assured them he would do good, as he had brought disaster, but they were to obey the social mandate and thus not arouse his anger again (8:14, 15). And yes, fasts prescribed for the four months would become glad, joyful, happy festivals. These celebrations would be realities if love for truth and peace was exercised. Finally, the community of restored covenant people would be joined by people from faraway cities and powerful nations and seek Yahweh God's favor as these people encouraged each other to do so (8:23).

Zechariah completed his proclamations of Yahweh God's jealous love and evidences of it; he presented a glorious scene of the kingdom of God. The restored community had a pivotal role. Zechariah had emphasized the role of the mediator repeatedly when he related what Yahweh God revealed to him in the visions. A wonderful future was set before the restored community. Covenant responsibilities were repeatedly held before them—truth (mentioned three times), holiness, faithfulness, justice, peace. The community with Yahweh God reigning over them, bestowing his love and covenant blessings upon them, had the potential and possibility to take a pivotal and all-encompassing role in the unfolding of Yahweh God's eschatological plan. Would the community carry out its role and receive all the attendant blessings?

An historical note. There is no record of Zechariah prophesying during the final two years of work on rebuilding the temple. Zechariah prophesied in 518 B.C. Ezra recorded that the temple was completed on the third day of the month Adar (March) in 516 B.C. (6:15). The preaching of Haggai and Zechariah had inspired and motivated the leaders and workers. The preached word proved effective.

NOTES

1. Peter Ackroyd has written that because of the variety of traditions and the intricacies of criticism of Ezra–Nehemiah one should not be surprised that many problems of Old Testament history elude acceptable solutions. *Exile and Restoration* (London: SCM, 1968), 138.

2. Ibid., 87.

3. Raymond A. Bowman is definite. He wrote that Ezra and Nehemiah unquestionably have been formed and transmitted by the anonymous person known as the Chronicler. "Ezra and Nehemiah," in *The Interpreters Bible,* vol. 3, ed. George Arthur Buttrick (Nashville: Abingdon, 1954), 552.

In 1968, Sara Japhet wrote that there were conspicuous stylistic differences between the three and that some parts exhibit actual opposition. Cf. "Supposed Common Authorship of Chronicles and Ezra–Nehemiah Investigated Anew," *Vetus Testamentum* 18 (1968): 371.

Later, writing in 1989, she gave her conclusion in clear language: "Having discussed the matter from different perspectives of an individual author and a 'school's, we now conclude that the answer should be a firm negative." She went on to write that the three books were written by different authors at separate—though proximate—periods in the Persian Hellenistic period. "The Relationship Between Chronicles and Ezra–Nehemiah," *Supplements to Vetus Testamentum* (1989): 312–13.

Then in 1994 she wrote an essay entitled "Composition and Chronology in the Book of Ezra-Nehemiah," *Second Temple Studies* (Journal for the Study of the Old Testament Supplemental Series) (1994), in which she referred to Ezra–Nehemiah as one book (which was divided in two by later traditions), 189. She reflects a semicritical approach in her studies; she seems to accept the text as reliable at times and then expresses acceptance of some critical approaches. I found difficulty in following Japhet's argument regarding Ezra as an historical person who wrote the book of Ezra, although I accept, on other grounds, that he was.

4. See R. Charles Fensham, *The Book of Ezra and Nehemiah The New International Commentary on the Old Testament* (Grand Rapids: Eerdmans, 1982), 2, who doubts Albright's view. Fensham also referred to Roland K. Harrison's view that Ezra and Nehemiah were responsible for their distinctive books. After briefly reviewing the three main views regarding authorship— (1) Ezra is the author of 1 and 2 Chronicles, Ezra, and Nehemiah; (2) Ezra and Nehemiah were responsible for their distinctive books; (3) the Chronicler was the final author of Ezra–Nehemiah—he adapted this third view, 3.

Loring W. Batten gave evidence of this controversy already occupying the attention of scholars before his time. *Ezra and Nehemiah,* ICC Series (New York: Scribner and Sons, 1913). He wrote: "The books of Ezra and Nehemiah were originally one," 1.

5. Ibid., 1. See also D. J. Wiseman's comment: "The Books of Ezra and Nehemiah have long been the subject of special and complex academic controversy." "General Preface," in Derek Kidner's *Ezra and Nehemiah* (Downers Grove: InterVarsity, 1979), 5.

6. Cf. my comments in *MROT,* 920–23. Various commentators such as Kidner, *Ezra and Nehemiah,* 13, accept this traditional view.

7. Japhet, in essays referred to above, and Brown in his commentary, have their doubts concerning the unity and reliability upon these supposed problems.

8. Robert P. Carroll in *Semeia* 59 (1992).

9. Ibid., 90.

10. Jacob M. Myers referred to the importance of gleaning (from sources) as much of the exilic and postexilic history as possible. *Ezra & Nehemiah,* Anchor Bible, vol. 14 (Garden City: Doubleday, 1965). He considered this account as reliable, thus affirming that the historical context of the prophets is also.

11. No attempt will be made to discuss the three concepts or strands separately or individually.

12. The term is usually translated as governor, but the term *pěhâ* is also translated as governor.

13. There is uncertainty concerning who Shesbazzar was. He is referred to as a *hannāśî* of Judah—a head, or prince. Because it was so indicated, it has been proposed that Sheshbazzar was "but another name of Zerubbabel." Cf. discussion of the identity of Shesbazzar by Kidner, *Ezra & Nehemiah,* 139–42.

14. Carol and Eric Meyers made what could be considered a rather rash claim, namely, that Haggai set the stage for a changing world order. Zechariah helped him. *Haggai–Zechariah,* The Anchor Bible, vol. 25B (Garden City: Doubleday, 1989), xlii. It can be said that Haggai's prophecy introduced a new stage in Israel's postexilic history. It is difficult to see how he initiated a new world order—one that influenced Persia, Greece, Egypt, and eventually the Roman Empire. Another voice that raises questions is that of Hayem Tadmos, who wrote an essay entitled "The Appointed Time Has Not Yet Arrived. The Historical Back-

ground of Haggai 1:2." Cf. Ki Baruch Hu (no vol. or date) 401–8. His point, if understood correctly, is that Haggai calculated the precise time for restoration and then began to prophesy. The text tells us God moved him to prophesy at the appointed time. The constant critical effort to say that the prophecies are solely inspired by men becomes an annoyance.

15. Carroll Stuhlmueller, *Rebuilding with Hope: A Commentary on the Books of Haggai & Zechariah* (Grand Rapids: Eerdmans, 1988), 11.

16. Pieter A. Verhoef, *The Books of Haggai & Malachi* (Grand Rapids: Eerdmans, 1987), wrote that "we may assume that he (Haggai) died soon after he delivered his last message or else he vanished from the scene." This assumption is based on the reality of Zechariah carrying on proclaiming the prophetic message.

17. It certainly was true that the remnant was living in turbulent times. It, however, cannot be assumed that this was the reason why there must have been divisions in the postexilic community that the prophets are said to imply and address.

18. Cf. Joyce Baldwin, *Haggai, Zechariah, Malachi* (Downers Grove: InterVarsity, 1972), 14.

19. Stuhlmueller, *Rebuilding with Hope,* assuming that the postexilic times provided the setting for the origin of Wisdom literature, found it of interest that there is in no way a concern for sapiential piety. He accounted for that by stating that Wisdom literature paid little attention to items such as the temple and its ritual salvation history or eschatology, 10. It should have occurred to Stuhlmueller that he presented a good reason for not calling for the postexilic times or the time of Wisdom literature's appearance.

20. Baldwin does refer to a local drought affecting the Jewish economy to which Haggai is thought to refer (Hag. 1:5–7), *Haggai,* 27.

21. Ezekiel prophesied this blessed future reality (Ezek. 47). Scholars who consider the postexilic prophets to identify with Ezekiel do not draw attention to this difference.

22. Baldwin, *Haggai,* 28. Carl Friedrich Keil, however, does not reject the idea that Haggai had seen the Solomonic temple but he points out that it cannot be inferred from Hag. 2:3. *The Minor Prophets,* vol. 2, trans. James Marten (Grand Rapids, Eerdmans, 1951), 167.

23. Stuhlmueller, *Rebuilding with Hope,* overstated the intent of Haggai when he wrote that Haggai identified himself with reestablishing David's authority. 11.

24. J. L. Koole, *Haggai* (Kampen: Kok, 1967), 7.

25. *MROT,* 794–95; *From Creation to Consummation*, vol. 1 (Sioux Center: Dordt, 1996), 206–7, 310, 402–3. Cf. General Index for numerous references.

26. Charles Simeon wrote, "he (Haggai) reproves them with just severity, and shows them that already God had inflicted his judgment on them." *Expository Outlines on the Whole Bible,* vol. 10, 8th ed. (London: Henry G. Bohm, 1847), 412.

27. David L. Turner refers to the remnant returned to Jerusalem as the "nation." *Dispensationalism, Israel and the Church,* ed. C. A. Blaising and Darrell L. Bock (Grand Rapids: Zondervan, 1992), 269. Blaising and Bock wrote in another context that Jews returning to Palestine in the 1900s establishing a Jewish state (nation) is the work of the Son of David. Christians should pray for this Jewish state. But they also wrote that Jewish believers in the Messiah are the believing remnant of Israel. The authors do not refer to this believing remnant as a nation or state. *Progressive Dispensationalism,* (Wheaton: Victor, 1993), 295–97. The authors express a hope that the believing remnant will in time become part of the modern Israeli state, in fact, that the state adopts the believing remnant's beliefs. Haggai certainly does not give evidence for this hope.

28. Thomas Moore wrote that the verbs Haggai used are in the form of infinitives which indicate that the action of the people, the work without profit, had been going on for some

time. *A Commentary on Haggai and Malachi,* reprint from 1856 edition, (London: Banner of Truth, 1960), 60.

29. Two Hebrew terms call for attention. *šiddāpûn* translated "blight" is a disease that affects the roots of plants and can refer to what happens to plants when scorching hot winds blast them. *yirāgûn* is translated mildew or paleness. The root of the term *yereq* means green, or greenness. Used in the same context as blight it refers to a plant disease. Its color may be greenish; most likely it will have a pale gray color as the mildewed plant dies.

30. Verhoef, *Haggai,* pointed out that the verb *nākâ* in the hiphil form in 227 places emphasis on what God has done. He struck them. The Hebrew term appears often in the context of Yahweh God executing the covenant curse, 126, 127.

31. Stuhlmueller suggests that the language Haggai used is reminiscent of holy war echoes from the books of Joshua and Judges. *Rebuilding with Hope,* 37.

32. This part of Haggai's fourth message was placed in the context of messianic eschatology; cf. point D.

33. It should not be forgotten that the community made up of descendants of the patriarchs included people from various non-Israelite tribes. Outstanding examples of these are Joseph's sons he had by an Egyptian wife, Rahab, Ruth, and some of David's warriors.

34. Covenanted, see NIV Berkley Version, promise, see RSV and NASB.

35. Cf. 2 Sam. 7:5–17; 23:1–5.

36. Cf. Baldwin, *Haggai,* 47.

37. Walther Eichrodt has written that the understanding of the covenant as an eternal and unalterable relationship of grace could be revived; the restoration of the temple represented unceasing covenant favor, and prepared the ground for a community of law. *Theology of the Old Testament,* trans. J. A. Baker, vol. 1 (Philadelphia: Westminster, 1961), 467–68.

38. Ibid., 2:60–64, 419.

39. Haggai repeated what Moses had proclaimed when he renewed the covenant with Israel on the east side of the Jordan before the Israelites took possession of the promised land (Deut. 28:1–14).

40. See my study of the messianic Mediator in the Prophecies of Haggai for further discussion of the persons mentioned here. *MROT,* 854–71.

41. Verhoef, *Haggai,* 101.

42. Koole, *Haggai,* "opniew . . . vooreenkeer [en wel bennenkort]." 64.

43. Ibid., " kostbaarheden," treasures.

44. Stuhlmueller, *Rebuilding with Hope,* may have spiritualized to an extent at least when he wrote that "the heart of Jesus becomes a new temple of worship where Jesus is the mediator of the new covenant (Heb. 4:14; 10:21) and the supreme high priest." 31.

45. I personally have spent much time in various nations as a "missionary." I found no desire for *the messianic Mediator.* When he was presented to the public in various contexts, there was little, if any, initial desire for Jesus Christ.

46. Curtis, *Haggai,* 77; Stuhlmueller, "Haggai's hope for the temple and for the Davidic dynasty never came literally true." *Rebuilding with Hope,* 38.

47. Meyers, *Haggai,* 83.

48. J. Ridderbos describes how bearers of signet-seal rings indicated an intimate relationship between the ring bearer and the one represented by it. *De Kliene Profeten Haggai Zacharia, Maleachi,* vol. 3 (Kampen: Kok, 1952), 29.

49. Keil, *Minor Prophets,* 2:214.

50. Ibid., 212.

51. Meyers, *Haggai,* 83, 84.

52. Chapter 30, I. B. See also my reference to this in *MROT,* 873, and a lengthy bibliography, pp. 882, 883, note 2. So also Michal Floyd's bibliography in "Cosmos and History in Zechariah's View of the Restoration," in *Problems in Biblical Theology,* ed. Henry T. C. Sun and Keith Eades (Grand Rapids: Eerdmans, 1977), 126, note 4.

53. Cf. chap. 31.

54. Joyce Baldwin, *Haggai, Zechariah, Malachi* (Downers Grove: InterVarsity, 1972), wrote that the book of Zechariah was an artistic whole, 70. Cf. her plan of Zechariah 9–14. 78–79.

55. H. C. Leupold, *Exposition of Zechariah* (Columbus: Wartburg, 1956), 19. Cf. also T. V. Moore, *A Commentary on Zechariah* (London: Banner of Truth Trust, 1958), who saw an exhortation to avoid their sins, 39.

56. Moses referred no less than eighteen times to the reality of Yahweh God's anger and wrath provoked by covenant breaking. Wrath: Deut. 9:8, 19; 29:20, 28; 32:22; anger: Deut. 4:24; 6:15; 7:4; 9:7, 18, 19; 11:17; 13:17; 29:23, 24, 27, 28; 31:29.

57. The text is clear and definite. The people themselves suffered just punishment. Zechariah stated the anger was with the people, the forefathers because of their sins, not as some would write: God hates the sin but loves the sinner. Cf. G.A.F. Knight, *A Christian Theology of the Old Testament,* 2nd ed. (London: SCM, 1964), 122.

58. *'ayyēk* is the lengthened form of *'ay* and places emphasis on the where. The answer is implied: "Gone, not here."

59. H. Veldkamp in *De Twee Getuigen (The Two Witnesses)* (Franeker: Wever, n.d.) wrote Zechariah's lesson in "kerkhistorie" (church history) brought a turnaround. The people's conversion was the fruit of the punishment, 51, 52.

60. *šābtî* is the first-person singular perfect of *sûb,* to turn back or return. To translate this verb as an imperfect, i.e., I will return, is incorrect.

61. Cf. A. L. Bartlett, "The Night Visions of Zechariah Against the Background of Conflict in the Early Post-Exilic Community in Judah," *Scrif en Kerk* 16 (1995): 1–15. Bartlett considered that the visions, not being in a priestly document, were not intended to return to the status quo of worship, but were intended to inspire hearers and readers to become involved in the process of changing society. Response: one should not negate the worship to enhance societal change; the two are inseparable, in reality, worship as Yahweh God ordained it is a vital aspect of societal change.

62. The color of the horses has given rise to various explanations. Three biblical passages speak of horses with various colors. Zech. 1:8; 6:1–6; Rev. 6:1–8. Each passage has one or more different color. In Rev. 6:1ff. the riders are said to signify various phenomena. Zechariah did not give such representations. Barry F. Peachey wrote an article entitled "The Horses in Zechariah and Revelation," *Expository Times* 110 (April 1999): 214–16. Peachey suggested that Bible translators knew more about Greek and Hebrew than about horses. He referred to Baldwin's discussion of the colors, *Haggai, Zechariah,* 138–40, and referred to some unlikely explanations. His conclusions include a statement to the effect that the colors may "have no meaning at all," 216.

63. Cf. Floyd, "Cosmos History," for his effort to outline Zechariah 1:7–6:1–15. He did not give details of personages seen in the visions but pointed out how at times a narration of visions was interrupted by exhortation, 131–32.

64. Floyd, seeking to employ historical and literary tools in a rather mild, nonforceful manner, included in his summation that Yahweh's activity with the postexilic community also "encompasses the whole world." Ibid., 143.

65. The phrase "raised my eyes" can be understood as a common formula to introduce a new vision. Cf. Leopold, *Zechariah,* 46.

66. The Hebrew term denotes a dissolution of the united condition and independence of the nation of God. Keil, "Zechariah," 2:239.

67. Baldwin, *Haggai, Zechariah,* 109.

68. The NIV translates terrify.

69. Cf. Ezra's account of how the opposition was terrified and made ineffective (Ezra 4:6–6:13).

70. For a discussion on the structure of this prophetic message, see Baldwin, *Zechariah,* 107.

71. Cf. Meyers, *Haggai, Zechariah,* "Most commentators . . . regard these oracles as complementing the first three visions," 172. As one studies various critical writers, one can receive helpful insights but also ideas that must be challenged. George Adam Smith very obviously interpreted Zechariah's visions and prophecies as coming from human insights influenced by social and international events. He wrote that the influence which molded the change that came over prophecy must be sought for in certain habits that the people formed in exile. "Visions of Zechariah," in *The Expositors Bible,* ed. W. Robertson Nicoll (Grand Rapids: Eerdmans, 1956), 625. It is true that one must understand the historical context in which Yahweh God revealed himself. Revelation did not come in a vacuum.

72. Baldwin pointed out that 2:8 [MT 2:12] is one of the most difficult verses in the entire book to interpret. The terms *kabôd* (glory? honor? insistence, heaviness) and *'aḥar* (after, with) are at the crux of the problem. She presented four possible interpretations: (1) after the Lord of glory sent me; (2) after glory, that is after a vision of glory; (3) with glory he has sent me; (4) with insistence (*kabôd* can mean heavy) he sent me. The NIV translates after he has honored me and sent me. This interpretation involves a future time. Baldwin preferred option 4. *Haggai, Zechariah,* 189.

73. "To go for" can be the same as saying "go after something to acquire it."

74. Leupold, *Zechariah,* wrote it should be seriously considered that the message to the nations was *to* them, not *against* them, 58, 59. Note that both *'el* and *'al* appear (2:8 [MT 2:12]) and 2:9 [MT 21:23]).

75. Isaiah had prophesied that plundering Assyria would be plundered (10:5–19), but also that nations would rally around the Root of Jesse as he reclaimed his people (11:10–16).

76. Cf. the eschatological events Micah included in his prophecies, chap. 22, Part III, B.

77. "*Hô* is hortative." Leupold, *Zechariah,* 58. "*Hôy* hardly means woe to the exiles." Meyers, *Zechariah 1–8,* 182; but see Baldwin, *Haggai, Zechariah,* "woe . . . an exhortation touched with a note of sympathy and pity," 108.

78. God's promise to Abraham, when he covenanted with him that nations would be blessed in him (Gen. 15:1–3), was fulfilled.

79. One should be hesitant to accept all that Kenneth L. Barker sees in this prophecy. He was correct to see the Abrahamic covenant fulfilled. To inject the prophetic "in that day" and "the great messianic future" which includes what he understands Daniel to prophesy, that is, the return of Christ to reign for a millennium on earth, is not acceptable. To do so is to place an unwarranted eschatological grid on Zechariah's message. "Zechariah," in *The Expositor's Bible Commentary,* 12 vols., ed. Frank Gabelein (Grand Rapids: Regency/Zondervan, 1983) 7:619, 620.

80. To consider Christ as judge is biblical. He spoke of himself when incarnate, as the judge (John 5:27; 8:16).

81. T. V. Moore, *Commentary on Zechariah* (London: Banner of Truth Trust, 1958) places the scene in the temple, where Joshua was officiating as priest, 62. Baldwin, *Hag-*

gai, Zechariah, also placed the scene in the temple but went on to write that Joshua "stood as a prisoner in the dock," 113.

82. Balaam, on the way to Balak, had one opposing him (*lĕśāṭān*). In this context it was the Angel of the Lord (Num. 22:22). David referred to his generals, the sons of Zeruiah, as his opponents in regard to Shimei's not being put to death (2 Sam. 19:22 [MT 19:29]).

83. Commentators refer to the court attendants as angels. H. Veldkamp, *De Twee,* 101; Baldwin, *Haggai, Zechariah,* referred to "angelic beings," 114.

84. According to John in the book of Revelation, angels served in various capacities. Cf. e.g., 5:11; 7:1, 2, 11; 12:7; etc.

85. Three Hebrew terms are translated "turban." They basically refer to the linen cloth wound around the head. Various references are considered; it was a sign of rejoicing or solemnity, as such an adornment for the priest and also for a bridegroom. It was translated as mitre or diadem, indicating royalty.

86. Curtis, *Haggai, Zechariah,* translated the active participle as "who delighteth," 150.

87. Cf. Myers, *Haggai, Zechariah*, 186.

88. Cf. my study of Gen. 3:8–4:25 in *From Creation,* 1:114–20, 127, 132.

89. Baldwin, *Haggai, Zechariah,* 115, gives a limited reference to the term *bêtî* (house), the temple. In this context the term *house* refers to the much wider and inclusive will and plan of God, and the temple rebuilding was but a small part of this.

90. Ibid.

91. Cf. my study of "the stone" in *MROT,* 880–82.

92. Myers posits the view that the identity of a memorialized one was inscribed but does not suggest who this was. *Haggai–Zechariah,* 210.

93. Keil, "Zechariah," 261.

94. Leupold, *Zechariah,* 78, 79.

95. Some translations (e.g., the Jerusalem Bible) do not mention channels, nor side bowls; reference is made to lips.

96. The term *mĭśiâh* is not used but the phrase *bĕnê hayyiśhār* (sons of fresh oil). Fresh oil was oil that had not yet been processed. For another discussion of this vision, see my study of it in *MROT,* 883–88.

97. These can be consulted but a final answer may not be readily accepted.

98. Michal H. Floyd has presented a unique exposition of Zech. 5:5–11. Cf. "The Evil in the Epoch: Reading Zechariah 5:5–11 in its Literary Context," *Catholic Biblical Quarterly* 58 (1996): 51–68. He considers this passage to present a vision distinct from that recorded in 4:1–14 and 5:1–4. He provided an extensive bibliography to indicate sources he approves of and those he does not. He accepted interpretations of terms and motifs that support his literary context and interpretation in distinction from historical, cultural, and phenomenological concerns. That a definite relationship between the messages of the visions is present is accepted. To interpret this in such a manner, however, that the conclusion could be established that the message of the vision is that "a commonly venerated Israelite goddess" had to be banished because Yahweh's worship could not be manifested in a feminine form is rejected. Rather, the idea of a female image representing divine royal rule in general and participating somehow in the representation of Yahweh God's kingship over heaven and earth could be accepted. Floyd came to this conclusion by his interpretation of the two women building, on behalf of Yahweh, a house in Shinar.

99. Vision 1 had red, brown, and white horses; vision 7 has red, black, white, and dappled (1:8; 6:2). In our study of vision 1 we concluded that the color had no specific meaning.

100. Some commentators translate "winds" instead of spirits, which suggest winds of heaven. Myers, *Zechariah,* 330.

101. Stuhlmueller wrote that "rough textual spots" were smoothed over by modern translators who follow ancient versions. He referred to three such supposed spots: the names are not identical in vv. 10 and 14, the Hebrew word order is "awkward" in v. 14a, and the final clause of v. 15 dangles. He concluded that these "blotches" result from oral transmission. *Haggai, Zechariah,* 96. In response, note that in v. 14 *Hen* is added, who may have been a temple person; the references to unusual Hebrew is seen to be efforts to find evidence for a critical reading. Cf. Baldwin's discussion of v. 14, *Haggai, Zechariah,* 137.

102. Ibid., 133.

103. Commentators, in view of what follows, i.e., reference to the Branch, discuss whether two crowns were made, one also for Zerubabbel.

104. Cf. discussion of v. 14 by Ridderbos, *Zechariah,* 100–105.

105. Cf. Keil, "Zechariah," 301. Kenneth Barker suggested that the crown in the temple was a reminder of messianic hope. "Zechariah," 641.

106. Most commentators make this point.

107. Cf. Adam Smith, "Zechariah," 637.

108. The names of the delegates to the priests have been understood to be Babylonian names, possibly of proselytes. Baldwin, *Zechariah,* 143.

31

The Golden Cable in Esther and Zechariah 9–14

I. Introductory Comments

II. The Integral Elements of the Golden Cable in Esther

III. The Golden Cable Explicated in Zechariah 9–14

IV. Joel's Agenda

31

The Golden Cable in Esther and Zechariah 9–14

Introductory Comments

The Little Book of Esther

"Tucked away in the Bible in an obscure corner of the Old Testament is the little Book of Esther." With this statement a commentator began his studies on the book of Esther.[1] This little book has drawn the attention of the Jewish people throughout the centuries because of its recording an important and crucial period in their history, 485–475 B.C. Christian scholars representing various theological preferences have also found that the book of Esther challenged their scholarly interests. Likewise, critical scholars of varied emphases have not over looked this little book.[2] Some scholars attempted to defend a mediating view between the traditional and liberal critical views.[3]

The Historical Setting

Someone who was a contemporary of the main characters in the book wrote it. The author is not mentioned, but various scholars have opined that Mordecai may have written it. The writer reflected intimate knowledge of the history of the covenant people and of the contemporary circumstances recorded in the book. Critical writers have attempted to discredit the unity and historicity recorded in the book.[4]

The events recorded in the book took place during the reign of King Ahasuerus, known as Xerxes I, who reigned from 486 to 465 B.C. as the king of the Persian Empire. Herodotus (VII, 8), recorded that Xerxes called his nobles together to consider a campaign against Greece.

This was the time of Vashti, the queen who refused to display herself before a drunken crowd (Esth. 1:12). She was deposed and Esther was chosen to be queen. Xerxes married her in 473 B.C. after he returned from fighting the Greeks who defeated him.

Esther did not initially reveal her true identity. She was a Jewess of the tribe of Benjamin (as was her uncle Mordecai).[5] She was given the highest position any woman could have had in the court of the greatest kingdom on earth at the time. She has been referred to as unethical for hiding her identity, becoming a member of a harem, marrying a Gentile, showing no mercy on Haman, and not observing Jewish dietary laws. It has been observed that in spite of these ethical and moral practices, Esther was not condemned by the author for shortcomings. Rather, the book was included in the canon because of its "significant theological value."[6]

Haman the Amalekite

Haman played a very interesting and integral role in the experiences of Esther and the Jewish people. Haman was identified as the son of Hammadatha, the Agagite. His father's name was not Jewish, but was likely Persian. The entire account supports the identity of Haman as a descendant of Agag, the king of the Amalekites. They had fought Israel in the desert (Exod. 17:8–10). Later Saul defeated them after a valiant fight (1 Sam.14:48). But Saul had not completely destroyed the Amalekites as he had been commanded (15:1–3) Saul spared "good things" as well as King Agag, whom Samuel then killed (15:17–35). An interesting question is: was the conflict between Israel and Amalek reenacted in the context of Esther's becoming and being queen? Was Mordecai, a descendant of Kish and relative of Saul, considered an enemy by Haman, a descendant of Agag the Amalekite who in turn was a descendant of Esau (Gen. 36:12, 16)? Did Haman *hēmâh* (be enraged) because Mordecai, descendant of Kish, refused to bow to him (Esth. 3:5)? Haman's reaction, according to the text, was because Mordecai was a Jew (3:4).[7]

The Feast of Purim

Scholars have attempted to trace the origin of the Feast of Purim. Was it of Jewish origin? Was it of Greek or Babylonian origin?[8] According to the biblical text, the Feast of Purim became an annual event because Mordecai wrote a letter to all the Jews in the provinces of "King Xerxes, far and near" to celebrate annually the feast of lots (Esth. 9:18–24). The term *purim* is the plural of *pur,* which means the lot. Haman and his cohorts had to cast the pur to select a day and month for the obliteration of all Jews. The lot fell on the month of Adar (3:7), the thirteenth day. Then an order had gone out to destroy, kill, and annihilate all the Jews and to plunder their goods (3:13–14). The Jews were permitted to strike back and won their right to life. So the lot, pur, was negated and the resulting festival was named Purim (lots).[9]

Evidence of the Golden Cable

As one reads the book of Esther, and consults the growing number of books and articles written on it, one can understandably be wondering why anyone would refer to the Golden Cable in the book of Esther. Writers do not seem to see it in the text. Some consider the book to basically deal with a nonprescribed religious festival. It was not included in Mosaic legislation. Some scholars have concluded that divine providence is the leading and uniting theme of the book. Thus the book calls for confidence in God in times of trouble.[10] The motifs, according to a writer, are banquets, kingship, and obedience/disobedience. The kingship motif in this context is strictly a human kingship in the lives of both men and women.[11]

The basic question to be asked is: what is the biblical-theological message of the book of Esther? What role does it have in the upholding and the unfolding of Yahweh God's redemptive plan and reign? A careful survey of what biblical theologies present in answer to these questions does not provide clear answers. Progressive dispensationalists do not refer to Esther at all.[12] Nor do some premillennial writers.[13] Some Reformed writers make no reference to Esther.[14] Nor do all the neoorthodox writers.[15] The lack of references to the book of Esther could suggest that it does not have canonical significance because it does not contribute to the understanding of Yahweh God's unfolding redemptive plan and purposes revealed in the Old Testament.

In this study, the contention is that the three concepts refer to realities functioning in what is recorded in the book of Esther. These three realities, the concepts forming the Golden Cable, provide the contexts for the themes various writers have selected. Hence, it is not incorrect to point out that kingship, feasting, obedience, providence, confidence, joyous assurance, oppression and the preservation of the Jews, hatred and vengeance, courage, and sacrifice are themes in the Esther material. These, however, are united and form a well-knit account when they are seen as based on and issuing forth from the three Golden Cable concepts—the kingdom, the covenant, and the mediator.

There is another reality that must be emphasized. The three Golden Cable concepts are crucial to the understanding of how the revelation in Esther provides an introduction to and a positive rationale for Zechariah's prophecies recorded in chapters 9 through 14. In other words, Esther provides the historical occasion and setting for Zechariah's later prophecies. Zechariah, the prophet, becoming advanced in years,[16] proclaimed the messages Yahweh God gave him to give assurance and confidence to the people. To allay fears his prophecies encouraged the Jewish people to resist the execution of Xerxes' edict. Zechariah gave them a vision of what their role was in the outworking of Yahweh God's redemptive plan and reign.

The Integral Elements of the Golden Cable in Esther

The Kingdom

The kingdom concept appears in various ways and numerous times. The term *melkût* (kingdom) appears thirty times. It is used to refer to the Persian Empire. Not once does it refer to the kingdom of God. The term *melek* (king) appears more than 230 times. It is used to refer to men who ruled over Persia, Media, Judah, and Babylon but never to Yahweh God the sovereign Ruler over the cosmic kingdom. The term *malkâh* (queen) appears twenty-three times, referring first to Vashti and then to Esther. Esther received full royal authority and exercised it (Esth. 9:29). This little book is a record of royalty and of the royal palace and gardens, of rich cloth and precious stones. It refers to royal banquets and dinners. But there is no direct reference to Yahweh God the sovereign Ruler of the cosmic kingdom,[17] nor is there a direct reference to the law of God, to prayer, or to God.[18]

The cosmic kingdom, over which Yahweh God always exercised his reign, is the all-encompassing context of what is recorded in the book of Esther. The biblical witness is consistent. Empires, kingdoms, nations, kings, queens, all persons with authority are integral aspects of Yahweh God's cosmic kingdom. Judah, and the king of Judah (2:6), were in the cosmic kingdom of Yahweh God. But there is only one indirect reference to the kingdom of Judah, a "theocratic" kingdom. This theocratic kingdom was not and is not an issue in the book of Esther.

The people who had been citizens of the theocratic nation of Israel/Judah are at the very heart and core of the Esther account. The political entity, the national form of government, is not an issue at all. The people represented the kingdom of priests although they were not organized in the form of a holy nation (Exod. 19:6). They were nevertheless kingdom people; they were a unique people, the apple of Yahweh God's eye (Zech. 2:8).

Another indirect reference to Yahweh God's cosmic kingdom was by means of describing the vast wealth, splendor, and glory of the Persian kingdom (Esth. 1:4). Queen Esther's wealth and splendor, the royal garments, the purple robe and golden crown given to Mordecai speak of Yahweh God's sovereign provisions for his servants who had a crucial role in the Persian Empire at the time.

Various writers, as noted above, emphasize that divine providence is the central theme of the book of Esther. This should not be doubted or refuted. The Jewish people were delivered in a wonderful way from the execution of the edict that called for their destruction. They were unexpectedly given the authority and ability to protect themselves and to destroy their enemies. They were given privileges they had not enjoyed before. Yahweh God reigned. He directed and guided the activities of King Xerxes, Mordecai, and Esther. Under Yahweh God's sovereign rule, Haman, his sons, his collaborators and would-be executioners met their death. One is reminded of how Yahweh God had assured Moses and Israel, that though they were comparatively few in number, they would conquer and defeat their numerous enemies (Deut. 7). That reassuring promise made and carried out centuries before was still the same. Yahweh God, the King, protects his people in difficult and threatening circumstances. He can and does because he holds absolute sway over the cosmic kingdom and over all that is involved in it. Thus his will, plan, and purposes are ultimately carried out.

The Covenant

The Hebrew term *bĕrît* (covenant) is not to be found in the Hebrew text of Esther. And one may have to search far and wide to determine whether the term *covenant* is mentioned in the contents and subject indices of commentaries and theological studies on Esther. These omissions do not prove or imply that Yahweh God's covenant with the descendants of Abraham, Isaac, Jacob, and his descendants had been forgotten. The very opposite is the wonderful reality. Yahweh God had assured the patriarchs that he would be their God and the God of their descendants for generations to come (Gen. 17:7). He had promised Abraham that he would have numerous descendants and through them nations would be blessed (22:17, 18). Yahweh God had said to Jacob that all peoples of the earth would be blessed through his offspring. Jacob was assured that Yahweh God would be with him and watch over him (28:14, 15). These promises had been repeated in various circumstances to his descendants. The book of Esther records that these promises were kept.

The Jewish people were under the rule of the Persian king. But that did not remove Yahweh God's care for them and his protection of them. His word to David was sure and abiding. David's son would have a kingdom forever. Yahweh God's love for him would never be taken away (2 Sam. 7:12–14). If this covenant promise was to be upheld and eventually realized, the Jewish people, through whom the promised Davidic Son would come, had to be preserved. The book of Esther records this preservation at a crucial time in the history of Abraham and David's covenant descendants.

Another important covenantal reality must be emphasized. Yahweh God had established the antithesis between the woman's seed and Satan's. He established enmity between them. This enmity referred to an unbridgeable gulf between the two seeds. In the course of the history, repeated attempts to destroy the woman's seed were made: the murder of Abel, the sinfulness in Noah's time, Jacob's treachery, Pharaoh's killing of the baby boys in Egypt, the constant attacks by Israel's enemies, the Amalekites, the Philistines, and the Canaanites. The nations that exiled the Israelites gave opportunities to remove the covenant people from the earth. The enmity, the antithesis, was always there—Satan, through his human agents, continually fostered the enmity.

The activities of Haman, the Agagite, revealed the ever-continuing antithesis between Satan and Yahweh God. As referred to in the preceding,[19] Haman could have had an historical reason to be filled with *hēmâh* (rage) (Esth. 3:5). Satan took advantage of this in another attempt to completely destroy the people who represented the seed of the woman. Thus he would keep from coming on the scene of history that one who would crush his head.

Satan's efforts, and his human agents, were not only covenant breakers, as demonstrated by their attitudes and activities, but they did their utmost to make

Yahweh God's covenant with the seed of the woman, with Abraham and David, completely null and void. The book of Esther is basically a record of Satan's effort, through Haman, to prevent the Messiah, the Christ, the Redeemer, from coming in the flesh to atone for sin and to deal Satan his sure and final death blow. Esther records how Yahweh God upheld his covenant and employed his agents for this.

The Mediator

The phrase "anointed one" or the term *Messiah* are not mentioned in the book of Esther. Neither is there mention of, or even a reference to, a type or an ancestor of the promised covenantal Redeemer, the Messiah. These omissions must not be understood as demonstrating that there is no messianic significance in Yahweh God's revelation as recorded in the book of Esther.[20]

References in the preceding have been made to agents employed in the dramatic events that occurred in the Persian Empire during the reign of King Xerxes. Haman did not in any way serve as an agent of preservation. He, however, as an agent of Satan, was integrally involved in the events that led to Yahweh God's victorious preservation of the Seed of the covenant. King Xerxes proved to be an agent in the preservation of the people. He gave the second edict permitting his first edict, that the Jews were to be killed, to become ineffective (Esth. 8:11). Thus the unsuspecting agent of Satan became a royal servant of Yahweh God and the deliverer of the covenant people.

Mordecai and Esther carried out their different roles as agents of Yahweh God. Neither was a direct descendant of Judah or David. Nor were they types of the coming Messiah. They, however, served as effective servants of Yahweh God in the preservation of the covenant people. They did more; they served, with severe threats to their lives, as means in the providential turn of events that led to the preservation of the Jewish people and their victory.

The Historical Consequences

King Xerxes, Queen Esther, and Mordecai were agents in Yahweh God's cosmic kingdom setting to preserve and protect the seed of the woman and to take their place in the unfolding drama of redemptive history. Esther became a wealthy royal queen (Esth. 8:7). Mordecai became an official spokesman on behalf of King Xerxes to the Jews (8:8, 9). The would-be killers of the Jews were put to death. The Jewish people were free to go about their normal lives throughout the Persian Empire. Mordecai, with regal authority, called for celebrations (9:20–23). The feast of Purim thus became a unique Jewish festival. The feast, however, should have great significance for all people, especially for Christians. It should serve as an annual reminder that under Yahweh God's providence the Jewish people were preserved. It is of great importance to all Christian believers that the Jewish people were preserved. Through them Jesus Christ came into the world, through them, the Scriptures (both Old and New Testaments) were written and initially preserved, and through them the Christian church came into existence. Yahweh God gave these great gifts to all the people of the world through the Jewish people and should be commemorated by Christians joining in the celebration of Purim.

The Golden Cable Explicated in Zechariah 9–14

Introductory Comments[21]

The apocalyptic character of biblical prophecy is very evident in this passage. Zechariah employed symbols and metaphors. These were not intended to be taken literally. They were taken from past covenantal history and present national entities. His hearers (and readers) could, on the whole, understand what he was saying. Zechariah had to speak carefully lest he offended the Persian satraps and cause more trouble for the covenant people than Haman did. So, by employing commonly used symbols and metaphors from Israel/Judah's past and present religious, social, and political life, Zechariah knew that the Persian leaders and population would not readily understand what was prophesied.[22]

The unity and authenticity of this prophetic passage have undergone various degrees of attacks and resultant sources are said to have been used.[23] A commentator has noted that there is no further reference to Zechariah, to Joshua, or Zerubabbel, or temple building, or that the temple was present (11:13).[24] That there are some differences between the two parts of Zechariah 9–14 (e.g., 9–11, 10–14), should be recognized. But these are not of such a character or proportion that each has to be considered as coming from a distinct separate source. Similarities can be pointed out. Each part is introduced by *maśśa'* (oracle). It has been correctly stated that the six chapters refer to war between nations and Israel, but do so in different ways.[25]

The specific feature of intertextuality is very prevalent. Zechariah demonstrated his thorough acquaintance with Old Testament Scriptures that obviously were available to him. Commentators refer to illusions, indirect quotes, and references from Amos, Micah, Isaiah, Jeremiah, and Joel.[26]

A final introductory comment must be made. The three Golden Cable strands are so closely interwoven that it is difficult to separate them. Together they present a very strong and clear message. In the context of the cosmic kingdom, the royal covenantal mediator is portrayed as the central reality. He will execute the plan and purposes of Yahweh God. An attempt, however, will be made to distinguish the three strands without detracting from their inseparable unity.

The Kingdom

At the very outset of this discussion on the kingdom it must be emphatically stated that Zechariah did not prophesy that the theocratic kingdom of Israel would be restored. A key statement is *wĕhāyâh yĕhwâ lĕmelek 'al kol hā'erez* (Yahweh will be King over all the earth) (9:9). He, and he alone, will reign over the land that once was the area of the theocratic kingdom. No reference is made to a Davidic person who will sit on the restored throne of David.[27]

Zechariah prophesied concerning the cosmic kingdom that included Judah, Israel, Greece, Hadrach, Tyre, Sidon, and the Philistines (9:1–13). In his sovereign power Yahweh God will execute his power over nations that oppose his reign. Tyre is singled out as an example. Her skillful work, silver, and gold will be burned. Her power on the sea will be destroyed. The Philistines will writhe in agony; they will no longer have a king or cities they can claim as their own (9:5–7a). Greece will not be the strong power over the land (9:13). Yahweh God, in his opposition to nations seeking to rule and control, will prove victorious (9:13–17).

Yahweh God is the cosmic King over creation. He provides rain (10:1), and he will overthrow false shepherds (10:3). His power extends over Egypt and Assyria, from where his dispersed people will come as Israel did from Egypt when they came through the Red Sea. It is Yahweh God who created the cosmic kingdom: the heavens, the earth, and all people in it. He will have control over war horses (12:4). He will demonstrate he reigns whether by sending earthquakes or by providing water to flow to the seas (14:8). He controls the plagues that strike his enemies (14:12–15).

The entire section pulsates with the reality that Yahweh God is King. He is actively reigning over the entire cosmos—the nations, the natural elements within it, and his people. He punishes. He spares. He gathers. He provides. He can and does execute judgment on nations, including his covenant people, for their disobedience and rebellion, but he delivers them in his own way and time.

Finally, Zechariah portrays a glorious scene. It has a futuristic touch. Not only will his gathered ones come together to worship *lîmelek yĕhwâ šĕbā'ôt* (the King, Yahweh of hosts) but also the survivors of the nations that once opposed and sought to destroy Israel (14:16). Zechariah added, "to celebrate *'et hag hassukât* (the feast of tabernacles)." Israel, to memorialize their wanderings, celebrated their deliverance from the desert. In like manner, when Yahweh God restores his people and gathers with them the survivors of former enemies, there will be a celebratory worship of Yahweh God, the cosmic Sovereign of the cosmos.

The Covenant

Zechariah mentioned the term *bĕrît* (covenant) two times (9:11; 11:10). In the first instance the phrase *bĕdam bĕrîtēk* (by or because of the blood of the covenant [with] you), reference is undoubtedly to the covenant ceremony that took place at Sinai. Yahweh God had confirmed his covenant with Israel (Exod. 19:4–6), and had sprinkled blood on the people to seal the covenant that had bound the people to Yahweh God and he to them (24:8). Because the people in Zechariah's time were sprinkled by that covenantal blood, they would experience Yahweh God's faithfulness.[28] Thus the reality of the abiding covenant Yahweh God had made with his people was emphasized. The people were gathered from dispersion (the waterless pit) in spite of their repeated covenant breaking because Yahweh God is a faithful covenant keeper.

The second reference is (Zech. 11:10) *lĕhāpêr 'et bĕrîtî* (to revoke the covenant). The verb *hāpêr* is the hiphil infinitive construct of *pārar,* which can be translated as violate, break, frustrate, make ineffectual. The question that has challenged commentators is: which covenant is referred to in this passage? Interpreters are quite agreed the phrase refers to the nations Yahweh God had employed in his dealing with disobedient and rebellious Israel.[29] If one recalls what the former prophets had proclaimed, the answer is clear. Isaiah prophesied that Assyria, a rod of God's anger, would be sent against Israel/Judah, which had become godless nations (10:5). Habakkuk had prophesied, speaking for Yahweh God, "I am raising up the Babylonians" (1:6). Jeremiah had declared that Yahweh God would hand over nations, Judah, Moab, Ammon, Tyre, and Sidon, to his servant Nebuchadnezzar, king of Babylon. "All nations will serve him" (27:6, 7). The term *covenant* is not mentioned. But the message was very plain. Yahweh God had a league arrangement with nations. They were called to execute the curse of the covenant upon covenant-breaking Israel/Judah. Moses had warned that Yahweh God would do so (Deut. 28:45–58). The restored community, threatened by the Persian edict calling for the destruction of all the Jews, were assured that Persia was not an agent to execute the covenant curse or any kind of judgment on them. Revoking the arrangement, the covenant, with the nations meant Yahweh God would no longer bring judgment upon the remnant community. Rather, he would uphold his covenant with his people, be their God, be with them, and carry out his promises to and through them.

The passage (Zech. 11:4–17), the context in which it was stated that Yahweh God abrogated his covenant with the nations, must not be understood to refer to the remnant community as a sanctified people. The people were referred to as a flock of sheep destined for "slaughter" (11:4). There was oppression in the flock. The rich and the leaders sought to use the flock to their own advantage. Nations would no longer be their threat, but their own leaders and shepherds brought disaster. These shepherds, however, would not remain in their positions. They would be removed. Another "shepherd" for whom a price would be paid would eventually give true shepherding care (11:13). Then a woe would be brought upon worthless shepherds (11:17).

In addition to the two verbal references to "covenants," one with Israel and one for Israel with the nations, Zechariah continues to unfold a basic theme of his prophecy: "The Covenant Still Stands."[30] At times in obscure phrases, at other times less so, but by implicit and indirect references, Zechariah referred to Yahweh God's keeping of the covenant with his people.

Yahweh God, speaking through Zechariah, proclaimed that those who are left still belong to God. Then he quoted directly, "I will defend my people . . . for now I am keeping watch," (9:7b, 8). These words follow the prophecy of a sure punishment, with destruction and mortal consequences for the nations surrounding Israel/Judah. This undoubtedly is a reference to the Davidic dynasty. Yahweh repeated his promise to David in the words *wĕḥanîtî lĕbêtî,* and I will guard[31] my house.[32] The reference to the Davidic house is preferred. The Davidic house was Yahweh's house through which the promised eternal Son would come. It should also be noted that in the immediately succeeding passage, there is a clear proclamation about him who represents and comes from the Davidic dynasty. This passage (9:7b, 8), refers to Yahweh God's covenant with David, and as such, to the people over which David's son reigns.

In the following verses (9:13–17), the reference is clearly to Yahweh God's covenant people. Yahweh God, the covenant Lord, will actually employ his people as an influence on and against Greece.[33] He, sovereign Yahweh God, will shield and save them; he will beautify them. The covenant people will sparkle as jewels. The young men and women will thrive as royal ones under Yahweh's care in their land (9:14–17).

The concept of the covenant, in fact, the reality of the influence of Yahweh God's covenant with his people, is pervasively present in Zechariah's later prophecy and is a major key to understanding what is recorded in chapters 10 through 14. The cosmic King, Yahweh God, will provide abundantly in the natural realm (10:1). In contrast, man-made idols are deceitful and cause people to wander as sheep without a shepherd. Therefore Yahweh's anger is against false shepherds. Yahweh God, as covenantal David had done (Ps. 78:72), will *pāqad* (attend to, give heed to, visit with loving care) his flock, the covenant people (Zech. 10:3). He will do more: he will *śām* (set, place, establish) his people with confidence and assurance among their opponents (10:3). Why? *Kî yĕhwâ 'immām* (because Yahweh is with them). The covenant promise given to Abraham centuries before stands. It will not be abrogated (10:5b). Being with them, he will strengthen them, restore them, and answer them. Their joyful children will rejoice in Yahweh. Although Yahweh chastened them, once restored they will rejoice for what Yahweh God, their covenant shepherd, has done for them. They will then walk in the way of Yahweh, that is, they will be obedient covenant people (10:6–12).

Zechariah the prophet set forth an idyllic scene for a faithful covenant people who were shepherded faithfully by under-shepherds. The tragedy was that the under-shepherds were unfaithful; cosmic natural elements burned them, pine and oak fell and pastures were destroyed as shepherds wailed (11:1–3).

The further tragedy was the covenant people, referred to metaphorically as the flock (11:4),[34] were guilty of much evil. Hence they were marked for slaughter, that is, for destruction. Their leaders sought to become rich at the people's expense. Yahweh God made it clear: "I will hand the people over." The ruthless leaders and unfaithful people eclipsed the idyllic future portrayed (11:4–6). A further reading of chapter 11 makes it clear that the basic problem in the covenant community was leadership.[35] Joshua and Zerubabbel were no longer present. Zechariah, the prophet, indicated that he was to assume a leadership role. This was not symbolic. The prophet, in these turbulent times when the Jews were under threat of death, undertook the task of providing leadership. He took up two symbolic shepherd staffs (11:7), and had three leaders, unnamed persons, removed (11:8). But the community did not support the prophet. He discarded the two staffs and on behalf of Yahweh God declared that he would let the people perish (11:9). Zechariah, who had attempted to shepherd the people, that is, provide good leadership, asked to be paid for his efforts. The thirty pieces of silver he received had to be discarded—thrown in the house of the Lord to the potter (11:13). But Zechariah was not finished; at Yahweh's command he had to provide instruments for a foolish shepherd who would misuse the flock. A strong woe was pronounced against these foolish shepherds.

Efforts to find persons who were referred to have been fruitless. That the restored community was spared death called for by Xerxes' edict is historically true. That the "flock," the covenant community, had unfaithful leaders and was itself guilty of rejecting Yahweh God's covenant shepherding is also an historic reality. New leadership was an absolute requirement. Yahweh God provided this thirty-forty years later in Ezra, Nehemiah, and Malachi.

The last three chapters of Zechariah change the emphases and perspective. The central concepts are victory for the covenant people and the Mediator's role in the lives of his people. And the presentation of the perfected kingdom under the reign of the Messiah concludes the prophecies. Notice should be taken of the presence of the three strands of the Golden Cable that integrally unites this concluding prophecy. While the kingdom and covenant strands are clearly present, the mediatorial strand stands out.

The Mediator

Zechariah had prophesied the Mediator as a humble royal one.[36] He was described as righteous, that is, he came according to and doing the will of Yahweh God. He came bringing salvation for his people (stated in militaristic political terms). He came very humbly. He came to fulfill the requirement that the blood of the covenant be poured out on behalf of "prisoners in the waterless pit." This language covenant people would understand. The Persian overlords would not likely do so (Zech. 9:9–17). Jacob had prophesied that the Ruling One would arise from Judah's tribe (Gen. 49:8–12). This prophecy was obviously fulfilled by Jesus on Palm Sunday (Luke 19:28–45).

The mediator was also typified by Zechariah the prophet. He answered the order to shepherd "the flock," the people of his latter days. They detested him (Zech. 11:8), and paid him off with thirty pieces of silver that he threw to the potter in the house of the Lord. He foreshadowed the betrayal of Jesus by Judas Iscariot, who functioned as an agent of the people and their leaders who despised Jesus (Matt. 26:14–16, 47–56; 27:5–10).

The second oracle Zechariah proclaimed in the days of Xerxes' edict is recorded in 12:1–14:21. The city of Jerusalem, rather than its inhabitants, is placed in the foreground. It is to become "an unmovable rock for all the nations." Central to the rock-like Jerusalem, its people, is the house of Judah (12:2–5). The strength of Jerusalem, the people it represents, is *yĕhwâ šĕbā'ôt 'ĕlōhêykem* (the sovereign Yahweh, their God). The people would be saved because the House of David would be like God. The following phrase states how their God appears and goes before them *hĕmal'ak yĕhwâ lipnêyhem* (like the Angel of Yahweh going before them) (12:7–9).

In the first part of this oracle the covenant people were assured that their sovereign Lord, the King of the cosmos, would defend, protect, and give them victory. He was the Rock who is the Messiah (1 Cor. 10:4), the Angel of the Lord, in the form of a cloud and pillar of fire, who led the Israelites to their promised inheritance (Zech. 12:7–9). That same Rock—member of the House of David—would undo all those nations (peoples) who sought to attack and destroy Jerusalem (the covenant people). But these people would mourn and grieve bitterly because their Rock, their leading Angel, would be pierced by the very people he came to shepherd, feed, protect, save, and guide to joy and peace (12:10–13). This prophecy foreshadowed the division that would exist within the restored community. There would be those who were with the one who pierced; there would be those who would grieve and weep bitterly because he, of the house of David, was pierced[37] (Matt. 27:5, 6; Mark 15:40, 41; Luke 23:26, 27; John 19:33).

In chapter 13 of Zechariah's prophecy three central points are stressed. First, the pierced Shepherd would provide the sanctifying blood that the people need. In picturesque language, a fountain is said to be opened to supply the cleansing means for the people. Second, a main defiling factor had been idols (13:2a). False prophets (prophecy) that had confused and corrupted the people would be removed. They who had so prophesied would be ashamed and deny they had prophesied. Families from which these false prophets arose were called to remove them (13:2b). Third, the striking of the Shepherd preceded the opening of the fountain. This striking would have a dividing and refining effect. Many would be struck down; one-third would be refined and tested. They would call on the name of Yahweh God and be heard. The covenant would be confirmed for them. Yahweh God will say, "My people," and the people will respond covenantally, "Yahweh is our God."

It seems difficult to correlate these three emphases at a first reading. Upon reflection, however, Zechariah can be heard to proclaim prophetically what was to take place. The Messiah would be struck; his blood would be shed. The blood of the covenant would thus be made available. The covenant people would be declared righteous (cleansed) and sanctified. The tragedy would be that not all of the covenant community, particularly the leaders (prophets), would acknowledge the stricken one. There would be division among the people who were scattered. Many would not be cleansed and sanctified. There can be no doubt that Zechariah was given the message of Jesus' trial, death and influence in the covenant community. The rejection of the redeemer Messiah was starkly portrayed in what could be considered tragic results—the death and destruction of those who reject him. The striking of the shepherd would have a redeeming result also. Righteousness and sanctification surely would be applied to many covenant people.

Zechariah concluded his prophecies with a definite reference to the future: *hinnēh yôm—bâ lĕyehwâh* (behold Yahweh God's day is coming, qal. act. ptc., stressing future continuity). This phrase emphasizes that Yahweh God has definite plans for the future (14:1a).[38] An attempt will be made to distinguish between the various activities/events that are portrayed.[39] First, the plunder, or spoils of war will be divided. The battle scene is that of nations gathered by Yahweh God to fight against Jerusalem. The nations will succeed in ransacking, raping, and dividing the people—half to stay, half to go into exile (14:2).

Second, Yahweh God will appear and fight against the nations and cataclysmic events will occur. Yahweh comes with his holy ones (14:3–5).

Third, on that coming day there will not be light, frost, cold, or daytime or night-time; in the evening there will be light. Also water from barren Jerusalem's hills will flow in two directions, in both summer and winter. Nature will experience changes (14:6–8).

Fourth, on that coming day, only Yahweh God will reign over the cosmos (14:9).

Fifth, topographical changes will take place at the time, effecting the Arabah, the rift, and Jerusalem will be raised up, with people living in it securely for all time to come (14:10, 11).

Sixth, a plague will strike all nations fighting against Jerusalem. Animals will be stricken also. Human flesh will rot, men will fight each other and people of Judah will do so also in Jerusalem. Great wealth will be collected (14:12–15).

Seventh, survivors of the attacking nations will join worshipers annually in Jerusalem (celebrating the feast of booths). Those not coming from Egypt will be punished.

Eighth, on that day holiness will be written on horses' bells. Cooking pots will become sacred bowls in front of the altar. Everything will be holy to Yahweh God. People will be also. No Canaanite, representing noncovenant people, will be present.

As written before, interpretations of chapter 14, with its wide array of features, vary dramatically.[40] All are agreed that there is an eschatological perspective. There is also a reaching back to various dramatic events in Israel's past. Examples suggested are Sennacharib's attack on Jerusalem, Israel's escape through the Red Sea, and David's flight from Absalom, which are said to be in the background of the split in the Mount of Olives. Commentators have found much intertextuality, that is, quoting directly or implicitly former prophets.[41] These features are cast into an apocalyptic setting.[42]

A number of aspects of this chapter must be noted.

First, the chapter intends to portray "an impressive picture of the power of Yahweh."[43] Yahweh demonstrated he is the sovereign King over all aspects of creation. He will cleave mountains and create a valley (14:4, 5). He will control days and seasons (14:6), and cause water to flow from hills that have no springs of fresh water.[44] The Arabah will be extended and Jerusalem physically raised to a higher level (14:10, 11). He will send plagues on nations as he did to Egypt (14:12, 13). Wealth will be collected under his reign (14:14). More, Yahweh God, will demonstrate his sovereignty over the nations and cause some members of these nations to become participants in Yahweh God's covenant people (14:16–19).

Zechariah did not specify precisely how and when Yahweh God would demonstrate his power, authority, ability, plan, purpose, and wisdom in effecting these great events, some of which were described as catastrophic. If the precise historical context of when this prophecy was annunciated is kept in mind, namely, Xerxes' edict, then one should have no doubt that Zechariah was comforting and assuring the covenant people. As in times past, so in the present and in the future, Yahweh God would reign supremely over the cosmic kingdom and all aspects of it. His people had to know they were secure under his sovereign kingship.

Second, chapter 14 emphasizes Yahweh God's call for holiness. This also is presented in an unusual manner. Moses had stated this covenant requirement plainly: "Be holy because I Yahweh your God am holy" (Lev. 19:1). Zechariah, however, portrayed holiness as not only personal. All aspects of Yahweh's cosmic kingdom were to be seen and known as sanctified to him. The covenant people had to live sanctified, holy lives. All that they interacted with was to be sanctified. Nothing was to be considered for common use.[45]

Third, there is no direct reference to priests, prophets, or kings as forerunners of the mediatorial Messiah. In the context of what Zechariah had prophesied before about the Shepherd sold, pierced, providing the cleansing agent (the fountain), and gathering and refining his covenant people (chaps. 12, 13), chapter 14 records the glorious result and all-encompassing sanctifying influence of the Mediator's effective role.

The Eschatological Perspective

Reference has been made before to the eschatological character of Zechariah's prophecies (chaps. 9–14). Two issues call for attention.

First, did Zechariah prophesy concerning a millennial kingdom to arise in the end times? Yes, say some biblical scholars. One wrote in his introduction to his comments on Zechariah 14 that "the ultimate goal of all history is the Lord's personal appearance and reign . . . the literal and full manifestation of his kingdom."[46] The idea of a literal kingdom on earth over which the Messiah will reign a thousand years is arrived at by means of a very literal hermeneutic and exegesis. This type of biblical interpretation does not do justice to the historical context of Zechariah's prophecies, or to the apocalyptic character of the prophecies. There should be no doubt that some elements of Zechariah's prophecies were fulfilled. Jesus entered Jerusalem riding a donkey (Zech. 9:7; John 12:12–15). Thirty pieces of silver were paid to betray Jesus (Matt. 26:14–16). The connection with Zechariah receiving thirty pieces for work done (11:12, 13) is not literal but is more an analogy. The reference to the fountain being opened for cleansing is not a literal prophecy of Christ's crucifixion. That there is a correlation, either by literal fulfillment or by analogy, does not mean that the entire prophecy must be interpreted literally.

There is a further problem. Zechariah did not prophesy directly that the Messiah would stand on the Mount of Olives and split it. The subject rather is Yahweh God, who gathers all nations *to fight* and to ransack Jerusalem. He who gathers is the one who is said to cause rupture of mountains and earthquakes (Zech. 14:2–5). Furthermore, emphasis is on Yahweh, the only name, who will be King over the whole earth (14:9). There is no direct reference to the Messiah. It is true, however, that when Jesus Christ ascended he sat at the Father's right hand. He was given the reign over the whole cosmos then (Acts 2:33). Furthermore, there is no New Testament reference to plagues and internecine fightings in Jerusalem in the context of the Messiah's second coming. Finally, there is absolutely no evidence in Zechariah that the king's reign over the earth would be for a thousand years. Rather, Zechariah sets forth the eternal reign of Yahweh God and the Messiah over the cosmic kingdom.

The second issue concerns the actual eschatological perspective that Zechariah set forth.

First, he implied that there would be an international political upheaval. Xerxes had endeavored to conquer Greece. Greece, however, is implied to be in charge in due time because Zion's sons will challenge Greece (9:13).

Second, the Messiah will appear humbly as king (9:9) and his coming will bring victory and prosperity in due time (9:14–10:7). Under his reign scattered ones will be brought in (10:8–12).

Third, before this reign of the Messiah is exercised from the Father's right hand, he will shepherd his people faithfully. This will be done to give contrast to faithless shepherds who desert the flock. As a shepherd among his people he will be betrayed and pierced (crucified). The ministry of Christ, which included exercising dominion over storms, bread, and evil spirits, will demonstrate his kingship.

Fourth, there will be a cleansing, sanctifying ministry. There is no reference to the Holy Spirit being poured out, but it is implied by the actual cleansing and by the gathering of people from various nations.

Fifth, the reign of Yahweh God by and through the Messiah will bring holiness into the kingdom. This holiness, to be initially evidenced in all aspects of life, will be fully demonstrated when all enemies, opposition, defilement in life, is fully and finally overcome.

Sixth, there is an implied perfect reign that will be exercised in accordance to Yahweh God's plan.

Finally, it must be repeated, in Zechariah's time the enemy seemed so strong. Death seemed imminent. Zechariah, in that context, proclaimed that the covenant promise for the covenant people would not fail. Yahweh God and his anointed were reigning and would reign. Opposition would be fierce at times. But Yahweh God did and would always bring victory as he reigned over the cosmos. In that *Sitz im Leben* the restored community could have assurance and confidence.

Joel's Agenda

It would seem apropos at this point in the study of the Golden Cable in the Prophets to again raise the question of Joel's place and role in the Old Testament canon. One scholar wrote that the Masoretic placing of Joel between Hosea and

Amos[47] lent to the predisposition for an early date. He went on to say that a great majority of critical scholars insisted Joel was written in the Persian period. He added, however, that a strong minority defend a preexilic date.[48]

In this study the position adopted and repeatedly demonstrated is that Joel was one of the first prophets to write. He covered a range of issues that other prophets referred to and/or developed.[49]

Zechariah repeated, or made reference to or developed, the following themes.

Joel had warned of local, national, and cosmic disasters. Zechariah referred to plagues and earthquakes. Joel called for repentance, obedience, and trust. Zechariah did not state these terms explicitly but the entire purpose of his prophecy was to inspire trust and confidence in Yahweh God and to turn to him. Likewise Zechariah spoke of Yahweh God's jealous love for his people (1:14), as Joel had done. Zechariah spoke of this love in a more stressful situation than pertained when Joel prophesied. Joel prophesied of blessings in the creational/natural realm; Zechariah did likewise (9:15–10:1). Joel had prophesied concerning the return and gathering of the covenant people. Zechariah's prophecies were spoken in the context of these events happening. Likewise, Zechariah expanded on the judgment to be executed on the nations and how this would have effects on the covenant people. Joel gave assurance of peace; Zechariah prophesied that peace would be proclaimed to the nations (9:10). Joel had spoken of Jerusalem as the symbol of Yahweh's presence over which he reigned. Zechariah was very explicit about Yahweh God's role regarding Jerusalem, assuring the people of his presence in the city that represented his people. Joel had spoken of water, living and constant, flowing from the temple; Zechariah also referred to water flowing from Jerusalem (14:8). Joel had spoken regarding the Day of Yahweh and all that it includes. Zechariah proclaimed that "a day is coming" (14:1). Joel had prophesied that judgment would fall on the nations and that many of the inhabitants would be included with the covenant people. Zechariah was specific: survivors from all the nations will go up to worship Yahweh (14:16). Joel had spoken eloquently about the pouring out of the Holy Spirit. Zechariah spoke of the Holy Spirit and referred to how the presence of the Spirit could strengthen, encourage, and enable builders to do Yahweh's bidding.

The conclusion is incontrovertible: what Joel had prophesied had come to fulfillment in various ways. Zechariah, however, repeated, expanded, and applied Joel's message. And as he did, he also indicated in various ways, explicitly or implicitly, how Yahweh God was faithful to his previously spoken word that prophets had continuously held before the covenant people.

NOTES

1. Ray C. Stedman, *The Queen and I* (Waco: Word, 1977), 7. Stedman revealed an evangelical perspective. Others who wrote with that perspective include the following: Alexander Carson, *Confidence in God in Times of Danger* (Sterling: GAM, 1990). Carson wrote, "The great design (of Esther) is to display the wisdom, providence, and power of God," 3.

Carl McIntyre, *For Such a Time as This* (Collingswood: Christian Beacon Press, 1946). McIntyre compared the Federal Council of Churches, the great enemy in Protestantism, to the adversaries of the Jews, 76, 77. A Dutch commentator, A. Roorda, in *Het Boek Esther* (Bredai: Traktaatgenootschap, 1912), wrote that Esther provided a necessary explanatory supplement to Ezra and Nehemiah, 5.

2. The Adventist theologian, Angel Manuel Rodriquez wrote *Esther: A Theological Approach* (Berrien Springs: Andrews University Press, 1995). Rodriquez wrote that the absence of the divine shifts emphasis to human causality, but considering the difficulty in interpreting Esther, he looked for the author's perspective and ideology and paid close attention to "certain literary features" and thus came to the conclusion that a theological understanding of the book should guide the interpretation of it; xi, 109–10. Authors who wrote with a critical perspective include Sandra Bette Berg, in *The Book of Esther* (Missoula: Scholars, 1979), who had as a primary aim to analyze the literary and stylistic features of the book, 16. She revealed an ambivalence. She paid full respect to literary and historical critics, but she also felt she had to honor the text and message as it had been handed on since its origin. Johanna W. H. Van Wyk-Bos gave evidence of wishing to find a biblical base for her discussion of contemporary issues such as feminism/sexism, patriarchy, prejudice, and oppression of Jews by Christians. *Ezra, Nehemiah, and Esther* (Louisville: Westminster/John Knox, 1998). She wrote that the book of Esther is "more clearly *narrative* than *history*. She defined narrative as story told in such a way as we identify fiction today, 104–5. Kenneth M. Craig, Jr., under the title *Reading Esther*, presented "a case for the literary carnivalesque" (Louisville: Westminster/John Knox, 1995). Craig followed Mickhail Mikhailovich Bahntin, who propounded a theory of literature referred to as "carnivalesque," the language of carnivals, 11–31. Gilles Gerleman in *Studien zu Esther* BKAT 21 (Neukerchen-Vluyn: Newkirchenen Verlag, 1960), who followed the recent critics who question the historicity of Esther, found a parallel between the story of Esther and the Exodus. Carey A. Moore, in *Esther*, Anchor Bible, vol. 7b (Garden City: Doubleday, 1971), wrote a section entitled "Support for Its Historicity," xxv–xliv, which began with the statement, "On the face of it, the story seems to be true." Subsequent to a short section on "Evidence Against Its Historicity," xlv–vi, Moore wrote that for him the contradictions, exaggerations and inconsistencies argue against the story being taken at face value. L. Lewis Beyle Paton, in the ICC Series, *A Critical and Exegetical Commentary on the Book of Esther* (Edinburgh: T & T Clark, first impression 1908, 2nd, 1951) continues to have writers who accept his critical approach to Esther. Paton wrote "the conclusions seem inevitable that the Book of Esther is not historical and that it is doubtful whether even a historical kernel underlies its narrative," 75. Paton did prepare a very useful study of the history of the text. A Danish author has stated the case as follows. "The text of Esther has a complicated history because of various Greek Translations." See Ben L. Sikfetzen, "From Story to Preaching," in *Alle der Ander*, ed. Else K. Holt (Frederiksberg, Denmark: Forlaget ANIS, 1998), 151–70. Sikfetzen correctly acknowledges that the Hebrew text is prior and basic to the various Greek translations that had alterations and variations, thus complicating the study of the original texts. W. Lee Humphreys wrote a review of recent liberal works. He saw an eclectic use of a range of literary methods and perspectives used in the study of Esther. "The Story of Esther in Its Several Forms: Recent Studies," *Religious Study Review* 24 (1998): 335–42. Humphreys did not state it, but his review indicates that various writers have predetermined modern preferences about biblical materials and they endeavor to find them in ancient literature.

3. Brevard C. Childs, *Introduction to the Old Testament as Scripture* (Philadelphia: Fortress, 1979), presented his view of the canonical significance of Esther. He emphasized the Festival of Purim as of major significance in the consideration of the canonical role and shape, 603–65. It would seem that his perspective on the Old Testament, as a book that developed in the context of the development of the believing community's desire and need for an authoritative Scripture results in his omitting Esther's canonical significance. Frederick Bush in "The Book of Esther: Opus non Gratum in the Christian Canon," *Bulletin for Biblical Research* (1998) correctly wrote that a serious misreading of the book of Esther tended to consider it as an unaccepted book in Christendom. But, Esther offers an insightful satire on the pagan world and presents a glimpse of the dangers Jewish people faced in the diaspora, 39–54. What Bush wrote is acceptable, but as will be pointed out subsequently, not completely.

4. Writers who have done this have a rather eloquent spokesman in Bernard W. Anderson, who wrote the introduction to Esther in *The Interpreters Bible,* ed. George A. Buttrick (Nashville: Abingdon, 1954), 3:823–32. Others who joined him are mentioned in the last part of note 2. Childs took a mediating position between "complete historicity" and the theory of a complete fabrication. *Introduction*, 601. A very helpful reply to the critic's presentations of doubting or denying the historicity of Esther was succinctly laid out by J. S. Wright in his essay, "Esther, Book of," in *The Zondervan Pictorial Encyclopedia of the Bible,* ed. Merrell C. Tenny (Grand Rapids: Zondervan, 1975), 2:376–80.

5. Writers who have attempted to present a type of mythological basis to the account have suggested that Mordecai is a corruption of Marduk, but Paton doubts if there is a connection. *Esther,* 77. Likewise Esther has been seen as corresponding to Ishtar, a Babylonian goddess, 79.

6. See Mark W. Chavalas, "Esther Theology of," in *Evangelical Dictionary of Biblical Theology,* ed. Walter A. Elwell (Grand Rapids: Baker, 1996), 208.

7. Rodriquez developed this view. *Esther,* 20–24, (Esth. 5:7–9). Craig referred to Haman as a "conniving dolt, a clever fool, who was portrayed as a man of distended pride who was often presented as a man running about." *Reading Esther,* 144–46. See also Berg, who wrote that the genealogies of Mordecai and Haman recall an earlier conflict between Saul and Agag. *Book of Esther*, 67.

8. Paton, after reviewing these theories, concluded that Purim was probably borrowed either directly from Babylonia or indirectly from Persia, *Esther,* 77–94. It is difficult to follow Craig's discourse on Purim in a carnivalesque manner; stressing "laughter" particularly, does not make much sense, *Reading Esther,* 147–51.

9. Berg, *Esther,* in a discussion of Purim, wrote that Purim is of primary importance in Esther, but that the term *pur* (often in the plural) appears infrequently, that the story does not require the festival to be named Purim, and questions about the authenticity of it (9:29–32), continue to be raised, 39–46. Moore saw three major steps whereby Purim became an important part of the Jewish religious calendar: the festal letter (9:22, 23); the Jews intent on celebrating the events of Purim annually; and the confirmatory letter of Esther to Mordecai. *Esther,* 97.

10. Roorda concluded his exposition by writing that the book of Esther is a "doorloopende lofrede" (continuous panegyric on the providence of God), 279. Cf. also Carson, *Confidence.* In spite of subverting the whole nature of Christ's house, God displayed his providence, thus giving confidence, 18.

11. Berg, *Esther,* 31, 59, 72.

12. Cf. Craig A. Blaising and Darrell Bock, *Progressive Dispensationalism* (Wheaton:Victor, 1993); Robert L. Saucy, *The Case for Progressive Dispensationalism* (Grand Rapids: Zondervan, 1992); J. Dwight Pentecost, *Thy Kingdom Come* (Wheaton: Victor, 1990).

13. Cf., e.g., Thomas E. McComisky, *The Covenants of Promise* (Grand Rapids: Baker, 1985).

14. Cf., e.g., Roderick Campbell, *Israel and the New Covenant* (Philadelphia: Presbyterian and Reformed, 1954); Gerhardus Vos, *Biblical Theology* (Grand Rapids: Eerdmans, 11th printing, 1980); W. J. Dumbrell, *Covenant and Creation*, (Nashville: Thomas Nelson, 1984).

15. Brevard S. Childs, *Biblical Theology of the Old and New Testaments* (Minneapolis: Fortress, 1993). Walther Eichrodt, in his two-volume *Theology of the Old Testament* (Philadelphia: Westminster, 1961), trans. J. A. Baker, referred to Esther in a footnote when he discussed Israel's "stubborn claim to sovereignty," 2:256. He also referred to Esther in a footnote when he referred to the turning from the heathen in contempt, 344. In another footnote he referred to Esther 1:14 when he wrote concerning the nobles closest to the king.

16. Zechariah was judged to be a young prophet when he began to prophesy. He may have been thirty years old, the age when religious leaders took up their official duties. This was in the year 520 B.C. The threat to kill all Jews was issued after Xerxes returned from fighting with the Greeks in 473 B.C. Esther had been queen for some time when the edict to kill the Jews was issued. Hence the edict went out sometime after 473 B.C. By that time Zechariah was approaching his sixtieth year.

17. Moore commented on the fact that Greek versions include references to God but the Masoretic (Hebrew) text never did. The conclusion is that where in the Greek text God is mentioned, editors inserted it. It was not in the prior Hebrew text. *Esther,* xxxii, 111.

18. Moore believes that the book of Esther is a "historicized wisdom" tale because Wisdom literature, as a rule, omitted reference to God. Ibid., iiiv, vi.

19. Cf. I.C.

20. Messianic significance was referred to in the preceding paragraphs. See also what I wrote in *MROT,* 920.

21. See my study of Zechariah in *MROT.* Note that on page 983 I wrote that Zech. 9–14 focused on the Messiah, his kingdom, and the covenant community's sanctified life. Cf. also the introductory paragraph on Zech. 9–14, 898–99.

22. Cf., e.g., C. Stuhlmueller, *Rebuilding with Hope, A Commentary on the Books of Haggai and Zechariah* (Grand Rapids: Eerdmans, 1988), who wrote regarding the apocalyptic forms, 115, 116, 154–57.

23. Ibid. Cf. references to Second Zechariah, 113–15. See also the lengthy introduction to the second part of Zechariah by Michael Smith Bewer, *Haggai, Zechariah, Malachi,* ICC (Edinburgh: T & T Clark, last impression, 1986), 218–59. Under his critical scalpel, Zechariah is quite severely dissected. Cf. Joyce Baldwin, *Haggai, Zechariah* (Downers Grove: InterVarsity, 1972), 62, 70, who discussed differences critical scholars have emphasized; she pointed out the similarities and concluded that the unified Zechariah should once again have a strong influence on the contemporary church.

24. Carl Friederick Keil, *The Twelve Minor Prophets,* trans. James Martin (Grand Rapids: Eerdmans, 1951), vol. 2. The second oracle is seen as containing "a more minute description" of how what is announced in the first oracle will happen, 320.

25. Cf. Stuhlmueller, *Rebuilding with Hope,* 114–15.

26. Baldwin, *Haggai, Zechariah,* 62.

27. Cf. J. Ridderbos, *De Kleine Proifeten, Haggai, Zacharia, Maleachi* (Kampen: Kok, 1952), 3:185.

28. Ibid., 132.

29. See Baldwin, *Haggai, Zechariah,* who limits nations to Jewish colonies scattered among the nations, 184. Bewer, *Haggai, Zechariah,* "a covenant by which the Jews were protected from other nations," 308. Keil, *The Twelve,* "the covenant made with all the nations" refers to a treaty "made with nations in favor of his people," 366. Ridderbos, *De Kleine,* vol. 3, God had given the nations the obligation to spare Israel, 156. Ralph Smith, *Micah–Malachi, Word Biblical Commentary* (Waco: Word, 1984), "It referred to Yahweh's covenant with the nations that would allow his people to go free," 270. These commentators reveal differing nuances but the basic thrust is that Yahweh God would no longer employ nations to execute the covenant curse on them.

30. Baldwin, *Haggai, Zechariah,* 87.

31. The verb *hārâh* has a variety of possible emphases. Depending on the context in which it appears, it could be interpreted as decline, bend down, encamp, to settle at. In the context of 9:1–8, the thought of protection is the preferred understanding.

32. It has been suggested that "my house" could refer to the temple, to the people, or to land in a general sense. Cf. Bewer, *Haggai, Zechariah,* who, as a critical literary commentator sees editors' influences in this passage but finally concludes that though house generally refers to the temple, here it refers to the "Holy Land," 269.

33. Xerxes did not succeed militarily against Greece, but the covenant people would influence Greece, not militarily, but as servants of Yahweh under the reign of his son, the cosmic king.

34. Commentators are challenged in an effort to identify properly the type of literature Zechariah produced. Was it basically poetic? Does the imagery of shepherd and flock, as used in other prophetic literature, indicate the use of metaphors, symbols, and images? Were these used because the restored community understood these biblical figures and their Persian lords did not? A good case could be made for this view.

35. Baldwin, *Haggai, Zechariah,* 179.

36. Cf. my discussion of the mediator's role in *MROT* 899–913.

37. Zechariah emphasized that there would be grief and mourning in every family or clan. The men and wives from clans would personally be stricken with grief.

38. See Smith, *Micah–Malachi,* 286.

39. Cf. what I wrote in *MROT*, 911–13.

40. Ibid., 911.

41. Cf. Smith, *Mica–Malachi,* 286.

42. Cf. Bewer, *Haggai, Zechariah,* who wrote that this passage has a decidedly apocalyptic character, 342. Few commentators deny this reality with the exception of some that try to read this chapter as a literal presentation of future events, or, as has been said, "as history in the making." For a radically literal history in the making interpretation, see Kenneth L. Barker, "Zechariah," in *The Expositor's Bible,* ed. Frank E. Gabelein (Grand Rapids: Zondervan, 1985), 7:688–97.

43. Bewer, *Haggai, Zechariah,* 343.

44. Ezekiel had set forth a similar result of Yahweh God's reign when he prophesied concerning water flowing from the temple mount and an ever-increasing flow as the water went through parched hills and eventually into the Dead Sea (Ezek. 47:1–12).

45. Here again is a drawing upon some aspects of Mosaic legislation calling for sanctity in all aspects of life and worship.

46. Barker, "Zechariah," 688–89. See also Blaising and Bock, *Progressive Dispensationalism:* "The Day of the Lord is the transition into the Lord's Eschatological reign on the earth. . . . In Zech. 14:9 . . . the Lord takes up his rulership as king," 226. Also J. Dwight Pentecost, *Thy Kingdom Come* (Wheaton: Victor, 1986), sets forth the idea of two ages, one beginning with the Messiah's first coming, the second beginning with the Messiah's second coming, this time to establish a universal kingdom, 152, 248.

47. Abraham J. Heschel listed Joel after Hosea. Cf. *The Prophets* (New York: Harper and Row, 1962), 501.

48. Brevard S. Childs, *Introduction to the Old Testament as Scripture* (Philadelphia: Fortress, 1979), 387. Childs did not state what his final conclusion was.

49. Cf. chap. 19, Joel: Setting the Agenda.

32

The Golden Cable in Ezra, Nehemiah, and Malachi

I. Ezra 7–10

II. Nehemiah

III. Malachi

IV. The End of Old Testament Revelation

32

The Golden Cable in Ezra, Nehemiah, and Malachi

Ezra and Nehemiah were led by Yahweh God to go from Babylon to Jerusalem approximately eighty years after the first returnees arrived in Jerusalem and began to lay the foundations of the temple to be rebuilt. It was in the seventh year of Artaxerxes who had succeeded Xerxes. The year was 458 B.C.[1]

Ezra 7–10[2]

The Historical Setting

Ezra was a priest, a descendant of Aaron's son Eleazar. He is described as a teacher well acquainted with the Torah. He became a man of many achievements; numerous writings are ascribed to him.[3]

King Artaxerxes was gracious and generous with him. He was given permission by letter to go to Jerusalem. He was given freedom to have priests and Levites accompany him. The king provided silver and gold and permitted Ezra to receive offerings from people to carry to Jerusalem for the worship of Yahweh God in the temple (Ezra 7:1–6, 13–20). Ezra was also permitted to take wheat, wine, olive oil, and salt for the Jerusalem community (7:22).

Ezra recorded that he gathered leading men from Israel to go with him. He listed the heads of families that went with him. Ezra had to make a special effort to convince some Levites to join the caravan (8:15–20). The total number of people who joined Ezra was calculated to number 1,513 males; with women and children included the number was around 5,000.[4] Ezra gathered them at a canal where the group camped while he organized the caravan. Ezra chose twelve leading priests who were given charge of the gifts, gold, silver, and articles of bronze (8:24–27). They fasted and prayed for a safe journey. No soldiers were requested to protect the travelers (8:21–25). They traveled the 900 miles from Babylon to Jerusalem; nothing is recorded about any special events along the road through the Fertile Crescent.[5] When the caravan arrived in Jerusalem, they rested three days; they worshiped, sacrificing bulls, rams, lambs, and goats. They gave the treasures for the temple to the priests. They also delivered messages from the king to local authorities, who in turn "gave assistance to the people and to the house of God" (8:31–36).

Ezra had to deal with the serious problem of intermarriage soon after his arrival in Jerusalem. Leaders in the restored community reported that some people, priests and Levites included, had defiled the covenant community by marrying women from surrounding groups and had joined in their worship (detestable practices) (9:1, 2). Ezra reacted with grief and self-abasement to this intermarriage and unfaithful practices of worship. He prayed, confessing that Yahweh God's commandments had been broken and acknowledged that Yahweh God was righteous (9:15). Shecaniah led in confessing the sin of the people and proposing that the people covenant before God to send non-Israelite wives away (10:2). A proclamation was made, calling all men of Judah and Benjamin to gather within three days. Disobeying the call would result in forfeiture of their property. Leaders decided this after Ezra withdrew. The people confessed their sins; they agreed without exception to send their non-Israelite wives away (10:12–17). A closing statement records that children had been born from these intermarriages. Nothing is recorded concerning the parental duties regarding them.

Other activities that occupied Ezra are recorded in Nehemiah's writings. These will be considered when that book is discussed. What calls for consideration first is this: are the strands of the Golden Cable present and influential in Ezra's account?

The Golden Cable

The Kingdom

There is no reference to Israel's former theocratic kingdom. Ezra arrived at and functioned in a religious community in which he was confronted by a vexing social and spiritual challenge.

The Persian king has a distinct and influential role. As the potentate of a vast empire he gave attention to the restored community in Judah and Benjamin. He made arrangements for Ezra to lead a caravan of Jewish religious leaders and their families to Jerusalem. He provided rich materials for the temple and provisions for the community. He is recorded to wish to know specifically what the spiritual situation was in the restored community (Ezra 7:14). He recognized and honored the God of Jerusalem who was Ezra's God (7:19). Likewise, he recognized the value of keeping the Law of God that Ezra knew so well and taught. He also called for obedience among the Jews to the Law of God; those disobeying were to be severely punished (7:26). The king's edict regarding obedience undoubtedly gave Ezra confidence to deal with intermarrying covenant breakers.

Summing up, there should be no doubt that Yahweh God, supreme King of the cosmic kingdom, ruled and guided the Persian king to carry out his purposes for Ezra and his people of the restored community. His preparedness to supply wealth and food for the Jerusalem people is also evidence that Yahweh God, the Lord over all aspects of the created universe, motivated Artaxerxes to be his agent in fulfilling the needs of the religious covenant community.

Ezra gave repeated expression of his full awareness that Yahweh God, the reigning King over the cosmos, was very involved in the affairs of his life and that of the people. His intimate knowledge of the Torah and the God who was revealed in the Torah (7:10) was powerfully demonstrated in his activities. When Ezra received the king's letter, he exclaimed *bārûk yĕhwâ 'ĕlōhê 'ăbôbênû* (Blessed be Yahweh God of our fathers) (7:27). What he proceeded to say reveals that he was fully aware that Yahweh God was the Lord of the king's heart. Yahweh God had put it into the heart of the Persian king *lĕpā'ēr*[6] *'et bêt* (to beautify or glorify the house of Yahweh God) that is in Jerusalem. Artaxerxes, led by Yahweh God, desired to do more than just honor Yahweh God. He wished to bring beauty, to restore the glory of the temple. Ezra understood Yahweh God's motivation of the Persian king's heart to bring glory to Yahweh God by beautifying his house.

Ezra also acknowledged that Yahweh God had given him "good favor" with the king, his advisors, and officials. He, the teacher of the law, experienced Yahweh God's *ḥesed* (mercy and steadfast love) through the royal favors he received (7:28).[7]

Ezra's acknowledgment of Yahweh God's gracious influence upon him and fellow travelers was expressed when Levites were brought to him to join the caravan (8:11). He readily acknowledged Yahweh God's grace upon those who obey him but divine anger against those who forsook him (8:21), and he readily confessed that Yahweh God had protected the caravan from enemies and bandits (8:31). These instances demonstrate that Ezra was fully aware of and truly believed that Yahweh God was absolute Ruler, Controller, and Guide.

The Covenant

The people in the restored community in Jerusalem, Judah, and Benjamin knew and understood what a covenant was (Ezra 10:3). They knew that by intermarriage the covenant Yahweh God had made with them was broken. The law Yahweh God had given, recognized, and stated as the basis for dissolving the illicit marriages had been clearly enunciated by Moses (Deut. 7:1–4). They undoubtedly knew what tragedy had come upon Israel because of Solomon's marriages with foreign women (1 Kings 11:1–8), who led him to worship Ashtoreth and Molech. Yahweh's anger with Solomon for breaking the covenant (11:11) resulted in the breaking up of the kingdom.

The restored community could also have been aware of the tragedies that followed King Ahab of Israel. He had done more evil than the kings preceding him. He married Jezebel, a Sidonian queen, whom he joined in worshiping Baal (16:29–33). Their son Ahaziah, who reigned over Israel two years, did evil and also worshiped Baal (22:51–53). Judah's king, Jehoram, married Ahab's daughter Athaliah and followed her worship of Baal (2 Kings 8:16–18). Their son Ahaziah became king and was influenced by Ahab's family, particularly by his mother Athaliah, granddaughter of Omri (8:25–27).

The intermarriages of the descendants of David with foreign and wicked wives had been, ultimately, a major factor in the punishment Yahweh God eventually executed on Israel and Judah. They were exiled. Now the restoration had become a reality and the temple worship of Yahweh God had been resumed. In this setting Yahweh God's covenant with his people and the law of Yahweh God, which was an integral part of the covenant, was disobeyed and broken. What could be expected? A repeat of the covenant curse executed on them?

When Ezra learned of the covenant breaking by intermarriage, two specific events must be considered. First, Ezra's prayer in which he confessed in shame and disgrace the guilt of the people (Ezra 9:6, 7). He acknowledged Yahweh God's grace in restoring the remnant to Jerusalem and the temple (9:8–10). He referred to the law that had been broken by the people before the exile (9:10–12), and the consequences of that sin. He asked: Will you, Yahweh God, righteous as you are, destroy us, leaving no survivor (9:13–15)?

The second event was the gathering of a large crowd around Ezra. They joined him in weeping and confessing their unfaithfulness. The people, led by Shecaniah, covenanted before Yahweh God that the foreign wives would be sent away.

The breaking of Yahweh God's covenant led to their covenanting before their Lord that they would honor his covenant with them. Yahweh God had kept his covenant promise. They had been restored from exile. They had broken that covenant by their covenanting with foreign women. To honor Yahweh God's covenant with them, they covenanted, and confirmed it with an oath (10:5), that they would break their sinful covenant with foreign women. The text records that in an orderly and organized manner, officials in the community appointed by Ezra led in the process of dissolving the marriages with foreign women (10:5–44).

A critical issue that is integral to the covenant Yahweh God had established pertains to the children. Yahweh God covenanted with Abraham and his descendants. Children born to covenant parents were included directly and immediately in Yahweh God's covenant. The question arises from the dissolving of marriages between covenant men and foreign wives is: Are the children of covenant fathers not in the covenant also?

A pressing issue in the interpretation of 10:44, is that the text is not clear.[8] Hence there are various interpretations but in the final analysis, all agree that the children of these mixed marriages did not fare well. No information is given concerning the care of them.[9] Ezra could be faulted for his stringency in applying the covenant law. He was described as a great zealot[10] for God and his law. The people, however, had confessed their sin. They admitted they had been unfaithful but there was still hope for Israel. This hope could be realized by sending all these women and children away. The people proposed this (10:3), and Ezra agreed to it. His mission was to apply the law to his people.[11]

The law of Yahweh God is eternal and applies to all ages. Circumstances, however, may demand varying specific applications of the covenantal law. In Ezra's time, when it was of utmost importance to develop a faithful covenant-keeping community, that aspect of covenant law forbidding marriage with foreigners had to be obeyed. But that historic application must not be considered as the rule for all situations. Paul made this clear. Being yoked with unbelievers should be avoided. But through marriage an unbelieving partner would be sanctified, *not saved* (1 Cor. 7:14). So also with children. A child born to a believer, even if the marriage partner was not, was still to be considered a covenant child.[12]

A final point: since Ezra did not reveal what relationship continued between the fathers and children sent away, it cannot be definitely determined that they were no longer responsible for their care, provision, and nuture. The possibility must be granted that they made some arrangement to carry out their covenantal responsibilities for their offspring.

The Mediator

The Davidic house, and its mediatorial descendant, has no great role in the book of Ezra.[13] David is referred to when a body of men who were to assist the Levites was appointed according to David's prescription (8:20). This reference indicates that David's past roles were still important for the restored community, particularly in relation to the temple. There is, however, not even a slight allusion to his kingship and his dynasty. There is a hint regarding the continuity of a faithful community; there is hope for Israel (10:3). But no reference is made to the necessity of the community's survival so that the promised Messiah could and would come through it. This lack of direct reference, however, should not be interpreted as there being no messianic relevance and importance to what transpired in the restored community when Ezra arrived there. It should be understood that the enmity between Satan's seed and the woman's was being activated. Satan was always active, seeking to destroy the woman's seed. Intermarriage could have an important role in Satan's efforts. The restored community had quite obviously become unaware of the absolute antithesis established by Yahweh God between Satan and the seed of the woman, the Messiah.

Ezra himself was not of the tribe of Judah, he was a priest of the tribe of Levi. He did not function directly in the sacrificial worship of Yahweh God. Others evidently offered sacrifices. Ezra was a student, a scribe and a teacher of the Torah. But as a priest he was an intercessor. His intercession on behalf of the unfaithful community became the pivotal event in the community's return to faithful covenant life, at least as far as marriage was concerned. Thus, as priestly intercessor, Ezra took on a mediatorial role, adumbrated, brought to expression in a shaded and outline way what Jesus Christ the Mediator, the effective intercessor does for his people (John 17:6–9; Heb. 7:25).

Nehemiah

Introductory Comments

The book of Nehemiah has been characterized in various ways. This is understandable because of the lively narrative it records.[14] The book reveals Satan's strategy. "Satan is a hater, a wrecker, and a destroyer." He is happy only when he can ruin God's work.[15] Nehemiah's doctrine of God reveals his unique sovereignty, holiness, compassion, mercy, power, infinite grace, and complete justice.[16] A brief survey of the contents will give evidence of other themes that characterize Nehemiah's writing. These themes do not indicate that an editor consulted various sources.[17]

Nehemiah commenced with an account of his grief when he heard of the condition of Jerusalem. He prayed for Jerusalem. As cupbearer to King Artaxerxes, he had an opportunity to speak to the king about Jerusalem. The king and his queen gave him permission to go to Jerusalem. He requested letters confirming he was sent by the king to be in Jerusalem. Opponents were disturbed. At night Nehemiah inspected the wall of the city and found big parts of it in ruin. Rebuilding began. Gates were built. Opposition increased. Workers were armed as they worked. The city had many poor people so Nehemiah helped them and accused leaders of oppressing their fellow citizens. Opposition continued but the wall was rebuilt. Nehemiah consulted records and ascertained which families had returned. Then Ezra was asked to read the Torah; he did so standing on an elevated platform. The Torah was explained; the people wept because of their sorrow but were enjoined to rejoice, for the joy of Yahweh was their strength. Later a day of confession was held. Israel's history was reviewed and Yahweh God's covenant making at Sinai was highlighted. A commitment to God's house was made. The new residents, including the Levites and priests, were given instructions where to live. Then the wall was dedicated. Nehemiah had to return to the king's service after twelve years in Jerusalem (1:1; 13:6). He received permission to return to Jerusalem a second time and found that reforms had to be undertaken. The temple needed cleansing. Levites and priests were not present at the temple. They were ordered to return. Trustworthy men were appointed to supervise the storerooms with grain, wine, and olive oil. Sabbath keeping had to be enforced. Nehemiah rebuked the men who married foreign wives and drove out the priests and Levites who had married foreign women.

Nehemiah's relationship to Ezra can be discerned by various incidental references. While Ezra did not refer to Nehemiah, Nehemiah did refer to Ezra. Ezra had gone to Jerusalem in the seventh year of King Artaxerxes' reign (Ezra 1:6). Nehemiah went to Jerusalem thirteen years later. Nehemiah referred to Ezra's reading of the Torah to the people (Neh. 8:1–18), while he was back in Susa (13:6). Once back in Jerusalem he dealt with problems that had confronted Ezra also, particularly in regard to intermarriage.

An interesting point is that in the original Hebrew Bible, Ezra and Nehemiah form one book.[18] This is evidence that the two leaders were considered contemporaries.[19] They served as religious leaders in the restored community. Ezra continued to serve as priestly teacher of the Torah. When Nehemiah arrived thirteen years after Ezra, he served in the capacity of administrator. They worked in their respective capacities; their concern was that the postexilic community continue as an authentic people of God, loving, serving, and worshiping according to what Moses had revealed as Yahweh God's will for his people.

Nehemiah had an important position with Artaxerxes, king of Persia. The king demonstrated a kind and understanding attitude to Nehemiah, who served as cupbearer to the king. That meant he was a high official whose duty it was to choose and taste the wine and then give it to the king. This gave Nehemiah frequent access to the king.[20] Nehemiah, in that capacity, gained the favor of his master and received permission to bring gifts and to lead a contingency of exiles to Jerusalem. He requested and received letters for the governors of the areas they would pass through and interact with in Judah and Benjamin. All people, including Persian officials, had to recognize Nehemiah's position as Artaxerxes' official representative.

Nehemiah was not given any specific instructions concerning the people in Jerusalem and outlying areas. He had heard from some men, who had come from Jerusalem, that the city wall was in ruins and that the people in the area were having trouble and were existing in disgraceful situations. The text (1:3) has been read to say that the report concerned people who had been left behind in the land when the last exile had occurred in 586 B.C. It has also been read to refer to the returned exiles who experienced difficulties because of the political and military turmoil on the international scene. This turmoil had drastically affected the returnees.[21] The people were defenseless because Jerusalem was not a secured city. Nehemiah, therefore, had a deep concern for the people's safety. He adopted a specific administrative leadership role. There was work to do. He considered he had been given authority to build Jerusalem because he had been appointed governor in the land of Judah.[22]

Commentators have selected various major themes from the book of Nehemiah: doctrine of God, passion for Scripture, prayer, and leadership.[23] It would seem appropriate to consider Nehemiah's account presenting the following factors that together present a unified account: (1) recognition of the authority of the Persian kings and Nehemiah; (2) the physical condition of Jerusalem and the need to rebuild its wall; (3) the Satanic opposition that had to be endured; (4) prayer as a constant source of encouragement; (5) the need to confront prevalent sins (e.g., regarding the Sabbath and intermarriage); (6) the need for the people to submit to leadership. These themes in Nehemiah's account should be seen as integral aspects of Yahweh God's cosmic kingdom, his abiding covenant with his people, and his agents who had to serve as Yahweh God's representatives.

The Golden Cable Strands

The Kingdom

Nehemiah demonstrated that he was fully aware of the reality and presence of royalty, royal authority, and kingdoms. He referred to kingdom (*malkût*), to kingdoms (*mamlakôt*—once), and to kings (*melek*—forty times). In the prayer of confession of sins, the people acknowledged that Yahweh God had given their forefathers, when they came to possess the promised land, the kingdom, ruled by King Sihon of Heshbon and of King Og of Bashan (Neh. 9:22). In that same prayer they acknowledged that they had had a theocratic kingdom with royal and priestly leaders (9:35). The people went on to confess that they were no longer a kingdom, but were slaves in the land given to their forefathers because of their sin (9:34–37).

The term *malkût* is mentioned when reference was made to priests who were recorded in the *malkût* of Darius. The term has been translated as reign (NIV, JB, NASB, KJ) in this context. The point to be stressed is that the priests were recorded as residing in Darius's kingdom. They were kingdom people—but of a foreign kingdom. They had lost their theocratic kingdom heritage.

Nehemiah knew his heritage. He mentioned King Solomon, who was loved by God, but as king of Israel, was led astray by marrying foreign women (13:26, 27). He also referred to King Nebuchadnezzar, who had taken captives from Jerusalem and exiled them to Babylon (7:6), as the king of Assyria had done years before (9:32).

A study of Nehemiah's references to kings and kingdoms reveals that kingdoms had existed and their kings exerted their authority and power. The kingdoms of Israel/Judah, Assyria and Babylon had ceased to exist. There was no longer a theocratic kingdom and Nehemiah made absolutely no reference to the possibility of it arising again. What this study does reveal is that Nehemiah was fully aware of the continued kingship of his sovereign Lord. He reigned, he guided, controlled, directed the kings and affairs of their kingdoms. Yahweh God caused nations to rise and disappear. He did so because he was the sovereign Lord over the cosmic kingdom that involved all aspects of creation, including mankind and its life.

A point should be made of Nehemiah's recognition of the kingship and authority of the Persian king. He did not rebel against him. Rather he served Artaxerxes faithfully as a servant of Yahweh God. Nehemiah, however, was in a position to appeal to and gain advantages from the Persian king's authority, ability, and power. He evidently recognized that Artaxerxes was a representative of Yahweh God under whom he could serve Yahweh God, the true and only Sovereign over the Persian Empire. Not only, however, over the Persian Empire. Nehemiah acknowledged and worshiped *yĕhwâ 'ĕlōhê haššamayîm* (Yahweh God of heaven) (1:5; 2:4), who *lĕbaddekā* (you alone) is Lord, having made the highest heaven, all the starry hosts, the earth, the seas, and all that is in them (9:6). Yahweh is God *min hā 'ôlām 'ad hā'ôlām* (from everlasting to everlasting) (9:15).[24] This only Lord, Yahweh God, is universally sovereign. The entire cosmos is his kingdom.

In a lengthy prayer of confession, the people acknowledged that Yahweh God had performed wonders in nature on their forefathers' behalf. He had divided the sea, drowned their pursuers, and provided shade and light (9:9–12). He had provided bread from heaven and water from the rock (9:15, 20). Yahweh God, the cosmic King, had given them a land as he dispossessed nations (9:24), and provided them with homes, orchards, vineyards, and wells. He had done all this to carry out his plan and to achieve his purposes. Yahweh God had truly demonstrated that he was great, mighty, and awesome (9:32).

Yahweh God, as cosmic King, also provided the restored community with a home and a city after they had suffered his just judgment. The Persian king had graciously provided wealth and supplies in response to Nehemiah's report on the trouble and disgrace that the people endured. The request for wood supplies to rebuild wall and gates was granted.

Yahweh God's reign over and provisions for the restored community were directly challenged by forces that represented Satan's parasite dominion. Various names were mentioned. Sanballat and Tobiah had official positions and felt disturbed and threatened (2:10). They ridiculed the builders (4:1–3). They gathered support from Arabs, Ammonites, and Philistines. Plans were made to attack and disrupt (4:7–9). Yahweh God frustrated these plans. With their Lord's care, protection, and provisions, the work in rebuilding the wall was completed.

Finally, it must be stressed that Nehemiah, an official in Artaxerxes' court and as appointed governor of Judah, much as he may have appreciated these advantages, nevertheless repeatedly called on the Sovereign of the cosmic kingdom. Nehemiah prayed repeatedly. The first prayer recorded began with "O God of heaven," followed by a humble plea for his ears to be open to prayers and his eyes open to see his people (1:5, 6). Nehemiah prayed that Artaxerxes would be inclined to hear and grant him his request (2:4). He informed the leaders in Jerusalem that the gracious hand of Yahweh God was upon him and thus he was encouraged to say, "Let us rebuild!" (2:18). Opponents' offers to help were turned down with the assurance that "the God of heaven will give success" (2:20). When ridicule and opposition became painful realities, Nehemiah prayed, "turn their insults back on their own heads and have them experience the results of their deeds" (4:4, 5). As actual opposition began, prayer was raised. Along with prayer, action was taken. Guards were placed. The omnipotent Lord revealed himself through his trusting and obedient servants (4:9). Nehemiah inspired his workers with confidence even as half of them worked and half defended.

Nehemiah, as governor, showed Yahweh God's compassion for the poor. They needed assistance to keep and maintain their homes and get food for their families.

Others had debts to pay on their vineyards and orchards. Some daughters had been enslaved. Nehemiah approached and reproached the leaders in the community for causing such misery. And as governor he never drew on the king's allotment for him as governor. He provided food for himself and for his officials. Thus the "taxation" and other requirements on the people were lifted.

Nehemiah prayed a short prayer a few times. He prayed *zākĕrâh lî 'ĕlōhê lĕtôbîyâh* (remember me God for good) (5:19; 13:31). Bible translators have preferred the term *favor,* which has a sense of grace implied, instead of *for good.* Commentators, however, have translated "remember me, God, for good." Questions have been raised. Was Nehemiah trying to build up a merit balance in God's ledger?[25] Did Nehemiah indicate anxiety that God reward his good works and should such a prayer be seen as "symptomatic" of a venal and legalistic religious characteristic of *Spatjudentum* (late Jewishdom)?[26] Should one be "apt to suspect Nehemiah of egoistic tendencies"?[27] These questioning commentators supply their own answers. Nehemiah wanted to receive favor from God; he worked on behalf of God's people, the carriers of his revelation.[28] He prayed this prayer professing sincerity in serving others for the Lord's sake[29] and proof of his genuineness as a servant of the servants of God.[30] These prayers of Nehemiah must be considered as genuine expressions of Nehemiah recognizing Yahweh God as the supreme Ruler over all. Nehemiah revealed he trusted God as a just judge, who sees and evaluates all that is done on behalf of Yahweh God's kingdom and particularly on behalf of his covenant people and their role in the carrying out of Yahweh God's purposes.

The evidence that has been gathered thus far clearly reveals that Nehemiah knew and considered himself, in his various capacities, as a servant of Yahweh God, Lord of the cosmic kingdom. He also revealed that he was convinced that King Artaxerxes was under Yahweh God's reign. The opponents were also and would not be able to thwart Yahweh God's purposes. He exhibited a confidence that Yahweh God upheld his covenant with his people.

The Covenant

Nehemiah referred to the covenant Yahweh God had made with Israel three times and once to the covenant of the priesthood. A careful study of each of these passages must be made if one is to understand and appreciate what Nehemiah understood concerning it. Nehemiah also demonstrated how it was the determining reality in the experiences of Israel.

The first passage to consider is Nehemiah's prayer.[31] He prayed when he learned about the trouble and disgrace of the returned exiles and the ruined status of Jerusalem. Nehemiah referred to the covenant itself and included specific references to aspects of it.

He addressed Yahweh who was the covenant maker and keeper. He is the God of heaven (1:5), the great God in might, holiness, and justice.[32] This God is also *hannôrâ'* (the niph. ptc. of *yārê',* to be feared). This niphal participle must be considered as emphasizing the continuous fear of God. Fear should be understood as reverence and awe that the knowledge and presence of God inspires. This God *`somēr* (is the always keeping one of) the covenant and (*ḥesed*) faithful covenant love.[33] As Yahweh keeps his covenant he demonstrates faithful tender love.

Nehemiah referred to those who are assured of Yahweh God's *ḥesed* (mercy and love). They are the ones who love him. This love is demonstrated by obediently keeping his commandments. Nehemiah thus adds a third aspect of the covenant, the Torah that included Yahweh God's instructions for all of life and specifically his revealed will, the law. As a covenant man, Nehemiah humbly asked Yahweh God to be attentive, to see and hear him as he prayed. Yahweh had promised to hear Solomon and would also forgive and heal.[34] Nehemiah knew what his covenant Lord had promised. This promise would be kept for a people who responded by repenting of sin and pleading for forgiveness. Nehemiah also referred to another aspect of the covenant, namely, the curse. The curse of the covenant, Moses had warned, would result in exile (Lev. 26:27–35). Nehemiah acknowledged that the curse had been executed (Neh. 1:8). The covenant people had been scattered. But Yahweh God had also promised to gather them (Deut. 30:4), and would bring them back to Jerusalem (Jer. 29:14; Neh. 1:9).

Nehemiah concluded his covenantal prayer by requesting success when he would request permission to assist the community in Judah and Jerusalem. He had prayed for four months (December 446 until March 445) before he had opportunity to approach the king. He demonstrated what a covenant man would do on behalf of the covenant people.[35]

Nehemiah's request was granted. He received assistance from Artaxerxes (2:1–9). Nehemiah was successful in his inspection of the ruined wall. In spite of opposition, Yahweh God enabled his city rebuilders to persevere. The gates were rebuilt (3:3–32). When opposition became more intense, Nehemiah prayed an imprecatory prayer (4:4, 5).[36] He prayed for the covenant curse to be carried out on those who opposed the work of the covenant rebuilders. He prayed that insults be turned upon them, that they be plundered as if taken into captivity, that their guilt not be covered up or their sins blotted out. He was not the first one to pray for the covenant curse to be executed upon fellowmen. David had prayed imprecatory statements. "Contend against those who contend with me . . . let them be disgraced and put to shame" (Ps. 35:1–8). He prayed that Yahweh would pour out his wrath (on my enemies and his fierce anger overtake them [69:24]).[37] Jeremiah also prayed or called for judgment on Israel's enemies.[38]

Nehemiah demonstrated an awareness of Yahweh God's covenant requirement regarding the poor. Mosaic legislation repeatedly called for consideration of the poor (e.g., Lev. 23:22; 25:47; Deut.15:7). He called leaders of the restored community together (Neh. 5:7, 8), and accused them of enslaving their poor fellow Jews and demanded that the poor receive back property, money, and food supplies (5:10, 11). He summoned priests, nobles, and other officials and made them take an oath that they would respond to the needs of the poor (5:12, 13). After rectitude had been made under his leadership, he again prayed for Yahweh to remember him as the covenant servant who saw and fearlessly carried out his responsibilities.[39]

After the wall had been completed, faithful men were appointed to be in charge of the gates. They were to be closed during the hours of darkness for security purposes (7:1–3). Nehemiah took a census so that Jerusalem could have sufficient residents (7:4–73). Ezra read the Torah after the resettlement had been accomplished. Day after day Ezra read; the people feasted when told not to mourn (8:8–12, 18).[40]

The reading of the law did lead to a confession of sin and an acknowledgment of how Yahweh God had confirmed and kept his covenant with his people. Ezra referred to the covenant made with Abraham (Gen. 15; Neh. 9:8). He reviewed Yahweh God's covenant with their forefathers who were delivered from Egypt, guided by cloud and pillar of fire, and led to Mount Sinai where Yahweh had spoken his will for covenant life and worship (9:9–15). The people confessed their fathers' unfaithfulness to the covenant because they were arrogant and stiff-necked (9:16–18). They remembered Yahweh God's compassion, his giving of his Spirit to instruct them, and the food and drink that was needed in the desert. They acknowledged that Yahweh God had subdued nations and given them the promised land (9:19–25). Again, disobedience was acknowledged; prophets were killed and blasphemy was committed (9:26–28). The forefathers were warned; the Spirit who addressed them through the prophets received no attention (9:20–30). They admitted Yahweh God demonstrated his covenant love by not abandoning them (9:31).

The review of Yahweh God's faithful covenant keeping that included carrying out his promises and executing the covenant curse produced the confession that Yahweh God had indeed been gracious and merciful (9:31). They also confessed that in all that Yahweh God had done, executing the curse, *atlâh `saddiq 'al kōl habba' 'āleûnû kî 'ĕmet 'a`sîtâ* (you were just[41] regarding all that came on us because you acted faithfully [9:33]). This surely was a covenantal response by the people made to their covenant-keeping Lord. Yahweh God, the covenant Lord, was faithful in keeping promises of blessings and carrying out warnings against sin.

Once the wall was completed, confessions were made and new residents were welcomed (11:1–12:26). Levites and singers gathered from Jerusalem and surrounding villages were organized into two choirs. Along with leaders from Judah (12:31), they led in giving thanks (12:40). Men, women, and children joined together in sacrificing and rejoicing (12:43). All aspects of the festival were carried out under the leadership of those who succeeded the leaders appointed by David and Asaph. Thus there was continuity in covenantal arrangements for worship and feasting.

Nehemiah was obligated to return to the palace in Susa. While he was gone, covenantal regulations and duties were neglected. When he returned, he led in a social and religious reform as called for by Mosaic legislation. Moses had been Yahweh God's spokesman to make known covenantal regulations. Nehemiah listed the reforms that had to be made. First, foreigners, particularly descendants of Ammon and Moab, descendants of Abraham's nephew, Lot were to be excluded from Israel. They had not assisted the covenant people when they came out of the desert but had hired Balaam to curse them (Num. 22:3–11; Neh. 13:1–3). The hard-heartedness and sin of calling for a curse instead of blessings had to be acknowledged and dealt with according to what had transpired centuries before.[42]

The second reform called for the "cleansing of the temple." Tobiah, an Ammonite official, had been given a room in the temple by Eliashib, who had been given responsibility for keeping the temple holy. Tobiah was thrown out (13:28), and the temple was purified. A third reform dealt with the Levites who had not been receiving their prescribed portions. This was also considered a neglect of the temple (13:10–13). A fourth reform dealt with Sabbath observance. Unnecessary labor in processing grapes and delivery of grain and other foods had to be discontinued (13:15–22). Merchants were forbidden to enter Jerusalem on the Sabbath but were to stay just outside the wall. The practice of intermarriage had continued. Israelite men married Philistine, Moabite, and Ammonite women. Nehemiah appealed to Yahweh God's punishment of Solomon to press upon the minds and hearts of the people how intermarriage led to covenant breaking (13:23–27).

Nehemiah was conscientious in correcting covenantal transgressions in the restored community. He attempted to be faithful to the Mosaic prescriptions for holiness in worship, business, and family life. In regard to intermarriage he did not deal with the problem as Ezra had done before him. It seems evident that Ezra had not been able to resolve the problem completely (6:18; 13:23–27). Nehemiah's efforts at covenantal renewal[43] led him to pray again for Yahweh God's remembrance of him (13:29). This prayer was offered specifically because he dealt drastically with the son of Eliashib the high priest. This priestly son had married the daughter of Sanballat, an enemy of the covenant people. The priest had defiled the priestly office and the covenant of the priesthood.

This covenant of the priesthood had a specific ordinance underlying it. Yahweh God had claimed the tribe of Levi for special religious services (Num. 3:1–13). Yahweh God had spoken clearly (3:12). They were to replace all the firstborn in Israel. They were to be bonded[44] to him specifically for religious service. The descendants of Aaron, Levites, were to serve as priests. Their fellow Levites were to assist them in various ministrations (18:1–7). A specific requirement for the high priest was that he marry a virgin from his own people (Lev. 21:14, 15). As priests, they were to set the standard for and be examples of sanctified living, particularly in relation to family life. This was an important aspect of the covenant Yahweh made with the priesthood. Their priestly covenantal responsibilities included dealing with sexual improprieties among the Israelites. Thus when a leader of the Simeonite clan brought a Midianite woman into his tent, he did this, evidently with defiance. Prior to his immoral act, Israelite men had begun to "indulge" in sexual immorality with Moabite women and Moabite idolatry. The leaders of these gross violations of covenantal requirements had to be put to death (Num. 25:1–5). When Phinehas, a grandson of Aaron, realized what the Simionite and Midianite woman were doing, he drove a spear through both of them (25:7).

Yahweh God informed Moses that Phinehas *hēšîb 'et ḥămātî* (has turned away my anger). The Israelites, as a bonded, united community, dedicated to Yahweh had to bear corporate responsibility. Phinehas removed the source of divine anger and punishment on the entire people. And Yahweh God commended Phinehas for his zeal, which was evidence of divine zeal (25:11). Yahweh God then added that the priestly bond was confirmed as a lasting covenant of peace.

Nehemiah gave repeated evidence of his knowledge of Mosaic and prophetic revelation. Hence he was on solid ground after he had banished the high priest's son and purified the priests and Levites "of everything foreign" (Neh. 13:29, 30).[45]

In conclusion to this study on the covenant in Nehemiah, it must be stated with emphasis that this book is a covenant treatise par excellence. Within the context of the cosmic kingdom, Yahweh God's covenant with Israel is a dominant strand. Nehemiah was a covenant-conscious man and the covenant promises, stipulations, and purposes were his driving motivation, his constant guidelines, and his clearly drawn parameters.

The Mediator

The third strand of the Golden Cable, the messianic Mediator, is not referred to verbally or indirectly. In the context of the biblical revelation, specifically in the context of the history of revelation, Nehemiah had a definite messianic role. Nehemiah, with Ezra, did very much to assist the covenant community to be the people of Yahweh God through and from whom the promised Messiah would eventually come. In other words, had Nehemiah not been concerned, had not prayed repeatedly, and had not with determination, addressed the needs of the community, humanly speaking, the community would have disappeared because of its ever-increasing unmoral character. Nehemiah was required for the maintenance of the covenant community. As an official in the Persian court, he had a position from which to gain favor with the king. As an appointed governor he had the authority to exercise leadership in rebuilding the walls and bringing security to the people. As a devoted servant of Yahweh God, he knew and understood the revealed will of Yahweh God for his people and the nations.[46]

The question pertaining to the messianic roles or officers must be considered. There is no direct or implied reference to the messianic person; that is, the narrower view of the Messiah is not presented. The wider view is present. The role of priest/teacher was occupied by Ezra, a priest. Nehemiah, who was not a descendant of David, occupied a royal role and carried out "royal duties" as governor of Judah. Hence it cannot be said that Nehemiah was an ancestor of Jesus Christ, the mediator. Much of his work, spiritual and moral, had messianic aspects and in that sense Nehemiah can be considered a foreshadow or forerunner of the Messiah.

An important point to stress is that whatever role Nehemiah is considered to have had in relation to the promised Messiah, he lived, worked, and served within the context of Yahweh God's cosmic kingdom and within the parameters of the covenant. Nehemiah was a covenant role model and a faithful kingdom servant.[47]

Malachi

Introductory Comments

A writer has opined that for much of its interpretive history, the book of Malachi has served as an empty glass into which scholarship at various times could pour their views.[48] The statement could be read to convey that scholars have paid little attention to Malachi's prophecy. The author, however, listed sixty-nine titles, books, articles, and dissertations, sixty of which were written and published in the past twenty-five years. No critical commentary, however, has included Malachi in the past ten years.[49]

Authorship

Scholarship, conservative as well as critical, agrees almost unanimously that one person wrote or edited the book of Malachi. He has been described as the "lecturer," a prophet who offers no prophetic personality as Amos, Isaiah, or Jeremiah did, a precursor of later Judaism, and as an artist who, like Rembrandt, worked with light and shade.[50] The evidence, admittedly somewhat scant, supports the view that the prophet who spoke and wrote this prophecy was an historical person named Malachi. The name can best be translated as "My Messenger."[51]

The Historical Context

George L. Robinson was apodictic. Malachi was a contemporary of Ezra and Nehemiah.[52] Scholars, however, are divided whether Malachi preceded Ezra and Nehemiah, prophesied while they were present, or came shortly after them. The range of dating thus is from 450 B.C. until 432 B.C. Baldwin wrote it is not possible to be specific.[53] That Malachi used the phrase *Yĕhwâ sĕbā'ôt* (Yahweh of hosts) twenty times, as frequently as Zechariah had done, does not give final proof that he succeeded him shortly afterward. That Malachi was a contemporary of Ezra and Nehemiah, however, whether before, during, or after their presence, should not be doubted.[54] His prophecy addressed the same issues that Ezra and Nehemiah had to address. It is my considered opinion that the last chapter of Nehemiah, written after his second return to Jerusalem in 433 B.C. (Neh. 13:6), presents an accurate setting for Malachi's prophecy.

Consider the issues Malachi addressed: a defiled priesthood, blemished sacrifices, family and marriage problems, financial and material obligations improperly assumed, Yahweh God not being seriously acknowledged as covenant Lord.[55]

Issues Critics Have Raised

Brevard S. Childs has written that Malachi has not received the critical scrutiny that other Minor Prophets have.[56] While he concurs with the wide agreement concerning the unity of the book, he nevertheless sees the book to be a collection of disputations that include glosses. A second issue pertains to the last three times the term *oracle* is used (Zech. 9:1; 12:1; Mal. 1:1). Is this use of the term evidence that these three are anonymous oracles, appended to the Minor Prophets? A third issue concerns the superscription indicating Malachi as the author. The fourth issue is the question concerning the book's original addressees. The harshness of some passages could indicate the addressees were non-Jews.[57]

An issue discussed by critical and some evangelical scholars pertains to whether Malachi was the last prophet. The contention has been raised that Obadiah or Joel were historically subsequent to Malachi.[58]

The Golden Cable Strands

The three strands are not equally dominant. They are, however, definitely present and serve to highlight the unity of the message[59] Malachi proclaimed in a number of discourses. Commentators have singled out specific issues he addressed. These are integral aspects of one or more of the three strands.[60]

The Kingdom

Malachi does not mention the term *mamlăkâh* (kingdom). This must not be construed to indicate that the prophet had no idea or thought about the kingdom of God. Evidence is present that the concept of kingdom was basic to what he prophesied, whether he was rebuking his hearers, speaking concerning the nations, or proclaiming concern about the messianic mediator.

The question to be asked—and answered—is what Malachi understood by the term *kingdom* and what it specifically referred to. He never made any kind of suggestion, not even an implied hint, concerning the theocratic kingdom that had been removed by the exile. As he did not give retrospective perspective, neither did he give any indication of a prospective view—of a future kingdom specifically for the Jewish people.

Malachi, beyond a doubt, prophesied with the concept of the cosmic kingdom in mind. Evidence for this is clear in the messages he delivered.

He quoted Yahweh God as saying *kî melek gādôl 'ānî āmor Yĕhwâ seba'ot* (for a King great [am] I, says Yahweh of hosts) (1:14). Yahweh God is the great King of what? A consultation of numerous commentaries has not given a clear, satisfactory answer. The passage is quoted but of what Yahweh God is king is not explained.[61] It is recognized that he must be acknowledged as a King, a great one, by people who bring sacrifices to him and who is feared by the nations. The question of why the curse, the fear of nations is not answered fully. Pusey made a somewhat fuller statement, quoting a source that spoke of God alone is Lord through his universal providence and his intrinsic authority.[62] Smith gave a fuller but incomplete statement. As King, Yahweh God enforced the curse because he was the great King who was enthroned in the ark of the covenant and this universal kingship of God was a present reality.[63]

According to Eichrodt, it was a human understanding that developed and came to the point of conceiving the kingdom of Yahweh subsisting from the beginning of time and already established at creation.[64] This statement is revealed throughout Scripture. Malachi gave evidence that his was the conception of the kingdom that Yahweh God revealed to him.

Yahweh God, the great One, is the Creator (Mal. 2:10). Malachi referred to Yahweh God as creator in a rhetorical question: *hălô' 'el 'ehed bera'anû* (Did not one God create us?) This God is one Father for us all. The question arose in the context of faulting Judah for breaking the covenant by idolatrous practices. The specific point Malachi was making was that the idols, no gods, were not their makers. Only Yahweh God is Creator of the people of Judah and of all people. Yahweh God is great because he alone is the Creator of humanity and the cosmos in which he placed them.

The one God, Yahweh, is great because of his love and his election of his covenant people (1:2). Malachi echoed what Moses had proclaimed: Yahweh God to whom belonged even the highest heaven and the earth and everything in it, set his affection on his people, loved and chose them (Deut. 10:14, 15). Yahweh God proved his love and absolute lordship by choosing Israel and hating[65] Esau. As sovereign Lord, Creator of all mankind, he deals with each nation as he deems necessary. The descendants of Esau, the Edomites, will experience the reality that Yahweh God is the cosmic King. They had been blessed with prosperity (Gen. 36:7, 8). Yahweh God had given Esau's descendants a specific land as their own. The Israelites were not to trespass on their territory when on their march to the promised land (Deut. 2:2–6). But they had a continuously raging anger and a flaming unchecked fury as they pursued their brothers, the Israelites (Amos 1:11). Yahweh God therefore, as King of the cosmos, turned Seir and surrounding mountains into a wasteland. When they tried to rebuild, Yahweh God demolished them. Yahweh God's treatment of Esau/Edom would raise this response: *yigdal yĕhwâ* (Great is Yahweh) (Mal. 1:5).

Yahweh God, via Malachi, made the apodictic statement *gādôl sĕmî balogôîm* (my name is great among the nations). These people beyond the borders of Judah would come to recognize and know that to Yahweh God alone is due the incense and pure offerings (1:11).

The great King of the cosmos—of the heavens and the earth and all that is in them—is repeatedly referred to as Yahweh *seba'ot* (Yahweh of hosts). The phrase is basically a cosmic kingdom designation. Yahweh is the absolute King, reigning over the heavenly bodies, over angels, over armies, over all that is included in the cosmos. And Malachi properly referred to him as *adonai* (1:11, 14). Yahweh, God of hosts, is the master, the Lord over all. He has the authority, power, and ability to reign over the cosmos. And as the reigning one, he owns, keeps, controls, and guides all aspects of the cosmos.

The great Yahweh God of hosts, the Creator of the cosmic kingdom, absolute sovereign ruling Master over all nations, loved and chose a people, the descendants of Abraham, Isaac, and Jacob to be his covenant people. This covenant was an abiding covenant and Malachi made it his great concern to have his audience know that the covenant with all its aspects was very much a reality in their time as it had been in the past and would continue to be for all time in the future.

The Covenant

Malachi mentioned the term *bĕrît* (covenant) six times (2:4, 5, 8, 9, 14; 3:1). A reading of Malachi could lead one to ask, "Which covenant did he mean?" Kaiser mentioned three possibilities, Mosaic? Levitical? New? (Jeremiah)?[66] He correctly answered that the content of these was a unity but there was a plurality of its forms. Baldwin has stated the case clearly. Fundamental to Malchi's teaching is the concept of the covenant.[67] Verhoef wrote that he shared Baldwin's view that the concept of the covenant "is to be regarded as fundamental to Malachi's teaching."[68]

Before commencing a study of the aspects of the covenant Malachi refers to, it is necessary to briefly consider three issues. One pertains to the covenant of creation. Was Malachi aware of the covenantal relationship Yahweh God had established at the time of creation? Does Malachi give any awareness of Yahweh God's creation covenant mandates: the cultural, the social, and the spiritual? The answer is manifestly positive. He spoke concerning the people's cultural responsibilities and their misuses in that area. He addressed the social particularly when he spoke of marriage and divorce. The spiritual mandate regarding the relationship of the people to Yahweh pervades the entire prophecy.

It must be remembered that the covenant Yahweh God made with Abraham and his progeny was an integral part of the creation covenant. It functioned within the prior covenant. The covenant of grace and redemption was Yahweh God's means of restoring his people to live and function within the creation covenant that Adam and Eve had broken in paradise. The second issue pertains to the question of the unity and structure of Malachi's prophecy. We have referred to scholars who uphold the unity of the prophecies. Two scholars writing about the covenant themes in Malachi concluded that Malachi 3:13–21 should be regarded as a later edition to the main body. And then they divide this edited part into two separate sections.[69] The reality is that the so-called second part also refers to the covenant.

A third issue relates to Malachi's method of addressing the people. He asked questions and raised objections; he raised accusations. Does this indicate that Malachi was dealing with the people as in a legal lawsuit? Previous prophets had spoken of a covenant lawsuit Yahweh God initiated against his people (Isa. 1:18; Amos 3:1, 2; Mic. 2:6–11; Jer. 2:23–25, 29–32). We must conclude that Malachi's style is fully in agreement with prophetic proclamation in thatYahweh God's people are brought into "court" and are accused of covenant breaking. Malachi, however, does not simply bring accusations; he in various ways demonstrates the basic essential nature of the covenant. It is a life/love bond that Yahweh God established and continues to uphold.

Consider Malachi's opening statement *'āhabtî 'etkem* (I have loved you) (1:2). This blessed truth was revealed when Yahweh God delivered Israel from Egypt and led them to Mount Sinai. There, while Israel was at the foot of the mountain, Yahweh God declared to them that they were *lî sĕgullâ* (a precious possession to me) (Exod. 19:5). Moses had reminded the people that Yahweh would keep his covenant of love and that he would love, bless, and increase his people who obeyed him (Deut. 7:12, 13). And he reminded them again of Yahweh God's love for them when he gave his final blessing to Israel (Mal. 3:3).

Throughout the generations, Israel had heard and experienced the love of Yahweh God. This love was what bonded Yahweh God to his people. It was this love that established and repeatedly confirmed the covenant. Yahweh God was the great Suzerain who bonded his people to him in love. In that same love he kept and repeatedly confirmed his covenant. Malachi could therefore say to obedient people who loved Yahweh God, *wĕ hāyu lî . . . 'ănî 'ō`seh sĕgullâh* (and they to me, or they are mine . . . and I am making or keeping them a precious possession (3:17). In this context the statement *'ānî Yĕhwâ lō 'šānîtî* (I Yahweh do not change) (3:6) Yahweh God is constantly the same; he is immutable in his person and character. Therefore his covenant is the same.[70] It never changes as to its basic character and aspects. Over time it had some alterations in form and administration, but never in character, intent, or integral aspects.

As we consider various aspects of the covenant as Malachi proclaimed, it must be understood that he did not follow the organized schema of the suzerainty treaties. But the basic elements are throughout the prophecies. Verhoef, for example, was correct to write, "The preamble, identifying and expounding the majesty and greatness of the author, the king, does not precede the message." Rather, he, the covenant-making king, is evident throughout.[71] Yahweh God's repeated reference to himself, via Malachi presents a vivid encounter between God and his people. Yahweh God, by his covenant, presented himself as a father and would have Israel recognize they are his sons.[72] Hence Israel was much more than vassal servants. They were taken in as precious children.

It is of deepest interest to uncover Malachi's rich awareness of Yahweh God's covenant with his people. We have discussed the author of the covenant and referred to his people with whom he particularly confirmed his covenant of grace.

The historical context of covenant making, confirmation, explanation, and application is always vitally important to understand. The *Sitz im Leben* of Malachi is clearly evident. He addressed the restored exilic community approximately a hundred years after the return of the first contingency. The temple had been built. Jerusalem had been made a secure city; its walls had been rebuilt. But the cultural, social, and spiritual dimensions of everyday life gave evidence of widespread covenant breaking. Ezra and Nehemiah had addressed some of these issues. Ezra, as a priest, and Nehemiah serving in a quasi-royal position as administrator, needed the voice of the prophet. And Malachi spoke Yahweh God's word plainly and directly.

Prescriptions were a basic element in any covenant. The Torah given at Sinai, along with all the explanatory laws and regulations for worship, were essential aspects of Yahweh's covenant with Israel.

Malachi addressed the prescription concerning sacrifices. Injured, crippled, and diseased animals were offered instead of the prescribed unblemished animals. Pure offerings and incense offerings were required (1:7–14).

Priests did not listen to or honor the Lord as required (2:2). The covenant Yahweh God had made with Levi and priests (Num. 26:12) called for reverence and awe. It demanded that true knowledge be preserved and taught. It was to be a covenant of life and peace (Mal. 2:3–9).

Young people were to marry only within the covenant community (Deut. 7). There was to be one spirit between husband and wife. And more, marriage was to endure. Yahweh God hated divorce.

Covenant people were to bring tithes and offerings (Deut. 15). Tithes were to be brought to the storehouses.

Covenant people were not to bear false witness or speak harsh things against their covenant Lord.

The covenant people were to remember the Torah with all its laws and decrees given through Moses.

Malachi made it very clear that covenantal prescriptions were not honored or obeyed. This reality brought another covenant aspect to the fore—the curse of the covenant. Yahweh God had warned that covenant breakers would have the curse executed upon them. Yahweh pronounced *'ārûr* (cursed) be the one who is a *nōkêl* (qal act. ptc. of *nākal*) (Mal. 1:14). The term in its participial form stresses that deceitfulness and craftiness was a continuous practice. The curse was pronounced upon unfaithful priests and their blessings (2:2). The whole nation, which was robbing God of his tithe and offerings, was under a curse (3:9). Yahweh God would strike with a curse those who rejected the one to come who would turn hearts (4:6). It is important to remember that the term *curse* (*'ārôr*) in Hebrew includes the idea of to bind. Hence when Yahweh God pronounces or executes a curse he binds that person under condemnation. To be cursed is to be bound under the wrath of Yahweh God. The curse is executed by Yahweh God when his love is offended and rejected as covenant breakers do. It is executed upon those who break covenant by refusing to obey and carry out Yahweh God's covenantal prescriptions.

Other vital aspects of Yahweh God's covenant were promises and blessings. Implicit in the statement, I have loved you, is the promise of continual love. This love would be demonstrated to those who obeyed Yahweh by giving tithes, offerings, and provisions for the storehouses. Yahweh promised to open the floodgates of heaven and pour out blessings. Yahweh promised to prevent pests who would destroy. He promised that a blessed people would be a blessing to nations. Yahweh God promised to return to those who, having turned from and disobeyed him, return to him. Yahweh God assured his people that he, the unchanging one, would keep his promise to Jacob that they would not be destroyed.

A strong promise was given concerning the coming of the mediator of the covenant. He would be a mighty agent for the continuity of the covenant from generation to generation.[73]

These promises emphasized two other aspects of the covenant. A covenant was confirmed by an "oath." Yahweh God did not sever an oath because his very word had the sure character of an oath. When he spoke it was a binding word; it was a sure reality. Note should be taken that the pronoun *'ānî* (I) appears six times and the long form, *'ānōkî* (I), that emphatically draws attention to the person Yahweh God who speaks. In addition, the suffix *ti o* (I), added to terms, appears repeatedly. Malachi strongly emphasized that Yahweh God spoke authoritatively. His word was his oath.

Another aspect of covenant making involved provisions for the future. It emphasized continuity that would be a sure reality through the mediator, the messenger of the covenant. The covenant would not fail and he would keep and fulfill it.

Three issues that Malachi included in his prophecies that have important covenantal implications require attention.

The first is Malachi's reference to the covenant of Levi (2:4, 8). Yahweh God had said that the "Levites are mine." Specific instructions had been given concerning them (Num. 3:11–13). Nehemiah had referred to the Levites not tending to their duties (Neh. 13:10, 11). He had dealt strongly with them for defiling the priestly office and the covenant of the priesthood and of the Levites. Malachi addressed the same problem and did so in graphic terms. He addressed the priests, reminding them if they were not faithful and obedient to Yahweh God, they were cursed and their blessings would be cursed because it was not in their hearts to honor God (Mal. 2:1, 2). Malachi reminded his priestly contemporaries of how their forebears had had the covenant of peace and life (Num. 25:10–13). Yahweh God still called for reverence and awe of his name. They had carried out their duties (Mal. 2:5, 6), but the Levites and priests had violated the covenant of Levi/priesthood. Therefore they were humiliated for showing partiality (3:9). This humiliation was symbolically portrayed by having the offal of sacrifices spread on the faces of priests and they would be removed, as offal was (2:3). With this removal the covenant with Levi and the priesthood could continue (2:4).

The covenant with the Levites and the priesthood was an integral aspect of Yahweh God's covenant with his people. Moses had made that clear. The covenant prescriptions for worship had called for faithful levitical and priestly service so that the people could and would worship their covenant Lord in a truly covenantally prescribed manner.

The second issue pertained to the covenant of marriage (2:14). A brief survey of the passage in which this covenant is referred to should enable us to grasp the full significance of what Malachi was preaching.

Malachi referred to the reality of the unity of mankind because of Yahweh God's creating us and thus being our common father. This unity, however, came to particular expression in the covenant Yahweh God made with father Abraham (2:10).

Judah, representative of Abraham's progeny, had broken faith, that is, the covenant. The people had defiled Yahweh's house by intermarriage. They were cut off even if they continued to worship by bringing offerings (2:11, 15). Yahweh God rejected the sacrifice and worship, and thus weeping and wailing on the altar was of no avail. Why does Yahweh God not receive what is offered? The offerer has broken faith by marrying an unacceptable woman. Yahweh God had united man and woman to be one flesh so that godly children would be born. So the admonition was given: guard your spirit and do not break your marriage. Then follows the strong statement, "I hate divorce." To divorce is to cover oneself with violence. Final admonition: guard your spirit and do not "break faith."

The common interpretation of this passage is as follows. Covenant life calls for faithfulness to the partner taken in marriage. To divorce is to break Yahweh God's covenant and desecrate his worship. Yahweh God hates divorce and the spirit that leads to it. Yahweh God insists that a pure heart and right spirit maintains the covenant of marriage and also the covenant between Yahweh God and his people.[74] This passage has given rise to a more detailed discussion.

Walter Kaiser saw two kinds of marriages. One was intermarriage with an idolatress, a worshiper of a foreign deity (2:11). Another was marriage between two covenant people that, due to the hardness of heart, was broken.[75] Yahweh God hates divorce; it disregards Yahweh God's covenant with his people.

Recent critical scholarship has drawn attention to what Beth Glazier-McDonald has written.[76] She reviewed various interpretations (mostly by critical scholars) of the entire pericope, 2:10–16. She also referred to those who take a literal approach to the passage, emphasizing that Yahweh God hates divorce. This literal approach too often does not include an in-depth discussion of the *bat-'ēl nĕkār.* This phrase can be interpreted as a foreign woman, or as a "goddess, or as a woman devoted to an idol god. The author appealed to Ezra and Nehemiah, who inveighed against marriage with foreign women. Thus the phrase should be interpreted as a "foreign idolatress." The children from such marriages, if any, were not raised in faithful covenant homes; hence Yahweh would close the womb of these foreign idolatrous women. Glazier-McDonald pointed out that not all Old Testament foreign women were idol worshipers; Ruth came into the covenant community. The basic problem she considers is that scholars have taken either a literal or a syncretistic approach. Stated otherwise, Malachi "was not dealing with a purely social offense, nor was he dealing with a purely religious offense" (1:10).

To present an in depth discussion of the various problems raised would entail too much time and space.[77] For this study, it is important to stress that marriage was and is a covenant ordained by Yahweh God.[78] It is furthermore an integral aspect of Yahweh God's covenant with his people. Marriage with foreign women, that is, women who were not taken into the covenant, as Ruth had been, was violating the covenant Yahweh God had with his people. Furthermore, to divorce the wife of one's youth, that is, a covenant female member, was not only a social sin, but also a religious sin. This sin was compounded if the divorce took place to enable the divorced husband to take a foreign, idol-worshiping woman.

As the Hebrew text reads, the phrase, *kî śānē šallaḥ* (for I hate divorce), gives expression to Yahweh God hating the breaking of the marriage covenant. The form of the verb stresses that God continuously hates divorce.[79] Some interpreters prefer to read the phrase as saying that if a man hates his wife, he can send her away.[80] This view is very inconsistent with the entire thrust of this passage and the testimony of the Old Testament.

It has also been pointed out, however, that if the Hebrew text is repointed to read what the Greek text says, then the reading would be, "But if thou shouldest hate thy 'wife' and put her away saith the Lord God of Israel, then ungodliness shall cover thy thoughts, saith the Lord almighty." This reading of the Hebrew text by Greek translators is said to show that the two clauses are parts of a coherent whole.[81] From a literary point of view this reading is appealing. From a textual perspective it raises a serious question. Did the Masoretes not understand what they were doing when they pointed the text? Did they make a mistake, writing *he* instead of *I* as the English text has it? And, is the use of two verbal nouns both stressing "ongoing" activity—divorce and God hating divorce—impossible? Is the liberty taken by NIV translators by rendering the next phrase that says, "and I hate a man covering himself with violence" any more unacceptable than to repoint the text in such a way that Yahweh God's reaction to divorce is omitted altogether?

Most commentators agree that Yahweh God maintains his covenant with both the obedient and disobedient. The marriage covenant must not be broken; one is not to send away the partner, the wife of one's youth, the wife of one's marriage covenant. To do so would involve breaking both the covenants.

The third issue addresses the reality of the antithesis that is inextricably involved in the covenant. As stated in preceding discussions, the antithesis was established at the time Yahweh God declared that enmity would exist between the seed of the woman and the seed of Satan. This antithesis was a hard reality throughout the entire history of Israel. Covenant keeping was directly antithetical to covenant breaking. This antithesis became particularly dominant between Isaac's two sons, Esau and Jacob. It continued throughout all of Israel/Judah's history. Malachi referred to this antithesis as he began his prophecies. The point to consider in particular is that this antithesis was not only established by Yahweh God, but also maintained by him. Malachi's statement is terse: "loved Jacob, hated Esau."[82] He went on to say that Edom would be called the Wicked Land and a people always under the wrath of Yahweh God (1:4). This maintaining of the antithesis is not an arbitrary or capricious deed by Yahweh God. Edom was in continual rebellion against Yahweh God. They, as sons of Isaac, were included in the covenant but they consistently and violently disobeyed and broke the covenant. They defiantly declared that though Yahweh God had crushed them, they would rebuild and continue in their obstinate ways (1:4).

The question to be answered is why Malachi commenced his prophecies with this reference to the antithetical relationship between Israel and Edom. The answer, as one reads on, seems clear. The people in the restored community were warned that continued covenant breaking, culturally, socially, and spiritually, made them as guilty as the Edomites. The antithesis between the Edomites and Israelites could and would also exist between faithful obedient covenant people and unfaithful, disobedient covenant people. As the covenant curse was carried out on the rebellious Edomites, so would it be on the rebellious people who were part of the restored covenant community. The antithesis was not only between Edomites and Israelites; it was also between the faithful and the unfaithful in the restored Judah community. Malachi stated it clearly. Yahweh God would have his treasured possession, they would be spared and receive compassion. But there would be a clear distinction between "the righteous," the treasured possession, and the wicked *bên 'ōbēd 'ĕlōhîm la'ăšer lô' 'ăbādo* (between those who serve [work for, worship] God and those who do not). Obedience rendered to Yahweh God and faithfulness to his covenant had been, was, and would always be the great dividing issue. Malachi's contemporaries had to be reminded and remember that Yahweh God maintained the antithesis and the consequences issuing from it.[83]

The Mediator

The mediator Malachi refers to is the messenger of the covenant—the Lord, who will perform purifying work as he executes his judgment upon covenant breakers. The prophet Elijah who will perform a task that was prescribed by Moses in the Torah will precede the covenant messenger. This forerunner will bring unity and harmony in families by his transforming work in the hearts of fathers and their children.

A number of remarks should be made concerning what Malachi proclaimed in each of his three "messianic" passages.[84]

Malachi 2:17–3:5. The immediate context of the phrase, "send my messenger . . . the messenger of the covenant whom is desired," is the query "Where is the God of justice?" This question was asked because of the perversions rampant in the cultural, social, and spiritual dimensions of life. The mandates of the creation/redemptive covenant were ignored and disobeyed. Faithful covenant people were said to long for the presence and work of the promised Messiah, who, according to previous prophets, would bring in justice (Isa. 9:7; 11:1–5).

Yahweh God's response, via Malachi, is *`sôlēâh mal'ākî* (the verb is an act. part. of *sālâh,* in the act of sending my messenger), who will prepare or make clear the way before me, that is, Yahweh God the speaker. Malachi made it clear that *ha'ādôn* (the Lord) is to be identified with the messenger of the covenant.[85] Yahweh God is distinct from the Messenger, the Lord. The deity of the Messenger is definitely stated here. Malachi went on to describe how the divine covenant messenger, the messianic Mediator, would execute judgment. He will be a purifying agent—like a refiner's fire and launderer's soap. Levites (and priests) will be purified, as will the people of Judah and Jerusalem as they bring acceptable offerings. There will be a cleansing. The antithesis will be evident. There will be the cleansed and purified ones. There will be judgment of many who *lô yĕrō'îmî* (not fear me). The term *fear* must be understood to include reverence, awe, and true worship. These non-fearing ones were particularly guilty of breaking the social mandate. Note that there is no reference to idol worship or misuse of Yahweh God's name. Sin against the first four commandments (the spiritual mandate) is not singled out. But sins against the fifth to tenth commandments, the cultural and social mandates, are. It is evident from Malachi that people do not fear and reverence Yahweh God or render acceptable worship to him are guilty of sins that are mentioned. These are sorcery, adultery, perjury, stealing from laborers (holding back wages), oppressing of widows and fatherless, and depriving aliens of justice. These evil deeds render acceptable reverence and worship of Yahweh impossible. They who are guilty of these sins are covenant breakers and are under the curse of the covenant. But the messenger of the covenant, the messianic Mediator, will execute justice and purify those who desire him.

The "messianic passage" setting forth the messenger of the covenant is followed by Yahweh God's stating emphatically, "I Yahweh do not change." Neither Yahweh God in person, or in promise, or in executing the curse would change. Yahweh would change his attitude and dealing with those who repented, gave their tithes (not robbing God), feared him, and communed with others who also did (3:15–18). But the curse would surely come upon those who said it was futile to serve Yahweh God. This prophecy concerning robbing God, complainers regarding futility, and communing with fellow servants, is followed by another messianic passage.

Malachi 4:1–3 (MT 3:19–21).[86] Malachi continues with what he had prophesied in the previous messianic passage (3:1–5). He spoke with assurance. The day is coming that will bring the purifying fire; it will be like a furnace with a fire burning stubble. It will be a complete purifying. The antithesis between the arrogant and evildoer (the stubble) and those who revere Yahweh God's name will become a clear reality. The Sun of Righteousness will arise, appear, and do the purifying. The sun is obviously a metaphor of the Messiah. He, as the sun, clears away fog and mist and gives warmth, growth, life, and blessings. So the Messiah will totally remove the wicked stump and root, and usher in righteousness. The Messiah would reveal and do the will of God; he would fulfill the promises of the covenant. Freedom and joy would be the wonderful realities he would bring. Amid all the joy,[87] Yahweh's righteous people would have a triumph over those who had done wickedly. Note must be taken, Yahweh God, through the messianic messenger of the covenant, would cause this trampling of the wicked amid the joy of being freed from sin and reckoned righteous.

The covenant promise concerning the messenger/mediator to come, and the blessings he would bring, is followed by Malachi giving a solemn reminder: *zikrû tōrâh Mōseh 'abatî* (remember, imperative, the Torah of Moses my servant), that I commanded him (4:4 [MT 3:22]). A redeemed, righteous, sanctified people could not forget what Yahweh God had given as prescription for covenant life. Recall that what Yahweh God had given as guidelines for covenant living were expansions of the creation covenant mandates.[88] Moses had not only given instructions for the redeemed life, but for all aspects of cosmic kingdom life and service (4:5, 6 [MT 3:23, 24]). Malachi concluded his prophecies by stressing another covenant promise. The prophet Elijah was to be sent and appear before the great and dreadful days of Yahweh God.

Some questions call for an answer. Why is the Day of the Lord described as great and dreadful? In the context of Malachi's prophecies with accusations of covenantal breaking deeds and the judgment to be carried out because of these, the coming of the messianic Mediator would include his administering judgment with justice. The purifying fire and soap would do their task. The evil and the good would be separated. Blessings would be given to some, but the sureness of the covenant curse on others could not be doubted.

A second question pertains to why Elijah was referred to as coming before the Day of Judgment. Elijah was considered the first great prophet. He boldly and fearlessly challenged Ahab and Jezebel. They were covenant breakers and Elijah waged a strong battle against them. He had been an agent of judgment. Malachi referred to him as representative of the last of the prophetic order that would come, challenge, and oppose the ways of evil that the Messiah would have to face and overcome.

A third question pertains to expectations. Did Malachi state the case clearly enough so that the covenant community was led to expect the coming of Elijah? The New Testament answer is yes. Evangelist Mark quoted Jewish scribes who said that Elijah must first come (Mark 9:11). And the disciples wanted to know who he was and when he would come. Scribes had described this second Elijah as one raising the dead, restoring manna, and solving questions raised by the Torah. In plain words, the scribes taught that the second Elijah had to be a precise and exact repeat of the first one. Malachi, however, did not refer to these detailed activities.[89]

A fourth question pertains to what Malachi prophesied about the turning of fathers' and children's hearts to each other. The last phrase of Malachi refers to the curse of the covenant again. It will surely come if hearts are not turned (4:6 [MT 3:24]). As Verhoef correctly stated, opinions vary concerning the correct understanding of this statement. He mentioned two. Many interpreters prefer the idea that holds that this second Elijah would settle many family quarrels caused by mixed marriages and divorces (2:10–16). This Elijah would introduce a new social order. Verhoef prefers the second view, that this Elijah will restore the Mosaic prescribed covenantal relationship between fathers and children.[90] Reference is particularly to the covenant confirmed at Sinai (Exod. 19:1–6), in which children were included with the adults (Deut. 5:1–5). Malachi referred to the Torah Moses had given that included clear covenantal instruction to fathers to nuture, teach, and train their children (6:1–11; 11:16–22). Having given these directions concerning the instruction of their children, Yahweh God added that long life would follow. Moses added, speaking on behalf of Yahweh God, " See, I am setting before you today a blessing and a curse" (11:26). Malachi quoted Moses. If parental instruction and influence were not exercised, Yahweh would execute the threatened covenant curse.

It is very interesting to note that the Old Testament ends with a specific instruction concerning the continuity of the covenant. Parental responsibility is to be exercised. Yahweh God's agents for the turning of the hearts of children to their fathers are the fathers themselves. They are God's appointed servants to hold the Scriptures before their children and teach them to know, understand, and apply all that it teaches to the generation following them. Implied in this passage is that the fathers themselves know, believe, and obey all that the Scriptures reveal.

Joel's Agenda

We return to the view some biblical scholars hold concerning the place of the prophecy of Joel in the canon and particularly in the history of revelation. The position set out and applied in this study is that Joel was the first of the writing prophets, not the last. A study of Joel leads one to see how he laid out the agenda for the prophets succeeding him. He did not, as it were, give a review of what the prophets preceding him had spoken.

Joel had warned of national and cosmic disasters to come. These had come. Malachi made no reference to these when he repeatedly reminded the restored community of the curse of the covenant to be executed on covenant breakers. As Joel had done, Malachi called for repentance and trust and spoke assuringly of Yahweh God's love. He did not refer, as Joel had done, to the future return and gathering of the covenant people. Joel spoke of the coming of the Holy Spirit; other prophets had referred to it; Malachi did not do so explicitly. Malachi did not refer to Jerusalem visited and spared as previous prophets had. As Joel, he spoke concerning the Day of Yahweh and all that was involved but made no direct reference to the coming of the messianic Mediator of the covenant and his predecessor. Malachi did not speak in general terms. He was specific. That messenger of the covenant and his predecessor were to be sent. Malachi thus emphasized what previous prophets had referred to. The Day of Yahweh was approaching. Yahweh God would be sending the promised covenant Mediator.

The End of Old Testament Revelation

In the previous paragraphs I made the case for considering Malachi as the last prophetic voice in the Old Testament times. Joel had introduced the prophetic agenda. Malachi concluded it by his direct references to the sending of the Mediator of the covenant.

The Apocryphal Material

In the 400-year period between Malachi's prophecy and the appearing of the angel Gabriel to the priest Zechariah and the virgin Mary, the Jewish community was active in various ways in their endeavor to resurrect the Jewish National State and to understand their times especially from a religious perspective. The scribes assiduously studied the Old Testament revelation. They wrote volumes of material in which they tried to explain what that Old Testament revelation meant for them, particularly for their daily lives and what to expect in the future. These writings contain a wide variety of literatures. Some is valuable from an historical standpoint. But there was no verbal revelation from Yahweh God. General revelation continued. In that setting special, verbal revelation was again given when the time had fully come (Gal. 4:4). And that time, according to Paul, was an evil age (1:4).

The Golden Cable Continued in the New Testament

The Golden Cable unites the New Testament revelation as well as continuing from the Old Testament.

The Kingdom

Matthew wrote concerning the king of the Jews. The wise men from the east had seen his star. Seeing the star, they concluded that a king had been born. Since the star shone over Jerusalem, the wise men concluded that the royal one born was the king of the Jews.

Two important points should be observed. The star was a cosmic phenomenon. The King of the cosmos controlled that star. Here is clear evidence that the cosmic kingdom was the context of what happened when Jesus was born. The next point to be observed is that Jesus Christ, born when the time had fully come, came as the promised son of David, the royal one, who was the promised king of the Jews, but not only of the Jews but of all who believed in him as King and Savior.

The Mediator

The promised Messiah was born. He was the descendant of David (Matt. 1:1–16). He came as the royal Mediator who exercised his royal power, his kingship, over water/wine, fish and bread, the storms on the sea, in the raising of the dead, in the casting out of demons, in crushing the head of Satan on the cross, and in personally rising from the grave.

The Covenant

The covenant continued as the redemptive and administrative means of the kingdom. Jesus Christ, the royal one, was the covenantal agent who fulfilled all the prescriptions of the covenant as well as the promises. More, he took on the curse of the covenant, thus freeing all those the Father gave him from that curse.

Conclusion

The Golden Cable's triple strands effectively served as the central and uniting realities of the Scriptures, both Old and New Testaments. Each prophetic book, each historical book, testifies to this central unifying reality. It also serves as the reality that united revelation as it came through the centuries of time. The Golden

Cable unites all of scriptural revelation. As time and stamina permit, under God's providential care and reign, the Poetic and Wisdom Literature will be studied. The evidence that the Golden Cable unites these to the other parts of Scripture will be demonstrated.

A final comment. The title of this study is *From Creation to Consummation.* Almost all the prophets, directly or indirectly, explicitly or implicitly, cover the entire range of the history of revelation and redemption. They, one way or another, cover the span of time from creation to the comsummation marked by Christ's second return. Malachi referred to creation. God created humanity. He made references to Moses and the prophets preceding him. He ended his prophecies by stressing that Elijah (John the Baptist) would come preceding the messenger of the covenant, Jesus Christ. Malachi's prophecies refer only to this first coming of the Messiah and what he will do. These activities will have definite influence on people in the course of history. There is no reference to the end of history. His task was to make a specific introduction to the first coming. This he did effectively.

NOTES

1. The date, 458 B.C., has been recorded by a wide variety of commentators. Cf., e.g., Derek Kidner, *Ezra & Nehemiah* (Downers Grove: InterVarsity, 1979), 10, 15. The date for Ezra's writing, according to Frederick Carlson Holmgren, *Ezra & Nehemiah: Israel Alive Again* (Grand Rapids: Eerdmans, 1987), xiii, is not acceptable, but he did agree that the "two books" (Ezra and Nehemiah) covered the period from 538 B.C. to 400 B.C. The date 400 B.C. stretches the time too far.

2. See the discussion of Ezra 1–6 in the first part of chap. 30.

3. Jacob Myers, *Ezra & Nehemiah,* Anchor Bible, vol. 14 (Garden City: Doubleday, 1965), lxxii, lxxiii.

4. Joseph Blenkinsopp, *Ezra–Nehemiah* (Philadelphia: Westminster, 1988), 160.

5. F. Charles Fensham, *The Books of Ezra and Nehemiah* (Grand Rapids: Eerdmans, 1982), 120.

6. The verb *pā'er* appears only in the piel; in the text it is in the piel infin. construc. The basic meaning is beautify, glorify. NIV translates it "to honor"; this term does not express all that the Hebrew term does.

7. See Stan Evers, *Doing a Great Work* (Darlington, U.K.: Evangelical, 1996), 70.

8. Fensham, *Book of Ezra* wrote: "We must accept that at the end of this chapter some corruption of the text has crept in," 144. Literally the last part of 10:44 reads "and there were from them wives and they put sons." Myers, *Ezra & Nehemiah,* states that this phrase makes no sense, 88, note 4. Blenkensopp, *Ezra–Nehemiah,* elaborated on various versions of this text, 200.

9. Holmgren, *Ezra-Nehemia* , 83.

10. H. Grosheide, *Ezra–Nehemia* (Kampen: Kok, 1963), used the word "ijveraar"—one who is very zealous for God, 275.

11. Kidner, *Ezra & Nehemiah,* 72; Johanna W. H. Van Wyk-Bos revealed a strong feminine bias as she concluded her study of Ezra. *Ezra, Nehemiah, Esther* (Louisville: Westminster/John Knox, 1998). She referred to the following: names of women are missing, the banished ones. Males who were responsible were given full publicity. Van Wyk-Bos asked,

why were the men not banished since they were responsible for the marriages? Men suffered emotionally; but women and children, weakest members of the group, bore the brunt of the sacrifice. She concluded "there is nothing good about this, and it is an example of a cowardly and condemnable behavior on the part of the male members of the community," 47. The author condemned Ezra from a contemporary context; she ignored the reality that the men were members of the covenant community by birth; the women were foreigners and not native to the community. The author also ignored what influence foreign women had had when they, by marriage, had become members of the covenant community. She ignored the covenant command given in Deut. 7.

12. Consider the case of Timothy (2 Tim. 1:5, 6).

13. Grosheide, *Ezra,* 11.

14, Raymond Brown, *The Message of Nehemiah* (Downers Grove: InterVarsity, 1998), 21, 22.

15. Cf. J. I. Packer, *A Passion for Faithfulness* (Wheaton: Crossway, 1995), 114–17.

16. Brown, *Nehemiah,* 17–20.

17. Myers, *Ezra, Nehemiah,* admits that there are not many sources in the tightly constructed document. But sources are discernable, xlviii. The truth is that the list of resources given does more to demonstrate the book's unity and authorship than its being a product of editors as Myers opines. Reference has been made in preceding chapters to the efforts of Sara Japhet to clarify the relationship of Chronicles, Ezra, and Nehemiah. Cf. her essay again, "The Supposed Common Authorship of Chronicles and Ezra–Nehemiah Investigated Again," *Vetus Testamentum* 18 (1968): 330–71. Also her later essay, "Composition and Chronology in the Book of Ezra-Nehemiah" *Journal for the Study of Old Testament, Supplement Series* (1994): 189–216. Note again the comment in previous notes regarding her changing views as she progressed in her studies.

18. Cf. Blenkensopp, *Ezra–Nehemiah,* 38. Cf. also H. H. Grosheide, *Ezra–Nehemia* (Kampen: Kok, 1963), who reviewed the time that they were united as the LXX also had. No reason can be determined why the books were separated, 2–4.

19. Holmgren wrote that Ezra and Nehemiah emerged as principal leaders in the pioneer community. He added that we do not know much about them because the books do not present exact history. *Israel Alive,* xiv, v. These comments indicate a low regard for these books as revelation. Thomas McCreech, in "Ezra and Nehemiah, Leaders in Restoration," *The Bible Today* 37 (1999), also wrote that it is difficult to identify Ezra and Nehemiah when they came to Israel and to establish the authority of the books associated with them, 201–6.

20. Kidner, *Ezra & Nehemiah,* indicated that the tasting was a proof that there was no poison in the wine. In this capacity Nehemiah could be an influential official. In the Assyrian court the cupbearer (or butler) was the chief minister in the court, 79, 80.

21. See Fensham, *Books of Ezra* 151, 152.

22. Loren W. Batten, *The Books of Ezra and Nehemiah,* ICC Commentary (Edinburgh: T & T Clark, 1961), entitled his comments on Nehemiah, "Nehemiah Becomes Governor of Judah," 182.

23. Cf. Brown, *Message of Nehemiah,* his section on themes, 17–25.

24. Ibid., 18.

25. Packer, *Passion,* 35, 125.

26. Blenkensopp, *Ezra–Nehemiah,* 265. He pointed out that if Nehemiah was legalistic, then Christian prayer could be characterized likewise. It is unfortunate that Blenkensopp takes the appearance of these short prayers as evidence of an editor's hand. He thinks such prayers were at the end of the memoirs.

27. Fensham, *Ezra and Nehemiah,* 199.
28. Ibid., 199.
29. Packer, *Passion,* 125.
30. Ibid., 35.
31. This prayer, according to most commentators, is a construction by the chronicler. It includes some "rich Deuteronomic phraseology." Myers, *Ezra & Nehemiah,* writes it was a prayer in conformity with contemporary usage. He believed that the Deuteronomist, as a person of critical imagination, had much influence. But that should not deny Nehemiah prayed this prayer, 95, 96. It must be stated emphatically that Nehemiah, well acquainted with what the Old Testament recorded regarding Yahweh's covenant with his people, was in a situation that led him to pray spontaneously as he did.
32. See Evers, *Great Work.* The biblical emphasis is on God's attributes of power, justice, and holiness when he is described as great, 105.
33. See Fensham, *Ezra and Nehemiah,* who correctly does not consider *hesed* (covenant love) to be an adjective of *bĕrît.*
34. Cf. 2 Chron. 4:14.
35. Evers, *Great Work,* 107. Loring Batten, *Ezra and Nehemiah,* was so bound to the Wellhausian textual criticism that he endeavored to find evidence for denying the authenticity of Nehemiah's prayer. In concluding his extremely critical remarks he wrote, "If Nehemiah recorded his prayer at all, it has been so worked over that the original cannot be recovered." Such a statement reveals the audacity of liberal critics.
36. An imprecatory prayer or psalm "constitutes a reply to national enemies and calls upon God to exercise retribution." R. K. Harrison, *Introduction to the Old Testament,* reprint (Grand Rapids: Eerdmans, 1969), 997.
37. Cf. also Pss. 109, 137, and for imprecatory sentiments expressed in Pss. 5, 7, 28, 54, 55, 58, 59, 79, 83, 101, 139.
38. Cf. Jer. 15:15 and 17:18: "Let my persecutors be put to shame."
39. Cf. comments on 5:19 in preceding paragraphs.
40. Scholars have noted that there is a thirteen-year gap between the time Ezra came and carried out reforms and his reading of the law (Neh. 8). Kidner, *Ezra & Nehemiah,* discussed various views concerning the gap, 150-52.
41. The term *ṡaddiq* as a rule, should be translated righteous. In this context the idea is that as God was faithful himself to his will (righteous); he demonstrated that in his relationship with his people, that is., righteous regarding himself, he was just punishing the people.
42. The discussion by Blenkinsopp of what is recorded in Neh. 13:1–3 raises questions about Edomites and Egyptians that is difficult to understand. Was Blenkinsopp seeking some evidence to discredit the text? *Ezra–Nehemiah,* 350–52.
43. See Fensham, *Ezra and Nehemiah,* for a discussion of the situation that developed while Nehemiah was back in Susa for a period of time, 266.
44. Within the covenant Yahweh God had established and confirmed with Abraham and his descendants, this priestly covenant was established. This can be understood more readily if one considers the marriage bond/covenant to be an essential aspect of Yahweh God's covenant with his people.
45. I had many commentaries to consult. Very few of them discussed this. Myers, *Ezra & Nehemiah,* referred to it briefly, 218. In previous comments on 10:33, 34, he had correctly stated, "The survival of the Jewish community depended on the maintenance of cultic identity and the rejection of compromise with the peoples of the land," 179.

46. Packer, reflecting on Nehemiah's role, wrote that one "need not suppose that Nehemiah enjoyed having to do any of the things" he felt responsible for, *Passion,* 193. But possibly he did because Brown correctly wrote that Nehemiah was an exemplary leader; he was earnest in prayer, treasured a deep personal faith, was dependent on grace alone, and was conscious of human accountability. *Nehemiah,* 254–56. Having such virtues and disciplines, one finds security in his Lord. This security is the root and fountain of joy.

47. Consult the brief study of Nehemiah in *MROT*, 924, 925.

48. Julia M. O'Brien, "Malachi in Recent Research," *Current Research: Biblical Studies* 8 (1995).

49. Ibid., 81, 91–94.

50. Willard P. Sperry, "Malachi," in *The Interpreter's Bible,* vol. 6, ed. George A. Buttrick (Nashville: Abingdon, 1956), 1161.

51. See Joyce Baldwin, *Haggai, Zechariah, Malachi* (Downers Grove: InterVarsity, 1972), for a succinct discussion of "The Prophet," 211–13. See also John Merlin Powis Smith, "A Critical and Exegetical Commentary on the Book of Malachi," in *Haggai, Zechariah, Malachi and Jonah,* ICC series, ed. S. R. Driver, A. Plumer, and C. A. Briggs, (Edinburgh: T & T Clark, latest printing, 1980). Smith wrote that Malachi is an anonymous writing; the name was attached to the book by an editor. The writer was a patriotic Jew, loved his country and people, and fervently hated Israel's enemies, 9–11. See C. F. Keil's rebuttal to that view. He argued for considering Malachi an historical person, *The Twelve Minor Prophets,* vol. 2, trans. James Marten (Grand Rapids: Eerdmans, 1951), 423–27. J. Ridderbos referred to some scholars who suggested that Malachi took the name as an official title, "God's Messenger." Ridderbos discounted this theory, *De Kliene Profeten,* vol. 3, (Kampen: Kok, 1952), 191. Paul L. Redditt, however, countered, writing that it would have been inappropriate for parents to name a child "God's Messenger." So he follows the critical scholars accepting the name as a title drawn from Mal. 3:1. *Haggai, Zechariah and Malachi* (Grand Rapids: Eerdmans, 1995), 151. R. J. Coggins had written previous to Redditt that it is generally agreed that Malachi is a later editorial addition. Coggins discounted it as a personal name, and agreed with most commentators (critical), that the book is an originally anonymous collection of oracles and that later the name was attached and became recognized as personal. *Haggai, Zechariah, Malachi* (Sheffield: JSOT, 1987), 73.

52. George L. Robinson, *The Twelve Minor Prophets* (Grand Rapids: Baker, 1960), 158.

53. Baldwin, *Malachi,* 213. W. H. Lowe, however, gave what he considers undeniable evidence that Malachi was Nehemiah's co-adjutor during his second visit to Jerusalem. Lowe lists the issues Nehemiah faced (Neh. 13) and the issues Malachi addressed. "Malachi," in *Ellicott's Commentary on the Whole Bible,* vol. 5., ed. C. J. Ellicott (Grand Rapids: Zondervan, n.d.), 598.

54. Pieter A. Verhoef, *The Books of Haggai and Malachi* (Grand Rapids: Eerdmans, 1987), wrote: "According to our date for his prophecy, Malachi delivered his speeches to the same audience to which Ezra and Nehemiah directed themselves," 180.

55. Because of these social problems, some scholars have taken a sociological approach to the study of Malachi. See O'Brien, "Recent Research," 89. One such writer is J. L. Berquist, "The Social Setting of Malachi," *Biblical Theological Bulletin* 19 (1989): 121–26. His study led him to conclude that a vacuum of political authority exacerbated the fragmentation of postexilic society. He detected three major groupings involved in social conflict. These, he wrote, were vividly apparent in the book of Malachi. The three were "The Pious Orthodox, " "The Skeptical Free Thinker," and "The Ungodly of Israel." These groups

were seen by some to have developed into Samaritans, Maccabeans, and Pharisees. Berquist saw Mal. 3:13–4:3 as especially illustrative of the three groups, but he characterized them quite differently. The inner group has exemplary faith. The second group are part of the in group who are doubters, and the third group are Jerusalemites, evildoers and arrogant. As Berquist proceeded in his presentation, he had to agree that parts of Malachi reflected a bifurcation, not a tripartite division. The issue of the character of the postexilic community calls for further careful exegetical and theological study. Berquist has made an initial contribution in which he, at times, somewhat confusingly, demonstrated that the spiritual (religious), social, and cultural dimensions of life impinge on each other.

56. Brevard S. Childs, *Introduction to the Old Testament as Scripture* (Philadelphia: Fortress, 1979), 489.

57. Ibid., 489–90. Harrison agreed that there is a problem regarding the prophet's identity. The addressee is clearly Israel, the restored community, as evidenced by the covenantal issues raised. The transmission of the unified text has left it in good order. *Introduction to the Old Testament* (Grand Rapids: Eerdmans, 1969), 958–61.

58. Jack P. Lewis, in *The Minor Prophets* (Grand Rapids: Baker, 1966), wrote: "It is not certain at what date Joel and Obadiah prophesied," 13. He therefore discussed them last, after Malachi. See section IV of this chapter for my view.

59. Robert Dentan, in his "Introduction to Malachi," *Interpreter's Bible,* wrote that there can be little doubt that the prophecies were produced by a single active mind, 1117.

60. A perusal of commentaries will give evidence of their varied perspectives. Lowe presented Malachi as a stern man who rebuked Israel for ingratitude to God who loved them, rebuked priests for sinful service, rebuked people for intermarriage and divorce, rebuked skeptics for the coming of the Lord, rebuked people for withholding tithes, and rebuked formalists. *Ellicott's Commentary,* 598–99. Ralph Smith in *Micah–Malachi,* in *Word Biblical Commentary,* vol. 32 (Waco: Word, 1984), sees six disputations regarding God's love, God's honor, faithlessness, God's justice, repentance, and speaking against God, 299.

61. A sampling of commentaries revealed the following. Robert L. Alden, "Malachi," in *The Expositor's Bible Commentary,* vol. 7, ed. Frank Gabelein (Grand Rapids: Zondervan, 1985), commented: "He is an absolute sovereign" and refers only to this God choosing whom he will, 713. Baldwin, *Haggai–Malachi,* in the context of the curse referred to God being feared, he is Lord God of gods, 232. J.M.P. Smith, "Malachi," referred to God as king of kings, a common biblical theme, 34. Dentan, "Malachi," God is the great king, a fact to which even heathen bear witness by the magnificence of their temples, 1130. Ebenezer Henderson, *The Twelve Minor Prophets* (Grand Rapids: Baker, 1980), did not refer to Yahweh God as a great king at all, 450, nor did Lewis, *The Minor Prophets,* refer to it, 82–86. Walter Kaiser, in *Malachi: God's Unchanging Love* (Grand Rapids: Baker, 1984), referred to other passages in Scripture that tell of God's greatness and that God is king. He did not say king over what, 50. Carl Frederick Keil in *The Twelve Minor Prophets,* vol. 2, trans. James Marten (Grand Rapids: Eerdmans, 1951), wrote that a curse was pronounced because of God's greatness and is feared among nations; he repeated the text. Lowe, *Ellicott's Commentary,* made reference only to what a subject would do to his king, 603. Ridderbos in "Malachi" discussed the curse at length but made hardly a reference to the great king, 203. Verhoef in *Haggai . . .. Malachi,* under a subheading "Cursed is the cheat," wrote in a short paragraph that God is feared among the nations because he is honored and acknowledged, 235.

62. E. B. Pusey, *The Minor Prophets: A Commentary,* vol. II (Grand Rapids: Baker, 1950), 475.

63. Smith, "Malachi," 316, 317. Smith referred to Walther Eichrodt who wrote that various Old Testament passages referred to Yahweh as king and that it was a present reality which effectively orders the world here and now. See Eichrodt, *Old Testament Theology,* vol. 1, trans. James Baker (Philadelphia: Westminster, 1961), 199.

64. Ibid.

65. The Hebrew term *sānī tî* (I have hated) has given rise to various opinions. Smith opined that the word should not mean hate in its usual sense but not chosen, repeated. "Malachi," 305. See discussion of Covenant for further discussion of the term *hate.*

66. Kaiser, *Unchanging Love,* 82.

67. Baldwin, *Haggai–Malachi.* She wrote the prophecy begins with Yahweh's covenant love and ends with a call to fulfill its obligations, 210.

68. Verhoef, *Haggai–Malachi,* 180.

69. Steven L. McKenzie and Howard N. Wallace, "Covenant Themes in Malachi," *Catholic Biblical Quarterly* 45 (1983): 549–63. They give two examples for their dissecting. The edited section does not refer to Judah, Jerusalem, or priests, and the first section deals with Moses, the second with Elijah. S. D. Snyman has challenged that view in an essay entitled "A Structural Approach to Malachi 3:13–21," in *Old Testament Essays* (Pretoria: n.p., 1991). Synman found that historical critical investigation of the passage had highlighted diversity. He, however, saw a remarkable unity displayed by the symmetrical pattern of the two parts.

70. Cf., e.g., Smith, *Malachi,* 299–300.

71. Verhoef, *Haggai–Malachi,* 180.

72. Baldwin, *Haggai–Malachi,* 216.

73. The mediator will be discussed more fully in the succeeding section of this chapter.

74. Various commentators accept this understanding of what Malachi was saying. Baldwin captioned her comments with "The Importance of Family Life," *Haggai–Malachi,* 237. Henderson understood that legitimate marriage where Jehovah had been witness had to be maintained; divorce was an abomination. *Malachi,* 454, 455. Pusey emphasized that unlawful marriages and divorce were a profanation of Yahweh God's holiness, *Malachi,* 462, 463.

75. *Unchanging Love,* 68–74. A. S. Vander Woude, "Malachi's Struggle for a Pure Community: Reflections on Malachi 2:10," in *Tradition and Re-Interpretation in Jewish and Early Christian Literature,* ed. J. W. Van Henting, H. J. de Jonge, P. T. Van Rooden, and J. W. Wesselhuis (Leiden: Brill, 1986). Vander Woude's first sentence, in his article, is "All commentators hold that Malachi's third prophecy (2:10–16), in its present form deals with two abuses in the postexilic community of Jerusalem and Judah: intermarriage with foreign women and divorce," 65.

76. Beth Glazier-McDonald, "Intermarriage, Divorce and *Bat-Ēl Nĕkār:* Insights into Malachi 2:1–16," *Journal of Biblical Literature* 106, no. 4 (1987): 603–11.

77. Readers can consult various commentaries for these, e.g., Verhoef and Baldwin.

78. A valuable contribution to the study and understanding of the covenant, and particularly of the "covenant of marriage," has been made by Gordon Paul Hugenburger, *Marriage as a Covenant* (Leiden: Brill, 1994). The subtitle of the work is "A Study of Biblical Law and Ethics Governing Marriage Developed from the Perspective of Malachi." It is *Supplement LII to Vetus Testamentum.* Chapter 5 presents a particular help for a student of "Marriage as a Covenant." Hugenburger reviewed and supported the five arguments that have been developed to support the view that Mal. 2:1ff. refers to marriage as a covenant. He reviewed the position of those who deny that it is and refuted them effectively, 27–47. In

his conclusion, he wrote, "It has been established that there is the plausibility that Mal. 2:14 identifies literal marriage as a [*bĕrît*] based on grammar and context," 340. Hugenberger has not come to this conclusion without awareness of some problems, e.g., did Ezra enforce divorce (Ezra 10:48), and what about Deut. 24:1–4, where provisions for divorce are given? Hugenberger concluded, after his lengthy study, that the perspectives of Malachi and Deuteronomy are not basically in conflict, 340.

79. Verhoef, *Haggai–Malachi,* 278. Note also Verhoef's discussion on the Masoretic punctuation of the Hebrew word for hate. It has led to varying interpretations of who the subject of hate is.

80. N. G. Swanepoel addressed this issue. "To Send Away in Hate or to Hate Divorce—What Does the Lord Want?" *Nederduitse Gereformeerde Teologiese Tydschrif* 36 (1995): 65–74. He concluded that to choose between the possibilities of reading and translating *kî `sanē `săllaḥ* is too difficult. The basic issue is with Israel's infidelity to Yahweh God's covenant with his people.

81. David Jones wrote an essay entitled "Malachi on Divorce: Who Hates What?" He drew attention to some textual problems that are evident in the Hebrew text and what the LXX records. *Presbyterion Covenant Seminary Review,* 15 (1989): 16–22. See also his "A Note on the LXX of Malachi 2:16," *Journal of Biblical Literature* 109 (1990): 683–85.

82. See the essay by S. D. Snyman, "Antithesis in the Book of Malachi," *Journal of N.W. Semitic Languages* 16 (1990): 173–78.

83. It seems that one should not accept what McKenzie and Wallace wrote: namely, that Yahweh God was in a real sense defending himself against charges by his people. *Themes,* 556, 557.

84. See my discussion of these three passages in *MROT,* 928–36. Note also the bibliographical data included in the notes. In the past decade, little has been written on the messianic concept in Malachi.

85. Commentators have discussed the references to three persons, my messenger, the Lord, and messenger of the covenant. Cf. *MROT,* 929, 930.

86. See discussion of this passage, ibid., 932–35.

87. Malachi referred to calves released from the stall jumping and leaping. This scene is very realistic. As a boy on a dairy farm, it was my duty to feed calves born during the months of November through January, when they were kept in stalls or pens. When the pastures had begun to grow by mid-February the calves were released to spend the daytime in pastures. It was a family joy to watch the running, jumping, prancing, freed calves. They made no effort to eat grass at first. They exuberantly delayed that for the "joy" at being freed from a pen.

88. The creation covenant spiritual mandate was elaborated in the first four commandments, the social mandate in commandments 5–7, the cultural mandate in commandments 8–10.

89. D. C. Allison, "Elijah Must First Come," *Journal of Biblical Literature* 103 (1984), discussed a number of the reasons why the expectation of Elijah was not a *novum* that Christians introduced. Allison pointed to various writings produced before Christ came that referred to Malachi's prophecy.

90. Verhoef, *Haggai–Malachi,* 342, 343.

Bibliography

Aalders, G.C.H. *An Exposition of Ezekiel.* Evansville: Sovereign Grace, 1960.

Aalders, G.C.H. *Daniel.* Kampen: Kok, 1962.

Aalders, G.C.H. *Ezekiel.* 2 vols. Kampen: Kok, 1957.

Aalders, G.C.H. *Obadja en Jona.* Kampen: Kok, 1958.

Aalders, Jan G. *Gog and Magog.* Kampen: Kok, 1951.

Ackroyd, Peter. *Exile and Restoration.* London: SCM, 1968.

Alden, Robert L. "Malachi." In *The Expositor's Bible Commentary*, vol. 7, ed. Frank Gabelein. Grand Rapids: Zondervan, 1985.

Alexander, Joseph A. *Commentary on the Prophecies of Isaiah.* Grand Rapids: Zondervan, 1953.

Alexander, Ralph H. "Ezekiel." In *The Expositor's Bible Commentary,* ed. Frank F. Gabelein, vol. 6. Grand Rapids: Regency, 1986.

Allen, Leslie C. "1 and 2 Chronicles." In *The Communicator's Commentary*, vol. 10. Waco: Word, 1987.

Allen, Leslie C. "Ezekiel 20–48." In *Word Biblical Commentary,* vol. 29. Dallas: Word, 1990.

Allen, Leslie C. "The Book of Obadiah." In *The Books of Joel, Obadiah, Jonah, and Micah.* Grand Rapids: Eerdmans, 1976.

Allen, Leslie C. *Joel, Obadiah, Jonah and Micah.* Grand Rapids: Eerdmans, 1976.

Allison, D. C. "Elijah Must First Come." *Journal of Biblical Literature* 103 (1984).

Althann, Robert. *A Philological Analysis of Jeremiah 4–6 in the Light of Northwest Semitic.* Rome: Biblical Institute Press.

Amerding, Carl, and W. Ward Gasque. *A Guide to Biblical Prophecy.* Peabody: Hendrickson, 1989.

Amerding, Carl. "Habakkuk." In *The Expositor's Bible Commentary*, ed. Frank E. Gabelein, vol. 7. Grand Rapids: Regency, 1985.

Amerding, Carl. "Habakkuk." In the *Expositor's Bible Commentary,* ed. Frank Gaebelein, 12 vols. Grand Rapids: Zondervan, 1979–85.

Amerding, Carl. *Studies in Old Testament Theology.* Dallas: Word, 1992.

Andersen, Francis I. "Yahweh, the Kind and Sensitive God." In *God Who is Rich in Mercy,* ed. Peter T. Obrien and David G. Petersen. Homebush West: Lancer, 1986.

Andersen, Francis I., and David Noel Freedman. "Amos." In *The Anchor Bible,* vol. 24A, general editors William Foxwell Albright and David Noel Freedman. New York: Doubleday, 1989.

Anderson, Bernard W. Introduction. In *The Interpreters Bible,* ed. George A. Buttrick. Nashville: Abingdon, 1954.

Anderson, Bernhard W. "What Does God Require of Us?" *Biblical Review* 11: 46, 47.

Anderson, Robert A. *Signs and Wonders.* Grand Rapids: Eerdmans, 1984.

Archer, Gleason. "Daniel." In *The Expositor's Bible Commentary*, vol. VII, ed. F. C. Gaebelein. Grand Rapids: Zondervan, 1985.

Archer, Gleason. *A Survey of Old Testament Introduction.* Chicago: Moody, 1964.

Baldwin, Joyce C., *Daniel.* Leicester: InterVarsity, 1978.

Baldwin, Joyce. *Haggai, Zechariah, Malachi.* Downers Grove: InterVarsity, 1972.

Barker, Kenneth L. "Premillennialism in the Book of Daniel." *Master's Seminary Journal* 4 (spring 1993).

Barker, Kenneth L. "Zechariah." In *The Expositor's Bible Commentary*, 12 vols., ed. Frank Gabelein. Grand Rapids: Regency/Zondervan, 1983.

Bartlett, A. L. "The Night Visions of Zechariah Against the Background of Conflict in the Early Post-Exilic Community in Judah." *Scrif en Kerk* 16 (1995): 1–15.

Batten, Loren W. *The Books of Ezra and Nehemiah.* ICC Commentary. Edinburgh: T & T Clark, 1961.

Beale, G. K. *The Use of Daniel in Jewish Apocalyptic Literature and in the Revelation of St. John.* Lanham: University Press, 1984.

Beale, Gregory. "The Danielic Background for Revelation 13–18." *Tyndale Bulletin* 31 (1980):163–70.

Beasley Murray, G. R. *Jesus and the Kingdom of God.* Grand Rapids: Eerdmans, 1956.

Ben Zvi, Ehud. *A Historical Critical Study of the Book of Zephaniah.* New York: Walter de Gruyter, 1991.

Berg, Sandra Bette. *The Book of Esther.* Missoula: Scholars, 1979.

Berlin, Adele. *Zephaniah.* The Anchor Bible, vol. 25A. New York: Doubleday, 1994.

Bernard, Alvin. *Insights into the Book of Daniel.* St. Louis: Publisher Bernard, 1993.

Berquist, J. L. "The Social Setting of Malachi." *Biblical Theological Bulletin* 19 (1989): 121–26.

Berrigan, Daniel. *Ezekiel: Vision in the Dust.* Maryknoll: Orbis, 1997.

Bewer, Michael Smith. *Haggai, Zechariah, Malachi.* ICC. Edinburgh: T & T Clark, 1986.

Biddle, Mark E. "The City of Chaos at the New Jerusalem: Isaiah 24–27 in Context." *Perspectives in Religious Studies* 22 (1995): 5–12.

Blackwell, Andrew. *Ezekiel: Prophecy of Hope*. Grand Rapids: Baker, 1965.

Blaising, Craig A., and Darrell L. Bock. *Dispensationalism, Israel and the Church*. Grand Rapids: Zondervan, 1992.

Blaising, Craig A., and Darrell L. Bock. *Progressive Dispenstionalism*. Wheaton: Victor, 1993.

Blenkinsopp, Joseph. *Ezra–Nehemiah*. Philadelphia: Westminster, 1988.

Bosman, J. G. "Shrif en Kerk." 16, no. 2 (1995).

Bright, John. *A History of Israel*. 3d ed. Philadelphia: Westminster, 1981.

Bright, John. *Jeremiah*. The Anchor Bible, vol. 21. Garden City: Doubleday, 1965.

Brown, Raymond A. "Ezra and Nehemiah." In *The Interpreters Bible*, vol. 3, ed. George Arthur Buttrick. Nashville: Abingdon, 1954.

Brown, Raymond A. *The Message of Nehemiah*. Downers Grove: InterVarsity, 1998.

Brownlee, William H. "Ezekiel's Parable of the Watchman and the Editing of Ezekiel." *Vetus Testamentum* 28, no. 4, 392–408.

Brownlee, William H. *Ezekiel 1–16*. In *Word Biblical Commentary*. Waco: Word; 1986.

Brownlee, William H. *The Midrash Pesher of Habakkuk*. Missoula: Scholars, 1979.

Brownlee, William H. *The Text of Habakkuk in the Ancient Commentary from Qumran*. Vol. 11 in Journal of Biblical Literature Monograph Series. Philadelphia: Society of Biblical Literature, 1959.

Bruce, F. F. *Israel and the Nations*. Exeter Devon: Paternoster, 1963.

Brueggemann, Walter. *Tradition for Crises*. Richmond: John Knox, 1967.

Bullock, C. Hassell. *An Introduction to the Old Testament Prophetic Books*. Chicago: Moody, 1986.

Bush, Frederick. "The Book of Esther: Opus non Graum in the Christian Canon." *Bulletin for Biblical Research* 8 (1998).

Calvin, John. *Commentaries on the Twelve Minor Prophets*. Vol. II, "Joel, Amos, Obadiah." Trans. John Owen. Grand Rapids: Eerdmans, 1950.

Calvin, John. *Commentaries on the Twelve Minor Prophets*. Vol. III, "Jonah, Micah, Nahum." Trans. John Owens. Grand Rapids: Eerdmans, 1950.

Calvin, John. *Commentaries on the Twelve Minor Prophets*. Vol. IV. Trans. John Duun. Grand Rapids: Eerdmans, 1950.

Calvin, John. *The Prophet Jeremiah*. Vol. 1. Trans. John Owens. Grand Rapids: Eerdmans, 1950.

Campbell, Roderick. *Israel and the New Covenant*. Grand Rapids: Eerdmans, 1980.

Campbell, Roderick. *Israel and the New Covenant*. Philadelphia: Presbyterian and Reformed, 1959.

Carlson, Frederick Holmgren. *Ezra & Nehemiah: Israel Alive Again*. Grand Rapids: Eerdmans, 1987.

Carroll, Robert P. "The Myth of the Empty Land." *Semeia*, 59 (1992): 79–91.

Carson, Alexander. *Confidence in God in Times of Danger.* Sterling: GAM, 1990.

Cassuto, Umberto. "The Prophet Hosea and the Book of the Pentateuch." In *Biblical and Oriental Studies,* 2 vols. Jerusalem: Magnes, 1973.

Charles, R. H. *A Critical and Exegetical Commentary on the Book of Daniel*. Oxford: Clarendon, 1929.

Chavalas, Mark W. "Esther, Theology of." In *Evangelical Dictionary of Biblical Theology,* ed. Walter A. Elwell. Grand Rapids: Baker, 1996.

Childs, Brevard S. *Biblical Theology of the Old and New Testaments.* Minneapolis: Fortress, 1993.

Childs, Brevard S. *Introduction to the Old Testament as Scripture*. Philadelphia: Fortress, 1979.

Chilton, Bruce. "The Son of Man, Who Is He?" *Bible Review* 12 (1996).

Chisholm, Robert. "The Everlasting Covenant and the 'City of Chaos': Intentional Ambiguity and Irony in Isaiah 24." *Criswell Theological Review* 6 (1997): 237–53.

Coggins R. J. *Haggai, Zechariah, Malachi.* Sheffield: JSOT, 1987.

Collin, J. J. *Daniel.* Grand Rapids: Eerdmans, 1984.

Craig, Kenneth M., Jr. *Reading Esther.* Louisville: Westminster/John Knox, 1995.

Craigie, Peter. *Ezekiel.* Philadelphia: Westminster, 1983.

Curtis, Edward L. *The Books of Chronicles*. ICC series. Edinburgh: T & T Clark, 1910.

Daniel-Rops, Henri. *Israel and the Ancient World.* Trans. K. Madge. Garden City: Doubleday, 1964.

De Vries, Simon J. "Festive Ideology in Chronicles." In *Problems in Biblical Theology*, ed. Henry T. C. Sun and Keith L. Eades. Grand Rapids: Eerdmans, 1997. 104–24.

Delitzsch, Franz. *Biblical Commentary on the Prophecies of Isaiah.* Trans. James Marten. 2 vols. Grand Rapids: Eerdmans, 1950.

Dell, Katherine. Review of Ben Zvi. *Vetus Testamentum* 45 (1966): 556–57.

Derby, Josiah. "Isaiah and Cyrus." *Jewish Biblical Quarterly* 24 (1996): 173–77.

Dillard, Raymond. "1 & 2 Chronicles." In *NIV Study Bible*, ed. K. Barker. Grand Rapids: Zondervan, 1985.

Dillard, Raymond. "Joel." In *The Minor Prophets*, ed. Thomas E. McComiskey. Grand Rapids: Baker, 1992.

Dillard, Raymond. "Remnant." In *Baker Encyclopedia of the Bible*, ed. Walter A. Elwell. Grand Rapids: Baker, 1988. 2:1833–36.

Dumbrell, W. J. *Covenant and Creation.* Nashville: Thomas Nelson, 1984.

Dumermuth, C. F. "The Good Threefold Way." *Asia Journal of Theology* 8, no. 1, 186, 187.

Dyer, Charles. *The Rise of Babylon.* Wheaton: Tyndale, 1991.

Eichrodt, Walther. *Ezekiel, A Commentary*. Trans. Casslett Quin. London: SCM, 1970.

Eichrodt, Walther. *Theology of the Old Testament.* Trans. J. A. Baker. Philadelphia: Westminster, 1961.

Ellison, H. L. *Ezekiel: The Man and His Message.* Grand Rapids: Eerdmans, 1956.

Elmslie, W.A.L. "The First and Second Book of Chronicles." In *The Interpreters Bible*. 12 vols. Ed. G. W. Buttrick. Nashville: Abingdon, 1954.

Elwell, Walter A., ed. *Baker Encyclopedia of the Bible.* 2 vols. Grand Rapids, Baker, 1988.

Evers, Stan. *Doing a Great Work.* Darlington, England: Evangelical Press, 1996.

Fackre, G. "Narration Theology." *Interpretation* 37, no. 83 (1983): 340–52.

Fairbairn, Patrick. *The Interpretation of Prophecy.* London: The Banner of Truth Trust, 1964 [1856].

Fasbroke, Hughell E. W. "The Book of Amos." In *The Interpreter's Bible.* 12 vols. Ed. George Arthur Buttrick. New York: Abingdon.

Feinberg, C. L. "The Rebuilding of the Temple." In *Prophecy in the Making,* ed. C. F. Henry. Carol Stream: Creation House, 1971.

Feinberg, Charles. "Jeremiah." In *The Expositor's Bible Commentary,* ed. Frank E. Gabelein. Grand Rapids: Regency/Zondervan, 1986.

Fensham, R. Charles. *The Book of Ezra and Nehemiah.* In The New International Commentary on the Old Testament. Grand Rapids: Eerdmans, 1982.

Finley, Thomas. *Joel, Amos, Obadiah.* In *The Wycliffe Exegetical Commentary,* ed. K. Barker. Chicago: Moody, 1990.

Floyd, Michael H. "Cosmos and History in Zechariah's View of the Restoration." In *Problems in Biblical Theology,* ed. Henry T. C. Sun and Keith Eades. Grand Rapids: Eerdmans, 1977.

Floyd, Michael H. "The Evil in the Epoch: Reading Zechariah 5:5–11 in its Literary Context." *Catholic Biblical Quarterly* 58 (1996): 51–68.

Ford, Desmond. *Daniel.* Nashville: Southern Publishing Association, 1978.

Fuller, Daniel P. "The Importance of a Unity of the Bible." In *Studies in Old Testament Theology,* ed. R. L. Hubbard Jr., R. K. Johnston, and R. P. Mege. Dallas: Word, 1992.

Gerleman, Gilles. *Studien zu Esther.* BKAT 21. Neukerchen-Vluyn: Neukirchin Verlag, 1960.

Gilmore, Alec. "The Voice of the Voiceless." *Expository Times* 105, no. 10, 303–5.

Glazier-McDonald, Beth. "Intermarriage, Divorce and Bat-El Nekar: Insights into Malachi 2:1–16." *Journal of Biblical Literature* 106, no. 4, 603–11.

Goldingay, John. "Hosea 1–3, Genesis 1–4, and a Masculist Interpretation." *Horizons in Biblical Theology* 17, no. 1 (1995).

Goldingay, John. "The Chronicler as a Theologian." *Biblical Theological Bulletin* 5 (1995): 99–126.

Goldingay, John. "What Happens to Mr. Babylon in Isaiah 47, Why and Who Says So?" *Tyndale Bulletin* 47 (1996): 215–43.

Gosse, Bernard. "Michee 4:1–5, Isaie 2:1–5 et les redacteurs finaux du livre d'Isaie." *Zeitschrift das Alteswissenschaft* 105 (spring): 98–102.

Gray, George Buchanan. *A Critical and Exegetical Commentary on the Book of Isaiah.* 2 vols. Edinburgh: T & T Clark, 1956.

Gray, George Buchanan. *The Book of Isaiah—i–xxxix.* Edinburgh: T & T Clark, 1956.

Greenberg, Moshe. *Ezekiel 1–20.* Vol. 22 of the Anchor Bible Series, ed. William Foxwell Albright and David Moel Freedman. Garden City: Doubleday, 1983.

Greenhill, William. *An Exposition of Ezekiel.* Avon: Bath, 1994 [1667].

Grogan, Geoffrey W. "Isaiah." In *The Expositor's Bible Commentary.* 12 vols. General ed. Frank R. Gabelein. Grand Rapids: Zondervan, 1986.

Grosheide, H. H. *Ezra–Nehemia.* Kampen: Kok, 1963.

Gurney, Robert. "The Four Kingdoms of Daniel 2 & 7." *Themelios* 2 (1977).

Haak, Robert O. *Habakkuk.* Leiden: Brill, 1991.

Hagstrom, David Gerald. *The Coherence of the Book of Micah, A Literary Analysis*. SBL Dissertation Series 89. Atlanta: Scholars, 1988.

Hailey, Homer. *Commentary on the Minor Prophets*. Grand Rapids: Baker, 1972.

Harris, R. Laird. *Theological Wordbook of the Old Testament*. Chicago: Moody, 1980.

Harrison, R. K. "Moab, Moabites." In *The Zondervan Pictorial Encyclopedia of the Bible*, ed. Merrell C. Tenny. Grand Rapids, Zondervan, 1975.4:257–66.

Harrison, R. K. *Introduction to the Old Testament*. Grand Rapids: Eerdmans, 1969.

Harrison, R. K. *Jeremiah and Lamentations*. Downers Grove: InterVarsity, 1973.

Hartman, Louis F. *The Book of Daniel*. Vol. 23 in the Anchor Bible Series, ed. W. F. Albright and D. M. Freedman. Garden City: Doubleday, 1978.

Hasel, Gerhard F. *The Remnant*. Berrien Springs: Andrews University Press, 1972.

Hasel, Gerhard. "The Dead Sea Scrolls Have Provided a Wealth of New Material for Reassessing Opinions regarding the Book of Daniel." *Ministry* (1979): 9–11.

Hauerwas, Stanley, and L. Gregory Jones, eds. *Why Narrative? Readings in Narrative Theology*. Grand Rapids: Eerdmans, 1989.

Henderson, Ebenezer. *The Twelve Minor Prophets*. Grand Rapids: Baker, 1980.

Hengstenberg, Ernst. *Christology of the Old Testament* and *A Commentary on the Messianic Predictions*. 4 vols. Grand Rapids: Kregel, 1956.

Hengstenberg, Ernst. *Christology of the Old Testament*. Trans. Theodore Meyer. 2 vols. Edinburgh: T & T Clark, 1868.

Hengstenberg, Ernst. *The Prophet Ezekiel*. Trans. J. G. Murphy. Edinburgh: T & T Clark, 1874.

Heschel, Abraham J. *The Prophets*. New York: Harper and Row, 1962.

Hinton, Linda B. "Ezekiel and Daniel." In *Basic Bible Commentary* (Cokesbury—no further bibliographical information is given).

Hirsch, Samson Raphaeil. *The Psalms*. New York: Philipp Feldheim, 1960.

Honeycutt, Roy L. "Hosea." In *The Broadman Bible Commentary*, vol. 7, ed. Clifton J. Allen. Nashville: Broadman, 1972.

House, Paul R. "Isaiah's Call and Its Context in Isaiah 1–6." *Criswell Theological Review* (1995): 207–22.

House, Paul R. *Zephaniah: A Prophetic Drama*. Worcester: Almond, 1988.

Hugenburger, Gordon Paul. *Marriage as a Covenant*. Leiden: Brill, 1994.

Hughes, Philip E. *Interpreting Prophecy*. Grand Rapids: Eerdmans, 1976.

Humphreys, W. Lee. "The Story of Esther in Its Several Forms: Recent Studies." *Religious Study Review* 24 (1998): 335–42.

Japhet, Sara. "Composition and Chronology in the Book of Ezra–Nehemiah." *Second Temple Studies* (Journal for the Study of the Old Testament Supplemental Series) (1994).

Japhet, Sara. "Supposed Common Authorship of Chronicles and Ezra–Nehemiah Investigated Anew." *Vetus Testamentum* 18 (1968).

Japhet, Sara. "The Historical Reliability of Chronicles." *Journal for the Study of the Old Testament* 33 (1985).

Japhet, Sara. "The Relationship Between Chronicles and Ezra–Nehemiah." *Supplements to Vetus Testamentum* (1989).

Japhet, Sara. "The Supposed Common Authorship of Chronicles of Ezra–Nehemiah." *Vetus Testamentum* 18 (1989): 330–71.

Japhet, Sara. *The Ideology of the Book of Chronicles and Its Place in Biblical Thought.* Trans. Anna Barber. New York: Peter Lang, 1989, revised 1994.

Japhet, Sara. *The Ideology of the Book of Chronicles and its Plea in Biblical Thought.* Frankfort: Lang, 1989.

Jeffrey, Arthur. "The Book of Daniel." In *The Expositor's Bible*, ed. George A. Buttrick. Nashville: Abingdon, 1956.

Jones, David. "A Note on the LXX of Malachi 2:16." *Journal of Biblical Literature* 109 (1990): 683–85.

Kaiser, Walter C., Jr. *Malachi: God's Unchanging Love.* Grand Rapids: Baker, 1984.

Kaiser, Walter C., Jr., *Back Toward the Future: Hints for Interpreting Biblical Prophecy.* Grand Rapids: Baker, 1989.

Keil, Carl F. "Micah." In the *Biblical Commentary on the Old Testament: The Twelve Minor Prophets*, vol. 1, trans. J. Marten. Grand Rapids: Eerdmans, 1951.

Keil, Carl F. *The Book of Daniel.* Trans. M. G. Easton. Grand Rapids: Eerdmans, 1949.

Keil, Carl F. *The Books of Chronicles.* Trans. Andrew Harper. Grand Rapids: Eerdmans, n.d.

Keil, Carl F. *The Minor Prophets.* 2 vols. Trans. James Marten. Grand Rapids, Eerdmans, 1951.

Keil, Carl F. *The Prophecies of Jeremiah*, vol. 1, trans. David Patrick. Grand Rapids: Eerdmans, 1950.

Kellar, Roger R. "Karl Barth's Treatment of the Old Testament as Expectation." *Andrews University Seminary Studies* 35, no. 2 (autumn 1997): 171–72.

Kidner, Derek. *Ezra & Nehemiah.* Downers Grove: InterVarsity, 1979.

Kidner, Derek. *Psalms 1–72.* Cambridge: Intervarsity, 1973.

King, Greg. "The Day of the Lord in Zephaniah." *Bibliotheca Sacra* 152 (January–March 1995).

King, Greg. "The Message of Zephaniah: An Urgent Echo." *Andrews University Seminary Studies* 32, no. 2 (1996).

Kitchen, Kenneth O. *Notes on Some Problems in the Book of Daniel.* London: Tyndale, 1965.

Knibb, Michael A. "You Are Indeed Wiser Than Daniel." *New Findings*, 399–411.

Knierim, Rolf P. *The Task of Old Testament Theology.* Grand Rapids: Eerdmans, 1995.

Knight, G.A.F. *A Christian Theology of the Old Testament.* 2d ed. London: SCM, 1964.

Koch, K. "Is Daniel also Among the Prophets?" In *Interpreting the Prophets*, ed. J. L. Mays and P. J. Achtemeier. Philadelphia: no publisher mentioned, 1985.

Koole, J. L. *Haggai.* Kampen, Kok, 1967.

Kort, Wesley A. *Story, Text and Scripture—Literary Interests in Biblical Narrative.* University Park: Pennsylvania University Press, 1988.

Kruschevitz, R. B. "Nebuchadnezzar as The Head of Gold: Politics and History in the Book of Daniel." *Perspectives in Relgious Studies* 24 (winter 1997).

Kuhl, Curt. *The Prophets of Israel.* Trans. Rudolph J. Ehrlich and John P. Smith. Richmond: John Knox, 1960.

Laetsch, Theo. *Bible Commentary—Jeremiah.* St. Louis: Concordia, 1952.

Laetsch, Theo. *Commentary on the Minor Prophets.* St. Louis: Concordia, 1956.

LaRondelle, Hans K. *The Israel of God in Prophecy: Principles of Prophetic Interpretation.* Berrien Springs: Andrews University Press, 1983.

Lasor, William Sanford. "The Prophets During the Monarchy." In *Israel's Apostasy and Restoration.* Grand Rapids: Baker, 1988.

Leslie, Elmer. *Jeremiah.* Nashville: Abingdon, 1954.

Leupold, H. C. *Exposition of Zechariah.* Columbus: Wartburg, 1956.

Levenson, Jon Douglas. *Theology of the Program of Restoration of Ezekiel 40–48.* Missoula: Scholars, 1996.

Lewis, Jack P. *The Minor Prophets.* Grand Rapids: Baker, 1966.

Lieb, Michael. *Children of Ezekiel.* Durham: Duke University Press, 1998.

Lim, Timothy. " The Wicked Priests of the Groningen Hypothesis." *Journal of Biblical Literature* 112–13 (1995).

Lindblom, J. *Prophecy in Ancient Israel.* Oxford: Basil Blackwell, 1962.

Locke, Jason W. "The Wrath of God in the Book of Isaiah." *Restoration Quarterly* 35, no. 4 (1993): 221–33.

Lococque, Andre. *The Book of Daniel.* Trans. David Pellaver. Atlanta: John Knox.

Lohfink, Norbert. *The Covenant Never Revoked.* Trans John J. Scullion. Mahwah, N.J.: Paulist, 1991.

Long, Brian. "Notes on the Biblical Use of 'ad 'olam." *Westminster Theological Journal* 41, no. 1 (fall 1972): 54–67.

Longman, Tremper, III. *Daniel: The NIV Application Commentary.* Grand Rapids: Zondervan, 1999.

Lowe, W. H. *Ellicott's Commentary on the Whole Bible.* Vol. V., ed. C. J. Ellicott. Grand Rapids: Zondervan, no date.

Marbury, Edward. *Obadiah and Habakkuk.* Ann Arbor: Sovereign Grace, 1960.

Marten-Achard, Robert. *A Light to the Nations.* Trans. John P. Smith. Edinburgh: Oliver and Boyd, 1962.

Martens, Elmer A. *God's Design: A Focus on Old Testament Theology.* Grand Rapids: Baker, 1981.

Mason, Rex. *Zephaniah, Habakkuk, Joel.* Sheffield: Academic Press, 1994.

Mays, James L. *Hosea: A Commentary.* Philadelphia: Westminster, 1969.

Mays, James L. *Micah.* Philadelphia: Westminster, 1976.

McComiskey, Thomas Edward. "Amos." In *The Expositor's Bible Commentary,* ed. Frank E. Gabelein, 12 vols. Grand Rapids: Zondervan, 1979–85.

McComiskey, Thomas Edward. "Micah." In *The Expositor's Bible Commentary*, ed. Frank E. Gabelein, 12 vols. Grand Rapids: Zondervan, 1985.

McComiskey, Thomas Edward. *The Covenants of Promise.* Grand Rapids, Baker, 1985.

McConville, J. G. *Judgment and Promise.* Winona Lake: Eisenbrauns, 1993.

McCreech, Thomas. "Ezra and Nehemiah, Leaders in Restoration." *The Bible Today* 37 (1999): 201–6.

McGrath, Alister. *A Passion for Truth.* Downers Grove: InterVarsity, 1996.

McIntyre, Carl. *For Such a Time as This.* Collingswood: Christian Beacon, 1946.

McKenzie Steven L., and Howard N. Wallace. "Covenant Themes in Malachi." *Catholic Biblical Quarterly* 45 (1983): 549–63.

McMichael, Steven J. "Did Isaiah Foretell Jewish Blindness and Suffering for Not Accepting Jesus of Nazareth as Messiah? A Medieval Perspective." *Biblical Theological Bulletin* 26 (1996): 144–51.

Meyers, Carol and Eric. *Haggai, Zechariah.* Vol. 25B of The Anchor Bible. Garden City: Doubleday, 1989.

Moore, Carey A. *Esther.* Vol. 7B of The Anchor Bible. Garden City: Doubleday, 1971.

Moore, T. V. *A Commentary on Zechariah.* London: Banner of Truth Trust, 1958.

Moore, Thomas. *A Commentary on Haggai and Malachi.* London: Banner of Truth, 1960 [1856].

Motyer, J. Alec. *The Prophecy of Isaiah.* Downers Grove: InterVarsity, 1993.

Mowinkel, Sigmund. *He That Cometh.* Trans. G. W. Anderson. Oxford: Basil Blackwell, 1959.

Moyer, J. C. "Philistines." In *The Zondervan Pictorial Encyclopedia of the Bible*, ed. Merrill C. Tenney and Steven Barabas. Grand Rapids: Zondervan, 1975. 4:76–77.

Murphy, Roland E. "Reflections on a Critical Biblical Theology." In *Problems in Biblical Theology*, ed. Henry T. C. Sun and Keith L. Eades. Grand Rapids: Eerdmans, 1997.

Myers, Jacob M. *1 and 2 Chronicles.* Vol. 12 of The Anchor Bible. Garden City: Doubleday, 1965.

Myers, Jacob M. *Ezra & Nehemiah.* Vol. 14 of The Anchor Bible. Garden City: Doubleday, 1965.

Nel, H.W. "The Davidic Covenant in 1 and 1 Chronicles: A New Theme for an Old Song." *Die Schriflig* 28, no. 3 (1994): 429–41.

New Bible Atlas. Ed. D.R.W. Wood. Wheaton: InterVarsity, 1985.

Newton, Isaac. *Observations Upon the Prophecies of Daniel and the Apocalypse of St. John.* Oregon Institute of Science and Medicine, 1991.

Nicholson, Ernest W. *God and His People.* Oxford: Clarendon, 1986.

Niles, D. Preman. "Called to be a Blessing to the Nations." *Asia Journal of Theology* 12, no. 2 (1998).

Noordtzy, A. *Kronieken.* Vol. II. Kampen: Kok, 1938.

O'Brien, Julia M. "Malachi in Recent Research." *Current Research: Biblical Studies* 8 (1995).

O'Kane, Marten O. "Isaiah: A Prophet in the Footsteps of Moses." *Journal for the Study of the Old Testament* 69: 29–51.

Olivier, Hannes. "God, as Friendly Patron: Reflections on Isaiah 5:17." *Die Skriflig* 30, no. 3 (1996): 2293–303.

Oswalt, John N. "Judgment and the Full Orbed Gospel." *Trinity Journal* 17 (1996): 191–202.

Oswalt, John N. *The Book of Isaiah, Chapters 40–66.* Grand Rapids: Eerdmans, 1998.

Packer, J. I. *A Passion for Faithfulness*. Wheaton: Crossway, 1995.

Pagaan, Samuel. "Apocalyptic Poetry: Isaiah 24–27." *Apuntes* 15 (1995): 14–27.

Paton, L. Lewis Bayle. *A Critical and Exegetical Commentary on the Book of Esther.* Edinburgh: T & T Clark, 1951 [1908].

Patterson, Richard D. "A Literary Look at Nahum, Habakkuk and Zephaniah." *Grace Theological Journal* 11, no. 1, 12–28.

Patterson, Richard D. "Holding on to Daniel's Court Tales." *Journal of Evangelical Theology* 36, no. 4, 445–54.

Patterson, Richard D. "Joel." In *The Expositor's Bible Commentary,* ed. Frank F. Gabelein, 12 vols. Grand Rapids: Zondervan, 1985. 7:230–34.

Patterson, Richard D. "The Key Role of Daniel 7." *Grace Theological Journal* 12 (fall): 245–61.

Patterson, Richard D. *Nahum, Habakkuk, Zephaniah.* Chicago: Moody, 1991.

Payne, David L. *The New Layman's Bible Commentary*, ed. G. C. D. Howley, F. F . Bruce, and H. L. Ellison. Grand Rapids: Zondervan, 1979.

Payne, J. B. "The Ark of the Covenant." In *The Zondervan Pictorial Encyclopedia of the Bible,* ed. Merrill C. Tenney, vol. 1. Grand Rapids: Zondervan, 1975.

Payne, P. F. Genesis in *The New Layman's Bible Commentary,* ed. G.C.D. Howley, F. F. Bruce, and H. L. Ellison. Grand Rapids: Zondervan, 1979.

Peachey, Barry F. "The Horses in Zechariah and Revelation." *Expository Times* 110 (April 1999): 214–16.

Pennybacher, Albert M. "The Two Micah's: Reflections on Integrity in Ministry." *Lexington Theological Review* 27, no. 2, 33–42.

Pentecost, J. Dwight. *Thy Kingdom Come.* Wheaton: Victor, 1990.

Polak, F. H. "Daniel Tales in Their Aramaic Literary Milieu," *New Findings,* 249–65.

Porteous, Norman W. *Daniel: A Commentary*. London: SCM, 1965.

Pusey, E. B. *The Minor Prophets: A Commentary*. Vol. II. Grand Rapids: Baker, 1950.

Redditt, Paul L. *Haggai, Zechariah and Malachi*. Grand Rapids: Eerdmans, 1995.

Ridderbos, J. *De Kliene Profeten Haggai Zacharia, Maleachi*. Vol. III. Kampen: Kok, 1952.

Ridderbos, J. *De Kliene Profeten Obadja tot Zefanja.* Kampen: Kok, 1949.

Ridderbos, J. *Het Godswoord Der Profeten.* 4 vols. Kampen: Kok, 1930.

Ridderbos, J. *Isaiah.* Trans. John Vriend. Grand Rapids: Zondervan, 1985.

Ridderbos, J. *Jesaja. Het Godwoord der Profeten.* Kampen: Kok, 1932.

Ridderbos. J. *De Psalmen.* Vol. II. Kampen: Kok, 1958.

Riggan, George. *Messianic Theology and the Christian Faith.* Philadelphia: Westminster, 1967.

Robertson, O. Palmer. *The Christ of the Covenants.* Phillipsburg: Presbyterian and Reformed, 1980.

Robertson, O. Palmer.. *The Books of Nahum, Habakkuk, and Zephaniah.* Grand Rapids: Eerdmans, 1990.

Robinson, George L. *The Twelve Minor Prophets*. Grand Rapids: Baker, 1960.

Rodriguez, Angel Manuel. *Esther: A Theological Approach.* Berrien Springs: Andrews University Press, 1995.

Rofe, Alexander. *The Prophetical Stories.* Jerusalem: Magnes, 1988.

Rondelle, Hans K. *The Israel of God in Prophecy.* Berrien Springs: Andrews University Press, 1983.

Rooker, Mark F. *Westminster Theological Journal* 58 (1976).

Roorda, A. *Het Boek Ester.* Bredai: Traktaatgenootschap, 1912.

Rowley, H. H. *Darius The Mede and the Four World Empires.* Cardiff: University of Wales Press, 1959.

Rushdoony, Rousas John. *Thy Kingdom Come.* Garden Grove: Presbyterian and Reformed, 1975.

Saucy, Robert L. *The Case for Progressive Dispensationalism.* Grand Rapids: Zondervan, 1992.

Scott, Julius L. "The Covenant in the Theology of Karl Barth." *Scottish Theological Journal* 17 (1964): 182–98.

Scott, R.B.Y. *Isaiah. The Interpreters Bible.* 12 vols., ed. George Arthur Buttrick. New York: Abingdon, 1956.

Selman, Martin. "Kingdom of God in the O.T." *Tyndale Bulletin* 40 (1989).

Shipp, R. Mark. "Remember His Covenant Forever." *Restoration Quarterly* 35, no. 1 (1993): 29–39.

Sikfetzen, Ben L. "From Story to Preaching." In *Alle der Ander,* ed. Else K. Holt. Frederiksberg, Denmark: Forlage ANIS, 1998.

Simeon, Charles. *Expository Outlines on the Whole Bible*, Vol. 10. 8th ed. London: Henry G. Bohm, 1847.

Skinner, John. *Prophecy and Religion.* Cambridge: Cambridge University Press, 1955.

Slotki, J. W. *Chronicles.* London: Soncino, 1952.

Smart, James B. *History and Theology in Second Isaiah.* Philadelphia: Westminster, 1965.

Smith, Duane A. "Kingship and Covenant in Hosea 11:1–4." *Horizons in Biblical Theology* 16, no. 1 (1994): 41–55.

Smith, Gary V. *Amos, A Commentary.* Grand Rapids, Zondervan, 1989.

Smith, George A. "The Book of Joel." In *The Expositor's Bible*, ed. W. Robertson Nicole, 6 vols. Grand Rapids: Eerdmans, 1947.

Smith, George A. "The Book of the Twelve Prophets." In *The Expositor's Bible,* ed. W. Robert Nicoll, 6 vols. Grand Rapids: Eerdmans, 1947.

Smith, M. P. "Micah." In *The International Critical Commentary*, ed. J.M.P. Smith, William Hayes Ward, and Julius Bewer. Edinburgh: T & T Clark, 1911.

Smith, Ralph L. "Amos." In *The Broadman Bible Commentary,* vol. 7, gen. ed. Clifton J. Allen. Nashville: Broadman, 1972.

Smith, Ralph L. "Micah." In *Word Biblical Commentary*, vol. 32. Waco: Word, 1984.

Snaith, Norman H. *Amos, Hosea, and Micah.* London: Epworth, 1960.

Snyman, S. D. "A Structural Approach to Malachi 3:13–21." In *Old Testament Essays* (Pretoria: no publisher, 1991).

Snyman, S. D. "Antithesis in the Book of Malachi." *Journal of N.W. Semitic Languages* 16 (1990): 173–78.

Soggin, J. Alberto. *Introduction to the Old Testament.* Philadelphia: Westminster, 1976.

Sperry, Willard P. "Malachi." In *The Interpreter's Bible*, vol. 6, ed. George A. Buttrick. Nashville: Abingdon, 1956.

Stedman, Ray C. *The Queen and I.* Waco: Word, 1977.

Stefanovic, Zdranko. "Daniel: A Book of Significant Reversals." *Andrews University Seminary Studies* 30 (summer 1992): 139–50.

Stek, John. "Covenant Overload in Reformed Theology." *Calvin Theological Journal* 29 (April 1994): 12–41.

Stek, John. "The Message of the Book of Jonah." *Calvin Theological Journal* 4, no. 1 (1969): 32–35.

Sternberg, M. *The Poetics of Biblical Narrative.* Bloomington: Indiana University Press, 1985.

Stuart, Douglas. "Hosea–Jonah." In *Word Biblical Commentary*, vol. 31, ed. David A. Hubbard and Glenn Barker. Waco: Word, 1987.

Stuhlmueller, Carroll. *Rebuilding with Hope: A Commentary on the Books of Haggai & Zechariah.* Grand Rapids: Eerdmans, 1988.

Swanepoel, N. G. "To Send Away in Hate or to Hate Divorce—What Does the Lord Want?" *Nederduitse Gereformeerde Teologiese Tydschrif* 36 (1995): 65–74.

Sweeney, Marvin A. "Structure, Genre, and Intent of the Book of Habakkuk." *Vetus Testamentum* 31 (1991): 63–83.

Szeles, Maria Eszenyei. *Wrath and Mercy.* Trans. G.A.F. Knight. Grand Rapids: Eerdmans, 1987.

Taylor, Charles L., Jr. "The Book of Habakkuk." In *The Interpreters Bible,* 12 vols., ed. George A. Buttrick. New York: Abingdon, 1956.

Taylor, Charles L., Jr. "The Book of Nahum: Introduction and Exegesis." In *The Interpreters Bible,* ed. George A. Buttrick, 12 vols. New York: Abingdon, 1951–57.

Taylor, John B. *Ezekiel.* Downers Grove: InterVarsity, 1974.

Thomas, Derek. *God Strengthens.* Durham: Evangelical Press, 1993.

Thompson, John A. "Obadiah." In *The Interpreters Bible,* ed. George A. Buttrick, 12 vols. New York: Abingdon, 1951–59.

Thompson, John A. *The Book of Jeremiah.* Grand Rapids: Eerdmans, 1980.

Thompson, Michael E. W. "Prayer, Oracle, and Theophany: The Book of Habakkuk." *Tyndale Bulletin* 44, no. 1 (1993): 33–53.

Torrey, C. C. *Pseudo Ezekiel and the Original Prophecy.* New York: Ktav, 1970.

Tov, Emanuel. *The Septuagint Translation of Jeremiah and Baruch.* Missoula: Scholars, 1976.

Trible, Phyllis. *Rhetorical Criticism: Context, Method and the Book of Jonah.* Minneapolis: Fortress, 1994.

Tsumura, David Toshio. "Ugaritic Poetry and Habakkuk 3." *Tyndale Bulletin* 40, no. 1, (1988).

Turner, David L. *Dispensationalism, Israel and the Church.* Ed. C. A. Blaising and Darrell L. Bock. Grand Rapids: Zondervan, 1992.

Van Gelderen, C., and W. H. Gispen. *Het Boek Hosea.* Kampen: Kok, 1953.

Van Gemeren, Willem A. *Interpreting the Prophetic Word.* Grand Rapids: Zondervan, 1990.

Van Groningen, Gerard. "The Sons of the Prophets." *Vox Reformata* 33 (1979): 2236.

Van Groningen, Gerard. *From Creation to Consummation.* Vol. 1. Sioux Center: Dordt Press, 1996.

Van Groningen, Gerard. *Messianic Revelation in the Old Testament.* Reprint. Eugene: Wiph and Stock, 1997.

Van Leeuwen, C. *Hosea.* Nijkerk: Callenbach, 1968.

Van Selms, A. *Jeremiah.* Vol. I. Nijkerk: Callenbach, 1972.

Vander Woude, A. S. "Malachi's Struggle for a Pure Community: Reflections on Malachi 2:10." In *Tradition and Re-Interpretation in Jewish and Early Christian Literature,* ed. J. W. Van Henting, H. J. de Jonge, P. T. Van Rooden, and J. W. Wesselhuis. Leiden: Brill, 1986.

Veldkamp, H. *De Balling Van de Kabaroe.* Franeker: Wever, 1956.

Veldkamp, H. *De Twee Getuigen.* Franeker: Wever, no date.

Veldkamp, Herman. *Dreams and Dictators.* Trans. Theodore Plantinga. St. Catherines: Paideia Press, 1978.

Verhoef, Pieter A. *Krisiswoorde in Krisistije.* Pretoria: N. G. Kerk Uitgewers, no date.

Verhoef, Pieter A. *The Books of Haggai & Malachi.* Grand Rapids: Eerdmans, 1987.

Von Orelli, C. *The Twelve Minor Prophets.* Trans. J. S. Banks. Minneapolis: Klock & Klock, 1977.

Von Rad, Gerhard. *Old Testament Theology.* Trans. D.M.C. Stalker. Edinburgh: Oliver and Boyd, 1962.

Vos, Gerhardus. *Biblical Theology.* Grand Rapids: Eerdmans, 1948.

Walker, Larry Lee. "Zephaniah." In *The Expositors Bible Commentary,* vol. 7, ed. F. E. Gabelein. Grand Rapids: Zondervan, 1985.

Wallace, Ronald S. *The Lord is King.* Downers Grove: InterVarsity, 1979.

Wallace, Wilbur. "The Coming of the Kingdom, a Survey of the Book of Revelation." *Presbyterion* 8, no. 1 (1982): 13–70.

Walton, John H. *Covenant God's Purpose God's Plan.* Grand Rapids: Zondervan, 1994.

Walton, John. "The Four Kingdoms of Daniel." *Journal of the Evangelical Theological Society* 29, no. 1 (March 1986): 25–36.

Walvoord, John F. *The Millennial Kingdom.* Grand Rapids: Zondervan, 1959.

Watts, John D. W. *Word Biblical Commentary, Isaiah 1:33.* Waco: Word, 1985.

Weima, Jeffrey. "What Does Aristotle Have to Do with Paul?" 32 (1997): 458–68.

Wenham, D, "The Kingdom of God and Daniel." *The Expository Times* 98, no. 5, 132–34.

Wevers, John. *Ezekiel.* Greenwood: Attu, 1976.

White, H. C. *Basic Forms of Prophetic Speech.* Louisville: Westminster/John Knox, 1991.

White, Hugh. *A Narration and Discourse in the Book of Genesis.* Cambridge: Cambridge University Press, 1991.

Whitley, C. F. *The Prophetic Achievement.* London: Mowbry, 1963.

Wilcox, Michael. *The Message of Chronicles.* Downers Grove: InterVarsity, 1987.

Williamson, G.H.M. *1 and 2 Chronicles.* In *The New Century Bible Commentary.* Grand Rapids: Eerdmans, 1982.

Wilson, Robert Dick. *Studies in the Book of Daniel.* Grand Rapids: Baker, 1979.

Wilson, Robert R. "Early Israelite Prophecy." In *Interpreting the Prophets,* ed. James L. Mays and Paul J. Achtemeier. Philadelphia: Fortress, 1987.

Wiseman, D. J. "General Preface." In Derek Kidner's *Ezra and Nehemiah* Downers Grove: InterVarsity, 1979.

Wolf, Herbert. "The Transcendent Nature of the Covenant Curse Reversals." In *Israel's Apostasy and Restoration,* ed. Avraham Gileadi. Grand Rapids: Baker, 1988.

Wolfe, Rolland. "The Book of Micah." In *The Interpreters Bible*, ed. Nolan B. Harmon, 12 vols. New York: Abingdon, 1956.

Wolff, Hans W. *Joel and Amos.* Trans. S. D. McBride Jr. Philadelphia: Fortress, 1977.

Wolff, Hans W. *Micah.* Trans. Gary Stansell. Minneapolis: Augsburg, 1990.

Woodard, Branson L. "Literary Strategies and Authorship in the Book of Daniel." *Journal of Evangelical Theological Society* 37, no. 1 (1994): 39–53.

Woudstra, Martin H. "Edom and Israel in Ezekiel." *Calvin Theological Journal* 3 (1968): 21–35.

Woudstra, Martin H. *The Ark of the Covenant: From Conquest to Kingship.* Phillipsburg: Presbyterian and Reformed, 1965.

Wright, J. S. "Esther, Book of." In *The Zondervan Pictorial Encyclopedia of the Bible,* vol. 2, ed. Merrell C. Tenny. Grand Rapids, Zondervan, 1975.

Wright, J. S. *The Date of Ezra's Coming to Jerusalem.* London: Tyndale.

Wright, John W. "The Legacy of David in Chronicles: The Narrative Function of 1 Chronicles 23–27." *Journal of Biblical Literature* 110, no. 2 (1991): 233–34.

Wyk-Bos, Johanna W. H. *Ezra, Nehemiah, and Esther.* Louisville: Westminster/John Knox, 1998.

Wyngaarden, Marten J. *The Future of the Kingdom in Prophecy and Fulfilment.* Grand Rapids: Baker, 1955.

Young, Edward J. *My Servants the Prophets.* Grand Rapids: Eerdmans, 1952.

Young, Edward J. *The Book of Isaiah.* 3 vols. Grand Rapids: Eerdmans, 1970.

Young, Edward J. *The Prophecy of Daniel.* Grand Rapids: Eerdmans, 1949.

Zimmerli, Walter. *Commentary on the Book of Ezekiel,* 2 vols. Trans. Ronald E. Clement. Philadelphia: Fortress, 1983.

Zvi, Ehud Ben. "The Authority of 1–2 Chronicles." *Journal for the Study of the Pseudepigraphy* 3 (1988): 55–88.

General Index

Scripture Index

Daniel

Hosea

www.ingramcontent.com/pod-product-compliance
Lightning Source LLC
Chambersburg PA
CBHW020945310726
48980CB00001B/55

* 9 7 8 0 9 3 2 9 1 4 5 2 1 *